For
PETER AND LARS FELTON, ELYSSA AND AMY THORP,
AND THEIR FELLOWS—
to whom all the Principals of this world
must answer.

INDISPENSABLE TOOLS

A Principal Builds His High School

DIALOGUES ON CHARTER EDUCATION WITH PETER THORP

Keith Spencer Felton

University Press of America,® Inc.
Lanham · New York · Oxford

Copyright © 2001 by
University Press of America,® Inc.
4720 Boston Way
Lanham, Maryland 20706

12 Hid's Copse Rd.
Cumnor Hill, Oxford OX2 9JJ

Library of Congress Cataloging-in-Publication Data

Felton, Keith Spencer.
Indispensable tools : a principal builds his high school : dialogues
on charter education with Peter Thorp / Keith Spencer Felton.
p.   cm
Includes index.
1. Thorp, Peter—Interviews. 2. High school principals—
United States—Interviews. 3. Charter schools—United States—
Case studies. I. Thorp, Peter. II. Title.
LB2831.92 .F45 2001   373.12'012—dc21   2001027402 CIP

ISBN 0-7618-2015-9 (pbk. : alk. paper)

*Education is learning to use the tools
the race has deemed indispensable.*

— Josiah Royce

CONTENTS

Part Three: SECOND SEMESTER

A PERSONAL PREFACE

Every reporter prepares in a special way.

To get ready to handle a year of weekly forays into the world of the high school principal, I did the obvious thing: I repeated the fifth grade.

Now, a repetition (or was it remediation?) of a primary year after the passage of forty-seven subsequent summers takes some adjustment; but the new tricks (new math, new metaphors, new heroes and new ways of presenting new morals to old stories) came easier to this aging returnee through the agency of his tutor—my then-ten-year-old second son, Lars, one of the class dons.   Of course, this regular presence at Charles R. Drew Elementary School of a figure with a white beard did not remain unconnected or unallied in the teacher's mind.   Teachers are not underpaid because they are foolish; and a very unfoolish Joy Otake quickly put her quintagenarian visitor to regular work—guiding study groups; arbitrating on the recess kickball court; narrative reading in the end-of-day floor circle; and, once every couple of weeks, presenting an hour's worth of etymological-history-for-the-fifth-grade discussions (etymology frequently being the wardrobe with which the Writer-Emperor clothes himself).   But however much I played the "paraprofessional," as teacher's aids are now called, I clearly ranked myself, at year's end, as the one in class who had learned the most.

By the time, the following year, that I "entered" Peter Thorp's Gateway High School (thus "skipping" four grades in a summer), I had acquired aspects of wisdom not available to me in 1952 (during that first pass through fifth grade).   I knew now, for example, that a school child could absorb ninety-eight percent of what you expected him to, even if reflecting back to you only two percent of it upon check-in.   I knew now that girls, maturing before boys, were still being required by some to perform the terrible social gymnastic of appearing smaller, while actually soaring (intellectually and physically) above their male classmates.   I felt the pain of budgetary penury, where every sheet of photocopy paper was carefully accounted for; and treats, if any there were, usually came out of a teacher's personal (and very modest) weal. Most revealing for my future time in the high-school principal's office—I realized that the authority vested in the school's leader was a gift of the governed, and attached by the most tenuous of strings. (At year's end, that grade school's principal, after only one year's tenure, was replaced.)

Before my fellow fifth-graders turned, magically before my eyes, into the over-six-feet-tall guys or the brash young women of high school age, I appreciated the great pressure known to all preceptors— namely, that there is no time to do anything, and everything must be done. (It was, to be sure, a sign of Peter Thorp's magnanimity that he accorded me one hour or more each week from his schedule.) [1]

There was, of course, another purpose in my visits to see the high school principal. Unlike my honorary fifth-grade status, helping create these dialogues was intended to make available to a wider audience a sequential glimpse at the inside of high school life; and for this I am the Reporter. And yet, here again, at this institution I remained also a father, with a child enrolled amongst the students at Gateway. Peter Felton, Lars's older brother, was, indeed, the original reason which had brought his father into contact with the school. Plainly, young Peter had needed a high school, and after a painful year in a public school with a student body numbering three thousand, new, charter-driven, student-focused Gateway fit the bill beautifully.

As a result, interspersed within the dialogues with Thorp would develop moments where the Reporter became the anxious parent discussing his youngster with the school's highest officer. These moments—when Reporter and Subject become Teacher and Parent— are not beside-the-point; and in fact, they serve a purpose; for whether as unique example or stand-in for all the student body, Peter Felton's shared experiences, noted with his permission, also have something to offer a readership.

That readership will have much future work, if it is to take to heart the many insights Principal Thorp's professional career offers. And in the end it will be the Peter Thorps, and no one else, who must be the standard-bearers for meaningful academic achievement, and who must motivate a citizenry to support them. American public school life, the cradle of our country's citizenship, bears (in addition to strain of mixed-metaphor) the burdens of being an inadequately-constructed

---

[1] Our meeting on Leap Year Day, 2000, chronicled in Chapter 14, is a case in point.

bridge. It will lie there and allow crossing on its back, provided the travelers keep moving and never, never sit upon it, in contemplative, absorbent, intellectual repose; for to do so is to be viewed as dead-weight, as mistaking its birds'-bones struts for a more secure *terra firma*. "Keep moving! Keep moving!" And so it is, from fifth grade to twelfth, and—"Quickly now!"—beyond.

I believe, after what I saw during these two years' return to a touch with public school life, that Peter Thorp's job—as leader and as teacher—makes him even more that bridge; I know also that he must surely use his time from lost sleep trying to figure out how to slow those kids down as they cross over him, enabling him to have with them dialogues of their own, and yet without causing them, or himself, to collapse.

It was thus no surprise to me when he revealed that his dream sinecure was teaching tiny children, in the lowest school entry levels. There was appeal and honesty to it, a place where, at the end of a teacher's work life, his own creative support could combine sweetly with a child's exuberant dash across the gorge.

KSF

San Francisco
January 2001

INTRODUCTION

What's on a high school principal's mind?

As he walks through the lunchroom, picks up a soda can on the school yard, meets with a reading-remediation service provider, hires a new resource teacher, and bones up on a school district issue for a presentation, what other "baggage" is he toting besides the programmatic pedagogy with which he was anointed before stepping out onto teaching's uncertain path?

This book attempts to fill in the picture of the principal—as thinker, planner, philosopher, psychologist, parent-surrogate, and leader of the teaching family and their flock. It follows one high school principal — Peter Thorp, Eastern-born, world-tramper, onetime Fulbright holder, archaeological student, experienced preceptor, longtime school administrator, and passionate historian—throughout a year in the development of what may be the most special opportunity in his life of work with students.

For Peter Thorp, who in 1996 was the comfortably-placed headmaster of a well-manicured and idyllic private school located on supple downs beside Santa Barbara's Pacific Ocean, the chance to take a risk—given Gateway's pedagogical "winnings" if the risk paid off—was too enticing to pass up. So, by 1997, he found himself in Magellan-like pose, in a distinctly urban setting, before a group of eclectic but determined parents of high school students, who had come together—all of whom had been dissatisfied with the education heretofore offered their youngsters. And in the charter school movement, as he would find, Peter Thorp was called upon to use a lifetime of skills for a task unlike any other from his canon.

The charter school movement in America is a radical departure from other ways of handling the dilemma of matching student to school. For a society long conservative in educational matters—and most educators, school administrators and concerned parents would agree that the bureaucratic glaciers called school districts operate with an energy level which at best could be called phlegmatic—the problem of placing students who did not find public school accommodating to their learning needs and patterns, but who could not afford (nor particularly desired) private schools, was formidable and unmet. With the advent of the charter concept—schools where individualized attention was possible, where lower teacher-to-student ratios were the norm, and, of seemingly greatest consequence, where public moneys backed the enterprise of such schools just as if they were "regular" public schools, an enormous opportunity opened up for addressing the dissatisfying and unsuccessful high school careers of many in America's cities.

San Francisco was just such a city. California, in a quandary formed in no small measure by the presence of two sequential two-term conservative Chief Executives, had stripped its schools to the bone. In every community of its model city by the Bay, schools built in the 1920s, 1930s, and beyond were in disrepair or closed. The rise of real estate wealth had a severe impact on zoning laws, which heretofore had protected neighborhoods against the incursion of entrepreneurial predation. The "neighborhoods" were gone; the schools, ghosts.

The 1980s and 1990s were a time of political reaction against the Governors Brown; the Republicans produced two successive two-term personages: One, George Deukmejian, was a former district attorney with a prosecutorial bent who won the first of two gubernatorial elections with tactics many felt were tainted by racism. Deukmejian was followed by one Pete Wilson, San Diego's maverick mayor whose mediocre talents inexplicably had taken him to the Sacramento statehouse via the U.S. Senate. Oddly, this conservative politician's qualities even lacked the charisma which so often "covers" leadership inadequacies.

Thus, for a great period of years, the schools of California were devoid not only of surface paint, but bedrock philosophy. Indeed, despite several high-profile superintendents of public instruction, secondary education in California seemed absent that ingredient of equal value to philosophical underpinnings: A champion. High schools, like society in general, were becoming polarized: In San Francisco, the elite upper-crust children (driven to academic neurosis by frenzied parents, many of them of rising minority ethnicity who were borrowing, rather than solving and replacing, the problems of the majority community) went to Lowell High; the low-income students were stuck with the schools assigned to their home zip code. In the middle, a great swath of earnest students, some with talent, some with learning disabilities, all with the need to match their natures to an appropriate school, but most meeting with frustration, were left hanging.

For many families, the charter school was the answer. Here—infrequently, and only after hard-fought battles—were created smaller secondary-level learning institutions which had the potential of offering attentive faculty; special needs attention; and concepts of community which were unburdened by gangs, cliques, and other impediments to safe, enlightened grasping of the meanings of socialization.

Such a dilemma, in this very city of San Francisco, befell a group of parents. Their solution—remarkable, under the circumstances—is told later on by Gateway Board Chair Lisille Matheson in striking detail. The effort of Matheson and her group of mothers made it possible for conditions to change, in at least one setting. The influx of the leadership of someone like Peter Thorp was a natural need, but by no means a guaranteed find. When they did find him, the prototype parental organization of Gateway High School had the link they would need to complete the circle. Peter came in, and, as one mother put it, "took over as the professional he is."

In doing so, Thorp, Matheson, and the successful school they have created in only two years has offered what that parent has described well: "a model for some major school reform."

When I first saw Peter Thorp, he was standing on a picnic table in a deciduous glen low in one of the valleys that make up the Presidio in San Francisco. This longtime military base, recently released by the Army under "downsizing" energies by the bureaucratic cost-conscious, was then at the beginning of its life of retirement uncertainty: Would this splendid acreage—despite its long military history one of the rare pieces of unbroken beauty right at the edge of the Pacific and overlooking the Golden Gate—would this place be used for the bolstering of the public weal, and become an art preserve or a community center, or a low-income housing facility, or a park? Or would it succumb to the acquisitive cleverness behind the flashing eyes of a faddist movie producer and a handful of politicians, and be ground under and exploited for its commercial gain? The setting's dilemma in some ways mirrored that of the families and school staff who had gathered in June of 1998, to get to know one another, and to take another step into the world of a charter high school. Parents lined up for hamburger patties with others new to them; and fighting the shyness which accompanies such "ice-breaking" moments, they very much wondered in their tentative conversations whether Gateway High

School, a new charter school, would in fact meet its promise of offering a sharp contrast to San Francisco's retinue of older schools—schools with pedagogic patterns unsatisfying to youngsters who, like these at the cook-out, decidedly "needed something different."

On the redwood boards of that picnic bench, Peter Thorp addressed the gathering. His full head of prematurely gray hair, his warm blue eyes, and a certain mellifluous sadness in his voice—a melancholy of tone, not of import, and certainly not restricting the enthusiasm he felt for his cause, the building of a new high school—lent a quiet urgency to his task of encouraging the troops. His presentation, like a stump speech in the woods of his constituents, was particularly affecting, and very much in keeping with his character; for it bore the earnest intentions of the program he wanted, through his school, to offer these seekers of a difference. And as he wound up his remarks, and descended the picnic table, he chatted individually with parents who stood in line by the pot-luck dishes and the relish and the buns. (The potato chips had been quickly devoured by the adolescents present, who had turned for new booty before Peter had finished his words of welcome).

In the months which followed, Gateway moved its initial student body of one entering freshman class of 100 from a temporary location in Newcomer High School (a former 1920s grade school on San Francisco's Jackson Heights) to a small three-storey brick building in the City's Inner Sunset District, which had formerly been a Depression-era elementary school called Laguna Honda School. Latterly housing a medical program adjunct to nearby University of California at San Francisco, Gateway's new home would provide transitional room for the newest freshman group (class entering 1999), the elevated sophomores from the initial group, and perhaps one more class on its way to a full complement of classes, before Gateway would have to seek out even larger quarters.

On the Sunday before the Monday marking the first day of school, Gateway's central "Multi-Purpose Room" looked more like the testing center at a paints plant. There, some of the same shy parents who had heard Peter's remarks at the picnic now stood on ladders, wore facial dust masks and carted sheet-rock scraps to the trash, and painted pipes on the ceiling. A side room still had spilled wash-water on the floor, but within hours it would hear Spanish being taught by Panamanian Ventura Rodriguez. The *ad hoc* paint crew generally exulted in the miasma of a shabby sense of unreadiness and utter excitement.

The project of creating a high school had begun.

Within months, the ever-growing faculty (honed and distilled constantly by Peter Thorp, despite an ever-present budgetary nervousness) would ignore light room dividers and classroom space resembling more a thespian fantasy than a permanent autonomy, and begin the process of offering a unique vision of secondary education to a strongly motivated and talented group of youngsters, students whose readiness for a special kind of school made the quickly-painted brick building's cramped spaces a repository for Thorp's faculty's rich loam of learning.

As free-flowing as his mind is, as artistic and creative and intuitive as his inclinations are, Peter Thorp has not spent decades as a school administrator without developing great managerial skills. And the best-managed of his concerns is his time. He and I met, weekly for sessions of one to two hours, for the months of the school year, and in his small but well-lit office, learned about each other and contemplated the scope of his task. And when each session's time had expired, he turned without a second's hesitation, to lend himself with full attention and vigor to the next, wholly unrelated task.

Within the purview of our discussions came every area of focus likely to befall a high school principal; and, because of his uniqueness as an individual, Peter revealed the breadth and depth of his mind as it approached his central professional question: How to offer a certain group of kids a high school education which will work for them (first, by treating them as individuals), move them along with positivism through the adolescent experience, and, without onerous and neurosis-inducing single-mindedness, prepare them for further education or a life in the commerce of society?

From our discussions eventually emerged several themes; there were themes also to Gateway's intentions, which were not always the same as our highlighted points, but which together with them excoriated the dimensions of Peter's fount of educational planning, and formed the basis of our dialogues. These themes, expressed in interrogative form, include:

• How does a school create a curriculum which will meet the exacting standards of the most demanding college preparatory programs, and still build in pathways for uniqueness of study and particularity of individual student need?

• How can a school provide resources to help students through the unpredictable and often fearful journey adolescence requires they take?

• What is the best use a school can make of outside learning resources—specifically, learning disability programs, remedial-education modules, assessment programs, and other relevant "imports" to give range and depth to the school's needs fulfillment?

• How can a school define its nature as an institution embracing diversity, community, tolerance, respect for others, integrity, and offer in its own performance the best role model for these qualities?

• How does a school create avenues within its structure to accommodate those whose perceived deficits—academic, social, personal—constrain a fuller growth?

These topics are thoroughly treated as they appear in the canon of Gateway's year. But by design this is not a book organized neatly into "themes." It is, rather, a witness to an educator found *in situ*. The context of his message stems from his daily experience on the job, and the text rolls along on those quotidian tracks. Although the dialogue project was designed to commence and conclude with the calendar school year—and, barring some additional task-tidying efforts it did— the full scope of the ideas generated by Peter's thinking courses onward, throughout the four-year high school experience, and much beyond. This is as it should be: *Indispensable Tools,* like all well-meaning journalism, is a product of its time, and some of the public events depicted in this book will be history by the time of its reading.

Each such historical incident, however, affected this high school principal in a critical way; and with history's inevitable revisitation, Peter Thorp's response to these problems should be instructive for other principals later, facing fiscal, pedagogical, assessment, sexual, and behavioral issues with the generations of students yet ahead. These issues and other fingernail-biting epochs color the cyclorama of Peter Thorp's year; contained now, a period after their appearance, they were then enigmatic, uncertain, and of concern. That concern is in force here.

Because the larger story of Gateway extends to others besides Peter Thorp, I ventured to other sources for historical or other information. From Lisille Matheson, Gateway's instigator and Board Chair, I heard a tale as exciting as any in modern education, about how a fistful of mothers, discontent to the breaking point with the lack of options available to their children, forged an alliance which would result, in relatively rapid order, in the institution through which their children are now coursing, and from which they will matriculate. Unrecorded but integrated throughout the process in the form of question-inspirations were commentaries from students. Kelly Oppermann is one such young person: A tenth-grade student at the school, her extraordinary energy, likeable nature, and overflowing mind helped provide the student perspective to some of the questions generated by discussions with her school's principal. I talked as well with a number of parents; the narrative draws in part from the effect of these discussions. But primarily, this book attempts to record the ruminations of a former history teacher, who had carried his vision of a special way of reaching adolescents along a career as a head administrator and ultimately into the unique setting of Gateway High School; and who, in his role as that school's leader (and urged by a relentless writer with a microphone), was willing to express those thoughts and offer them for public perusal.

Thorp's considered expressions form a marketplace of ideas of extraordinary richness and excitement. And although his own modesty would likely not permit his saying so, his ideas are provocative, and, at their best, assure parents and students alike of the presence of the invaluable and uplifting feeling of *possibility*. As Gateway's gifts to its students will prove, what is indispensable amongst the tools of learning of the school's originators is an ability to stay focused, to drive one's ideas forward through an unceasing and not-always-identifiable adversity; and never to lose sight of the fact that learning is sublime, and that through our children we hold the future in our hands.

Chapter One

BREAKING THE ICE,
AND SETTING THE SCENE

"Baby boomer parents function a lot through guilt. Both parents are busy, busy, busy working; so if they have the financial means to provide things for kids, like piano lessons and soccer and all that sort of thing, they do that instead. And the parental guilt of being not at home results in more and more stuff that the kids get involved in, and they become psychologically exhausted. Then, more and more effort comes from parents to prevent their kids from failing in any capacity, and it feeds this kind of cyclical problem. The benefit of risk-taking is that you fail every once in a while, and you learn to come to grips with failure. What's education if it isn't making mistakes? And some baby-boomer parents who try as hard as they can to keep their kid from experiencing failure. And to me, it's a mistake. It's a mistake for parents to protect their kids from failing. Because failure's going to come; and if failure comes to people for the first time when they're thirty-five, they're going to become permanently demoralized and dysfunctional. If, however, the failure comes for the first time when they're eighteen, or worse yet I suppose, fifteen or sixteen, they're going to commit suicide, or get into drugs, or whatever it might be. You know, the best education in the world is to have your kids fail a whole lot!"

14 December—*Our first session revealed a highly agitated principal, a man frustrated with the drogues on his school's—and education's—forward thrust.*

As we talked, the areas of importance began to have identities attached to them. If we didn't resolve these dilemmas, at least we unmasked them, for purposes of our dialogue.

But first: The business at hand was to see what we already knew— to give the "statement of undisputed facts," as the lawyers say—and then make an attempt at unmasking the man himself.

FELTON. Who is this Peter Cahill Thorp?

THORP.   To answer that question, I go back to the fond days of yesteryear in college. I graduated in the spring of 1970, the year of the Kent State killings. I'd entered college fully intending to major in political science and then head off to law school; and at some point during that time, probably beginning in sophomore year and certainly by halfway through my junior year, I realized that political philosophy was not the course I wanted to take. I'd begun to take art history classes, and halfway through my junior year switched my major from political science to art history. The reference "A degree in art history" was a questionable commodity, even back then. So I graduated in the spring of 1970 with not a light plan in place.

I was enormously fortunate to have been identified as one of the graduating members of my class whom a particular teacher—in fact, dean of the freshmen—had identified as someone worthy of this very intriguing fellowship called the Thomas J. Watson Fellowship— "Thomas J. Watson" as in IBM Thomas J. Watson. The only limitation on this fellowship is that you cannot attend the University. It's completely independent study, and totally consistent with the 'sixties and early 'seventies concept of the "*Wanderjahr*." And I "wandered" all "jahr." When I finally reported in, the title of my topic was "A Human Scale in City Planning in Europe," which sounds relatively esoteric. My research methodology was basically going to sit in a lot of cafes in a lot of main squares, and drinking a lot of beer. And assessing human scale.

I learned a lot, and it was really intriguing. And had I been in a position to afford it, I would have thought seriously about going to graduate school in city planning and architecture. But I didn't have the money, and I also continued to be befuddled by life in the late 'sixties and early 'seventies.

Then, an art history professor with whom I'd studied got permission to begin an archaeological dig in France, in the summer of 1970. And so I began my *Wanderjahr* with four weeks in Southern France working on this dig, and ended, in my thirteenth month, doing the same thing. Those two summers formed such an extraordinary experience, so much fun, and so interesting that for the next three years I really worked odd jobs to make enough money to get myself back over to France. I was a security guard, I drove a cab, and eventually became the assistant manager of Martinetti Liquors and Grocery in the north end of Boston.

So I sold jugs of wine to little old Italian ladies and fancy prescuitto sandwiches to newly-born yuppies for three years, and I would quit every May and go to Europe for the summer, and they'd rehire me every September. Eventually I got tired of my mother weeping about her son the college graduate cutting cold-cuts for a living. And I started going back to graduate school. I went back part-time, primarily to get my credential to teach in the public sector, because I was a public school kid, and I'd gone to college with a lot of private-school people who were not from my background. Also, my parents were private school teachers. But the closer I got to the reality of settling down in getting a real job in teaching, the more I queried them and others about the field. The ability to teach in college—having been a pretty good athlete in college—seemed to indicate the natural choice of a private school teaching position in a boarding school or private school, and that's what I ended up doing.

FELTON. How did it happen, specifically?

THORP. On top of all these concerns, in the spring of 1975 I was newly-married. So the pressure was really on! I sent my resume to a bunch of folks, and this school in Colorado Springs at the foot of Pike's Peak felt that a grizzled ex-hockey player who still had all his teeth and enough experience working behind a liquor store counter and driving a cab—which, by the way, are the two best professions to get an unofficial degree in psychology—seemed to match what they were looking for. So I headed off to Colorado Springs, to begin what I thought was going to be a two-year jaunt. Eighteen years later, I finally came to the conclusion that I was a Westerner, and I wasn't going home again. So the boarding-school venue then became my professional career. Eventually I ended up a history teacher and thus converted art history into real history.

One of the things that intrigued me about the West—especially about kids in the West, and particularly the Rocky Mountain West—is that people in the West are more willing to take risks. And as a Bostonian, I felt I'd come from a place where I don't think people are as willing to take risks. In fact, I think the New England area is the least risk-taking area. It doesn't surprise me that the center of venture capitalism is Silicon Valley. So being in the West was really fun—

working in an environment where both schools and kids were really open to trying new things and take risks and developing the attitudes which I really hope to foster here at Gateway. The risk for me was to go up or down the food-chain, depending upon how you look at it, from classroom teacher to department chair to academic dean to assistant head of school to eventually wanting to become headmaster of a school. And in order to do that, I had to leave my school in Colorado and go somewhere else. So I was very fortunate to land a position as headmaster of Cate School in 1993. And Cate was an extraordinary school.

FELTON. Located—?

THORP.   Just outside Santa Barbara, in Carpenteria. It's up on the mesa, just this incredible place—one of the most selective schools in the country, with one of the most impressive college placement records.

FELTON. How old is the school?

THORP.   1910 was when it was founded, and it was founded by those who started many boarding schools in the west, these flinty New Englanders going out to the West. One Curtis Cate founded this school and he was the head for forty years, and when they wheeled him out into retirement, they named the school after him. It was called the Santa Barbara School prior to that.

FELTON. But forty years were not in the cards for *you*—?

THORP.   After five years, a sort of harmonic convergence took place, or disharmonic convergence might be a better way of describing it, not the least of which was turning fifty and especially not the least of which was that my marriage fell apart. And so it was time for a change. I made the decision to resign; I announced that in January of 1997 and then finished up in the next eighteen months. That gave the school enough time to find my replacement.

FELTON. Which puts you either back in the cab, or still slicing presciutto.

THORP. Yes! Of course, I didn't have something for my next profession, and I looked far and wide. I put over 50,000 miles on United Air Lines between January and March of 1998, and I literally looked from New York to Hong Kong. I interviewed a number of times in schools in the Far East, and I was interested in working there, because I had done some work in the Far East, and had experienced my Fulbright there for a summer. I didn't want to go as far away as to Hong Kong, for I had by then been divorced, my older daughter was graduating from high school, where I was the head, and going on to college, and so I didn't want to go too far away from her. To make a long story short, it came down to choosing between Gateway and a school in New York, just north of the Manhattan. It was a very prestigious place; and of course my daughter wanted me to take that job, because I would have been right close to her—

FELTON. She landed where?

THORP.   She's at Barnard College. She's a sophomore there. And the chronology was right: On a Monday, Lisille Matheson, Chair of the Board here at Gateway called me to say, "We've made our decision. We want you to become the founding head of the school at Gateway High School." I said, "Thank you very much, I'm getting on a plane on Tuesday, and am flying back to New York to do my final interview in New York, and I'll let you know when I get back."

I found out later that Lisa's interpretation of that response was "Thanks, but no thanks. And indeed, I started feeling that this job in New York for all sorts of reasons seemed to be the right choice. I went back there and interviewed for a day and a half of what was actually my second visit. So this was the final step of the minuet. I did that and then I flew back, and I flew back out West. That was on a Friday, and I had a long plane flight to sit there and think about it.

Somewhere over Nebraska, I said to myself, "Nah. This isn't right. New York just does not feel good. I've been there, I've done this, I've worked with these kinds of faculties, I've worked with these kinds of issues, I want something new and different."   And I concluded: "I want to try this Gateway." And so I got back, and called Lisille on Saturday, and told her, "I'm yours."   She was pretty thunderstruck, as was I. Because in part—and to bring this whole thing full circle, in part given that my roots are Irish Catholic Bostonian, I'm not genetically inclined to be a risk-taker. And this was a big risk. And *is* a big risk. But I finally had to "put up or shut up," and after espousing this for many years with kids, I finally decided that hey, maybe I should try this risk-taking stuff and see how it works out. And boy, did I get it!

FELTON.   Yes, you did! But at least as far as geography was concerned, you'd already tasted Colorado…

THORP.   Yeah. And Colorado is a very easy place to fall in love with.

As I noted, scale is something of which I'm very conscious. And the scale in the West is so grandiose, so "sublime," to use a good art-historian-critical term, that to me it's really overpowering. And at the school in Colorado I would walk from my place to the dining hall and have Pike's Peak off in the horizon over my right shoulder, and I would look to the south, to what we called the Spanish Peaks, which were about 120 miles away as the crow flies. And again, it was like standing in Pittsfield, which is at the western edge of Massachusetts, and seeing what's called the Prudential Tower out of the tallest skyscraper in Boston, which is 120 miles away. Now, in that part of the world, scale is—if you can look past the trees—you can see a little bit. So scale is something that is very important to me. Horizon is something that is very important to me. And I didn't know that until I lived in the West. The scale—and the peace of mind—to be able to see the horizon is something that is really important. And again, at Cate, my house was in a place enabling me to have a commanding view of the Channel Islands out in the Pacific. Not to mention avocado groves, and flower groves.

So of a number of lessons I learned in the West, one of them is risk-taking, and the second is that tradition is both reaffirming, but also confining. I learned risk-taking, I learned scale and space; and that is something which has become very important to me. And one of the very first things I did at Cate was to set up a study where we rewrote the mission of the school. And I wanted to make some reference to the beauty of the place, in the mission, and a lot of Cate people didn't want to do that because it wasn't part of the mission or the goals stated as to what the mission is, but they saw it as more of a reality in which we worked. And my point was that it was so integral to our mission that our experience at Cate would not be the same if you picked the school up and moved it to Fresno. The mission simply would not be the same thing. So I'm very attuned to that sort of thinking.

The third lesson I learned living in the West, particularly in New Mexico—Santa Fe became the favorite watering-hole for those of us in Colorado Springs, when we had some time—was the real spirituality, the spirituality of space and sky and color and land. I'm on the board of trustees of a school called the Native American Preparatory School, which is right outside Santa Fe, which is the second most interesting school in the country after Gateway. And so I get to go back to New Mexico four times a year and experience the spirituality of that space.

FELTON. Another Easterner named O'Keeffe managed to do all right there.

THORP. Absolutely! And seeing her as an art historian, I believed her art changed not only in terms of subject matter, in the sense of working with things in New Mexico instead of Manhattan, but one of the things which changed was scale. Her paintings were of a style in which scale really took over her work when she moved to New

Mexico. I mean, how could it not, for somebody who was so observant as she was?

FELTON. We've placed you now as a school head. I'm curious: I notice that about every seven or eight years, my college alumnae literature announces that the President is saying what a wonderful time he had, and that he's leaving. And I wonder—is that a kind of average tenure in an executive position in an academic institution? What motivates that choice of job? And then, what propels its occupant in another in that direction so soon?

THORP. You're right to raise that as a question. About ten years ago, the average tenure of a headmaster of a private school was less than five years.

FELTON. That's all?

THORP. Yes. It's a function of a number of things, and here's an illustration from today: All this morning I was downtown at a principal's meeting involving all the high school principals, which happens once a month. And between the two of us: They're profoundly depressing, because these are really wonderful people, they're good-hearted people, they work hard. But lo and behold!, this morning, a guy announced his retirement. As he said, it was time, and there was some retirement financial opportunity going on right now in the State Teacher's Retirement Association. But his real point in his words this morning was: "I'm tired. I've got friends who are dying of heart attacks, and I don't want to do that. And I get in this for kids, and I'm tired of the crap I have to put up day-to-day in my work for kids. The paperwork."

What depresses me when I go to those meetings is—well, what I'm wallowing through in this pile of paper on my desk—is the amount of incredible paperwork that one has to process. And in looking over your questions about what is my vision for Gateway, one of the things I was concerned about as I was attending a school board meeting is: To what extent are charter schools—and to what extent is Gateway specifically—going to be compromised by external forces in the political process, and a kind of regression to the mean that always seems to happen in biological spheres?

Somebody said to me recently that they know a lot of heads of schools—we were talking about the private school world—and none of them is happy. For example, there is a dramatic increase in the amount of legal minutiae that one has to put up with. There is a litany of paper you've got to submit, things you've got to be responsible for. And the whole idea of educating kids just dissipates because of the amount of time and energy and money and resource that's involved in the paper trail. And the paper trail is so out of control now that it's lost its purpose. I understand you need to keep track of kids, and I understand you need to keep records, and I understand you need to be able to lead in a legal and ethical way. But it's so complex now that it's not serving the purpose for which it's originally designed. And special education is a good example of that: It's just so totally blown out of proportion in terms of all the requirements that one has to follow, that the effort becomes following the requirements, rather than accomplishing what you're trying to do in terms of special education. So a lot of principals and a lot of heads of schools are cashing in their chips.

There was an article in this past week's edition of *Education Week*, about how difficult it is to attract superintendents to the school system. You think the life of principals is short; the life of superintendents is unbelievably short!

FELTON. That was a real firing situation, wasn't it? Involving former San Francisco Superintendent of Public Instruction Bill Rojas?

THORP. Yes—I keep stupidly asking myself: Gee, Peter, would you ever be interested in becoming a superintendent of a school district? And so far I'm able to say to myself, "You've gotta be crazy to do that!"

I've got to believe the average superintendent's tenure is not much more than two years on the average, and in some schools, they go through superintendents of schools like baseball managers on a losing team. This situation was crazy: Bill Rojas, the guy who was superintendent here in San Francisco who went to Dallas, is going through it there. Within two months of his time in Dallas, they called for his resignation over stuff which was meaningless. He's a guy whom I have very high admiration for in a lot of ways. And he comes into a school district just absolutely falling apart, and says, "Okay, I've got an idea as to how to fix it." And he gets hammered in doing it. Now, he probably did it wrong in terms of style, because he is fallible in his approach. Still, within two months they're calling for his resignation!

So it's really changed; and I think that even though a lot of improvement has taken place in getting rid of the old generation of autocrats, I think a fair amount has been lost because people are looking for "quick fixes," too quickly. There's nothing like a baby-boomer parent to extract a quick fix; I would get phone calls from a parent on his way to the airport saying, "I've got five minutes; let's take care of this problem."

You know, he's revealing his generation—of which you and I are a part—that fails to recognize that when it comes to kids and their development, "fixes" aren't that easily accomplished.

I give a talk on statistics about the baby-boomer generation. And one of the points that I make is that baby boomer parents function a lot through guilt. Both parents are busy, busy, busy working; so if they have the financial means to provide things for kids, like piano lessons and soccer and all that sort of thing, they do that instead. And the parental guilt of being not at home results in more and more stuff that the kids get involved in, and they become psychologically exhausted. Then, more and more effort comes from parents to prevent their kids from failing in any capacity, and it feeds this kind of cyclical problem. The benefit of risk-taking is that you fail every once in a while, and you learn to come to grips with failure. What's education if it isn't making mistakes? And some baby-boomer parents who try as hard as they can to keep their kid from experiencing failure. And to me, it's a mistake. It's a mistake for parents to protect their kids from failing. Because failure's going to come; and if failure comes to people for the first time when they're thirty-five, they're going to become permanently demoralized and dysfunctional. If, however, the failure comes for the first time when they're eighteen, or worse yet I suppose, fifteen or sixteen, they're going to commit suicide, or get into drugs, or whatever it might be. You know, the best education in the world is to have your kids fail a whole lot!

FELTON.   Well, how insidious, how contributory, is the fact that they may feel guilt, they may worry about failure, but they're not going to give up on their six-figure salaries to stay home and work with their kids?

THORP.   One answer is to see the problem as having stemmed from a political continuum. Reagan came into office and overturned the Rooseveltian revolution of the 1930s, the idea that government is good for you, and that government is going to be helpful to you. As people came out of the Second World War, all the good feeling, the feeling that we in government are in this together, all that went out the window, too. Reagan made government the bad guy. And that's the way it has stayed to today. The consequence of that is that our government has become dysfunctional and our politicians have become defensive. They also possess a remarkable lack of courage in the political arena and that has had a profound effect on education.

So one issue is Reagan's accomplishments in turning people off to government. The second issue is that the 'eighties turned our society very quickly into an acquisitive society. The cynicism of Watergate combined with the failed idealism of Jimmy Carter, to produce what's left, which is an attitude of "I'm going to concentrate on me, and my personal status and my personal wealth," and suddenly the tech industry takes off and people can make that kind of money. The kids have suffered as a result of this, and you can see it in all sorts of ways.

FELTON.   Well, to focus right here, let me put it this way: Do kids come in here in their designer jeans and their hundred-dollar shoes? Or is there an inroad opportunity for values to be set right here, at this level, so they don't develop those values?

THORP.   No, this is not a school where one sees designer jeans very much, and partly that's a reflection of who we are and the profile of the kids that we have coming our way. I would say, however, that where the consistency comes between the Gateway kid and the situation we've been talking about is that I don't see kids having goals that are much beyond next week. And again, it's really easy for somebody my age to look back and convince myself that at the age of fifteen, I had goals. But I do remember at least thinking about what I wanted to be. And what I wanted to accomplish. I don't remember thinking so much about how much money I wanted to have. And what I wanted to own. I mean, I was definitely the child of Depression-era parents, who were obviously—well, that whole generation's psyche was scarred by the Depression to where it wasn't acquisition they were concerned with, it was preventing loss.

So through no fault of their own, our kids here are caught up in a short range, kind of myopic sense of what's valuable in the world. And one of our tasks here is to try to open kids' eyes not only to other possibilities and other opportunities, but also to long-range goals. And I think, frankly—this is what I believe—to reopen them to the potential of youth, which is inherently more idealistic and less cynical and more interested in making a difference in having a productive life. That it isn't automatically: "I want the hundred dollar basketball shoes,"—which are probably now a hundred and sixty dollars. But I don't know if we can. They've been corrupted.

FELTON.   I fear so.

THORP.   I suppose one could now write the twenty-first-century version of the eighteenth century *Candide*. Where it was once the corruption of the church, now it would be—you tell me: The Internet, or Reagan, or Home Shopping Network, or whatever it is. So we have our work cut out for us on that.

FELTON.   That makes me wonder: My eleven-year-old, who loves basketball—when he's watching Michael Jordan selling something, does he see a guy kind of having fun and winking at everybody? Or does my kid see Jordan's aura more seriously imparted as a commercial overlay?

THORP.   The simple answer to your question is: "No, kids are not drawing the lines." And there are subtle symptoms of the problem to which we are all susceptible. As a parent I suffered two great defeats with my second daughter. The first—well, I swore that my daughters would not be taken in by the "Barbies" phenomenon. I swore that wasn't going to happen. And I lost that "big-time." Of course, happily, both of them have moved beyond it.

The second defeat—and one that was even more painful—was my younger daughter's fascination with professional basketball and Dennis Rodman, whom I think is the Devil incarnate. And I don't think she was just tweaking me. I don't think she was one of those Newtonian forces moving in opposite directions that kids get involved in; I think she did not understand why I so completely objected to everything this person stood for, with the one exception that he happened to be able to rebound pretty well. And it drove me crazy.

I suppose the third thing I was defeated about was that both of my kids had really liked rap music. I don't have a problem about the music, and when I was a kid I swore that I would never get mad about my own kids' choice of music. But when rap evolved, I found I had to deal with both of them about the idea of giving misogynist messages as music. I ask them, "Doesn't that bother you?" And they say, "Oh, you don't understand," or "They're not serious, you're just interpreting." I keep hammering: "This is not good stuff!" But I've lost on that one big-time, too.

FELTON.   You don't hear rap artists saying, "Just kidding, just kidding."

THORP.   I see the world through political lenses and, patently, we have lost moral leadership. I'm not calling for the return to the days of Cotton Mather, but I am saying that with moral leadership, some of these issues can be addressed. This is the consequence of the Monica Lewinsky matter.

Despite the obvious stupidity and inappropriateness on Clinton's part, the real cost of the episode with Monica Lewinsky is that the leader lost the opportunity to do something that very few Presidents in the twentieth century have had, even few Presidents throughout our history, and that's to have a second term. If you go back and look at Presidential administrations, with the exception of Johnson, most Presidents really made their contribution in their second term, because they weren't running for reelection. Clinton was all set up to have the opportunity to make a difference; and the difference that he was set up to make was, I think, in education. He was set up to demonstrate some political courage. I write speeches for Clinton in the shower in my head, and they run: "This is what you should be saying—'We need to change our educational system, and you parents need to look at school people in a different way and you need to look at parenting in a different way. You can't expect schools to be social service agents, which is really what they've become. And somebody's got to take responsibility for this—'" and then I envision the whole list of things I think he should have been insisting upon. And he lost! He lost the opportunity to use the bully pulpit to address the issues that I think are fundamental to this society. And I think it's a real tragedy.

In fact, it is *the* political tragedy of the second half of the twentieth century. And from World War II to Clinton, here we are. What we have at work right now is almost what I would call moral anarchy. It's not that people are immoral or amoral; it's just that what we're losing is common voice.

Hirsch's book on cultural literacy—does that ring any bells for you? E.D. Hirsch, I think it is. He came out with this book seven or eight years ago, about cultural literacy. You have a list of about five hundred things, and the notion ran, "If you know this point, you're culturally literate," and it moved like a game show. The problem is that people missed his point. His point was not so much, "If you don't know these five hundred things, you're illiterate;" the point was, "We need cultural literacy to communicate with each other. We need to have a common language so people will understand reference and nuance, and be able to communicate more effectively.

When I say things in class like, "This is going as quickly as a 78 record," as you can imagine that reference doesn't register. Or if I use a Shakespearean reference, "hoist by your own petard," chances are that few of these young folks are going to get it. Then you start seeing the evanescence of even more common phraseology. And the consequence of that is, I believe, a breakdown in communication. Historian Arthur Schlesinger wrote a book a couple of years ago which addresses that issue: "How," he asks, "do we celebrate diversity and difference?" You refer to some of this on your list of questions which we'll hopefully get a chance to talk about. How do we have this diversity, and yet at the same time not have this kind of centrifugal breaking apart in society, in a way where there are no common links?

Certainly one of the lessons I've learned at Gateway in the time this school has been going, has to do with cultural values I took for granted, which really aren't there.   And it's been a wake-up call for me; it's actually reframed my job and my task in terms of what I feel I need to work on.   The answer to the preview-list question you ask about whether I   see Gateway evolving a certain way, or whether I see Gateway as just another school with an interesting twist to it, is: I'm not sure.   In part, this is because the idea of the school is formulated without really knowing the raw material which was going to be walking in the door of the school.   And now that we have a better sense of the raw material, the program is evolving, to respond to it, which means different approaches, but which also means different assignments.   And one of these is to deal with kids on values.

We got a telephone call from a parent just yesterday, about something introduced in a sophomore humanities class.   The teacher used scatological terms, and the parent was wildly upset.   I'm not critical of the parent for being wildly upset, but it's an issue for us in terms of being more sensitive to that and conscious of that.   Still, the subject treatment this way, I'm sure, had literary merit in a way that it was not an inappropriate thing to be talking about in a classroom.   But it's that kind of culture clash where—I guess I'm hoping that I'm going to be able to be courageous, I guess that's what I'm getting at, hoping that I won't be lobotomized or emasculated every time I go through this.   But there isn't a meeting that I go to in the school district where— to keep my metaphor going—I don't feel I have to rise to assert that courage.

I was in a meeting this weekend of the California School Boards Association with two members of the Board of Education here in San Francisco, talking about charter schools.   The Board members were highly critical of the charter schools—and actually highly critical in a way that I could understand.   But I wanted these people to be pushed, to take risks!   I said, in effect, "Show me that the public schools are working as they are."   I don't think they can; and they need to take the risk of accommodating us, by letting us prove our worth!

And that's why I'm doing this.   I think it's a better way; not that I have miracles, or not that anybody here does; but I just think that trying new approaches is going to be helpful.   And might make it.

FELTON.   What will you accomplish in some of these areas? Will you allow for growth and breadth in thinking here which will seek the liberal-arts-interdisciplinary-wide- studies idea that we experienced, which were earmarks of our own education?   Can you plant this idea, set a place for it, and create a vacuum which can be filled by a growing cultural vocabulary?   Can you avoid being—"hoist on your own petard"?

THORP.   I don't know. I hope so. At school this week and last week, we're celebrating the four religious traditions that coincide religiously and culturally.   They include Hanukkah, and a Kwanzaa celebration which I thought was going to wreak havoc; and we're hoping that somebody is coming to talk on Ramadan. We came to the conclusion that we couldn't require attendance, that we were restricted merely to *offering* the kids the opportunity to attend those assemblies, because we are the public sector. And it killed me to do that!

FELTON.   Did you nonetheless get a turnout?

THORP.   Yeah. We held them in our twice-weekly assemblies, adding: "If you don't want to attend, you have that option."   And the first time, before the Hanukkah one, somewhere between thirty and forty kids got up and left.   That was about fifteen percent of the students. Twenty percent. The second one, which was Kwanzaa, was smaller, and I suspect the next one might be smaller still.   And again, I appreciate that this fits in with the whole public area. But if every such issue has to end up as a Supreme Court versus ACLU case of "religion in the schools!," a lot of instructive and enlightening opportunity for fifteen-year-olds to grow will be lost. I fully support the stand that the public schools should not promote religion. There's a case in Texas right now where they're arbitrating whether they can have prayers before school football games. That's fine to debate. But the fact that I can't require my students to sit there and learn about Hanukkah and other traditions is upsetting!

It would not be the last issue to upset Peter Thorp.

We adjourned—to go celebrate Kwanzaa, and Hanukkah, and Christmas, and Ramadan.

Chapter Two

PROBLEMS IN EDUCATION—
AN INITIAL SURVEY

"The panic in part is brought about by an increasing realization that a hell of a lot is being done in education where nobody knows how to identify what works and what doesn't work. The second point is: It's the panic of "cover-your-ass" as the goal, and not "Let's not worry about how our mistakes have made us look, but rather let's figure out what good education is all about." And point three: Doing this search, this scrutiny for revelation in a particularly diverse cultural world, will require a level of risk-taking, a willingness to make mistakes, and a faith in learning from mistakes that the "cover-your-ass" school of life doesn't allow for...."

"Now,...in terms of professional development, ...you also have to be really self-critical. The best teachers are reflective, and the best teachers are self-critical, and constantly dissatisfied with what they're doing. And so there's this incredibly complex balance between satisfaction that what I did was good, and dissatisfaction that what I did wasn't good enough. A recipe for therapy if there every was one!"

31 December—*On the last day of the year, and the last day of the nineteen-hundreds, Peter Thorp and I continued our stock-taking of the future of education generally, and charter education in particular.*

Before we parted from the initial session the week before, Peter had given me to read the Education Week *article on former San Francisco Superintendent of Public Instruction Bill Rojas' troubles as Dallas' new—and newly terminated—schools chief.*

FELTON. I read the Rojas article, and some of the other pieces in the journal, and I came away with a sense that in this whole—if you will forgive the use of the word—"industry"—

THORP. No. It's a word that should be used more.

FELTON. —that there is an undercurrent of panic—

THORP. Yes!

FELTON. —a sense of lack of control that just jumped out of the writing. It's hard to describe how it happened; it probably happened because people were attempting to write in a methodical and matter-of-fact way, but about things which, as I say, there felt to me to be this thinly-cloaked panic.

THORP. I think you're absolutely right about that. And it is the panic spawned by the several sources: It is the panic which comes from greater knowledge, if that makes sense. "Ignorance is bliss"; and in the educational world, until the last ten years educators have been pretty ignorant about what works and what doesn't work. And thus in the attempt to find solutions, there were generated extraordinary misdeeds all carried out under the guise of good education. One of these was the English boarding school educational milieu, to which Curtis Cate was connected. One was the male-dominated education in so many of the so-called "prestigious" schools in early- to mid-twentieth century America. Another was to apply educational techniques which appealed to certain neurological profiles—which condemned some people to a blue-collar life instead of a white-collar life. So the panic in part is brought about by an increasing realization that a hell of a lot is being done in education where nobody knows how to identify what works and what doesn't work.

The second point is: It's the panic of "cover-your-ass" as the goal, and not "Let's not worry about how our mistakes have made us look, but rather let's figure out what good education is all about." And point three: Doing this search, this scrutiny for revelation in a particularly diverse cultural world, will require a level of risk-taking, a willingness to make mistakes, and a faith in learning from mistakes that the "cover-your-ass" school of life doesn't allow for.

And so the panic that you see in the faces of educational bureaucrats, which says: "Make sure that nobody does anything which falls outside the law, or falls outside the political weather vane," results in mad action that forces educators to scurry around like hell to come up with some kind of deflecting response such as "Get rid of that issue, and get rid of that messiah, and get rid of these 'emperor's-new-clothes' questions, until life settles down again."

It's the panic of the lawyers running the world, rather than the people who should be running the world; and school boards and boards of education and superintendents spend a fair portion of their waking hours thinking about which shoe is going to drop next, or what lawsuit is coming their way. And there is an incredible panic as a result of that.

And it's the panic of the control issue, that everything has spun out of control. And the truth is: It has! Boy, you really touched a nerve here! Based upon my observations in the last year and a half here, increasingly kids realize they have the power in schools. And they are willing to do things or not willing to do things, depending on what the issue is. You and I would never even have dreamed of acting outside the boundaries, or not responding to directives. But today's kids do, and in certain ways, they are able to get away with it.

This is the issue in the Decatur-Jesse Jackson confrontation. There, the school board suspended a pair of youths for two years for an infraction. Jackson defended them. I'm not going to say that I agree with that school board's decision to suspend those kids for two years. I mean, two years in a high school life is a kind of a death sentence, if you will. But on the other hand, Jesse gave the wrong message. Particularly to kids who probably needed some wisdom and guidance about what's appropriate behavior and what's not appropriate behavior. So there's the panic of the captain of the ship not only having plenty of time to see the iceberg up ahead, but being a leader who suddenly goes to the wheelhouse and realizes that the rudder's broken, and that he can't steer the ship out of the way of the iceberg. And the result is— incredible panic.

I think the people who are least panicked are people who know exactly what they want—the status quo, or their status quo, or at least their perception of the status quo. And they're going to do what they think is necessary to preserve their niche in this educational world in a way where they're not going to be sensibly challenged to think outside the blocks, think creatively, be reflective, be self-critical in a way that's going to produce better educational systems. I'll cite two examples:

One is that schools of education, in my opinion, are for the most part a joke. The people who run them are in league with politicians in a way where because of the credential certification requirements in states for public school teachers, you have an industry which has—to use an economic marketplace term—very little demand. It's like the Department of Motor Vehicles. If the DMV existed within market forces, there probably wouldn't be a DMV.   The reason these schools of education exist, and the reason they're able to exist in the sloppy way in which some of them operate, is they have a market.   There are all these people who want to teach in public schools, and they're required to complete credential programs.   The other status-quo preserving entity, at least in California, appears to be the California Teachers Association.   That entity seems most interested in legislation which will preserve schools the way they've been, and it doesn't seem to be equally aggressive in developing legislative initiatives which will get at some of the key issues in education.

So: There's a lot of panic out there, indeed.

Another unsettling issue is the whole college enrollment / admission situation.   And I'm thinking again as we talked last week: All you've got to do is look in the eyes of a seventeen-year-old senior applying to college, and there's *real* panic!   When you have four thousand or seven thousand or whatever the number was of 4.0 grade point valedictorians being turned down by Berkeley, something's wrong with the system.   If these kids are worthy of going to Berkeley, what's the problem with the supply-and-demand?

Now, I think the good news eventually—and it may cost us a generation of kids—eventually the satellite campuses of the University of California system are going to get much closer to Berkeley than they have been.   I think that certainly UC-Santa Barbara has really ratcheted up in the last decade.   Certainly Governor Gray Davis has many extraordinary problems, and there are many others, but quite generally I think the Regents are beginning to recognize that you can't put all your money in the Berkeley basket, you've got to spread the wealth around, so you distribute the interest around.

Finally, there's panic because I don't think the Federal government knows what the hell it's doing. This morning, the Federal judge in Ohio overturned the voucher law in Cleveland.   And so creatively-thinking people don't say, "I support vouchers," but at least they're striving for a creative approach to the problem of how to get quality education to a wider group.   And there's the panic of, "We can't do it, because the Court says you can't do it."   It's like the Supreme Court in the 1930s that drove Roosevelt crazy, given some of the things he was trying to do.   Yep, there's a lot of panic.

FELTON.   Well, let's go back here a moment, conceptually. Earlier today, you suggested something that I don't like to think is operative.   We all know that intellectuality, the world of ideas, moves forward by people like Einstein and Bucky Fuller; but we also know that these special people move along in their very small capsule, and they have an enormous miles- and years-long metaphorical rubber band behind them, which is tied to the slower society; and that band eventually tensions and pulls society up to their level many years later. We understand that this is the relationship between genius and all the rest of us. But what you suggested, it seems to me, was that educators, who should be somewhere between the two—

THORP. Yes...

FELTON. —instead are acting more like lower- to middle-level Government Services workers at a VA hospital or a post office who are playing it safe, who have done the math of their job, and have made the calculations to decide just how much effort they need to put out each day without working up a sweat, and then multiply that times forty years. And I shudder to think that an educator would consider behaving in that way. Now let me read you the question I wrote after I read the Rojas piece—and it relates to you: "How does a far-thinking administrator become effective in a professional environment of lemmings and sheep?" I think of the affirmative action issue—where do you look? What are you going to do to be more at the forefront, and yet not constantly be disappointed or demoralized?

THORP. Well, let's take one case again and see. My criticism of the California Teachers Association, for example, is not in any way a criticism of *teachers* who are members of the CTA.

FELTON. Sure.

THORP. But it's a criticism of the organization that I think has lost sight of what the goal is. To be fair to teachers at this level—and I know that your question speaks to administrators—but to be fair to teachers, what I don't think has been lost is the passion of Socrates for education, the passion of making a difference in kids lives. To the contrary, one can make the case, I suppose, of saying that the commitment and the dedication and the passion is greater now than it's ever been because the hurdles are bigger than they've ever been, as are the challenges and the obstacles and the resources. So for people who are "hanging in there" in educational circles, their sense of "calling" almost in the theological sense might even be stronger than it was previously. The criticism therefore needs to be doled out equally to those forces of society which have contributed to teachers feeling unsupported. And in innumerable ways, people support things that get in the way of kids' lives.

FELTON. Yes.

THORP. So from my perspective, the question you posed—if I can rephrase it in such as way as to leave it consistent with your intent—to me the teachers' dilemma boils down to a personal and professional satisfaction at one level, combined with the sense of making a difference and having an impact. To me that's all jumbled together; I wouldn't be doing this if I didn't want to get personal and professional satisfaction and also wanted to make a difference.

Partly, it's a function of maturity or age, if those are synonymous, where the patience of age may help one weather the storm of lemmings and sheep. But also, however, you run the risk of losing sight of the essence of your mission, and compromising too much. And I've got to tell you that's something I wrestle with a lot personally. One person's compromise is effective political strategy. Another person's compromise is cashing in your chips, and losing sight of your mission and your real purpose for being there. And I'm constantly trying to figure out where a decision I make falls on that spectrum. And I'm very mindful of either a particular decision in which I might be compromising my principles for reasons I think are appropriate, and then I wake up the next morning saying, "I can't believe I did that!" But the one frankly that's more insidious is a series of small decisions after which I wake up three months later, and say: "I can't believe I did that; I can't believe this is now where we are!," as a result of that. That equally is of concern to me.

Still, the personal and professional satisfaction component which keeps somebody like me going is, I suppose, a very personal thing. I don't know what it is. For me it can come from having a good conversation with a kid, from a good day at school, from a relatively minor moment—or "teaching moment," as I call it, because I do recognize after this many years that the payoffs in education are very seldom immediate. It's very seldom that a kid comes up to you at the end of a class and says, "You know, Mr. Thorp, that is a really profoundly life-changing experience I just had in your classroom!" I haven't had too many of those in twenty-five years. But I *have* had letters ten or fifteen years later—which said, "You know when you said this to me twenty years ago? It really changed my life."

FELTON. That's great!

THORP. —And you say to yourself, "I don't even remember the incident." But you get your satisfactions where you can get them; and it provides security, it provides satisfaction, it provides sanctity, if you know you can go to a place in a profession and get satisfaction. I am both self-critical and externally criticized at times for the amount of time I spend on daily stuff in school, and being the advisor of a group of student advisees, for example. And I do it for a whole bunch of reasons, not the least of which is the selfish need I have to take an interest in the kids. And that's why I got in this business, not to deal with school work!

FELTON. We've mentioned Rojas. What about education at the top levels?

THORP. There isn't really insightful leadership at the national level on these questions. I like Vice President Al Gore, I think Al Gore is a fine person, I think he'd make a fine President. But I don't see a tremendous amount of creativity in his educational plan, which is more the typical Democratic "We'll-throw-more-money-at-it." And some other names from the 2000 Presidential Campaign come to mind. But whoever makes it to the end of the race has to be a reformer! And how does somebody who wants to be a reformer hang in there? And more importantly, I suppose: How does he appeal enough to get chosen?

I teach about reformists in history. One of the great moments I ever had in education was when I was teaching a U.S. history course line, and a high school junior in my class wrote a seventy-five page paper on the Populists. It was a phenomenal piece of scholarship and an incredibly interesting story. He knew far more about it than I did! And he taught me a lot, and got me very interested in the story of the Populists, which was this agrarian reform movement that was very interesting in the 1890s because of its interest in combining the forces of the downtrodden against the forces of the entrenched or status quo. And so these seven Democrats tried to bring out the reform movement. And the Populists got crushed. And then where it gets really interesting, and where this student's paper took it, is through the eyes of a guy named Tom Watson, who was one of the leading Populists at the time, who had been the most ardent supporter and ally of various civil rights actions. He saw the interests of the white farmer and the black sharecropper, so to speak, in common. And yet, he ended up becoming the most ardent Negro-baiting racist in the early part of the twentieth century that you could possibly imagine!

I hope there's some clarity in the point that I'm making: There's one story of what happened to a reformer. It was this incredible attempt to do a lot of good. And the Populist platform of 1892 and 1896, looked at today, makes us say, "Wow, if we'd only done that then, we'd be in a hell of a lot better shape now than we are on civil rights, and various other issues!" But Watson became so embittered by his inability to change the system that the pendulum just swung in the other direction and he became this ardent racist, and one of the worst extreme ones. I hope that something comparable doesn't happen to me; I guess that's the point that I'm trying to make! I hope I don't get to the point where I'm so frustrated and disgusted where my pendulum swings in the other direction. And I'm not sure I could speculate what direction that would be.

But I could certainly see myself having greater longevity in the school were I to have more time to try to take some of the ideas that I've got in my head and apply them on a broader scale, to speak and write, and to try to influence legislation. I just don't have time for it now. So I have to be satisfied with the good things that happen on a daily basis. I'm also the kind of person who is patient enough with the foibles of others, but I'm sometimes too tolerant of people who are in the position to make change and don't, whose political agenda, in my eyes, is anti-education, or anti-kid.

And to Rojas' great credit, and I admire him for it, he has zero patience for that kind of inaction. That makes him a weir of ideas, and it also heats the firestorms that he gets involved in. I admire that.

FELTON. That kind of dilemma begs a central question: Can you behave outlandishly if you have great ideas and you want to bring them out, or are you smarter, craftier if you aim for a lower profile? Does Rojas, or even Jesse Jackson—will that kind of individual be more effective than say, former UCLA basketball coach John Wooden?—whom nobody would look at twice, and yet who was an extremely effective leader?

THORP. They are all reformers. Reforming is complicated stuff. Particularly in a society that isn't frankly sure what it wants out of its educational system.   Richard Hofstader, one of the great political historians, essentially made a career as an intellectual historian, on the premise that America is basically an anti-intellectual society. I think there's a lot of truth in that. There's a lot of value in that. I think the practical tinkerers of the nineteenth century are now the venture capitalists in Silicon Valley. They were inspired by their education, but not necessarily because of it. Not everybody thinks you've got to go to college to be successful, and Bill Gates is on the top of that list. A certain percentage of folks don't see the link between college opportunities and other options in life, because they really haven't had exposure to a belief that would give them access to that.

But let's balance: To be sure, a whole chunk of people who don't value education or intellectual pursuit on its own merits, shouldn't necessarily be criticized for feeling that way. And I think that's where college folks need to start doing some reflection, ranging from that point we talked about—four to seven thousand 4.0 valedictorians get turned out of Berkeley—what does that say?—to the frustration at the college level about the percentage of kids coming your way who can't write their way out of a paper bag. What does that mean? The job description of a typical full professor in a college is sheer fraud. That's my opinion as a tuition-paying consumer of private college education right now. That duplicity drives up the cost of college tuition in a way that is scandalous. I can't think of a better word. And it's no wonder that college professors don't have a whole lot of influence in this society as college professors. I don't see a whole lot of influential reformers from the college ranks standing up and talking about education. I mean, who talks? College professors have influence when they become Cabinet members, when people like Robert Reich leave whatever they did and do that; but where's the college voice in the educational reform? There's former Education Secretary William Bennett, who's using the bully pulpit. And there are folks like Bill Rojas, and the current Secretary, Riley, a wonderful human being who's stuck in an Administration which has lost its influence. They're all in a situation where the Federal government is this civil service, that has a Republican Presidency going in one direction, and a Democratic Presidency going in another direction, and it basically just "does its own thing."

So there aren't real educational reformers out there in a way that you see in some areas of life, particularly business and industry, who are really willing to ask the hard questions. Again, as I said last week, that's the real tragedy of the Monica Lewinsky situation, because we're going to have to wait for the next Administration, and that Administration's second term, before we're going to get some leadership. So there goes another eight years, or two high school generations worth of kids before we get on.

Can I say one more thing about this? The other part that's scandalous is that it is remarkable how little attention is being paid to the increasing gap between the rich and the poor in this society. And education's failure to address that is unbelievable.

FELTON. Perhaps poverty is inspiring to monks; but not to teachers—?

THORP. There is an expression in Mandarin Chinese, which says teachers are the gardeners of the nation's flowers. Now, there aren't too many expressions like that in American English—except maybe "You reap what you sow"!

Part of that panic we were discussing is also the recognition of the value of a good teacher—Gore said this in the Presidential campaign's early debates—he said something like, "We need to get so many hundred thousand or millions of excellent, high-quality teachers in the schools." And he's right; but now, how are you going to do it? You're not going to do it if you pay teachers what we pay them. You're not going to do it if every time the teacher tries to impose a set of values, he or she gets called on the carpet. You're not going to get the kind of quality people in the profession that you need; not that way. And the panic that I feel, frankly, or part of the panic that I feel, is trying to attract good people into education and learn to keep them. But there's a challenge in keeping people around, particularly the people who are the kind of people you want in a school, who have other options for themselves, either other schools that could be more exciting, or other businesses.

The real challenge is: How are you going to keep good people in education, when there are all the reasons for them not to stay in education? It's a huge challenge, and it's one that I think about on a daily basis. And at Gateway, that challenge is how to keep the people here, and how to make them reformists to the point where reform is their instinct and their mission. An interesting phenomenon. And make that mission worthy enough so that they'll also want to hang around for a long time.

FELTON. When you hire a teacher, what do you look for?

THORP. Education isn't very complicated in my book; it really isn't. If you put good adults in a room with kids and let them go, good things happen. It may be overly simplified, but it's the real essence. It's not gimmicks, it's not gizmos; it's good people. And that's what I try to hire in schools, and I gather I've been pretty successful at that. But trying to keep them around is a challenge, in a profession that does not have a whole lot of external rewards. Part of the maturity issue, in terms of my own "How-do-I-put-up-with-the-lemmings?" stuff, is simply that over time you develop a capacity to reward yourself, and to pat yourself on the shoulder in a way that probably doesn't happen as much in other industries. There, the paycheck is more the reward, and the business is more the reward, and the profit margin and the bottom line are the sole concerns.

Here in education it's much less tangible in that sense, and therefore much more amorphous. So if you can't develop an ability to say, "That was a good class," or "I handled that incident with that kid well," it can be a pretty unrewarding experience. The paycheck doesn't do it, and as I commented before, you won't be walking out of class that often saying, "That was a great class." You've got to be able to reward yourself.

Now, the flip-side to me, in terms of professional development, is you also have to be really self-critical. The best teachers are reflective, and the best teachers are self-critical, and constantly dissatisfied with what they're doing. And so there's this incredibly complex balance between satisfaction that what I did was good, and dissatisfaction that what I did wasn't good enough. A recipe for therapy if there every was one!

FELTON. Do you like the rapport you have with your teachers here? Can they come into you and say, "Dammit, I really blew it on one problem today! It didn't work!" And not feel: "He's the boss. I better not tell him that...."?

THORP. I have mixed results on that. My biggest weakness as an administrator is in this area. Not wanting to—I should double that negative—Not *not* wanting to have that kind of relationship. I mean, there are some people for whom that kind of self-confronted dilemma is not even on their radar screen. But I need sometimes to help people understand that they can have those conversations in an unthreatening way. I am told that I can be a pretty intimidating person; and when you're intimidating, even when it's unintentional, and you also have the power of your position, it further complicates things.

I also have to be very careful in another way. I have to bring in my own insight on occasion, which is the insight borne of experience, to say to a teacher, "This happened to me twenty years ago, and this is how you should handle it." But I don't want that individual to walk out of a conversation like that feeling that they were wrong in not seeing the solution, or that the Principal was that much more insightful than they were because he had the solution. And so I work hard to try to resist what is a huge genetic predilection on my part, which is to be a problem-solver. I'm an excellent problem-solver; and if somebody comes in to me with a problem, I'll say: "Here are some purported solutions, let's try this..." I love solving problems, but what I've had to learn is, often people just want to come in and get a concern off their chest, or talk with you. They're not looking for solutions but are simply desirous of stating a feeling and then carrying on with things. I tend to want to leap up and say, "This is great! Let's look at this, and why don't we look at this!..." And I've learned that I can thus overwhelm people with insights or problem-solving approaches.

FELTON. So—leadership is an ongoing issue—?

THORP. The door's literally open all the time, and part of my effort to do certain things that I do in the school is to be doing as many of the same things as folks are doing, so I can understand what they're trying to do, and I also in return have a kind of credibility that I wouldn't have if I weren't doing some of this stuff. But my biggest Achilles' heel as an administrator is that kind of personal connection.

I've wrestled with this a lot over the years, and it continues to be something that I have to think about a lot. I mean—I don't think this is obvious; but I'm actually a very shy and introverted person!   And so for me, it's work to engage in that kind of a conversation. It's not bad work, it's not something I in any way dislike; but it's work, it's not my way to relax if I have to go to a party. Parties are *hard* work for me! My way to relax is to sit in a chair by myself and read a book or a magazine and just kind of restore my spirit—from inside. I've gotten as far as I have and am in the position I'm in and have been able to do the things that I do, including stand up in front of people and speak in a relatively relaxed way; so therefore some adjudge that I must be a very extroverted guy.   If I find I'm not making that kind of personal connection, I therefore assume it must be because people don't like me or are not interested in me, when in fact it's probably because I'm really shy. This was one reason I was not a good match with my first wife.

FELTON.   In the world of theater and film production—a world very much hierarchically ordered—it's very easy for a director to give a line reading, to say, "This is how you should think about this, this is how you should say the line, this is how you should play the part. Now do what I do." It's a hell of a lot harder to be Socratic about it. To take a back door approach, and pull someone in. I completely understand your personality and your leadership style, because one of the first things I felt on acquaintance with Gateway—and my son's mother felt the same—was your availability as a person. You know the French translation of that word is, richer: *disponibilité* as a concept is a so much larger concept than being "available" to someone; and your aura carries that extra meaning.   It's there despite any uncertainties you might feel about your persona, and that obviously registers with people.

I wondered about something connected here, in the sense of how bureaucratic works best. We tend in society to see an administrator or a superintendent as the CEO; but this is actually entirely the wrong kind of model. I mean, it's true if you're in the business world, you can say: Well, Charles E. Wilson ran the Air Force, therefore of course Charlie Wilson can run GM, and he ran a Cabinet post, and he could probably have run Campbell Soup just fine.   And he did not have to have any interest in internal combustion, or tomato puree, or anything else, even jets.   But he was able to be executive in all those spheres. But we as a public don't tend to want that.   So if a Rojas stands up—if somebody with ideas stands up there, it just might be that nobody will pay much heed.

THORP.   What you're asking is the question of leadership. And leadership involves not so much intellect as it involves being connected. One of the huge figures, one of the people I admire in the twentieth century, is Roosevelt. Now I don't think FDR could be accused of being an intellect really; but he had enough breeding that he could carry off a dinner party. He was someone who connected to people. And Clinton has perhaps had the ability to connect—not surprisingly, especially with women. There are women I know who have been in his presence who just come away "ga-ga." He has less intellect than charisma, for sure, but he seems to have that kind of influence.

This is a nation that appears to be best led by people who are able to touch the masses in a way that some of our brightest, most capable people—President Carter being one of them—were unable to do. And speaking personally in a sense, I know I'm a pretty bright guy; I'm not the brightest guy on the block by any stretch of the imagination, but I also have some pretty clear thinking about educational issues, and I can hold my own against most thinkers in education. On the other hand, the real question for me is my abilities to lead people to the mountain, or the valley, depending upon which direction we're going. And I think a lot about this sort of problem. The American people develop more passion about people who are less threatening to them than people who manifest a challenge. This is either because their ideas are threatening—Carter's "malaise" comment to some extent is an example—or who are threatening to them because they're coming from a place that few people can relate to; there is an intimidation factor in that. And what I don't think has happened in American education is the advent of a terribly sympathetic educational thinker who's been able to connect with people in a way that would get them excited about *real* educational reform.

It's the real question for education. Can we produce somebody who knows enough about education to reach the people in a way that they haven't been reached, to restore some of the sanity to a world which *was* sane forty years ago. And that's where we need an educational leader who is not a college professor, but is somebody who can get to Joe Six-Pak and say, "This is what you've got to be a part of in order to make schools different."

And frankly, one of the reasons why I think the charter school movement is full of hope is because I think the kind of people who come to charter schools are the kind of "Joe Six-Pak" folks, who are real middle-class folks who are working for the best for their kids. And I think this movement is starting to unlock some of that support for education. I mean, I don't know if I'm a good example or not, but when I speak to our parents, people seem to respond to what I'm saying, and think that what I'm saying is interesting and insightful tells me that somebody like me with a broader national impact could in fact make a difference.

In my weak moments, I think, "Okay, what I should be doing is running for office, and really see if I could change things in a legislative way." Then I get sober very quickly and realize what a sad idea that is! But true leadership is something I think a lot about, and meaningful, day-to-day and leadership is something of which I have some big doses, but also have some big gaps. And I admire people who can connect with other people more easily than I can.

FELTON.   Well, the essence of a point you made about the connection with the student five years later, who said to you, "Look what you did for me!," is that it doesn't happen very often. Clearly, the unhappy corollary to that is the teacher who cannot see the deleterious things that are happening that he'll read about, rather than be told—and not in a letter from a student.

Let me ask the question which is actually the question down the line with which we want to finish this book: Do you think you'll want to go back to teaching when this is over?—when the balance of your active work life is complete?

THORP.   I'd love to teach first grade. I'm utterly unqualified to do that, but I would love to teach kids who have yet to be touched by the withering hand of cynicism. And by the time they get to the ninth grade, particularly in the city, they're pretty cynical. You can't be a good San Franciscan and not be cynical, it seems to me. Which is too bad. It's kind of a down side of the wonderfulness of this city, that I think the typical San Franciscan is kind of cynical.

There is a U.S. History textbook, by Thomas Kennedy and Thomas Bailey. In a chapter on the Antebellum South, the whites loved the Negro as an individual, and hated him as a race. In the North, they loved the Negro as a race, and hated him as an individual. And there are parallels in education to that!   I'm trying to get people to understand that you can love kids as an individual and still kind of throw up your hands about "these teenagers, what has God wrought!" There'll still be satisfaction out of working with kids; it connects all this, and makes education really satisfying. But the idea of teaching at the first grade level is the most interesting one to me.

FELTON. Combating cynicism surely ranks as a positive goal.

THORP. The cynicism in San Francisco is far more *ad hominem*, I think, than back in New England, where you have this kind of regional cynicism that says, this is the hub of the universe, so therefore anything beyond our immediate purview is second-class at best. In San Francisco, that New England cynicism is combined with a very strong notion of "I am my brother's keeper." And here in this great Western city that feeling is even refined further: It appears to me that there is much less of "I-am-my-brother's-keeper" sense to it, and much more of a "We're-all-equal" stretch to it. There is this kind of regional difference including cynicism, and there's a lot of cynicism in this city. And that pervades the educational setup as well. For thirteen-year-olds coming up, they're kind of cynical. And I'd like to change that sense of things

FELTON. Well, go down to Van Ness and look at the building— a school, which now houses the offices of the School District. This mausoleum once was filled with young voices, and now looks like a bunch of dirty needles in the dust.

THORP. Which will collapse on itself.

FELTON. You talked last time about risk-taking, and we've touched on it today. How do you impart that value to kids—kids whom you want to teach to have inspiration, to be able to jump off in a daring way—and yet you want them to be tempered by maturity when that comes along? You've really embraced that idea, and it's a hard idea. It's the age where you really can make the demand, but there may not be the tools yet to enable them to pick up your challenge.

THORP. I'll give you a quick answer, even though it deserves a long one. The best outdoor educator I've ever seen at work is a guy with whom I worked in Colorado Springs. This is somebody who has led an expedition to Everest. This guy is a world-class mountaineer. His outdoor education is such a valuable route to personal growth and education. He has said that the trick with kids is to put them in situations where they perceive risk when in fact there is none. He means, you can have them hanging from a wall—which seems an incredible risk—when in fact there is no risk, because every conceivable safety precaution is in place. And you can take that statement, and figure out ways to apply it to all sorts of other venues of education.

To me, it can help define what education is all about. To a kid in a math class, the perception of risk might be in taking a different route to a geometry solution, and yet having created a situation where there is no risk, either because you've trained the kid so well that you know he or she is going to get to the right answer, or because you've created a climate where an answer is utterly wrong, but the kid is going to come away feeling fine about that, because of the support of the environment. Then you have things humming in life, and you have a good situation.

And I would have to believe in your own experience that you can probably flash back on some incidents in your own education where you were put in risk-taking situations which you either succeeded or failed in, but probably gained from moving through the risk, even though in retrospect you might have recognized there was less risk in that situation than you thought. And maybe that was the case because you were working with a good educator, who set it up that way, and whatever he or she was doing, it was in a way to help you have that feeling without truly running a risk of humiliation or injury.

That to me is a definition of good education.

Chapter Three

DRAWING UP THE CONTRACT

"A good test of the success of Gateway High School is going to be whether or not we can create a culture within which kids take responsibility for other kids. I mean, literally, not responsible in the sense of "I'm my brother's keeper," as much as to see that they can play an important role in the growth and development of kids who follow them. Because kids—when the going gets tough—most kids are going to turn to other kids first, rather than to adults....

"[K]ids are being asked to grow up a lot quicker than they're developmentally prepared to do. And one of my goals is to try to help kids be children as long as they can be children. One is really swimming upstream to have this attitude. And one of the reasons you're really swimming upstream is because that's where peer pressure takes them. And more often than not, even non-malevolent peer pressure is peer pressure to be older than you are...."

"So how do you connect with kids?....The reaction of too many parents of our generation is to wash their hands of the problem. They say, "Here are the car keys"—which in a way just says: "Take your developmental problems elsewhere...."

7 January—*Any charter school, including Gateway High School, begins its existence when its precepts are formally codified in what is variously called its charter, or charter statement, or mission, or* mission statement. *In the education world of Peter Thorp, inherent dignity obtains to the phenomenon of being a student; and one of the ways this status is solemnized is by stating it, in a formal manner. Such a statement—as in any vow or proclamation—also operates in the manner of a contract. It announces intention; it defines terms; it swears allegiances; it identifies ideals; and, in an understated way, it rues transgressions.*

On the morning of the seventh day of January, our next colloquy, I entered the Principal's office in his absence. There, on one wall, appeared a poster-sized sheet of paper, presentation-style. It bore the following handwritten legend:

<u>CONTRACT</u>

What is the agreement which needs to be made?
What issues need to be addressed in the contract?
    (Homework; behavior; attendance)
What are you committed to?
What is the school committed to?
What are the consequences of meeting the terms of the
    contract?

I pondered the questions, and the tenets behind them. Is this, I wondered, a matrix for initiating student responsibility? What group had met in this office, the Principal's inner sanctum, and attempted to define the commitment and consequences of being in this high school?

We would talk about the roles and responsibilities not just of students, but of all personae in the classroom.

FELTON.   If I were to put my money on one of the best general outlets for educational information, it would be National Public Radio. A recent program touched on some of the material we've dealt with, and specifically with areas you've commented on.   This program presented an interview with Vartan Gregorian.

THORP.   Former President of Brown.

FELTON. Yes.   He's now the President of the Carnegie Corporation.   I'd like to select samples of his responses to Reporter Scott Simon's questions, and assess your commentary on Gregorian's point of view.

This scholar moves through viewing education today as training, due to technology.   He comments that a teacher in 1950 worked knowingly and methodically—from an established textbook, but that today's revolution in communication, technology, pop culture, and so forth, makes that impossible. In effect, he says, that cultural speed has robbed the teacher of his authority, his solidity.

Simon asks: "What about students? How is the role, what it takes to be a student, changed?" And Gregorian answers: "Students are much more adult now. They come to school with much more experience. Much more traumatic experiences: abuse, loneliness, poverty." This, he asserts, affects the exalted position teachers once had in our society. "Of all the professions I know," he says, "that is noblest of all, because it deals with the future, it deals with potentiality. But gradually what has happened in our society, and students are aware of this, we value not who you are, but more and more, what you have. And as a result the teaching profession does not get well-paid.... So students are noting the teaching profession not to be an ideal profession for them to go into." Gregorian sees education nonetheless as a lifetime learning endeavor and adventure. "And that's good," he says.

He concludes with this comment on the question you've raised— about shared cultural language. As the interviewer posits: "Are the number of common experiences and points of knowledge we have decreasing in the expanding welter of knowledge?"

Vartan Gregorian's response is pithy: "It's very hard now to have a kind of common cultural text or vocabulary that ties the nation intellectually....You only have four years in college to cover so many texts. Now, we would like you to know about American heritage. We would like you to know about the multicultural nature of America. We would like you to know about Western Europe. We'd like you to know about ancient Greece. There is so much to know now, and so little time. So as a result, one of the things we should watch out that we do not transform everything into a Reader's Digest.... I was taught that the only thing we have to worry [about] is your mind. Youth, beauty, fortune, everything is ephemeral, but the only thing that has no depreciation is one's mind. And nobody can rob you of ideas from inside—from the kind of inner joy and internal joy of being and becoming, that culture and civilization and thinking gives us."

When you hear that, are you heartened or depressed?

THORP. Well, I suspect it comes as no surprise that I agree with most of what he's saying, and certainly with the thrust of what he's saying. There's no question in my mind that the teaching profession has devolved in respects over the last half-century, both for external reasons, and internal reasons. I think the teaching profession has done things that has lessened its respect, not the least of which most recently is cheating on the New York Regents test, or that something like 75 percent of the teachers failed the Massachusetts Teachers' Competency exam. So then it becomes a self-fulfilling prophesy. Another Public Radio figure, Cokie Roberts, commented just the other day about the Congressional version of this. Ratings are highest in the polls when Congress is on recess. Probably, teachers are highest rated during the Summer.

So there's no question that that's the case. The thing that's interesting to me is what I would call the "Balkanization" of schools. I don't think it's so much that we're losing a common literacy, as I referred before, as much as what we're having is multiple literacies. "Literacy" might be an exaggeration in some case; but we're having multiple cultures at work again, with "multiculturally diverse schools," and that sort of thing. But I really talked about something more profound, and to appreciate it you go back to the mid-nineteenth century. The whole point of McGuffey's Reader was to teach *reading* and to teach *values* in one feal swoop. That probably held true, until at least the 1930s, and in some respects beyond that to the 1960s. It really wasn't until the 1960s that the dogma, or the didactic nature of our American education was exposed and rejected—for better or worse. And here we are thirty or forty years later thinking, "Well, maybe it's for the worse."

The issue that this society faces is an historical issue—trying to balance the conflict and consensus forces that existed in society from the experience of being essentially a nation of immigrants. By "immigration," I mean either literal immigration, or this almost "internal" immigration, in the form of phenomena like the civil rights movement, where people came from one place to another, either geographically or in terms of their status.

So what we have, and certainly what we see here in the schools, is Balkanized values. Again, it's true of every school in the country that you've got different cultures at work here: You have a teacher culture, and you have a kid culture, at the very least—and you hope that they intersect every once in a while.

But what's interesting to me is to watch the multiplicity of "kid values" which are, I think, more well-formed, and also more inflexible, among these kids at the age of thirteen and fourteen than I think was the case for us. But I've got to believe, looking through the lens of many years, that when we were thirteen and fourteen, we were still more *tabula rasa* than kids are today. And the challenge of being a high school teacher today is that the kids' minds are less open. It's true, in perhaps a less critical way, of classical music. And it's also true of the advent of two different interpretations of history. But to get to the salient differences, we need to launch into the issue of empathy.

Empathy is a huge issue in schools; it's a huge developmental issue for teenagers. Teenagers aren't supposed to be empathetic. I understand that, because they are experiencing such an egocentric developmental stage. But one has to hope they are working through that, to the point where they then are becoming empathetic, or can become empathetic, because they will have gotten through the egocentrism, and now recognize, "Okay, I'm all right; and maybe I know myself well enough that I can put myself in somebody else's shoes." That kind of cultural commonality is, I think, what's at work in schools.

Forgive the political reference, but I think this problem can be recognized in our political process. I was listening to the New Hampshire debate of Republican potential candidates for the Presidency; I think politics contributes to the unwillingness of politicians to take stands, courageous stands. And one of the reasons why you find it hard to take courageous stands is, it's hard to build any kind of consensus in this society. There's no majority; it's a set of single-issue group minorities that are sort of put together.

As an historian, my references are at the ready! And one of the great works of American historical literature is James Madison's Federalist Papers, Federalist No. 10, which talks about the whole issue of faction. It's a fascinating piece of analysis of how societies work, and how the majority and minority work. A second historical example is the Compromise of 1850, where they were trying to figure out how to make California a state, and California was going to come in as a free state and that was going to upset the whole balance. And Henry Clay figured out that there was no way we were going to achieve compromise on this issue—and five other key issues that were part of the thing. He was also bringing in Texas as part of the deal. This was the organization of the Western territories. So rather than trying to get everybody to agree to the five principles and vote on that, he figured out they needed to take them one at a time. And so the Compromise of 1850 is a misnomer, because it wasn't that—it was five separate votes, and you could bring together enough minority opinion at this point that it got passed.

So at the risk of sounding like a Conservative here, there is reason to be concerned that the society has lost a cultural glue. While this point of view shouldn't stultify or preclude or exclude those who are different—something disavowed because of the 'sixties—I nonetheless think we have lost the opportunity to capitalize on a sort of common experience as empathy forming, where educators can count on a certain openness to attitudes in their classrooms, and capitalize on that. A teacher might need to go further back in the process to restabilize before starting the education process.

FELTON. You bring up some points that conveniently segue into the next area I want to talk about. Let me build a situation:

I've had some experiences with my own son which have reminded me keenly, as we're all experiencing, that the teenage world is a separate world, or more precisely, a separating world. In a sense, an argument, an analogy can be offered, suggesting that teenagers are a kind of a foreign species, almost a "foreign body" that's rejected by the organism of society until we in the larger society develop some sort of "anti-rejection" mechanism. I wonder if the role of the teacher, who has to fight against that, is in part to remind us that we all were in that stage of existence once and that today's students are going to metamorphose into something else. I'm really interested that despite our overview of understanding, we stay at a remove.

There's a fascinating short piece in the *Journal of the American Medical Association's* overview of abstracts, called "Diagnosing Pediatric Pain." It talks about a scale, in the medical model, which was developed to enable you to assess pain, to discern pain, in kids. And in one sense, of course, that's a methodological approach, to help that particular diagnostic problem; but what that said to me was, "My God! We need some kind of translation device to be able to discern this most basic of emotional responses in one early stage of people who are a member of our own species!" And this reminded me that there was a remove at that stage, and that we also have the remove in respect to teenage life—that despite what happened to us, we seemed to get away from it.

This empathy issue is "front-and-center," I know, in Gateway's current quandary over the mix of its students and the surrounding community—a classic "Town-Gown" problem. Neither group seems empathetic.

One Friday night, while I was cooking dinner, my son Peter was listening to this whole roster of television shows which is pitched to teenagers, called "TGIF." The sponsors are acne creams or other adolescent-focused products, so basically the whole night's given to this age group. And I overheard a kind of set-up, a little "teaser" for a show coming up; and the teaser featured a mother and a daughter. And the dialogue, with dramatic music behind it, showed the mother confronting the girl, saying: "Are you having sex with anyone now?"

So I came out after a while, and said to Peter: "Do you think it's the right of a parent to ask a teenager whether he or she's having sex?" And he said, "Nooooooo." I said, "Okay. Do you think it's the prerogative of a parent to ask a teenager whether, if that teenager is having sex, he or she is taking appropriate safety precautions?" And he thought for a minute, and he said, "Yessssss....." He was willing to give that.

Now, he measures all his words. And like all kids, he wants to make certain that he's playing both ends against the middle with me, that he represents himself, but he wants to see how he can best acquit himself of Dad's point of view. Well, we had a kind of discussion that carried on in that theme. I then asked: "What do you think the administration of Gateway would do if a girl in the school became pregnant?" And of course, he said, "I knew you were going to ask me that!"

THORP. He had you figured out.

FELTON. Yes, sure! That's his job, isn't it? "Well," I continued, "all right—tell me what they would do." And he said, "Well, it depends. If it was a good student they'd probably say: 'This is too bad. Take some time off.'" I responded, "In other words, they'd be gentle and forgiving...?" And he said, "They'd be—nice." I then said: "What about another kind of student?" "Well," he said, "If it was, say, a kind of scuzzy girl, they'd probably say: 'I can't help you. You'll have to leave and deal with it.'" And I said, "Well, would you agree that the good student probably has personal resources and strengths to handle the solution?" "Yeah." "And a student who's sort of bordering on delinquency might not have those personal resources for handling the problem?" "Yeah...." "Then doesn't your view of the probable reaction they would have would possibly reverse what's really needed in the situation?" And he said, "Well, maybe, yeah."

And of course this inevitably hearkened back to our discussion about kids having power: How can we get closer, have our own empathetic resources come to our aid to deal with these young people who populate your school, not cut ourselves off, give them the freedom they're yearning for, allow them that development that's happening, and at the same time maybe keep the structure we want?

THORP. A big question! Well....to go back to your metaphor about the transplant and the rejection: I'd reverse it. It isn't *we* who are rejecting teenagers; it's teenagers who are rejecting *us*. And they should.

FELTON. Go on.

THORP. It's developmentally appropriate for teenagers to go through a stage where they're rejecting their parents. And adults in general. Because what they're doing is trying to define themselves, and they're trying to define themselves in opposition to the world within which they exist, which is primarily family and school. And so the pushing-away part is maddening as hell, but developmentally appropriate. And the parents who can't see that are pouring gasoline on a fire, because they're not recognizing that it's a natural process. It's not the kid is rejecting you, the parent, in that circumstance; you're *supposed* to be rejected, that's part of the drill here. And what we're concerned with: It's true here, as well, with educators. Educators need to depersonalize adolescent rejection; but it's really hard! And if you think it's hard for a parent, which it is, to depersonalize, it's also hard for a teacher to do it, and it's especially hard for a teacher who cares a great deal, to have a kid "blow you off," so to speak.

So how do you connect with kids? I mean, how do you—you know, high school is in full swing right when this is happening, and you can't say, "Okay, the solution is to start high school at the age of eighteen, when they've finally gotten through that developmental stage."

First of all, what has to happen is the recognition of the process on the part of the adult. And the balance for the adult, both parent and teacher, comes in setting limits, but doing it in a depersonalized, de-emotionalized way. That's the top job of being a parent and being a teacher. And it's damned hard, and there aren't too many guidebooks to doing it. And of course, the reaction of too many parents of our generation is to wash their hands of the problem. They say, "Here are the car keys"—which in a way just says: "Take your developmental problems elsewhere." So point one: The parent needs to figure out how to set limits, and yet to do it to the extent that's possible where the child understands why you're doing it and that it's coming from love and support, and to try to *de*-emotionalize it.

And point two: Look for allies in the process. And allies can be found in a variety of places. In some kids it might be the scoutmaster, for others it might be the priest, rabbi or minister. For others, it might be the coach, or the music teacher or horse-riding instructor, whatever it might be. When they're a little older adolescents, it might be the employer. Most interestingly, the real agenda in this process—the personal agenda for the parent—is trying to figure out whether or not your son, or anybody's child's peers, can be allies.

That to me is real interesting; and a good test of the success of Gateway High School is going to be whether or not we can create a culture within which kids take responsibility for other kids. I mean, not responsible in the sense of "I'm my brother's keeper," as much as to see that they can play an important role in the growth and development of kids who follow them. Because kids—when the going gets tough— most kids are going to turn to other kids first, rather than to adults.

To go back to your example, if a kid is pregnant, if a kid at Gateway gets pregnant, I'm not going to be the first one who knows that. A kid's friend is going to know that. And that young friend is put in an unbelievably important position about giving advice. And of course, he or she is totally unprepared to do so.

So part of what I hope will happen—not through immaculate conception, but rather through part of the programmatic stuff that we're wrestling with—is how to develop a program where kids feel that they are in a position where they can help somebody else in trouble, and feel responsible for doing that. And I want them to be able to work with the adults in that process. I've seen it work. I've seen it work really well.

FELTON. Do you mean it more in a concerted or formal conflict resolution sense? A *program* to do that? And if so, is that in place at Gateway?

THORP. Yes. It's not yet in place here. But the program that I'm most familiar with is the one that existed at my previous school, where there were ninth and tenth grade programs, and the seniors were teaching assistants. The ninth and tenth grade classes worked with faculty, and played teaching assistant roles, and assumed a fair amount of the teaching responsibility. But they were there especially to serve as a support device. This was important at school, of course; but a lot of the issues they dealt with were in the home. Cross-parental supervision entered in here. We wanted parents available as resource models.

The students were also trained to recognize that they weren't just kid advocates, but they were also there to work with the faculty to keep the channels of communication open. This is all under the heading of alliances. Geopolitical child-raising.

FELTON. When we started, when you were talking about the gutless politician who equivocates rather than being courageous, that caused me to think of the teenager who becomes rigid and dogmatic and doctrinaire, and says, "This is the way it is!" because he's foundering, and needs something really just to say, "Here it is...." It seems to me that when there's this kind of flux—which is a good word to describe the adolescent experience—there still ought to be a way for all the repositors of wisdom, to *engage*, to be able to pull. The fact that this "purveyor of wisdom" might be the parent simply underscores that he or she will need to take time out from being winsome to being a disciplinarian. Oughtn't there be a way to do this?

THORP.   I think we need to come to grips with influences that are so pervasive. And to do some reflection. I think some decades or even centuries from now, we're going to look back at this period as a time when child-rearing was not at its apex as a science. And that's not to say it was great during the Middle Ages, either; but I think there are compelling historical reasons why people are confused about how to raise children. It's been true for a long time; but I think there are some unique aspects to the confusion.

One influence we've touched briefly upon is the baby-boomer/parent generation level of permissiveness which is developmentally inappropriate and confusing in its intent. This is influence number one. Influence number two, of course, are all the other influences, the societal influences, violence—I could go on down a great list, but the two that bother me are violence and misogyny.

There's no question in my mind that kids are equipped with experience and language of a level of adult sophistication much sooner than they should be. They possess this awareness much sooner than they're equipped to deal with subtleties: They aren't discerning, for example, of the difference between flirtation and sexual harassment. Or: The difference between biological identification and misogyny. And the difference between Arnold Schwartznegger as cartoon character and Arnold Schwartznegger as violent predator-cum-killing machine.

I'm not a Freudian, but there's a Freudian recognition of the impact of culture upon development. And I think people need to take some responsibility in this. Just a single, even simplistic, glance is illuminating: As an educator, I see the consequences of kids who are latchkey kids. I see the consequences of kids who are sneaking into R-rated movies at the age of ten. I see the consequences of kids who are listening to misogynist music—and again, the list goes on. Now, I believe as an educator one primary purpose is to share values and teach values. I don't back off from that; and maybe that's where I'm a little bit different; but I sure realize that, for an increasing number of kids, it's a bigger row to hoe than I thought it was going to be.

Ten years ago I was in Fiji right at the time they were debating whether or not they were going to allow television. And my response was: "Don't do it! Don't do it!" And they did allow it, and within a year they had a coup! Television is—television for the "unfiltering"— for the person who cannot filter—is pretty nasty stuff. And powerfully influential stuff. And we see the statistics, and see where kids average six hours a day of TV. That's a hell of a lot more time than parents are spending with them, but the simple nature of the fact is that people have to put bread on the table. So we're entrusting our kids to being raised by people I'm not sure we really want to have them raise them.

So kids are being asked to grow up a lot quicker than they're developmentally prepared to do. And one of my goals is to try to help kids be children as long as they can be children. One is really swimming upstream to have this attitude. And one of the reasons you're really swimming upstream is because that's where peer pressure takes them. And more often than not, even nonmalevolent peer pressure is peer pressure to be older than you are.

FELTON. Let's explore for a moment your point of "letting them stay children longer—and let's think of the analogy of a broken limb, or some injury, which heals over, but at times of stress later comes to the surface again. And in the new crisis, the person drops back to that stage. And of course, a "skipped" stage is an example of a paucity, a hole that is going to haunt someone later.

I'd like to touch upon divorce as an influence in adolescent behavior, and as a symptom to be considered in all developmental stages we've discussed so far—identification, empathy, and so on. I have a very mature eleven-year-old, and a kind of taciturn, ambivalent sixteen-year-old. And there's a kind of natural centripetal energy to be buddies, to tend to want to "equalize" rather than maintain the stances that were the nuclear stances before a divorce interceded in our lives. I enjoyed that at first; but then I realized that that's a trap, and a trick, and I get caught up in it, and there are moments when it comes time to be the disciplinarian or whatever calls attention to that, we go back to that injury. But those fissures, those injuries that those kids sustained because of the divorce or whatever, are going to re-emerge; and their efforts to surmount it by being "older" is not going to help.

THORP. Well, Freud, of course, would say that divorce has removed the Oedipal rivalry. So now you're able to be buddies at a time when in a way you weren't otherwise. But more often than not it's a very dysfunctional bonding. Parents in a rancorous divorce become really dysfunctional around children in terms of their need to "get at the other," the ex-spouse, through the kid, or outdo the other spouse through the kid, or outdo the other spouse through the kid. What's common is the opportunity for greater closeness between single parent and children than might have been the case when everybody was living under the same roof, all "lovey-dovey." But there can also be some real dysfunction in that. Certainly that was true in my own experience. I mean, I have a better relationship with my two daughters now, than I did when we were an alleged family unit. And while I certainly don't advocate divorce to get to that point, a lot of good can come out of it in terms of putting an end to the pain.

I don't know if it's more powerful, one gender more so than the other. You've got sons, I've got daughters. Maybe in circumstances like this, it gives the father that much more opportunity to have time or make time with sons, and reconnect that way. I don't know. I had to meet this morning with a student's parents, separately, parents who are going through a divorce, and things were so bad we had to start from "day one" in the situation.

There's nothing to add to that, except—there's always opportunity in crisis, I guess. There's a Chinese character that puts those two terms together.

FELTON. Before we leave today—the California Governor has addressed some educational issues recently, in his "State of the State" address. Do you believe his concept of incentives will offer any meaningful succor to the teacher's lot?

THORP. You're talking about teachers' supplements?

FELTON. Supplements, and the mortgage support the Governor has offered teachers, and all of those things that were inducements for a teacher candidate to complete a credential.

THORP. I'm less sad about the credential incentive in part, because it could help address the very real teacher shortage that is already here, and is going to increase. I'm sadder about the thousand-dollar scholarships Gray Davis is offering to kids based on grade point average. Was it not to be distributed on the basis of Star test results?

FELTON. That's right.

THORP. As someone else said—Talk about rewarding the already rewarded! This will only reach the top five percent. And from the educator's point of view, we have all taught what is arguably the most frustrating scenario: The incredibly bright kid who will do a bang-up job on the Star Test, but won't do anything in class! Seeing that student profile rewarded is going to grate on some educators. Not that every kid doesn't deserve a reward, but you know—once again, it's a simplistic political solution.   It's sad that artificial inducements to teachers have to be considered in order to get people into teaching.

FELTON.   Well, we have to leave the teachers for now—while they're down!

Chapter Four

DEPRESSION, IDENTITY, AND GROWTH

"....[W]hen a kid is a quiet loner, it's really easy to jump to the conclusion that the kid is depressed. "Why," you ask yourself, "would any kid want to sit in the corner eating lunch by himself or herself? Must be depressed!" Well, maybe the kid just wants to sit by himself or herself....

"So we have to be careful. And it certainly speaks to the need of schools, especially in the public sector, to have counseling resources to address this question, both for the kids involved, and for the adults involved. This is because the kids need that kind of support, and the adults need the support to try to separate the real depression from the pseudo-depression, or the falsely-perceived depression. With this support, and invitation to insight that can follow, you can reach those kids in Columbine, Colorado, who killed twelve other students and themselves. You can get to guys like that because you will have the resources to get to them. Because those are the kids who really *are* depressed...."

"The psycho-emotional health of American teenagers is, I believe, more precarious as a society than most observers are aware....Schools are not designed to be inclusive communities....by the time you're getting to the secondary school, the typical school is a narrowing experience, rather than a broadening experience.

11 January—*A framework was being laid down to support this book's thesis, which is that a particular charter school, with a particular* *leader, was opening up new ways of growing, not only for its adolescent constituents, but for the larger community of educators, parents, taxpayers, and Board-level members of education's official world.*

It was important at this stage to learn more about the inner workings of the new school itself; and Peter would direct my attention to the people who had hired him ("Lisille Matheson, the Board Chair, and others, I think, will be able to speak with great passion and eloquence to [the school's beginning process]"). But before meeting Lisille and others, it was important for Peter Thorp to address the essential tenet of Gateway's charter—namely, that children were different, one from the others; that the school was required to celebrate that difference socially and culturally; but that it was required also to exploit that difference professionally, for the very benefit of the student who exhibited that uniqueness—each student, every student.

FELTON.   I want to throw a new feature in here, because I sense your mind would be very receptive to this approach. I'm going to call this the "Off-The-Wall" question. And we'll have one of these every so often, because even though they may not seem to be right on target, they may stimulate.

THORP. Sure.

FELTON. But another query first: We were talking a lot last time about empathy, about its developmental role, and, actually, empathy as a chevron, as an indicator of a stage of growth attained or not attained. You had mentioned that the empathy problem also had political implications. It also occurred to me that it certainly had psychological implications, in development.

One of the things that I know from my own experience, is that empathy is one of the first things to be abandoned when depression hits. We don't have strength to take that extra measure of "turning the situation around," in a depressive expanse.   I'd be interested in knowing what you feel about adolescence and depression. I'd be very interested as to whether that phenomenon is an overtly-considered element of discussion amongst you and your group, or whether it is simply something you deal with in a more unspoken way.

THORP.   I was going to wait for the "off-the-wall" question as well.

FELTON. By and by!

THORP.   Okay, then.   My response needs to be predicated by the fact that I'm not a psychologist; and so this is very much an amateur's "take" on adolescent depression; so put it in the appropriate context.

I think that most teenagers experience depression.   Can one segue from that and say: Most people experience depression in their adult lives?   I don't know.   But I think the existence or the presence of depression among adolescents or an adolescent is not in and of itself alarming.   And whether or not it's the kind of supercilious, "zit-in-the-middle-of-the-forehead" depression, or whether it's the almost-developmental presence of depression as a consequence of a certain stage between childhood and adulthood.   That's the stage where one is shifting from anything being possible to a stage when you come to grips with the fact that not everything is possible, and finding peace with that.   This is this terrible stage called adolescence, where you face a lot of rejection.   It's the rejection of asking a boy or girl to dance, or even to being rejected—a San Francisco example—being rejected at the school you really want to go to for high school.

So adolescent depression is almost redundant, at one level. Obviously, it becomes alarming when it becomes pervasive in a community; and you know as well, for example, as, for example, that the amount of adolescent depression among Native American teenage populations is pervasive community-wide.   Obviously, it's alarming if it's a pattern or an extent of depression in a certain individual.   And I've been repeatedly fooled, in my capacity as an educator, by kids whom I've thought were either *more* depressed than they were, or *less* depressed than they were.   And it is a function, I think, of the remarkable resilience of the human species, and the adolescent human species, to deal with depression in a way that—I mean, almost in a Darwinian sense, in a way that will ensure the survival of the species— the species being teenagers!

It's also a reflection on the adolescent ability to combine their newfound powers of manipulating the society around them.   And the first level of this society is their parents.   In this manipulation, the depression gets retooled to look different from what it is, because they don't want their parents to see it.   They often assume—incorrectly, in most cases, I'd like to believe—that their parents aren't part of the solution, but are part of the problem.

I've also leapt to conclusions about a kid being depressed, and of course in independent schools, or schools where you pride yourselves on knowing your students, sometimes you can know them too well, or think you know them so well, when perhaps the problem is you're not "giving them space." So when a kid is a quiet loner, it's really easy to jump to the conclusion that the kid is depressed. "Why," you ask yourself, "would any kid want to sit in the corner eating lunch by himself or herself? Must be depressed!" Well, maybe the kid just wants to sit by himself or herself. It's Freud, again: Maybe a cigar is just a cigar.

So we have to be careful. And it certainly speaks to the need of schools, especially in the public sector, to have counseling resources to address this question, both for the kids involved, and for the adults involved. This is because the kids need that kind of support, and the adults need the support to try to separate the real depression from the pseudo-depression, or the falsely-perceived depression. With this support, and invitation to insight that can follow, you can reach those kids in Columbine, Colorado, who killed twelve other students and themselves. You can get to guys like that because you will have the resources to get to them. Because those are the kids who really *are* depressed. So it's a tricky, tricky question.

As I say, I've been wrong as often as I've been right in terms of identifying kids' situation, and then to try to respond appropriately. I think an element of depression pretty much affects all teenagers, and most of it's pretty short, and relatively without permanent consequence. But there are a few kids who don't come out of those issues. And training educators to recognize the difference is part of the challenge we face. And as you might expect, most schools have a pretty high number of student-to-counselor ratios, to the point where the counselors really can't be effective. And more often than not, therefore, it takes a crisis, a psycho-emotional crisis, to generate the response from the system. And by that point, it's either too late, or again, even if it isn't too late, and that kid gets treated appropriately and well, it still leaves kids who are on the "depression fence," where Day One is normal depression and Day Two they're kind of slipping off the fence, because of something they think is really serious; and some kids unfortunately don't get the attention they deserve.

And of course, at the other end of the spectrum are the kids who are dying from family circumstances where their parents are so constantly looking for depression all the time that depression becomes fashionable! These parents see it as a way to explain normal teenage *angst*, and the developmental challenges that one faces in one's adolescent years, wherein not everybody can make the varsity baseball team, and not everybody's going to make the honor roll, and not everybody's going to get into Stanford.

FELTON. One of the things I notice sometimes about Gateway is that it has a kind of "Situation-normal-all-fouled-up" anxiety level some days, where everybody just has too many things to do, and they're running around like those grim characters in a George Grosz drawing, with people just too locked in this state, to be able to see: "Hey, this might be a problem erupting here; something's emerging here," in the way of a youngster with a developing serious depression. Is it your—is it a normal experience, or would it be certainly expected, that a teacher would come into your office and say, "Coach, we've got a problem over here, I think," or "I want to talk to you about this"? Would that be routine?

THORP. Well, sure. And it's a function of teenagers, it's a function of the population we have, it's a function of the amount of observational data we're constantly drawing in, it's a function of the way we care about kids, that we're not going to let things slide. It's also a function of, "We're not where we want to be." We're not yet where we want to be on emotional health, the psychological health issue, and I believe we have a surprising number of kids who come to us psychologically unhealthy. That's one of the lessons that I'm learning.

FELTON. Surprisingly high?

THORP. Yeah. And it's very easy for people to say: "They're all screwed up before they get to us, and look what we have to deal with!" That's not my point, although I feel that way at certain times. My point is that in dealing with this new population of kids, in a new job for me, I'm surprised to hear their stories! We hear them, when they're comfortable enough with me or the other adults in the school to start sharing those stories. And sometimes, the stories are not pretty: You know: We have some single-parent families, where spouse A simply moves into another house in Pacific Heights, and we also have the scenario where spouse B moves into a flophouse somewhere, and the kid ends up in a one-bedroom place with Mom and Mom's new boyfriend. We're expecting that kid to have those momentous interruptions in the quality of his or her life, and yet we insist he also do college-level work!

So—the psycho-emotional health of American teenagers is, I believe, more precarious as a society than most observers are aware. There are a lot families whose kids are struggling through the years of adolescence, doing the absolute best that they can, given their circumstances. And despite this effort, the "best that they can" is falling short, in terms of having their children emerge from the teenage years the way we want—with strong self-esteem, strong coping skills, strategies to address the complications of life, ambition, hope, confidence, and all the kinds of things you want your kid to have in his teenage years. It's a challenge to me to recognize the extent to which that's the case.

Now, of course, educators are critical by instinct. You know, if you said to me, "Well, Peter, of the 192 kids you have in the school, how many of them do you think have complicated psycho-emotional profiles?," maybe the number's going to be twenty percent. And so you might say, "What's the problem? Eighty percent of the kids are fine!" And the answer might be, "Yeah, but..." It's not the eighty percent of the kids who bear the brunt of this flawed development, or have to come in so I can listen to their stories.

This speaks in part to something we're wrestling with as a school, which is the allocation of our resources appropriately across the spectrum of our kids. I think it is an absolutely fair criticism of us that we are allocating a higher percentage of our resources to kids with troubles—and I used that phrase, as opposed to "troubled kids," if you see the distinction there—than perhaps makes sense for us. We need not to lose sight of the other percentage of kids who are going through normal teenage depression or anxiety or joy or discomfiture, whatever it might be. We must not over-allocate our resources in such a way that we miss the boat with those kids.

FELTON.   In many arenas, especially in a pressured world, the baseline of expectation is perfection. And if anyone slips an iota beneath that, it is a failure, it is written off, it represents a terminal problem. Nobody sees the eighty percent who were absolutely fine, who probably performed even better than some sort of normal mean. So it seems that society at large has picked that up; it's more of the "whip-cracking" problem that society has now, and perhaps we need to acknowledge that attribution of part of the stress.

One of the things I notice about Gateway kids: I don't know if I'm here more or fewer times than most people who have a reason to relate, but the behavior almost uniformly that I've seen bespeaks really good, solid, mental health. You can tell! I mean, you do make your own litmus after a while, and you have to depend on it; maybe you inflate its worth. But everywhere here, the way I see couples relate to each other—it's so open. I get a really good feeling. There are really good examples of that. There are also people who are quiet; but there's something that's very strong about that as well.

THORP.   It's helpful for me to hear that observation.

FELTON.   Is it?

THORP. Oh, sure. It's very helpful.

FELTON. Good. When I first came up today, kids were coming back from lunch. And there were two very dramatic examples of kids dealing with the rain and with the afternoon. A young couple came by, and they were joined by Evan, one of my students; and their whole body language and their way of relating was just so easy and comfortable. They weren't particularly engaged in conversation, they weren't apart; they were just sort of there, together. And sometimes, certainly, with a couple, there's touching, and sometimes there's just being in a group. And you can see the community experience in this much space, in an environment or a circumstance which does not call for any conscious awareness of it. It was telling.

One of my questions is about the "Town-and-Gown" issue. It would be very interesting to follow how the school attempts to deal with this issue, or sees it mature into a kind of fluid way of handling it.

THORP. Yes. It's not the only story of Gateway, by any stretch of the imagination; but it will be one of the key stories of Gateway. I mean, if I were writing my own book about all this, you know—there are the "Seven Levels of Troy" stories of Gateway, not the least of which is at least a couple of chapters about facilities, development of program, development of how we're trying to create the learning community that we are. But clearly, this question of having commit to this community, and having this community become a place that kids want to commit to, that kind of tautology of community, I think, is going to be if not the key story, certainly one of the top five key stories of this school.

FELTON. We will follow that. Let's earmark that point; but now, here's the "off-the-wall" question. It's a way of tying in some of what you were saying about your own personality:

I think, as I've said, we've seen some students who are bold, and outgoing, and charming and approachable. And that's very rewarding to see. But there are also some others, and I want to try and focus for a minute on these others, and tie them in with some of the comments you were making about empathy, and how you describe yourself, as someone actually who feels diffident, and in some ways perhaps at a remove—I'm not casting that in stone, but just as a way of positing here—.

THORP. No, that's what I said.

FELTON. Fair enough.

One of the ways psychologists try and teach us is a healthy way to connect, to go about adding other people to our personal society, is with eye contact. And yet my sons—and it's really true of both of them, even though they're very different—as well as some Indian tribes and other groups, shun this eye contact, and even disparage it as being confrontational, and even aggressive. You'll also remember that psychologist, a lady named Patterson, who compared the way two boys interact with the way two girls interact, where the girls are intense and facing each other one on one, and the boys are kind of next to each other, tentatively and obliquely. My view has always been—excepting for a minute that we're not talking about pathology, or evasion, or that kind of motive—if you see that, such supersensitivity really is akin to the old Native American idea about photography, of that frontal invasion as a way of capturing the soul, which is to be disparaged. With my sons, at least, I identify this kind of obliqueness in part with a certain creative personality. I think that particular reticence has a certain creative component to it.

I said "in part," though; and in my older son's case, this phenomenon exists also because he has an aural orientation, rather than a visual one. And we've determined that with testing; and he really relates best in that way, with physical obliqueness; in fact, relating "head-on," is painful for him. So obliqueness for him is not avoidance; it's actually a greater, more active contact.

I heard a program which discussed Jose Senemago and Günter Grass, the last two Nobel laureates in literature. And a participant in that discussion referred to a statement of Senemago's, which was: "You need exile in order to be creative." And in my way of thinking, the kind of diffidence that you've expressed, that you have, and that kind of oblique-but-still-supersensitive connection that my sons have with people, through that tendency to avoid eye contact, is actually an intensively active creative streak, in which the heartbeat of that personal contact is quickened in a way to urge the participants to find a creative engagement with it. And out of that comes the nature of the participants.

So to my question: How can personal traits, such as diffidence, introversion or ultrasensitivity, and these aural and visual and other sensory acuities, not uniformly be viewed with suspicion, but instead be brought more to the fore in dealing with teenagers, and promoted when they would encourage creative growth, instead of simply set aside when a more familiar factor is required to define a problem? And how can this, in its own way, build and bolster the worth of those qualities, and at least offer an alternative to the ethos our teenagers are getting out there on the street—which is, "Competitive at all costs!," "Up

Front!" "Strive to be the best!" "Captain-of-Industry is where you've got to go!" and that kind of concept of goal orientation for these kids?

THORP. What a great, great question! Let me respond in this way:

I just met this morning, totally spontaneously, with a fellow who runs a school back in Maine called the Hyde School, which is a private boarding school, and which actually has a couple of campuses, and they're getting started in the charter school movement. To sum up that school's mission much more briefly than it deserves, it's a school that's all about *attitude*, rather than aptitude. I don't know much more beyond that, although I know the boarding school world. It's a school that's really dedicated itself to making a contribution to character education.

Schools are not designed to be inclusive communities. Schools are designed—and I'm speaking of secondary schools, obviously—schools are designed to prepare kids for college, and preparing kids for college is a really rather narrowly defined prescription. Schools are designed to keep kids in school, past a certain age, also. Schools are designed to socialize, acculturate; schools are designed to promote the values of the community—all of which, and I could go on, all of which is saying that by the time you're getting to the secondary school, the typical school is a narrowing experience, rather than a broadening experience.

It is also the case that the message that kids get more often than not is: *"Don't take risks. Risks are not good!"* And I don't mean the kind of risk like drinking and driving. It's the kind which suggests: "Don't take that class which you think you might not do well in; it's not a smart move." And so, the educational world is not, on average, designed to embrace creativity. Because creativity taken to its logical extent pushes the limits of the bubble. And strains the resources, if you will, and also challenges people to understand and evaluate things that they may not be capable of understanding and evaluating.

I remember sitting in a faculty meeting, ten or fifteen years ago now, a three-hour faculty meeting debating the ethics of spell-check on computers. I mean, it was tremendously heartfelt! You can imagine the meeting: There was the chair of the English department saying, "Over my dead body!" And the point is: Creative people push the envelope. Creative people are ahead of their time. Creative people don't want to operate within the system. And systems are called "systems" because they're *systems*!! And most systems are not designed to allow for a great deal of creativity.

But I think yours is an amazingly provocative question, because it speaks to the heart of what the American schooling experience is capable of producing. And I don't have the answer to it, because on the one hand, we finished last in math tests when we're stacked up against Hong Kong, and Singapore, and all these other places. On the other hand, when you add up the Nobel prizes, there aren't too many flowing to Singapore and Hong Kong and those other places! So one has to be a little bit careful about drawing sweeping conclusions condemning the American educational system.

But there's no question that creative people have a harder time working through the school system. It's the reason why art teachers in most schools have this amazing chip on their shoulder—understandably so—that nobody appreciates them. In fact, they are second only to librarians in that feeling. The librarians have this pathological feeling that nobody appreciates them. And, they keep it up long enough that nobody does appreciate them.

But art teachers understandably feel undervalued, and the mistake that educators have made, and especially with systems that cut out the arts programs, is that the art teachers are trying to tell people that creativity should be valued rather than viewed with suspicion. Unfortunately, most art educators haven't adopted the right vocabulary. And they haven't done a good job of getting that message across. That's why we have an arts program here that we're paying a lot of money for, that technically we don't have to have as part of our program, but we're doing it because we want to make sure kids have at the very least a typical outlet that one would have through an arts program. We don't believe, of course, that that's the only way that you foster creativity.

I think what I'm hearing you ask also is a broader question: How can schools not only allow for, but celebrate difference and being different? And that's a tough one, because it brings us back to something we talked about earlier, which again is that there is never only one culture in a school. There are many cultures operating simultaneously, and where you have a terrific school—and again, I'm part of one now, and certainly have been part of one in the past, and the one in the past most recently certainly had a much longer time than Gateway as it was—it was a school that had a culture where the kids were really good to each other. And amazing in the fact that the students valued that component of the adult culture, that they accepted it as well. Having said that, there were plenty of examples where kids were not good to each other, and the kids were kids.

But difference is viewed with suspicion, and again, you know, I'm an historian, and so we start rattling off this list of historical examples where if people had only stopped for a minute and listened to the Messiah, maybe—or John the Baptist—maybe things would have been a little bit different. Or if they had listened to various people who came along at times and tried to change society for the better, or tried to show people a different way of living, maybe things would be a little different. And of course, it's ironic in this society, a nation of immigrants, where difference is viewed with such suspicion. And that's really one of the themes in American history, what I call "closing the door behind you" theme, where you get yourself in there and then you slam the door shut!

So for the Peter Feltons of this world and others, my hope at the very least is that he feels as if he's in a school where he's allowed to be different. That's Step Number One. And then we hope he'll get to the point of feeling that he's *encouraged* to be different, and not just left to be different—for then you get idiosyncratic, you get the student who's the stand-up comic, you get the iconoclast and you get the anarchist. But he should be encouraged to be different, because in his difference lies his strengths, and he'll be able to capitalize on them. And—I mean, you just taught me something about your son, which I'm now going to be much more conscious of: That when he's not looking at me, he's doing that as an effective interpersonal device for him, because visual images are staccato—or a better word is noise. And he needs to depend more on his aural input, or aural receptors. That is something that I didn't know, and that 99.9 percent of the population would never even think to discriminate between in trying to understand why somebody might be behaving in that way.

It's fascinating, actually. Eye contact is fascinating to me; and the lack thereof is fascinating to me.

FELTON. One more notion about the school, just for whatever it's worth to you: I had two experiences in my own past, that taught me to develop a way of noticing—I was immersed in two kinds of environments that were very telling, and they only later made sense to me in this way. One of them was that from about the age of three until eleven or twelve, I grew up in Oak Ridge, Tennessee. And—

THORP. Glowing in the dark!

FELTON. Something like that! And then, I had the Grinnell College experience. But the interesting point about Oak Ridge—and what I believe is mirrored to an extent in the diversity of Gateway—is that the community was this most incredibly perfect social weave; the guy who owned the house across the street was an unemployed garage mechanic who slept all day in the front yard; his neighbor was a Nobel laureate in physics; that fellow's neighbor was a former moonshiner; and *that* guy's neighbor was the psychiatrist for these incredibly high-powered people coming in from Europe and the East Coast for the Manhattan project! And of course, Grinnell had its own sort of experience because, over the course of time, when faculty families would move in, they would become part of the community. So you had agrarian, bedrock, good solid people from the Midwest, and then their neighbors, people from any manner of place who were academics. And it formed the same kind of place.

So I developed a notion of this kind of neat-mix world, or a kind of hybrid vigor, that really became an ideal learning state. Because by its very nature, it gave a dimensionality, which forced you in one way or another whether you were aware of it or not, to be aware of differences of perspectives, commonalities, and all of that. The idea of a special place.

And I think Gateway may be that for a lot of kids. I certainly think it relates to something you mentioned last time—the idea of this being the focus for these kids right now. School is the focus; this is a pretty big part of their lives. This particular school, I think, can do that in a really good way. And as I look through here, as I look at my son's teachers, the kind of available and engaging persons they are and the kind of subjects they're presenting, really offer a lot. It's a very sophisticated curriculum that kids can get. And if they get it through teachers like these, who have a terrific presence, I think that will be wonderful. It makes a big difference. And when I see some of his teachers in action, it reminds me a lot of some of those earlier living experiences, with people who had to accommodate, and put together these differences.

THORP. True! I think there are two forces at work in taking advantage of difference. There is the "difference shows up on your doorstep" difference; and there is the "difference of you showing up on somebody else's doorstep" difference. And I suspect that for you, your sensitivity to that difference was in part, and maybe in large part, a function of the fact that you're the one who moved around, and found yourself in different circumstances, and had to adapt.

And so for some of our kids, the fact that they're in a school with kids from seventy-nine different middle schools is for many of them an opportunity to take advantage of that kind of difference. But for some of the kids, they're not taking advantage of that. It's a simple observation. They can still be "themselves," as they were last year, and for years before that, because they haven't had to pick up and go to a place and survive, live, in a different environment that really challenges their previous existence or level of comfort. And this is so although it's not enough—it's necessary but not sufficient, I guess is the way to look at it.

To build a school like this, where you have all these different demographic profiles is fabulous! But you've got to continue to take it beyond that, and figure out, "Okay, now that we have got that raw material, what can we *do* about it?" And you just can't let it happen that it will spontaneously combust, and that kids are going to reach out and say, "So you're different from me? Wow! Let's have lunch!" There has to be more work in making that happen. And that's one of the things that we look at and try to figure out strategies to have that happen.

FELTON. Let's take one specific issue, just to tie things up, as we've learned a fair amount about the school in the process. In your letter of last week to the parents, you presented the idea of "The Getting-Ready-For-The-Next-Step" process. What is that all about? What are your ambitions for that, what are your notions about how you think that's going to work?

THORP. It's partly a response to the perception, the realization that there are a lot of kids who are not ready. And when I say "not ready," it doesn't mean that what I'm trying to do is to ratchet up the rat-race of the college application process even more, by getting them frantic a year earlier than they should be frantic. But again, what I realize is the world that I came from in education was able to act based upon the assumption that kids were coming to that world having "bought into" the steps. "Yes, I'm going to college." "No, there's no other option." "Yes, it makes sense." "Yes, I'm going to do what I need to do to get into the best college I can"—all that sort of thing. Not true of a fair chunk of our kids, for reasons that I'm still in the process of figuring out.

This all, of course, points to the college preparatory class. Our college prep class is typical in its adherence to the Gateway philosophy of appealing to a broad range of styles and, in this case, interests—for the kid who is ready for it, it's going to be: "Okay, let's get started in a gentle, introductory fashion, and get you to start thinking about 'The List,'" as it's called—Schindler's list taken in a different direction! We say to them: "Let's start getting honest with your parents about the financial factors which are going to come into play, and start figuring out what are we going to do about it now, in terms of pursuit of financial aid;" and "Let's start talking about the fact that whether you like it or not, there's a college application process which is probably for most of you the first marketing experience you're going to have, and guess who you've got to market? And what are you going to do to 'market' yourself?"

So for some it's a very practical head start on the process. But for some others—and it's going to be very interesting to see who ends up in the class, because, as you might have guessed, the kids who have signed up for it for the first time through tend to fall in that former category of kids who are thinking about college. Those are the kids to whom it occurs, "Aha! This is an extra boost." And the kids, frankly, for whom the course was really designed were the kids who haven't seen the value of what it is they need to do. But what I'm appreciating about the sign-up, and I'm still marketing the class to some other kids, is that I want that mix, because I want some kids to feed off other kids.

FELTON.   Will you be handling the chair?

THORP.   Yeah, I'm the teacher.

FELTON.   Good!

THORP.   It's a selfish way for me to get back into the classroom. It's also a need that I have seen that needs to be filled, and I'm the one with the most free time to do it.

FELTON.   One more observation: It occurred to me that you had mentioned that when you return in a larger context to teaching, you're going to do it with very young kids.

THORP.   Well, I would consider doing it with them.

FELTON.   And it just dawned on me that last year, the National Teacher of the Year was a Kindergarten teacher. And I know that another woman—a very interesting young woman, who won the Pulitzer in Theater, was a Kindergarten teacher who wrote her winning play as a sort of exceptional experience, had no intention of going on with dramatic writing, and was going to return to her Kindergartners as fast as she could! And I just thought that was very interesting, that we're getting away from the idea that that level of schooling is babysitting; and we're going a long, different way with it. I mean, forgetting Montessori's furrowed brow for a moment, that dismissal was the prevailing attitude.

THORP.   Well, two responses to that; and I really appreciate that you called it up, for it reminded me of something I meant to say earlier, in response to the creativity question.

Mel Levine, who's on our Advisory Board and who's this developmental neurologist-pediatrician of whom we think very highly—I remember him saying once in one of the many sessions of his

I've attended over the years, that speaking to the issue of SAT scores, there is no correlation between high SAT scores and happiness in life. In fact, if anything, there's some evidence that there's an inverse correlation between those two. There's no criterion by which you can sort of say, "Aha! This is going to be a successful adult. Because look at this factor!" But he added that there is one possible exception, and that is: There seems to be evidence that happy adults spent an inordinate amount of time as children in creative play.

FELTON. Really!

THORP. And the second thing I was going to say: It is my belief, that I need to modify into a more diplomatic way of expression at some point, that the quality of teaching and the level of education, meaning primary, secondary, are inversely correlated as well. That the worst teaching takes place in college, and the best teaching takes place in Kindergarten.

I really think, and it's one of the things we're trying to address as a school, that something switches between elementary school and God-only-knows what happens in middle school; something switches between elementary school and high school in terms of the obsession with content at the high school level. This is understandable up to a point, but this narrowing concentration is something which results in a different kind of person coming to the profession, with a different kind of mission, and making a different kind of attempt. And I think such an individual misses out on the importance of the interpersonal relationship between teacher and student.

My alma mater has this shibboleth it enjoys, about education: "The true education is a student on one end of the log, and Mark Hopkins"—who was this kind of revered nineteenth-century teacher at Williams College— "...and Mark Hopkins at the other end of the log." That's Williams' idea of the ideal vision of education. Well, it's nice when you can afford that, but it still speaks to the issue that it's a mistake, in my opinion, to overlook the relationship aspect that speaks to the ability of a teacher to have an impact on a kid. That if teachers feel that they're—at the secondary level, and certainly at the college level—if they feel that the impact they're having is as a result of the content that they're disseminating, I think they're making a mistake. Or I think they're overvaluing that, and their undervaluing other forces at work.

For me, when I go back to Williams, the old professors that I look up are people whom I loved. And that's something that we're trying to create here. And probably the biggest frustration for me, and where I have to be careful about reminding myself that I'm the adult in this, is when kids spurn my affection. It's when I'm just trying to reach out to a kid and say, "I'm here for you, and I'm supportive, and I have something to offer you." And the kid says, "Get away," that's frustrating. But I'm beginning to learn why they feel that way.

I can learn here, too.

Chapter Five

NEURAL PATHWAYS AND
OTHER ROUTES TO THE GOAL

"[W]ith each individual kid, the best perspective is the parents' perspective. Those situations where we have worked through an issue most effectively, and with the best results, have been those times when the partnership has worked well. And those circumstances which are probably most frustrating to us are those situations where we and the parents can't 'get on the same page.' A lot of finger-pointing takes place in circumstances like that. It's certainly not unique to Gateway or other schools, where if your various constituents aren't able to arrive at some kind of consensus in a situation, the situation will remain unresolved."

18 January—*A month or so into the first semester, Gateway introduced an outside service agency called "4WD"—a catchy shorthand for "Forward," as in "forward thinking."*

"4WD"'s stated intention was to offer a pilot program of reading readiness through phonological processing remediation to any Gateway student in whom preliminary assessments had detected demonstrable vision, literacy, or information-processing deficiencies. The pilot program—one "4WD" had derived from their own successful elementary-school program of similar design—would be introduced at the school and made available to any student with a diagnosed need, who wished to participate. In exchange, "4WD" would gather relevant data from the process, and use that data to refine their "package" before putting into place a wider, concerted marketing plan.

As "4WD" shared ideas in common with Mel Levine and other theoreticians of neurologically-based learning studies—all of which seemed formative to Gateway High School—I wanted more information from Peter Thorp about it.

On this meeting's occasion, Peter kept me waiting for some stretch beyond our usual starting time, as he dealt with the parent of a prospective student admittee. And—although as friendly as ever—he seemed distracted as we begin an abridged session. There was also discernible in my subject's attitude a new component of energy—a kind of inexplicable, subrosa *static. The causes of his concerns were not immediately evident as we got underway.*

FELTON. I know a man who's a psychologist, a Ph.D. and a Licensed Clinical Social Worker. And in discussing adolescents with him once, he stopped abruptly in our conversation, sort of drew himself up, and said: "The more I practice, the more I believe that problems in kids are the result of the varieties of neural pathways."

What was interesting about hearing that statement come from him is that this was a deeply humanistic person, and a humanistically-oriented psychologist, who would not immediately leap to this neurophysiological conclusion if he didn't have some compelling sense of its determinative involvement in behavior. And I know in my own sons' development, very clearly one can find places where you would seek to answer some kind of problem or trick or lack of development, or convolution that took place, by thinking neurologically. This may, indeed, be true of everyone.

I would like to tie that psychologist's remark to two phenomena: One is the school's focus on the so-called 4WD Program, and how you think that might link and how that's an expression of a way Gateway goes about dealing with certain problems. And the other is something that you said in passing, to which I responded but which we didn't explore in depth. It was that you felt there was "a surprising number of unhealthy kids who come here." I wonder if you meant that in any way connected with this statement.

THORP. The statement by the counselor?

FELTON. Yes. How might it relate to neurological problems, or needs which would result in some of those kids seeking the help of a program like 4WD?

THORP. Well, probably the most enlightening moment of our last session for me was your comment about your view of how healthy the kids are. And that kind of snapped my head a little bit; because it is good to have that kind of fresh perspective. People in schools—people in education, I think, in general—spend a lot of time "tree-watching and forest-forgetting." Or overlooking. And that's especially true in a school like this, where we advertise, if you will, that our commitment is to a personalized approach. And so you spend a lot of time working one-on-one, or some small combination of people to address situations. And of course, in any kind of community society, aberrant behavior tends to draw attention more than normal behavior. So for someone like me to say, "I see a surprising number of kids with unhealthy profiles or issues," probably is (a) an exaggeration; (b) reveals my own predilection to want to see each kid perfectly formed, perfectly happy, and to have no obstacle in life; and (c) may fail to recognize how wonderfully healthy some kids are, given how much junk they have to deal with on a daily basis. And if they weren't so incredibly healthy, they'd be—you know, fill in the blank: chronically depressed, suicidal, runaways, murderous! And any or all of the above.

So it's interesting to be reminded that as a professional, you've got to constantly check in with yourself, to make sure that your perspectives are not being skewed for one reason or another. And it sure as hell is helpful to have outside perspective come in. That's why I do believe—and I'd be curious as to your response on this—what I'm doing in the admission dog-and-pony show—I talk about partnerships. You've probably heard me say it, maybe even with your first exposure to Gateway. Of course it's a marketing thrust. But I believe it!

FELTON. Yes.

THORP. —And we're going to do our job more effectively when we have outside perspective. Of course, with each individual kid, the best perspective is the parents' perspective. Those situations where we have worked through an issue most effectively, and with the best results, have been those times when the partnership has worked well. And those circumstances which are probably most frustrating to us are those situations where we and the parents can't "get on the same page." A lot of finger-pointing takes place in circumstances like that. It's certainly not unique to Gateway or other schools, where if your various constituents aren't able to arrive at some kind of consensus in a situation, the situation will remain unresolved.

So it probably would be advisable for me, in one sense, to back off from that statement I made a week ago, about a surprising number of unhealthy kids, and to recognize that I can't lead to a generalization because I really don't have all the data I need; and secondly, even if I did, I might have to say to myself, "Look, Thorp! You've been in these schools long enough, and you can walk into a school, and you can "smell" a school with problems. If you drop me into the middle of a school I've never seen before, I can tell you about it.

So I do believe that we have a surprising number of unhealthy kids. But I need to be careful not to act on that generalization in a way where I overlook how healthy some kids are. I don't usually subscribe to all this "generational" talk; but in looking back I don't think that I had to be as resilient as kids in this age are. We had our problems, for sure. But I don't remember—and maybe it's because I was blessed by a childhood where, you know, life was okay for me for the most part, and so again I can't generalize from my own experience. But I do think generationally, we didn't have to be as resilient. And these kids do have to be resilient. And they're pretty good at it!

Now, I'm a long way away from your original connection about neurological functioning behind all this, so help me link that, if that would be helpful to you.

FELTON. All right. Let's link it this way: Another parent and I were talking last night, and she was going back a little bit into the history, as she knew it, of Gateway, talking about the advent of your own tenure here. She was talking about your coming "on board," and she had spoken about all the wonderment and the effort of two people named Lisille Matheson and Joyce McMinn and some others who formed the charter Board; and she said, "Then, when they found Peter Thorp, and he came on, his professionalism kicked in and things just soared from there!" That basically was her point.

Now, for the purposes of my comment, let's assume her remark was not adulation, but objective observation. It's interesting, therefore, to me that if you have a leadership and an administration of quality; and a faculty with the same virtues; and a parent body which is behind you and which has needs and is seeking a certain kind of educational attainment for their kids—very concerned, very caring; and a board of governors who are also concerned—you're not going to have all of those major parts of this organism, and not also have the other element, the student body, similarly cast. Taken another way: You're not going to have a "healthy" group of people promoting this enterprise, and then have the other side, the object of your attentions, not also be that way. It simply couldn't cohere as an organism unless only as a severely dysfunctional one, or unless it was a "crack outfit" of teachers and counselors with a totally different mission, that of being devoted to a full load of pathological students. So I conclude that by its nature, it's not unhealthy.

Another observation: I see the Gateway kids at lunchtime. And I hear an entirely different way that the sexes communicate with each other. It's much less—that interaction has almost none of the component of gender anxiety or cautiousness that would have marked our era. It's people *talking* to each other. Now, no one forgets that young teenagers aren't very "gender-concerned"; but nonetheless, that contact is so much healthier, if you will, so much more direct and matter-of-fact, and will lead them into, or down the paths toward citizenship and all those virtues that we want to inculcate in them. And it's really striking; you can hear it, and you can see it. The "games-playing" almost is not there at all. It's simply direct, one-to-one. To me, it was astonishing.

THORP. Have I mentioned to you a video called "The American Dream at Groton"? It speaks to this issue, which is the multi-layered cultures in an organization like this, and in a community like this. It goes back to the expression the "melting pot/salad bowl" issue in American history. And clearly, at one level, an orthodox Sephardic Jew community, just to take an example, has—one would argue—fewer cultural issues than a multicultural organization where all say, "Every culture will be celebrated and affirmed." Well, great! But what does that really mean? It's remarkable when the cultures intersect, and it's difficult when the cultures don't intersect. I'll try to explain.

The reason I was late getting going on our session here today is because today's challenge greeting the Principal upon his arrival was a situation of a student's assertion of sexual harassment. I was just meeting with a student who alleges—and I'll put it that way for now, since I haven't had the change to get any of the other side of things—who alleges some pretty direct and specific sexual harassment on the part of another kid. And without completing my initial investigation, I feel that kind of culture you described, in its sensitivity, a case of harassment is really debilitating to it.

FELTON. Sure!

THORP. —And really frustrating to somebody like me.

There's a concept in city planning called "collective irrationality." And the concept is that the sum total of a series of rational decisions is irrational. For example, in Los Angeles, it is a rational decision to get in your car and drive to work every day. But the sum total of those hundreds of thousands, millions of rational decisions is collectively irrational, because everybody makes a rational decision and yet it takes you forever to get to work, and causes the pollution problem, and all that sort of thing.

And what I wrestle with here at school is whether or not we are being collectively irrational, and whether or not *I'm* being collectively irrational, that I'm condemned to be a Rooseveltian, in the sense that I believe that I can influence people. Not in a negative way, I'd like to believe, but the fact that I have insights and thoughts and values that can positively impact people. And it's happened frequently enough that I can continue to believe I can have that impact. And where this speaks, is that it's really hard for me to come to the conclusion that I can't sit down with a kind one-on-one, walk a kid through a scenario such as I'm going to have to deal with with these kids in a sexual harassment situation, and have them leave that conversation, like St. Paul on the road to—you know, an epiphany experience. And where that rational approach on my part may be collectively irrational is that I'm failing to recognize that by not dealing with things in a broader way, and by believing in an individual's potential for evolution, for change and the potential to get it, I may be underestimating the damage that it's doing to the community. In this instance, I'm talking about a young woman and other young women who, I have to believe, are sitting back and watching to see how the school will respond to this incident. And if the school responds appropriately enough, that's going to be reaffirming; and if the school responds inappropriately in their eyes, then I've further exacerbated the situation. Even when they may have no clue as to how appropriately the school has responded. And that's one of the things you weigh in schools—which is, the individual civil rights of a kid, so to speak, versus the community's need to learn, and to grow, as a consequence of action.

It brings us back in a way to *The Scarlet Letter*. Did the Puritans have any right moves, so to speak; were the Puritans in any way wise in their approach, which was to publicly humiliate people. A friend of mine, an American director of admissions in a boarding school in Saudi Arabia, was forced to attend a public beheading.

FELTON. My God!

THORP. That's the way they do it. And as horrible as that is, it is a graphic illustration of my point. One of the things we wrestle with is how to educate a community individually and collectively. And those two things don't necessarily go in sync.

FELTON. How, tactically, do you plan to go about resolving the harassment allegation issue? I mean simply, in the rudimentary sense: Will you meet with parents? How do you foresee this will have the best way of working out?

THORP. I guess it's sort of a three-step process. It's investigation—and assuming investigation in terms of the allegation.

It's response—and one person's response is another person's punishment, which is the institution's response to the situation. And then it's education—both individually and collectively. Each one of those steps has its challenges, as you might have gathered; because more often then not, in an investigation, unless you have a witness to it, you have the "he-said" "she-said" situation. And particularly, as we all know, in many schools, in areas of sexual harassment, you really get bogged down with the "he-said, she-said" scenario; and the response/punishment part becomes critically important for us, because in the incident of sexual harassment, the way the school feels about how serious that is, it can get escalated very quickly into a question of whether or not the student should be remaining in the school.

And that brings us right to this "collective irrationality" scenario." And of course, depending on the decision you make in step two, it has an impact on step three—that is, the education. If your decision is only to eliminate the problem by expelling the kid, obviously there isn't going to be a whole lot of personal education. But you would like to think that the kid would get the message that this is so serious that he had to leave the school, and therefore he would never do it again. Well, maybe one in a hundred kids would have that reaction to it. But of course, then it's the community education that becomes important, and if you allow the kid to remain in school, because of other circumstances, or because you feel that the kid has the potential to learn, and reasons of that nature, then of course you have the possibility of greater education for the kid, and of course for the community as well. It is a tempering of your response, and tempering the justice and mercy part, which brings us all the way back two thousand years ago. And the school is nothing but a fancier Old Testament world here! An Old Testament World with computers. And that's tricky stuff. Really tricky stuff!

It transcends a whole lot of things like Algebra 1 and Spanish 1, things like that. And it puts all that stuff in perspective. Because if you're the young woman who feels that she's been victimized by sexual harassment at ten o'clock in the morning, by three o'clock in the afternoon it's pretty hard to be concentrating on Algebra.

Your original question was about the neurological basis for all this?

FELTON. It was!

THORP. Well, part of the response to that question is: It sort of depends upon where you're coming from. If you're a behaviorist, then you think that the brain controls everything. If you're a Freudian, it's the groin that controls everything. So, take your body part, and define your school of philosophy.

This is actually a very timely question, because last Friday, the faculty met with Dr. Mel Levine, whom we've talked about a little bit, and about whom you've done some reading.

FELTON. Yes.

THORP. He has devised two categories which he holds as a template against a given institution. When he came here to the school to meet with us, we posed the question: Is Gateway really a "Schools Attuned," or an "All-Kinds-Of-Mind school?"—the two labels that his organization created and is trying to figure out whether they apply to Gateway. And he sort of "wet his finger" and stuck it up in the air to see, metaphorically, which way the wind was blowing. I couldn't be here with him because I was away in Mexico. But I met with him last night, to follow up on that question. And I think as a result of the meeting last night, the two organizations became closer to each other, rather than more distant. I believe that by listening to our faculty, and listening to the questions that the faculty posed to him, he was able to understand their commitment to wanting solutions to difficult educational problems.

My thrust with him yesterday was to emphasize—and I put it a little more diplomatically and subtly than this—that I think his organization needs Gateway as much as Gateway needs his organization. This is a real school with real problems, with a nature of problems and a level of problems that are typical in traditional and established schools, but also of course manifesting problems that are a function of our newness. So in some ways, we have more problems than a school that's been around for a while. It also means, however, that we aren't encapsulated or encrusted with the solutions to problems that might have worked when they were implemented, but are no longer viable solutions—even though many cling to them. We're the kind of organization that people look at superficially, and say: "It's pretty quiet here," which is like Custer going over the last hill, and saying, "Well, it looks pretty quiet over here on the prairie." And when you take one more step, you better perceive what the problems are. I stressed to Levine as well that we are not so encrusted with solutions that we can't steer a new course pretty quickly.

So it's interesting for us to come at a really complex situation, where Mel Levine's approach is very much neurocognitive. It's all neurocognitive. And he's brilliant at defining and isolating and recognizing that. Our experience is that we see neurocognition in socio-economic contexts. And whether or not it's diet, as you once suggested—and as I think it is. I'm amazed by two aspects of our kids' physical health. One is how poorly many of them eat. Both in terms of "at all," and "what" they eat. And I'm amazed by the number of kids who have said, in passing, how poorly they sleep.

FELTON. Really! At this age?

THORP. Yeah. At this age. I'm probably generalizing unfairly, I haven't done a full survey, but we have a significant number. And I don't know what significant is, but it's at least ten percent, and I believe it's more than that—who don't sleep well. And there's probably some fair correlation between the kids who don't sleep well, and the kids who don't eat well. You've got the "double whammy" there.

So it's interesting to me that a school which began its vision with really an essentially neurocognitive mission—different learning styles, "all kinds of minds," creative pedagogical approaches, to address these different nervous styles—has taken on with this the challenge of neuro-cognition and socio-economic and, frankly, political contexts, which makes it enormously more complicated. And again, therefore, this is why I feel that Dr. Levine needs Gateway as much as we do. It's rather an "If-you-can-make-it-here-you-can-make-it-anywhere" approach to things: If we can figure out an approach in this school, then I really do think we have a model to provide to others, which is one of the missions of the school.

As I may have commented earlier: One of my many campaigns in this whole effort to challenge the educational diagnosticians, and the educational therapists, is to step outside their lucrative private practices that many of them are involved in, and to see that they have a public mission, which is to share their expertise and support with a broader socio-economic range.

I didn't see the paper this morning, but I was listening to National Public Radio on the way over, and there was some report out in the last day or so further explaining the gap between the rich and the poor in this country.

FELTON. Yes. We have much to discuss about that gap.

THORP. And you may also have seen in the paper in the last couple of days—yet another manifestation of that, which is kind of an interesting beginning of the Millenium—which is the "computer gap," as one aspect of it.

FELTON. The so-called "digital divide."

THORP. But I also believe that there is certainly an educational gap—or an educational services gap—between those who have and those who don't. And one of the things that we're trying to accomplish here, is that you'll get a full range of educational services, depending upon what your needs are, where money is not a barrier to you. Now, I'm not so naïve as to say that that's an impossible goal; because no matter what you provide, somebody with money can always get something more. But I want this school to be a place where any kid, no matter what his socio-economic circumstances are, no matter what he or she has concerns about, that student can get a full range of services. And in that sense, we're combining the mission of a school founded on a neurocognitive strategy with a school that now recognizes that you've got to do that hand-in-hand with recognition of a wider range of influences and stimuli. These are the things which cause fourteen-year-olds to be the people that they are. And that's why they present to you the kinds of challenges they do.

As I think I may have said in one of our earlier sessions, and what I hope our faculty and I communicated to Mel Levine, is that in fact, the school already has been wonderfully successful with the profile of kids for whom the school was designed. I don't know whether I see your son Peter in that category, but I'm thinking of a half dozen kids right now who have been real frustrated in other situations, who have learning disabilities, and who have come to us and have been remarkably successful. We're doing what we said we would do!

Where our mission has become much larger and more complex, and therefore more difficult, is this: We have a wider range of kids coming our way, whose profile is a combination of neurological challenge and other challenges. And if you can strip away the other challenges, the neurological stuff is—I was going to say, "Remarkably easy." That underestimates it. It is certainly *attainable*, when you have a school that's staffed by the remarkable people on this faculty, who are committed to trying to have kids be successful. It's really an amazing thing. And it's not a school that has the kind of "Harvard Law School first-year" mentality for life, which suggests without stating it that part of the goal of the first year is to weed out all but those of the "Officer-and-a-gentlemen" approach; but rather, the goal is: Every kid will be *successful*.

So there is indeed a real neurocognitive element in this. But it's more. And that's been part of my input to it. Of course, some people hearing me speak in this sense would say: "Come on! All that reveals is how naïve this guy was, and how unusual his previous experience was, where he was in this rarified world of small boarding schools." And while there's truth in that, I'm not an inherently naïve guy. I claim, too, that what I'm offering is a level of insight that may cut across a wider range than simply Gateway; and it thus can become a model for a wider range of schools which is part of its public mission.

FELTON.   Donna Stravinski, a parent here, said it for you: "This school can become a neuropsychological model—not a 'special-ed' model. Gateway is a model for some major school reform."

What I also hear in this—and we can discuss it further—is that Gateway, by dint of design, intention, genius, newness—neophyte status, too, has the license to operate by the seat of its pants, without being tied down to anything traditional or sobering or off-putting or delimiting. On the other hand, whenever you get some of these classic problems, such as the harassment issue which fell in your lap this week, it's going to age everybody very quickly, and some of the pedagogical tendrils will be reaching down to other, earlier-rooted, places. So it's hard to know; it's a tricky problem.

THORP.   It is. And it requires constant attention and vigilance.

FELTON.   Let me tell you where I would like to have gone, if we had had some time, and we can pick these up next time:

One of the things you alluded to just a few moments ago—your St. Paul allusion—referred to something from last week's time I wanted to talk to you about, about your own responsiveness to kids and theirs to you. I wanted to deal with that. I'd like to talk more about when kids come of age philosophically, as well as morally. And some of the implications of that which I feel are worth thinking about.

THORP.   It's a new semester, ahead!

FELTON.   A brave new world—?

Part Two:

THE NUTS-AND-BOLTS OF GATEWAY

A Prefatory Note

Three Key People—
One Who Got It Started;
One Who Feeds Its Coffers;
One Who Finds Its Students

At this stage in my researches—approaching the midway point of the school's academic calendar—I thought it propitious to carry out two background scrutinies: The first was to talk with some of the other people critical to Gateway's structure. And the second was to arrange to get more of an exposure to the inner workings of the school classes themselves.

As in any organization—and much as it caused a few frowns from time to time—Gateway inevitably and necessarily has evolved from an idea gestating in the minds of a handful of disaffected mothers of high-school aged students, to have emerged, in full form, as a bureaucracy. Even if human and approachable, and certainly reformist in character, Gateway nonetheless within two years based its working patterns on a traditional hierarchical structure and organization.

Three of the key individuals in that structure shared ideas and history about the school's roots and ongoing function, and in doing so gave dimensionality to Peter Thorp's reportage from "the top":

Lisille Matheson was one of the original founders of the school. For the first two years as Gateway built its substance, she served as its Board chair. Her work as initiator and guiding director conveyed much of the spirit which brought the school into being, and still, in its second year, was seeing that it did not stray from its assigned compass readings.

Gale Mondry, a lawyer seeking refuge from the world of health maintenance organizations and their legal infirmities, would also be a Gateway parent by the beginning of the school's third year. Gale is the school's Director of Development, and successfully has steered private patronage and commercial treasuries toward Gateway's development funding, in ways far beyond the imagining of the first gathering of mothers who hired Peter Thorp before there were funds to pay him! And

Meghvi Maheta, too young by a decade-and-a-half for any dual role of maternity at Gateway, capably engineers the process by which inquiring parents, District lotteries, and other means provide a student body of choice at the high school.

Their conjoined functions, and their candor, helped give dimension to the picture of Thorp, of Gateway, and of San Francisco's brave new educational process. So I planned to ask essential questions of each of these functionaries, the answers to which, I hoped, collectively would describe our field and ground:

- How did Gateway begin, and what kind of needs urged its advent?

- How did Peter Thorp come into the picture, and what do his qualities tell us about the School?

- In selecting a student, what does that choice say about the philosophy of Gateway, and what does it portend for its survival as an institution of learning at this level?

Acquiring the answers to these questions would broaden understanding of the school at large, and add, from others' eyes, more color to the portrait of Peter Thorp.

Chapter Six

THE BOARD CHAIR:
SPEAK SOFTLY, AND CARRY
AN ABSOLUTE CONVICTION

"You know, another founding mom has a daughter here. And I know that that mother's hopes for Gateway took fire with her child in mind, and we talked about this a lot; the fact was undeniable that we got into this because we saw the needs of our own children. But it's grown so far beyond that. It's no longer about her daughter or my son: It's about *these* kids! And *this* school! It's really about what this community needs. I tell prospective foundation donors that—the fact that now there are only two hundred. But our work and their money will grow to help thousands!"

Lisille Matheson, a trim, attractive woman who could easily fit in with a gathering of her daughter's fellow dancers, is otherwise as unimposing as her mission was grand. Not quite shy, but, like others at Gateway a bright person who contained her exuberance until prompted a bit to reveal such strong feelings, Matheson was an ideal choice to be the school's first Chair of the Board. As such a position—and the hard and unstoppable work she did to create the school which selected her for it—would suggest, Matheson possessed pronounced qualities of leadership; but as many connected with this particular school exhibit, her personality and the kind of leadership which it generated dovetailed perfectly with Peter Thorp's and others of the administrative body at Gateway.

We met, on a rainy San Francisco afternoon on the day following the school's first semester finals, in the office of Gateway's Director of

Development. There—Ms. Matheson taking the Kennedy rocker, and I the Arts and Crafts lounger—we talked about School Boards, parental determination, and the tide which, largely through her efforts and that of others, was rising for this new and progressive institution.

I asked what drew her to the radical stand regarding deficits she and others felt characterized public high schools.

"We took a radical stand, that's for sure."

And as for the choice of Thorp?

"I think that we had a stroke of good fortune when Peter Thorp applied for his position. We had a lot of great candidates, but also a lot of mediocre candidates. For us, it was such an unknown. And for the people applying, it was such a career risk, to take this on, and such a big job. Because not only are you forging new ground politically, and educationally, but you're forging a lot of new ground in just starting in school. That's a hard enough job as it is.

"There were four or five of us, all really hard workers who are all on equal ground: I happened to emerge as the Chair of the Board, I think, because I had more time than some of the other people. And I had—once the core group were there, I had reached out to a few other people, who made a big, big difference. So I sort of was just by chance, or "by hook or by crook" I sort of was the one who people were coming to ask some questions, because they were my friends, and I had asked them to help out on certain particular things."

What was the early structure like?

"When we started out, we were a committee, we weren't a board. We were a committee of some people who felt strongly that the San Francisco community needed another option [for high school education] in this city, needed more high schools that didn't focus on the "cream of the crop," but rather focused on all kinds of kids coming together in a very supportive environment and learning from each other. And that that kind of community was lacking. I think that we have a lot of schools—independent schools, private schools—that choose "the best and the brightest." And they're great, great schools, and those kids are going to do well no matter where they go. But I didn't—*we* didn't feel that there were enough schools that kids who were "B" and "C" students, some kids who have some learning differences, but can still do well in a college preparatory curriculum, were getting a fair shake out there. In fact, they were not getting a fair education at all.

"So our thinking, of putting high-functioning kids, middle-functioning kids, kids with learning differences, all together in a very cooperative, supportive place, where their individual learning styles—and everyone learns differently—were celebrated and supported and understood, was a really important goal. Then—we met with a lot of principals and headmasters: Several at local high schools, and even one principal from an elementary school. That may seem odd, but elementary school heads are concerned about where kids are going to go, how to place them in high school. It was a valuable contribution.

"Shortly thereafter, when Gale Mondry, now our Director Development, joined us, we just sort of made this transition to form a Board of Trustees. Others of that original group were terribly important to us in those early days.

When were those "early days"?

"In June or July of 1997, we were incorporated. And that was the transition of going from a committee to a board. The next move was to talk to yet another group of heads of schools and see about putting in a learning center."

From there, 'networking' contacts became operative, in rapid succession. An advisory group developed. Kathleen Alioto, a very visible member of a famous San Francisco family, came into the picture.

"Kathleen had a lot of ideas for us. She was really committed to public education. So she really said, 'You know, I love what you're doing, and I'll advise you in any way I can; but I want to do it with public schools! I'm doing public education.' And we were not sure then what we were doing."

The group started going to some independent schools. One friend, a member of nearby Marin Academy's board, advised, as Matheson put it:

"'Go to the head of our school, and talk to him. We're looking for a population of kids who maybe aren't diagnosed, but they have some learning differences. And we need to figure out how to support those kids.' Then suddenly, people from every school we canvassed recognized that there kids with learning disabilities in those schools, and they began to hire learning specialists, and write a big grants, and get moneys to put learning centers into those schools.

"Now, most kids at these schools were very high-functioning kids. But three years ago, nobody was willing to take the risk of lesser-performing kids. Then Kathleen Alioto finally said to us: 'You know, let's sit down with Bill Rojas, Superintendent of Public Instruction, and let's talk to him about what he sees.' It seems—and she knew this—that Rojas had just had some meetings with Mel Levine and he had set up some meetings with his public school heads. And Mel wanted to do some brainstorming about strategy for kids in the public schools. And we were pretty discouraged at that point. We were thinking: 'Well, what are we going to do? How are we going to make things happen?'

By now, it was January of 1998—a point of stasis, of quandary for the founding group. They had made great strides—from a handful of mothers with issues, to a school's board applying for a 501C3 school status, within a nine-month period. Still, they needed something dramatic, something formative, to take place. They decided to get a little track record selling their idea.

"We had nothing to lose, really!"

So, the person they made their sounding-board was San Francisco Unified School District Superintendent of Public Instruction William Rojas.

It was a brilliant strategy, even if fallen into innocently. The first question they posed was about a trial effort to put a learning center in one of the Superintendent's public schools. Rojas thought otherwise. He was positive, and pointed; and in advising, he set the Gateway Board on its true course:

"'No,' he said; 'don't do that. Because then you'll have to take the teachers that we give you. You'll have to take the people who have seniority, who want to be there. Make it a charter—because then you can hire the teachers whom you want, and you can run the school the way you want to do it. And I'll support you if you'll make it a charter.'"

Rojas went on in that meeting to define the problems.

"He told us the two big issues we were going to face were facilities and insurance. We asked what he could do about that. There were problems, bad timing conditions, that sort of thing. But he said he'd put us on to his 'facilities guy,' and then stood up. Ending the meeting, he said: 'I'll send a letter for you, and give you some entrees to other places around the city, and let's see what we can do.' And he added: "I'll also give you one of my associate superintendents to work with you on writing a charter.' So you know, we really got lucky! This was amazing!"

"As it turned out, this associate superintendent had already been named as sort of the 'charter school liaison.' It was a woman named Laura Brecker. So following our Rojas meeting, we went right next door into Laura's office, and met her. She was enthusiastic, and set up an appointment for the next week. So—I mean—it was honestly almost like the decision was made for us!"

*Still, a couple of good breaks were on the very small positive side
of things. The negatives were still formidable.*

"There were a lot of times in the early days when I thought it
wouldn't fly. But once we met with Rojas, the door opened. At the
end of that first, critical meeting, one of us even asked him to be on our
board—and Rojas sat there, and looked around, and then said, "Okay."
I would never have dared ask him that! But one of us did. That's the
kind of mix we needed of people to launch this school. The
personalities needed to be so much 'in sync,' and they were!"

*Then the speed increased. A foundation friend of Matheson's told
her:*

"Send me a proposal right now. What you need is money to start
up. You need money to search for a head, and you've gotta have a
secretary, and a computer...." And we had nothing! Literally! I went
to a friend of mine, who's the Director of Development for another
school, and I said: "What—what do I write!?" And she just started—I
whipped out my yellow pad—and she just started telling me what to
write. And so I wrote it all down, and I sent it in, and we got seventy
thousand dollars!"

*That would hire a head, and get an office together, and give them
something every bit as important:*

"It made us feel professional, you know?"

*Wasn't it true, though, that at that stage, their impulses did not
find them focusing on the charter experience?*

"Not initially. No. That came about after our research, after doing a
lot of talking to people in the community, after, you know, really seeing
what the need is in the community. And what we could accomplish!
And what kind of support we got. I mean, when we 'walked through
the charter school door,' the support from individuals and foundations
just mushroomed! The support was because they realized that this is a
school for all kids! That this was a school we can get behind because it
wasn't just a school for the lucky bunch who can pay fifteen thousand
dollars a year. And especially foundations like this; not only because it
was public education; but because it was going to make an impact on
public education. You know, this was a model—that maybe our public
schools can look at and say, 'This works!'

"So, when that first grant check came in, though, you know—I was
"freaked!" I mean, I realized, now, this was *other people's* belief in
our dreams. And it's a big responsibility, you know? The next time I
felt scared was when we hired Peter, and I realized this was
somebody's career on the line. He took a big leap."

Somehow, the work got done. The charter was penned, reviewed, rewritten, finalized. People got used to each other. The ideas, once fanciful, were getting real.

People grew.

Then came the night of crucible: The Board of Education was to approve or disapprove the school's charter.

"That was a very difficult process. It was the fourth time I 'freaked.' The board people made us work really hard, and jump through a lot of hoops. And at the time, I was infuriated, I was annoyed. I look back on it, and I think: I respect them for it. We needed to do what they asked of us. Things like: 'Get out more in the community. Do you think this is going to be just a bunch of your kids in this school? How are you going to change your curriculum? You're going to need to change your curriculum right away; make some changes in your reading list.' Things like that.

"Leading up to that meeting was clearly the most frenzied period of our process. My husband had an office in our home, downstairs. We moved him out, and took over that office. So that became the Gateway office. And it was our office for probably eighteen months."

Many of those charter rewrites took place there, over four months. Then they submitted the charter in May, 1997.

"By law, the Board of Education is supposed to meet on your charter within thirty days of submission. But they were negligent. It took more like ninety days. And we were really on 'pins and needles.' I mean, we were trying to move forward, we were still working on a building. We had a building out in the Sunset District of San Francisco, on Quintara, that had been assigned to us at that time. So we felt that wasn't a worry; but we were not sure if we could recruit kids, or if we could hire a head, or really move forward in any way on this school, until we were further in the charter approval process.

"We were assured by some people in the District—not Board members—that we would have the charter approved early in the fall. And we would be ready to open in September of 1998. Well, in October of 1997, we finally met with the curriculum committee. And we thought it would be a 'slam dunk.' Well, that's when they made us jump through the hoops."

The "hoops" were held high: Curriculum design and changes recruiting; meeting "diversity" balances. With Thorp around, the hiring process began in earnest. The ever-present budget issues needed constant attention. The curriculum required three meetings with the Board of Education's Curriculum Committee. Finally, that august board declared they were ready to go to the Board for a full vote.

Matheson and her own board felt that once that happened, they were assured approval. After all, Rojas was behind them; and it was Lisille's sense of things that he had been "helpful in pushing it forward for us."

The final approval? Almost an anticlimax.

"I was prepared," Matheson recalls. Rojas chaired the meeting; suddenly, he announced: "We're coming to the new charter school, Gateway..." And I stood up, ready to go up to the microphone to make my plea. And I was shaking. And Rojas said: "Well, this is the proposal; all in favor, say Aye." And Bam!—it was done. I never had to say a word! I sat back down. It was so fabulous for me, because I didn't have to make my speech."

But there was no time for celebration. Now the hard work really came:

"I thought: Now, we have to do it.!' And all the while, simultaneously, we'd been recruiting kids; gathering resumes of heads; we'd been raising money. So, finally, it was like—Okay! You can put your foot on the gas, because it's January, and we're opening in September!

The major issues, minus charter approval, still loomed: A head of school needed to be chosen. The site needed to be occupied. And true to expectation, the promised facilities were revoked. The School District reneged on its assignment of the little schoolhouse on Quintara. And Peter Thorp, found in a spurt of luck and hired on a promise and a prayer, would start the year without a school!

"Which," *Matheson added with a smile,* "makes me admire Peter Thorp even more: That he jumped into this ring with that issue looming."

Somehow, despite this setback, alternative plans were made, and the School Board was held to its commitment for a school. The one chosen at the last minute—long after Thorp arrived—was Newcomer, a disused 1920's elementary school in the Jackson Heights district of San Francisco which like so many of the city's wealthy areas, had abandoned the need for little schoolhouses, and left them empty where they sat. Newcomer was the District's sop, a backhanded congratulatory gesture.

Gateway would make the best of it. In Peter Thorp's office, the new principal placed the two wooden armchairs acquired in past positions, with their stately schools' logos carved in their backs, inside the meager executive space of his new school—a school which was far from boasting a logo, and barely possessed a chair to put it on. And when school opened, even those horrors of the first weeks came, were absorbed, and passed.

But the San Francisco Unified School District was, and remained, the "bête-noir."

Matheson says Peter still spends an inordinate amount of his time working on rectifying issues with the School District. And she wishes that weren't the case; because, quite simply, in her words: "He needs to run a school."

What other concerns are on Matheson's mind at present?

"We want to be more out in the community, we want to be more a-lot-of-things. But there just isn't the time for that. Gale Mondry, another one of our original Board members who's now the Development head for the school, puts it very well when she says: 'Let's not worry about getting out in the community. Let's worry about making what we have here great! And when we have it great, then we'll worry about that other stuff.' You know, she really puts that great vision to it; and she's right!

Of course, a major difference between those early, formative days and now, that they were off and running, is that what the school had now is unassailable: There was a quality faculty in place; a student body; a track record; a couple of full years under everybody's belt. The annoying problems that were going to haunt the school and come back to remind everyone of the "old days" were perhaps still a bit in the future—like the site problems will be when the school grows. That will remind you that it wasn't all over; and meanwhile, there was a great elevation in public regard, wasn't there?

"Yes! I mean, people now say: 'Wow, Lisille! Gateway is a force! Gateway is something to be reckoned with, in this city now!" And it's going to be more. It's going to be a lot more, because we have some plans now, and are working a lot more closely with Mel Levine on projects, that are going to put us on the map in a big, big way. Especially if we do it well."

Mel Levine was a topic by itself. Who was this psychological phenomenon whose program the faculty—and Peter Thorp above all— extolled, and with whom these school leaders sought identity? Many student profiles indicate that Gateway had an extraordinary group of students. There was a case to be made that every one of them would have come here because of "special needs," but they're not needs that describe debility necessarily; they might just describe unusual personality. Eccentricities, uniqueness in nature and approach of people toward living. There was, indeed, an astonishing strength in this group. They're healthy; their interaction is direct....

"They're inquisitive!"

Yes, they were inquisitive. It was an enlivened group. Of course, all of the cliches about teenagers applied; these kids were not free of "teenagedom." But there was something special here; and this might be linked with terms like "LD" or "special ed"—as a misrepresentational way of being linked to concepts of deficiency, rather than simply individual characteristics. Didn't she think this was plausible? Even a liability?

"Well, that's very much in the spirit of what started this whole thing. It is that kids, especially adolescents, who don't do as well in school for whatever reason, as some other kids, have strengths in other areas.   Or in some area.   And they have a lot to offer a school community.   And just because they're not making "A's" but instead they're making "C's" doesn't mean they can't be part of an enlivened and exciting school curriculum and school community. They must be part of those, because they bring a whole other vision and view of the world!"

"But there are a lot of kids whom you might call 'mainstream' kids here. They have strengths and weaknesses, just like the academically-weak kids have strengths and weaknesses.   But families choose Gateway because it feels safe, safer than some other public schools out there. Part of this is because of small class size. You know, you got a lot more individualized attention; you don't 'slip through the cracks,' as easily. And—most importantly: It's a *community*—and if you value that, you're going to kill to get your kid into that school!"

"We had a board retreat recently, and one of the facilitators' questions was phrased something like: "When was the most challenging moment in the last year, or school year, or since the school opened?" And I was the first one to speak, and I said, "They occur every single day."

There were keen reserves in Gateway kids; they were resourceful. Did they ever ask themselves: Why do I not feel that I fit in? or, How can I best exercise my uniqueness?   Or, "How can I assess and serve my instinctive needs?

"See what the humanities teachers do in their classes. And it's a knock-out! What they ask of students, and how hard they want them to think.

The week before, one of those humanities teachers had been working with a student, and seeing them hearkened to the school's unofficial slogan, "One student at a time". The body posture of these two people—a young fellow with his teacher sitting next to him— revealed their intense common work on a lesson. The teacher's interest removed the hierarchical structure of teacher/pupil. And one could really feel it. Those who knew Gateway's faculty knew that that feeling pervaded the larger list of teachers.

Matheson agreed, and tied in teacher success with the legendary Mel Levine.

"These teachers *are* incredible! And they care. When Mel Levine was at school here last week, he told me how much he loved meeting with our teachers! It seemed so interesting for him, so informative, so uplifting. 'You know, ' he said, 'I could tell—I heard their frustrations: How do I make this kid get this?—How do I do this? And I told him it was more than faculty frustration. They're worried! 'Am I good enough? Am I a good enough teacher to help these kids do it?' They're worried, and they care about these kids!"

That frustrated faculty was also a noticeably young faculty. This fact alone had drawn fire.

"On the other hand, these are people who are not set in their ways," Matheson replied. "They're open to new ideas about education. And that's what we're all about. Strategies for running a Learning center, shaping the curriculum, and things like that—Mel will be a real support to the faculty. And the faculty's really open to his input."

But what about a critical view of an outsider—especially one with a high profile as a daring innovator? Will Levine be a strong, ancillary figure in an advisory capacity to steer the faculty and the Learning Center director in that direction? Or is there is a risk that a kind of unfortunate, associated "cult of personality" would come in? In other words: Will there be an identification of Gateway with this fellow, with this philosophy, in such a way that it could have any kind of deleterious consequences later? For example, if there is somebody who doesn't like him. Somebody who says, "Ahh, yeah, they followed Gurdjieff, too..."?

"I wish one of our other founding mothers was here. She's good at answering questions like that. Mel said at our meeting: 'If they're open to my support and interest in the school, I want to do what I can to—and put in programs that can be helpful.'

"On the other hand, he's—well, he's getting to be a 'big' guy. In the nation, you know. And he's got a very powerful board behind him, that is steering a lot of his dreams to get his philosophies more—what's the word?—inculcated into many different communities around our country. But Mel gets turned on by the one-on-one. He's working hard on making a lot of his things more accessible to more people. Meeting with a kid, one-on-one, that's a thrill for him. Meeting with our faculty, he was turned on!—by the real problems."

Were there not also practical considerations? Levine was, after all, based in North Carolina. How could the distance factor be overcome? Long-distance love rarely worked.

"Well, we haven't figured that out completely yet. He and his board, what they call the 'All-Kinds-Of-Mind' board, want to open ten 'Student Success Centers.' Right now, they only exist in Chapel Hill. The first satellite center, outside of Chapel Hill, which he wants to open is here in San Francisco. Which means two things, from our point of view, I think: One, that Mel, and more of his really carefully-trained people, will be in the Bay Area, and two, that they'll be some collaboration regarding that. We'll have more access to him. And our kids will have more access to him."

Gateway was also trying an on-campus assessment program, run by a scientific institute. "4WD" was a computerized testing assessment program that its originators were going to install here, with its module for assessing reading, and comprehension, and aural and visual acuity in approaching information. A selection of about fifty students in the group were initially chosen to start off. Ultimately, the whole school would go through that program.

"That's our whole intention—that everybody is assessed, for their strengths and weaknesses."

Matheson's instincts and impulses for starting Gateway stemmed from her personal intensity, and as much from her maternal concern. An older daughter—a straight-A student and a dancer—was on her way to college. But a younger child, a son, had long stimulated thoughts of a Gateway-like place. It didn't exactly work out as planned.

"My son is one of those kids who works really hard, to get the B-minus, C-plus. Really hard! And he does have some learning differences. He's very capable of doing college preparatory work, and he wants to go to college! But I mean, he also hates school, because school is hard. For my son, academic work is just like hell. So, Gateway was very much conceived with my son in mind. He was entering the ninth grade, and started here at Gateway. I really believe in this school, and I believed it would be a good place for him. But what I misjudged is that he needs a place of his own. And he needs a place that *he* chose, not that his mom chose for him. So his time at Gateway was doomed from the beginning. His dad, my husband and I, talked about it a lot, and we just said, "Look, we have to do what's right for him.' And we talked to Peter Thorp a lot about it. Yeah, that was a real disappointment."

Matheson fell silent a moment.

"You know, another founding mom has a daughter here. And I know that that mother's hopes for Gateway took fire with her child in mind, and we talked about this a lot; the fact was undeniable that we got into this because we saw the needs of our own children. But it's grown so far beyond that. It's no longer about her daughter or my son: It's about *these* kids! And *this* school! It's really about what this community needs. I tell prospective foundation donors that—the fact that now there are only two hundred. But our work and their money will grow to help thousands!

"I guess—this school is really a work-in-progress. And Peter Thorp and our Board all agree: It will always be a work-in-progress! It needs to be."

This notion brought the discussion back to the Principal. Matheson's enthusiasm had not dimmed. "He just has these wonderful combinations of—a self-effacing quality, and a humility that's really there, it's bedrock; and yet he has a public persona, that can rise to the occasion. He's brilliant, and yet he's—you know, he understands it all from the hard-slogging daily grind as a teacher, to what you need to do when you hold his office. It was a wonderful find.

"He's a great problem-solver. A great administrator. He has his weaknesses, though. But I tell him that all the time! And *we* do, too. The Board—everybody."

The Chairperson of Gateway High School's Board of Directors looked pensive for a moment; almost wistful.

"I worry that we are squandering his talent, because, many ways, he's so bogged down with so many details, that I say to myself, 'My god, this is not the best use of your great skills!' He's also human; he's had some personal unhappiness, and has wrestled himself with real human problems. I think he learned a lot from that unhappiness. That's helped to make him a great dad, too, by the way. He has the most wonderful two daughters. And they have the warmest relationships. That's another thing, I think, that personal unhappiness—it made him stand up and say: 'This is important.'

"I saw this in him after we hired Peter. And it really made me happy. It was sort of like this extra gift we got; that he really cares about the kids. Even in the first interviews, he just focused right in on them."

What was her own tenure? How long would her own official capacity last, and then what did she envision beyond that?

"Well, I see that I'm going to be here for a long time. That's for sure. Whether I want to or not! Because I believe I'm still needed here! At the end of our fiscal year, I step down as the Chair. And that absolutely is needed, and is appropriate. And the Vice-Chair will step up. So I'm working hard right now to have a really well-oiled machine for her. And I'll stay on the board. I imagine I'll volunteer sometimes, as Peter's assistant! So I can just stay on as the thorn in his side, for a long, long time!"

Said thorn—Thorp—interrupted at that moment, with a word to his Board Chair that a new bookkeeper was about to be hired. Lisille Matheson smiled at him, nodded silently, and Peter moved on. I noticed at that moment how wan her smile appeared—and yet, how much impact it had when a beat let it sink in. It was an apt image of the strength inside her—the kind of strength that produced new schools where before there had been nothing but unhappy stories of students thwarted from chronic inattention to academic and personal needs.

The buck—passed by school boards, and superintendents, and overwhelmed administrators, and undernourished teachers, and schools woefully inert—stopped here, in this office, in the lap of this woman.

Already, in her eye, could be seen the concern: What was the next student problem? Time to go work on it.

One student at a time.

Chapter Seven

THE DIRECTOR OF DEVELOPMENT: PARTING A WISE COMMUNITY AND ITS MONEY

"You don't have to be perfect to be wonderful."
— *Gale Mondry (referring to Peter Thorp)*

It takes a special combination of personal traits to be the one who goes out into the community, "beating the bushes" to find the funding to float the enterprise. Some do it "hat in hand," with a plaintive Oliver-Twist "Oh- please,-sir!" feel to the approach. Some do it Fuller-Brush-Salesman style, with a gregarious smile and a "brush-up-your-life!" invitation. Gale Mondry, former attorney and mother of four, has done it for Gateway, to great effect, with a keen intelligence and polished professionalism. She has also applied that quiet demeanor that bears the hint of a great, momentarily-sequestered power within, which the potential donor feels wise to let lie.

This might be seen as the lawyer in the lady; after all, depositions are not accomplished nor trials won without at least an implied threat of a big stick behind soft speech. With Mondry, as with any good attorney who tries to stay a few steps ahead of the other person in the equation, her face smiled in a way which, remaining sincere, kept mirth from invading the eyes, no matter that pleasantness took shape about the mouth. A forthrightness erroneously conveyed at first a quality of discomfiture; but I soon saw it as merely a clue to a sea change in the dynamic of her presentation. Her manner had a way of suggesting that thinking about her words was something given effort—not that it was difficult, but rather that she wanted the words to be right.

Such a personal presentation is not mere mannerism, nor idle consideration. And to be sure, nothing about Mondry is mannered nor idle. To fund successfully a brand-new school takes a dogged approach, by a fundraiser dedicated to enabling the donor to appreciate the worth and seriousness of the project. The fact that this Development Director is bright and experienced in professional settings far from the halls of ivy has almost guaranteed that the funding resources she approaches do not need to tarry over questions of "whether," but can move right to "when" and "how much."

Others at Gateway had suggested Gale was the initial contact with Peter Thorp, and an early champion of his candidacy for the school's leader. I wanted to know how this came about. And as I learned, a series of events had to coalesce in order for his appropriateness to the position, his availability, and Gateway's attractiveness as a possibility, to come together to bring him in.

How did somebody like Gale Mondry manage to slip the bonds of the legal world, and come into this kind of life?

"I never worked for very long as a private attorney, in private practice. I worked for Stanford University in their General Counsel's office, as part of an educational institution. And then I went to work for California Pacific Medical Center, where I was their General Counsel. And I enjoyed both those jobs; I liked being part of a problem-solving team. That's sort of what I enjoyed; I never was in love with the law, as a body of knowledge. And in fact, I was always a generalist and kind of a generic problem-solver. I always—if you needed a really technical look at an arcane area, I always referred that out. That 'wasn't my thing.' So my coming here might not be the stretch that you think.

"And then when I left California Pacific Medical Center and did become "of counsel" to a law firm downtown, that was never anything I liked all that much. I was actually doing more community service than I was law. I got on some boards of organization, was at the Jewish Community Center, was on the board there. And they didn't have an executive director, nor did they have a chief financial officer. The organization was really in crisis, losing hundreds and hundreds of thousands of dollars a year, and it was really a great experience to be part of turning it around.

"And doing that made me think, 'You know, I really like this more than law. I like being a problem-solver, and I love being a part of an organization in transition. Because it's so satisfying to feel that you can make a difference.' And while I was doing that, I found I had some time for more activity. So I got involved with Gateway, through—I had lunch with the head of Lick-Wilmerding High School in San Francisco; my husband teaches there. At the time I was pondering: 'I can't go back to work right now, because this Jewish Community Center is taking a lot of time. But it's not taking so much time that I don't want more to do.' And the man from Lick-Wilmerding told me he had met with these people who were thinking of starting a charter school. Well, I've got some kids with learning issues, so that resonated with me; and I knew how happy Bruce, my husband, was as an educator.

"Then, after I'd been working on the Board of Gateway, my other involvements lessened—the crisis at the Jewish Community Center improved, and the place began really working well. I felt frustrated not working again; I really *liked* working, I really liked having a place to go, I liked being responsible—not just giving my opinion, but actually having to carry some things out. So I took stock: I'd done a fair amount of fund-raising. And writing a grant isn't that different from writing a legal brief. You know, you've got to advocate for your organization. And then I began to think: Gateway really needs a development director! And here's an organization I know pretty well, and one I believe in."

Mondry was no stranger to children, having four of her own. Did she have any kids here at Gateway?

"No. I have an eighth-grader, who's applied here. I hope she'll come. She's kind of uncertain whether—she's never been in public school. And she's uncertain about whether she wants to be at a school where her mother is. And I can understand that. So Gateway is one of her top two or three. But the choice is hers, if she's accepted—and I don't know whether she'll come.

"My oldest child is a senior at Lowell High School, what is pretty generally thought of as the city's toughest academic high school. And then I have two children at the San Francisco Day School, one of the most competitive private elementary-middle schools. One youngster is in sixth grade, and one in fourth grade."

Your predilection for problem-solving should have, if nothing else, caused you to be able to work hand-in-glove with this man Thorp. Peter certainly prides himself on also having those qualities. As he's described it, he feels that his best attributes, the best "go" he gives something, are his approaches as a problem-solver. But it's also sometimes a liability for him—that those talents might not be what a situation is called for, if he's having an interaction with someone who's troubled. Maybe they don't need to hear, "Well, if you do A, B or C..." Maybe they just need to hear—

"*Do* it!"

Yes. Tell the story of Peter Thorp's beginning acquaintance with Gateway.

"We had formed a search committee, and it was late. We'd committed that we wanted to open in September, which I remember being a little nervous about, whether we'd be ready. And it was about January. The search committee formulated two ideas. One was: We couldn't afford a 'head hunter'; we were going to have to do the search ourselves. The other idea—also largely controlled by budget—was that we should therefore limit the search to California.

"Next, we decided that the number one desired quality was that we wanted an educational leader. We wanted somebody who could really create a quality school. And we wanted somebody who believed in Mel Levine, or if not already knowledgeable about him, was someone eager to learn. We felt that the mission of the institution as we had developed it resonated with the Levine ideas. We wanted somebody who had experience in secondary education. We didn't feel like we should really take a flyer on somebody from business who wanted maybe to do a career switch.

"So we put ads in some of the California education periodicals. We made contact with the Unified School District, although we were not really sure how widely they publicized the job, to be honest with you. We didn't get one applicant that way.

"Then we contacted the different schools of education in California: Stanford, San Francisco State, University of San Francisco—the ones up here. That turned out to be the way Peter heard about the job. After that I got a listing of the California Association of Independent Schools, and the heads of all those schools. And I wrote a letter to almost all of them, saying we had this job opening, and attaching a job description. It was one which was well-written, I thought. And then—a good move!—we also attached copies of two letters, one from Dr. Rojas, who was then Superintendent of Schools, in which he endorsed Gateway, writing about how great Gateway could be. And we included one from Mel Levine, where he also said this could be a model school.

"I sent these to the heads of all these schools, not thinking I'd get a response from even one of them! But I did figure maybe I'd get an answer from a person in a 'number two' position, who was ready to move on, ready to move up. And so I asked them if they knew of anybody, to circulate it to someone they thought interested and qualified for the position. And we got about forty applications."

A good response!

"Yes; but some of them had problems; you know, they didn't have the secondary school education, or they were getting their Principal's Certification, and they had no track record of any educational leadership. There were perhaps seven or eight that we considered seriously.

"When Peter's came, I couldn't believe it! I mean, I was just very surprised that someone who was the head of the Cate School would be interested in this job. It seemed like such a shift. He had a beautiful letter, and had attached an equally beautiful statement of educational philosophy. He talked about how every child should be cared for and loved. My guess was he didn't put it together just for this presentation; it was probably something he had worked on for a while.

"So I called him, and then he called me back. And I said: "Are you really serious about this? Is this for real?" And he said: 'Well, yeah! I mean, I'm looking at a lot of other things, too, but—yes.'

"We decided as a search committee to interview five people. And Peter was one of the five. And we had a very good interview with him. He was knowledgeable about Mel Levine, and very responsive, personable, inspiring—you know, all the things. I had some reservations, and I think some other people did too: He'd never worked in the public setting. And he seemed so sophisticated, and so intellectual, that I wondered: Would this 'play' with our kids? Would he find it satisfying himself? Would they connect with him? I believe, actually, that he had that reservation himself. The only other concern was the lack of experience with our population. And then we all pondered the issue of how serious was he? Would he really make this move, or would he back out? Or find something else that was less of a jump but also exciting to him? It was clear he had some other opportunities.

"The number two person for the job was nowhere near as inspiring; but this guy had different talent from Peter's. He was from the city; he knew all the School District people; Rojas liked him. He had worked with the types of kids who come here, for quite a while. He had a whole cadre of teachers with whom he'd worked. He was quite confident that he could quickly pull together a team of people. *But*—he was not as thoughtful as Peter. He didn't have the depth, he didn't have the presence. He was younger, and he was not as inspiring. We definitely felt Peter was much more impressive.

"Still, we worried: Peter didn't have the experience with our kids, he was totally immersed in the boarding school environment—and I mean, you can't come up with a more elite environment than Cate. And for him to commit to us, he would be making so many changes.

"So we interviewed those five, and quickly got it down really to the two. And then we had a long discussion, and everybody felt that Peter was the one we wanted. But now *he* wanted some additional time, as I recall. Not long; but now it was March, and we wanted to have somebody on board before we accepted our kids. Because otherwise, we figured we wouldn't get families and kids to come; they wouldn't take us seriously, if we didn't have a Head.

His request for additional time was troublesome:

"Do we give him the additional time? Right then I would have bet that he wasn't going to take the job! I kept reminding myself that it wasn't clear that he could transfer to this environment, it wasn't clear that it would work.

It could appear that he was just working "against type," to get some kind of stimulation by the fact that this is set up in a way strange to him, to give an opposing feeling—didn't she agree? And his understanding of how people come from a different background, is obviously useful to him. And he can work without a terrible need to identify one way or the other. Had she considered him from that perspective?

"Look: To me, the story of Gateway really is *his* story. *That's* the interesting story! And a couple of other things have impressed me: One is, how much he loves the classroom. You know, you can't get him out of the classroom. And I think that's great! That's great for the teachers—you know, he's the backup physical education teacher, he's teaching his college counseling course, he's teaching—"

Right now, he's also the temporary math teacher.

"—Yeah, the temporary math teacher—you can't get him out! And it's a wonderful role model, I think, for the faculty. You get a lot of heads that never go back into the classroom, once they get out—and here he's basically been a teacher for most of his career. It's not like he was one of those people who quickly jumped into administration. And I think you'll see that if you watch him. He really tries not to isolate himself. I think he really loves teaching, and loves being around kids.

"And the other thing that's been amazing to me is how well he's adapted to what I imagine to be a really different situation. I feel it myself. When I was a lawyer, I had all these support systems. You know, I didn't do my own Xeroxing, I didn't do my own filing—I didn't have to make my documents look nice. And the same thing at Cate; he had a whole cadre of people to call on for those tasks. Whereas here, he's moving furniture here, he's fixing things that break. Every time a student's having difficulty, he's in his office. So it's interesting to me that he can go back to being very 'hands-on.'"

What about the board of Education? It's well and good that the people who hired him like Peter Thorp; but what about the brass downtown?

"I think—I think they like him a lot. He's actually done a good job—I don't think he saw himself in this role, but he says he actually likes it a little bit, because he's a political "junkie." But he's seen as what he is, which is a really solid educator who adds to the resources of the District. I mean, charter schools are part of a larger political framework, and it has been an issue which has divided the Board; and they've had some pain from it.

"You know, you go through so many hoops with the Board, and then you just end up getting annoyed. So we'll see. I hope it works. I think there are risks out there for us. Definitely. But the Board's not known for making tough—I don't think it will come from them. It might come over finances, or demographics—you know. I don't personally think they will pull the rug out from under us."

Any criticisms of Peter Thorp? It's nice to feel a leader's the central focus of a "love fest." But that's not reality; and school-managing is nothing if not reality, no?

"Well...He's not perfect. Believe me, he's not perfect! You don't have to be perfect to be wonderful—that's my motto!

" I don't think he really likes fundraising, you know? So that's an issue. And he's got so many other things to do, that he spends very little time on it. And so sometimes I feel like I should be pushing him more to spend more time. But I'm there—the fundraising's going very well, and I'm very respectful of all the other things he's got to do. And—he can give a great speech. So, that's—you know, when people <u>are</u> exposed to him, they come away very impressed and excited, and that's more important than the amount of time he spends on it.

"But yes, I think some people would say he takes too long to make decisions. And some would say he talks too much, he should listen more. I think he's doing a great job. But that's not to admit you won't find people who don't have criticisms of him. I think he's done really well with the faculty, and I think most of the students—and he's done well with the kids of color, you know? I think they see him as an advocate for them, in general. I think he's been too busy to do the mentoring of some of the younger employees here, that would be ideal. That kind of work really all rests on him. I mean, he is our mentor-teacher. He is our senior academic. And he hasn't had much time for that. I'm sure he'd say that, too.

"And so—you know, I don't know that he's given it the younger faculty the 'tender loving care' that some of them need, or want. But he's certainly working hard! And, you know, the place is chaotic! Which is not surprising for a new institution. Some people feel like maybe more attention could be paid to creating systems, and structure. As opposed to "ad-hoc"-ing everything. Some of that falls on him; some of that falls on all of us.

"But—we're growing! And the start-up years are hard. But I think Peter is wonderful, and that's one of his attractions. You don't find a lot of men who are that self-critical, or men who will use emotional language to talk about things. And Peter will. It's rare, I think, in a man. And it is so appealing! It really is. It's one of the reasons he's so successful in giving a talk, because he's not—you know, he may see himself as a problem-solver, but when he actually speaks, he's pretty good at appealing to emotions. From what I've seen, he can make the tears come to your eyes, and it's not because he's so logical that that happens.

"We see it in working with him. And the students, in their own way, see these qualities, too!"

On this last point, I would find out for myself.

Chapter Eight

CLASS TIME

"In class is where it all comes to bear. And this is true for teacher and student alike. It's where 'the rubber meets the road.'"

— Peter Thorp to a visitor to the College Preparatory Class

What's it like when the Principal is in charge of the classroom?

Being in a class taught by Peter Thorp is probably as close as any participant in it is likely to come in knowing what the little Presidential terrier Fala must have felt like during Roosevelt's Fireside Chats. There, in focus at one end of a large conference table, sat the man with the "All-Is-Forgiven" voice, beckoning with smile and warmth of word for every student to feel welcome. There—serious when required, and inspired to impish humor when he desired—the class leader, as with FDR, let it be known that if you were here, you were special; if you were here, you had something important to say, and his intention was to listen. And if you were here, you could take away with you ideas that might resolve a quandary or two, or perchance even change your thoughts and alter your life. For this was a college-preparation session. And in very real, measurable ways, Peter Thorp was as critical to the future of these youngsters as the four-term President had been to his wider flock.

In this installment of his weekly hour-and-a-half time with the college prep group, Peter reviewed initial mailings received by the students from college inquiries, and used the promotional material to show how colleges, like students, try to "put their best foot forward." Using the very literature the colleges had just sent the members of his class (a mailing prompted by an assignment earlier in the sessions), he showed that the choices the colleges had made in developing their promotional photography—including ethnicity of both students and teachers, the ambience and "feel" of the physical environment, and other subtle selling points of this first-impact level of college outreach—told as much or more about the institution than the accompanying written "sales pitch" or even an on-campus meeting might convey.

The man who as a senior high school student had declined Harvard's welcome to come to its hallowed halls also exhorted these fresh-faced, earnestly-concerned and imminent higher-education applicants that when the time came for college visits, to go not at the "great times"—the magnificent foliate fall-time, as displayed in an almost preening way by all Ivy-League-looking institutions—but during the worst weather of the year. "If you like your choice when it's freezing or steaming and wet as hell with humidity," he said, thumping the photos of autumn's loveliness," think how much you'll love it when it looks like this!" Trust your senses, he told them, and *use* them— sight, smell, taste, hearing, touch—to learn about this place.

Later in the session, he went over a college application form, line by line, and opened up for the trembling novitiates an understanding of the perspective of the particular college, "what they are looking for." He talked about the mandatory and all-important student essay, about how revealing it was, the essential litmus for the college administrator in getting a bead on what was inside an applicant's mind and heart. "You'd be surprised how many students have others write their essays," he said.   He then urged these youngsters to bring themselves the challenges of the essays, with the four varieties invited by the admissions applications:

- *Evaluate a significant life experience;*
- *Discuss some issue of personal concern and importance to you;*
- *Present a view of a significant person in your life;*
- *Describe a fictional or historical character who has had a profound influence upon you.*

Within moments, Peter had encouraged sophomore Cynthia Diaz to present such a precise and vivid story of having risen to a personal challenge that "had we had a tape recorder here, you could have taken what you said, word for word, and had a ready-made essay!"   And Bombay-born Amy Mehta's immediate notion of presenting the influence of Buddha upon her young life won approbation from the gray-haired man sitting opposite her:

"Great! Let's talk!" he appended to the close of her tentatively-expressed, but heartfelt notion of an essay idea.

Throughout the hour and a half, on every face, there were palpable feelings of belonging, acceptance, trust. For some—perhaps for the first time—there arose the possibility of hope in the fearful college process.

The qualities of making young people feel at ease, and making their time bear the weight of purpose without being ponderous, are gifts which I discovered Peter brings to teaching. And as I sat, "auditing" his college preparatory class of five bright, attentive young girls—all of whom wore Third World faces, faces "of color," as we now say—I remembered for a moment the rare sparks from long-ago classroom days, when my own meager retinue of inspired teachers lit a fire in the temporary modular prefabs which were my own halls of high school academe in Los Angeles forty years before. Those historical moments of inspiration were notable for their sheer paucity. Now, today's youngsters—or some of them—had a chance, in this old concerted Depression-era primary school, to feel the flame of possibility again.

In the year to follow Peter Thorp's college prep group, he would hire a new teacher to handle these concerns full-time. And in Maria Victoria Rosero Rivera, he would find exuberance, enthusiasm and no mean flame of Latin fire, to keep the student college curiosity at high-point. But the teacher inside the Principal, the man's pedagogical core, had been tapped, and would need another outlet.

That next year would find Peter back at the blackboard, chalk in hand, teaching Advanced Placement U.S. History. Predictably, Thorp would be unorthodox.

"Okay," he would begin the course. "I want you to consider this proposition:

'The Constitution of the United States is inherently anti-democratic.' Right?"

It would prove for this longtime preceptor an exciting way to get out of the Principal's office; at least, for a few hours, anyway.

And now, with Gale Mondry's perspective to help sharpen my understanding of Peter's arrival on the scene, and his own classroom manner strongly imprinted on my mind, I had one other stop before I returned to focus on the school figurehead himself.

Chapter Nine

NEW BLOOD

"My feeling is you bring kids who can feel successful and are set up to succeed, but also are diverse. And there are kids out there who are like that, you must find them and you get them to come here. The problem in San Francisco is that there are schools who have a ton more money, and resources, who want the same kids...."

"What I *do* have, I think, is I have some sort of ability to form a relationship with somebody even after only knowing them for ten minutes. And so the kids who really are looking for that relationship, with the teacher, get really excited about Gateway, and Gateway really is about relationships between teachers and kids, and kids and kids...."

"This is a very exciting place. It has a lot of areas to improve. But—I don't know—I think the issue with charter schools is that everyone wants to fix something, or change something, or be a pioneer. But sometimes you just need to get down and do the work, instead of thinking about it! And sometimes you're getting down to doing the work so much you *can't* think about it!"

It is by fortuitous design that one of the first people a prospective Gateway student will see, upon making admission inquiries to Gateway, will be Meghvi Maheta. Her first distinction—and only dubious one—is her title, the longest at the school: Gateway Director of Community Outreach and Enrollment. *Most at Gateway get to the point of the lofty title by referring to her simply as "Admissions Director." But far more important is her function in a modern San*

Francisco multicultural environment; for Meghvi is the quintessential embodiment of "diversity." Her rich East-Indian complexion and eyes and a smile which create an atmosphere of immediate acceptance and comfort, Meghvi is still aware of being in her mid-twenties and thus only about a decade older than the students.

But what a difference a decade makes!

This former Stanford Student Body President's engaging approach to people helps her to present the school's offerings in a light every bit as attractive as she is. Holder as well of a Stanford Masters Degree in Education, Meghvi is ideally suited to evaluate families and students who apply to Gateway. Her background includes political science and biology, and her student work at Stanford culminated in presiding over a fund-raising project which created an astonishing six-figure endowment for the class.

Given her expertise, and the long mid-year months of effort to accommodate the growing number of people who are seeking the kind of education Gateway offers, it is all the more surprising to find in Meghvi one of those administrators who knows where everything is, and who—surely not always conveniently—is asked to find every wayward paper, or to make the critical connections between people who relate to the school. This bedrock efficiency makes her a mainstay, without which much of the administrative apparatus would find functioning a "harder go."

Meghvi agreed to see me only after the weeks in March—hectic weeks for the Admissions Director, charged with student selection for the 100 members of the incoming class—were behind her. Now, blaring some upbeat music from the next office "because I miss the energy of the students!," she had been in meetings all day, even though this was "vacation" time.

How did a person like her fall into the Admissions Director position? The question embraced awareness of her Principal's notion about the concept of a "chevron," a calling-card that administrators or teachers possessed by dint of having gone to a university like Stanford. It gave, as the phrase had it, a certain cache.

"I wanted to be a politician when I was in high school. I was very intrigued with the inequality. I mean, that issue itself has always been something that touches me. I don't know why; my parents didn't feel like they have ever been discriminated against because they're Indian. They think: If you work hard, that's all you need to do. I have a family background where we need to help those who are underprivileged.

"So, I went to Stanford thinking I wanted to be a politician, and I majored in political science from my freshman year. I loved the classes I took. But as I was getting closer to graduation and becoming friends with people who were interested in education, I started realizing that there was a lot of inequality just before kids get to colleges. Or even before they get to high school. So I started an interdisciplinary program with my area concentration on how race and gender and economic status affects a child's ability to learn. The central question for me was: How can a kid walk into the room and already feel like he's a low-status kid without having anything happen to him?

"Codifying that concern made me decide that it was too early for me to leave. I wanted to learn more before I left. It's hard to leave kind of this welcoming, warm place where people are always challenging each other. And the stress of real life isn't there; it's the stress of: 'What are we going to do now? How are we going to fix all these problems?'

"So I stayed and got my Masters in Education. I was really looking at status, but also doing some focus, a focus on higher education. The problem, though, is after my second quarter of my Masters' program, I basically had taken every class in education I wanted to take. Because I had started taking them my sophomore, junior years. I could go to the graduate school and take my classes if I wanted to. So I think at point I thought: 'Gee, I'm really tired of this subject! I don't know if I want to do this the rest of my life. What am I going to do?!'"

And then a problem emerged. What was that?

"A school like Stanford can tell you you're really good at everything, but they don't tell you what you're *especially* good at doing. So I left with the M.Ed. degree, but saying to myself, 'What do I *actually* want to do? I don't really know.' And in a flurry of anxiety, I applied to businesses, to educational research places; to 'think-tanks!' And I went home and did a lot of soul-searching, reconnected with my family, and also volunteered in a kindergarten classroom. And that was what made me think, 'Maybe kids on a kind of one-to-one basis.... And with my interest in ways to change the system, it became more sensible to see how that happens at lower levels. And being in a kindergarten classroom and teaching a kid to read, you start realizing that's really exciting, to go from the bottom up."

And somewhere after this stage—Gateway called? Not quite: A roommate had a fiancé who knew Peter Thorp's fiancée. Without trusting 'networking,' Meghvi's name carried anyway, on this ad hoc "significant-other" grapevine. Thorp put her off, begging he was too busy to see her. By the time he did, she was concerned he had no interest.

This fear—and Thorp's disinterest—evaporated when they met: He hired her on the spot.

Was it with the admissions directorship title, in this role?

"This title—a longer one—and this position—a huge one! Except I was doing fund-raising as well. Despite titles, everyone wore multiple hats in the early days. And the pressure built before I started. They all said: 'Everything's going to be better when Meghvi starts!' They did that with everyone—and it just made the new guy that much more nervous!"

What was the first problem she encountered?

"I realized enrollment is not an easy thing in San Francisco. There are too many schools, and too many consequent difficulties attached to the kinds of kids you have, diversity being one. San Francisco is one of the smallest communities and everyone knows everything about every kid who comes to Gateway. So it was right away a full-time job. I gave up fundraising; and by June, Gale Mondry came in as Director of Development. And it's more than a full-time job for her. Nobody could really do both, I think."

Mondry was a good choice, didn't she think? After all, she had been in the working world for a longer period of time than most Gateway staffers. She had more contacts—an essential tool for that kind of work.

"Well, I don't think they were ever thinking of me as the Director of Development at all. Which is ironic, because that was actually how I got my foot in the door to come to Gateway. They looked at my Stanford senior class fundraising experience, because it was a pretty big campaign—the largest, in fact, in the history of doing campaigns with students."

You mentioned your own family background, and your consciousness about diversity. How did that play out in your dealing with people here? Had there been specific issues with individuals, with families and personalities and not just numbers, where your own depiction of diversity had been a factor?

"Yes and no. Last year I really had a lot of pressure for diversity. And this year, too. But last year I was new, it was my first job out of school, and in faculty meetings, faculty members would raise the issue: 'What about diversity?' And it would make me very nervous, because I felt like it was a personal attack. You know, it was as if they were saying: 'Our class wasn't diverse enough.' And in fact, in recruiting, I went to one school in particular and tried to get as many kids to apply to bump up those numbers. I felt like I was doing the right thing, because there were a few kids we didn't take; I felt they weren't ready to be in this environment. But I definitely did feel that pressure to get those numbers up! And the Board of Education, and even our own Gateway Board looks at those numbers and starts asking questions: 'How come this number is low, and this number is high?' And then in faculty meetings everyone's complaining about the skill level of our students being so low. Now, they happen to be the same kids!

"And the teachers were saying: 'These kids have no skills, why are they here?' I don't know; it's very much of a 'Catch-22.' My feeling is you bring kids who can feel successful and are set up to succeed, but also are diverse. And there *are* kids out there who are like that; you must find them and you get them to come here. The problem in San Francisco is that there are schools who have a ton more money and resources who want the same kids.

"This year I felt like I was much more competent. My priority was getting kids who can handle our course load, who want to be in a program where they are motivated to succeed, and they have to work hard. But who also bring that diversity component."

Let's have an example.

"Peter Thorp and I were talking last night about it. About twenty out of every hundred of our kids who are coming in next year are African-American. That's really high! But our Latino population is twelve. Out of one hundred! Well, he said: 'How do you feel about that?' I said: 'I feel excellent. I feel we are trying to establish a culture, of getting work done. And I feel like kids who are coming who are diverse and strong kids.' And that's what you want to show as examples of success. You don't want to set the kid up to fail; and you also don't want to say that the only diverse kids we can find are these kids with, you know, very, very low math skills. Because that's not true, and it's just furthering a stereotype that shouldn't be around.

"So—yeah, diversity is a big thing. And it's a personal thing, because the purpose of this job is to make sure we hit every community in San Francisco."

Was she not allowed to view the school population as a whole? This present year's class is very heavily-weighted for Latinos.

"Our Latino population is high for this school, but for this class it's *low*. And the African-American population for this school is not very high; but for this class it *is* high. So to me the big picture is this: In three years, you're going to have a whole school of kids committed to excellence. And that's what's more important; diversity comes when you have a good school. Diversity is an important part of being at a school, because that's how you learn how to interact with other people. But if the people you interact with are constantly lower-achieving kids, then that's how those stereotypes are formed in other kids' heads."

Some ethnic groups in this area seem to have been able to remove themselves as a group to be viewed as an ethnic minority, or a group to be given handicap in a certain way. Did this phenomenon alter her qualitative view of the ethnicities of applicants?

"That's called the 'model minority theory.' They made themselves into models. And at our school, actually, Chinese students are under-represented. According to their population. And it's interesting, because I don't think the Board of Education really cares if they are or they're not. I mean, they don't really worry about the Chinese population, and I think they should. They should be worried about whether these Chinese students are getting a well-rounded education and what the effect on them is from being with other kids who are not of their background.

"So—the question often unspoken is: Is there a model minority? And what does that mean for those Chinese or Asian students who aren't doing well? I'm not really excited about putting any sort of stereotype on any ethnicity, because I have it. I have a certain ethnic background, I'm East Indian, my parents were born in India, and I was born in California. And I walked around constantly feeling like there are expectations for me one way or another: 'You're born in America, so you should be doing this. But you're also Indian, so you should be doing that.' And I don't think there's much, you know—the feminist Indian women are emerging! I think it's really surprising, because I think it's breaking this expectation."

What is the dynamic, or the energy, or the chemistry or the intuition, or whatever it is, that happens between Meghvi Maheta and an applying student, that gels and causes that student to come here?

"I don't know what it is. I think there is a lot of anxiety, I think that kids are looking for someone to give them the answer—that this school is right for you. And I think the kids remember our interactions, because it's this heightened awareness of themselves; they're really worried that whatever they do, they're going to screw up, or think: 'I must have said the wrong thing!' or whatever. And I think my goal with every student, whether they're 'in' or not, whether they're accepted to come or denied, or they don't enroll is at least to let them know that I understand where they're coming from, and that they're valued. So, what's hard is making a huge value judgment on them, whether we take them or not. And a lot of times a rejection translates into: Their skills are just not up there enough. And we don't even have very strict criteria!   We give them two years' grace period on some subjects, because we think that we can do that. But whose awareness is even more heightened, because they know that they're not performing at the average level, or even right below average level.

"I don't know if that's answering your question.   Are you asking me, what is the chemistry between a kid and me?"

In essence, yes. After all, didn't something special need to happen here, so that a kid whose academic record is a mess, but who's a sharp kid, who could contribute, who could be turned around in the areas of deficit, would be spotted by somebody who carries some inspiration in with the job?

"I don't know if I have that yet. I definitely didn't have it last year. Any kid who could make me cry in an interview, it was very hard to say "No" to! And Peter will tell you, that was quite a lot! Some of them would walk out, and say "Thank you for this interview," and I'd say, "Thank you for coming," and then I'd go into the bathroom and come out an emotional mess—! And you know why? It's because think every person in this world has a story. And some of these stories are really tough!

"What I *do* have, I think, is I have some sort of ability to form a relationship with somebody even after only knowing them for ten minutes. And so the kids who really are looking for that relationship, with the teacher, get really excited about Gateway, and Gateway really is about relationships between teachers and kids, and kids and kids, and all that. And so I think that is where the inspiration lies.   That the teachers are really excited to get to know kids.

"But I don't really know if I have what you think I have, which is this 'eye,' because even if I did, it doesn't make a difference, because we use a lottery process!   It's not like I'm picking these kids; I basically am facilitating this process, which is grueling and devastating to three or four hundred eighth-graders, so they can be told whether they're good enough to come to this school. And I don't know—I don't know how much I really like that process. But I *do* think that there's a chemistry between Peter Thorp and me, that's different from how people in our roles interact at other schools."

What was the first class for which you were the 'midwife'?

"The freshman class this year. I came in at the end of November, 1998. So there already was a class, the first class. Of course, everything that year, I'm given to believe, was pretty much one long running panic."

There is a pattern here—charming in a way, sort of 'engagingly desperate'—in which a lot of people at Gateway say: "There is a crisis, and it's hopeless, we're all doomed!" And then they just pick up and keep going, and are there to deal with the next crisis. And the school is still in a great state of flux. There are a lot of issues that the students feel, about the stability of the faculty, and clearly issues that the faculty feels that have to do with the students—all of which is just normal school life. But maybe at this stage of birth, it's tricky, or unnerving.

"I think until we get a senior class, until we have a full school, we're going to have a crisis every day. Because every year, something is going to happen here. It's kind of what I like about being here. It's also what I don't like. I like the fact that one day I came to work and I saw Peter trying to unhinge a classroom door because it was locked, and an art teacher needed to get in, and I spent an hour and a half trying to help him do that. And he did it! So I like that.

"The first day of work, I came in a—not really a suit, but it was kind of like a suit, and nice sandals. And I got to school, and the director of the Learning Center said to me: 'Oh, good—you're here! You're going to go with Group C.' And I said, 'Excuse me?' And he said: 'It's community service day. You're going to go feed people in a soup kitchen.' And I'm looking at what I'm wearing, and—I mean, it was almost to the point where I was a little disappointed, but it was also a feeling: 'This is crazy! This is great! Let's get right to it!'

"But it also makes it hard to function as a school. And I think that Peter is really resistant at systems, as I am in my own life. But I see how it breaks down, on a day-to-day basis, how things aren't working well. And I think we can't expect our kids to make adult decisions, so we have to put a system in place for them. They are guided that way. I think that we can set our kids up to fail in any aspect—in cutting class, in being late to school, in treating other people disrespectfully—we can set that up, if we wanted to. And not that a system is the answer; but it's really important to have something in place. And I think the crises will happen, until we have some sort of way to prevent them, and then deal with them effectively."

Peter Thorp, it was important to note, talks about dealing with all levels of problem. There is the small crisis—a skateboard infraction— or a large issue—a painful deliberation over a need for a student's expulsion or suspension that's wracked the faculty.

"Problems will always come at all different levels, you know. And it's really hard to distinguish what kind of problem will have the most lasting effect, if not handled well. The *truly* big ones are: 'How come kids aren't respecting their teachers? How come kids can't stop talking when a teacher's teaching? What about our culture allows a student not only to get away with it, but to think it's okay?' We need to figure out how we're going to deal with the big ones, and not just get wrapped up in the small ones all the time."

Still, you're the one at the gate, arbitrating who's here and who's not. And student behavioral issues seem to command center-stage most of the time, no?

"I think the reason for misbehavior ·is not because these kids are bad kids, but because a lot of them had nothing to lose when they came here. And a lot of them were looking for a Lowell High—a school at the top of recognition—but they wanted a smaller one. You had two distinct populations: Kids who want to do well, who came from private schools, from parents who didn't want to pay for education anymore and whose youngsters either didn't get into Lowell because they missed it by a couple of points, or wanted that smaller setting—they're here, and they're doing well.

"And then we have kids who, I think, for the most part are this very diverse group of kids, who could have gone to other San Francisco high schools like Balboa High, or Mission, or Galileo, and decided instead: 'I've nothing to lose, I'll start this new school, this is really exciting, and adventurous, and I want to do it!' Or sometimes it was because their middle school counselor said: 'You should really go to Gateway, this will be different.' And without really knowing what they were getting themselves into, they said 'Yes.' And now they came here, and they don't really understand the concept of loving to learn; or creating relationships with teachers; because in most high schoolers' minds, teachers are supposed to be enemies!

"And then you have the middle ground, kids who don't fit into either category. They're actually the group of kids I'm most bonded to. They have that spirit of adventure!—and risk-taking. I kind of feel like I'm one of them, I feel like I'm going through my sophomore year right now, this month, this very time of deciding! I kind of feel like I'm in their class!

"So it's an interesting mix. But I feel that this year it was really clear that the kids who are here to do well, and want to go on to college and are really worried about their grades, don't want to be in the classes with kids of lesser focus or ambition. They really want to be in classes where kids all want to learn. Because they see others' distraction as a detriment to their own learning."

Is it that divisive? One class from another?

"One of my best 'finds' was a girl who told me: 'My math class is filled with kids who talk all the time, and don't really want to be there to learn. And I'm not like them; but it's really hard to be different in a class like that.' And that's what concerns me. Because I spend all my energy, and anything I can possibly do to convince kids to come here. And I think: 'What's the use of bringing them here, if they aren't even set up to be successful by their peers?' Which is why I'm putting a priority more on academic strength than anything else."

It sounds a little like the "first-child" syndrome. But discerning these priorities in admissions lead us to the lottery system. How does that requirement jibe with selectivity, with a school's own choice preferences?

For the first time, Meghvi hesitated. She smiled softly.

"I have to be careful here, because it's very legally-driven. Basically, we ask for applications. And the reason behind that is to weed out those kids who just want to sign up to go to a school. Because we want to make sure that they understand what Gateway's about, and they want to be here. And also to see any serious 'red-flags'—either in behavior or in skill level. We need to know up front if they're just too low for us even to be able to help them.

"So our process is not to be exclusive; not to take out the kids we want, but to take out the kids whom we just don't think will benefit from our program. Because of the skill level, or their behavior, and in some cases I guess the behavior issue is more for our own benefit. But we're just too new to take on so many risks. And we have already. So the goal is to have as many kids in the lottery as possible.

"And then, what we did this year—which I feel is a better example of a year, and I think it will be the beginning, the precedent that's set for our admissions—is that we picked out those kids who have a priority in the District. The District gives priority to certain groups of people, people who live in three different zip codes—I think it's 94134, 94110, and 94124, I believe. So those kids from those zip codes are prioritized; siblings are prioritized; and students who are eligible for free- or reduced-lunch are prioritized. This year, we just took them out; and those kids automatically got in. If they made it in the lottery, and if they had a priority, they were in. And then we picked the remaining. For one hundred spots, you kind of want to admit a little bit more. We admitted sixty more, as a beginning of the year, because we think sixty of our kids who were accepted probably won't come here.

"And then we had a wait list of kids who made it in the lottery, but weren't picked. And we had sixty-six kids on the wait list. Of those sixty-six, about maybe thirty have gone to other schools, and thirty are very, very much wanting to be here. Clearly, for me the worst part is the 'deny' part. Because I don't like telling parents that their kid didn't get in the lottery. I don't think it's really a good idea, either. That's kind of how it goes.

"I still think, although this year was a little bit more of a trying year—I think that if a kid really wants to be here, and has the profile of a kid we could take, they will get in. But they may not get in in March; they may have to wait to get in in June, when off the waiting list."

Peter was dealing with a letter from a parent of someone who had not gotten in, one day at the beginning of one of our dialogues. His letter in response was much more perfunctory or bland and impersonal than one would have thought he would have done, given the kind of person he is.

"His response to their letter?"

His response to the parent's lament that his kid didn't in, and not quite understanding why. His answer was pretty much the "canned"— you know—"So many applied; we can only take so many" idea. Now, perhaps the truth is that that's pretty much all he can say, without opening up a situation that's fraught with more heartache, if he were to pursue it with "Let's see what we can do," and all of that. He can't do that, can he?

"It isn't always smooth or cut-and-dried. Today I had a mom come in, and try to get her kid in. She only applied to Lowell, and didn't get in. A single parent, parochial school—she's earning all A's. And the mom has been here for eight years from Russia. I told her: 'Your application's very late; we've accepted kids, and then we have a wait list of about thirty or forty, and your student, if she were eligible, which she looks like she is, would be after that.' And the mom was saying, with a very hushed voice: 'Please! Please help me! I'll do whatever I can!' Then she added: 'Ms. Maheta—I'm going to Russia in three weeks, I'll bring something back for you!'"

A bribe!?!

"That's the second time or third time some distraught parent has offered something for admission to their child. And I said—I think the only thing you *can* say is: 'I hear your frustration. I can imagine how painful it feels. But I cannot do anything.' And I kept trying to convince her to get an alternative, because I said: 'Look: Your student looks like a very good student, and the chances of her getting in over someone who might have classroom behavior issues or bad grades are high. But you do not want to be in a position come September of not having a school for your child, because you 'put all your eggs in one basket.'

"Of course, just by my suggesting that they have an alternative, she was very nervous. And yet, that's all you can say. And there are many days which end with that kind of dilemma."

What resources do you draw upon, to sustain your mood and energy after such situations?

"Last year, Peter was helpful in giving me a lot of guidance; but nobody can really tell you how to do your job. And I came home one night, and I just started crying, I couldn't stop crying for an hour. Sometimes a denial means a kid will go to a school with gangs. But— one must be positive, of course. And the good part of the job is that you're helping people. It's nonetheless hard to forget that the bad part is that you are oftentimes taking away any possibility that they will have a really strong high school career. Because Gateway is so far removed from the gang scene, from the idea of not-having-the-right-status scene, and it's really just a kind of haven for kids who are at risk in any way."

Now that fact, certainly, is one of Gateway's strengths, isn't it? And accounts for so many kids here?

"This is a very exciting place. It has a lot of areas to improve. But—I don't know—I think the issue with charter schools is that everyone wants to fix something, or change something, or be a pioneer. But sometimes you just need to get down and do the work, instead of thinking about it! And sometimes you're getting down to doing the work so much you *can't* think about it!"

In summing up, let's return to what is arguably the current operant philosophical theme, not only at Gateway but at all schools in this and many other school districts: Diversity.

A while ago you mentioned your close identity with the classes you're building from student applicants throughout the community. And perhaps unlike many admissions directors, your background qualifies you for exceptional sensitivity to the issues surrounding racial and ethnic distinctions. What about your own "diversity" issues? Are there any? If there are, how do they fit in with your feelings, your professional judgment, and your effectiveness?

"I don't know if there is any resource that makes it easy to fit in when you're not white, or when you're not in the majority. I'll give you a case in point: A group of us where I live had a party for one of my roommates last night. And we talked. She said, 'You know, I don't have any non-white friends.' It's always interesting when I look around the room and realize that I'm the only non-white person there. And now that I think about it, last night was a testament to that. My other roommate, who is Egyptian, and I were the only non-white people there.

"And it's almost scary to me because I don't think that people who are like those at that party ever really think of me as being different. Because I don't think of myself as being different. But there are certain cultural things that we will never have in common. And will never be able to reconcile. In my family and in my life I didn't feel like I really needed to make a decision. I just was whoever I was, and that was okay at the time. And yet, there's a connection that will never be made. Sometimes it's as simple as listening to an old song, and hearing someone say: 'Oh, yeah, my parents used to listen to this singer!,' and I don't have that. The culture that parents have when they interact with people like my friends, and the way that *my* parents interact, is much different from the way that my roommates' parents interact with me. Just a different cultural way being. It's just something that another person can never be a part of; so no matter what you say, how you describe it, words cannot explain it. A culture that is not as complex to you, not as mysterious, is naturally easier to understand in some ways.

"One of my black friends who went to Stanford had a different idea about this. He said: 'You know, it's curious to me that every time I'm with friends, I realize they're all white. And sometimes I really feel like it's a noticeable quality, and sometimes I don't.' Now, his roommates are all much more diverse, but they're not Stanford grads. They have much more diverse circles of friends, and I think, to some degree, when they come over, it makes my one roommate from Maine, the one we gave the party for, feel a little—not uncomfortable, exactly; but she's just not as excited about them. She's not as *present* for them.

"And I don't think this fellow meant it as a *race* thing; in some way, I think it's just the circumstance making him feel: 'You don't look like me, and I don't know how comfortable I feel being around people who don't look like me.' And that, of course, is the whole thing that's bringing us all to head with each other!"

Does that give you clearer indications of what path to take in your school position?

"I don't know, I'm not sure. But I do know this: It makes what we do with this issue at Gateway all the more important!"

Of these three key office-holders at Gateway High School, Meghvi Maheta—the first to meet the students—had the last word. The consequences of her student selection, and Gale Mondry's capable fiscal embellishment, and Lisille Matheson's steerage as founder and Board chair, broadened awareness of the complex interconnections which together made up a new charter high school.

If the school as of the day I left Meghvi's office was growingly complex, its intricacies paled in comparison to the forces to which it would be subjected in the new semester which loomed.

A deep breath was in order.

A Note at First Semester's End

On Thursday, 20 January, twenty days into that new calendar with its unaccustomed chevron "2000," the initial semester's final examinations were completed at Gateway High School.

By all accounts, this first measurable academic period spent in the old Laguna Honda Elementary's building had been a great success: Students had formed friendships; teachers had stretched their pedagogical wings; parents had been invited to jump on board and help reinforce the bulwarks of education; the prestigious outside services of a learning researcher had been enlisted to crystallize Gateway's focus on individual student information acquisition patterns. And a gambler—Board Chair Matheson's confidently-conscripted headmaster from distant parts—had quietly brought to the streets of San Francisco an approach to education with a psychological walk which to those who would experience it was a sure-footed swagger.

Had anything happened out of the ordinary?

On the face of things, perhaps not: Young people had fit into their roles as high school freshman and sophomores. Teachers had planned course structures, soaked themselves in learning theories, exposed themselves to enlightened viewpoints from many sources, and thence turned to prepare, with their colleagues, to continue the good effort, the hard effort, the sometimes-exhausting effort, in the awaiting half-year which would start without fail the following Monday morning.

What had devolved within the growing outlook of Gateway's preeminent educator, Peter C. Thorp? Did he still carry his convictions about young people? Did he still want to teach very young children, when his administrator's roles came to an end in some future time? Did he still believe in it all?

A revealing event had taken place the previous October, when the school year had only been coursing for about a month. An evening meeting in the school's Multi-Purpose Room was in process, a collective of parental committees. It was late, and the fifteen or twenty people there—with their "liaison" roles, and their "student activity" reports, and their "budgetary" or "computer list" assignments—had debriefed each other and were winding down. And then Peter Thorp, the school's principal, walked forward to the focal point of the circle, and sat down. He appeared casual, yet curiously restive. He began to talk; it was conversational, but came from deep streams.

He talked about kids' learning styles, about the mildly-controversial subject of how much homework high school students should be asked to produce. He talked about the differences in maturation between a ninth grade student and a tenth grade student. He entertained parental comments about the acquisition of good or bad study habits, and extrapolated from the anecdotes a number of watchword points about expectations—realistic expectations comfortable for parents to hold, and points about those expectations which would lead to frustration. Peter spoke in his quiet voice, to a receptive group, for the better part of a half hour. And then he stood, and, smiling, walked from the group and the meeting closed.

Nothing he had said was remarkable, or precedent-setting; but two things happened which were noteworthy. The first, so simple and baldly symbolic, could have been overlooked: At one point, striving for physical comfort in a straight-backed auditorium-type chair, Peter altered his position to posit his six-foot frame upon it in the least ungainly fashion; and as he did so, his checkbook slipped the confines of a back pocket, and fell to the floor. There, for the preponderance of the time he spoke, it lay between the prongs of the chair's legs. And only when he was finished talking, did an alert parent notify him to retrieve this resource of a bank account, which he did in one movement, and with a distracted grin. It was an obvious inference to draw for anyone who saw the incident that to Peter Thorp, the least important part of his work was the check which Lisille Matheson's bookkeeper created for him at the end of a month as Gateway's leader.

The second incident—even less obtrusive than the first, but of such a wider meaning, was that something in Thorp's presence—his message, his manner, his very voice—had brought forth a sense of reassurance, and had engendered a feeling to that group of parents, a low glow, a quality of good will and purpose and positivism which was of such greater, lasting value than the routine exchanges of information necessary to keep committees on track.

And now, three months later, a milestone had been reached. For all those students, a unit of study had become historical, factual, verifiable, and a part of their records. And as trendy as adolescents like to be, things of permanence hold great meaning for them. I doubted that Peter Thorp had thought about his checkbook since then; but I knew without doubt that he had thought about homework, and learning styles, and the concern on parental faces, many times since then.

And so, at the end of that last long morning of the first semester, Kate Graham, Gateway's Academic Dean, and Tara Kini, that teacher who had worked so intensely to help a lone student struggling with his studies, walked together in the light rain toward Irving Street to seek a bite to eat and a sanctuary for their animated conversation.

On that same afternoon, outside the school as the dark-haired teacher and the pretty young dean disappeared down the walkway, a tenth grade girl called out to her boyfriend to be at telephone's length, that evening, "—without fail, y'hear!"

And also that same afternoon, Peter Thorp—father of two and pontiff for one hundred and ninety-two academic acolytes—prepared for yet another visit by the scrivener with the tape recorder; a new candidate for a staff position; a night-and-a-day or more of test grading assistance to his faculty; and a new semester's renewing cycle of teacher's meetings, curriculum preparation, beginning classes, youthful faces, questionable answers, and unanswerable questions.

Part Three:

SECOND SEMESTER

Forethought

During the panic and irrationality surrounding the Lindbergh kidnapping, a flamboyant retired school head who fancied himself percipient offered his services as a "go-between," to be entrusted with making the initial contact with the child-stealers' representative. Taking the sobriquet of "Jafsie" (from the initials of his name, John F. Condon), the former principal did not hesitate, in pursuit of instructions for a money "drop," to meet with a mysterious figure in a graveyard. Historian Joyce Milton, in her book *Loss of Eden, A Biography of Charles and Anne Morrow Lindbergh* (1993) writes of the encounter:

> *Seconds after Condon entered the cemetery, he saw a man waving a white handkerchief. He approached and found himself sharing a stone bench with a muscular, clean-shaven man who held up his coat collar to shield his face. Condon had not spent three decades as a high school principal for nothing. "Take that collar down and be a man," he scolded.*
>
> *The stranger complied.*

Chapter Ten

HEARTS COMING TOGETHER

"The part you call "comfort with ambiguity" is not something that schools are set up for. Ambiguity is seen as incomplete answers. Ambiguity is seen as not mastering the content. So, one of the things that has to happen is that schools *need* to be comfortable with the ambiguity. And of course, that ranges from "Is it right to steal if you're starving and have children?" to five hours' worth of faculty meeting last night deciding whether or not a kid should remain here. It is connected, in my opinion, to a misguided rush to excellence that dominates our language. In a way, I think people have lost sight of what excellence means and doesn't mean. Not only the illogical "Lake Wobegon" effect of everybody "being above average," so to speak, but—to ask it: What does excellence in a school mean? To me, a school is excellent if it's just loaded with mistakes....."

"By the time a kid is eighteen, you've got a pretty good sense of what that person's going to be like in adult life. Can he change? Sure; but it seems to be a pretty good predictor. And so, those years between ten, twelve, fourteen—especially between fourteen and eighteen—are critical years in the development of a belief system. And schools are not equipped—and that's not a criticism of schools, it's a criticism of society—for the most part, to devote the time and attention we need to giving kids proper guidance in the development of their own belief systems."

27 January—*San Francisco's winters try their best to accommodate the moods of an urban, sophisticated and always-desirable coastal* cosmopolis, *and so the millenium-turning season brought just the right measure of rain to steep emotions in melancholy, along with the perfect* *temperature for letting things keep going (snow and ice are dictionary concepts here). It was also not surprising that, between seasonal emotional "highs" and finals-time anxieties, the beginning of the second semester would bring with it a lessened enthusiasm, and a need to regrease the skids for the ongoing task of learning.*

When Peter Thorp and I sat down on this date for our regular session, his evocation of our mutual joke about this being our weekly "therapy session" lacked the fullest irony or eye-twinkle we usually accorded it. My accommodation to his long face—("It seems to be one of those days!)," followed by my inelegant but sincere offer for him to "Spill your guts!" found him ready, spiritually, to do so. As I would learn, there were several very compelling reasons for his distraction.

It will also be remembered that, as part of a Gateway family, this Reporter and his son handily serve here in an occasional role of example. The available exemplars were brought into play in this session; but the real onus was on Peter Thorp—and the session proved a crucial one for assessing the psychological stamina of the Principal.

THORP.   We've had a very emotional last fifteen hours, even longer than that. We had a faculty meeting that went from about 2:45 yesterday until about 7:30. And in that five hours—whatever the math is—we talked about five kids.

FELTON.   Wow!

THORP.   Which is a function of a number of things: It's a function of how deeply we care about the kids. It's also a function of the dysfunctional nature of educational conversations about kids, and how you could possibly spend that much time talking about that limited number of kids. And it's mostly a function of the incredible emotion that swirled around.

To get right to the point: We were reviewing five kids who were on academic probation coming into this semester. Our concern was whether or not to allow them to stay here at the school. In two of the kids' cases, the recommendation was that they ought not be allowed to stay at the school. Now, I've been through this enough at my previous work in boarding schools, where everybody picks up, moves on, and life goes on. But in the short run, it's very emotional on all parts, and particularly when the school is trying to build its culture. In the first kid's case, we spent an hour and a half on her alone. But the conversation was as much about who we are and what we care about, and what we are as a school, as it was about her specific case. And we had to thrash through those questions in order to make some sort of thoughtful, reasonable decision on her.

So there were a lot of emotions swirling around. And of course, because it just happened last night, we're still in the "thick" of it. The kids at issue don't know our decisions yet. Not only the student body at large, but these two kids don't know it. So it's not over, yet.

FELTON. I assume that since these kids were on probation, there had been some history to it. Was this meeting therefore a kind of "court of last resort," well into the time when the serious decisions have cut themselves out clearly?

THORP. It's the classic Solomonic position of weighing the interest of the individual versus the interest of the community.

FELTON. Expand on that.

THORP. That's what these decisions were about. And it's further exacerbated by the—"tendency" is not a strong enough word, but the Pavlovian response is probably too strong—by the desire on the part of educators to save every kid who comes his or her way. And very much a function of that for even those of us who know that you can't do that. You just can't. That is still very much tempered by the thought: "But if they have to leave here, what are they going to?" And what they're going to—in both of these cases, what they're going to, we believe, is so much worse or potentially worse, that staying here—well, you have the sense of having condemned them to a life of lack of opportunity and at least as much misery, if not more. And when it comes down to the final vote—"All those in favor of this resolution"—you can see the agony on people's faces. And I can tell you, it was pretty "heavy" last night.

FELTON. Meghvi Maheta relates a similar reaction—a guilt reaction, really—when turning down a kid for admission whom she knows will end up in a gang-ridden school.

THORP. These are real problems, and real people involved, for all of us. But this situation was more than agonizing, it was also dysfunctional. By that, I really mean "inefficient," in terms of spending that amount of time on those kids. After all, a different school with a different *ethos* would have given about three and a half minutes on each of them, because the conclusion was so clear-cut and so obvious. Each sophomore had an eighteen-month history, including last year. Eighteen months of nonconformance; a very clear expectation as to what they had to do to stay here, and they so totally fell short of those expectations that again, if we'd spent three minutes on it, we couldn't be questioned for not having given it due deliberation.

FELTON. Well, it seems to me that in that deliberation, that kind of democratic community of you and people who teach here, you took a very generous stance in which you really wanted to seek every possible dimension. Even if decisions are ninety-nine percent made by crisis time, you wanted to hear it one more time, to see what you could find in it in the way of redemption.

THORP. Yes; very much so. And of course, there was individual investment on the part of certain teachers. And what's particularly emotional for me, is that one of the two kids is my advisee. So, I wasn't just wearing my "Principal's Hat." And different people in the room had different levels of investment in the kid, some really didn't know the kid, because they teach only ninth graders, and the kid was a tenth grader. Thus they haven't really crossed that kid's path. So their decision was much more "clinical," if you will, not cold-hearted, but clinical, rather than emotional. And of course, the great balancing of the needs of the individual and the needs of the community—all the people who are not present, and particularly the parents and the rest of our students, those, those two constituencies most strongly, are saying, "Goddammit, get rid of these kids! These kids are the ones getting in the way of the rest of our kids' learning!"

FELTON. I can imagine.

THORP. And *they* deserve our services and our support as well. That's in the end why we made the decision we did. If this was the Oxford tutorial system, we wouldn't have to worry about anybody else. We would—the effort instead would have been trying to figure out another way, to try it one more time, one more approach, one more cajoling, pleading, confining—you can make a list of the strategies. There was commitment to do that. You might wonder, when one kid's faculty constituent said: "I volunteer to be this kid's mom from eight in the morning until 4:30 in the afternoon, and this kid won't go anywhere without me." Or, "I will sit with this kid, and have him check in with me twelve times a day to insure he's in the right place."

FELTON. Well, you'd be forgiven, if on no other basis, for having the posture that you were trying in every way to get a return on your investment. It's a lot of time to spend on a couple of kids—that's two, two and a half percent of your student body.

THORP. Yes—which means we didn't get to the other three, by the time 7:30 had rolled around. We pretty much had all run out of gas at that point. We didn't get to the other people, and so we're trying to do that by E-mail. But—back to our pursuits.

FELTON. Well, Peter, I hate to hold your hand over the flame; but these in fact *are* our pursuits! One of the things I wanted to do today was to tell you that this session should really conveniently wrap up the first semester. And actually, we're on point with this discussion. In our process we want to do just what we're doing, in our laying down some philosophical thought, and tracking some issues, no matter how painful they might be for you. The story of these three students' misfortunes certainly is one; it will be worthwhile to check the ramifications of this situation down the line, or see if there comes any similar experience. We can hope not.

Another issue in progress—and, by way of a compliment, a change of tone: I thought you took a quick and definitive handling of all the issues surrounding the sexual harassment situation. It seemed a great example of "leadership on the spot" by what I understand were buzz sessions, bull sessions—however you want to characterize them—last week, and calling in some outside expertise to bring the student body into a position of focus on it. Can you tell me a little about it, what prompted that, and was it successful? How do you feel about it?

THORP. At the risk of bursting your bubble, I had nothing to do with it! We had originally intended to have that day be "Career Day"; and the truth of the matter is we didn't get things together quick enough to make it work, for students or teachers. Have you seen a set of Gateway grades?

FELTON. Not for this semester end. But the first quarter grades, yes.

THORP. First quarter. All right. To enable the teachers to write extensive individual comments, we give them a day off, a professional day to do that. So it leaves us a skeleton crew to marshal the rest of the program. And we had planned to do this special program, and it didn't happen. So there we were, at the beginning of the week, saying to ourselves: "Okay, we've got Friday, and we've got kids showing up; what are we going to do?" And that's really what led to "Don't we think that it's time to take advantage of this day to focus in on some of the issues which have been bubbling up over time, and more immediately, in the days preceding it?" So that's how the sexual harassment evaluation events happened.

I was actually—again, to further burst your bubble—I was one of the more cautious people on this. In part because I've dealt with other sexual harassment cases and I get paid to be the most "savvy" person around here in terms of legal issues and other ramifications that follow. And I've also been around enough to know that sometimes the last thing that a kid who has made an accusation about sexual harassment wants to have happen is some sort of public big deal made out of it. So we went through that, and got a series of meetings going with a couple of kids involved in that incident. This was on Thursday, before the Friday of the event. We let them know that this was happening anyway, and assured them it really wasn't as a result of the issue that they personally had raised. And of course, a young person is going to believe some percentage of that, but not all of it.

FELTON. True.

THORP. The day itself was great. And here are a couple of anecdotes from it: There was real concern on the part of a number of the people that we would, in fact, be exposing some girls who had the courage to step forward in the recent days, to make some accusations. "Oh," they might have thought, "So this was where it was going, for them to make a public deal out of it!" And so it was my job to set the tone of the day. And I did, with small groups. The point that I tried to make was that every once in a while we give ourselves an opportunity to do some community-building, that this was not academic, but still very important core issues of the school. Not the least of this issues is how we treat each other. So that was really my theme for the day, trying to make it broader than the sexual harassment issue, or cross-gender issue, or same-sex harassment issue.

And I used the example from last year that I may have told you about, in one of our conversations: About the day after the Columbine incident?

FELTON. We've mentioned Columbine in a limited way. So you might develop that a bit for us.

THORP. Columbine? Yes. Of course, school happened for us the morning after the murders there. And again, I take zero credit for this, it was really the idea of our Assistant Principal. Spencer Tolliver came to me right away the first thing in the morning, and said, "Peter, we have to start the day with an assembly." And so we did. We got in a circle; and I said something, and Spencer said something, and we had a moment of silence, and we sent our prayers and thoughts to the people of Columbine. And then we began a conversation, or invited kids to join in a conversation about how things were going here at the school. And—yes, Columbine was bad, and yes, those kids were gone, and that sort of thing; but what was behind Columbine? We understand, from what we then knew from the news, that here were two kids who for some reason had taken this unspeakable action in response to having been harassed or teased, or not treated well at school. And how do we feel about that at Gateway? We spent a few minutes—

whatever it was, thirty minutes—of very powerful conversation with kids sharing back and forth their observations of how in most cases they had felt that people hadn't been kind either to them specifically or they had witnessed unkindness, in other events.

And—most powerfully—one kid in particular spoke, and apologized for being disrespectful or abusive or teasing other kids; he said: "I really didn't mean it. And I want you to know that; I also didn't realize how hurtful it was." It was an incredibly powerful moment. And I cited that moment recently in a speech, noting that we didn't want to take advantage of Columbine in the situation, but that in talking to the ninth graders and the new tenth graders about it, here is one of the things that the discussion evoked; and it was really one of the most important days of Gateway's history, with this morning assembly.

And that's what we're trying to do today with these assemblies, to take time out from the day-to-day stuff of what we do in classes. To spend some time building community, and talking about what's getting in the way of building community, and what's contributing to building community. And to engage in conversation which will help us take advantage of what we're doing right, and address what we're doing wrong. And which we hope will take place in an atmosphere of trust, so people will feel like they can say what's on their mind. And as you probably heard from your son, we set it up—we did a couple of sessions. We had a woman from the Rape Crisis Center come speak. We asked her to speak specifically about what sexual harassment is. And then we had this police officer, who was a woman assigned to schools, and we've had her in a few times—she's become "our cop," so to speak. And she was great; she did this kind of rambling presentation ranging from "Here's my gun" to "Here's my life story growing up in the Cabrini Green Projects in Chicago," and you know, going to jail herself, and now here she is on the street as a cop. And she was very articulate, a no-nonsense kind of person. The students are hugely impressed by it.

And then we finished the initial gathering, and the students broke into groups, male/female. And I and another faculty member went with one of the groups, and set up some conversations. The key question in each group was: "What do you want the girls to know about you, as a boy?" and "What do you want the boys to know about you, as a girl?" And then when we came together after lunch, we exchanged some of those observations. It was really quite open in the single-gender session, and more closed when we got back together again. But nevertheless there was some good conversation back and forth about issues of communication and misunderstandings between the sexes. It was done in a way where the kids came out of there feeling good that they had a chance to speak about it; and a number of kids came up to me afterwards and said, "We've got to do this more often." And we should, and we will.

So it was a good community-building day. But it's the kind of thing where one has to be realistic that we haven't cured anything, by spending one day on it.

Peter Felton was a very bold and active participant. Did he share that with you?

FELTON. Well, he shared something. But I'd like to hear more about your observations; and then I'll tell you what he shared. It was kind of symbolic.

THORP. Sure. I was very impressed with his willingness to put himself out there. And I don't teach Peter, and I haven't had that much contact with him, but he seems a pretty reserved guy, in many ways. Yet—he was the least reserved guy of the day, at least in my group; and I dealt with half the kids. And I was impressed with that. I was quizzical about why he was. And I was curious about what his motive was. And I hadn't had a chance to speak with him about it. And I was also concerned about some of the things that he said. And it's clear—I mean, this is my interpretation—it's clear that Peter is wrestling with how to establish positive relationships with the opposite sex.

FELTON. Absolutely right!

THORP. And it's clear that he's not succeeding. And it's clear that he's really frustrated. And it's clear that he's trying; and it's clear that he's in this kind of maelstrom of emotions that need to get straightened out sooner rather than later. And I'm a little concerned that his comments were seen as so outside the pale that for a guy to take a risk of revealing himself in terms of some very personal feelings that he expressed!— all appropriate, but in doing so he ran the risk of being absolutely unproductive in terms of what his goal was. Is that consistent with what he said?

FELTON. That's consistent with Peter in the larger sphere! You see, what I take out of that: Peter—not to dwell on him, but—

THORP. No, this is part of the story.

FELTON. —But his thinking is often like someone who's running so fast that he trips over his feet. Peter does that, emotionally. He gets going with something, and then he suddenly finds that he's sort of overbalanced, and other things come out that are really sitting back there. And it sounds as if that's exactly what happened in these meetings.

He's very forward and straight about his feelings, his frustrations that he doesn't have a girl friend, that he doesn't seem to find anyone— and despite all of our ways of trying to mollify all that, and set it into perspective, he still feels it keenly. And the truth of it is that Peter's got a lot of maturing to do before he will make himself attractive in that way. So I'm not surprised that this is the case. But—I talked with him here, on a lunch break, when I was here to see someone else.

THORP.   It was that day, right?

FELTON.   It was that day. He told me a couple of things very quickly. He didn't really take the time to expand, and I haven't seen him at any length since then; but one thing he told me very proudly was that he was in *your* group. This meant a lot to him. And the other— which I tried to read what it meant, because it could have meant two things with Peter—I made a note on it—he said this as if it was a key emotional revelation, he made this comment: "Do you know?" he said, "Peter Thorp pronounces it '*HAR*assment!'"   And I thought about that; for with Peter, things like that aren't inane little comments. With Peter, that could mean two things. It could mean simply that he had heard the other, incorrect pronunciation, which many people use, and he wanted to let me know he was being "lexicological." Or—it could have been his way of saying: "You know, I really saw things in a new way!"

THORP.   Interesting. Yes. A kind of signal there.

FELTON.   That's right. When I next work with him, I can find out which it is. And of course, I hope it's that he got some insight. I don't know if there was opportunity for feedback, just within the context of the group expression; but I'm sure he benefited from that session. And he'll talk more about it when he's absorbed it. But I think you're right.

THORP.   It will be interesting to see what he says to you, to that question, "Did you get feedback, or what did you get out of it?" As I say, he was an incredibly impressive contributor, in terms of not only the frequency of what he said, and the forcefulness with which he said it, but also to push the conversation to a more honest level.

FELTON.   Yes.

THORP.   And of course, the thing with adolescents is: Being honest is a *big risk*! Especially when it involves issues of boyfriend-girlfriend or gender issues. And so my observation on that is that Peter was a great contributor that day, but not a great listener. But as you have enlightened me in previous conversation, it's not always "what-you-see-is-what-you-get" with Peter.

FELTON. He's very "up-front" about things. There are some things which are almost charming in a way. We'll walk down the street, and he'll take my hand, the way he did when he was a very young boy! Or he'll kiss me when we meet, which is lovely that he has retained that affection and trust, and will do that. Or probably a more revealing example, and something I can't imagine having said to my dad—when he went through puberty, there was some occasion when he said, casually, "Oh, say, Dad, do you know, I'm getting pubic hair." Just as if he said, "I wore the blue shirt today." And that's—he's completely comfortable with that. So in a sense, he views himself as an "open book." On the other hand, the "book" is a really very convoluted story. And so I'm hoping that there'll be some growth there.

THORP. Another young guy—a very large black kid—probably had the most poignant moment today, when we were in the group session. He talked frankly and movingly about being teased. And you can imagine, with his size, how much teasing he's faced in his life. We were talking about talking itself, communicating. The concern of the girls in the group, expressed to the boys, was: "What we want from you is that we want you to reveal your emotions more. That's what's wrong with boys. Please reveal your emotions." Okay, we've all read the books—you're right. But the young fellow I mentioned—in one incredibly powerful moment he said, in effect: "You don't understand: If I reveal my emotions, and how I really feel about the teasing I've experienced in my life, you're gonna get a set of emotions that you haven't bargained for." The point he was making was: "I keep things inside because I don't want to share my pain with you; and if I share my pain with you, you're going to get a S_{name} of pain which you don't realize." And of course, the girls' response to that is: "Tell us more! Share more! It's good for you!" and all that sort of thing. Well, there's the battle of the sexes.

But the contrast that I'm making is that it was an utterly poignant self-revelation, which actually elicited applause when the guy was finished. Applause of support and sensitivity, to him. Whereas Peter's remarks didn't elicit that same kind of support, because his comments sounded more accusatory than self-revealing, when in fact they were profoundly self-revealing. And one of the things he said—I mean, he commented very strongly in both the all-boy session and the group session—on what he wanted from girls. He said—and I was puzzled by this—he said: "What I want from girls is when you break up with me, or when you spurn my advances"—and those are my words, not his— "Don't do it by saying something duplicitous like, 'Oh, but you'd be much happier with Mary.'" Be *direct* with me! Don't try to make me feel better by giving me this phony soft letdown!" And I thought: "Yeah! Why should somebody have to experience the falsehood of the kind of line which says, "Well, you're not good enough for me, but you're good enough for my best friend"? And he was saying: "Don't you understand, women, that I can see right through that!?" And, of course, what I heard was not only the point that he was making, but I heard what was behind the point: He has made overtures in some number of cases, whatever it is, to try to make a connection in a relationship and has been spurned. And has felt not handled well by whoever the young woman was who, rather than being direct with him, shunted him off with the sop: "Well, there's somebody else out there for you."

So: It's a surprise, sometimes, to see such strong feelings emerging in a young person. What's so important in this age group, when those feelings are expressed, is to respect them; and the only way to do that and know what is best to say, is something one won't know until the situation arises. Just think of the kids first. It's perhaps the only guide.

FELTON. Your harassment workshops utilized the large, central space called the Multi-Purpose Room. Are the twice-weekly student assemblies you hold there generally perfunctory scheduling occasions for announcements, or are there moments on a regular basis where it's warmer, in the manner of a Amish service of sharing? Do any routine meetings have the character where they could lead into the kind of group experience you just described in another, more crisis-promoted context?

THORP. Yes; but not frequently enough. And it's a function of planning time as much as anything. In fact, Assistant Principal Tolliver and I were talking about this for tomorrow; it's a function of the rapid pace of life in schools, where suddenly here it is Thursday afternoon, and we have an assembly tomorrow morning, Friday. What are we going to do?—which is not an excuse, but it's an explanation for it. How that kind of lack of planning can take place.

That's one answer. A second is: Unfortunately, it's become a time where too often, the assembly has been used for negative messages about our culture. For example, we're wrestling right now with the fact that there have been a number of thefts in this school. And—this is killing me, Keith. It's just absolutely ripping me apart, that I can't— that kids are being abused, hurt, bothered and wronged, by a relatively small core of kids; and yet, we can't be everywhere at all times. So, Spencer Tolliver and I are talking about whether or not tomorrow's assembly becomes the "theft" assembly. Because you can't ignore it.

FELTON.   Yes.

THORP.   And yet—we all get grumpy when the assemblies are grumpy. And the best assemblies we've had have been those times when there has been some community action, two of which were where two of our students sang. In two separate assemblies, some students presented musical numbers. They brought about a great, uplifting moment.

So we need to develop a curriculum for the assemblies. We have curricula all over the place. And one of the curricula to develop is a curriculum for assembly. So we really have a strategy and use that time we have together. Because otherwise, whatever the law is, available junk fills available time. And we have plenty of available crap in terms of announcements. And we have many cultural announcements. So: One of our goals is to use that time more effectively.

FELTON.   You mentioned Columbine. The Felton family's first foray into the Gateway family—a meeting for prospective parents— was right after Columbine. And two of the students, two young women who were standing and presenting their thoughts, mentioned the assembly where everyone was together on that. And tears came to their eyes when they did; it had been very recent. It was hard.

THORP.   I was not prepared for how that impacted our kids. For me, it was a challenge, a terrible tragedy which you can't really just park in your "emotional parking space," in a way that you could deal with it.   Our kids came to school that Friday with the question uppermost: "Will it happen here?" As you could image, I had a huge rush of phone calls from parents, saying: "What are you doing for security at the school?" And it's kind of a terrorist answer that you hear from the federal government, who says, "Look—if you have a committed terrorist who's willing to die for his cause, there is *no* way you're going to stop him." And I sure as hell wouldn't say this publicly, but if somebody wants to get into a school, they can get into a school!

But these kids were really frightened, and really disconcerted, and it was so good that we had that assembly—even if it had been far more perfunctory and less profound, it was really important to have it. I've learned how anxious kids are.   I don't remember growing up as an anxious kid. But these kids *are* anxious.

FELTON.   Let's jump for just a minute to some fiscal talk.

Tonight, the President is going to talk about the State of the World. The State of the Union.

THORP. I'll be in rapt attention on that.

FELTON. I daresay. He's going to give his education emphasis. And obviously, Clinton is going to have his stance; Vice President Gore is talking about 100 million dollars for education. Governor Davis is out there today, at Washington High in San Francisco, trying to look like a good guy. I'm interested in how this strikes a man like you, when you hear these things. How does a principal, sitting in his school, in his city, a long way from there, react to that? Do you think it is sloganeering? Do you think it is heartfelt? Do you get out your list and start making all of your needs clear so that when that money just rolls in, you can handle it? What happens? Is it negative? What do you feel about it?

THORP. My primary reaction is my stated feeling about the dearth of courage in the political arena. I'm as disgusted with whole driven policy developments as I am with single-issue policy people. And that's why I'm outraged at Jesse Jackson's position in Decatur, Illinois—not because he was fundamentally wrong, but rather because in the past, he's been a healer. He's now been terribly divisive, in a situation that would have benefited enormously from healing. I mean, the Decatur Board of Education was wrong to expel these kids for as long as two years; but they sure as hell were not wrong to expel them. That was necessary.

The polls indicate that among the American *populus*, education is one of their great concerns. Thank God! And—so at least, we've got the right compost heap, maybe, to generate some political activity.

The frustrating part of it is that we have a mindset of both immediacy and quick-fixes that lead to such things as: "The way to fix education, the way to measure that we've fixed education, is through test scores." And—I'm trying to think of a good example of it—it's not unlike these Taiwanese buildings we hear about in earthquakes; until the earthquake comes, they're real fun to look at, decorated with all sorts of neat finishing touches, but they don't have one ounce of rebar in the walls.

And it's the same kind of thing regarding education: How can you expect that the problem's going to get solved because you measure standardized testing, when you can't fix the foundations? So people are coming at it from the wrong point of view. And again, I think I've told you my feelings about the real Monica Lewinsky crisis, and now I'm going to be real curious to see. Because what politicians—and you mentioned three really good examples, Democrats all, at one level, but coming at it from slightly different perspectives—none of whom, in my opinion, has the courage to get at what the issues are. I'd love to see a politician really take on the educational program. I write speeches in the shower all the time, and I never mail them, on thinking that if people could recognize that by the time you get them to high school, it could be too late. I mean, as I've said in previous sessions, that's one of the things I'm wrestling with, is—how much can we really do, by the time they get here?

Okay; the implication of that question is: Pump the money into pre-school, into Head Start, child care programs—to give everybody an opportunity to challenge the country to support teachers in a meaningful way, by giving them salaries that they can really live on. And don't do it with the carrot-and-stick approach of: "We're going to give it if you pass this test." If somebody's been in your school system for twenty years, and you haven't dealt with it, then it's you're problem, not the teacher's problem. Pay him a decent wage. And—as in the Decatur situation—the community standards and the school standards are not together, there is a need to make sure the community and the schools have their values aligned.

There is also this "zero-tolerance" policy. Well, what does that mean? To me, it means this piece of your community will have no tolerance for behavior that appears to be acceptable, or at least allowed, in another segment of your community. So you don't have your community working together. And as you've heard me say in a previous conversation, but to try and put it somewhat delicately: Why don't the Democrats have the courage with the other glove, to say to the teachers, "You know, you're responsible for policing your profession. If you don't like other people policing the profession, then somebody else is going to have to do it." And those are the kinds of political messages that I think are ridiculous.

So, in sum: I'm thrilled that education really is at the top of the California Governor's agenda. And I think it will in fact be an issue in this national campaign. And Clinton would like to do something for education in his last months in office. He won't; but he's going to try something real serious. And I think there's some hope in the sense that the Republicans don't want to be put in a position where the Democrats will say at election time: "Look, these guys voted against whatever the issue is: A stand on supporting teachers." So, there's a chance that crafty Democrats can bring the Republicans along on this, because this is the time when the public wants to see something done on education.

FELTON. Let me explore one limited aspect of testing. This week produced the Stanford 9 results in the Bay Area. I'm wondering how you'd respond to something else that's happened. I see it, and I wonder if you do.

You're a San Francisco high school principal and you're watching his television set, just to relax, and here comes an ad, for the "Sylvan Math Course." And here comes another one called "SCORE." These are programmatic outfits, commercial products, set to take your student and get him where you want to get on math remediation. And I even saw one on the Internet, called "Caplan," which—

THORP. —"Full-stop shopping."

FELTON. Yes! And one of their pitches, one of their inducements was that this is an aspect that is attractive to realtors. Realtors can sell houses in communities, because those communities are able to show higher test results! I'm overwhelmed. I wonder how you feel about that?

THORP. Welcome to the painful real world of educational shopping. It's—it is to me, depending upon my mood, it's either uproariously funny, or profoundly discouraging, that people would put such stock in test scores. Now, there you have in the paper that Lowell High School in San Francisco got the highest ranking. Well, if they didn't, there ought to be a federal investigation as to why they didn't! And there was the city's Balboa High School, in this morning's paper, discovering that they didn't get scores, because they didn't have kids take the whole Star test. The former principal was kind of saying, "Gee, I thought we did." And in fact a real bungle took place on that.

It's just so misguided, to focus so exclusively on test scores. And yet, it's understandable. This is, you know, the American passion today—to look for easily-solved problems, or easily-identifiable criteria where one can feel like he knows what he's talking about. "Well, this must be a good school, because it has high test scores." Or: "This is how I'm going to be a good realtor, and I'm going to let people know which neighborhood in my city has the best school because it has the highest test scores." Well, I don't think Peter Felton—if I may use Peter as an example—would be best served at Lowell High School. Let's say Lowell was a neighborhood school rather than a magnet school. So I don't think your realtor would necessarily be doing you a service, if you were moving into San Francisco today, to say, "You've got to live here. Pay the extra money to live here, because Lowell's the best high school."

The second issue on this, of course, is that it simply underscores the incredible unfairness of how one's socio-economic status contributes to one's opportunities in life. And unfairness is too weak a word. That's something that people need to stand up to and the politicians need to address. And I'm actually hopeful that Clinton might make some references in his State of the Union speech along those lines. I do know that he's proposing a ten-thousand-dollar tax credit for college tuition, which is going to help the middle class. Maybe he's going to talk about some funds for schools to have more placement classes in the high school, or better facilities, or whatever it is. Those are the kinds of things that make a difference.

As to test scores:

The test scores are (a) a false measure of educational value. It's not that they're utterly false; but they're false to the extent to which they're abused. And (b) we create a political agenda which sure as hell trickles on down here to Gateway, which puts incredible pressure on us.

One of the reasons why I'm probably looking slightly frazzled, in addition to the other things we talked about, is I got a phone call from the District yesterday, saying "I just want to let you know that on February 15, you guys are going to be called in front of the Board of Education to do a presentation about your school." And I also happen to have known, from someone who had the "inside scoop," that the members of the Board of Education right now are at war with each other. And one of the things that they're at war about is charter schools. So this guy who called me said, "Gee, we want it to be as painless as possible." And I'm saying to myself: "No, you don't! I know what's going on. I know that there are some members of the Board of Education who want the scalp of at least one charter school, and the rest of us are going to be dragged into it, because if they go after one, they've got to go after all of us, to make it look like they're being even-handed about it.

And of course, they're going to establish some criteria about the diversity question. In my opinion, Gateway has the best diversity of any school in the city. That's not going to fly at the Board. I'm going to try and make that case and I'm going to stand up to them when they say, "Well, you don't quite understand what we mean by diversity. We mean what's your percentage of African-American and Latino students at this school?" And I'm going to say: "It's just like it is here in the city, and that's the way it should be." And then they're going to get all over my case on that.

FELTON. That's something you felt sometime back, too.

THORP. We're not perfect. But we're providing a certain level of service, that apparently wasn't that well provided in San Francisco up until this point, which is to have people say, "Yeah, I think I'll send my kid to a public school in this city..."

The other problem with statistics is they're used to support political agendas, rather than the other way around. It should be that political agendas are spawned by an analysis of valid data which would help you say: "Okay, we really need to do this!" And that is happening in some cases.

FELTON. I'm not trying to make you feel worse about this, but—

THORP. You can't!

FELTON. Right! But do you think this is a "done deal," and they're just playing out the little drama?

THORP. No. No. But what I fear is that—I mean, I'm not afraid that they're going to pull our charter. I can't believe that they would do that. But what I fear is that they're going to put constraints on us in a way that's going to insist on *their* point of view rather than what *we're* trying to do; and that's going to turn us into just another old school. A Lowell school. And that certainly is not what I'm looking for. I don't think that's what the city needs. Now, again, that's somehow—and given that this only happened yesterday afternoon about this time I obviously haven't gathered my thoughts about it—but somehow, I'm going to have to go in and try and make a pitch along those lines. And what this guy who called said was: "Just go in and tell them basically about diversity." And I said, "Fine." But somehow, I've got to figure out the way to get the message across without being aggressive about it; because then I won't have any leverage. And I really think it's important that they hear what I think is important in the schools on this issue.

So mark your calendar for the fifteenth of February!

FELTON. It sounds like running for Congress—you've always got to be selling yourself!

THORP. Yeah. But you know, it's part of the drill.

FELTON. Well, let's go to something nicer, though probably not as consequential: I wanted to update you that I'm canvassing others here to give them an opportunity to contest the rumors of your popularity. I started with a great meeting with Lisille Matheson, the Board Chair.

THORP. Great. She's an incredible woman. Incredible!

FELTON. So I gather. Well, it turns out she feels the same about you. And I felt in truth that she had a really good, strong bead on you. She sees your qualities—and she understands your frailties. You're a dimensional man, you've had some unhappiness in life, and you've learned how to use that to your advantage in your own growth. And she also understood exactly what I meant when I referred to you as an artist. She said: "Absolutely. And he's a wonderful father as well."

THORP. That's the best news. I'll tell her to call my kids and tell them.

FELTON. Well, that's exactly where I'm going with this point!: She grasped your humanity. And if that is palpable to the people who come in contact with you—then I do think back to that time when we talked on January 11, when you made that comment about reaching out to a kid and being told, "Get away." You were just starting to say that you were beginning to learn why they feel that way. And I don't know if you feel like talking about it, and you don't have to excoriate your soul. But I'm just wondering if there's a direction there that might—

THORP. No. I'm happy to talk about that, because that's—I really thought you were going to use a different example. That example actually is not one that I feel such a sense of personal shortcomings. If I'm understanding your example correctly, the failure of kids to respond to my outreach is, as I see it, more of a function of their inability to trust an adult reaching out like that, than that it's *me* reaching out like that.

Now, again, clearly the fact that I'm the Principal, for some of the kids, is part of it; clearly the fact that I'm a man for perhaps some of the young women may be an issue; clearly I'm not twenty-three. I mean, there are all these kinds of components where I may in fact not be the "right one" to reach out. And also, clearly, I tend to reach out intellectually more than I do emotionally, and that may also be a barrier to a kid—or anybody—feeling: "I can connect with this person, I can allow this person into my realm of thinking in a way that I'll trust him not to abuse my faith." That's probably far less than you had in mind with the question.

FELTON. No, I get a good sense there.

THORP. What I thought you were going to ask me was when I talked to you about the challenges I've had over the years connecting with other adults. In schools, with faculty—do you remember that?

FELTON. Yes. But this was not that. Any notion of that was extinguished by the encouragement at finding you which Lisille Matheson had, and knowing right away that "the math was there." And it's very interesting, both from the standpoint as I see it, of her responsibilities and her personality, and your responsibilities and your personality, that these are highly insightful, capable working people who go after problems, but do it from the standpoint of a very unassuming, very low-key approach.

THORP. She's an incredible boon to me. And the board that I work with is the best board I've ever worked with or served on.

FELTON. Really! Why is that?

THORP. Because they're everything you want; they're supportive, their worker bees. And they don't sit there and say, "Do this, do this"—they roll up their sleeves and help as well. They care deeply about the school, and most importantly, they're not wrapped up in their own egos. Which unfortunately tends to be the reason that boards become dysfunctional before long.

FELTON. Let me pick up on something you just said in another context. You mentioned the "intellectual" versus the "emotional" component of your behavior. And that really prompts another question I had:

I ran across a new study in which the polarity distinguishing, as the study put it, "emotionality versus rationality," had new meanings, with the emotional being given a negative connotation, and the strain put on the rationality, to focus there. And I've been thinking about this in connection with what we're trying to do with kids, what the educational process at this age level is attempting, most demonstrably here at Gateway. We've accepted somewhere around the age of ten, twelve, or fourteen years as the age of the dawning of moral consciousness. And I'm curious about when you feel a philosophical consciousness develops. I have a way of viewing that, and I'll mention it, because it deals with that rational versus emotional side of kids.

Some of the work I've been doing on a project dealing with Albert Speer has reminded me again of the impact and the richness of the "Plato's Cave Allegory," as a learning matrix. It seems to me that that, and other legends, have a power of mystery, and they extol mystery, in every sense of "not knowing." Or even, if you will, as far-fetched as the Catholic concept of "mystery" is, as an idea—that richness of what we're not certain about. There's the question of "reality versus illusion," all a component here. And how a youngster will develop a kind of balance between a confirmable reality, and a speculative reality. And again, we seem to emphasize the "confirmable," we're looking for the "factual," we're looking for the concrete.

Well, I'm unsettled by that emphasis. I'm still pursuing when the kid encounters an abstract world. And there are tons of examples of everything we do in other perfectly routine kinds of aspects to our daily living, such as black-and-white versus color, the notion of theater, as the old cliché goes: Theater is lies like truth, lies about truth, it's a fictional situation which tells something deeper and real.

I guess the question out of all of this that I'm looking for is: How is all of this development of an apperception of the world best shaped, by people like the preceptors here, for grasp by an adolescent mind? And what, in essence, is offered to kids in the form of an intuitive way of perceiving and analyzing, as well as a systematic way of doing it? I think kids obviously are exposed to some kind of abstract thought throughout—religious families promote the idea of a God concept, and kids wrestle with that, I presume. In other ways, the language, the culture, development of tolerance, of a nonjudgmental point of view toward others—all of this might or might not be based on how they interact. And we might want to shape that based on something that's less concrete and more abstract. So I've distilled my thought down to the fact that I know we want to inculcate this scientific mind in students with a logical predisposition to an orderly way of thinking. But what about giving them an equal chance to develop a way of accepting what I'd call a philosophical disorder, and encourage a kind of philosophical scrutiny accompanied by a direct, or a willful, or in a sense a positive delving into *uncertainty*?

My last point: How do we make the young mind comfortable with learning and thinking as a producer of the *unanswerable*, as well as learning and thinking as producing a *solution*?

THORP.   Well, that'll take a few days!

The quick response to that is: Okay, that's *algebra*. For many kids, the leap from arithmetic to algebra entails an awful lot of what you're describing. And I know that it's so much more than what you're describing; but it's what separates some kids from others, I think, in their ability to master algebra. It's also, on a broader plane, that kind of goal—and if I heard you correctly, the part you call "comfort with ambiguity" is not something that schools are set up for. Ambiguity is seen as incomplete answers. Ambiguity is seen as not mastering the content. So, one of the things that has to happen is that schools *need* to be comfortable with the ambiguity. And of course, that ranges from "Is it right to steal if you're starving and have children?" to five hours' worth of faculty meeting last night deciding whether or not a kid should remain here. It is connected, in my opinion, to a misguided rush to excellence that dominates our language. In a way, I think people have lost sight of what excellence means and doesn't mean. Not only the illogical "Lake Wobegon" effect of everybody "being above average," so to speak, but—to ask it: What does excellence in a school mean? To me, a school is excellent if it's just loaded with mistakes. And of course, that would require a long explanation for the person who was avoiding me. But I think you understand what I mean.

FELTON. Yes.

THORP. And so, school culture needs to change, where kids can feel that it's okay not to know the answer, either to the question of algebra, and "What do I do when I don't know the answer?" and "Do we have a college where the kid feels comfortable trying to get the answer?"—by raising his hand in class, or by coming in after school, knowing that a teacher will in fact be there, or is interested in working with a kid after school, all that sort of thing.

It's also a function of asking the right questions. And again, one of the things that I've learned is that in the public sector, as opposed to the private sector in schools, you are constricted to having a more narrow range of conversations than you are in the private sector. And maybe for the better; I'm not going to make a qualitative judgment about that, although my bias, I'm sure, shines through. So that, for example, when right before the winter vacation we had those series of assemblies, great assemblies where we shared various religious traditions, we had to allow kids to get up and leave. That killed me!—but we did it. And, you know, in retrospect, I don't know if it was the right thing to do.

Your son Peter will experience, here in the second semester in his humanities class—an initial unit where our focus is comparative religion. That's what our study is going to be in Sophomore Humanities. And if you haven't gotten it yet, you'll get a letter shortly from the teachers, sort of saying, "We're doing this, and we hope it's okay, and you won't be too mad." But we have the need to do that. So, part of it is: There's a constraint on the questions that are allowed to be asked, in schools about religion, which I think is belligerent. It's further complicated by the fact that there is a knee-jerk reaction that "values education" in schools runs the risk of "values indoctrination." When was it?—ten, fifteen, twenty years ago?—I don't know—the whole fashion in schools was "values education." And that ran aground on account of the question: "Oh, by the way: Whose values?" And my response to that is: "*My* values, goddammit!" In the sense of: If you put me in the position of the principal of your school, then I've got to believe that you appreciate my values as a human being. But is it not the case that in fact there are in this culture, some common values? And that this isn't "We're all going to celebrate Christmas," but rather it's: "We're going to be nice to each other." And that's a value that I don't feel one should back away from. Even if being nice to each other means a conversation like: "You can't use that language." "Well, I get to use it at home, and my parents say it's okay." "But you can't use it here."

So—back to my point about cowardice—there is cowardice on this issue, of philosophical development. Because if you study—and God forbid you should be condemned to go into the School of Education—if you study "wounds taxonomy," as it's called, the highest level of the pyramid of thinking is evaluation. The next highest level—the kid level—is synthesis. But when you get to evaluation, you get into the key stuff. And—

FELTON. Sounds like Maslow's hierarchy of needs.

THORP. Yeah. There's a connection, or at least, a parallel structure. So it balloons, and approaches a neurocognitive level. And this is the nature of learning that should take place. But the highest level of intellectual activity is when you are able to make a judgment about something. Because you not only have the data, that kind of low-level, and eventually you'll be able to synthesize different points of view. And now you can draw your own conclusion and make a judgment about it. So it's a sort of intellectual hierarchy. But of course, given what it is, it really then provides a springboard into the development of belief systems. And there's no question in my mind that we have, as a species in this country, a higher percentage of, shall we say, "developmentally delayed" folks on that pyramid than would serve us well.

I don't know, we could reach some sort of silly conclusion on that; but I do think we're heading in the wrong direction as a country. As a country, we're not doing a whole lot of evaluation. It's not a particularly reflective country. Whereas in the Depression, maybe—not having lived through that—I think there was a level of reflection in the Depression, out of necessity—arguably, a level of reflection in World War Two, out of necessity; and I think in my own experience, a level of reflection in the '60s, partly, quite frankly, because of the reflection caused by drug-altered conditions, partly playing the game of evaluation in and around the Vietnam war. And I imagine our generation probably was overly simplistic as we look back at it, about some of the issues that were going on then.

Actually, the best example of this is not really Vietnam, but, some time later; Cambodia and the killing fields. Why wasn't this country outraged, and why didn't this country stop and do something? And my response is: Because we learned the wrong lesson from Vietnam. And our generation was responsible for learning those wrong lessons. So—

there's not a whole lot of evaluation, not a whole lot of reflection—not a whole lot of time for reflection, it seems. And not a whole lot of necessity for reflection, in this booming economy.

FELTON. Yes!

THORP. It's not too far away from the mentality of Calvin Coolidge's "The business of America is business," to the mentality of James Carvil's "It's the economy, stupid!" And I'd like to say, "It's the values, stupid!" But nobody wants to go there.

FELTON. To me, the most disheartening thing about philosophical education—I mean, a philosophy of education, if you can call it a philosophy—is that it does go to that mentality of: "Just keep 'em going through; let's just worry about the tests. And let's not get into any of that amorphous stuff." It's just a real change.

THORP. And it's really a shame, in the years of adolescence, because these are the years when, as you said, I forget how you put it— ten, twelve, fourteen, when moral development is taking place—it really gets fixed at the conclusion of adolescence. By the time a kid is eighteen, you've got a pretty good sense of what that person's going to be like in adult life. Can he change? Sure; but it seems to be a pretty good predictor. And so, those years between ten, twelve, fourteen— especially between fourteen and eighteen—are critical years in the development of a belief system. And schools are not equipped—and that's not a criticism of schools, it's a criticism of society—for the most part, to devote the time and attention we need to giving kids proper guidance in the development of their own belief systems. And that's not to suggest we should tell them what their belief systems should be. But to challenge them—and frankly, it's the reason why I love to teach history, because that's the way I do it. As a vehicle for evaluative reflection or ethical education. Just through the lessons of history, and what better way to do it? I mean, what better way than to put the kid on the spot, and say, "Give me the answer to this question. What would you do in that circumstance?" Or, What should you have done? Or, Why didn't we do something to stop the killing in Cambodia? If you had been present, what would you have done? What would you have done if you had "Sophie's choice"?

FELTON. A couple of comments on that. Peter did mention to me that the religion unit was going to start. But the way he said it—in a very typical "Peter" way, with a little bit of apprehension, was: "Ah, now we're getting into some religious stuff. I don't want all that 'Lord' talk, and all that prayer stuff." And I said, "Wait a minute, wait a minute! First of all, the state won't let you do that. You don't have to worry about that, no one's going to approach that; there are laws against mixing those two things." Peter prides himself—and it's deserved—on a very thorough knowledge of geography. So I said: "Here's a chance for you to enhance that, because you'll learn what the Moslem world is, and you'll learn what the Catholic world is, and you'll learn where the Hindu agglomeration is, and the whole geopolitical and religious conflicts of ages; and as you can look on the map and figure it all out, it's going to excite you! Don't worry about it. No one's going to make you say The Lord's Prayer, or whatever you don't want to do!" But that was his first reaction.

I was interested that your initial response to my question about speculative thinking was about algebra. I hadn't really thought about that. Peter's younger brother, my sixth-grader, is in a school where he has a keen math teacher. An extremely sharp woman who's a Russian *emigrée*, who speaks five languages. She'll teach very thoroughly a lesson in advanced math—and I'm not even familiar with what they're doing, but it's algebraic—and she'll make sure that every kid gets it, she'll go through whatever they're proving, to see every kid gets it solidly. Then, at the end of that unit, she'll say: "Okay: Now I'm going to show you how we would solve it in *Russia*." And she'll give an entirely different approach and proof to the same problem! And I just love that! She doesn't dwell on it; but she gives them that dimensionality, to say: "There's an alternative belief here. There's a different way of doing—"

THORP. —Something that allegedly is fixed. That's wonderful.

FELTON. It *is* wonderful. And that's what I miss about it; how do you develop a concept of alternative beliefs, if all you're hearing is—not only "the party line," but you're hearing a very denatured party line.

THORP. Tell Peter to talk to me about geographic determinism. When I teach U.S. history, I love being outrageous in U.S. History, and I have the kids work through two theories during the study of U.S. History; and I'm only half-joking, when I say I'm intuitive, and they both have to do with the Civil War. One is: I have them write a paper responding to the thesis: "The Civil War was caused by rocky soil in the North."

FELTON. Great!

THORP. —Now, that isn't geographic determinism; but the second one I have them do is: "All the history books are wrong; in fact, the South won the Civil War."

FELTON. Those are great challenges!

THORP.   They're effective questions to get the kids to look at truth, and—especially the second—to look at truth through new eyes. I mean, frankly, it's also how I entertain myself.   And I think as a teacher, one has to be able to entertain oneself at various times! So for me being a contrarian serves many purposes.

The other one I really love to do is the proposition: "The Constitution is in fact an anti-Democratic document." I have great fun with that.   That's the 'sixties guy in me who will never go away! I probably will tread more carefully teaching that unit in the public sector than I did in the private sector.

FELTON.   Yes! Will you have a chance to do that here?

THORP.   To teach? Well, we're in the negotiation stage right now, with our full-time faculty on this. But I'd like to be able to teach the Advance Placement U.S. History section. I don't have enough time to teach more than that. And that's what I should teach. Now, there are some other folks who might be interested in doing it, although obviously I have the most experience in that field.

FELTON.   As you look back over the semester, what are your triumphs? What are your failures? What are you excited about—I mean what just kind of jumps out at you? What still stings?

THORP.   It's a remarkable group of faculty.   Flawed as any faculty are, and we can go back to what we said at the beginning of this afternoon—flaws though they are, they are the flaws of incredible heart. One of the great triumphs is that this is a remarkable group of men and women who are knocking themselves out to help kids, and have them be successful. And where there are flaws, both in terms of their own experience and this kind of setting—public school—it's true that they would not necessarily have this kind of experience teaching in "special-ed" circumstances—they're remarkably dedicated to developing skills. Last Friday when they all met with Mel Levine, in a very impressive way, they said to this guy: "Look, this is the kind of stuff we're wrestling with, and we want answers to this, and you can help us out."

On a personal level, one of the great triumphs is just being in this building. Most people don't know the full story of what it took to get into this building. Now, some people do know about the two thousand hours of volunteer time; and the glorious part of that is how incredible and permanent that is. But people don't know how close it came to just running out of time, and running out of gas. So that's a great triumph. It was a quiet triumph, but our back was to the wall, and it was that close! That feels really good.

Another personal triumph—and I'll get to the "stings" in a moment—was that—a personal triumph also is that in the past six months I've had more opportunity to be a spokesperson for charter schools, and education in general. But even in other settings than this one, people seem to think that I'm someone who has interesting and intelligent things to say. And I'm finding myself in a position where I can maybe have an impact. But of course, the tension in that is that the moment I'm away doing that, is a moment I'm not here. And it's a constant balance.

The "stings" really are that we still have yet to create student cultural balance within the school. That's it. We just haven't succeeded in building the kinetic energy, I guess it's called—where enough kids will just go on in a life of their own, alone. There is too much hand-holding that needs to take place, and too much negative Chee, that Chinese concept, being spent on having kids "buy into" what we're doing. And it's draining to all of us, and it's draining to kids. The kids have "bought into" the culture. And that, more than anything, is of greatest concern to me. Because for a number of the kids, we are really at the point of saying, "You know, it just isn't going to change." And we're sort of back to last night's faculty conversation on expulsions.

And that raises all sorts of questions, about who are the kids who aren't making it in here, and why aren't they making it in here? And what are your support services for all that? So, of all the shortcomings of the school—that's it. There are still plenty of things that need to get done—curriculum development, I could make a long list of stuff that's unfinished at this point—but in terms of reflecting over the first semester, it's great to look like a school, and feel like a school, and to be in a building, and to have new carpet—it may seem like silly stuff, but you know just what that feels like, and why I'm commenting about that. But it also—we're not there yet.

And we're not as far along as I thought we'd be. At this point, by this year, I thought we would have the sophomores more "bought-into" the program, as college looms closer. And I thought we wouldn't have as long a period of time as we have had with some set of the ninth graders, to buy into our program simply because we had had a year to "market" ourselves in a way where we felt we did it effectively; and we did do it effectively; but you're never going to have total control over what somebody's hearing you say. We're saying, "Don't come to Gateway unless you're really committed to a college preparatory program," and they have to appreciate what that entails.

So there's work still to be done, and gains still to be made. We're heading in the right direction, and we're doing it, again, with a remarkable group of people investing in this school. And that's not just the faculty; it's the Board of Trustees and the parents, who really want this school to succeed, and want us to be successful, and wants the kids to be happy as they should.

Actually, I don't feel that I've capitalized on that good will and that energy to the full extent. We can talk about why that's the case; but there's even more good will than we've been able to capitalize upon. So I'm hoping that good will elicits even more good energy!

Chapter Eleven

THE PRE-STORM'S MELANCHOLY QUIET

"The trick about being an educator—and this is really me!—is: Who are you going to be? Are you going to be 'Mr. Chips'?—you know, this totally selfless person who at least for a couple of generations of educators seems to be the ideal? It doesn't work in the 'Me Generation' at all. Or are you going to be 'The Prime of Miss Jean Brodie'?— the co-dependent, psychologically-damaged preceptor, what a colleague of mine calls 'pathologically charismatic' people in education? Or are you going to be something else? For me, one of the challenges throughout my teaching career, and this gets back to what I was saying about the way I do or don't connect with people, is to find the right balance between 'thick skin' and 'thin skin.' You can't make it personal with kids. But how do you *not* make it personal? You can't overly personalize it..."

"I think what makes a good kid is not too much different from what makes a good educator: A willingness to be stretched, a willingness to be challenged, a willingness to accept defeat not as crushing defeat, taking things away, as: "Okay. Didn't make it this way; time to try it a different way." I think what makes a good student is—well, frankly, it's a hard question for me. It's a great question. What I think makes a good student is good parents. And that is not a socio-economic variable, in my book. Some of the best kids we have here in the school come from the most modest socio-economic circumstances. And some of the most screwed-up kids we have in this school come from the highest socio-economic circumstance. Gee what a surprise that is!"

4 February—*As the session began, it was clear that Peter Thorp was* *visibly upset.   This powerful alteration of his expression was emphasized by his unusual appearance in the office in a suit and tie— he had attended the funeral of one of Gateway's trustees.*

He shunted this palpable dismay swiftly when, before we began, a young student and his older family member came into the office to retrieve a compact disk player which had been the source of discipline, with the Principal acting as temporary custodian. When the repentant music-lover had contributed his part to the episode's review and concluding admonitions, and he and his monitoring relative had left the room, Peter fairly slumped into the captain's chair marked "Cate School." I slid into the captain's chair marked "Colorado Springs," and, wordless but with cliché arched brows, invited the Principal to unleash the floodgates of private agony.

I had been worried about Peter's possible frustration with the seeming circularity of my questions (actually different ways of approaching a problem, to achieve dimensionality). Peter accepted good-naturedly the fact that this meant he was the "piece of wood" in a whittling exercise. I then told him of the general office agitation which had preceded his return from the memorial. Peter—always attuned to ambience and its meanings—perked up.

FELTON. I have never seen the place "jumping" the way it's been jumping in the last hour or so.

THORP. Is that right?

FELTON. Yeah!

THORP. "Good jumping," or "Mexican bean jumping"? Or—

FELTON. No, it was good jumping.

THORP. —Or maybe Mash Pit jumping?

FELTON. No; very good jumping, in fact. It was a good energy. Maybe "When the cat's away…"? In any event, that has to do a fair amount with some of my questions here.

THORP. You would have made a wonderful Medieval confessor. Just throw out the key questions, and let the sinner spew!

FELTON. Since you've said that, I'm going to jump to a recent report. I heard a news filler item that came over the wire just like this: "There has been a sixty percent drop-off in confessionals to priests—"

THORP. How apropos!

FELTON. —And the news went on to say, "A priest is creating a new plan to make priests available by the hundreds."

THORP. Yes?

FELTON. And my question was: Who's hearing people's troubles instead? Is it psychologists and psychiatrists? I doubt it's too many mothers; maybe some mothers. Is it Dr. Laura?—Frazier Crane? Or—is it *teachers*? What about teachers? Could they, or should they, fill that kind of a role? Are they a valid target for unburdening? Are they available because of the conceits of the position that they want to hold? Are they also available for this other level, and is it necessarily a good idea? How does it work?

THORP. Well, there's a great question!

FELTON. The question really is: "What's a teacher for?"

THORP. I trust you will not be surprised to hear me say that Yeah, a teacher's for that, for making themselves available for the children with whom they're working, be they three years old or eighteen years old. And that is very much at the heart of what I'm trying to do here. Remember, though, that every teenager, at one time or another, makes it difficult to like him or her. But you've got my point. For me, a primary criterion in hiring is: Pick somebody who likes kids.

That doesn't mean coddle; it doesn't mean inappropriately develop relationships of a kind of co-dependency that you see oftentimes in educators. But it means: These people *like* teenagers—and love them enough to be there, both in the "shoulder-to-cry-on" and the "footprint-in-the-seat-of-the-pants" aspect of parenting. The term that most of my educational career was built on at boarding schools is the term "*in loco parentis.*" Now, some say, "Well, that's boarding school, and they're living with you," and that sort of thing. But when you think about it— just do the math—here in a school like this, we're "loco-parentising" seven or eight hours a day of the kids' lives. I bet you I'm spending more time with most of your children than you are.

FELTON. I'm sure.

THORP. And to me it therefore falls short to believe that schools aren't a place where counseling opportunities are legion.

Paragraph Two is: But boy, oh boy!—do some kids bring a set of suitcases of emotional baggage that challenges even the most committed and able educational organizations to meet the needs of that kid. And I'm sure that most of what I've said at this point is that the extent of some of the emotional baggage that kids carry transcends the expertise or the devotion even in a school like this. And the hardest thing for an educator is knowing when to say "When." He must know when to say: "I can't meet that kid's needs for him, so therefore it's not just a one-on-one conversation; it's time to get the school counselor involved. Or, it's time to get the Principal involved. And of course, you take it to the next level, and it's the *school* coming to the decision that we can't meet the needs of that kid, but the kid will be better served in a different situation. That's what's hard.

There's no question in my mind that teachers have replaced priests, to go back to your original structure; but—I guess this is sort of serious!—but we don't have excommunication up our sleeve. Nor, let alone, Hell. So the ability to effect change is more challenging in that we have to rely almost solely on interpersonal connectedness and trust, than was certainly the case in the Catholic Church when I was going to confession. I don't know if you put the question this way because you know that I was one of those fallen Catholics—!

FELTON. No, not really!

THORP. —I'll tell you a quick story: I was an altar boy for ten years, and I went to confession the second week of October, 1962, which was the Cuban Missile Crisis. And there were the longest lines I had ever seen in church.

FELTON. Really!

THORP. —Because everybody thought that we were going: "Poof!"

FELTON. Unbelievable!

THORP. And there were long lines at the confessionals. So I've done that routine. But again: A few "Hail Marys'" at the altar took care of it, or some real finger-wagging, or the "You better stop it or you're going to Hell" kind of stuff. It worked for a little while. With teachers—it's all going to work if kids trust adults. And that brings me back to something I've probably said after every one of our sessions, that's kind of the central theme: Why is it that kids have that trust, in some cases, and don't have that trust, in other cases? What are the variables? Is it the "adult" variable? Is it the "kid" variable? A little of each? If I could be a sage sitting on the mountain top and figure that question out, I'd be writing books!

Did that answer your question?

FELTON. Yes, indeed, it did. Since our last meeting, when we talked a certain amount about my son, I turned to a number of issues naturally flowing from that idea, that had to do with feelings. The question regarding teachers as priests being one; because certainly that kind of confessional bond—and I did mean it in the lower-case "catholic" sense—brought out some other interesting things.

The first few weeks we had our colloquy in place, and I had the Gateway Photo Club running well, and some other activities rolling, the excitement at Gateway generally was palpable. It felt very good; it was rich, and it was immediate. You came in the door, and—just like today, there were a lot of things going on. Perhaps not as kinesthetically as it was today, but still going on.

THORP. Timing is everything.

FELTON. —And then, one day I came up here, and there was a change. I approached a couple of teachers, whom I thought had known who I was, and asked how I could get hold of one particular student. And my question brought out in them an aura of nervousness. And I thought: "Oh, gee, I didn't want to cross the barrier of confidentiality that's there, and I assume they understood that I wanted to communicate with the student for a legitimate reason." But nonetheless, that suspicion was there. And that started me thinking. Then later, in our session of that week, there were a number of tedious and nerve-wracking concerns on your mind that we had talked about. And at that point something just struck me: Those women weren't being rude to me. They were being part of an *organism*; they were reflecting the nervousness of general, institutional concerns. And their concerns in some way represented whatever the issues were which in that time period had kept the faculty engaged, or were heavily involving you. And it was fascinating to realize that this indeed *is* an organism. It works perfectly well; and if the head is upset, the limbs are going to twitch! Something is going to happen.

THORP. Response?

FELTON. Please!

THORP. You touch on a key issue of leadership. You touch on a key issue of effective leadership. You touch on an issue which, for me, is an issue about my own leadership. And it's one that I don't think I do as effectively as some other leaders; and that is, to find the right balance between personal accessibility—and I don't mean the ability to walk in the door—but the ability to "get into" me, to find out who I am. And the ability not to make people nervous with what's going on behind these eyelids when I'm thinking about other concerns.

I'll share with you something I've said to three other people today. One of my strengths as a person is that I'm a problem-solver. I see a problem, I love geometry, I see a problem, and I say: "Let's just figure out a strategy." I love architecture, which to me is one of the great visual problem-solving phenomena. Now, this orientation is a blessing; but it's a terrible curse at the same time, because you begin to see the world as a set of problems that need to be solved. First, I believe it's more of a male issue; if a female significant to a particular man comes to him sharing a problem, most guys—and I'm an extreme guy in this way, although I might be a bit more feminine in other ways—most men take the metaphorical gear shift, ram it into fifth gear, and zoom out, with: "Okay, let me solve this problem!" When, in fact, all the woman may have wanted to do was just share the problem, and just walk away and say, "I got it off my chest," or "Just talking about it helped me think about how I might get out of this problem." So, any time somebody walks inside the door with a problem, my reaction is: "Gee, they're not getting their money's worth unless I solve their problem for them!"

This is particularly so right now. I don't think we've got time to get into this; but there are some serious matters coming down from the School District that are making me nervous as a son of a bitch. And I'm really wrestling with how much to share, and how much not to share. And wrestling with how to share what I do share in as least an *angst*-producing fashion as possible. And behind these relatively calm bloodshot eyes is a guy just riddled with *angst* right now. I don't know if that's clear when you walked in here—

FELTON. Not in that sense. But I knew something was awry.

THORP. —if I was giving you that nod. Okay. So, I'm good at not revealing; I'm good at holding it in.

FELTON. Yeah.

THORP. But—a real personal revelation: The hardest part for someone like me in that circumstance is: "Who *do* I share it with?" For some folks it's a spouse; for some folks it's a dog. Or, for me, I have the blessing of Lisille Matheson, who just is incredibly supportive. But something I wrestle with is, as you put it: When the head moves, the limbs twitch! And I want the people on the staff to be fully involved in the process of building a school and recognizing that. And I also have to be sure that I give them enough credit, as working professionals, that they can handle it. Or, I need to give—I need to have enough sensitivity that "Yeah, they can handle it—but not today." You know? And again: Timing is everything, in some ways.

You have correctly sensed that this is an organic setting; this is an organism, as I think all schools are. And like any organism, it's subject to stimuli. And it reacts to stimuli, whether or not it's the stimulus of warmth and sunshine, both literally and metaphorically; or whether or not it's the stimuli of abrasion and irritation that causes withdrawal, like a paramecium here. Sometimes people don't understand how quickly schools react to stimuli.

Now, most people who follow schools know—especially in a small school—that the character of a senior class can be dramatically different from year to year. It's really interesting to watch, where this year's senior class is so unlike last year's senior class. But this is a school that has moods.

FELTON. Moods?

THORP. Moods, yeah. And you've seen some of that. You've experienced some of them. Depending on the time of year and what you've observed, there are some common phenomenological observations one can make. There is a phenomenon in the schools that, for want of a better term, I would call: The post-Christmas blues. The first week of January is a lousy week in most schools. February is universally the lousiest month in schools throughout the land. It's true in boarding schools—especially true in boarding schools in the Northeast—kind of a "Ground Hog Day" scenario. And therefore, lo and behold!, that's why there are a lot of conferences in warm places for headmasters of boarding schools to go to in February. They're not dummies!

FELTON. Ah!

THORP. So, there are biorhythms in schools. Natural biorhythms that, no matter how you slice it, they're going to be felt. A couple of weeks ago we were in the biorhythm of the stress of final exams. It affected both the faculty and kids, and was really stressful. We're in a different biorhythm right now because the faculty has kind of recharged its batteries to say: "Okay, we've got to push on, and we're expected to push on with some clear direction and focus." And a reflection of that renewed focus is that we're now going to make some decisions about some kids, in asking them to leave the school, that shows real consistency with our mission. Of course this has some sadness to it—I told you last week about this seven-hour faculty meeting. But there's also a sense of resolve that we had to do it, and—this is a terrible metaphor, but it's Friday afternoon—we had to cut out the cancer in order to allow the organism to continue to exist.

So you'll see those moods. And I emphasize that we're very subject to moods. Sometimes I will underestimate my own moods. One of my weaknesses as a leader is that I'm much more cerebral—I think I told you this—I'm more accessible cerebrally than I am emotionally. You've probably experienced that. I'd like to think that I'm a pretty upbeat guy to talk to; but I haven't revealed a whole lot emotionally, although I haven't held it back. You probably know me a lot more intellectually than you do emotionally. You actually probably know me a lot more emotionally than most of the people in the school! And it's not as if I consciously keep it in; it's—you know, it's the way I was brought up, or my neurological wiring, where I try to say to myself: "It's not relevant. What's relevant is—what am I thinking?"; what's relevant is: What's this problem I've got to solve, you know? What's *not* relevant is: How I'm feeling about things. "How am I feeling about things? Why, I'm fine, you know; I get paid to be fine."

A case in point: I'm going to be here all weekend working. Am I thrilled about that? No, I'm not thrilled about that. But I don't have a choice. I'm not whining about it, but I've got to do it for this school. And that's no reason for pity; I make my choices, and this is it.

So—you're absolutely correct, that schools have psychological profiles. And if the schools aren't conscious of that, they're kidding themselves if a psychological profile doesn't bubble up in the grass roots. The salient question is: Do you want to create your own psychological profile, and have a healthy psyche, or do you want to have the psychological profile created in the state of anarchy, so to speak, which develops in whatever way it's going to develop. And then you have the inmates running the asylum. Which, frankly, I think, is not atypical of a lot of schools.

FELTON. Yes. Now, if we follow that logically—and it would be my bent anyway, to view it this way—that biorhythm is felt in every cell of the organism.

THORP. You bet!

FELTON. —And the youngest kid—well, you have big kids here, but if this were an elementary school, I would maintain, although I couldn't prove it, that the youngest kid would pick that up.

THORP. Definitely.

FELTON. It would translate into his or her own way; but it would be picked up. The most complicated adult decision-making process idea by someone on your level, would be picked up by that littlest kid here, in his way. Teacher's behavior or whatever.

THORP. That's right. Kids have teachers absolutely figured out. On some days, far better than the teachers have themselves figured out. They're always watching.

FELTON. Yes! Just one comment, and then I want to show you how amazingly you've anticipated, or taken us already to some places I wanted to take you.

I—not to draw too brutal an example of it—but I hope that there's a way, when you approach that problem-solving, or the need to work the weekend, or problems like that, that it is not like the old somewhat dated cliché of the physician who has to be God at all times, and then ends up on morphine, having given himself some from his own supply, because he can't deal with things. And—I'm glad you mentioned

Lisille, and some other moral support people, because everyone's got to have a recourse.

THORP. That's an issue for me. I've mentioned more than once that I've been described as a "workaholic." And who knows what that term really means; but I sure know that I'm working harder than any one human being should be working, I guess. You know, but I'm a big boy, and I make my choices. And I sort of knew what I was getting into—well, really, if I'd really known—who knows!—but I'm into it.

And—well, let me share with you this anecdote; it may seem like a *nonsequitur*, but I've got to share this with you today, because it happened today. And you can put it into the right context. I shared it three or four classes ago, and each one of those three or four classes is so much in my head. It speaks to this question about why I'm doing this:

We have lab period here, on Fridays. And I've been working with this group of kids who are hanging by various thin threads in their time here. I put this group together after the first quarter grades, because these guys, with three exceptions, are in doubt. So we said, "Okay, if we're going to have these kids make it, forty-five minutes, or fifty minutes with the Principal once a week might be a good dose." So we did it and the point was, it was reality therapy. I told them: "You guys really need to understand how close you are to having to leave this school. You've got to understand." And I drew graphs about levels of expectation, and I showed the slope of that curve versus their curve of improvement. And then I said, "You're telling me you're improving; and I'm showing you in simple mathematics terms—the slope of my graph of increasing expectation is steeper than the slope of your improvement; so in fact, the gap is getting bigger rather than narrower."

So today, we had our first session. And about six of them showed up; and I remarked, "Look, you guys, we need to talk about whether or not we're going to keep doing this. I've been working with you, and I think each of you is a nice person. But I've seen your grades at this end of the first semester as compared with the first quarter, and I'm feeling as if my efforts didn't make much of a difference. The grades aren't very good! Some kids did worse; but my point now is, I think I wasted my time. And I want to listen to you tell me whether or not you think I'm wasting my time." And I added, "It's not that I think working with you guys is a waste of my time; but I'm saying I'm feeling ineffectual. And I'm feeling ineffectual in part because you guys didn't 'buy into' the reality therapy I was trying to give you, and you still hung onto some old habits."

So we went around the room. One of the kids happened to be the only freshman in this group. Most were sophomores, and that shows they were given more time to turn things around and these guys really *were* hanging by a thread, and two of them are leaving; two of them are the ones whom I talked about last week. So this one kid was the only freshman, which tells you what kind of shape he was in at the end of the first quarter! And his name was José, and when it came to his turn, I said, "Okay, José, you tell me whether or not *you* think I'm wasting my time."

And he said, "Mr. Thorp, you're not wasting my time." And I said, "Why is that?" And he said: "You need to know that when we started this, I looked at you and I said, 'Okay, here's another one of these white guys who's going to give up on me, the inner city kid, faster than you can shake a stick." That's perhaps not his phrase, but that was the point he was making. "—And I've seen guys like you"— again, my words, but his point—"I've seen guys like you, and you give up on inner city kids like me. And you need to know: You didn't give up on me. You need to know how much that means to me. You need to know that I *did* improve. My teachers are telling me that. And I know that I'm not perfect, and I know you're not happy with my grades, and all that. But you're *not* wasting your time."

That meant so much to me! And it means more to me every time that I tell it; and I've had three occasions today to tell that story. And I've got to go find that kid. I'm going to connect with him and tell him, "You need to know the impact you had on me by saying that. You need to know how powerful, what an impact you had on me, in sharing that anecdote." And it also is part of my faith in that group.

I think I may have told you my experience from a year ago, with the African-American father? I had written a letter—and boy, you send those letters, and you wish you could take them back!—I'd written a letter which had all the appropriate language: "If So-and-So doesn't improve—and he doesn't have enough credits, and he's going to have to go to summer school, and he's failing his classes—he's going to have to leave Gateway or he's not going to be able to come back here in the fall." And because the kid was my advisee as well, I added the sentence: "It really pains me, or frustrates me—" something like that, "—to see Joe throwing his life away like this." Bad sentence!

The father came in—and he was infuriated! And he told me what infuriated him: "You don't understand how happy I am that my kid even comes to school most days. I don't care how he's doing in classes. You need to understand that I'm so happy that my kid is a good kid, that he's not doing drugs, that he's not in a gang, that for you to say 'He's throwing his life away,' you don't get it!" And he was so right!—that I didn't get it. And here I have my values, and I was shoving them down that family's throat, saying, "Schooling, schooling, schooling is what matters." Now, again, I'm reflecting, I'm not going to sit back and say, "Oh, so if you're an African-American kid from the inner city nobody should push you academically. No; that's not the point at all. But I learned from that family, and I sure as hell learned from that kid today, that, you know, there really are cultural chasms that us Honkies need to be paying a whole lot of attention to, and need to be listening a lot more than we're telling! And this was an example.

We began this monologue with which question? I'll try and bring it back!

FELTON. You're doing just fine. We don't need to tie it up neatly. Everything you've said today has been as if you've read my next question. And here is that question:

This whole subject heading, just to share my notes with you, says: *"Peter Thorp as Responsive Instrument."* One of things about you I believe *is* your sensitivity, is your way of receiving the stimuli in the world about you. I feel that pattern from you, even though you've made the comment about your intellectual functions and your logical predispositions. I want you to try and describe that human instrumentation which is what you were—or, as I put it, "What is your version of Peter Felton's sideways vision? How do you read people?—do you read them silently?—do you absorb them in general in a wholesale way?—do you let your subconscious or unconscious do it?—Do you have eyes in the back of your head?" What do you feel, as a person, are the ways your tendrils go out and apperceive somebody else? No matter that your modus is logical or factual or systematic.

THORP. I'm a complex and sophisticated guy, who can be unbelievably naïve at times. I'm inherently inclined to trust, but as a good child of the 'sixties, I'm not at all surprised when I'm taught to distrust. In other words: When I begin a connection, an involvement with somebody new, they start with one hundred percent, in my book. And it's only when they teach me, through action or inaction, that I should be less trusting of them that the ratio starts going down a little bit. It's particularly true, and where I'm incredibly naïve, with education. To me, the only thing that counts is whether or not it's in the best interest of the kids. It's the only thing that counts. And I couldn't give a damn about anything else.

Right now, a whole lot of stuff in the School Board is flaring up, and it's *not* about kids. For some people, in education in general, in this city in particular, and in this school district and Board of Education even more particularly, it's not about kids. And I now know that. I know what we're up against more clearly than I knew even two weeks ago. And certainly moreso than I knew eighteen months ago.

So, I'm this package of contradictions—sophisticated and worldly, and reasonably intelligent, and that sort of thing; but fully prepared to find that I'm totally naïve.

That's why I spoke at one of our admission open houses about my outrage with the term "gifted and talented education." I think it's unconscionable that some mindless bureaucrat came off with an expression like that. So I've been taught, at a relatively old age now, that maybe I should be a little less naïve, and maybe I should be a little less trusting, than I'm inclined to be. Life sometimes has winners, and sometimes losers. But when it comes to kids, dammit, it ought to be all winners! And people ought to be trying to figure out a way where it doesn't have to be a win-lose situation. That's why this school is not designed to become a school where we're skimming kids off the top, which we could do.

And too, my training as an art historian makes me tremendously sensitive to visual stimuli. I loved art history because studying it in college, I learned to *see*. And so I'm very sensitive to visual stimuli, and very aware of body language. I'm very tuned in to people; and if you ever had the chance to watch me working at a parent conference, I'm very good at managing those kinds of conversations. Because I can tell at the slightest shift of position whether or not a kid is telling the truth, or whether or not the kid is holding back because he doesn't want to say anything in front of his parents, or whether the parent is misrepresenting things to us because they feel they've got to inflate things in front of the principal. So I'm very savvy that way.

Do you remember the Thomas Bailey remark I mentioned in which he wrote, "In the South, the white people love the black man as an individual, and hate him as a race. And in the North, they love him as a race and hate him as an individual"?

FELTON. Yes.

THORP. Now, here's the intellectual link: I love people collectively, and I love kids collectively. And I love adults collectively. But it's harder for me to love people individually. My work—God, I'm sounding Biblical here!—My work is with the masses! Someone said to Mother Theresa, "How could you save forty-five thousand people?" And her response was: "I pick them up one at a time." In essence: "I started with one, and a number of years later, somebody told me it was forty-five thousand."

I see the world in broad strokes. And that's what enables me to be a thinker. But at various times, I get really fascinated with detail. Back in my history, I had the position at a school of Academic Dean, which is Kate Graham's job here. I loved doing a schedule, because it was most nearly like a crossword puzzle. A real, finite, intellectual, roll-up-your-sleeves challenge. And it was tough, but it was really fascinating. But I also get bored with details very quickly. And it's a real weakness of mine, particularly in this field, where unfortunately, some of the people I have to work with, outside the school—all they care about is numbers, and they don't care anything about what I've been talking about in this session that is the heart and soul of this school. So, I've got to be careful about that.

So: The way my tendrils go out to people is in groups. I take enormous pride in the role I played in hiring the faculty that we have here at the school, where collectively they're a great group of folks, and I'm content to sit back and watch them at work. I haven't made tremendous friendships with any of them individually—which is in part because of the nature of this position—but I see it collectively. And with the kids, again, partly a function of time and job description and all that, I have less time to connect profoundly with individual kids. But I *want* to connect profoundly with the whole school, and I direct my speeches and comments during school assemblies toward that goal, and sometimes I "hit." But I also know with kids that, particularly with the principal of the school, he's given very few opportunities to make connections. And so I work really hard to take advantage of those quick moments when they happen. When I'm walking around the school, I'm constantly taking advantage of "connection moments," in a way where a youngster, I hope, leaves saying, "the *Principal* just spoke to me, and the *Principal* knew something about me personally."

Tell me if this sounds manipulative: I do that not necessarily because I want to connect with the kid personally, as much as I want that kid to feel that this thing called the Principal cares enough about him or her to want to know this about him, or to say this to him, so the kid will feel good about being here in this school. Does that distinction make sense?

FELTON. Sure! It makes perfect sense. Well, the best example I can give you to reflect upon that happened just today, just before we set forth here. Because its dynamics had some impact. When Richard, the student whom you saw before we began today, came in to get his radio, you accomplished everything you needed, to remind him of the problem, assess it historically, see whether the parameters of remediation had been met, and call attention to his deficits in meeting the agreement; and yet you didn't do it in any kind of way to denigrate him, make him feel bad. You called attention to his lack of having picked up on the first instance of the transgression; but—nothing was "torn apart" here. You maintained your contact with him. And just like the positive aspects of the situation you related about the black student and his father, you maintained them in this instance as well. No damage. It was a positive thing. And he—I don't know him—one would hope that he will ruminate on this conversation, this minute-and-a-half—he will go over it and over it and over it, and posit it from his point of view, and yours, and that of his dad; and he will try and understand that. And every time he does that, and he'll do it a few times, I don't know how sensitive he is, but if he does it, he'll do it a few times, and every time he'll come up with: "Peter Thorp is okay. He's a good guy. Here I am, I'm still in the school, my radio is mine again, and now it's up to me." He will have learned from it. It was a successful interaction.

It also—and just parenthetically here, for whatever comment down the line you might want to make—it occurred to me that it was in such beautiful opposition, in the kind of problem it was, from what I know of your other problems today. Maybe not today; but I read in the Gateway Newsletter that a trustee has died—that sets up a whole range of problems, maybe not pressing, maybe so—and then this incident. And it occurs to me that these are Georges Seurat's "dots," you know, and they're making an image here.

THORP. "Teaching moments." The principals of schools get only teaching moments, they don't get teaching periods.

FELTON. Ah!

THORP. —Forty-five, fifty minute periods, for the most part. So you've got to get pretty good at taking advantage of those "sound bites," snippets of time.

The other thing you have to learn in education—this gets back to something you were getting at earlier, in terms of the biorhythm of the school: Frankly, I think what we are wrestling with in our essential biorhythm is whether or not the faculty and the kids *do* like each other. This is a critical issue right now. And the challenge of hiring these wonderfully outstanding men and women of the faculty that we hired here is that they'll be successful buckaroos in their own right, and they want these kids to be successful. And like me, they value education, and like me they get frustrated when kids don't seem to value education. And they haven't had, perhaps, the experience that I had this afternoon with this kid, who said "Okay, Gringo, you didn't give up on me; and that meant something to me." And in turn—Wow! That meant something to *me!*

The trick about being an educator—and this is really me!—is: Who are you going to be? Are you going to be "Mr. Chips"?—you know, this totally selfless person who at least for a couple of generations of educators seems to be the ideal? It doesn't work in the "Me Generation" at all. Or are you going to be "The Prime of Miss Jean Brodie"?— the co-dependent, psychologically-damaged preceptor, what a colleague of mine calls "pathologically charismatic" people in education? Or are you going to be something else? For me, one of the challenges throughout my teaching career, and this gets back to what I was saying about the way I do or don't connect with people, is to find the right balance between "thick skin" and "thin skin." You can't make it personal with kids. But how do you *not* make it personal? You can't overly personalize it.

What I did consciously try today to do with that youngster and his music machine—and what you're not aware of is that we had a couple of conversations prior to that, and the thing has been sitting in my office for a couple of months now—what I consciously tried to do was to remind him of an incident those two months ago now, that says in effect: "Okay, the water's under the bridge, but there's still something to be learned in this." And thank you for picking up on the fact that I didn't want to do it through personal humiliation, because that doesn't get anything.

Right before I began this session, though, I was next door with another kid whom I jumped on during assembly today. Ask your son about this. Again, I was making my usually impassioned speechifying—in fact, about this trustee whose funeral I was at today, that's why I'm dressed like this. This guy was Dr. Zuretti Goosby, who was a real pillar in the African-American community. Mayor Willie Brown spoke at the funeral, and it was powerful and impressive. This guy Goosby was really interested in life! And I was saying to the students: "You ought to know that this was an example of the kind of people who associate with Gateway, particularly those of us who are African-American in the audience, and here is somebody you might want to find out more about, and I put something on the bulletin board outside about him—" And this kid kept chatting away. And he was an African-American kid! I just reamed him out. I said, "I can't believe that you're not listening to me, because I'm standing here, telling you about someone who paved the way to make it possible for you to go to a school like this." I was furious!

FELTON. I bet you were!

THORP. —And I'm not sure but what an impartial observer would have said: "You really humiliated that kid. What you did was out of line, because you should not have humiliated that kid in front of the rest of the school like that." And I'm curious as to what your boy Peter's reaction was to that. Because I don't know if what I did was right, but I was angry! And I let him have it. And I was angry, and affronted, not only because he was interrupting me, but because he wasn't listening to something that I damn well thought he should have been listening to. So the issue for me is trying to find that right balance between opening oneself up personally and not.

The other thing today—I mean, it's been a big day, as they all are—you can pick any day of the week!—the other thing today was that I told one of my young advisees that he had to leave the school. And it broke my heart!

FELTON. I'm sure it did.

THORP. But he made it easy for me. He made it real easy for me. And sometimes kids do that. Not because he was trying to make it easy for me, but sometimes you've also got to realize that kids can rise to the challenge to handle defeat and trauma in a way that we might not give them credit for. So, finding that balance is critical.

There's a guy named Doug Heath, a former professor at Haverford, who may or may not still be alive. His life's work is on vocational satisfaction. And he did a lot of work on schools, particularly independent schools. He had set up this paradigm where he'd give the faculty a list of a hundred fifty adjectives, and say, "Check off all the ones that apply to kids in your school." And then he'd give the kids the same list, and say: "Check off all the adjectives that you think apply to your school." And what you hope would be the case is that the lists would be common. And the one school where I was where we actually invited him to come do this, it was a real offset between the faculty list and the student list. And he came back after doing his analysis and said, "You guys don't like your kids."

FELTON. Wow.

THORP. And he was right. And it wasn't that we literally didn't like the kids; it was that we had an incredibly powerful, talented faculty which was dealing with a bunch of kids who, in those days, didn't necessarily want to be in that boarding school, and weren't "getting with the program." That was the tension. And that's what's at work here, at Gateway. Not in a huge way; but that's one of the dynamics, one of the biorhythms that we're dealing with.

And of course, for the Peters in this school—and Peter may or may not be a good example of this—the kids who are not in that category, who are causing the faculty frustration and *angst*, they're sitting there and seeing the biorhythm, and saying to themselves: "These guys don't like each other! And if they don't like each other, maybe they don't like *me*." And "they" might be the faculty or the kids. In other words, it's not a happy place if I'm seeing unhappy people.

And so one of the challenges for the second semester here is to make this a happier place. And again, that's not a privilege I trust you'll see. If you took that statement out of context, you might say: "Gee, the Principal said one could make this a happy place, but for me that's not a rigorous education!" Nonetheless, I'll tell you: Happy schools are ones where a rigorous education *can* take place.

FELTON. It's curious; one of my questions here was actually a contract of a high school that's probably more appropriate to our generation than theirs. I've notice that I don't feel any of the superficial social dynamics here that I did in high school. There's no—with the possible and quite benign and charming exception of Gus Porter, the Student Body President—there's no "Big Man On Campus" here. Kids approach you, as I've said, whether they know you or not. Nobody is a strutting Homecoming Queen with her nose in the air. There may be some who are, of course, more trying than others—people have variations on the tediousness of personality. But—as I've said before—they're a highly *available* group of people. And I can only take my own presence to be a measure of that, because I'm clearly not a teenager to them; but I don't feel I'm an enemy to them. And the response in these kids is really pretty interesting.

I don't know if kids in general are like that or not. I suspect that at the dysfunctional high school, which this is not, there would be just a bunch of jaw-draggers who will never communicate and just want to get up and get out of there while the bell is still ringing in their ears, they want to be on the street. And that's not the case here. I just see it every time. I saw it upstairs, waiting for a humanities teacher. And one of the Spanish teachers gave the kids a break, and they were out in the area in front of the other teacher's office, doing wonderful things! And then the Spanish teacher "whistled," and they all went back in, and everybody had a very positive feeling. They related to me—and some of them I know now. But some of the ones who *don't* know me related to me! I don't think any of that was possible in the years I was in school. And—maybe that's just why. I mean, maybe it was just a whole different time.

But I'm wondering—one of my questions here, which we've covered somewhat, was: "What makes a teacher?" And now that leads to another, which is: "What makes a *student*?" What makes these kids feel this way, feel this comfortable?

THORP. Well—

FELTON. Parenthetically, before you start: I think part of the reason is sitting in your chair. So it ties back into that discussion.

THORP. Yeah, maybe. As comedian Johnny Carson used to say, "If you buy the premise, you buy the bit." And I'm not sure I buy your premise, if I'm reading your premise correctly, that Gateway is better, because Gateway doesn't have "Big Men On Campus," so to speak, and I recognize that's an oversimplification of what you said. In fact, Gateway *needs* a few "Big Men On Campus"! What we really need are some *role models*. We need some powerful kids who are going to help the faculty get over the cultural hump we're still not over yet. And what's interesting is that among our boys, some of the most powerful kids are the ones who have demonstrated their power—on a few occasions, positively and productively, and they've had a tremendous impact. Some, unfortunately, have demonstrated negative ways. In some instances profoundly negative ways, and in other cases less negative ways. So in fact, we need those "Big Men On Campus." And as you describe Gus Porter, he has all the potential in the world; but his sweetness and his gentleness might not get him there as quickly as we would hope. Still, I have evident excitement and confidence that he's got a lot of talent to carry him there. So—it may just come down to the issue that we continue to be a young school.

Now: What makes a good kid?—wow! What a question that is! I can tell you this, I think; most schools would answer that question with: "The kid is cooperative." "The kid doesn't rattle the cage." And I would say, "Okay. But what else? Is that enough?" And a lot of schools would say: "Yeah! That's enough. You know—we want to keep our kids cooperative." And again, as I've made reference to this before: It's the theory behind that book, *Horace's Compromise* by Ted Seizer: In effect—"You don't hassle me, I won't give you homework." You know: "I won't press you." So what do you get? Everybody cooperates with each other. That's the contract, Locke's Social Contract applied to twentieth- now twenty-first century schools in America.

I think what makes a good kid is not too much different from what makes a good educator: A willingness to be stretched, a willingness to be challenged, a willingness to accept defeat not as crushing defeat, taking things away, as: "Okay. Didn't make it this way; time to try it a different way." I think what makes a good student is—well, frankly, it's a hard question for me. It's a great question. What I think makes a good student is good parents. And that is not a socio-economic variable, in my book. Some of the best kids we have here in the school come from the most modest socio-economic circumstances. And some of the most screwed-up kids we have in this school come from the highest socio-economic circumstance. Gee what a surprise that is!

It is the kids that you can clearly recognize—kids who have come through a maelstrom of infancy/toddler/entry level/early adolescence relatively unscathed. And you gotta believe that a hell of a lot of credit goes to parents, and a hell of a lot of credit goes to the educators who are doing their work. But what's tricky about high school work is: You're presented with pretty well formed organisms, and your ability to "remold the clay," the Gene Pitney Guide to High School Life"—the ability to remold the clay is a lot less than at any other stages. And yet, perhaps, the impact of the remolding of that clay is more profound, and even greater, and even more life-changing as a consequence.

And so therefore—to come back around to what makes a good teacher—you've got to be pretty strong, as a teacher in high school, in a school like this where you have a commitment to try to change kids' lives.

It's really telling: We're being visited next Wednesday by five or six members of the School District staff. And the word on the street is: They're gunning for us. They're gunning for *all* charter schools. And they're going to come in here and turn over every rock they can turn over, so they can write a report that says: "Charter schools don't do this, don't do this, don't do this." Not the least of which is: "Charter schools don't meet the curricular standards." And it's going to be really hard for me not to not say "You're damned right we don't! And the problem with you guys is all you can think about is these ridiculous standards that don't mean anything!"

First, you must appreciate that I'm not going to say that; and second, there is value to having standards and goals and objectives and lesson plans and scope-and-sequence, and all that kind of educational jargonese. In fact, there's solid value to it. But I'm going to work as hard as I can to get them to engage in a conversation about *real* education. And I'm not terribly optimistic that I'm going to have the quality of communication and conversation with these people that I have with you. These people are the School District, and the School District is predisposed to want to demonstrate that we're failing. *That's* sort of what's on my plate at this point. And the next ten days are going to be critical to the life of Gateway.

Why do I say that? Because the week after that, we go before the Board of Education. And again, the word on the street is: "They're lying in the grass, waiting to take shots at charter schools." And my work is cut out—*our* work is cut out; for it certainly isn't all falling on my shoulders. But I will need to take great care to make a convincing and compelling case for what we're doing, and you know me well enough to know that it takes time for me to develop that. It's a lot more subtle than something like Star Test scores. So it's going to be interesting for me to convert however many hours of discussion you and I have experienced to ten minutes of sound-bites, which is how much time I'm going to have, on February 15, before the Board of Education. I've only got that long to tell them what this is all about, and why they should support us.

FELTON. My parting comment has been deflated by what you just told me. I feel badly, because I thought it would be a kind of boost—

THORP. It'll be a boost. *Anything* will be a boost!

FELTON. Well I hope so. But I don't know. You threw a new factor in here. Up to that comment, I was going to say: "Well, buck up, because I know a man who specializes in counseling high school personnel and adolescents; and when acquainted with your quandary, and the do-or-die dilemma of the upcoming Board meeting, his immediate response—and here's a guy who's in tune with all the schools, because that's his practice—his immediate response was: "Oh, he's got nothing to worry about, because they can't yank his tag without yanking all charter schools' tags"—

THORP. Sure. He's right.

FELTON. —And I thought, "How wonderfully comforting that will be for Peter, because they're obviously not going to blow the whole thing out of the water." Now what you're telling me is that that's *exactly* what they're going to do!

THORP. *Au contraire, mon frère.* Here's my prediction: They won't do that. What they're going to try to do is to peck us to death, like ducks. They're going to insist that we follow curriculum laws that we have no interest in following. And my prediction also is: They're going to go after us on the facility issue. They're going to allow us to stay here in this building one more year, ideally, but that they're going to make it nigh impossible for us to stay here beyond next year. Now, we may not want to stay here beyond next year. But that would be what we're likely to get. And—to bring it back full circle—it's all politics. And it's *nothing about kids.*

FELTON. That's right.

THORP. It's nothing about kids. I told Lisille today: It's probably the worst—on one level, Keith, I shouldn't even be saying this to you, because in addition to being a good friend, and someone with whom I'm working on a project, you're also a parent of the school. So the last thing I want to do is alarm you; but I'm letting my hair down, and hope that you'll keep it between the two of us.

FELTON. Speak.

THORP. I mean, if this really gets out of control, and it may make it impossible for us to continue, I'm going down in flames, and this school district won't know what hit them. I don't think they've ever dealt with somebody like me. Again, I may be real naïve about that; they might eat up guys like me and spit 'em out all the time. And maybe they do; but I'll expose this school system in a way that they'll regret that they messed with me.

Now, one could say: "Okay, and so what will that get us?" And the answer is not a lot. It would simply be the last gasp. But in the meantime, I'm just as passionate and committed about making those allotted ten minutes have an impact. I'm going to figure out ways to tell stories about Gateway that transcends statistics, so they can feel the heart and soul of this place. I'll talk about our late Board member Zuretti Goosby, whom they've got to sit up and listen to, because he's somebody in this community who did a hell of a lot for the schools before these people decided to join the school board. So it's going to be fascinating. But it's going to be a real fight. A real dog fight.

FELTON. They don't chew up and spit out guys like you all the time because you doubtless know—even though I don't think you've lived in San Francisco all that long—that this wonderful place to live, this absolutely idyllic place, is made up on the administrative and political level of people who play the game, and get along by going along. And they're not a very illustrious group. And that's the "small-townness" of San Francisco, that every once in a while will show its head. When the Bank of America just tips a little bit to one side, you see that it's really pretty provincial here. And the city's run by provincial guys. So you're not something they're going to be familiar with. You're constructed on a much grander scale than the mayors and supervisors and School Board members of quaint little San Francisco with its daydreams of swashbuckling Barbary Coast—and I say that as a native, and with love. I hope you don't ever have to be in the position of giving them hell; but if you do, I'm glad that you're the one doing it.

THORP.   Well, I've no interest in doing that, because all I want to do is make the school a success. That's all I care about. But I'm not going to roll up and play dead.

Forgive me, but I'm going to beg your indulgence to say: Can we not meet again until after I get through the next couple of weeks?

FELTON.   Any way I can help advance that, including being in the shadows.

THORP.   Well, I may actually call upon you in a variety of capacities. I may throw a speech at you, if I have time—

FELTON.   Absolutely. Anything I can do.

THORP.   —And have you on call for February 15, Tuesday night, at the Board meeting, where there'll be some amount of time for the public to comment after people like me get to comment. And of course, what's tricky about that: I'd have you do it in a second—this just shows you what it's all about—I'd have you do that in a second, if you were African-American. But the fact that you're white, you might not be my first candidate.

FELTON.   Sure. I understand.

THORP.   I'd love to put you up there, as someone who knows about the school. All the charter schools are kind of coordinating and trying to figure out how to do this all together—

FELTON.   I think you're right.

THORP.   —And one of the knocks on Gateway, that we know about, is that they think of us as this kind of "private school in public school clothing." So we've got to get our African-American and Latino people going.

It's all politics, isn't it!

Chapter Twelve

IN THE GLADIATORS' PIT—
THE SAN FRANCISCO UNIFIED
SCHOOL DISTRICT BECKONS

"What I think I'll specifically point out on our list of courses, toward the bottom, is a course in neuropsychology—a class we actually call 'Psychology' that all ninth-graders take, so they understand the workings of the brain in general, and the workings of their brain in particular. Because the central premise of our school is that if you help kids understand how their brain works, they're going to help their teachers teach them that much more effectively...."

"It is our hope that over the next five years, we're going to take and build on the successes we've established already, by completing our program—a program, again, which combines a traditional college preparatory curriculum but done in innovative fashion, one in which we continue the outreach to all the communities in San Francisco, particularly those areas that have been underserved. And we will seek to balance innovation in our program with tradition, as any good college preparatory program should be. And we will continue to meet or surpass standards, and we hope that in fact we will become a national model that will make this city proud."

For good reason, Peter Thorp's adrenal system was in "high gear" for much of the ten days which followed our February 4 dialogue. His parting comment to me, at the doorway—"I'm gonna be here all weekend!"—and a corollary question, almost desperately voiced: "Do you know a program called 'Power Point'?" summed up his expectations of preparation for the hearing on February 15: It would require midnight oil and weekend water to get him through.

Along with the aptly named computer program (supplied with love, determination and involvement by his fiancée), Thorp would continue, as he always did, to minister to his flock, counsel the teacher, gently chide the wayward radio-listening student, and guide his college prep class into the next underground tunnel designed to lead (light-years hence, to these tenth-graders) to the baccalaureate. But for all those ten days, Peter had one developing idea in his mind—the only one, he knew, which would keep him from "going down in flames": How to convince—not dramatize, not dazzle, not overwhelm, but *convince*—the Board of Commissioners of the San Francisco Unified School District that Gateway Charter High School, a dominion of a score of teachers and less than ten score students, deserved a reprieve from the death knell that, "on the street," was their surmised, projected, and feared fate.

On the night of February 15, 2000, as Commissioner Frank Chong, the Meeting Convenor, brought to order the Board, the five presenting charter high school Principals, and the gallery of supporters, parents, teachers and staff boosters, part of the suspense was broken and the air cleared by his opening remark in which he announced that the five-year renewal of all charters had been granted.

But, following the applause which greeted this welcome news, the gas jets were re-ignited under the seats of the school heads, who sat before this Board, squirming or fiddling with computer-projection machines, and sifting through the miasma for the karmic calming they still would need. The squirming was not mollified by the statistical information provided by Dr. Roger Tom, Associate Superintendent, who informed the Board—with an intended *sub rosa* tenor of alarm—that the number of charter schools statewide had grown from 102 to 250.

In the District itself, he continued, this number had grown from one to five, and that within the last two weeks another six applications had been announced or submitted by interested groups or individuals. He took pains to relate, under the heading of Policies and Regulations on Charter Schools, that "Though the District has been guided by State legislation on charter schools, it has not formally adopted School District policies and administrative regulations on charter schools." District staff has, he assured, been working on such regulations, and their findings—and presumably recommendations—would be presented to the District's Curriculum Committee "in the coming weeks." The five District schools now under question were the ones chosen to be heard this evening, Gateway included. Expected highlights from these charter school representatives would be "reports on the history of the charter in the District; the charter school life cycle from the presentation of a petition to the request for a charter renewal; the profile and academic performance of each charter school."

To add to the layer of statistics initiated by Dr. Tom, his report was followed by that of Dr. Ritu Khanna, Director of the Board's Research and Evaluation Committee, who presented an overview of the Academic Performance Index (API) and Data Gathering and Reporting Issues/Recommendations. Following on a handout syllabus which featured a grid delineating schools on one axis and academic subject categories on the other axis,[1] scores in each category were compared between the individual school under examination, the School District "norm," norms from San Francisco generally, and State norms.

Spectators could readily appreciate, in Gateway's column of comparison, that the school exceeded not only the District's own parameters for various measures of academic course testing results, but that it measured well against its "competition"—other charter high schools under scrutiny. But Dr. Khanna's pure-vowelled East Indian lilt carried in its pronouncements the clear message: This was to be an evening of statistics. The quiver was defined: Test measurement. The arrows within would need to be sharp, to reach the hearts of Commissioners, and deflate the puffed-up front of their attack.

Board Member Jill Wynns (from whom and about whom more would be heard), in questioning Dr. Khanna, expressed concern that the evaluations of all the schools were not codified and "consistent and in the same time frames." The feeling from this Commissioner was that there was not enough policing guaranteed of Charter schools to satisfy her.

The agenda for the meeting was billed, in a clipped fashion, at the head of a Meeting Agenda which was passed around by the Associate Superintendent:

San Francisco Unified School District
Board of Education Committee of the Whole

---

[1] These appeared under the heading "San Francisco Unified School District, Stanford Achievement Test, Ninth Edition, Spring 1999, National Percentile Rankings, Elementary Charter Schools/High Schools" Charter Schools."

Mid-Year Report on SFUSD Charter Schools
Tuesday—February 15, 2000, 7:00-0:00 p.m.
555 Franklin Street, Board Room

Brought before this tribunal, as Commissioner Chong announced, were a total of five charter school principals. Each would be allotted ten minutes to make a case. Each was to address the question: *"To What Degree Has the Charter School Been Able to Fully Implement the Provisions of Its Charter from SFUSD?"*

Peter was preceded on the podium by Mr. Tom Wheeler, whose Kindergarten-through-eighth grade school, ("We have a staff of three," the young man with the pony-tail length hair and earnest face announced proudly, "—an administrator, a secretary, and myself") was under fire; and by Dr. Barbara Karvelis, whose Kindergarten-through-fifth-grade Edison Elementary was disadvantaged in presentation by the luckless caprices of uncooperative projection-throwing equipment.

And when Dr. Karvelis, making the best of things, thanked the Board and withdrew, Commissioner Chong pushed the button on his microphone, and, face rubricked by the "On-light" of the modern board room's public address system, intoned:

"Next I'd like to ask Dr. Peter Thorp, the Principal of Gateway High School, to step forward and offer us his presentation."

The senses-sharpened man in the blue suit, with the wavy gray hair and the dead-serious blue eyes who sat next in line at the Principal's table, stepped to the podium, oriented his machinery, and became in every sense Gateway's leader. As such, he would prove again how deserving he was of the absolute faith of his own Board's chair, Lisille Matheson, who from the gallery's Plexiglas chairs watched along with Gateway's Development Director, a Gateway ninth-grade humanities teacher who was planning a summer wedding, the parent-supporter of the junior varsity basketball team whose son that week just before playoffs had broken his arm, the two tenth-grade mothers who edited and published the Gateway Newsletter, and the Reporter, whose tweed's breast pocket had retired its handkerchief that evening in favor of a small tape recorder.

Responding to Chong's final salute of "Welcome, Peter!," Thorp began:

> Thank you, Mr. Chairman. While we're taking a moment to set up, I'd like to take a moment publicly to thank Mr. Tom [Dr. Roger Tom, Associate Superintendent of Schools] for providing us at Gateway and at all of the charter schools very clear directions for this

evening. We certainly thought that we were responding to what the Board was expecting of us last April [at the previous meeting] and what were its wishes. We want to be sure that we are answering the questions you want to ask. We are hopeful that the data we are providing tonight will in fact speak to the questions that you're asking—specifically, whether or not we're meeting the terms of our charter.

Gateway is proud to be part of the San Francisco Unified School District in educating this year about 190 kids in grades nine and ten as we grow to our full capacity of 400 kids in grades nine through twelve eventually.

The initial statement of Gateway emphasizes appropriate aspects of what high school education should be, and you can see this on our descriptive slide. As we talk about the school being a model program, one committed to academic excellence, a school that's defined by its attention to the individuals at the school—personalized education, in the context of a rigorous curriculum. We hope, in the capacity of educating kids in a ninth-through twelfth-grade program, to develop the skills and habits and knowledge that will help them be successful in post-secondary education and beyond that.

Gateway is utterly committed to reflecting the face of San Francisco, and that is one of the fundamental premises of this school—our commitment to diversity; and you'll see some statistics in just a moment that speak to our efforts to create appropriate outreach to all the middle schools in the Bay Area. We understand there are about 110 middle schools, counting all the venues in San Francisco.

Gateway is also a school that believes that a high school program should educate kids to develop in the cognitive realm, in the affective realm, and we are committed to the values of personal integrity, responsibility, and respect for others. And we hope that because of this education, and as a result of this education, our students will contribute to their communities in every way they can, and wherever they end up. Tonight, very briefly, we'll walk through the profile of Gateway, after its first year and a half, we'll show you the test results that come from our very first year of existence; we'll show you some of the resources we're bringing not only to Gateway but are being shared throughout the District; we'll speak specifically to the Board Resolution of January, 1998, which authored our charter; and we'll also talk about what we're hoping to do in the next five years.

As you compare Gateway's enrollment by race and ethnicity to high schools throughout San Francisco, you'll see that we have a higher Latino enrollment than the typical high school in San Francisco—however statistically, about the same level in African-

American enrollment. And the specific anomaly at Gateway is that you'll see that our Chinese enrollment and our Other-White enrollment are essentially flip-flopped based on what you see in other high schools based here in San Francisco. We employ a Director of Enrollment whose job is specifically to go out and talk about Gateway in the middle schools throughout the city, and spread the word about what this school is, and to try and attract families from across the socio-economic spectrum to our program. Using two statistics that further measure socio-economic diversity: You'll see that using the Cal-Works descriptor, that Gateway is slightly above the District average. And we are below the District average for Free and Reduced Lunch, although it is our belief that our figure of about 33 percent underestimates the true number of students at Gateway who are eligible for a Free and Reduced Lunch, because we're having trouble getting some of our statistics for some of our students, a few of whom come from out-of-District, and some come from parochial schools, and we don't yet have the data on them that would indicate whether or not they're eligible.

Gateway's central mission, in addition to being a college preparatory school, is in fact to demonstrate that, as we say, students with "All-Kinds-Of-Minds" can be successful in a college preparatory program. More specifically, by the terms of the charter that this Board of Education approved, 25 percent or more of our students should be special education students. As you can see from this chart, our enrollment is essentially three times the enrollment of special ed students in the District. This figure of 25 percent, which may not be consistent with figures that are in your packet, is the result of the following: About 15 percent of the students of that 27 percent are in fact students who come to us with IEP's. The balance of those students making up the 27 percent are students who have specific cognitive and learning disabilities through other measured tests, either through the public or private sector. We have therefore in our enrollment of about 190 students, 51 students who either have an IEP or have a specifically-documented learning disability. In addition to those 51 students, approximately another 50 students are students that we're working with whom we have through our work with them in the last year and a half—or in some cases who are new to us in the past six months—we've identified learning issues that we believe might in fact become learning disabilities as they pursue their studies further. So we hope that you'll believe that we've met the terms of our charter on this.

One of the specific points in our charter, and one of the aspects that you wanted us to demonstrate to you is that we are providing a rigorous program, as you can see, comparing our graduation requirements to San Francisco Unified's—we essentially have the same requirements or greater requirements; and of course, we will be responsible in conducting courses to make sure that our students have met the terms of the University of California A through F requirements, so they can matriculate on to UC or Cal State schools—or whatever other school they want to attend. What I think I'll specifically point out on our list of courses, toward the bottom, is a course in neuropsychology—a class we actually call 'Psychology' that all ninth-graders take, so they understand the workings of the brain in general, and the workings of their brain in particular. Because the central premise of our school is that if you help kids understand how their brain works, they're going to help their teachers teach them that much more effectively.

A specific part of our program is an interdisciplinary emphasis, because we believe both from a content point of view, students will benefit from seeing connections in their work; and from a neurological point of view, we believe that students will benefit when they can see that the work they're doing in one class can be reinforced in another. We're essentially committed to ensure that the students at Gateway graduate at the end of our four-year program having been exposed to the full range of voices that they have available in literature and history and a full arts program, in conjunction with the San Francisco Arts Program. And much of that is not only the doing of art, the creating of art, but the study of art as it relates to various cultures as well.

What is seen, then, is that we have a relatively traditional college preparatory program in terms of the courses that students are expected to take. Yet, in fact, what makes Gateway different, and we hope you see, is that we are trying in a series of innovative approaches, we hope to demonstrate that, as the District has called for in its own study, that special education students can be fully included in a college preparatory program. That "special education" is not a place where students are sent, but a service that they receive—we hope, in the same classroom. It is our particular focus that one of the best things that you can do for any student is identify that student's strengths; because we believe that every student has strengths, and that the teacher will capitalize on those strengths to help the student and his or her teacher to work on areas that need improvement.

One of the things that marks Gateway's approach is that we develop appropriate accommodations for students. It is our belief that you need to provide multi-modal assessment for students, so that you don't penalize the student who might have tremendous mastery of content, but might have difficulty expressing that on paper or verbally, and so provide that student with another option to demonstrate that mastery. We use technology extensively, particularly in our Learning Center, which is at the heart and soul of our program; and we see technology, again, as another vehicle to provide support for students whose skills in a certain area might need specific technological support, be it a laptop computer, be it a reading machine in the Learning Center, tapes which will enable them to turn in their answers verbally, for example. And finally, we are very excited about continuing to capitalize on District resources. I want the Board to know that the Special Education Department of Ms. Medrick has been particularly helpful to Gateway and supportive, and we have a wonderful relationship with the Special Ed Department. And just this past week I want to salute Maria Santos and her staff for coming out to the school and spending a full day at the school doing a visit and assessment, and giving us a report written relatively quickly—which I thought was really terrific as it underscored those things which we think are strengths of the school, and helped us to focus in on areas where we believe that we need to improve, as well. So she did a great job.

The scores that you see are from last year, when we just had ninth grade, and approximately 92 students taking those tests on the Integrated Writing Assessment. You'll see that Gateway students scored essentially above the District average; our median was a score of 4, whereas the District's score was 3. I do these comparative statistics not to demonstrate or make a point that Gateway is outperforming the District; that's not the point, but to demonstrate that as part of the District, we are being held accountable on specific scores, and we want you to know how we stack up against that set of numbers that you're most familiar with.

Our Stanford 9 results also indicate that our students are performing above the District averages in most cases. I'll take the math score, which is the one where we are slightly below the District average, and talk about it a little bit because I think it's important that we all take these scores and put them in the proper context. Our math score, which is a mean on this test, as all the Star tests are reported—if you look at the median math score at Gateway, it's actually quite a higher number, well into the mid-60's and close to 70. What that means is the bottom quintile of scores for the students who took the math test was really very low, and brought down the mean to that level. And this is something that we are working on very specifically, because it's certainly our new knowledge that a number of students coming out of the middle school lack the arithmetic skills needed to be successful in Algebra I, which is a District goal, of course, to be having all ninth graders taking Algebra I. And so we're working very hard; and Dr. Santos, and her staff, I think, will be helpful to us to develop a program where we can figure out how to help students be successful in Algebra I and in overcoming their weak-arithmetic-skills background.

More specifically—again, to take numbers and really look at them carefully—looking at that math score once again, it's very important to understand that the Superintendent's top priority was to ensure that certain populations, certain under-served populations in the District, were being served well. If you look at these four categories of students: African-American, Latino—limited English proficiency and special education students—all improved dramatically in their test scores after their first year at Gateway.

One of the things that we're most proud about, both locally in the Bay Area and around the country are the number of people who take an interest in Gateway as a model school, and we are proud that we are bringing these resources to the city through Gateway. And you can see that list, and if you have any questions about who they are, of course, you can ask me afterwards. I'm trying to do this as quickly as possible.

The four terms of the Board Resolution of January, 1998 are listed here; and my hope is that I have addressed them, albeit quickly, in that we have created a diverse student population, and developed a program with appropriate rigor. That we are in fact meeting the terms of our Memorandum of Understanding that we worked out with Mr. Palatsios in the liaison office for the charter schools, where we have been appropriately prudent in our fiscal expenditures, and in our financial reporting, and that our risk management is appropriate. Third, the requirement was that we enroll our students in a lottery, something that we are doing, and we are working very closely with the Educational Placement Center and Jennie Horn and her office. And finally, we are working very closely with the Facilities Management Office in the District. We hope that the Board of Education will believe that we've developed a "win-win" situation whereby being present in the former Laguna Honda elementary school, we are housing a quality program that's associated with the District, and one that's generating rental income back to you as well.

It is our hope that over the next five years, we're going to take and build on the successes we've established already, by completing our program—a program, again, which combines a traditional college preparatory curriculum but done in innovative fashion, one in which we continue the outreach to all the communities in San Francisco, particularly those areas that have been under-served. And we will seek to balance innovation in our program with tradition, as any good college preparatory program should be. And we will continue to meet or surpass standards, and we hope that in fact we will become a national model that will make this city proud.

To add just one thought: Two weeks ago I had the honor, and I would say the sad honor, of attending the funeral of Dr. Zuretti Goosby, who is really one of the giants in this city in the last fifty years, and a gentleman who was on our Board of Trustees. And at his memorial service, someone remarked,

Zu will be remembered as a loving husband and father, as a person who was committed to bringing about change by being part of the system, striving to improve societal equality as it fell down racial and socio-economic lines; as an advocate for those who were not on an even playing field, particularly in education; as a person with wonderful humanity, who treated everyone with respect because he genuinely respected them; as a person who inspired others to take on causes bigger than their personal lives.

That's what San Francisco is all about, that's what this School District is all about, and that's what Gateway is all about.

As it would turn out, Peter's remarks were the moral highlight of the evening. The remaining principals told of good works—Mark Kushner's Leadership High School had hit good strides, but had lost its landlord, and now had to fight the baneful, rudimentary-issue real estate battle all over again. And a representative of Life Learning High School, a vibrant, cookie- and idea-wielding firebrand substituting for the school's leader, Ms. Teri DeLane, described astonishing achievement in social rectification of its students in the form of a very different student body comprising post-reform school/jail/delinquent students located on the unusual school's Treasure-Island 1939 World's Fair site, who had recanted their life of gangs and drugs, turned the corner on the lives, and were placing their values on education and community. Peter's discussion, however—crisp, factual, but regaling Gateway's virtues without braggadocio—essentially removed any doubt that the Board would be bound to continue Gateway's charter.

At the end of it all, Peter Thorp and Gateway's threatened charter would survive this one fight. There would be no need to ride education's stricken airfoil down "in flames"—at least not yet. In fact, quite the opposite climate prevailed at Peter Thorp's presentation, and its reception: His was an air of cool collectivity of wits. He delivered his message sagely, skillfully, and succinctly, as requested. (The clock is such a sacred regimenting device for committee bureaucrats the world over.) And, as if in gratitude for his permitting the Board to retain its dignity when it had appeared to behave like a small dog yipping at the heels of the smilingly innocent Charter High School, The Board permitted the pronounced applause of the gallery of supporters, and even—by addressing him as such—gave Thorp an "honorary

Doctorate" for his elevated stature in accepting and meeting the challenge of the Board's backstage, wily pinprickers.

If there was controversy during the evening, it came from not from the likes of Principals like one Peter Thorp, but from the likes of a School Board Member, one Jill Wynns. It was Wynns who earlier had called attention to her perceived need for closer scrutiny of uniform standards for charter schools, through a tighter evaluation process. And it was Wynns who now used excessive commentary time accorded the Members (an evening Commissioner Chong had clearly characterized at its beginning as a "listening time" for Members) to descry wastage in the schools.

Wynn, reduced now like the Donitz Post-Nazi Government to retaining scrappiness in the face of clear defeat, first questioned Edison School for the technicality of its charter, and questioned as well whether that school in fact legitimately fell under the aegis of SFUSD support. The Board member then turned to advocacy of larger schools for the total student body, rather than the many smaller schools which is the pattern for charters. Why, pray, did Wynns want to extol the virtues of larger schools—the time-fatigued tradition in education for decades?

It's nice to have smaller schools, she suggested. "But the price of that—the price of that in money—is that we cannot afford a lot of other things that we could afford if we had larger schools....Having this number of schools has been at the expense of many things that other schools frankly have. It has been at the expense of elementary school libraries; it has been at the expense of school nurses, of school psychologists, counselors—"

At this point, the Chair interrupted to caution the Member her time had expired. Wynns, irritated at the interruption, plowed ahead, warning charter holders that further funding requests would be taken under the advisement of this perceived paucity of funds. She concluded by requesting a tighter relationship between charter schools and the District, with fiscal concerns its goal: "What we need to demand that our charters do is to participate in some kind of formal, organized learning and communication back and forth. And then, frankly, that—and everything else we do—is something that has to be paid for. And I think has to be borne as much by the charter schools as well as by the District."

Unlike the ovation which had greeted Thorp and other presenters, the Commissioner —who at last had felt she had her say—had one lone set of hands clapping in support of this acerbic call for belt-tightening at Charter's expense.

And on this note of acerbity, the meeting drew to a close.

As a deliberative body, *"The San Francisco Unified School District Board of Education Committee of the Whole, in its Mid-Year Report on SFUSD Charter Schools, that Tuesday, February 15, 2000, at 7:00-0:00 p.m. at 555 Franklin Street, Board Room,"* received the word from Gateway's Principal and his colleagues facing the sword, smiled politely, bowed skillfully, squabbled briefly amongst its own family, and adjourned, with all decorum in place and personal dignity—all, that is, which met the eye—unruffled.

A POSTSCRIPT—At about that moment when the meeting had grown restive, and the Chair had interrupted School Board Member Jill Wynns's harangue against the abusers and wasters of pencils, the city's largest daily newspaper, *the San Francisco Chronicle,* was being unloaded from the fleet of square blue step vans all over the city. There, throughout the community, tied in bundles for newsstands and unmanned kiosks and the paper routes out in the Excelsior and St. Francis Wood, awaiting for the morning coffee or the streetcar crowd was the *Chronicle's* inside section called "Bay Area and California."

And if Jill Wynns had had access to a newspaper from this delivery, at the time she was berating her fellow board members for fiscal excess, then about the time Life Learning's spokesperson was handing out her good will-gestured red-cellophaned cookies, School Board Member Wynns could have found the piece at the bottom of page one, by Chroniclers Phil Matier and Andrew Ross, under the subhead "Travel Tips." In all likelihood, Ms. Wynns would have been even more distressed by this copy than she was by having have been interrupted for overtime talking:

> With all the problems facing the San Francisco schools [the piece led off], it's nice to know that the hot talk between board members these days isn't over something frivolous like test scores. It's over something really weighty: each other's travel expenses.
>
> Particularly the expenses of San Francisco School Board member Jill Wynns, who really gets around...

Matier/Ross went on to catalogue Wynn's junket-hopping over an eighteen-month period, featuring a trip-a-month at an aggregate expenditure of $18,000. The itinerary would have sent the zircon sparkling on the squash blossoms of any travel agent:

Wynn's most far-flung jaunt was in July and August, when she flew off to Osaka, Japan, for two weeks as part of an educational exchange.

But her busiest month was October, starting with a four-day National School Board Association conference in Philadelphia, followed by a three-day Great City Schools conference in Dayton, Ohio, followed by a five-day Unified School Districts labor-management meeting in Boston.

In January, she attended...

In March, she flew to a two-day...

In July, she jetted off to a three-day...

....followed by a four-day....

The writers concluded their subject's agenda:

Overall, Wynns, who has been on the board eight years, spent nearly as much on her travel [this year alone] as the $22,000 spent by the other six school board members combined.

Her response?

"I don't think [the other board members] travel enough."

Matier and Ross are professionals, and their piece characterizes journalism, not smear. They concluded by leading the reader toward the proper litany of issues involving Board President Mary Hernandez, who was on one side of the issue, against Wynns in the other faction, which had ousted ex-Superintendent Bill Rojas.

It's hard to feel that the muckraked and unseemly scenario rises to the level of smug, *arriviste* status suggested by the refinements in the redecorated Board Room. But—as former archaeological-dig participant Peter Thorp could have attested, many modern cityscapes bask in the sun while astride the bones and stones of the darkened subterranean killing fields of forgotten jousts from just such unremembered battles of complaint-and-redress.

One wonders whether Wynns, or the entire San Francisco Unified School District Board, would have been comforted by a report which came out the Friday following their Tuesday meeting. Standard & Poore, the assets-evaluating folks, have announced a new scale—the Standard Education System ("SES," in America's acronymic mania). To go into effect within a year, first in the state of Michigan, the SES— "applying the principles of Wall Street to the measurement of your school tax dollar"—promises to be a rating of school districts. Its parameters measured: Where money is spent; what the outcome of such expenditures portends for students served; a basic student demographic study; a measure of how this money affects the learning environment. Billed as "an impartial comparison over time to see what works, and what doesn't,"[1] the SES is by their own terms an analysis of what the public is getting for their educational dollar. As is "standard" for "Standard & Poore," they profess objectivity and independence.

Perhaps Commissioner Wynns will book a trip to S&P's home offices for examination of the process, as a junket for preemptive involvement. Even if she does, it should be emphasized that the intention here is not directed toward embarrassment or even exposure of one of the Board's "squeaky wheels," or even of the tempting rectitude supplied by Matier and Ross's refusal to supply that wheel some much-needed grease. But there is good reason to note that, even if no longer sporting bowlers and watch chains—and obviously, no longer being exclusively male—local San Francisco political figures (which must include members of any prominent, deliberative commission handling public funding) have been in sniping battles since long before the 1906 quake temporarily humbled Bagdhad-By-The-Bay's prominent citizenry.

"*Plus ça change, plus c'est le meme*," Voltaire famously noted. (He would have thought no less had he lived to enjoy a subscription to the "Chron.")

And as if to exude a well-earned sigh of relief: Within two days of the positive reception at the Unified School District, Gateway High School emblazoned a red-and-white banner across the Depression-Era Brick façade on Seventh Avenue, covering the lettering from the long-defunct Laguna Honda Elementary School with the proudly-proclaimed new legend (preceded here by a repertorially-added oath):

"THIS, BY GOD, IS *GATEWAY HIGH SCHOOL!*"

In the age of the Internet, another proclamation—the Latin of Peter Thorp's own school days—also came to mind:

Quod Erat Demonstratum.

---

[1] National Public Radio report, "Morning Edition," Friday, February 18, 2000.

Chapter Thirteen

POST-MORTEM:
THE MIGRAINE-SWELL OF REFLECTION

"[The Board's attitude is] the classic example—and my own lens for seeing this is the social-scientist's lens—it's the classic example of the response of the status quo to reformers. And it's the classic example of the nervousness about the new or the unknown. And the classic profile, I guess, of starting at the point of suspicion, rather than embracing the unknown to find out when it's no longer worthy of being embraced. Then, change it, as opposed to the other way around...."

"[Being a teacher means] you have to be very observant; and it also means you have to establish criteria that are going to help you define 'satisfaction.' If you walk into class every day thinking, 'I'm going to change these kids' lives,' you're setting yourself up for frustration.

"I think in one of our previous conversations I've talked about my own journey here, and both my strengths and weaknesses as an educator over the years, feeling that I am a persuasive person with kids. I don't feel that in a manipulative way, but in the ability to really sit down and have a heart-to-heart communication. And in fact I'm having lunch with a kid tomorrow afternoon....I mean, I'm going into it thinking: 'I'm really going to straighten this kid's life out, which is a mess!' And she's probably going into it thinking: 'I'm getting a free lunch with the principal—and he's not going to do anything to my life!'

So the trick for educators is to figure out how to be satisfied."

23 February—*It would be several days before I sat down with Peter again. But through other communications, I expressed to him my* *pleasure at his bravura performance on the night of the School District Meeting. He was palpably relieved, both at the reception his defense of Gateway was given, and at the passing of the pressure. It would not, he cautioned me—and events immediately proved him right—be the last concern the school would have this year from the city's educational governing boards. But we could find momentary relief under the shelter formed by the retrenchment of the side in opposition to schooling.*

A few nights later, Peter met with some of the hard-core parents at what had come to be called the monthly "Parent-teacher" get-together. He outlined some of the concerns which lay ahead—"journeyman" problems, on the order of the acquisition of school lockers, the functioning of committees, and—not routine—the matter of admission procedures, which (with the city's lottery in effect) would determine how many of the 325 new applications would be welcomed in as the 100-member freshman class of 2000-2001.

The next day, our dialogue began on simpler issues.

FELTON.   I had a whole series of questions about the Board meeting, and some other materials, as well. And I think I'm going to abandon them, and instead ask you to deal with two or three questions about the meeting, and mainly open it up to your random thoughts about it, for I'm as interested in that as anything else.

Regarding the Board of Ed session, I have your formal presentation; but I don't have what you *feel* about it. And I'm interested in your telling me what all of that did to you, and what you think it did for the school. Other than the charter extension, what is the immediate impact on Gateway?

THORP.   The first effect of the Board meeting was the Board's strategic retreat to a less-vulnerable, less public attack plan. What I found out is that the fight shifts now to a Subcommittee Meeting. They will try to go at us from that level.

FELTON.   Is that more of the "duck-pecking"? Or does it have another purpose? And before you respond, the Board meeting prompted me to want you to speak a bit about some of your heretofore unelucidated views about the whole ethnicity syndrome, and what they're really after there. I have statements from you, and I know Meghvi's view; but it's a little unclear to me. Some experience from some other schools suggests to me that it's not quite so easy to discern. It's not, for example, a matter of a school's having a head who is of a certain ethnicity, something like that. It has subtler suggestions; and I'm interested in that phenomenon.

THORP. This question, of course, is one we could spend the next three weeks on. So I'll try to be precise and crisp.

I think what one observes with this School Board is a frame of mind and approach to diversity which is the precise problem faced all the way from the San Francisco School District to M.I.T.—namely, diversity is seen as an end, and not a means. And that's the problem. The School District would be completely satisfied if on that chart I put together for the meeting we had the kind of diversity that they want. And, of course, the "they" part then gets broken up into more subtle subtexts, because the various members of the board have different understandings of "diversity." And what I find ironic about part of the thrust, is that I have evidence to believe certain members of the board would be pleased if the school were ninety-nine percent Latino and African-American kids, or even ninety-nine percent African-American kids. And then we would be a school that was serving the under-represented, or under-served, or poorly-served segments of San Francisco and parts of its population.

Were we to do that, I would say, I would venture to offer that we would not be a particularly diverse school. The point that I was trying to make at the Board of Education meeting –and you can tell me whether or not I had success—is that Gateway's representation is more typically diverse than some of the schools in the city, than most of the schools in the city. That is because the school more accurately represents the "face" of San Francisco than some of the other schools do. And for me, therefore, diversity is a means to an end, and in order to have that means in place you have to have in fact a diverse population. For me a diverse population is non-exclusive, so that you're bringing in representation among all racial and ethnic groups— and also different economic levels. And of course, Gateway's mission speaks to the question of another definition of diversity that gets lost— or doesn't get lost, it doesn't get thought about!—which is intellectual diversity, or neurocognitive diversity. And we think that's important as well.

Again, my frustrations about conversations on diversity is that people check both their intelligence and their courage at the door when diversity becomes the topic. Because unfortunately it's become so riddled with tension agendas, political correctness, and so on, that it's really hard to get beyond a certain point. Some people have enough courage to get up to a certain point, and then when the going gets tough, off it goes. Then they step back. And of course, that's the very point that the next step has to be taken in order to figure out: "Okay, what *do* you do?"

The underlying text from those who challenge Gateway is that Gateway is skimming the cream of the crop off the top, in that we're a kind of a private school in public school clothing. What I was trying to show at the Board Meeting the other night is: That ain't true! And I don't care what your perception of the truth is, here's the truth! And if I can't move you from this impression of Gateway, after showing you the statistics, then what the hell am I left with to convince you that your impression of the school is inaccurate, and therefore your opinion of the school is inaccurate, and therefore you're putting us in a bad position because you're not judging us based on the facts. This was a great deal of my reaction throughout that whole process in the presentation the other evening. In some cases, I was preaching to the choir, but in more cases I was preaching to—I don't know what the counterbalancing expression is!—to people who have pretty much already decided that we're not diverse enough, and, that we're too elitist, despite the facts they're shown, and despite the thrust behind our mission.

And as you know, the District is just befuddled by the legal challenge that it's faced; and I don't criticize them. Again, under Rojas, the goal of this District is an eminently worthwhile and noble goal, which is: Let us construct a system where we will not create *de facto* segregation. And the more as we knew, growing up, that segregation was in fact *de facto* and not *de jure* segregation. And San Francisco could fall prey to that very quickly, just given the neighborhood aspect of San Francisco. It was not unlike Boston, where I grew up, which of course is neighborhood driven, and where the trouble began with desegregation in the 1960s.

So the goal is worthwhile; and they're really hampered by the current legal climate in terms of affirmative action or consent decrees, or encountering racial profiling. So it's a tough spot. But having said that, I think more people need to do some thinking about how diversity is a means to an end, other than an end. And certainly at Gateway, we make it clear in our mission statement that the reason we ascribe to the theory of diversity is not to be just "politically correct," or to respond to the pressure that you've got to do that in this district, but because we believe that there's a benefit with diversity. And incidentally, this is the same reason why I have strong feelings about fraternities.

FELTON. Can you draw the parallel a little more sharply?

THORP. Just take fraternities as a metaphor and apply it to the schools—the problem with fraternities is that they are not only anti-intellectual, but they are "stultifying organizations" rather than "growth-enhancing" organizations. And a school that is not diverse is a school that is a growth-stultifying school, rather than a growth-enhancing school. Our basic belief is: You grow from difference. Again: It's Martin Buber's *I and Thou*. There's got to be a "thou" for the "I" to grow. And it's much better when the "thou" is different.

So we have a rationale to our diversity which is: You're going to grow more, because you're in a situation, with this population and this school, that through our curriculum, consciously causes you to study other voices and other cultures. And you're doing that with kids who may represent those voices and cultures. Just one of the things we do in assembly is to speak to the issues of diversity. We believe that our kids are going to come out having taken advantage of the fact that they're in a diverse population. What I wish is that there was more discussion in educational circles about what you do with the diversity once you get it, as opposed to saying: "Okay, we're diverse, and there you be." For the real test is: What do schools do for the minority kids who are there?

At my former school in Colorado, we were very eager to develop a successful program for Native-American kids. And for years it was a total failure; we had kid after kid come through and we at the school either voluntarily withdrew them, or ended up with them being thrown out for one reason or another. And in retrospect, it was because the school didn't support the kids, and their needs. One of the ways you do that is you build to critical mass. And so for the Ward Connerlys of this world, you need to understand that critical mass is a phenomenon where if you really do want to build diverse communities based on merit. I don't disagree with that as a philosophy, but it's a hell of a lot harder to build that kind of community while being conscious of the fact that it's really difficult to be one of a single archetype, a single type in a community. And we learned in this school in Colorado—a school where we had 120 kids—that until we had nine Native-American students one year, it was a failure. And the year that we had nine, it was a huge success. Because these kids could look and say, "You know, there's somebody else like me."

It was also—here's a quick story just to give you a sense of gringos like me needing to be much more mindful of things that make a difference: I'll never forget this young Native-American woman who was one of the first two Native-American women to graduate from the school; it was an incredible moment, and they were dressed in their Navajo dress for graduation, and it was really something special. She was a very shy and withdrawn kid who had spoken with me no more than a few times over the three or four years that she was at the school. She told me right before graduation: "You know, Mr. Thorp, I was frightened to death coming to this school." That didn't surprise me. Then she said: You need to know that I came real close to turning right around and driving right off campus and never enrolling in the school. But the reason why I made it past that very first moment, when I almost left before I got there, was this: As I drove onto campus, right next to the library was this cedar bush. And cedar is sacred to my culture, and that said to me: 'It's going to be okay here.'"

FELTON. Wow! What a story!

THORP. That's the kind of *benefit* of diversity and *challenge* of diversity, rather than just throwing up charts and graphs, that—you know, here is the sense of it!

FELTON. Well, I have a charts-and-graphs question that relates to what you just said. But first, just a couple of reactions: Grinnell College, in 1960 when I started, was liberal in attitude, well-meaning in attitude. And just as blind as anybody else in practicality. There were two—I don't know how many Black students they enrolled that year, but two of them—one from Chicago, one from somewhere in Alabama—were in my dorm. And Grinnell thought that the two young men naturally would want to room together.

THORP. Oh, my god.

FELTON. —And these two guys went along with it, but you know—come on!

THORP. When was this? Nineteen—?

FELTON. September of 1960. They should have known better than that. Even then. But it was their assumption, their own biases, that they couldn't see. The things die hard in the most "enlightened" of us.

THORP. The reason why I pinned you down on the date is if the year had been *1968*, and they *didn't* room together, they would have taken as much crap for *not* rooming together—

FELTON. That's right! Just those few years later; you're exactly right. Well, about statistics—it's funny: Obviously, you had to skew your pitch to the School Board—

THORP. I resent that remark! What a thought!

FELTON. I'm sure you do! I know in that Board-of-Education arena, statistics constituted the *lingua franca*: That was what they wanted, that was going to "make or break" your case, unfortunately.

But one of the questions on my longer list about the School Board was: Ms. Santos, is that her name?—the Board lady who came here to "look around"? I'd like to know really what she saw. But even before you answer: I don't understand how anybody could have even a five-minute experience of Gateway and think that you were running a Groton-type fancy private school here. Gateway is *not* a private school! This is not a cushy place with a bunch of "frat boys" running around. And how could anybody make that mistake who worked for a School Board at all? That's astonishing to me. That you would be pigeon-holed even for a minute. I wonder if her report allayed some of that suspicion? Or fear? I wonder also whether the weight of the statistics which you were able to mount in criticism made a difference?

THORP. Maria Santos was terrific. And I publicly acknowledged her on purpose.

FELTON. Yes, you did.

THORP. Obviously, it was also a political purpose. But it was also because she did a terrific job. And she and her team were appropriately praising and appropriately critical of what we're doing and where we are. Where they were appropriately critical was in their comments that we need to develop a tighter curriculum in certain areas, particularly in math. And they're totally right about that! Totally. No doubt about that.

Where they were praising was particularly in the humanities, and they took the time to break it down into the elements of what we're doing there, in terms of the relationship between teachers and students, in terms of quality of service the kids were getting. And we feel that that's appropriate praise for us. So I impressed that for the most part they came away with good impressions in a relatively brief snippet of life at Gateway.

Having said that, the one quarrel I have with their report is that they saw classes being conducted in what they described as "a more traditional way"—more teacher-centered than student-centered, less group work than not, tables arranged in—and they made a big deal about the table arrangements!—tables that were kind of traditional in their arrangement, and were not conducive to the group work. Okay, I have to accept that on that particular day, they did not see a lot of group work. I would say that there is merit in the criticism in the sense that we may not be doing as much as even a year ago, as much as even we should be. But they clearly didn't see the full range, or an appropriate percentage, shall we say, of what we know we are doing. And even on that day, there were some group things that did take place right in front of their eyes that they didn't comment on. So it's an example, of course, of where all of this sits—and it hearkens back to the diversity question: Your perceptions depend upon the lenses through which you're looking.

The issue for us right now with the District, is: Given increasing inspection of charter schools and increasing tension on the part of District-and-charter schools—and this is the "pecking-ducks" issue—they're trying at the very least to suggest making the curriculum overlap to an extensive degree with the San Francisco Unified. And what I've been doing today is E-mailing messages back and forth to Mark Kushner, my opposite number at Leadership High School, because a new proposal is going to this District Subcommittee on Wednesday night with new policies, one of which says "Charter schools curriculum will meet the standards and requirements of the school district."

Now, it's a vague-enough phrase and in one way could be interpreted loosely to say: "We just want to make sure that the kids are taking math and science and other statewide requirements." Okay, terrific; we are. But if the phrase is interpreted in a strict constructionist way, which is, "Oh, no, no—you've got to do the courses in this order, and you've got to use these textbooks, and you've got to have the kids take Driver's Ed at Gateway—then they're asking us to do something which violates my thinking about the spirit and the letter of the charter school bond. So—

FELTON. It reverses the comment the Board lady made, that all public schools should mirror the charter schools experience, because she thought it was so wonderful; whereas what they're saying about the curriculum is the opposite.

THORP. It's the classic example—and my own lens for seeing this is the social-scientist's lens—it's the classic example of the response of the status quo to reformers. And it's the classic example of the nervousness about the new or the unknown. And the classic profile, I guess, of starting at the point of suspicion, rather than embracing the unknown to find out when it's no longer worthy of being embraced. Then, change it, as opposed to the other way around.

FELTON. It's interesting, and an important verification of that, that when your statistics showed that Gateway's students were vastly superior, all the responsive commentary offered by the Board last week was: "Wait a minute! We'd rather just see an *incremental* adjustment here." In effect, she was saying: "We need to get used to this, we need it to be gradual in fact." Which is absurd! I mean, students' results have made quantum leaps here. And it was obvious—you showed them that. Perhaps when you very modestly didn't rub their noses in it too much—

THORP. On the contrary, I tried to make a special point of saying, "Look, we're not saying that we're better than the District. We're just saying, Here are our results, and we're giving you some comparative data."

FELTON. I'm going to try and grab another idea here that actually winds up something that we were talking about last time. We were discussing biorhythms. Another idea occurred to me. And don't get this wrong; because this example would make it seem as if I'm talking about pathology here, and I'm not. I don't know if you remember this; but it was my impression that when they first started using the Minnesota Multiphasic Personality Inventory a lot, they came to the astonishing conclusion that penitentiary guard staff and the prisoners they were guarding had exactly the same profiles.

THORP. It's a syndrome.

FELTON. Yes?

THORP. Well, I mean, it's sort of like the Patti Hearst thing, you take on your captors' personality.

FELTON. Oh! I hadn't thought of that element. That's very interesting. I was thinking it meant more that despite society's clear moral distinctions, whatever would motivate one to be deviant would also somehow, maybe with one little idler gear thrown in—

THORP. And I think that's a perfectly proper permutation and corollary to that.

FELTON. But what I wanted to do—and otherwise as I said, ignore the pathological intimations of it—

THORP. I think I know where you're going with this—

FELTON. Yeah, I'm sure you do! I think of the teachers—we were talking about whether the teachers and the kids here like each other. And in that kind of rhythmic way, I see syncronicity, syncopy, whatever you want to call it, that brings them together in the way students vibrate, in much more of an important way than when they *don't* come together with a teacher.

When Lisille Matheson and I were talking, we were extolling the virtues of the faculty, and I said: "Let me leave you with the thought that as a parent, if anyone ever talks about the "too young faculty" here, as a parent I always ask myself, in one way or another: "What if my kid were in a terrible emergency. Is there anybody there, in all those faces, whom I would have the confidence to say he could turn to, and know that that person would instantly give him his or her all?" And—

my god—you can just go down the line here! There isn't a person on the faculty who wouldn't turn and help. And that's astonishing to realize."

And of course, she strongly agreed.

Now, I *feel* that way; that's my sincere view. But my point here, is: I also think that the *reverse* is true. I think your kids would do anything to help these people who are teaching them. And that doesn't mean that someone's not going to snarl at a putdown at the end of a class, or however he perceives it, or—go through human experience. But the basic bond is clearly there; and it may never make a tinker's dam of difference to someone sitting down there on a school board. But it certainly is going to make your life enriched, and better off, because of that.

THORP. I hope you're right.

I just had lunch with a faculty member, as I'm going through a series of meetings now, talking about this year and next year. And this faculty member is really wrestling with the difficult choice about coming back next year. And I think there are two fundamental issues. Of course, each faculty member, for his or her own reasons, financial or whatever, professional decisions—the bottom line is totally personal. But in my role as head, I have to find common themes in this capacity that—for this teacher there are two issues. One is: Fewer of the kids seem to be prepared for a college preparatory program. And this is a college preparatory school; and there are few opportunities where he's getting the satisfaction of doing what he knows is college preparatory work. And secondly, he says: I'm spending too much time in negative "Chee,"—too much negative energy, with things ranging from incessant note-passing with kids who are immature, to more confrontative behavior, with a class exchange like: "Stop doing that." "How come?" Or, "Put your head up." "Well, why do I have to put my head up? I'm listening."

And this teacher is really wrestling with: "Is the mission of the school worthy enough—and for me is the potential of the school, the success of the school both great enough and soon to be realized enough for me, that it gives me reason to want to come back knowing that the skill level of the kids is lower than this person anticipated—that indeed, all of us anticipated!" And can I reconcile the fact that there are too many kids who are not with the program in terms of what business, of course, school is?"

In working with this distraught teacher, my attempt was to help the person understand that one of the great challenges of being a teacher is: You've got to figure out how to reward yourself. Because there aren't as many rewards coming your way as there are at least in some other circumstances, where it's either the big bonus, or the big salary increase, or the easily-identifiable "bottom line" business concept of meeting a quota. And there's not even the feedback of "customer satisfaction." If I'm a massage therapist, I get customer satisfaction feedback usually pretty regularly. Not as a teacher.

One of the real challenges of teaching, in addition to the bimonthly paycheck (which is an insult more than a pat on the back), is that real, meaningful satisfaction is incredibly delayed satisfaction. And for immediate feedback, you've got to work hard to find it! That means you have to be very observant; and it also means you have to establish criteria that are going to help you define "satisfaction." If you walk into class every day thinking, "I'm going to change these kids' lives," you're setting yourself up for frustration.

I think in one of our previous conversations I've talked about my own journey here, and both my strengths and weaknesses as an educator over the years, feeling that I am a persuasive person with kids. I don't feel that in a manipulative way, but in the ability to really sit down and have a heart-to-heart communication. And in fact I'm having lunch with a kid tomorrow afternoon—

FELTON. Why, that's great!

THORP. —Well, we'll see. I mean, I'm going into it thinking: "I'm really going to straighten this kid's life out, which is a mess!" And she's probably going into it thinking: "I'm getting a free lunch with the principal—and he's not going to do anything to my life!"

So the trick for educators is to figure out how to be satisfied. And I think what has depressed this industry, or what has caused the depression in the industry, is that there are fewer and fewer sources of satisfaction. And that's why we have a high turnover rate in the industry; that's why fifty percent of the people leave in the first couple of years of being a teacher.

I think a relative few—or a relatively small percentage will find the right sources of satisfaction, find the secret of professional vocational satisfaction. Because this is what you are going to have to do in education. Some number of them stay in teaching out of inertia. Some number of people stay in teaching out of the security of getting a paycheck every couple of weeks. Some number of people stay in teaching because of the time off, which is pretty cool. And—believe it or not, I'm still responding to your "bonding" question—

FELTON. Right, right!

THORP. —And actually, as a result of this proposed lunch with the student, I was thinking about this as I walked to the office, although I wasn't sure you were going to ask about this issue. To bring this full circle, what I wish the Gateway kids would understand and what I'm going to ask parents to do is this: We really need to have our parent body, and ideally our kids, letting our teachers know how much of a difference they are making. We really need to come up with ways to honor the faculty's contributions, beyond the celebratory things that are happening already in terms of dinners and such. But insofar as the parent organization goes, I think what we need to have happen is a kind of letter-writing campaign. This needn't be in the sense that one teacher suddenly gets forty letters on one day, thinking "Where does all this come from?" and sees they're all Xeroxed versions of the same thing. But one of the other things I realize—and this is another piece of information that is teacher-related—one of the kids came up to this teacher within the last couple of days, and said to him: "You're not leaving next year! All the teachers left on us last year. You can't do that!"

And on the one hand, the teacher felt great about that, but on the other hand, I think he was appropriately tempted to say: "Well, get your friends to start doing what we need to do around here, to provide me with that level of satisfaction."

So I don't disagree with your premise, that the kids would do it as well; but I think the kids—because they're only fourteen, fifteen—understandably don't recognize the impact upon their teachers of their poor behavior or their apathy toward schoolwork. Nor do I think they fully appreciate much of the impact they could have if they really let the teachers know how they feel. Of course, that's a lot to ask; but it's something that I'm really wrestling with, because some number of our faculty are really wrestling with that question, too. They're knocking themselves out; and when you do that you've got to feel that you're doing it for good reason. And not feel that either you're making a difference because the educational program is so sound that you're not challenged, or you're making a difference with kids who have reached you on an individual level. But I'm not sure that any of those will happen.

FELTON.   Well, I think that with youngsters of this age, there seems to be a progress of growth into emotional maturity which is: First, you conquer the hyperbolic exclamation. And only down the line do you find yourself capable of expressing heartfelt emotional feeling. And I daresay I can see, with some exceptions, it might be difficult for them to express that sentiment to a teacher. And it's too bad. In that sense you're right.

THORP. But in a sense I'll make the issue as well. I could go take at random a certain number of kids. And I would say, each one of them would be able to come up with an example where he would say: "Oh, I did that, Mr. Thorp! Here's what I did." And the adult would have missed the point. For the adult would have not recognized that the kid really was saying, "Thanks," or "I really appreciate what you're doing," or "That was nice," or "You helped today." This is because kids don't do such things in a direct fashion. They do it in an oblique fashion.

FELTON. Yes.

THORP. And it's also not particularly fashionable to compliment the teachers.

One of the things I was working on with this teacher was trying to help him understand: "You know, you've also got to be looking for it. You can't forget the signs." For me, I just watch how kids look at me or don't look at me when they walk by me. And in some kids I don't see any variation at all; but in some kids I'll see real variation from one day to the next. In seeing who I am, in acknowledging my presence. And some of the same kids will do both of those. And there's a lot to interpret in those kinds of kids.

This youngster I'm having lunch with tomorrow is really painfully aware of my intervention. In two weeks, she hasn't looked me in the eye at all. And when through a conversation with one of her parents, I got the word back that this lunch was what *I* wanted to do, I realized that the kid wasn't going to be bright-eyed and bushy-tailed in my presence. But my real fear is that she's not going to be able to respond to me at all. The way I'm looking at it is that I'm going into it to give her a pretty firm message: That "One the hand we love you to death, and we want you to be here; but if you keep on doing what you're doing, you gotta go. We're here to help, and this is an important time of your life, but it's equally important that you've got to go to class." And she's not doing it. And sympathetic as we are, supportive as we are, you've got to go to class!

FELTON. You've got to go to class. Well, she may be there only with—as you've mentioned before—the fact that you paid attention to her. Even if it was unpleasant, or had, you know, tension to it, it was attention.

FELTON. In your own life, did teachers have a vital impact?

THORP. My connection with education, my reason for getting involved with education was very much a personal connection to teachers in my life that made a difference. It wasn't principals! It was my seventh grade geography teacher; my ninth grade biology teacher; my tenth grade geometry teacher; and my twelfth grade physics teacher. All were people in my life whom I respected enormously, and admired what they were doing in the classroom, and I certainly appreciated that they had my needs in mind when they worked with me.

FELTON. Did they feel your appreciation by dint of your enthusiastic performance, or from your expression of it?

THORP. I think I was probably too immature as a person to state it. But I have to believe that my seventh grade geography teacher understood what a great teacher I thought he was.

FELTON. I would like to introduce here the use of a very elaborate kind of "visual aid" to understanding the mission of private schools, which you have made available to me. You asked me to look at a film about Groton, the New England prep school attended by Franklin Roosevelt and others of stature. I did, and it was highly illuminating. We might touch on it in several contexts throughout our process.

For today, something I heard this morning hearkened back to having seen this film on Groton. I picked up a little story this morning on the news, a feature about an elementary school in Falls Church, Virginia. It's called "Bailey's Elementary" and their whole focus is on inclusion, rather than elitism. They have people there—little kids—representing eleven different ethnic backgrounds. And at Bailey's, they don't see these students ethnically; they see them *lingually*. They say that there are *languages* here, different languages—in their term, "language minorities." And they work with that, rather than with terms like racial minorities, ethnic minorities, or educational minorities, disability, dysfunctional minorities. The teacher expressed their mission in a very revealing way: She said, "Our goal is to go from learning to read, to reading to learn." And making that transition with those little kids' lives is very important to this. She says: "If there are groups of kids with deficits, we don't isolate them or single them out in groups; they don't have any kind of group identification with a liability. Today it might be Marta and José and Ivana who are my group for now; and we're working on this project. And tomorrow maybe one of these kids will go elsewhere in the room because he jumped the hurdle, and the others will stay with me because today this is my *new* group." It had nothing to do with inferiority or superiority, or any of that. It was fascinating, and, I thought, innovative.

The question that school's technique generated was: Why was it so difficult for Groton or other schools everywhere to find a similar new way of thinking about kids? Why is it so different, maybe even on a high school level, unless the obvious answer is simply that kids at this particular school's age are so *tabula rasa* that you can damn well do as you please? I don't think it was that; I think it was parental attitude. It was a very exciting view. And then only a night later, another item appeared in the news bearing, totally the opposite message. This was a very worrisome report that drugs such as Clonadine and Ritalin and anti-depressants and other pharmacological solutions are being given to very young kids.

THORP. It's true, and it's frightening.

FELTON. Yes, it *is* frightening. These reports show such totally different approaches. And the consequences are so obvious, because when they land in *your* bailiwick, one group is going to go in one direction, and the other group is going to go in the other.

THORP. You know, as a social scientist, one wonders what the proper role of the community is. One wonders the extent to which the community is stultifying. Taking Groton, for just a moment—and I know you have a larger context for its discussion later: Groton has a community, an amazing community. Groton has tradition; it's a school which understands its traditions and its values. But to what extent does tradition get in the way of progress, the ability to absorb difference, diversity? In my own sphere of influence, I compare it with this Native American Preparatory School in Santa Fe. Their Board, on which I serve, was deeply concerned with how well their kids were going to do in college. Those students are going to have less of a track record in terms of substance, although from a marketing point of view, you can imagine the school's going to champion its college placement. They've already had one of these confrontation scenes about a decision made at Harvard to accept one of their students. Well, Harvard and any other college are falling all over themselves to get the Native Americans into their schools. But the catch was—these schools wouldn't give them any money! And so my point to these kids is that their college counselor is so well poised to look the Director of Admissions to Harvard in the eye and say: "Don't you dare accept my kid if you're not going to support the kid!" And the counselor can really put the pressure on them to see if he's going to be successful. I'll find out shortly how many kids have made it through their first year of college, and I expect some attrition.

FELTON. Why is that?

THORP. It's a big issue in Native-American post-secondary education. One thing you might not know: Prep schools often base acceptance on the realities of cold, hard cash. And one of the things that I dealt with at Cate, in the admissions process—and I'll put it less diplomatically than I would in front of a committee—is: "Who are you going to accept as fourteen-year-olds who as sixty-year-olds are going to give you a lot of money?"

FELTON. This is a consciously-posed question?

THORP. Well, even at Berkeley, as we saw last year, it should be merit-going, but wait a minute—there's a whole category of people getting in because of their connections and their wealth. So, if anybody doesn't think the issue of the ability to support the school doesn't influence admissions decisions, then they're not paying attention. And again, given my own slight Marxist leanings in certain ways, I like having fun with this question: "Okay, if that's true, then let's really look at who is likely to give us money!" And if a kid got in in part because his family had means, and then they intimated when they came across as that "We'll support you," and then they didn't, they heard from me, saying "Wait a minute, here! This is part of the drill here!"

But it was more interesting from an intellectual point of view to watch the families of inherited nineteenth-century wealth in the 1980s and 1990s want to get their kids in based on the fact that they had means. It was a sham, really, when you realize in fact that their means had pretty well been piddled out by the last two or three generations that hadn't done anything worthwhile except spend the nineteenth-century generated wealth! It was *those* families who created the Grotons, and to a lesser extent Cate. And it was nineteenth-century wealth that allowed somebody to walk into the school no matter what an idiot the person was, and get enough of an education to be less of an idiot, to get some sort of a job to survive, and have enough people propping you up to make you look successful. To put perspective on it. And to pose the question: "Ahh-ha! The kids whom we ought to be accepting now in the 1990s are fourteen-year-old geeks who at the age of 25 are going to be multi-millionaires because they founded Microsoft; so don't you think we ought to be a little—?" And you can imagine some of the old-boys sitting around the Cate Board table just exploded when I would make that point. "What do you mean? That's not what this school is all about!" they would throw back at me. But my philosophy was: You create that kind of community with the idea of longevity in mind. But if you talk about a school as a family, which I do a lot, it means you've got to *act* like a family. If there's a family in the school that's been a good match, then when the next kid comes along, that kid gets special attention. I believe in that; and I'm happy to say that Williams College believes in that. I don't know what Grinnell's policy on that is, as for legacies, but Williams is very much that way. But it does get into the issue of a school's values.

FELTON. And you don't have any qualms about that?

THORP. I think there's merit in the idea that you connect with a family, and that connection should continue under normal circumstances. One of the big issues in the day schools here, the private day schools, Hamlin and Towne School, is they might have one kindergarten with twenty-two openings; let's say they have two classes, making forty to forty-five openings. If they have twenty-three younger siblings, fine. You can imagine that there are only twenty-odd slots left for the other two hundred people who are trying to get their kids in.

FELTON. Thinking of schools and costs: Standard & Poore's, the bond ratings people, have a new school measurement scale. It's, in their words, "A rating for schools, and it's to see where we spend the money, what the outcome of student demographics, the learning environment." They propose to do everything with kids that they do with bonds. And, they also want "To use the analytical tools of Wall Street to assess the return on school districts' investment." When I heard this report, I got a distinctly "eugenics" feeling about it, and I just wondered what you might have heard about it, whether this was something that your friends down at the School District are going to jump to use, or what.

THORP. Well, I can tell you the best thing that came out of that School Board session the other night was the statement by School Board member Juanita Owens, who said: "We ought to have all our schools do this."

FELTON. Yes. That's in my notes; I was glad she said it, too.

THORP. That was by far the best remark, and I hope that's something that they ask them to do.

FELTON. Let me ask you one more question, which you already partly answered—in reference to Mark Kushner, Principal of Leadership High, that other charter high school in San Francisco whose under threat. Are you getting a good—between you, amongst the five of you—are you getting a good mutual-support group going here? Can you work together as a sort of "side"? Partisans in the struggle?

THORP. Yeah, we are. We're not doing it as much as we should; and we tend, because of the nature of what we do anyway, we tend to be very much of a reactive force, unfortunately. When the trouble starts, we tend to sort of corral the wagons. And of course, there's a difference between the elementary school situation and the high school situation. Within the elementary school—the whole problem is the Edison Elementary School. And you could probably hear that the other night. The Board is not supportive of a "for-profit" run school. And I'm not going to disagree with that. I would just say, "Do it your way and see if you could do it better," rather than just saying, "By definition it doesn't work." But anyway, there's enough difference in who we are; and even the last school, the Life Learning Academy—their situation is different enough from ours. So in the long run what that means is that Mark Kushner and I are really close in terms of what our needs are.

And where that gets a little bit tricky is that unfortunately there is a little bit of rivalry; it doesn't come up very often, but we do compete for the same students. And right now we're in this kind of "rats-in-the-lifeboat" scenario, where it looks like he's going to lose his facility. As he said that night. So we both are very careful to preface statements at various times, with: "I don't want to do anything that would hurt you...but on the other hand...." We're working very closely again today. We sent E-mail messages back and forth like crazy about this set of resolutions that are going to be presented to the Board. And we have a couple of serious concerns and reservations ourselves. Trying to strategize how to get out—that's what I just said in an email to him. Saying: "Don't you think we ought to get a meeting with this guy, Roger Tom? He was the guy who led the School Board discussion at the beginning of the meeting. This way we can sit down in the meeting and say: "Look, you're out of line here. This is why." And: "Won't you change the basic resolution?" So we work pretty closely together.

Are you asking also about a personal support group?

FELTON.   I really wasn't; and I imagine a certain amount of camaraderie would generate that anyway. But if there is one, I'd certainly be interested in hearing about it.

THORP.   There is one. What is nice is that in this area, there is a group called the Bay Area Schools' Head Association. "BAYSHA," or something. And they've been nice enough to ask us to participate as members, and they're a great group of people who get together once a month or so. Unfortunately, I'm not going to be able to make the meetings, I'm usually too busy. But the couple times that I have, it's nice to sit around with a group of heads, and share stories about our life in schools. Because only heads of other schools can understand what you are going through.

FELTON.   I'm sure!

THORP.   Anyway, in the case of Mark and me, our experiences are so much different from their experiences.   There is also a group called The California Network of Educational Charters, which is the governing body for charter schools.   So I've added something else to my plate!

Chapter Fourteen

CREATIVE GENIUS *VERSUS* SLOGGING STUDENT

"One person's creative genius is another person's pain in the ass. And I think starting as early as elementary school, schools are designed to be less tolerant of creative genius than they should be. And creative geniuses are too quickly seen as pains in the ass. The kid who becomes bored in school, because he or she is bored in school, develops a natural human response to boredom, which is stimulation! That kid will seek stimulation. And because the kid isn't getting it in whatever's going on in the classroom, the youngster will begin to operate outside the classroom—not in a physical sense, but as the class cut-up, or in daydreaming, or whatever it is...."

"[There is a] myth of public education in this country, that 'public education needs to be the same for all.'....It's an unhistorical myth, and...I believe it's an unproductive myth. And somebody needs to have the courage to stand up and say: "No! Not every child is going to get the same experience, because in fact, different children need different experiences....That's why we have the Bronx School of Science; and that's why we have the School of the Arts here in San Francisco; and that's why we have magnet schools, and that's why we have boarding schools, and on and on....And it's not true in the history of school law and development that the intention of school people was that every child would have the same experience."

29 February—*Almost nothing went "right" on this day. For starters (which we would not learn until later), in the morning, in a* *faraway Michigan city, a six-year-old first-grader brought a pistol to class and destroyed the life of a classmate. Had the two people sitting in the Principal's office of Gateway High School in San Francisco solemnly evaluating the vicissitudes of charter education been aware of this devastating fact at the time, it would surely have affected what, for Peter Thorp , was an already compromised morale.*

The tragedy in Michigan notwithstanding,, Principal and Reporter probed, and furrowed, and posited, and reflected.

Every successful dialogue works as a more or less sane version of a folie-a-deux: *In intense synergy, two persons share the impetus for the dialogue's movements. In a dialogue such as this series, there were actually "four people" involved—The Principal of Gateway High School, a Reporter, and also one Peter Thorp and a parent named Felton; and part of the dialogue's functioning depends upon which persona(e) advanced at which time. This slightly schizoid consideration was necessary in order to maintain the proper traction— the "sobriety," if you will—of the experience. A "controlled schizophrenia" of reportage-advancement works if, like a rocket's propulsion system, it stays a hair under volatility (the rocket's forward thrust being gained by its fuel remaining a "controlled explosion). Now, on Leap Year Day, a matter of note arose between the "junior" members of the foursome: Felton, who was the growing friend of the man Thorp, had become concerned with the effects of strain upon his subject.*

Peter was a supreme juggler. He maintained at any one time, in the air above his energy vortex, a range of problems. His solutions to them—some spontaneous, as he would point out during the day's session—often were adventitious. I came to see that his mind worked in the same manner as the randomly—assigned information storage on a computer hard disk. Whether this example is prosaicism or quintessence is open to debating tastes; but the spinning encyclopedia of neuron-firings which buzzed all the time above the Principal's head could be gathered by him, at the propitious time, and reassembled at lightning speed for the purposes of informing and directing his discernment.

But being a walking (if lower-case) Solomon has its consequences, and takes its toll. And I was beginning, with my own rougher "floppy drive" of a mind, to understand that Peter was in need of succor, of some form of emollient to sustain the whirling, incessant pressure for ingenuity which, in a very real sense, was his job—his occupational albatross.

I knew that art history was a part of his emotional bulwark which he valued perhaps more than any other. I also knew that the neurosynaptic experience which takes place when exposed to color— especially in the form of the visual experience of art—had at the same time an elixir-like, calming effect upon the brain. At the risk of being a bit manipulative (but with a therapeutic salubrity as my high-minded goal), I resolved to create, during the breaks in his day which our meetings represented, a moment at their beginning which would be neutralizing of jarring stimuli. A moment's appreciation of something visual would then enable us to attend to the sober strings of our pedagogical concerns. If my scheme worked, it would operate much like the alternating scenes of the Globe's Shakespearean performances of the 1600s, in which stagecraft required a short scene in a small balcony, to cleanse the spectator's mind of the bloody battle just seen upon the main, lower staging space, before returning to it, and its necessity of laying forth an acceptable arena for an idyll or a tryst.

As it happened, I was the parent-advisor for Gateway's photography club (called the "Photo Session," in wry, one-syllable-briefer homage to Alfred Stieglitz's famous Photo Secession of the early 1900s). The day before this meeting with Peter, I had worked, one-on-one, with a particularly gifted student photographer named Evan. So my first of the new pattern of "neutralizing" imagery represented a series of photographs drawn to illustrate eye-brain interactions, how we perceive, and how that interaction enables us to perceive differently. I had hoped that this might evolve naturally into an opening discussion of different ways a principal might work to obtain a favorable, different perception of the intentions of charter school leaders.

Peter not only enjoyed the diversion—and I saw some of the furrows lift from his countenance—but he participated, sharing two photos from his own history, of Chinese scenes of great beauty and power he had made in his Fulbright years in the 1980s. His work had all the impact of any good photographic depiction of peasant life, including repetition of visual gesture, and intense human feeling.

So, our session began well enough in my newly-structured "visual calming ground." And it progressed to a session filled with event and meaning. This notwithstanding, it was a session destined constantly to be interrupted. The persons whose needs broke into the discussion were valuable, however; for their insistence brought the quintessential picture of the Principal in his job, pivoting from this pillar to that post, trying—as Peter Thorp says frequently—to be a problem-solver; for Gateway High School, the problem-solver.

As these interruptions so graphically depicted the vagaries of Peter Thorp's professional school day, note of them as they occurred will be illuminative of Peter's unrelenting job's demands. Even with these frequent interruptions, however, the two convoking searchers— one Baby-Boomer, one War-Baby, in a school of Millenium Teens taught by Generation-X'ers—probed ahead.

In setting up the tape recorder cables, I noticed, under Peter's credenza, a series of large and well-used skateboards. After the previous experience of the young fellow whose radio had been confiscated, I reasoned that these were simply impounded spoils of student-teacher warfare, paraphernalia at issue in some way.

My mind shifted from skateboards to the initial questions I intended to pose; they related to meeting the special learning needs of the youngsters. Even outside my own family's interest in that problem, I had an involvement to illustrate. I began by telling Peter how I had connected with the one youngster whose photographic interests had shown him already to be—in that word loathed by at least this one educator—"gifted":

FELTON.　　There are a zillion ways we could start this session; but I guess one thing I'd like to tell you about is one thing I'm doing here at the school. I thought you'd want to know, because it's interesting.

Your "advisee," Evan Alsnauer, could not make the schedule for the regular Photo Group meetings that we have. I liked him enormously when I met him; but when I saw his work—I had asked the students to bring in whatever they'd done—I saw that this was an astonishingly talented kid. And then I wanted to pursue it. Now, when we could not pursue the schedule—

INTERRUPTION #1—Peter wants to arrange to send a fax of a confidential nature to a colleague, following up on a two-hour-long conference telephone call of the previous day. The office at the other end won't let him speak to his intended recipient; this disconcerts Peter, who insists on a direct acknowledgment by the man that he and he alone will receive the fax. At last, the staff is made to understand Peter's unwavering needs; they promise cooperation; we return to the dialogue, as Peter's secretary begins the faxing process.

THORP.　　So, anyway: Evan Alsnauer.

FELTON. We worked it out. He had another commitment, and we worked it out that, because I so missed his contribution to the group, I arranged to meet with him the day before the rest of the group met. And we had our first session yesterday—

THORP. One-on-one....

FELTON. —A kind of tutorial. And it was wonderful. An interesting thing happened when I spoke with his mother. I expressed this scheduling dilemma, and my desire to have him in the group; and she was very glad that I did. Photography was obviously something that he'd spent a lot of time with.

And then she said—and I thought this would be interesting to you—one parent to another, one Gateway parent to another. With the kind of embarrassment that one would give to someone totally unaware of this school; she said: "You know, actually he has some learning dysfunction." And I think she expected me to respond: "Oh, well, then, the hell with him. This is all off." And what I said was: "Well....if he didn't, I imagine he'd be pretty lonely there!"

THORP. He'd be in the short lunch line!

FELTON. Yes! He would! And then she relaxed; and we worked it out. But it's been interesting, by dint of the way he responds. He's really an instinctive photographer. And I gave him a series of images—it's not a test, it's just some examples that I use. These have to do with perception; how we see, and what the brain does to help us orient to the visual image. That excited a whole range of things that he and I then went on to talk about. I don't know if you've ever seen his portfolio. It's not big; but it's—wondrous! So we're going to pursue some more.

THORP. Well, that's great. And thank you for working with him in that way. He's a kid who is struggling with the issues of: "I can't do math, period!" But for a kid to say that, and also say, "I'm worthy,"—it's like Leonardo's perspective; here's a kid who doesn't miss mathematical points. But his computational abilities are not what they need to be; so he's really struggling. And also a reflection, I think—this is somewhat superficial, but I think it's on the right track—of his impulsivity, which provides on the one hand, enormously profound gut reactions to instant images, which is fantastic, but which isn't the kind of learning methodology or learning profile that's great for sitting down and working through a math problem, where each step of the puzzle is dependent upon your success in the previous step of the problem, so to speak. So—I don't know how good you were in math, but certainly I can imagine some correlation between the genius of impulsivity and the creative act of impulsion and gut instinct being somewhat inversely proportional to the methodical requirement of problem-solving, car repair—you can make your list on and on—of what learning style would be best suited to a certain task, based on sequential thinking. This is in great contrast to instinctual response to image or stimulus, whether or not it's visual stimulus.

And I think that our kids have much more exposure, much more opportunity to respond impulsively than I think was the case for us. But I don't know that. I mean, there are all these trite theories now of too much television, and what that does to kids, and so on. I do think there is some truth in the statement that this generation of kids has a higher visual acuity than you and I did; because I think they're looking at a lot more images than we did; and in fact, the images are being played out to them in increasing levels of sophistication, be it a video game that gets more complicated with each advance. But I also think that our kids have more opportunity to be impulsive, which is good in some ways, and of course problematic in other ways. They're not—it's not the good old nineteenth-century school of "You should be seen and not heard;" it's kind of a Baby-Boomer idea: "Kids have First Amendment Rights, too!" That—to stress the point a bit—they can sort of say whatever they want. So, yes, that's great for Evan. It's wonderful because it's providing him a vehicle to realize a real success that wouldn't be the case otherwise.

INTERRUPTION #2: Confirmation came of Peter's fax.

During this time, Peter shared with me his self-described "school of averages" photographic renderings: "If you take enough photographs, eventually you'll get one you like."

The two he showed me were both likeable, indeed. Both of China, one depicted the early-morning T'ai Chi ritual exercises around a lake in Hong Jo, with Peter's pleasure at my delight increasing as he pointed out a tree which mirrored the movements of men. And a second—and my clear favorite, although one he had not enshrined with quite the reverence as that given the exercisers— taken through a bus window at a young peasant seated on the ground, in communion with an elderly man. The unmistakable visual referent to the mentor-disciple relationship—complete with the young man's face disturbingly serious, and the wise elder's face a round moon of delight at the attention of the Ansel Adams in the passing bus—made the photo a strong statement. When we talked about them, he said Hong Jo was a place where Mao had located a country retreat, in his heyday. "On earth there is Beijing; in Paradise there is Hong Jo," he quoted to me. The Paradise in the stylized dance rituals of T'ai Chi was as movingly dramatic as any modern dance moment; but the earthiness in the old Buddha's round face was for me an even truer Reward. (In fact, in the spirit of our earlier exchange, Peter mused that he'd love to show the student Evan the two peasants' photo, and ask him what he thought they were "talking about.")

This interruption—both the telegraphed work message, and the aesthetic respite—passed, and we moved on with our dialogue.

FELTON. Just one last note on Evan, because it did have to do with math: I asked him if he could solve a problem that I don't know the answer to. I said: "You know how fast light travels?" He didn't, but he knew it was fast. I told him; and I then added: "If light can travel that fast, 186,000 miles in one second!, why is it that a lens that is four inches long, if you make the same lens or even expand the lens just another four inches, the light weakens by a factor of one half. Now, that light is going to travel that four inches just as fast as it does up in the heavens; but then, why does it lose half its strength?

It's a question about optics, that I don't understand, because I understand only what a slogging photographer knows about optics, but not what an engineer knows. And it's a question that he moved around in a pretty interesting way, though I don't know whether he hit it or not. But it is an interesting question about what's happening when the light value falls off by many factors, and the photographer has to compensate accordingly. In just this little space of a longer camera lens, what's really magnified is not the image but the variable choice of decisions the artist must make.

THORP. Well, that's great. You're opening up all kinds of little doors for him.

FELTON. Just one other question, that you just raised now, about impulsivity in responsiveness. I remember the shibboleth that I didn't learn until it was almost too late: "Trust your first answer." Which is kind of an appeal to impulsiveness in the mind-body-brain-eye reaction experience that should come to one's aid. And then thinking of kids responding in class: In our generation, a student would have factored in so much in the way of anxiety, about what was expected to be the response, and what was remembered from studying, and other mental impositions, rather than the encouragement just to be impulsive and say what comes to mind. And I don't know where this group—Gateway's student body—is on that.

THORP. Let's put it this way: One person's creative genius is another person's pain in the ass. And I think starting as early as elementary school, schools are designed to be less tolerant of creative genius than they should be. And creative geniuses are too quickly seen as pains in the ass. The kid who becomes bored in school, because he or she is bored in school, develops a natural human response to boredom, which is stimulation! That kid will seek stimulation. And because the kid isn't getting it in whatever's going on in the classroom, the youngster will begin to operate outside the classroom—not in a physical sense, but as the class cut-up, or in daydreaming, or whatever it is.

I think impulsivity is a reflection on new ways of looking at things, and new responses; but it's seen as *normative* behavior, in an environment where creative genius works—to wit: Your work with Evan in this circumstance. And it's seen as *aberrant* behavior where conforming thought processes are what are sought and valued. And for example, in a math classroom, impulsivity is not what the typical math classroom is designed to celebrate, or to cherish; it's "Know your drills, know your tables, know the processes, know the solution—" and moving up the scale of hierarchy in terms of things that are called for. And only when you get to certain levels of mathematics will the teacher sit back and allow the people to be creative.

Well, what about the kid who all along has been coming up with these incredibly creative solutions? My partner's son right now is just a brilliant little guy! But he can't do his math tables. And he can't do the kinds of things that are required to be considered a success in math; and so he seems a problem in school; and it's a kind of spiraling phenomenon where he's told: "You're a problem." And he answers, "Why am I a problem? I'm really interested in this stuff!" "You're a problem because you're not doing it the way you should be doing it." "Well, I've got a *better* way of doing it, in my eight-year-old-mind, and why should I be doing it your way?" And you can see how that kind of spirals out.

So—a kid like Evan—not to make too much of him—but a kid like Evan responds, as somebody would, to being put down, so to speak, for one's creative impulsivity, creative genius, by figuring out: "Okay, I've got to subvert my own way of looking at the world, or my own ability to interpret in the way I want..." Some kids will subvert their own instinct, thinking: "Okay, I know what the game of school is; I know what the goal of school is, and I value what I can get out of this, which is the next step; so, okay, I'm going to play the game." Other kids say: "I don't value this, but I'm going to follow the path of least resistance so I don't get yelled at every day in school." That's said by probably the great majority of kids, and those are the kids like Evan, for example, who use dress as a way to express themselves creatively. He walks around with that hood pulled up over his head as a way to kind of get himself where he wants to be, and keep out the things he doesn't want coming in.

So—I feel for people like that, because I don't understand them. Because I'm not an impulsive person, I think. We've talked about this—in fact, I'm pretty damn sure I'm not an impulsive person. To the contrary, and here's another set of—

INTERRUPTION #3—The Chairperson of Gateway's Board of Directors, exhibiting the great flexibility for which she was known, entered the room wearing a different "hat"—this time as lunch courier, attending to the gustatorial needs of the man she had placed in charge of the school. Lisille Matheson handed Peter a wrapped mid-day meal, which, begging my indulgence, he began to consume.

I have the peculiarity of seeing great dignity in such gestures as this; and the Principal of the school, grabbing a quick bite at our session from lunch just brought him by the school's Board Chair, brought no less admiration from me of him (and her) than had his appearance several weeks earlier before the San Francisco Unified School District's sitting Board. No repas au déjeuner of Charles DeGaulle's cabinet (at which Le Général himself used to serve the soup) would have impressed me more. Sometimes, the act of eating is humbling, for it states the hidden case: This is basic animal behavior! It refreshed those in the room, and aired out the headiness.

Peter checked again on the progress of the confidential fax, and answered another aide's query about a teacher's mileage chit and a question about an admissions matter. Then we continued on, between bites (of that lunch which itself would not be consumed until several more interruptions had transpired).

THORP. I'm not an impulsive person. In fact, I don't think most educators are impulsive people. And it's the beauty of the sound, rational, thoughtful mind. Again, educators as a species are not particularly impulsive people. They pride themselves on their ability to work through to the point of Ph.D. theses, which nobody cares about except this thoughtful person. And it's also why you have educators "doing their thing" in a very thoughtful world, and you have people out making a lot of money who are making impulsive split decisions in the world of technology, who are *not* in education, and for whom educators drive them nuts! This is partly because educators say: "Come on, already! Get on with it!" They *don't* say: "Well, on the one hand, there's this, and on the other hand, there's that; and of course, if you look at it this way—" You know, we're sort of trained to help people look at all sides. And in fact, I think increasingly the world is going to reward impulsive people and less so methodical people. I don't know if that's good; I don't know if we're going to be a better world because of that; but—and I'm as guilty of this as anybody—I don't think schools fully recognize the need to train kids to be impulsive appropriately. Because there sure as hell is a fine line between being the venture capitalist and making the right call in inventing things, and holding up a Seven-Eleven, to put it at the other end of the spectrum. Or, to behave impulsively—well, actually, let me do a much better analogy: There's a difference between the venture capitalist and the day trader. And schools need to help kids figure out how to match up their impulsivity with an appropriate goal and an appropriate restraint. And there are a whole bunch of day traders who are being incredibly successful because it's the right match; and what I read about is a whole lot of day traders that are losing thousands of dollars and their whole life savings pretty damn quickly.

   FELTON.   Well, I agree that it's a desired goal to develop—to use your term, a more "appropriate impulsivity." But we're also going to have to raise future teachers who are going to have to systematize five classes worth of starting at the beginning of the book and working our way through the end of the book! So somehow, each style has to accommodate the other in some respect, or there's going to be hell to pay.

   Now I suspect, just parenthetically—going back to your partner's very bright eight-year-old with his math class quandary—I suspect that if he's as sharp as I am completely willing to believe after a short exposure to him—even though he may not understand it, something in his thought process must communicate to the pleading face of his teacher: "I'm just not ever really going to get through to this person what it is that makes me tick. So—if I don't say anything right now, it's just because I haven't the vaguest idea how to deal with it. I don't really want to do it her way; and he can't understand my way to save his life; so I'm just going to have to pass for now and we'll hope that it comes to me tonight!" You know? My younger kid has somewhat of the same problem.   And other kids whose intellect is so stratospherically removed from their age level have that problem.

   THORP.   Yes. And they lack the—

INTERRUPTION #4 was the summa of the art of distraction. Once it was initiated, it required that Peter and I terminate our meeting for the moment, so that he could impose his authority on a situation of urgency, confidentiality, parental distress, student grief, and, I am sure, more. In the words of the teacher who brought the dire matter of a young girl's emergent problem into Peter's office: "I worry about her safety."

When Peter returned from his intervention, his mood continued to be high, signaling to me that his problem-solving side had risen to meet the crisis. I in turn took a moment to let him finish his lunch, while I cancelled a meeting of a portion of my photo group, and then we settled in for a hoped-for unbroken conclusion to our session.

His response to my series of questions at this time revealed how wrong I was to think he was rolling on a "high plateau."

FELTON. I want to do some "cut-to-the-chase" stuff," which is fine because they are sensitive issues, but they also will accomplish our curricular goal of following the progressive course of problems. Whatever you'd care to relate about them, there are a number of issues here, and I'll just put them all out:

One is to inquire whether there is any movement or development with the teacher who was concerned about staying, about whom we talked last time. Another issue, with a similar sensitivity, is embraced in another follow-up question: What transpired at the lunch you had arranged to have with the problematic student, the one with whom you needed to communicate some messages about her continuing at school? And another is sort of a departure on the teacher issue, insofar as you'd care to share.

THORP. Well, I'll talk about the student lunch first.

Actually, it turned out not to be lunch, because she ate before I had a chance to get her, and I said, "Hey! You just blew a free lunch!" I had such a profound and wonderful impact upon her that, within forty-eight hours, she had run away from home.

FELTON. No!

THORP. In fact, in all sincerity, I think we actually had quite a good meeting, and a meeting-of-minds; but it's just a continuing reflection of the lives that kids lead are multifaceted and multidimensional and multi-compartmentalized. And we had worked out a modus operandi for her at Gateway during this "lunch," and something blew up again at home. And it blew up to the point where she's left home. And we haven't seen her at school; and she was on the streets, the last that I heard. Now, this is the news as of yesterday morning. So I don't know what's transpired since then.

FELTON. How old a kid is she?

THORP. She's a sophomore. Fifteen. You know, as I think of one of my themes, my comments all along: Most kids are making eminently rational decisions in their heads. And so was this one! It was eminently rational, for this kid, to leave home and start living on the streets. And to her, she was going to "a better place" than home was. Of course, that tells you what her home was like. But I guess it also tells you that her behavior at home had resulted in a choice: "Either curtail this behavior now, or you're out." And the behavior was pretty egregious, as I understand it, in that she and her friend broke into her own home, if you can believe that, and had some kind of alcohol-laden party on the premises of her own home. And one of her parents came home and responded to that by "flipping out," as one might. And that was apparently the final blow-up. So I don't know where she is, what she's up to, or how well she's doing. I'm frightened for her; so you can imagine what her parents are feeling. Even with all the combined guilt and anger that all gets interwoven in a situation like this.

FELTON. So it sounds as if she didn't even really have an opportunity to share with them the effectiveness of her meeting with you.

THORP. Well—even if this hadn't happened, I don't think she would have. I mean, basically, what she was looking to do with me was negotiate a truce for the next couple of months: "If I just do this, can I stay here until I start pursuing my Graduate Equivalent Degree, and emancipation—are you familiar with that concept?—

FELTON. An emancipated minor?

THORP. Right. That's what she wants to do. So you can chalk that one up to a no-life-converting experience!

On the teacher matter: I've had a whole series of meetings with teachers this week, because this is the time of year for that; so to be honest, I don't remember which teacher I was talking about, and kind of what the scenario was for that issue.

FELTON. You very circumspectly did not identify the teacher. But—my notes indicated this was someone who was not certain he wanted to stay; and you and I extrapolated from that into a discussion of teacher satisfaction. But I know this individual was very torn. And—now I'm editorializing—but I imagine he came to you about this, in the classic "cry-for-help," to try and get some persuasion to stay, and you described very realistically what the situation was like, that the decision belonged to him. And I just wondered whether that decision had been made yet.

THORP. No. And now I know who I was talking about. The person is wrestling with options, both with all sorts of Gateway variables, and primarily with Gateway variables; but also the kind of "life options" that we all deal with in terms of a commute. This is one of our teachers who lives in the East Bay, and an option has come up for him that—there is an opening, and therefore a possibility of a job with a school that's about three minutes away from his house. So there's that issue.

Having said that, he's really torn, because he sees better now than he did a couple of months ago, in the depths of his frustration, that there is greater opportunity; we've made some changes in some class line-ups that have been very positive. And basically, he's of the kind of mind that says that you really need to give two years to a situation before you make a decision, because it really needs two years.

I, for my part of the conversation, tried to be encouragingly realistic, which is probably an oxymoron. Both to be encouraging about the school, and encouraging about his place in the school, and his impact on the school, and he's a person who underestimates his impact on the school. And at the same time, to be realistic; because I don't think it's fair to anybody to sell him a "snow-job." And I can do that. And to help him identify the right questions, and put aside some of the wrong questions, or at least arrange them in a hierarchy that makes sense in terms of what the real triggering points are.

So who knows? I mean, a lot of it depends on whether he would be offered the other position. His feeling—his final statement to me about that was: "I really would like to stay a second year, and I really appreciate this conversation, and I really love my colleagues here, it's a great group of people. But I don't know, because if I don't go for this one position, and a year from now I decide that Gateway wasn't the right match me, am I going to be kicking myself in the ass that the one time I had to go for this job, which is such a right job for me, that I will have blown my chance to do it?" So there's that component of it as well. The timing of things. So we'll see.

FELTON. Decision-making! There's no way to get advanced degrees in decision-making. There's no way to learn. Because it just doesn't allow for it.

THORP. I told you the story of my decision to take this position—

FELTON. To come here? Yes.

THORP. Did I tell you the "over-Nebraska" part of that? That's my point here, for this fellow. Teaching's hard enough; but at some point you go with what you've got. And if you'll remember from what I said earlier, this is from a guy who's methodical to the point of killing something!

FELTON. Well, I'm glad you honored that feeling.

INTERRUPTION #5—During Interruption #4, a sweet-faced young boy named Anatoly whose English was tinged with Slavic sounds had asked me, in Peter's absence, if Mr. Thorp would be back, as he had promised the boy he would lend him a book. The youngster returned now, and, sheepishly, knocked on the door and despite discomfort, reminded his Principal of the promise. I recognized him as a student from one of Peter's college-prep classes. "I need some information on scholarships," he said. The Principal allowed the lad to come back and use the book in question, but not take it home. The pressing need for financial assistance gave the boy no choice; he thanked the school head and left. I then turned the conversation back to its pre-interruption concern: The teacher with the uncomfortable decision about staying.

FELTON. Do you feel, if the teacher leaves, that this in any way represents a personal failure on your part?

THORP. Sure it does!

FELTON. You think it does.

THORP. Sure. Totally. And that's—and if he were hearing this conversation, as based on what he said to me in my talk with him, he would say, "Oh, no, no, no—that's not true!" But call me whatever, I totally feel that it reflects on me in a way where I lie awake thinking, "What can I do differently? What could I have done differently in the circumstances?" You know, if I had paid more attention, if I had rearranged the classes earlier; you know—if, if, if, if, if!…..Would it have made a difference?

And eventually, I'm able to step back, and come up with an explanation for why somebody would make that choice. And again, just with the few details I've given you, one could come to the conclusion: "Of *course* he's going to look at that other situation; who wants to do the Bay Bridge commute or the Bart commute every day, when you could be going to a school three miles away from home, and life would be a lot easier! And who wants to choose creative evolving chaos over well-ordered smooth-operating efficiency in terms of this other school being around a long time, and its being a private school, and therefore incredibly selective in its kids, and so—and my point eventually is: "Okay, you've got to make your choice." And what I try to do very, very hard in the hiring process—which is what I'm involved with right now; that stack of folders in the corner is files of candidates whom we're talking to—what I try to do in the process is be as clear as I possibly can about what Gateway is and what it isn't. And put people through the mental hurdles of asking: "Do you really want to teach in a school like this? It's a public school, public kids, facility-challenged, and all sorts of things." And try to find people who are committed to this venue.

And in this person's case, I think the commitment certainly was, and, I think, still is there. I think the personal failing I feel is that this teacher hasn't received enough support either to recognize fully the contributions he's made, or to give him more opportunities to feel satisfied than he's felt. Whether or not it's that we should have yanked people out of his class, or we should have booted people out of school, or whether we should have systems in place where the kids' behavior truly is being modified, rather than just responded to—those are the things I really wrestle with. You know—it's kind of a "captain-of-the-ship" issue, that ultimately it's my responsibility. I don't see it solely as my own job, but I'm the one who's got to answer to my bosses, the Board of Trustees, the parents, and so on, if we have high faculty turnover two years in a row. It doesn't reflect well on the school, and in the eyes of a bunch of people who are sort of watching the school it will appear Peter Thorp makes all the decisions, or that the school is what Peter Thorp thinks it should be.

I'm really the embodiment, the only person someone can turn to and say: "What's the answer? What does this mean for my kid?" And—well, you're a parent, you're sitting in front of me having much greater insight about the workings of the school because of these conversations; but, you know, you, too would be entitled to say, "Hey! So what are you doing about it, Principal?"

So, yeah; it has a real impact on me. And both in a professional and a personal way. It's probably the most discouraging moments for me, when somebody walks in and says: "I'm not coming back." There are, of course, some people who, in all honesty, if they walked in and said "I'm not coming back," I would say, "I think you're making the right decision." But not the case in this business. There's what's called "positive and negative attrition." Both kid-wise and adult-wise.

This is a school that you've got to buy into—you know, not only buying into—not only buying into admission, but buying into what we could call the "life cycle" of a start-up operation. And I've done that, rightly or wrongly; and part of my fear is that by buying into it as completely as I have, it's very easy for me to develop blind spots, and very easy for me to not recognize that the typical person probably *isn't* as committed to this venture as I am, and therefore does waver sooner than I might, or does get discouraged sooner than I might. And also, the typical faculty member is less experienced than I am. And so I have a bit of a perspective when things happen that don't go well, I can either put it into a context, or I can draw on my reserves of experience that say, "Yeah, it happened. But I remember the day when I *did* have lunch with a kid, and it did turn out to be a more productive experience than this one the other day.

So yeah, it has a huge impact on me. And this was not a good one.

FELTON. I wish I could comfort you in that.

THORP. Well, thanks, I appreciate that. I just—and I talked about this in one of our early sessions, about leadership style, where one of the things that I reflect about is I need to do more in that kind of personal connection to help people see me as greater support, or be able to say: "Hey, I need one of those 'lifetime-experiences' examples that you have in the back of your head that helps you get through the day; share one of those with me!" And I don't do that as much as I should.

And again, it's very easy for me, particularly these days—and you see what I've been doing with the School District, and that sort of thing!—to justify everything I'm doing. And yet the cost of losing good faculty is very high in the cost on the kids. It's interesting, a couple of kids said, I think maybe to this faculty member: "Are you coming back next year? Are you coming back?" I think it was this guy. And to be honest, I don't know what the teacher replied; but it wasn't definitive one way or the other; it was a kind of "non-answer." And the kids added: "Don't leave! All of our teachers left last year! Please don't leave!" So, it has an impact on the kids. Very much so.

FELTON. Well, one positive turn on that—I guess—

THORP. Yes! Give me one!

FELTON. —The negative one being the little coda from Commissioner Kelly following the Board meeting presentation, right at the very end he expressed concern about attrition of teachers.

THORP. Yeah. That's right.

FELTON. I was pleased to learn something about your teacher hiring process. A candidate came by to place his name in consideration for a teaching position while I was outside your office this afternoon. Apparently, I learned, you involve all the faculty. Everybody gets a chance to put in one's two cents. I think that's remarkable.

THORP. Really?

FELTON. Yes, I do. The opportunity to be a part of the evaluation of one's future colleagues, which is such an important consideration, is, I suspect, rarely given in schools. I think it's a wonderful idea.

THORP. Yeah.   It's standard-operating-procedure in private schools. I wouldn't say that everybody does it; but in a boarding school, for example, when people come and interview, the interview is two and three days long. You come, and you have lots of people to meet, and you meet the kids, and you see activities. You might spend a fair amount of time in a dorm to see what dormitory life is like; things like that.

To me, it makes total sense, because it's just the right thing to do, to have the people who are part of the team get a sense of the kinds of colleagues that they think would be right for the school. And they have full rein to say whatever they want, in the interviews, in terms of: "Here are the challenges," or "Don't come here!" or whatever the extreme position might be. It's also slightly selfish on my part, that it's always nice to be able to say, "Well, *I* didn't hire the person! *You* all said that this person would be great!" So there's a kind of "sharing responsibility" aspect to it.

But it's just right to do. And the one area where I *am* pretty impulsive is in hiring people, and making decisions about whether I think somebody would be right for this school. I can come to a conclusion pretty quickly; and that's not capricious or arbitrary. I can smell a good school from a mile away; and I can smell a good teacher from at least a half a mile away. But I value the process, because I really do value people responding to my initial impression, to confirm it or not. And we actually had a couple of candidates come through this past week where most comments were totally consistent with what I predicted people were going to say about this person; but there was one set of comments about one of these candidates which I hadn't predicted, and hadn't been aware of. And in fact it was said by a couple of teachers, which tells me that it was a legitimate issue. The comment was: "This person doesn't seem to listen very well." And the fact that this person was interviewing for a counseling position made that a big point. And the fact that more than one person said it, caused me some concern. There are other complications of the person's candidacy; but that became a big concern.

FELTON. To be sure.

THORP. But it's also a way—you know, the more you can have your faculty involved in institution-wide issues, the more it helps them to understand the issues. So we try to get the faculty involved in the enrollment process as well. Because it's easy for a faculty member to sit back and say, "How did this kid get here?," or, "Why don't we have more X, Y and Z?" And if the faculty member is part of the process, they'll understand what efforts are being made to accomplish that goal and whether the efforts have succeeded or have fallen short, and the person will have a better perspective on it.

All these lessons come from the perspective of a very young Turk, when I started my teaching career, who was critical of just about everything the administration of the school I started out at was doing, because—"Well, of course, they're all screwed up, and they don't understand that I have a much better way of doing it. And why are they doing it that way? And why don't they listen to me?" You couldn't have been a citizen of the 'sixties without feeling that way, and I sure played it out on my first teaching position.

FELTON.   That was your first teaching job, not your assistant headmaster position?

THORP.   No, no. I'm saying I was the young Turk faculty member who with a bunch of other people did crazy things, and thought that we were just being great, and we were really stupid! And we of course didn't recognize that experience on the inside does have some value!

INTERRUPTION #6—One of the skateboard jockeys presented himself, hat in hand, to collect his steed, only to be told by Peter: "You can't take it with you, because I'm confiscating it for a while, because you let someone else use it in school." A grilling of the reckless rollerman ensued. Peter ended up changing his mind, as an act of faith in the boy's probity and surprise at learning of his friend's misprision. "I don't want to have to distinguish between one skateboard and another," Peter said; "I can't tolerate people pulling them out and using them at school. Okay?" This ended the conversation and the miniature trial. I felt it entirely reasonable that a man in his mid-fifties should not be required to learn the fine points of skateboard manufacture in order to earn his pay as Principal. As he ushered the boy out, the co-conspirator suddenly appeared at the door; Peter charged the first boy with bringing the Principal's sober and considered judgment to the other youth.

FELTON.   Let me jump from this place to note some kind of impressions about what's on the airways, what's in the newspapers. I caught these items—and they're a set up to other concerns:

There was a bulletin in California news that "Charter schools are more prevalent..." and it went on to define them as "...schools created by parents and teachers." Just a little note which took as long as I just took to say it. Another one was to note that "San Jose's first charter school, called "Downtown College Prep" is in process. There were—as you certainly can imagine—all kinds of different levels of reports on Proposition 26, the ballot initiative reducing the public vote requirement on school bond measures from three-fourths majority to a simple majority. And also in the course of the last week, there were questions about the Title I measure signed by President Clinton to support public schools, to increase parental involvement. A measure to devote lottery proceeds to textbooks. A number of issues I mentioned briefly last time on an issue facing the University of California's Santa Cruz campus about whether the narrative evaluations would survive; and the faculty said "thumbs down" on it. That spelled the end of written evaluations.

THORP. "We don't want to spend the time writing those things!"

FELTON. —That's right! And a very interesting student interview following that decision, saying, "My God! That's why I came here!"

THORP. Sure.

FELTON. —And now they've done it in. Another issue which was totally unrelated: "California high school diets—high in fat, sodium, preservatives."

THORP. You should see what they bring in.

FELTON. I'm sure! I'm sure it's ghastly. Another note that daycare centers are now connecting with Burger King.

THORP. That's interesting! I'm not sure I've seen that one.

FELTON. —Which is also horrifying to think about. And then the last one, and my question from all of these: On a news program from last week, the local public television show from Northern California which is in the "Washington Week in Review" format, this one, even though local, featured Leon Panetta and Henry Cisneros, former Clinton cabinet officials. And a quote from Panetta: "You can't work on the local end level and not realize that what happens in Sacramento or Washington will affect *your* school." He went on to say: "Getting involved, and building leadership, are educational imperatives." Now all of that—

THORP. You mean, being involved in building leadership?

FELTON. Building leadership in the schools, was imperative for educational institutions. All of that, which were either news reports from one medium or another, throughout the course of the week—anybody who walked in here from Mars would certainly feel that education was an important issue, a probing substantive matter that concerned the whole population. Anybody hearing all these news items would say: "Gosh, this population is really concerned about this. There is a lot of fire under everybody's butt." The truth of it is, it's all a battle! You've got a battle against the School Board; against a community not disposed on any level to finance education, despite what lip service is given it. National bureaucracy you're battling; you're battling against standardization on testing and curriculum, school expectations. How does all this leave you feeling? I mean—if every day you've got to put on the armor, and figure strategy—what will be your posture, in fact? Are you going to battle until the end? Are you going to try and find a new approach? Are you—— suppose the "giving in" posture is just to get through it. But that's not your style; so how are you going to deal with it?—with this climate?

THORP. The simple answer is one you've already posited, which in effect is: "Are you going to struggle with it, and work through it?" And the answer is: "Yeah." I mean, as I've said in previous sessions, I have my competitive blood boiling over this, just in terms of the Gateway component. I have a meeting tomorrow morning at the School District, where I'm dealing with the Associate Superintendent about a set of proposals about charter schools, and there are two or three of those proposals which are really problematic. So we'll see how it goes tomorrow morning.

FELTON. Good. Can't help but be smoother than the last one.

THORP. I hope people at the staff level will respond to being further educated about why these policies are ill-advised. I'm not terribly confident that that's going to happen; but I'm doing the appropriate protocol, which is: "Okay, deal with staff first, and see if you get satisfaction there. But if you don't get satisfaction there, then start going above staff's head and going straight to Board members, and doing my laundry in there—

INTERRUPTION #7—The owner of the second skateboard came to retrieve his possession, which Peter refused to give him, "because of what happened in math class." The bad news was received well: "Okay. I'm fine with that," a youth said, showing Gateway's widening range of cooperative spirit.

THORP. Returning to the Board problem: I won't hesitate to go above this person's head to the Board, and I won't hesitate to put this person in a bad position if I have to do that, to get things done.

I think there were many permutations of your question, and I'm trying to remember them all. You also posited: Would I do it a different way? I don't know. That's the simple answer. And in part that's because I don't know what's a different way. Everything I'm doing I see as a different way. And yet, at the same time, I'm also hesitant to do it in an entirely different way because of the risk involved. And one scenario there is just to make a public pronouncement about these unsupportive, ill-advised, unclear people I've had to work with, and say to the San Francisco Chronicle—"Can you believe this?" I'm not ready to go that route, because that's really where you burn your bridges.

But I can certainly see scenarios where that would be the only recourse that would have an effect. And if they were to try to not renew our charter, I certainly wouldn't hesitate for a second to go that route.

One of the ways that Clinton could have provided leadership to education would be his acknowledgment of educators, saying: "It's time that somebody stood up and pulled the plug on the myth of public education in this country, that public education needs to be the same for all. That's a myth." It's an unhistorical myth, and at this point, I believe it's an unproductive myth. And somebody needs to have the courage to stand up and say: "No! Not every child is going to get the same experience, because in fact, different children need different experiences. And we certainly have programs throughout the land that are based on that fundamental premise. That's why we have the Bronx School of Science; and that's why we have the School of the Arts here in San Francisco; and that's why we have magnet schools, and that's why we have boarding schools, and on and on. And for those of you out there in Videoland who rail against "gifted and talented" programs because they are elitist, and throwing up democracy as your rationale for being opposed to the "gifted and talented" programs, they're fundamentally missing the point of the Founding Fathers in terms of their interpretation of democracy. And it's not true in the history of school law and development that the intention of school people was that every child would have the same experience.

It would take a hugely courageous politician, and, I'm suggesting in the other permutation of the Monica Lewinsky story, only a second-term President who could stand up and say: "You know, folks, you really have it wrong about schools. And the reason why we're talking about charter schools, and why we're talking about choice among schools, is that we really want to restore a fundamental right in education, which is that parents and families ought to have the right to choose what education works best for their child. The paradox of public education is that it's become precisely the opposite of democratic; it is *anti-democratic and monopolistic,* and it bears all the facades of Standard Oil in terms of its control of the marketplace. And furthermore, it's the worst kind of monopoly, because it's not even sensitive to prices as a "free-market monopoly" would be, like Standard Oil, because it's a *government* monopoly, and you know, you can't put a stop to it, so to speak, because you can't *not* buy the product. And even Standard Oil as a monopoly had to be somewhat sensitive to the concern.

The education issues—even on the campaign trail—finagle around the edges, and don't get to the heart of the problem. And for most people, the answer is pouring more and more money into the system, which is great news for an educator, particularly here in California. But more money isn't going to solve this problem. If you buy the premise of public education, in terms of the way it's presently constituted, you won't go to the heart of the problem.

FELTON. I have a particularly jaded point of view which comes to mind at times like this. I ought to abandon it, because it's from an earlier stage of my intellectual evolution, and it probably doesn't hold water any more. But it's still—

THORP. Pre- or post-Grinnell? Or mid-Grinnell?

FELTON. Around the time I was at Grinnell. It's a sort of Marxist extrapolation: Nothing will happen in this society until someone can make enough of a profit off it to be satisfied. For example, we will cure breast cancer when the profit is satisfying enough to those looking for profit, and not before. So, to use charter education as a football: Charter education starts over at one pole with its extreme cutting-edge, avant-garde thinking, radical thinking. And then over on the other pole, in the year Two-Thousand-Whatever, is "Charter Ed Chic." And in between, on this curve, is your struggle; but at the point at which a profit will be turned in our free-enterprise system here, it'll be accepted, and acceptable, and then we'll go on to other things. Just as: I have absolutely no doubt that within an astonishingly short period of time we could solve breast cancer as a problem, if someone can make a huge profit off it. There is absolutely no doubt in my mind. So as a jaded notion, it worries me, because it means that society has to course through the curve with an ingenious and remarkable idea, until it is a commonplace or an obsolete idea. And accepted by most people.

THORP. I think another corollary to that is: Problems aren't even realized until it's a real crisis. It's sort of a "flip" definition that it's a recession when your neighbor is laid off, and it's a depression when *you're* laid off. And clearly, Roosevelt, I think, was the last President, the most recent President, to be able to connect to the people in a way of "Wait-a-minute-let's-think-about-this."   And "Wait a minute, we're in a tight fit," and "Wait a minute. We really might have to do things differently."

I think Reagan had that same kind of communication potential. But I think he used his communication for the wrong stuff, which is: "Wait a minute, let's figure out how we can all get our little piece of the pie here!" And Clinton, whom I also think had the possibility with some segments of the population—particularly and ironically the African-American portion of the population—was uniquely positioned to be a voice that would bridge gaps across races, because he was the, I think, the first "Black" President.

So we really need two things: We need the coming together of the circumstances and the purpose to deal with a problem; and we need a good crisis! And no crisis appears ready to happen in the economic picture, and no crisis seems to be happening in "good old" foreign policy. That's unusual, for you can count on something to happen about every twenty years to blow up things, to cause people to focus on, and say: "Gee, we really need to come together on this!"

So the question is: Where are you going to find your crisis? And the truth of the matter is: I think this *is* a country in crisis. And you know me well enough to know that that's the lens that I see the world through. It's this problem-solving lens; and you can't be a problem-solver if you don't have any problems. It's like being a faith healer in a land of no faith.

But I do think that the country is in crisis. And we sure have a generation of kids in crisis.

INTERRUPTION #8—Peter Thorp's assistant announced the arrival of the next parental-student crisis personae, waiting outside. He indicated this was our cue to find the moment to stop and place our outrage on hold for another week.

THORP. I am concerned that there is this huge divide in this country, and I am concerned that with the number of kids who are killed, and the number of kids who are making terrible choices, with the dissolution of the family—the list goes on and on and on—that we really need a powerful leadership, and I don't really know who of the people poised to try could provide that leadership. We need leadership in a time, particularly where the schools are broken, and it's clear that most bureaucracies, most educational systems, are—in a very good-hearted way—trying to survive! And if you're trying to survive, you're not trying to think about breaking new ground.

This time, with parents pressing in the outer room, the Principal interrupted himself.

Chapter Fifteen

A NATIONAL AWAKENING TO CHARTER SCHOOLS

"[A] fourteen-year-old's perspective, is: 'Gee, won't it be nice to go to a school where I'm going to be known! And I'm going to be cared about! That's what these adults at this school seem to be talking about.'

"[W]hen the kid actually gets into that situation, his response becomes: 'Ain't no way I'm letting you into my world! I'm keeping you as far away from who I am as I possibly can.' So you have that dynamic at work from the kid's point of view, which is the kind of abstract, going-to-a-small-school and being-in-small-classes where you have these good relationships with adults. It seems really cool, until you find that there is a certain percentage of kids whose behavior says: 'You want to know about what!? You're inquiring as to why I don't seem to be 'up' today, and you want me to tell you why I'm depressed!?—or why I look depressed?!'....Unfortunately for teenagers, they are put in the position where they have to prove the negative, sometimes. And that's really hard to do.

"Teenagers are swimming upstream. And of course, it's like pouring gasoline, because then they get defensive, and then they don't have the maturity to try to work out how to make the guy in the corner feel more comfortable. 'Why should I?' So—to me, it's a fascinating dynamic, which a school with a good program can address, and I've seen addressed a lot, by the time the kids are eighteen.

14 March—*One of the themes which coursed through our dialogues had to do with communication—human contact. It was approached* *from different standpoints—contact between students and teachers; between teachers and Peter Thorp; between the Principal and individual students; between Thorp and his interviewer. A dynamic of human interaction which I believed colored all these relationships actually came to the fore as an issue for discussion with Peter following the second meeting of the San Francisco Unified School District Board (its subcommittee meeting of 9 March). This had to do with the subject of* expectations.

It was my belief that role-playing provided templates for behavior, to aid everyone in a school environment. This role enactment, as any psychologist would attest, included anyone from the President of the School Board to the newest ninth-grader. One of the "jobs" I believed Peter and I had in our dialogues was to remove ourselves as much as possible from the act of role-playing, so as to free our minds and our emotions to address delicate or uncomfortable issues, those which had hindered the Charter cause, as well as those suggesting progress and triumph.

In the "one-on-one" forum, our ability to function in this role-free way was put to the test, on our March 14 meeting, by our focus upon issues both personal and educational.

I had planned to begin the session with a question that might have taken us either of two ways—that is, it might have invited Peter to feel more comfortable with personal information; or it might have made him protect his private side. It was one, as I told him, which I'd wanted to put to him for weeks, and we'd always moved to other areas of discussion. Now, I needed just a word from him, about his romantic life.

After the first School District meeting, Peter's fiancée Donna and her son Boone had "become real" to me. I wanted to know what kind of woman gave this man's life special meaning, and what feelings he had about becoming a father-figure to a young boy, at this stage in his life, and with his own responsibilities to children having coursed away from the fathering of girls, to being the paternal force helping to guide 200 high school students.

My question would have to wait, however. For when I presented myself to begin our meeting, Peter was saying goodbye to four visiting Japanese educational officials, and their Consular Office guide. When introductions (featuring some language lag) were accomplished, Peter asked for my views as a parent about the Gateway Charter experience. His guests offered polite attention, as I extolled the school's virtues, and emphasized that the most important role for a parent, as I saw it, was intense involvement, coupled with a determined effort to remain objective, see the student body at large, and not relate to or respond to school issues in the narrower emotional channel of one's own child's interests.

When Peter had seen his guests to a taxi, we regained our dialogue postures. He was greatly energized by their visit.

FELTON. So, you're back to a hectic pace here.

THORP. Yeah! That's the way it is, you know. I keep saying to myself: "Well, today will be a little slower." Or: "This week will be a little slower." Forget-about-it! I mean, it's always something.

FELTON. You've just attended a Board meeting of your New Mexico school. How was it?

THORP. A totally fascinating experience. Their school's in a tough situation. And I ended up being kind of the focal point of trying to resolve a situation. This particular Board of this particular school is split down the middle of a question. So it was going to come to a head; and sure enough, it did. It was an incredibly political and gut-wrenching experience, because I had to push an issue that was painful. And it got done; but it wasn't a whole lot of fun doing it.

I'd hoped for a long time just to read into the record, quite literally, the agenda when we had our last parent meeting. Just to give some color of what those things are about. There were issues ranging from the purchase of school lockers and Gateway sweatshirts, to the legal fine points surrounding the charter approval, and the seismic sanctions on the school's very building. I wonder if you had any reaction to what differences, if any, you feel in relating to a group of parents, from what your other experiences here are. And I'm mindful of the idea of "partnership" between parents and school leadership, which you've just expressed to your Japanese visitors a few moments ago; I wonder if there's anything else which differentiates that kind of everyday-issues meeting from any other experience you have with the parents, and how you see that functioning.

THORP. Meetings with parents are among the highlights of my experience, truly. They are very gratifying meetings in that people are taking time out of their busy lives to come over here and sit down and listen to me talk about some issue, or to ask questions themselves. But even the more difficult meetings we've had are gratifying, for I think we've succeeded in creating a sense of "we're all trying to accomplish the same goal." And what I alluded to with our Asian visitors is that in most cases it doesn't start from ground-zero in an adversarial kind of relationship, but rather from wrapping our arms around the parents and saying, "Hey, you're part of the team, here, and we want you to be part of the story."

And I think that for the most part, parents are ready to believe that, and, frankly, eager to believe that. Then the proof of the pudding is the extent to which we keep them believing that we *are* acting in the best interests of their kid. And even in those most difficult circumstances—and there was one today—which, because of this meeting, I couldn't be a part of—where we needed to say to a parent, "Time to go"—the parent didn't see us as the enemy. At a meeting last week, when the parent and I were both present, the parent turned to us and literally and figuratively threw up his hands and said, "What do I do? Help me! Help me come up with a solution! We were hoping Gateway would be a solution, in that our student would turn things around, but he didn't—so help me figure out some other solution."

So it just underscores to me the great reservoir of good will that is out there among parents, who want the best for their kids, and will eagerly work with the school, to try to see that happen. And again, it's particularly gratifying in that they seem to trust us. I don't think that willingness is typical, as I hear it from my colleagues who are principals of other schools. That's where I was all morning, a three-hour meeting with principals, which I finally mustered up the courage to go to. Normally, there's kind of a basic posture that as soon as parents get involved, it's going to be complicated, more complicated.

We have an example tomorrow. We have an IEP meeting—you know what that is?

FELTON. Explain. Spell it out for the record.

THORP. IEP is "Individualized Education Plan," which is what has to happen for a kid to get special education services. And you've got to have these meetings to get a kid those special education services. And once a kid has an IEP, they need to be redone every three years, or renewed every three years. We have one coming up which is a renewal. And I just got the word from our resource specialist here, that the parent is bringing "an advocate" in with her. I don't think that means a lawyer, although it could mean that. I think it means somebody who is—whose business is child advocacy, of which there's a big business. And that's fine; that doesn't bother me. If the person gets ridiculous, I'll tell the person that he or she is ridiculous. But to me, it's fine that a parent turns to support because—off the record, I think this parent is a little unraveled, in life, anyway. She's actually been in one of our most difficult parents, just because she's inclined to be totally untrusting, and I had a couple of difficult conversations with her throughout last year. But even she's at the point where she doesn't see us as the "bad guys" or as evil. I also think this is a big enough deal in her life, and taking care of her kid is her sole focus, that she wants to be sure that she doesn't get bamboozled.

FELTON. What consequence could her confusion have?

THORP. Most infrequently, a parents will feel insecure enough, or combative enough, that he or she will have a lawyer in attendance at a meeting with the Principal. Yet, even in a situation with a "legal eagle" looking at us, that's fine with me. I've been there, and I know when we're doing it right, and I know when we're not doing it right. And also, I can listen. We're in a position where we can change some things if we're not doing what we're supposed to be doing.

So the parental component of this is really one of the joys, not the least of which is all the parent work which is done. Again, it happened this weekend. I wasn't here, but a whole bunch of folks were. Parents came, and they cleaned up the place and did a whole lot of things, and had the place in much better shape than it was prior to last week. So the parents are a great part of the story; and I think the parents are a great part of the charter school story. And those Japanese Ministry of Education folks were pretty savvy about that.

FELTON. Yes? They actually made a reference to the parents' involvements?

THORP. Oh, yeah. Very savvy. And I'm fascinated—and I slipped it into my conversation with them, and I hope they know I was very serious, if you heard me, that I'd love to come to Japan and talk to their charter schools. And I would. But it's incredibly interesting that they're thinking about that. That would be a huge reform of the Japanese system. So it's interesting that they're doing that.

FELTON. It will be interesting to follow that up.

THORP. Yes. I'm hoping to keep "e-mail" connected with them.

FELTON. Keep me posted.

One of a couple of areas that I wanted to cover today has to do with the fact that last week was a sort of "big press week" for charter schools. There was a feature television piece; there were a couple of feature newspaper pieces that touched on some of the problems that we've talked about. For example, the MacNeil-Lehrer News Hour did a feature on charter schools last Friday, March 10.

THORP. The school district in Washington, D.C.?

FELTON. Yes. And I'd like to abbreviate some of the running commentary from that program, and ask you to try and hear it as the average listener or viewer would encounter it. Some of the commentary, I think, contradicts what we've come to understand out here on this coast; and I'd be interested in what you have to say.

Here are some excerpts—and, I caution, they are *just* the highlights:

A mother says of charter schools: "I like their curriculum; I like the things that they do, the things that they teach, and the behavioral rules that the kids have to follow. I like that."

The narrator says: "Because the school runs its own financial affairs, the Principal can hire and fire teachers without going through the bureaucracy downtown. And his staff can decide how and what to teach....Edison Friendship has all the autonomy of a private school. But it isn't: It is a public charter school, paid for with taxpayers' money."

The director of the D.C. Charter School Board clarifies the funding: "The Charter School is a public school that operates independently of the traditional public school system. It is publicly funded; it is accountable to a public body. But it is operated without the red tape and the bureaucracy of the traditional public school systems....The number of Charter schools has grown from just one in 1992 to over 1700 in 25 states today...."

And the narrator adds: "Today almost one out of every ten kids in the public school system attends a charter school....Critics of charter schools also say because teachers don't have to be certified, there isn't enough control over the quality of teaching. And they say, Charter schools hurt the traditional system, because each child who reads takes more than $7,000 in pupil allotment with them to the charter schools.....Educators from all over the country are following what happens here closely, to see if Charter schools can undermine traditional public schools at a time when aggressive attempts are being made to improve them."

The Washington, D.C. Superintendent of Schools has weighed in at this point—on the conservative side. But we don't hear strongly from her for a while. Meanwhile, that Director of the D.C. Charter School Board describes an example of the conflict of charter *versus* public school: "It's a dilemma: How do you put a brand-new charter school which is authorized to fully occupy its building, in the same building with a school with 500 kids, which is what the school system says they want, and that school would appeal directly to people who don't like charter schools! That is a prescription for failure, for tension, and for a not-very-good learning environment."

The narrator continues: "Now the debate has turned ugly. A group of teachers representing about half of the teaching staff at Paul has charged they were threatened with their jobs if they didn't go along with the charter school plan."

We turn to the Washington, D.C. Superintendent—one Arlene Ackerman. Ackerman's words to this point have played some classic "divide-and-conquer" and fear-spreading kind of rhetoric. Now she goes for the jugular: "And so we need to be careful. I mean, charter schools are relatively new, they're untested, we don't have a lot of data about results, and I think this is one of those initiatives that, while it certainly has a lot of benefits, we need to move slowly with them. And we need to make sure we're holding charter schools accountable for the same kinds of results and high standards that we're holding public schools accountable for, as relates to student results."

The narrator concludes: "They may not be new; but the charter schools are rapidly becoming a popular alternative to the status quo. Surveys continue to show parents...are frustrated with traditional public schools, and impatient with efforts to reform them."

That's their piece.

THORP. Well, that's it all! I mean, there isn't an issue they didn't touch on!

FELTON. Yes. But if you were sitting out there in that audience, and you'd never heard of a charter school, and all of these issues were taking place, and they characterized the schools as they did, and it had that sound, as it did in several instances that charter schools have it pretty "cushy," they're not obligated to obey the law, and tow the line the way some of our tax-paid public schools are—what would you feel?

THORP. Well, like anything, my feeling would depend upon the context. We haven't met since the recent Primary Election, right?

FELTON. Right.

THORP. I am distressed that Proposition 26, authorizing a simple majority vote to carry school bonds instead of a two-thirds majority, went down to defeat. And it's hard for me to believe that people would have voted against it, except when I'm staring at the statistic: That only 25 percent of the voting population in California has a kid in a California school. There it is, seen in that vote percentage.

So, if I'm sitting there as a retired person, in an audience, living on Social Security, and looking at city services, I'm saying: "Damned right! They're sucking money out of the public sector, and it's public money and it's not accountable, and I don't like the way that smells!" If I'm a public school teacher, I'm also sitting there, saying: "Damned right!"—and as you may know, the school that they were talking about first, an Edison school, is one of the for-profit ones, which I think adds a whole other layer of controversy, as it does here in San Francisco as well.

"*But*—if I'm that last parent at the end of the NPR story, I'm sitting there saying, "Hallelujah! I have a choice for my kid, that I think is going to make for a better situation than the other choices I had!" Now, in her case, apparently, she was able to come up with six thousand bucks to pay whatever private school tuition situation she was in. But that's, I would have to venture, the unusual person in the Washington, D.C. public school system, or the Washington, D.C. area.

So it's all context. As I'm sitting there listening to you read that transcript—because I could anticipate the points they were bringing up, I was shifted into a different mode; and I was listening much less to the sentences, because these are not new arguments. What I was really looking for were the *words*. And I was just listening for words. Now, if I'm a member of the Modern Language Association and doing this, I'd say, "Okay. Take this and read it backwards. Pay no attention to the context; and look for the words. Okay? It's all about words. Find the sentence where it says, "The charter school '*undermined*' the public schools." It's all about language.

A case in point: The other night at the School Board Subcommittee meeting, I stepped up to the microphone to answer the question about the right of teachers to return to the district. And Commissioner Jill Wynns wanted to put a five-year cap on that, and I said, "We don't have a problem with that." And I added: "We have no problem with that, although I would remind the members of the Curriculum Committee that in fact the teachers in charter schools are still teaching the kids in the San Francisco School District"—

FELTON. That's right…

THORP. —And her response was: "Yes, I'm aware of that." Well, that was a little interchange there, that kind of underscores some of the positions on this. And some of the language. What frustrates me in all this, Keith, is—like the "diversity" questions—people check their brains at the door on this. And my response to some of the issues in the television show you quoted is: "If it's a conversion school, let them convert on their own. If they want to do it, and the teachers want to do it, fine! But the real solution—and why I'm designing Gateway *this* way, and not as a conversion school—is: *Start a new school!* And then you know that you're dealing with a situation where you're not trying to chain somebody, who's already in place, to do something differently. It's "I'm going to build a new place," and if you build it, they might come!

But—and this is what drives me crazy—I'm going to the School Board meeting tonight, at Everett Middle School, they meet every second and fourth Tuesdays. And tonight is the first reading, the first official reading of the Gateway Charter Approval. I'm going to see if there's any comment that's made, or any shenanigans.

But it's always this language of "we....they..." We. They. And this morning, at this Principals' meeting that I attended, I got a copy of the budget report that the Budget Office gave to the School Board a few weeks ago. It points out a line item in there, it's a specific point: They've got a twenty-one-million-dollar budget, and actually it's far more than that—a multi-multi-million-dollar budget. They make a point of iterating an extra expense next year of $186,000 for charter school supervision. And pardon me if I can be blunt, but this is the same school district where a janitor had earned $55,000 in illegal overtime pay. And yet, they're making a deal of $186,000 of charter school tuition. Okay, fine! My point is: Nobody is calculating how much money we're bringing into the school system, because we're bringing kids from outside the district back into the district! You know? And we're not getting every one of those dollars, I guarantee you! A fair percentage of those dollars are sitting down at 555 Franklin, at the School Board, and we're helping them out! So fine: We're costing you $186,000? Start subtracting from that the money that we're generating for you and bringing in!

So people indeed do "check their brains at the door." And also, like anything else, it's a political agenda. To go back to your question: It all depends who I am sitting in that audience listening to this, as to how I react to it. And I think, to make a bit of an intellectual leap here—it's why the National Rifle Association can get away with what it gets away with. Unfortunately—and this happens in the Proposition 26 issue, and this happens in other school-related issues, and it's also what's happening with the charter schools—you have a much easier time painting the "new" as scary, the "unknown" as scary, than the known. So the charter school movement starts with the disadvantage of being the "unknown," the "untested." I want to fall down in laughter over one of the last statements a person made in the News Hour piece, about "Well, the charter school is new and untested, and we have to move very carefully." Well, fine. But the premise of that is What? Because the system is working otherwise?! And the charter school is a threat to that!?? Come on, already!

As Franklin Roosevelt said, in the darkest days of the Depression: "People don't eat in the long run; they eat in the short run." Well, kids don't go to school in the long run, they go to school in the short run. So don't give me this crap about "We've got to move slowly to do it." The system requires, in some parents' opinions, pretty radical change.

I got a call from a parent who sounds like he has a lot of means and influence and pyrotechnics, etc., who's calling me to pick my brain because he wants to start a new school. And I don't think it's going to be a charter school, and it might not even be a private school, but possibly some kind of home schooling situation. But gee, what a surprise!—it's a parent who has a kid with a learning disability, who's frustrated that the kid isn't getting the right services, and he can't stand the thought of it going on any longer. I don't think a parent like that is wrong to sit there and say: "I can't wait." And compare that with the remark on the MacNeil-Lehrer program, saying: "We have to move slowly, because it's untested—"![1]

So, aside from my investment in the charter school issue, there's just my kind of intellectual investment in political debate; and I'm becoming increasingly impatient with idiocy. And there's just too much idiocy out there.

FELTON.   That's a public view of charters here. Let's go back a moment, to take advantage of your recent visitors here: I'll be interested to see what Japan does with the charter possibility. Because if you look at Japan, Japan is the exact antithesis of this problem here, of dragging your butt, and going through the meaningless debating suggested by the Washington, D.C. charter story.   In Japan, in contrast—one day, you know, as they might say, "We are in the second millenium of our Feudalism, and then all of a sudden we have to be in the modern world!…We have to adjust.   One day, our Emperor is God—and the next day he's just another bloke!…We have to adjust. One day we have two cities sitting on the edge of our island, and the next day they're blown away!…We have to adjust.   And the Japanese *do* it like that, and they don't look back, they just keep chugging.   And if they do that, maybe those people who were visiting from the Ministry of Education will go back home and say: "What we've been doing in Japan is stupid; and now we're going to do charter schools."   And it'll just run as smoothly, as, say, their industrial change that took place a few years ago, and it won't be any problem.   Because even though things last a long time there—a "long time" in *our* vocabulary —when they change, they do "180's."   Or at least, right angles, you know?

---

[1] Neither Thorp nor Felton, nor, possibly the speaker of these sentiments in the story, could foretell that their originator— Arlene Ackerman—would become San Francisco's Superintendent within months.

They move, they make a difference. So it will be very interesting to see that.

THORP. I'm not sure I share that opinion. I agree with you that there have been these profound moments in Japanese history when they required 180-degree change. But I think the change has come with a fair amount of underlying scar tissue. And it will be very interesting to me to see whether or not the Japanese system is altered in a way that I think is the idea behind American charter schools. This idea is: "Listen to the voices at the grass-roots level." Japan is a very hierarchical society. And so there's this counter-cultural issue behind the charter school movement in Japan, where grass-roots programmatic development is something that is less likely to happen there than it is here; and this makes it even more interesting to me that the Ministry of Education is talking about it. I asked them the question: "Who's doing this? Are you guys out ahead of the curve?" And they said, "Yeah, we are."

So there are some interesting buckaroos, obviously, in their Ministry of Education, that make me think about the system. But not unlike the American situation, the reformer curriculum is just the tip of the iceberg; the reformer program is just the tip of the iceberg. And what they're going to experience in Japan, in my opinion, is if they're going to push forward on this reform, they're going to challenge the hierarchical structure of Japan, where, as you may well know, the whole issue of "getting to University" is the thing; and once you get to University, you're set. You never have to do a lick of work the rest of your life! Certainly not in University.

And that's why you have so many Japanese kids committing suicide, because that's when the "rubber hits the road," in high school. And the reform situation here is all the more interesting, because once again, it requires that we know what really is the purpose of the American public school. That's the question that charter schools are challenging. And very few people are talking that conversation. It's all around the edges, which is where most of the conversations in this country take place. The basic question really is: "What is the purpose of education in a democracy? And what's the purpose of the American public educational system?" And very few people—especially politicians—are willing to take that on.

FELTON. Well, your earlier comment on language was really appropriate to that board meeting last week. Because it's a model of how a bureaucratic organization attempts to keep things at a very low level and to keep either inflammatory or significant meaningful issues from rising too high to the surface. And every time one of those issues—such as the one you pointed out, about who's paying the bills here—came to the fore in that meeting, someone would come up with a kind of "shape-of-the-table" question. For example, there was the calendar issue, debated *ad nauseum*: "Are we going to call it 'work day' or 'Tuesday?'"

THORP. Could you believe that?

FELTON. It was disheartening to see my school board wasting that kind of time. Well, let me jump here, because I want to turn to another issue.

I had an interesting discussion with one Peter Felton, our erstwhile Gateway sophomore we use from time to time as a representative student whose experience we examine. This discussion was about role expectations. And I'm interested in what the Principal thinks about some points which emerged.

The basic theme was his general feeling—which is a strong feeling—that teenagers are maligned as a group. And he's feeling this very keenly.

THORP. And with good reason, goddammit!

FELTON. We walk down the street, this sixteen-year-old and I, and people will go by, and their conversation, which gets ellipsized by distance, is: ".....and those teenagers!...." And Peter will turn to me and say: "See! See!" So we have this issue.

He and I talked a little bit about how stereotypes come about; and then we had an interesting discussion about the assigning of roles. We talked about how in families it happens all the time: One kid will be the "good kid" and one kid will be the "bad kid." And how the family, if has any spark of life at all, is going to realize that, so that it will then assign compensating and balancing roles to those kids, so as to give some sort of sense of balance to it so the family can go forward.

Peter and I talked a bit more, and we talked about stereotypes. And I tried to urge from him a comment about why stereotypes continue, when by and large, they've been shown to be specious. And he didn't come out with the one element which I wanted him to say, which was that there was a kernel of truth in each one.

THORP. Right. Exactly.

FELTON. And we talked about his immediate stereotypes—the people who disparagingly say "Teenagers!" Or the stereotype of the merchant in the little store who's convinced that every Gateway student who goes in there is going to rob him blind. And how those can be broken down and how he and his fellows can deal with them.

Then I gave him a kind of definition of a stereotype—not a definition, but an explanation—as being the handiest means of dealing with the problem of making sense of a disordered world. And that you've got to grab onto something; the merchant will grab onto what he can, to deal with what he sees as a little crisis developing. And the teenagers who see the world maligning them feel the same way.

That's pretty much what our discussion was about. But I wondered whether this dynamic manifests itself here at Gateway. I wondered if there are "easy traps" to codify ways of viewing the students here, or viewing the teachers here, and how a school can avoid the pitfalls of characterization of kids as either "good" or "bad," or "leader"/ "troublemaker" roles. Peter shared with me some recent impulsive-behavior problems that had befallen a few students last week. And he introduced that because I think it meant something to him, given what we were talking about, that one's expectation for somebody may have some other elements enter in that show you that there is no simple way of seeing things in people's behavior or interaction.

How would you reflect upon any of that?

THORP. Lots to it.

Did you ever see the movie "The Paper Chase," about Harvard Law School?

FELTON. No; but I did see John Houseman's television series based upon it.

THORP. There's a reason that college professors teach in this antiseptic style—in other words, not invaded by the germs of humanity—in that it keeps the issues away. It keeps the individual issues away. One of the things we trumpet about Gateway—and I was up really early this morning reading a whole lot of applicant files, I read about forty files here this morning—and almost without exception in the essay part where the kid is asked "Why do you want to come to Gateway?," they make reference to the small classes.

Now, I don't know if that's because we fed them the answer, since when we're doing our "dog-and-pony show" we talk about small classes, so that you'd have to control for that in an analysis. But I think there's some percentage of response that says: "Yeah, it seems as if that would be good for me." And the interesting dynamic in this, from a fourteen-year-old's perspective, is: "Gee, won't it be nice to go to a school where I'm going to be known! And I'm going to be cared about! That's what these adults at this school seem to be talking about."

What gets really interesting is when the kid actually gets into that situation, his response becomes: "Ain't no way I'm letting you into my world! I'm keeping you as far away from who I am as I possibly can." So you have that dynamic at work from the kid's point of view, which is the kind of abstract, going-to-a-small-school and being-in-small-classes where you have these good relationships with adults. It seems really cool, until you find that there is a certain percentage of kids whose behavior says: "You want to know about what!? You're inquiring as to why I don't seem to be 'up' today, and you want me to tell you why I'm depressed!?—or why I look depressed?!" So there's that dynamic at work.

The more interesting dynamic—the dynamic that relates to the professional teaching—is the challenge for the Gateway faculty, to know how to balance individual case studies with archetypes. And adults trying to solve problems look for patterns and predictability. It's transference—pick whatever term you want, it's synthesis, it's transition—it's being able to learn from incident "A" and to apply those lessons to situation "B." And so when we meet as a faculty, we're constantly talking about individual kids. But it doesn't take long before somebody throws in either an impression, an analysis, a conclusion, or an adjective that is drawn from the person's other experience. Oh! What a surprise! That's why you look for experienced teachers, because they've been there before.

So the trick, again, is to find a right balance, in the individual profile *versus* an archetype. This is something I learned in the world of private schools, where you exercise your ability to get to know the kids, and boarding schools, where I've worked, where you get to know the kids better than most parents have. You really get a sense of kids, particularly in the teenage years, because most teenagers figuratively run away from home, and obviously a few do literally! But you know, they spend their whole time trying to keep their parents out of their world. And in school, they can't do that as easily.

What I would tell the faculty in the boarding school where I used to work, is: "Look, one of the great things about Cate is we know the kids so well." And invariably—and I mean *invariably*—we'd have our first Parents' Weekend, during the second week in October, when the kids had been with us for six weeks. And the parents have come for the first time to a boarding school's Parents' Weekend, and by Sunday—the weekend being Friday, Saturday, and Sunday—by Sunday they're walking around with their jaws hanging, saying: "I can't believe how well you know my kid!"

It was a wonderful experience, because you'd see these parents totally in awe of the situation. Now, what you *didn't* tell them was: "Of course we know them well, because it doesn't take long to figure out what makes a kid tick when you've got him twenty-four hours a day, and you see them in those situations where some of their security is stripped away, and some of their pretense is stripped away."

But the point is, and what I would say to faculty is, one of the great things about a school like this, and why people spend the kind of money they do to send their kids to such a school, is you get to know their children, and the parents feel that their kids are in good hands. The danger, however—and this is really the point—is: "You as professionals can think that you know the kids too well. *But*—I remember two years ago when we had a kid like that, and this kid is showing the same kind of signs." And there's a high percentage of accuracy and truth in that; but there are enough examples of where the stereotype is applied far too early, or far too comprehensibly, and you miss the signals. You might miss the fact that: "No, this is not a stereotype; this is a kid carrying a unique set of issues. And so—pay attention!"

The professionals at Gateway are really wrestling with that, partly because we're trying to invent archetypes. In other words, we're really trying to develop patterns in kids, so we can be mutually informative, and potentially develop this model school. There, we could stand up in front of some professional forum and say: "Look, here's what we've learned about this particular learning profile." A stereotype! It's a very interesting challenge in education, I think, is to learn when to apply the stereotypes, because they *do* have nuggets of truth. And I've said in many of the meetings I've had with parents this year: "Look—I've been in scores of these kinds of meetings before, and that's not to say that your kid is just like the kid I dealt with ten years ago. But I'm telling you, I've been there, and I know what you're going through, and I know what the situation is."

And yet, by the same token I need to be very careful not to assume that I've got the right answer every time, simply because it's looking like a horse, and sounding like a horse. It might be a zebra! And of course, for kids, you know—the adolescent years are so judgmental! Internally, externally, collectively, individually—everything is about judgments. And when a kid feels he or she is being judged, or is in fact being judged, they respond. And if they think the judgment is unfair, they respond understandably, and I feel in a rational way, which is: "You have me pegged! You're stereotyping me!" Or: "You're stereotyping teenagers!" Or: "You're not listening!," to whatever the response is. And sometimes they're totally right.

On the other hand, sometimes they're wrong, and sometimes they miss the point that in fact, what the adult is doing in calling in a stereotype, is to say: "Look—you need to know that you're not the first kid going through this set of problems. And there is experience out there which will help you get through this period"—assuming for a moment that it's a difficult period, but it doesn't have to be a negative situation. There are things you can bring to bear in your life which will assist you to move through this era, whether it's Thanksgiving with an extended family that you don't want to spend time with, or a year and half of acne, or whatever it is. Because previous experience *does* have value. This is a theme that we talked about previously, that there is value in tradition. And there is value in stereotypes connected—not directly, I guess, but at least they're linked in the kind of "internet" sense—to tradition, and to values, and to community. And to all sorts of things.

I mean, "stereotype" has a kind of pejorative connotation to it, doesn't it? Okay. Well, I think there's a whole industry called "psychotherapy" which deals in stereotypes. It's an industry that's trying to come up with answers that tend to have a kind of stereotypical—what's the expression for manic depression now?—bipolar disorder. Or EDD. Again, to bring this to Gateway: Mel Levine rails against neurological stereotyping. His whole philosophy is what I call the "snowflake theory" of neurology—that every brain is different. I'm already thinking of my leadoff assembly speech for next year, and I may talk about the "snowflake theory" of neurology.

So, stereotypes have value. To me the issue in stereotyping is: It really depends upon the power of insight and the power of reflectivity, and the power of adaptability of the stereotyper. At what point does a stereotyper realize that the stereotype does not apply? It's Huck Finn, you know? And it's desegregating the Army, and it's teenagers walking into the corner store. Unfortunately for teenagers, they are put in the position where they have to prove the negative, sometimes. And that's really hard to do.

Teenagers are swimming upstream. And of course, it's like pouring gasoline, because then they get defensive, and then they don't have the maturity to try to work out how to make the guy in the corner feel more comfortable. "Why should I?" So—to me, it's a fascinating dynamic, which a school with a good program can address, and I've seen addressed a lot, by the time the kids are eighteen. Partly through the "trial by fire" of the college application process, where the kids are forced to look inwardly, and recognize: "Hey, pal, you're applying to college. You're *not* going to be stereotyped. You 're going to be looked at as an individual, and you're going to see if you measure up to what this school is talking about." And even in that area, we can talk about various unfair issues that kids think about the college process.

In the first couple of classes of my college preparation class, I told the kids if you really want to get into Harvard, or Stanford, you have to be from Wyoming, you have to play the piccolo, and you have to tell the college you're going to major in Egyptology. And then they'll take you in a second!

FELTON. Ahh, the ideal candidate!

THORP. And we're having fun! But it's a classic example of this school having taught me more than I've taught this school, in learning just how distant these kids are from the world of the college process. It's been fascinating.

FELTON. Well, your point is a really interesting one, about experience being the difference to a teacher. And it's really the medical model, too: You know, you depend on the doctor to have listened to or palpated eight zillion chests, and to know all of those sounds—but you also need him not to get desensitized to that. So that he can use experience and information effectively.

THORP. Yes. One of the issues this morning at this educators' meeting was all about special education. The District is under federal watch right now, and we're going through this step-by-step process that's going to take place, about compliance with special education. And a good portion of the conversation was about "the brown folders." Apparently, the "brown folders" are the Special Education files, and that shows you how much I know of the situation. They've got to be "just so," and during the first week in April, the Feds are coming through San Francisco schools looking for the brown folders. That's okay, because the District's been out-of-compliance on the brown folders. But one of the principals raises her hand, and says: "Yeah, I understand that; but my problem is I can't get the brown folders from the District. Every time I try to get my IEP folder, my special ed folder for the kids in my schools, I call the District and nobody can find it."

And that's true of us. We don't have a certain percentage of our IEP folders, because the District can't find them. So, you know—the amount of energy that therefore is spent on a brown folder issue is energy that could be better spent on some of the key issues.

FELTON. In concluding now, I'd like to invite you for next time to put some more human interest on Peter Thorp.   The big School District meeting downtown, the first one, gave me a chance to put faces and character to your fiancée Donna and her son Boone.

THORP.   Right!   Boone's a piece of work, isn't he?

FELTON.   He is.   We talked a little bit about him, actually, in connection with some of his math concerns.   But I'd be very interested if you'd give a sense of what his mother's all about, and how she fits into things.

THORP.   Sure.   I'll be glad to.   After all, she's my only claim to having a life!

Chapter Sixteen

MONK'S COWL AND CELLULAR PHONE

"I think we're at another turning point [in scholasticism], where the Medieval/Renaissance university is being challenged by Cyber College. And it's being challenged not only in terms of the methodology, I think it's deeper than that, in the sense that I think for the first time the inherent, intrinsic value of the educated mind, the education being, person, is being challenged. And I don't think the educated mind has much of a response to that challenge right now.

"...One has to fall back on a value judgment....It's kind of a "because" answer: "Well, what's the value of a liberal education? Why is it so good?" "Because." And I don't think that's going to be good enough, you know. And—at the risk of sounding like H.G. Wells, here, I think there's the potential for an increasingly small class of educated people over the next chunk of time, say, century, who are the keepers of educational tradition, educational knowledge if you will—you know, knowledge for its own sake—who will either be exalted as priests, or will be ridiculed as cranks. Or isolated as hermits. Not unlike the Irish monks in one sense....

"[W]here the computer revolution is really shaking things out, with yet-to-be-determined results—is that the inherent, intrinsic value of education in and of itself as an end and not just as a means to an end, is being fundamentally challenged. And these kids here at Gateway insist—I mean, I hear it in the kind of remark like: "Why do we have to study this crap!?" And I don't think it's necessarily fair to respond: "Because." Or: "It's good for you." Or: "Any educated person needs to know this." There has to be a better answer to that."

21 March—*Two of the oldest shibboleths to dog American children, from the Biblical epoch onward, are the exhortations: "Do unto others*

as you would have them do unto you," and "Turnabout is fair play."
They emerged, unspoken but real, in the Principal's office on the
occasion of this dialogue. For something in our normally pleasant
sparring set off Peter Thorp on this particular day; and the result was
that the pursued became the pursuer.

Perhaps, on the one hand, it had been the letter he was writing
when I arrived—to a parent, who had sent in a sensitive, even hurt-
filled query seeking explanation about why his son had been rejected by
Gateway. Peter held up a hand, remaining concentrated over his
laptop-generated response. ("These are the hard ones," he mumbled,
finishing typing; his response seemed an admitted inadequacy to
assuage the family's feelings, but, I knew, was simply part of the
process. In a better world, one given to Peter's sensibilities would
have taken the man to lunch, and dealt with School Application Grief
one-on-one, in a more meaningful way of comfort.)

Perhaps, on the other hand, it was the plumbing bill, which was
presented to him in his office as I was setting up the tape recorder, by a
huge, sweating work foreman dressed in what the French call "bleu de
travail." The dialogue, which my machinery was not yet prepared to
immortalize, went something like this (the blue-clad workman
opening):

"Yes sir! My man said you had a question."

"You bet. It's a pretty simple question. How in hell do you think
I'm going to pay a twelve hundred dollar plumbing bill!"

"Wellsir, I can go over the problems with you..."

"Isn't it normal to check with the guy footing the buck as you go
along and find problems, rather than hitting him with a statement like
this when the damage is done???"

"'Damage' was why we were called, Mr. Thorp," the big man
replied, placing his fifteen-stone bulk in the Colorado Springs
Boarding School Captain's Chair I had planned on occupying. "But
let's look at that bill—"

This was followed by a detailed account of what surely is normal
and expected from every toilet in every high school in America: Bad
valves, followed by half-replaced valves from a previous visit to try to
effect repair, followed by fully-replaced fixtures; then digging out
mounds of gravel from every toilet. Common, everyday stuff in the
plumbing world.

"But—in every goddamn toilet in the building?!!" Peter said. (I
hoped he wasn't whetting his rhetoric, to be aimed later at me.)

"Well....Look, you're a regular customer—"

"You bet I am! This is—what?—-your fourth visit!?"

"—Let me go over it with the bookkeeper, and I'll get back to you."

"Get back to me!"

The man of lead took his leave.

His replacement in the Captain's chair, slighter by a hundred pounds and armed with a tape recorder instead of a Stillson, slid into place, faced the Plumbed Principal, and assessed how much true damage—not monetary, but philosophical—the visitor from the trades had wrought. Peter looked tired; shouldering one more burden, I had come to be aware, was simply what one did in this job. And, to add more pebbles to the water closet's valves, the subject of a plumber's fiscal impudence would play in our later discussion. But when, a moment later, he looked up at me, his ballasting smile, a bit rueful now, had returned. I attempted to reinforce that good feeling with my reaction to his recent college preparatory session, which I had attended.

FELTON. First, Let me attempt to clear your mind with pleasant thoughts: I realize we've never really talked about your college prep class. I thought it was just wonderful!

THORP. Oh, good! I'm glad you liked it. Wasn't it fun?

FELTON. It was indeed. In fact, Peter, until I sat in on that class, I had begun to feel that despite my exposure here to some very bright students, I hadn't experienced a setting with a real academic feeling. And your class had it: A small, active, enthusiastic group of students exploring an idea with a preceptor. It was really strong. And I came away feeling: "How lucky these kids are!—that you're who you are, that you take the interest, and that you've focused on them for this purpose. And to demystify, and detoxify—"

THORP. Right! That's the operative word.

FELTON. —detoxify the stuff that comes in from colleges in the application form, and make it approachable and palatable—it's so necessary; and it's a godsend that you do that. I was really pleased to see that.

THORP. You should have been in my afternoon class. One kid told me he probably was going to drop the class. Because it's made him too nervous.

FELTON. Is he a kid who has borderline qualifications for college, or is he strong academically?

THORP. He's pretty strong. Which speaks to the anxiety level among kids. He's a kid from, I think, relatively high-pressure parents, who has a learning disability, and that's why he's here at Gateway and not at one of the private schools. He may have an older sibling who's been through this. And this boy may feel: "Oh-oh!—I know what lies ahead for me, which is wrangling with my parents on this. And this is just bringing this up much sooner than I wanted to." That may be an interpretation, and it may be totally wrong; and it may be that I'm doing it in a way which is working with that class you saw, and it isn't working for him in the sense that it's increasing his anxiety when he's thoughtful enough to do the research.   And recognize that— "Whoops!—these scores aren't necessarily what I think I'm going to be getting." So we'll see. I told him to talk about it with his parents, and let me know on Thursday what he's decided. I think he's probably going to drop.

FELTON.   Well, that's a damn shame. Still, if he wants a future, the problem isn't going to go away.

THORP.   Right.

FELTON.   Well, with that in mind, I want to talk about variations on the college theme.   Variations relevant to our discussion of the contemporary computer culture.

A recent forum featured a number of college presidents, including a guy who is the President of Tufts, a guy named Arthur Levine, who's head of the Teacher's College division of Columbia—

THORP.   Columbia, yes.

FELTON.   —And the President of Golden Gate University, and some other people. The gist of the conversation was: Schools as we know them are not going to be around much longer. What's really going to be chugging out the degrees are going to be *commuter* schools, with their loss of intimacy, and an increasing emphasis upon "cyber learning," and use of the computer at home.

What bothered me about this is that both Arthur Levine and the guy who was President of Golden Gate University, and to a certain extent this fellow from Tufts, didn't sound terribly upset about all this! They thought this was just a fine idea. Now, I admire people who roll with the times, and can "wear the latest style" and be just as true to that style as they were to the last one—but it dismayed me to hear so much about a kind of willingness to turn one's back on all of the kind of enrichment that enables us to have what you were describing about knowing kids after six weeks at boarding school! That's gone. I mean, neither place is Williams, and neither place is Grinnell; and that's fine. But even kids at State colleges whom I knew in the 'sixties and 'seventies and 'eighties who were attending there had a little bit more of a feeling there of: "This is home. This is our *alma-mater*-to-be.

We're proud of it here, and we love it here." Rather than just this—Ethernet anomie.

THORP. I think you've identified what I consider to be one of the key issues in higher education, post-secondary education, that's going to get played out within the next quarter century. And that issue is: Is post-secondary education going to become the "secondary" education of the twenty-first century? In other words, moving from the eighth-grade education of the nineteenth century to the secondary education of the twentieth century—and let's assume for a moment that that is the case—let's assume that the continuing existence of such organizations as City College, and especially cyber education, is going to be a college degree accessible to a wider range of people. These are people who are now being put off by cost factors, primarily, or work/class scheduling issues, so that within the next twenty-five years, anybody—and I mean *anybody*—who wants to get a college education, or a post-secondary education, can get it.

The question becomes: Is that a good thing or not? And the natural answer is: "Well, of course it's a good thing! Because, you know, we'll be the first society to have such a widespread level of higher education that nothing but good can come from it." But—*au contraire, mon frère!.* I think not.

To some extent, it will continue—and this I think is really the interesting question in education right now—it will continue the gap between the "have's" and the "have-nots" educationally. This is not far away from the problem of the infamous "digital divide." And there's no question that that exists. To me—where I thought you were going to conclude, or what I thought you were going to quote from Levine or somebody else, is how important it remains as to where you went to school. And how do institutions like Princeton—we'll lay off Grinnell and Williams for the time being—how does an institution like Princeton look at the thought of "cyber college," so to speak?

Now, on the one hand: If you're the President of Princeton, you're saying to yourself: "Whoa! I've got to be careful, because no matter how they slice and dice it, a year of cyber college is going to cost a hell of a lot less than the $32,000 I'm charging right now, and there are a whole lot of people who are going to say: "Is the $32,000 worth it?" And the answer to that is: "No, it ain't worth it!" Because—you know, and obviously there are going to have to be some stages of working out the kinks in cyber curriculum—but given most of the classes one takes in college—Psychology 101—why couldn't you get Psychology 101 on cyber space, and learn what you need to learn in Psychology 101? And how many of us really remember what we learned in Psychology 101 anyway?

So the question becomes: "Why shell out thirty-two thousand bucks, or an-inflation-plus adjusted thirty-two thousand bucks over the next two years, in a place like Princeton? And then you have a couple of divides, one of which is: Williams and Grinnell get to say, "Because you can sit in the classroom at the feet of So-and-So Professors, who are full professors but who are devoted to undergraduate education, or, in the Williams expression: "That is Mark Hopkins and the log." Have I told you that quote?

FELTON.   Yes you have, and in fact, Arthur Levine, without attribution, gave the log line.

THORP.   All right. There's that. But a place like Princeton doesn't even necessarily have that. I mean, let alone a place like the University of Michigan, which is essentially a research institution. So what do they have to sell, for their thirty-two thousand bucks? A B.A. degree. Well, you can get that in cyberspace. Not necessarily close student-faculty relationships, that some might be able to survive. What do they really have to sell? *Connections!*

And it's a reality about schooling that causes the insanity of the college application process, where people think there are only a hundred good colleges in the country, and everybody applies to those hundred good colleges. It isn't true. And that's coming from somebody who had the benefit of attending not just one of the hundred best, but one of the twenty best, in my opinion. And who would argue that, in fact, an education in a place like Williams *is* worth the thirty-two thousand bucks. Because of the intangibles that go along with it.

So what does it mean? A lot of it means asking a question: "What's the point of a post-secondary education anyway?" And I think that question is going to get played out. So what's the point of a bachelor's degree? You know. What's the point of liberal arts education? I think increasingly, the liberal arts degree is—well, I was going to say is viewed as a kind of anachronism; but I think it's encouraging is that we hear every once in a while somebody from the "techno" world pop up and say: "I want to hire liberal arts graduates because they can think, or grade, or problem-solve," whatever it is.

So if I'm the Provost of a college or university, I'm sitting here this afternoon scratching my head, saying: "Are we going to be here ten years from now?" And "Is there going to be a market for our product ten years from now, that we can out-market cyber college?" I mean, hell, the schools that are cutting costs by having three, four, five, eight hundred people in Psych 101, you know—I could stay in bed, and not have to change clothes and shave, and get the same experience as a class like that. So, are the colleges that are going to survive the ones that advertise classes of twelve, fifteen, and that kind of relationship? And how can we afford them anyway?

I think it's really interesting what's going to happen. I haven't talked yet about whether I think it's better or worse. But I sure do think an issue on the plate. And I think the question, "Does somebody need to have a B.A. to go to graduate school?" is a question that's going to be answered. I mean: Why? You obviously would answer in terms of: "Are you really prepared?" But what about somebody who demonstrates: "I don't have a B.A., but throw any entrance examination you want at me, and let me take it, or let me show you my personal dissertation, which makes it clear that I ought to be in your engineering school." Why not?

FELTON. Well, until fairly recently, at least in the Great State of California, you could "read for the Law" and not have a fourth-grade education. If you could pass the Bar, you were a lawyer!

THORP. Is that right? I didn't realize that.

FELTON. That's only stopped within the last four or five years. But I think that's an exception. Most entering medical school freshmen have been past the fourth grade.

THORP. If part of your question is: "Is it a good trend?" I'm going to cop out a little bit and say: "I sure think it's going to be interesting!" Because I think on the one hand, the more widespread literacy, or post-secondary literacy is, I think, exciting.

To bring it back to local issues, Gateway is trying to play a relatively small part in that, by spreading post-secondary education to a wider group of kids. But for what reason? You've kind of thrown up a mirror to me; and do I say to myself: "Well, okay, Peter, how come you're doing this? Are you trying to give kids from the Mission the chance to go to a place like Princeton, so they can get connected?" Or, some other reason? And I don't know! It's interesting to me, for example, when we do our "open houses," our admission open houses, people have read our brochures, and without exception, anybody who has chosen to comment on our faculty says: "Wow! What an impressive list of people!" Well, look, the only thing they know from that cursory a view is what colleges the faculty attended! Really! What they're truly looking at is: They're all Stanford grads! And if you graduate from Stanford, you've got to be impressive.

But I'd say that while there may be some literal truth in that, there's an *exalted* truth in it, for sure. And yet, it's like dealing for the big Arthur Anderson consulting firm, or the big law office in town. The list goes on and on. If you walk in the door with your degree from Cal State Hayward, *versus* the person sitting here with the degree from Stanford, well, you tell me how that is going to go.

FELTON. Sure.

THORP. So—I think it's going to play out with a whole lot of other issues: The "Digital Divide," the educational divide. And, I hope, with an intersection with a Presidential leader at some point in the next quarter century, where we really can devote our resources to trying to narrow the gaps in our society. And by doing that, not only the greater access to college would be possible, but the idea of connectivity would be one based on merit, and not based on pedigree.

FELTON. After this forum on cyber education, the President of Tufts said, with more optimism than he expressed for anything else: "You know, not only is cyber education going to be what we're going to expect and look forward to here, but as far as I'm concerned, *corporate training is as good as institutional educational learning!"* And he felt that what those bright, enterprising guys who learned how to tie a tie, and can get a job in a monolith, can pick up on the job, is every bit as efficacious as anything they're going to get out of the Halls of Ivy. It's certainly going to be more practical, and immediately useful, there's no question about that; but those guys—and the son of the geek you were referring to—I'm not sure I want any part of. And I shudder to think that my sons will rub elbows with them in school! And compete.

THORP. Why is that?

FELTON. Because in my estimation these are narrow people, people who acquired a minimum of breadth of understanding and experience and depth and insight, and because they acquired enough of the "dance steps" and the vocabulary of the business or commercial or "high tech" worlds to be able to purvey that into a position of authority and a sense of well-being—and a somewhat smug superiority—that therefore, they're "off and running." And I find such people repugnant enough for me to disparage their company, and question both their motives and their true contributions.

THORP. Okay. And so, to press you on this a little bit—what I'm hearing you say is that you don't like their values.

FELTON. Sure. I think that's a good summary.

THORP. Okay. And what I'm hearing you say is that you believe that your values are more worthy, more appropriate—I'm not sure what the right term is, than their values. So the question becomes: How come? Why? Who are we to judge? Who are we to think that our values are superior? What I hear you criticizing is a kind of narrowness, in all of our discussions on this point. And my question to you has to be: What has the world gained from breadth?

FELTON. Well, let me try to approach it in this way—and I'll tie this in with the little experience you had here picking yourself up off the floor after getting that plumber's bill.

One of the truly memorable moments in my life came shortly before my marriage to Peter's mother. My father and my aunt—who were performing the role of my parents, as my mother was dead—arrived for the first meeting with my fiancée's father, and his wife—who were serving the role of her parents, since her mother was dead. Their name was Kennedy—

THORP. His second wife?

FELTON. His second wife. And I know, because we had been staying with the Kennedys, that there was a certain amount of trepidation about this meeting. And the trepidation revolved around the fact that "Mister" Kennedy, who expressed this trepidation, was a plumber; and he felt, somewhat anxiously, that this put him in a position of social disadvantage when he had to meet "*Doctor*" Felton, a world-renowned physician who had been decorated by Presidents!

And the truth of it was that, even though neither of them knew it at the time, and Mr. Kennedy has since died, his estate that he left is probably as large as any "professional" man's, because he had been an immensely capable tradesman and a very shrewd Scot, and took care of every penny he earned, and he earned every damned penny honestly. And the truth of it also is, the values in the lives of those two men—if anybody asked "Is there anything wrong with the values of this person who followed a trade?," the answer would certainly be "No!" Because I think there was something admirably humble by nature in his life. It wasn't that his values were more solid; it was that there were fewer circuitous routes through his excursion than through a professional's. Now, later on as he aged he became bitter, and he became more "Scots" and hence a little unpleasant; but he was unassuming to the end. And my dad would be among the first to acknowledge that there's no reason to assume *he's* better than anybody else. And there are other values that he's expressed throughout his life that are not dissimilar to yours, in that he was an educator for fifty years, and considered himself first a teacher! Still, he's wrestled, I believe, with things the plumber didn't. It was a striking moment.

So—I don't make quick judgments, I think, about certain ways of seeing people as having differences. But I have been in a number of settings where I have felt the superiority and the smugness from people who assumed I couldn't understand possibly what they were talking about. And I've also been in places where brand-spanking-new Bar-accredited attorneys, of one day's legal service, came aboard law firms at the age of twenty-five, making three times what I'll ever make, their first day in practice. And—just as some guys would throw the mortar board in the air at graduation, these people throw any humility, any ability to perceive and empathize with other people, automatically as a matter of course, as a matter of the notion that "We're all equals as humans"—they throw that in the air.

So I have some unpleasant feelings that form prejudices in this direction.

THORP. But you've acknowledged them both as personal. And prejudices, as in "pre-judge," as in "conclusions based on what you think your priorities should be."

FELTON. Yes.

THORP. And the question we're wrestling with is: "Is it in fact the case that those values are superior to the value of—what— vocational ambition/monetary success, which is I think in part what's behind your abhorrence of the more narrow path that—am I reading you correctly on that?

FELTON. I think—I'm trying here to distill this down, trying to find what really is pushing this point of view; and I think it's that I don't believe that one's harnessing of his personal growth to help him be a contributing member of society can be done in a formulaic and programmatic way. I believe the formulaic is easier to do if you are a son or daughter of Silicon Valley, and you say, "I'm setting my sights on that billion, and I'm going to get there by these determined stepping-stones, and I'm smart enough to do it, and I know the courses in programming, and so on—and I'm *going* to do it!" If it's that easy, then I feel even worse about the human race. But to a lot of people, it *is* that easy.

To me, and seen through my perspective, based on experience, and based on what I'm attracted to in others: The way you become a contributing member of society is by—is by *failure*; is by wrestling with one's own personal problems and the problems of society together, and by continuing to thrust your face out into the cold wind.

THORP. Take it one more step: You've described the methodology or the path by which one would be a contributing member. But what *defines* a contributing member? What's the result of a contributing member's efforts?

FELTON. I think the results are a substantive, essential enrichment and betterment in the lives of others brought about in part by your intervention or involvement. And I qualified it in that way so that we don't say that the man who made your computer has enriched your life; because that's not what I'm talking about.

THORP. Is Bill Gates a contributing member?

FELTON. I think he's like—the old joke about the huge animal who can eat whatever he wants—I think Bill Gates can call himself whatever he wants. I don't feel that he is a contributing member; at least, not in the way I'd like to feel. I feel that he's—he's special in one way only, I think. And that is that he was an *Ur*-person, he was a progenitor of an era the way the Beatles were progenitors of an era. And you might not like the Beatles; but they undeniably were the defining line which separated an epoch from the immediate past and into the future. I think Gates did that. And I think he's formidable. And I probably would have liked him more than I would have liked Howard Hughes; or John D. Rockefeller; and *certainly* more than I would have liked Henry Ford!

THORP. What about Andrew Carnegie?

FELTON. Carnegie, I think, would have been like Tolstoy. He would have wrestled to the end, with things inside. And therefore I would have empathized. I would have been able to attach to him a little better. Certainly what he did with his money underscores that.

THORP. Well, thank you for humoring me in turning the recorder in the opposite direction. Number one, because I was curious in what you had to say; but again, thank you for allowing me to probe in a kind of academic sense. Because I—to me, getting back to your original question—I do think we're at a seminal moment in history, and certainly educational history. When we go back, you know, following the decline and fall in Rome and the seminal moment was a couple of Irish monks hanging in there and writing enough to keep track of things, followed eventually by Renaissance thinking about the role of the educated mind. Which essentially—I mean, colleges and universities today are essentially Renaissance models. I mean, there isn't a hell of a lot of difference in it, in fact some look like they looked five hundred years ago!

I think we're at another turning point in—or at least the possibility of a turning point—where the Medieval/Renaissance university is being challenged by Cyber College. And it's being challenged not only in terms of the methodology, and I suppose one could make a case that Cyber College is this year's version of a Xerox machine, which is that year's version of a ditto machine, which is that year's version of the Irish monks, going back. But I think it's deeper than that, in the sense that I think for the first time the inherent, intrinsic value of the educated mind, the education being, person, is being challenged. And I don't think the educated mind has much of a response to that challenge right now. Because—and that's sort of who you were, in your comments there—because one has to fall back on a value judgment, because I don't think, frankly, you can fall back on tangible results, so to speak, of a kind of three-times-making-more-money on the first day of law practice. Nor can you necessarily fall back on "We're more likely to change the world in a positive direction" arguments, because there are plenty of examples of where narrowly focused people—Bill Gates—have had a greater impact on the way the world conducts itself than you or I have. Or many a liberal arts person.

So you fall back on the value. It's kind of a "because" answer: "Well, what's the value of a liberal education? Why is it so good?" "Because." And I don't think that's going to be good enough, you know. And—at the risk of sounding like H.G. Wells, here, I think there's the potential for an increasingly small class of educated people over the next chunk of time, say, century, who are the keepers of educational tradition, educational knowledge if you will—you know, knowledge for its own sake—who will either be exalted as priests, or will be ridiculed as cranks. Or isolated as hermits. Not unlike the Irish monks in one sense.

And coming full circle: For better or worse, there seems to be much greater pressure on the link between education and something else: Net worth; salary; results; change in the world; winning law suits; building buildings, whatever it might be. And the liberal arts position of the inherent value of education really runs the risk of becoming extinct, or isolated. At least, narrowed down. And what is that going to mean?

FELTON.   If all that we feared losing was the more esoteric side of intellectual conviviality and an ill-disguised sense of preciousness about our perceptions and the magnificence of our wisdom, I wouldn't miss liberal arts thinking too much. But, it seems to me that if education has done its job, then maybe there would have been more of a chance that people who fell into Sunnyvale's offerings might instead have pondered: "What about architecture? *There's* a career where my scientific bent will be needed every day, and yet my humanity will also be required of me, constantly. And I can put the two together in a magnificent way that might benefit people and it might not, depending upon how I feel about it at the time; but it will certainly be satisfying to most of the impulses that I feel as a human being." Why aren't there more areas like architecture to attract people? Hell, it's got it all!—even on their terms: It's got money, it's got prestige. Besides, it's one of the few fields where you can be called a *visionary!*—and receive accolades on that score.

I don't know. In my simplistic mind, it tends to make me see things very cynically, or rather, to see people who are happy to take that easy path to some rather mercenary or otherwise objectionable goals, as being cynical. And that makes me feel crestfallen about where we're all going. And when I come here to Gateway High School—even though things are pretty fast-paced, and you can't be in the way, it's still a hell of a lot better feeling than in some other places I have to go every day, where I don't feel as good! Because what's behind all this is that there are 192 litmus sheets from which you can get a fair measure of what's happening here. And that's very encouraging; it's enlightening; it's revivifying, or rejuvenating. And it also brings me back to some of the original values that Howard Bowen at Grinnell and some other people were talking about; and I never really thought they were talking through their hats. Any more than I think you are.

THORP.   So how come all these Stanford graduates are going to "dot-com" organizations and not teaching? I mean, they've got your values. They went to an institution that has those values.

FELTON.   My first reaction, as the possible explanation, is that they're—twenty-one, twenty-two, twenty-three?—and anybody who was born in 1971 is not, for better or worse, going to have the perspective of a kid born during the early years of the war.

THORP.   Which war?

FELTON.   Who was born within a year of Pearl Harbor—

THORP.   Oh, okay.

FELTON.   —As I was. And it's just not possible. No matter plumber or physician; no matter what.

THORP.   Yeah, I agree.

FELTON.   It's just not going to happen. I'm not laying a condemnation of a group by saying that. I don't know how old the director of Admissions, Miss Maheta is; but she's probably not over twenty-five. And yet, I think she's one of the wonders of the world. And it isn't because—what she brings to the school didn't come out of her Stanford degree. It comes from her bedrock decency, her inviolable value system.

THORP. But I bet, and this is just a guess, I bet there isn't a night she falls asleep where she doesn't say to herself: "All my friends are making two and three times, twenty times what I'm making. And here I am busting my ass doing all these things."

FELTON. Well, it *is* hard. Because it means that she will—she'll be doing this a lot longer. And some of those people will be on beaches a lot sooner.

THORP. But you see, the thing is—I'm not trying to put you on the spot. But in asking you to speak to that, if—it helps me to think about this very issue myself, because I wrestle with it. It's interesting to listen to your words; I mean, you use very pejorative words for people who make the other decisions. You describe it as the "easy" and the "cynical" path. I would think, I would venture to say that the successful venture capitalists of this world describe people who become educators as a career as following an easy path. Particularly a college professor. Christ, I mean, you teach three or four classes a week, you sit around and you smoke a pipe in a tweed jacket, and correct a few papers here and there, and go to football games, and you know. *There's* the easy path! So why, for you, is the non-liberal arts choice an easy and cynical path?

FELTON. Well, let me make sure that I express myself well in one area. In fairness, I don't think it's easy to get up every day at six, and put on a suit which you hate, and shine your shoes and have a real slick haircut, and go out and kiss corporate ass. That's got its own tedium. You have to be a highly-motivated individual to do that. So, in a sense, I have a begrudging respect for people who would choose that. I have great respect for *anybody* who accepts a huge challenge and goes out and works tirelessly to do it. Even if it's for something that I don't particularly—that doesn't particularly reflect my values. But what I meant about being born in 1971 is—I—we've touched on this a long time ago, I think—

THORP. Or actually, it would be 1977.

FELTON. Pardon?

THORP. It would actually be 1977. Those kids would be twenty-three.

FELTON. Oh, my god! That's right. Well—*tant pis!*

THORP. You rest your case, huh!

FELTON. Yeah. I—I begin to feel we're speaking different languages.

THORP. Aha!

FELTON. And the weight, the *opprobrium* of the generation gap really began to be felt on this boy's shoulders when those became the values, and the automatic shared ideas weren't there. And it came home literally—you can't often pin it down to one moment, but I think I can.

I was on a crowded streetcar coming out of the city. And two young girls, who could have been in your school here, were talking. They were particularly attractive and charming. And they were talking about what kind of marriage mate they wanted. They were not—you know—hippie, punk; they were nice-looking working girls. And I felt, "Well, this will be interesting." It was right in front of me; and you listen.

THORP. Sure!

FELTON. And one said, "What kind of man are you looking for? Who do you want to bring home to your parents?" And with a wistful look of longing, the other girl said to the first, "I think—I'd really like—to find—*an investment banker!*" And I thought: Holy God!

THORP. She's no dummy!

FELTON. Perhaps not. But I still expected, in my idiotic senility, to hear at least the "Big Three"—you know, "I want to find a doctor, I want to find a lawyer, I want to marry—" I doubt she would have said "professor," but she might have said something that would have had the connotation of that which society reveres on the highest planes. Instead, her "mark" was this kind of bishop in the pagan church of venture capitalism.

THORP. I think you've crystallized the issue: That probably back as far as the Old Testament, there have been references to "generation gaps." I think we're talking about something different now. And I don't think it's just a generation gap. I think it's a cultural gap. I think we have a cultural gap, which is a *values* gap, taking place in this society. And I think it's probably happened since the Beatles. I mean, not only did you define the Beatles in your own earlier reference, but I think that's really when the cultural gap started. And the baby-boomers who were the babies, at that point, are now reaping the benefits of what they sowed. And they are also reaping the benefits, or the consequences.

And I think what we have is a cultural gap which causes communication breakdown, and causes a values breakdown, and a values gap. This is a theme we've talked about before; but not quite in this way, I think. Where for the first time—there are all sorts of historical references, but—it would appear that in the post-Industrial age what you have is a new generation in fact speaking a different language, and a language, in some cases, of words that are different, but more importantly, of course, the language of values—that what counts, what matters, and what matters less. And it's only going to evolve further, I think, before it settles in, in one way or another. And it will also evolve for people like you and me, who see the intrinsic value in intellectual pursuits that doesn't generate investment income in and of itself; we're going to be increasingly seen as irrelevant. And humored, as nice but irrelevant people are in any society. Not—what's the word I'm looking for?—not *suppressed*, per se, but humored. As kind of the quirky uncle in the corner of the room.

It is an issue that I think affects education, and this brings us back to this thing that we talk about periodically, about what's going on here at Gateway. It is that you don't have educational "re-use"—a term I use pretty loosely. The Governor of the State of California, the Secretary of Education of the State of California, the Superintendent of Public Instruction are all talking so much about liberal arts values. And what they're talking about is performance-based schools. It's the language of the stock market applied to education. But it's being pushed in a way that runs counter to the liberal arts education. And maybe with some good reason.

But I don't want people to be fooled into thinking that—you know—standardized tests, standardized tests and test-score performance based education is consistent with, certainly, a Deweyesque approach to life, let alone an Aristotelian approach to life. Let alone Erasmus. Let alone all sorts of people who value education for its intrinsic value. It's intrinsic merit.

And so the question we have to ask ourselves is: "*Is* there any intrinsic value in education?" And you and I are both going to cling with our fingernails to the face of the cliff, saying, "Of course there is! Of course there is! Of course there is!"—as our fingernails scrape lower and lower down the wall. But *is* there? Does your attractive working class girl have it wrong? I don't know.

And I tell you: I can't sell the value of education to these kids at Gateway. With very few exceptions. And that class that you attended—we weren't talking about the *value* of education, *per se*. I mean—they're as close as you're going to get; but for them, it's very much a vocational path. As it should be! I mean, college isn't the ivory tower. But they're not talking to me, or they're not taking this class because they're dying to take liberal arts education. You know, for them it's a necessary step on a journey to some amount of personal satisfaction.

FELTON. Well—I can certainly see that getting into college is an onerous task, a daunting task for young people who have been spared that kind of bureaucracy by and large. So I can see that they would be practically-minded there. But what would happen if you came into work one day, and by design, sodium pentathol were spread everywhere in the building. And then these kids were asked: "Why do you come to school?" How many would say: "I'm here because socialization which takes place daily is the most important element of my life right now." And how many would say: "I'm really charged by ideas, and I get then when I talk with Ms. Barty, the math teacher, and Mr. Rodriguez, the Spanish teacher, and Mr. Thorp, the Principal." And how many would say: "The law says I have to be here right now"?

THORP. I'll do it in a different order, okay? Sixty percent of the kids would say: "I'm here because I have to be." Thirty-seven percent of the kids would say the first one, which was—?

FELTON. Socialization.

THORP. —"Socialization," okay? And three percent would say: "I'm here because I love to be challenged by the pursuit of ideas."

FELTON. Wow!!

THORP. Now. Obviously, that's a specious argument, in the sense that the way we even set it up, most kids wouldn't know how to respond to that third category, the pursuit of ideas. Either if you offered a fourth choice, or rephrased that one to say: "How many of you are here because you know the value of education and want to get an education?" the percentage would be much higher. But again, the way *they* defined education is as a means to an end, and not an end in and of itself.

FELTON. Well, I do think this is the striking difference.

You know, I worked for years, following graduate school, at UCLA in the Department of Psychology; and my shop was responsible for producing the department tests, and for providing their security. So I was kind of a "mark." And it resulted in some troubles associated with it, as some students tested that security.

It happened that UCLA was entertaining a large influx of Iranian students at the time; it was pre-Revolution—just at the end of the Shah's power. I made friends, if that's the word, with a couple of young kids who were brought in as work study students. They intrigued me as a group, they intrigued me as a culture, because they were attractive, they were bright as hell, and they had the greatest carborundum-hard-edged goal orientation I've ever seen. One of them, determined to get his B.A. but despite speaking five other languages, not competent in English enough to pass 101, was the capper: He would leave a classroom in the middle of a test, on the other end of

UCLA, and come all the way down to my workshop and say: "Can you stop a minute? I need the answers!" And I would say, "Razi, I can't do that! This isn't the way it works here!"

Once, I asked him: "How is it that when I'm going down the road, and I come upon this huge rock in the road, and it's an emotional rock, I get depressed and I go home and drink my Scotch bottle dry, and then I try, and call some friends, and then maybe by the next day I'm ready to face it? But when *you* get to that rock, what do you do?—you look at that rock, and say: 'Will I get around it better if I go over there? Or will I get around it better if I go up over there? Or if I just climb over the top, will I get around it better that way?'" And he smiled and replied: "I don't think about it. It's just another rock in the road."

That kind of reasoning leaves me speechless. The man of emotion and intuition can't hold a candle to somebody who has a kind of—not knee-jerk, but a kind of very-easily determined path, in terms of the alternatives that he will ponder in deciding how to go about getting over the obstacles in his road.

THORP. I have an American example of that for you: It's why Harry Truman was considered to be a great President and why Adlai Stevenson never got elected.

FELTON. That's a really good example. You're absolutely right!

THORP. And it's the issue that I face as an adult. And the issue I'm facing in my career is that teaching is a profession which is attractive to somebody who's not a risk-taker. And I'm not saying that all teachers aren't risk-takers; but I am saying that if you're not a risk-taker, teaching can be an attractive profession. And it goes back to the simple tenure laws.

It's also why venture capitalist businessmen have little patience with academics. Because they see them as caricatures in some ways: It courses from "Yet another Ph.D. thesis that four people in the world are going to read, and only two of them are going to care about!" to the paralysis of thought which probably is a distinguishing characteristic of a liberal arts institution. And by paralysis—perhaps I should rephrase it; not "paralysis of thought" in the sense of no new creative thought. To the contrary. But "paralysis" of *applying thought to action.* Which I think is at least an Achilles' heel of the life of the academic. The academic has tended to look down his or her snooty long nose at the plumbers of this world, Mr. Kennedy, and got away with it, for a long time. So that the Mr. Kennedys of this world would walk into that meeting, feeling as if they had to carry their hat in their hand, and be deferential. When in fact, the Mr. Kennedys of this world should have been looking down *their* noses at the academics. I don't really mean that; but what I think has happened more recently—and where the computer revolution is really shaking things out, with yet-to-be-determined results—is that the inherent, intrinsic value of education in and of itself as an end and not just as a means to an end, is being fundamentally challenged.

And these kids here at Gateway insist—I mean, I hear it in the kind of remark like: "Why do we have to study this crap!?" And I don't think it's necessarily fair to respond: "Because." Or: "It's good for you." Or: "Any educated person needs to know this." There has to be a better answer to that. We did talk a little before about the "cultural literacy" issue. E.D. Hirsch's book had five hundred "things," which the cultured person should know. And it was typical of this country that people zeroed in on this almost like a game show: "How many of these do you know?" And they missed his point. They missed his point, which was: "In cultural literacy the word was 'literacy'—not cultural, so-to-speak—" In other words, the concept relates not to how much you know, but whether or not you can communicate across this culture and other cultures, and that's where things are drifting away.

So the—if the liberal arts professors of the world have to justify their existence, the way that they ought to be able to do that does not lie in the intrinsic value of education, the value of a liberal arts education, or, as we've talked in a previous conversation, this thing called "the love of learning"; it should in fact be: "It is critically important that a society be culturally literate. That there be an ongoing language which encourages communication, stability, connectivity, to get itself through the very difficult times that any society is going to face, some more difficult than others. And the reason why society is poised for some serious negative stuff is because we are not as culturally conversant, or as culturally literate, as we were once.

And that doesn't mean we're dumber. To the contrary. We're far better educated. But we can't communicate. And that's where the liberal arts organizations of this world need to establish themselves and find their nature. We are the keepers not of the sanctified, sanctimonious set of pieces of knowledge. We are—and again, this is the "priest" reference—we are the sustainers; we are the nurturers of the language that binds this society, and the communication which makes this society stick together. And lacking us, lacking this tradition, lacking this glue, this society is going to spin in centrifugal force in a way that will result in—what? I'm not sure. Balkanized America? Pretty possible; certainly socio-economic Balkanization, which is well underway.

And so, to come totally full circle on this discussion: I don't think the liberal arts tradition is an anachronism. But I think it runs the risk of being viewed that way unless it wakes up to the fact that a lot of people are passing right by it, and saying: "You're irrelevant!"

FELTON. Well, let me throw out one other question, that might just be a lament:

THORP. And justifiably so!

FELTON. When I went to work for a law firm in April of 1982, I had had no real exposure to lawyers. And in my *naïveté*, I said to myself: "Gee, I'm going to read up a little bit, so I can converse when I get into the law firm." So I did what any naïve liberal arts person does: I read up on a couple of heroes.

THORP. Who were they?

FELTON. The first was Clarence Darrow!—

THORP. One of my favorite people!

FELTON. And the other—whom, it should be remembered, was a Grinnellian—was Joseph Welch.

THORP. Oh, really. I didn't know that.

FELTON. Yeah. So I felt "well-prepared" to go in, because I had reacquainted myself with two wonderful human beings who as lawyers had made formidable contributions to society, and to history. And I met all the lawyers, but I didn't find one who had the vaguest ability to focus intellectually outside the narrow range of his expertise in law. And I guess the classic awareness of that was when one fellow came up to my desk, and noticed the book that I was carrying to read at lunch, and he said: "Who's this guy?" And I said, "Whom do you mean?" And he picked up the book and read the name of the author: "Who's Somerset Maugham?"

Well, you know, once again—he was toting around, I don't know, high six figures every year. *He* didn't need to know who Somerset Maugham was, to succeed, and to feel that he was a productive human being. But at home, when that man went home—did he just sit in front of the game show?— and I don't mean "Jeopardy!"—what happened to him?

I regretted, I lamented the loss of these people, who were trying to do something professionally that involved the intellect, and yet had missed the point of that "breadth" question. And I see that breadth as personally enriching, personally nourishing, to have that curiosity, and to do something with it. These men didn't need that. But the consequence was that outside their immediate professional sphere, the light went out of their eyes. And I felt terribly for society—if that doesn't sound too "purple" to say!

THORP.   So then what you need to do is to—to exalt the value of curiosity, in pursuit not for reasons of dilettantism, but for some other value.

So have we sufficiently trashed the whole liberal arts tradition here?

FELTON.   I don't surrender! But clearly, the job for the liberal arts tradition is to find that niche, to survive, and to see what it's truly going to become, and to wonder if we have enough years left to enable us to come full circle, when maybe this might be rather an interesting thing to do, again.

THORP.   Obviously, I feel the value of that tradition. But I do think academics run the risk of being marginalized. In fact, I think they have already. And I'm not so sure that they're paid much attention to today. College is—it's a commodity; but enough people right now are still in enough position to pay all that thirty-two-thousand-bucks bill.

I can tell you of one last example that's interesting: There was a session back in my independent school days where somebody generated a list of all the private schools in Los Angeles, published from the Los Angeles *Times* of 1938, or sometime like that. And of all the schools that were on that list, only two were in existence in 1970-, 1980-whatever it was.

FELTON.   Is that right!

THORP.   So it's easy to sit back and say: "Of *course* we're always going to be here." In a school like Cate, there is no reason to think that that school would ever go away. It's kind of refreshing, at Gateway, where you never quite know if it'll be there from one day to the next!

Chapter Seventeen

WHEN HONORABLE MEN DISAGREE

"[S]chools don't do enough…to have a kid feel the satisfaction of mastery, and the satisfaction of expertise.…[W] hen they've really taken a quantum leap forward toward mastery of something, what can a school do to help a kid enjoy that moment? And too often it's: "Do tomorrow night's homework." Too often it's: "Okay, run the next chapter." That's something that this school, I hope, one day, will have resolved better than most schools."

"What's the nature of schooling? And what's the role of school in this society?"…. Should they be transmitters of cultural values? Should they be *in loco parentis*? Should they be the locus of societal programs addressing various forms and levels of dysfunction? Or— should they be, simply, the locus of intellectual pursuits and not as an end, the love of learning issue, but as a *means* to an end?….

"So context is everything; …And one of our challenges is that we've authorized our kids to be vocal here, and to be part of the conversation of school and to build programs and to talk about the neurological profile. But…we've underestimated the degree to which kids don't have context, or don't understand context, and therefore don't know yet how to communicate appropriately their needs. They just hear the first half of the sentence, which is 'communicate your needs,' and they don't hear the word 'appropriately.'"

27 March—*At Eastertide—Gateway's ten-day Spring break in school activity—something happened to Peter Thorp, and to our communication.*

It started with an issue in the office after our last meeting, in which some women staff members bantered with Peter: A remark of his about the way he and I had scheduled our next meeting raised the suggestion of an issue of sexism. (He had remarked that a man would have announced his unconcern about a specific date in the way I did, whereas a woman would not.) The staffers picked up the point, and "did not let him get away with it"; but the more important event was my glimpse of a momentary dropping of the veil of adulation accorded him by his underlings.

I noticed something different as well in his responses to my challenges on the subject of the inordinate rise in importance of computers in schools—"cyber ed." This slight alteration in his focus on our subject matter—and his now continually repeated tardiness in keeping our appointments—gave me pause. It would have consequences for the sessions left to us on our project.

This development did not deter me from awareness of the fact that it was my job to learn as much as I could about all *the stresses in my subject's work life. That was the nature of our task—to create a book detailing all the events, high and low, which impinged upon his daily conduct over a year in the Principal's role. His seeming lapse of concentration was no exception. I would try to explore it; for it bore upon his accomplishment of his goal as surely as any Board of Education dictum, or any teacher's leaving, or any student's struggle in the classroom.*

My early arrival this day had taken me to a nearby coffee shop for some caffeine to help go over my notes. At a table sat Peter and Spencer Tolliver, the school's Vice Principal. The senior man, noting me, attested to his effort to keep the appointment. I drained a thermos of dark roast into my cup, and pointed toward the parking lot, my halfway house on the way to the world of Thorp.

Peter arrived, about twenty minutes late. We began. It was Monday of the vacation week; but Peter opened with curiosity about my presence the day before, on campus, with the student Photo Group. One had the choice of viewing his query as pleasantry, or micromanagement. Knowing Peter better now, I took it to be a third alternative: Like a sometimes-overlooked younger sibling, he simply didn't like to be left out of things.

Our opening discussion about a student photo project grew into an exchange on pedagogy.

THORP. What are you doing here on a Sunday?

FELTON. The Photo Group had a great day yesterday! This was our Polaroid workshop.

THORP. Interesting!

FELTON. I'd been wrestling with what to do to get this photography club off and running, given no facilities. Finally I realized that the only way that I was really going to get to these kids is not if we sat around pining for a darkroom, or going through all the delay of using a film lab. So I just went strictly to Polaroid. I got a complete contingent of old Polaroid cameras, and it worked like a top.

THORP. Great!

FELTON. Everybody got involved in it. We had four different assignments, and broke into groups of two students. And even though not everybody came whom I thought would come, some came whom I didn't think would be there. We use worksheets; they have instruction before the task, and they have a space to fill in responses after exposing the photo but before processing the image; and then they process the image, and then they have a space to write in responses after they see the image. It's a project based on work Minor White did at M.I.T. in the 'sixties—one of the projects which brought him to Ansel Adams' attention.[1]

The students are free to write anything; and I encouraged a lot of "feeling" writing. But what happened was kids would take photographs, and then give intense work!—maybe ten minutes at a time to a written response. And I thought: "This is great, they're really plumbing some depths, here." But when as I looked over the papers, I saw they'd largely just written: "The photo was darker than I thought it would be." Just a simple idea. And those are all valid, too; those are all fine. I would have liked to see more of an emotional response; but they were really working hard. So I was very pleased with it.

THORP. The students always cry for more extracurricular activities. I'm glad you're helping provide them.

FELTON. On another topic, I saw—with great effort at self-control—the first of a two-part film documentary series, which you might have caught, on the "Digital Divide." Are you familiar with it?

THORP. No.

FELTON. Well, it was a good thing you didn't see it. It would have just upset you. It was a very well done Public Broadcasting show; and in this first part, they tried to balance it between teachers

---

[1] This project—a pedagogical model—is described in detail in Chapter 21.

who were highly driven toward computerization, and those who said: "Wait a minute! Hold on!" It wasn't evenly balanced; but there was some challenge to the idea that the only way anybody's ever going to learn anything from now on is computer-driven work. And I wrote down a series of quotes from the show; it's astonishing how little some people understand not only what pedagogy means, but even how to mount an attack.

The worst seems summed up in one instance. It portrays a school called "New Technology High School," in Napa.

THORP. Oh, yes.

FELTON. Frightening! Basically, the school heads want to build a technology center and give kids high school credit for doing what is actually job training. And everything is geared toward that goal. In the opening shot, the principal brings a group of dignitaries through, and the narrator, in voice-over, kicks off the description: "Education can't get much more digital than it does here. This is New Technology High School in Napa. New Tech is an experimental school with 220 students, and 280 computers."

Then the principal takes off. He addresses the visiting group: "The mission of New Technology High School is to prepare our students for high-wage, high-skilled jobs of the future." That's *his* order of importance. "We entered into conversations with our local business community," he continued. "What we found that they really needed was an academically prepared student that also had technology skills, that allowed them to communicate effectively with an information-based work environment."

So, a lot of jargon, a lot of high-tech—and, incidentally, a lot of bad grammar from the head of a school! And then some kids talked about how wonderful this is. And it really felt like—it felt like a cult. It felt like some kids had been brought in and they were lost, and they didn't know how to learn before, but now—

THORP. You mean unlike the charter school cult!?

FELTON. Well, look—you walk through here, and this is a school. There's somebody up in front of the room with a piece of chalk or a marking pen, saying, "You know, you've got to get these verbs down," or "You've got to do this," or "You've got to get this equation," or "Here's how this physical principle leads to that one in our science project—"

THORP. I'm going to have to get a couch in my office. Because the longer you and I meet, the more depressed you're going to get, with all this stuff of education, because a liberal arts guy is a pretty extinct buckaroo!—or endangered, at the least.

FELTON. Well, I think that's terrible! But I'll leave it off with the last quote from this film, which is the most chilling quote of all. One of the teachers at "New Tech" says—as she's standing over a couple of kids who are at keyboards and entranced by the monitor's image: "Teachers don't look at students as students *per se*. We try to look at them as perhaps our co-workers, that we're here to supervise, and help to do a good job"!

THORP. Why is that chilling?

FELTON. It's chilling to me because it negates the entire developmental stage in which role models are helping those who have acknowledged, and are acknowledged by dint of their very age, to be in transitional phases of growth, not "adult business" life, but childhood or adolescent learning life. And the distinctions are important because the child's age should inaugurate the transposition out of the family environment with parent figures, into the school environment with the development of transference of attachment onto the mentors, and only thence out into the community at large. Extremely important stages! And this film just dismisses all that, saying: "We'll all just treat each other as colleagues." Well, students and teachers are *not* colleagues! And to foster that view just underscores the duplicity of it to a degree which I feel is unconscionable.[1]

THORP. Well, you know how I think, but allow me to be artificially provocative for a moment.

FELTON. Go ahead!

THORP. You know, maybe a school like this is going to push the envelope in terms of the big question, which is: "What's the nature of schooling? And what's the role of school in this society?" Should schools be the following: Should they be transmitters of cultural values? Yes or no. Should they be *in loco parentis*? Yes or no. Should they be the locus of societal programs addressing various forms and levels of dysfunction? Or—should they be, simply, the locus of intellectual pursuits and not—given one of our previous conversations—as an end, the love of learning issue, but as a *means* to an end?

What in fact *is* the purpose of education? We talk about monopolies in various ways, whether or not it's Microsoft or the California Teacher's Association. I think—depending upon one's

---

[1] When posed with the example, and Thorp's responsive question "Why is that chilling?", Meghvi Maheta exploded: "'Why is that chilling?'!—where's the *moral education!!!?"*

predisposition—everybody has some discomfort with monopoly in one way or another, for the reason that it cuts down on choice and options for flexibilities. Is it not the case that the public educational system is a monopoly? And is it not the case that it's the most far-reaching monopoly of any organization that exists—even though the most complicated and dysfunctional monopoly!? You know, in some ways, it's the most powerful of monopolies, not unlike the Defense Department, because it both has power it wants and has additional power thrust upon it that it doesn't even want. It's the budget where the Pentagon people are trying to say to the Air Force: "We don't want those planes!" And the senator from wherever is saying: "You're going to get them anyway!" This describes a monopoly that is dealing with such important issues in lieu of the right people who ought to be dealing with it.

Again, I'm being somewhat artificially provocative here: Do you want that teacher, do you want any teacher, replacing you as a parent? In a perfect world, wouldn't every kid be home-schooled? Up to a certain point, maybe? You know, in a sense, they are.

FELTON. Right.

THORP. —Up until age five, which I think we all know is a pretty critical time. And so: Is it so chilling for a school to say, as did Calvin Coolidge in the 'twenties: "The business of America is business"? And is it so wrong for a school to say: "The business of this school is schooling"?

FELTON. No, that wouldn't be wrong. Because then the business—the quote would be within its own quotes. It would be someone saying: "I'm going to use this metaphor of business." But they're *not* using this as a metaphor at New Tech. They're saying: "This *is* business! This is the vestibule of the 'big room' called business." And—

THORP. What's wrong with that?

FELTON. A couple of things. First of all, there would be nothing different between that school and this school, which was an opening question of yours, if one condition obtained here: If there were no room for or tolerance of the differences between—and the uniqueness of—your teachers here. You can go through your faculty; and if instead of celebrating *their genius at being themselves*, and hence bringing in really important and varied dimensions on education, you said subtly or overtly in your direction to your faculty: "Homogeneity is the key here. This is the Army, except we don't wear quite such starchy uniforms. And you must look like each other, and you must act like each other." And the uniformity of this kind of thinking is what I think of as dangerous.

The other thing that I think happens here is that I believe being *in loco parentis* is, in fact, a natural condition whether you're in the second grade, when the teacher who might be female is almost immediately a kind of intuitive substitute for a mother; or whether you're Keith Felton and his Photo Group student Kelly Oppermann, in a Gateway parking lot looking at some photos from the Group Project—there's a kind of natural instinct to use that individual not only in the mentor role, but in the kind of maternal/paternal role. I don't think it's necessarily negative, I don't think it's bad; it may end up just being neutral. But what is key about it is *the education process*. And this role casting is just one more way of achieving and advancing learning.

But as I thought through our conversation last time, and as I saw this film on the "Digital Divide," what seemed to be the essential difference is this: To me, the most valuable thing that happens here at Gateway is that just like that church across the street, although in a less formal way, this school has proclaimed: "We have had a ceremony to make this place a kind of hallowed ground. We've sanctified it for a special purpose, and have attempted to imbue it with a kind of special feeling which will only really happen when we practice in it what we're here to do. We have *consecrated* this place; and as a result, the feelings and attitudes you bring here, and we want to bring to you, will create a transformational environment. So that you will experience something here in a special way that will charge you in a way nothing else could, and you will go out into your life, taking this as part of your development, and do something with it. And it might be to go right to those businesses that New Tech is dealing with; and it might be to become a teacher yourself; and it might be to do whatever is the current version of the Peace Corps. Doesn't matter to us; *this transformational experience* is what is critical to us, and what we think is critical to you. And we're going to work on that."

And that special quality is very much like a liturgical space, or a theatrical space, in that it is the momentary suspension of certain other parameters so as to focus, so as to concentrate. And I think it's critically important.

THORP. Yeah, though I see very different functions that—I think the liturgical space is the closest analogy. Because I don't think there's any church in the world, whether or not one defines Taoism as a church, or the closest aberration to that—that believes fundamentally in heterogeneity. That the very definition of church—theology, belief—s stepping some number of steps toward homogeneity. Where I think the analogy of the theater doesn't hold true is that it doesn't require that, because it truly does suspend time and belief, and substitute role-playing for that. I think a school is much closer to a church than it is to a theater. And I think the—one of the great shibboleths, myths, fabrications, possibly untruths of schools is the extent to which heterogeneity furthers inculcation of appropriate beliefs.

So how do you deal with that? You deal with that in—you get schools defined around certain missions that get to select the people who are appropriate to their mission—private schools, parochial schools—who reach out for diversity in a way that they sincerely see the benefit of bringing in other voices; but you know for damned sure their intent is to have those voices meld into the dominant culture. It's (a) the American Dream at Groton, it's the Jo Vega[1] issue; or (b) you get the public sector, at an extreme where there's no values discussion because nobody has the right to ram his or her values down my kid's throat. And so they become—what would be the word?—"a-ethical."

And then there are some schools, of which the one you're questioning is one, in which the resulting desired inculcation of beliefs is a function of the degree to which the heterogeneity can be turned into a force of progressive momentum and power, rather than an obstacle to be overcome. And it's a huge, huge challenge. But there's an underlying ethic, which is that there are certain universal values which hold true! And that brings us back to the digital high school, with the statement being: "Oh, yeah? Not with *my* kid, you're not!" And: "What I want out of my kid is that she knows calculus or computers!" There's no difference between the New Technology High School and Lowell High School. Okay? There's no difference between that and, arguably, St. John's College—which we have or have not talked about?—

FELTON. No.

THORP. St. John's College, in Maryland and Santa Fe, it's the campus of the "Great Books" program, kind of the Balloon, if I remember the name, idea toward—I mean, it's *the* haven of the liberal arts. It's Samuel Johnson, a math teacher here at one time, who was a product of that school and why he tried to teach geometry in the way that he was teaching it. But even they, through what you would espouse is Nirvana!, from the liberal arts perspective, have a very clear

---

[1] Groton and Vega are discussed in Chapters 24 and 25. Vega, Hispanic and artistic, struggled at Groton, feeling perennially out-of-place.

point in terms of what they're trying to do, which is that the life of the mind is inherently valuable.

Now, again, this is not fair to them, but I have this image of St. John's that if every alumnus or alumna of St. John's ended up sitting on a mountain top contemplating his or her navel, they'd be thrilled! That they had done their job. So—I turn any questions, as you know, into political issues easily, and this to me is one of the interesting historical/political issues in this country.

When one teaches U.S. History, one can teach it from essentially one of two perspectives: The story of America, the story of the United States, is the story of "conflict" or "consensus"—and you can see the kind of left or right spectrum in that. And you know that I teach the conflict approach. It's fun to teach, when the opening line is: "The Constitution of the United States is inherently an anti-democratic document." The "consensus" perspective, which most people would prefer be the story of American history, but as a teacher is a lot less fun, frankly, holds tremendous value because it's the question of the distribution of power.

There's a really interesting book written about the advertising business called *Captains of Consciousness*. This famous book was about advertising in the 1920s when advertising was really born. And it's essentially a Marxist interpretation or approach toward the role of advertising. And the basic point—and you can take that and put it next to the Great Gatsby—is this interesting juxtaposition of the "American Dream" issue. You know, the "American Dream" is either a false goal because it's kind of perverted, a kind of Fitzgeraldian component of things, or the "American Dream" is made available just enough by the Captains of Consciousness to make sure that we don't have a revolution. And so the whole theory behind advertising in the 'twenties, particularly given that it followed immediately upon World War One and the Red Scare—was to get the masses back on board on the "American Dream" so they're buying Model T Fords and not throwing Molotov Cocktails!

The history of the twentieth century, through the eyes of this Marxist, is what business does! Business keeps people sucked into this American dream, and they've been damned effective at it. And they've been so effective at it, they've known, to varying degrees, when to let up a little bit. And eventually, they have known to allow women into the fold, so to speak, in a way that was not true before 1950, and arguably, I suppose, before 1970. And of course, the smug posture of the Jovian Captains of Consciousness would be: "Well, we let them in, and they're doing it just like we did. We did it!" As opposed to something like Allan Goodman would argue, which is: "Women need to change the fundamental nature of work." Or: "Women have the potential to change the fundamental nature of work." And now, it's just: "They're doing it better than men do, but they're doing it in that style!"

Similarly, people who have been historically excluded from the power capital are being allowed access to that, but are coming in not in a conflict stream, but in a consensus stream. And the inherent question in this emergence is: "Can somebody be truly different in this society, and make it? And attain a position of—I don't know if it's wealth, or respect or power or whatever would make somebody truly different?" It's pretty unusual for that to happen.

But as a parenthetical note: A number of books were written in the 1920s where Jesus and Moses were cast as businessmen. Probably the most famous book was written by a guy named Bruce Barton, of BDD & O?—the advertising agency—

FELTON. Yes!

THORP. —And that's what the first "B" is—Bruce Barton. It's called *Moses, Persuader of Men.* The whole thesis of the book is that Moses was the best real estate agent in history, because he got a whole people to pack up and head over across the seas to "do its thing." And the book *The Man Nobody Knows* was a book about the life of Christ, and Christ was analyzed as a businessman. Here's somebody who took twelve people and changed the world. It was sort of Microsoft, two thousand years ago!

And believe it or not, this ties in right with what you said at the beginning of our session. This is what the "Digital Divide" is all about! It's access to power, assuming again that you see that the lens with which I look at the world exhibits that point of view. If that is what people aspire to—and I'm making no value judgment about whether or not they should; and I'm not even sure they do, although my antennae tell me people look for wealth, not so much to exercise power as to have comfort—then that's where the digital divide is such a key issue. And that's where this school you saw the show about which upset you—a private school, I'm guessing?

FELTON. I believe so.

THORP. I mean, it would be interesting to know, whether that question—if the entry into that school was completely unfettered, in one's socio-economic circumstances, then it gets very interesting. If, on the other hand, it's a private school and you've got to pay tuition, and it's self-selecting, if it's just enhancing the digital divide—or even if it's a private school with a wonderful scholarship program, then it's saying: "Come with me, come this way, down the consensus road." And what this society has yet to come to grips with is: Can you be really different, can you have fundamentally different values, and have as many options and as much choice? Can you walk into a job at Merrill Lynch with—I've drawn a total blank on the term—Rastafarian hair—called—what—?

FELTON. Dreadlocks.

THORP. Dreadlocks! Thank you. And the answer is: "Not if you want the job, you can't!" And the question then is: "Why does it make a difference?" Particularly in a business which has so little, if any, face-to-face contact—what difference does it make?

Now, again, if a dreadlock-wearer was selling Bibles, it might be a different story, going door-to-door. But what difference does it make? Why are these criteria exercised over and over? Why do I regard a job application from a graduate from Stanford differently than I do one from somebody from Sonoma State? It's because I'm predisposed to certain value judgments about what that means from the "get-go." Like any intelligent person who has stereotypical baggage, there's usually some truth in what you might be able to assume about Person A and Person B in that scenario. But I'd better be damned sure that I'm not overlooking the fact that the person was at Stanford because he came from wealth, and "got in" that way, or he came from "basketball," and he might be a terrible teacher; whereas the person from Sonoma State is knocking him or herself out to get even that much less expensive degree, and might be the world's best teacher.

FELTON. I'm going to challenge one part of that response, and then ask you some questions about it.

First: You of all people—if those two candidates for the job sat there, and the guy from Stanford—or the woman, whoever it happened to be—clearly had a drug problem, or wasn't awake that day; and the person from "State College" was just on top of things, and showering you with really creative ideas, and had a very upbeat personality, you're going to make a decision that's not derived just from their resumés. There are some people who wouldn't; but I—certainly, I don't think this would be your problem.

Now, to the substance of your very pithy response: I think that with certain exceptions in our country's history, the way I see, it I think your interest in power is quite *à-propos* here. I see most situations from the standpoint of how people acquire power, and retain power. There are some times when I don't understand American history. I don't understand how women, who had—what?—four years of "Rosie the Riveter" opportunity, immediately then handed it back to the other gender and said: "Okay, we'll go back and lie on our backs, literally, or we'll go stand in the kitchen, and return this role to you which we have savored now, and learned a lot about, and learned about ourselves for four years while you went somewhere else." They did give it back. And then we had the 'seventies, and the "glass-ceiling" idea, and we had the "women-should-be-men-without-penises" idea, but in every other respect they were going to be men, because they wanted to have this power, and all that.

But I think society has its own threshold of tolerance—which has a curve that sometimes is up, and sometimes is down—for allowing us to have certain eccentrics in society, whose presence will drain off that challenging energy.   And this gives us—this allows us to have Buckminster Fuller, and Frank Lloyd Wright, and Russell, in England, and Spock and Pauling—and we're able to have these people because we can do two things: We can begrudgingly respect them, and we can make fun of them. But whatever they do, they will drain off a lot of the intolerance which we are now going to put in most of our energy, hard-core, toward getting people to shape up and conform.   And that's regrettable, because those five people I named probably will do more than as many millions in advancing some pretty important values.

THORP.   That's why Jesse Ventura, the Governor of Minnesota, will get a hell of a lot of votes for President, and Ralph Nader won't.

FELTON.   That's true. That's exactly right. Yeah. We just can't afford that; that breaks the bank. That goes against our grain. And along that line, probably the most negative and unpleasant-to-deal-with situation of a guy who's going to have a huge influence, is—the "doomsday doctor"—

THORP. Kevorkian?

FELTON.   —Who's now just—you know, we finally "dealt with that," we found a way to throw him in jail and leave him there. So— I'm worried about that.   But coming back to the school idea, the problem with this New Tech school, as I see it, is the material focus, rather than the philosophical focus. When I studied theater, the idea— even though it has a little bit of a precious element—the old *cliché* you learn about theater is: "All you need to have theater is two boards and a passion!"   In other words, you have to have ideas!—and all the rest doesn't matter. But what you absolutely must have to have computer literacy—as they like to say—and relevant acumen, and the ability to put it all to work for you, is a huge retinue of constantly-changing equipment, and a certain doggedly-pursued knowledge of incoming programs. A software-dependent thinker must *never, never* get off the treadmill.

When I worked for that law firm—about the time when computers began to take over everybody's desk—I saw two things happen that really disturbed me: One was that people who could not communicate to each other, one-to-one, who were the office "curmudgeons," did find, by living a life of e-mail, that all that sociopathy when with other human beings was sidestepped, for they could sit by the hour and have conversations which came out of a machine!

The other phenomenon which I found curious was that people who had not either had the opportunity or had not taken the opportunity to acquire a certain level of expertise could acquire a computer skill with a relatively short amount of diligent effort and time. They became important to the office, because they had this very limited, manageable skill. And I think those people liked the feeling that they were now the "experts," even though their range of expertise was quite narrow. It was a useful skill, yes; but it was in truth nothing that any number of people in the building at the same time could not have acquired themselves. And I thought: "Something's wrong here." The whole idea of this quickly-grabbed expertise has subtly contributed to the greater computer emphasis in our national life.

THORP. What's wrong with either one of those things? On the one hand, to turn it around, what you defined is a vehicle to give voices to people who lack voices—who were ill-powered to engage in conversation equally with people who were more facile. There was an article in yesterday's New York Times, about Wake Forest, which was one of the many colleges to become computerized; and they were talking about this class, where every student has a laptop. And many of the classes are conducted in silence, and it's all done in chat rooms. Which is an interesting development, particularly when you start weaving in the research on gender bias in the classrooms, where in seminar classes, men tend to dominate unless you have a facilitator especially sensitive to that, who manipulates and manages the conversation so that that doesn't happen. Or you have kids from a cultural background, or if you get a teacher—I used to work with someone who would just leap all over a kid. This person had serious issues as a teacher, anyway; but I remember him taking on an Asian kid about not speaking up. And the Asian kid needed to say: "Hey, you jerk, my culture says *not* to speak up, especially with a teacher who is viewed as esteemed. So I don't have the problem—*you* do, because you're injecting your cultural expectations on me, without being aware of my culture."

So on the one hand, you've got an avenue for voice for people who might have been "dis-voiced," in that sense. And the second point that you make is something again—and I'm not being artificially argumentative here, but what's wrong with the thought of expertise? Even narrow expertise. I mean, why not? It seems to me that one of the benefits of the technological revolution, and I really do see it as a benefit of the technological revolution, is that all sorts of people have been given avenues for success which didn't exist before. It's an avenue which is very different from many which have existed before, where your success level is pretty much a function of initiative level. And speaking of the American Dream, there it is! Again, the interesting juxtaposition is, you know—the "Freaks and Geeks" issue, and it's why the Microsoft-*versus*-U.S. Government lawsuit is interesting, and why Bill Gates is interesting, and so on. And— Whoa!—look: For the first time, the Groton-schooled Averell Harrimans of this world, the way they maintain power, which was in the clubs of Princeton, is being absolutely threatened by the Bill Gateses of this world, who have no desire for that old world—and in fact, see that club as not only anachronistic, but as counter-productive, and maybe with some good reason! For as they see it, power is much more accessible to a broader swath of people than it ever was before.

If you buy into the "Captains of Consciousness" theory, the Captains only let enough power out to keep people suppressed. Whereas, technology is to some extent power-neutral, or again, the danger of consolidating power is even greater with Bill Gates, who could be King of the World if he wanted to! But nevertheless—and this is picking up on what we talked about last week—you and I share the potentially ill-advised, misguided, anachronistic perspective on the world, that the value of the mind has inherent value, even if unexercised in a way that produces better stuff for the world! And it's pretty intriguing to be challenged in a way where Bill Gates says, "Get out of the way! You guys can sit around having these interesting Ph.D. discussions on all sorts of minutiae, but forget about it! I've got more interesting things to do, and I'm going to change the world!" And college professors and people like you and me, sit there, sputtering: "But—but—but—but—! What about the Greek classics!? Or, what about the Victorian novel?! Or what about—What!?"

Here's my point in all this, Keith: The issue I have with that school you don't like is not that it's trying to train kids for a meaningful role which might produce two houses and vacations and money and a

Porsche, or just the comfort of putting bread on the table and the security of having an income so one can have a family and be a good person and a contributing member, I have no problem with that. In fact, parenthetically, one of the things I wrestle with here is to what extent does Gateway have to do some vocational training? No—the issue that *I* have with that school, and the issue that I have with that teacher's quote about "colleagues", is: "Is the school value-neutral?" That is what technology is. And where we've seen the problems with technology is that too many people are given access to unfiltered information, either that is inaccurate—"The Holocaust never happened"— or they're being given access to information that's inappropriate to them, developmentally, or culturally, such as pornography.

And where are the values coming into play? What's the value with that kid in Florida having been hammered for sending that threat over e-mail, if Columbine hadn't happened? I mean, what about people who shut down the system in that barrage a couple of months when they flooded various important websites like AOL, with "Spam," or whatever the word was—that shut them down? I heard a report where somebody well-known in the computer industry said; "You know, this is actually kind of cool! Because it's giving a message to the big shots that you don't run the world."

To me, the really interesting aspect of this question that we've been coming at in a variety of ways, is: What is the role of values in a school?

FELTON. I think that *is* the question. I'm just not sure your position as stated supports that point of view in the end.

THORP. Let me add one thing.

One of the interesting things about education, and one of the things that we're still wrestling with here at Gateway, is the "satisfaction" question. When are we as adults most satisfied? To speak personally: I'm most satisfied when I think I've accomplished something. In my vocation. I'm most satisfied when I have the skills, that is, the expertise, to do something that I know is an accomplishment! And that ranges from running a school, to—back in the days when I was doing it—filing down and resetting my spark plugs.

I think one of the mistakes that schools make is that they deny kids too long, particularly high school kids, the feeling of expertise. And it's—and I've been guilty of this for most of my years as an educator— it's the holding out of a desire to end mastery. It's kind of Charley Brown and Lucy, you know—where she would pick up the football every time he would run to kick it. And teachers kind of pick up the football every time the kid just gets there, and—"Whoops!—the football goes, and you've got to do this problem now! Okay— whoop!—but you've got to read this next chapter!" What schools don't do enough with, and what this school doesn't yet do enough is to have a kid feel the satisfaction of mastery, and the satisfaction of expertise. Now, we can recognize that fifteen-year-olds aren't going to be expert at too many things; but in those moments when they've really taken a quantum leap forward toward mastery of something, what does a school do to help a kid enjoy that moment? And too often it's: "Do tomorrow night's homework." Too often it's: "Okay, run the next chapter." That's something that this school, I hope, one day, will have resolved better than most schools.

FELTON. Well, I think you have a much better chance than most schools at doing that. Some of it is out of your control; and the most magnificent thing that could happen—not without consequence, but probably—is if you could get a lasso around all of the problem called standardized testing, and just lift it out, and throw it away, and open up all that time to focus on critical issues. The problem I have with forcing people to find a rather limited niche of expertise—and "expertise" is in quotes—is that I don't think it has ultimate satisfaction. I think there are two directions you can go: You can say: "I want to find out what's inside these people, and I'm going to have to work to do that. But when I discover their uniqueness, I will then really be able to build all kinds of worlds with and for them, by doing that." Or, saying: "I'm here, this is what I'm offering, I've set up the premise, to suit my needs. Who is swimming up this stream, and will conveniently fall into the role that I have here? I need somebody to do this task, and I need somebody to do that task." A limited point of view.

A small example—which I haven't explored too much, except I've been thinking about it—my photo student, Gateway sophomore Kelly Oppermann, has a quite passionate interest in collecting antique porcelain figurines. That's a very important thing to know! And if I were her main teacher, I would want to translate that little fact into something very practical and applicable to her enjoyment of whatever my subject is. And it doesn't have to do with figurines; it has to do with a student's inclination, and her attraction to that idea. The teacher's job is to search out the student's realm, take cognizance of its elements, and change and modify them in a fruitful, pedagogically productive way.

Now, in a business, there's probably not time for that; but a good person, a personnel manager, still can learn to say: "That guy likes to sit on his desk, rather than in a chair. How can I use that to help him work in this environment, and make this a better environment for other people?" It takes an inspired head to come up with that question, and most people in business aren't good at that, and aren't going to do that. Most of them aren't even looking up above the papers in their hand. So—that's what makes me wonder, when I hear the "my-student-is-my-colleague" stuff.

Let's jump. We'll doubtless come back to some of that.

Based on a radio report of this morning, Palisades High School, outside Los Angeles, suspended some kids today for having created, and run, and dispersed, an underground newspaper which featured some profanity. Those kids were suspended.

Suppose that had happened at Gateway: What would the Principal have thought or done, in a similar situation?

THORP. I've been presented with that challenge already. I mean, not that specific one, but a permutation of it. What I can't answer right now, and what I would have to check, is there is some very specific case law about this right now. And—gee, what a surprise!—the ACLU is all over that sort of thing from a First Amendment point of view. There have been a number of cases that have been decided about kids' First Amendment rights, in terms of school newspapers, yearbooks, and that sort of thing.

It's that issue; it's also the "cocaine" image in the yearbook. And the one that I had to deal with a couple of weeks ago is this play that's being developed here at Gateway in the sophomore drama class, where kids are writing their own script, and a kid came to me with a line containing four-letter words in the dialogue, and made a passionate plea for not excising it, because it was language appropriate to the dialogue, and language which made the dialogue more powerful. And I excised it.

My rationale is: This is a school, this is not society, this is a school that stands for certain values, and this is a school where it will not publicly support things that it believes run counter to those values—one of which is profanity. And I'd be the first to admit that I'm not a saint on that issue, and I run the risk of being called a hypocrite on that question. But I'm not going to fail to challenge a student who is engaged in activity which results in something running counter to our values.

One of the cultural values that this school is going to stand for is sportsmanship. And if we get ourselves in a situation where either our players, or more likely, our fans, are behaving in ways that I consider to be unsporstmanlike, we're going to do something about it. And boy, oh, boy!, is that going to be a challenge, given the issue of sportsmanship in this era.

So—you know, without even having seen the Palisades High newspaper or what the profanity was, I think the principal was completely within his or her rights to say: "It's not okay." Again, I don't know the case law, I don't know of the facts whether the kids did it on their own—you know, did they Xerox their own copies at Kinko's, that sort of thing, and hand it out—who knows? Then you get the question: Could the current events club distribute an Amnesty International poster or a KKK leaflet and that sort of thing? That's when it starts to get to be a problem.

But I believe it is connected to what we've been talking about, which is that schools can't be "value-neutral." Maybe one day we might be able to be, if the rest of the society wasn't "value-confused," at the very least. Schools need to be riddled with values, particularly if we continue to go in the direction where people will make choice about the schools—schools of choice, charter schools being one of them, where you say: "Hey, don't come here if you don't like the school's values! Go down the street to that school which has a different set of values, which is happy to have someone with that set of values."

So I support that principal's action, even in balmy Southern California.

FELTON. Our friend Peter Felton provoked a similar situation for me. He wanted to be in the Gateway Talent Show which took place recently. He has a unique, a very British, sense of humor.

THORP. It's a very adult sense of humor. And that's going to be a real strength to him when he's an adult. But it's problematic when he's a kid.

FELTON. It's very problematic. He wanted to do a routine based on the Robin Williams film called *Good Morning, Vietnam!* Williams does this routine in the film where he talks about Nixon coming to visit the troops. And he sets it up, and then caps it with the line: "Yeah, the Big Dick will be here tomorrow!" And Peter wanted to do that line. So I took a practical stance. I said: "You're really just asking for unnecessary trouble. Because nobody is going to remember Robin Williams, and Vietnam, and Richard Nixon—they're only going to remember some kid standing up there saying, "Big Dick!" And they're going to take it the wrong way. So just do yourself a favor, and find some other way to do that."

His solution was not to do the thing at all. Not even to be in the show! So—

THORP. It's all context. And that's the hard part. We've gotten at least one call this year—one I took from a parent who was very unhappy with some materials from one of the community resources. It was poetry which was pretty raw, and the person was outraged that we would be reading this in class. And I've got to be careful about that, because you and I, perhaps—our natural inclination is to honor the intrinsic value of recognized literature. And clearly, the context of this was not Howard Stern shock theory, reading some scatological passages so we could chuckle about it; it was in the context of whatever the study unit was. So it was perfectly appropriate educational context.

On the other hand, we read about that teacher down in Los Angeles somewhere, who was suspended for showing the film "American Beauty" in class. Because a good school system, and most school systems, have a policy against "R"-rated movies. Is that okay? I can't say that it's not okay. And arguably, freshmen and sophomores anyway shouldn't be seeing R-rated movies, because you have to be seventeen, or some such age, to see them.

FELTON. Yes. Sure.

THORP. Or maybe even twenty-one. So there's an issue there. Schools have to be really careful of the context in which they do things. And that's where kids make mistakes. Because kids don't have as much context, personally. And kids don't think about context, so much. And context can be viewed both as a life skill, from a Freudian superego point of view—that kind of context. But also it could be from—I mean, arguably, politics is *all* about context. And context ends up being compromise, and your whole life's career as a politician might be to achieve compromise when in fact, all you're doing is sacrificing your principles over and over again. And at what point do you say: "No, I'm not going to compromise on that! No way!" And out you go from getting that fever.

Kids just don't have context. And Peter is a kid I think who has less context than some other kids do, even at his age. There's a more narrow vision on his part—which again, is probably going to be and already is a strength of his, in so many ways. But as we talked some number of months ago about his role in the sexual harassment group discussions we had here, he made a number of comments which were very adult, and very poignant and very revealing and very courageous.

But he missed the contextual setting, in a way where they didn't have the impact that he hoped they would have. And as a consequence—and again, I mean, one of his strengths is he's perceptive-intensive about that, and so he knew that was the case, I believe, which increased his frustration level probably more; and in fact, he was genuinely expressing frustration and openness to engaging in dialogue about "How I feel? Tell me how you feel"—and when he didn't get many takers in response to that, my guess is it increased his frustration level, and he was kind of left making comments like: "Why? Why don't people understand me? Why didn't they get it? Why didn't they respond?"

FELTON. Yes.

THORP. And in part, it's because his comments were more adult, more provocative, more "out-there" in terms of the general nature of what the topic meant to us; but also because he doesn't see the context of the issue. And that's typical of groups of kids. Some folks don't see context because they've never had to see context. Maybe it's because either their family circumstances are such that they don't have to worry about context.

And here's one Peter would love: My fiancée Donna's son Boone had a "play date," as they call it—a term that drives me crazy!—with another kid yesterday. She took the two of them to the movies. And she was driving the car around, and headed in toward a garage, and stopped and looked back and said: "Oops, I can't go in here. It cost seven bucks for parking." So she started to back out, and the kid who was there as Boone's guest turned to Donna and said: "Well, pay the seven bucks and go in and park!"

Now, this is a nine-year-old kid saying that. And Donna said: "I just wanted to smack the little bastard!" So here's a kid who is completely and totally unpopular at school. And Boone, who is Donna's son, is also somewhat of a fringe element, and they hook up at those moments at lunch when people look around and see who else is sitting by himself or herself at the table. Boone's lack of context is an obliviousness to the concerns of others, the needs of others; but he clearly has—and adults can see this—he has a sweet and gentle obliviousness to bumping into people that are there, which is one of his neurological phenomena. Whereas this other kid, his lack of context has manifest itself in a way where he's utterly obnoxious, and comes clearly, as you have discerned, from a background of enormous wealth where money is not an issue. Donna went on later, to get them some snacks, and she said; "I'll get you one thing, and you can share it." And he said: "I'm not sharing! I want this!"

FELTON. Wow.

THORP. And you can imagine what Donna's reaction to that was. Everyone else says, "Aw, it's just a kid." But she wants to smack him. I imagine the problems that kid's going to have in school, and already does, clearly. The parents have kind of thrown up their hands, gotten therapists, and said: "What are we going to do with our poor kid?" And the answer is: "Maybe start teaching him some contextual value about money," because the kid was given, I believe, fifty bucks for the day! You know, they said: "You're going to the movies, here's fifty bucks, take care of it."

FELTON. My God!

THORP. So context is everything; timing is everything. And this is a school which is also trying to teach kids. And one of our challenges is that we've authorized our kids to be vocal here, and to be part of the conversation of school and to build programs and to talk about the neurological profile. But we've let the genie out of the bottle in some ways, or opened Pandora's box is probably a better way of putting it, in that we've underestimated the degree to which kids don't have context, or don't understand context, and therefore don't know yet how to communicate appropriately their needs. They just hear the first half of the sentence, which is "communicate your needs," and they don't hear the word "appropriately."

Chapter Eighteen

THE MOUTHS OF BABES

"Is the charter school movement putting out the right marketing message? And if so, how can we reinforce that?....If not, why not? And what *is* the right marketing message?"

4 April—*One thing I suspect Peter Thorp had forgotten—and which even I forgot from time to time, despite my efforts to uncover such secrets—was the fact that despite his protestations, he had a private life.*

While I waited for him to come from his office, invite me in and begin our two o'clock appointment, the time evaporated. I enjoyed conversation with the receptionist—a young Yugoslav émigrée, who would soon leave her position to seek her fortune in filmmaking—the time crept dangerously toward the point where not enough would remain to complete a meaningful interview. I had a photography group meeting with students planned to follow our dialogue session; now—with half the 1.5 hours eaten away by Peter's attention to a meeting with other administrators—the pressing need of that gathering would eclipse my meeting with their Principal. The situation—which had happened several times—left me feeling irritated, and helpless.

Surely, I told the apologizing receptionist, he must have had some crisis. In the meeting with him, I learned, were the Assistant Principal, the school counselor, and the Academic Dean. This was not a time to press—more than the one interruption I asked her to carry out—an announcement of my presence. But when at last the meeting ended, and a chagrined and embarrassed Peter invited me in, I would be made to realize that what had detained me, and disconcerted the higher echelon of Gateway's leadership, was not a school crisis at all. Not, that is, in the strict sense of the word.

Peter's private life, it appeared, had come up from behind, and landed a blow. Crestfallen, red-eyed, and not at all the stalwart figure whom I'd watched speak with great Gateway boosterism at a school assembly only the morning before, Peter repeated his apology. I closed the door, made as fast a setup of machinery as I could, calculated how to abridge my session's plan, and ultimately listened to him explain an agony he had obviously not been prepared to carry.

FELTON. Let me save the "ponderous" questions for our next meeting. And use this—as Jung would say, this "wonderful opportunity!" to do just some "rote" business, some smaller points that I wanted to fill in—

THORP. "Chinking," as we call it in the log cabin business.

FELTON. "Chinking?" Ah! I guess I can see that. Well, that's what we'll do.

When we left off a couple of sessions back, I wanted you to carve out an impromptu ode about your lovely person Donna, and her meaning in your life. And even though I now know a little bit about her son Boone, I'm kind of curious as to how that relationship works out. Is it a "stepfather surrogate" relationship? Is it a friendship? Are you there as a family member "without portfolio?" How do you view that whole constellation?

THORP. I've got to tell you—you're catching me on a rough day. I have had one of those phone calls that I was just listening to again as you came in. It was a phone call from the head of the school where my daughter goes. She has some serious concerns about staying there. And it's likely that she's going to leave. So I'm kind of dealing with that kind of family stuff right now. So your questions are right in line with the theme of the day!—

FELTON. Well—I appreciate your telling me that. If you would rather flag the whole session, we don't have to—

THORP. No, no! I'm fine. And I'm perfectly—

FELTON. I'm so sorry!

THORP. —I just want you to know that that's governing my head right now. And it's just the kind of thing that one deals with as a parent, and—could have an influence on the way I respond to your question.

Where does one start? Donna's a fascinating person who has a great combination of what I would call "white collar intelligence" and "blue collar work ethic."

FELTON. Wow! That *is* a combination.

THORP. That could be seen as an aspersion in all sorts of ways! Anyway, the result of that combination is that in many ways she's ideally suited to what she does. Like all of us, I suppose, we go back and forth on the question: "Is this the right life's work? What if I've got other choices?" "What if—" "What if—?" You know. It's not just "the grass is greener" syndrome. It's the luxury that our generation has that our parents' generation had, which is the luxury of choices. I think our parents' generation, particularly the Depression era, had, my parents had, and I trust yours—

FELTON. Indeed.

THORP. —had fewer choices. And the question—and this is not unrelated to teenagers—the question in that sort of circumstance is: "Who has it better?" And the simple answer is: "If you've got more choices, that fact, by definition, is better." But not necessarily; because one of the things that has evolved from that is less institutional loyalty, which may or may not be a good thing. I mean, obviously, the extreme examples of –in my own parents' case, my father's insistence that my mother would not work is something that proves it's great that that ethic is pretty well gone. Similarly in schools, the first school I worked in, commemorated on the back of the chair that you're sitting in, talking to some of the "Old Guard" faculty who had arrived in those first years of the 1930s when the school was established, it was made clear, and I think maybe explicitly clear, to the faculty wives that they would not work. And their purpose was to be around school, available, and the proverbial "to pour tea." It was not appropriate for them to have jobs outside of the school, because that's not what a boarding school was all about.

So we have all sorts of choices. And this is related to Donna, in a sense that because she's a very talented woman, she has a lot of choices. And the choice that she made three years ago, to leave the law and to go into education was a choice that she was really excited about, and really enjoyed; and she then made the choice to leave education and go to somewhere else, which then got intermingled with her decision about me, and my decision about her, because she had pretty much made up her mind to leave a school called Midlands, and then we intersected with each other, and sort of planned to "run off together," so to speak. And she's fallen back into the law, and fallen back into the same field, and she's fallen back into the firm that she worked with two jobs previously.

She's very talented at what she does. And what she does is kind of nasty work, which is negotiating on behalf of her clients, which are typically public agency, school boards, and community college boards and that sort of thing. She negotiates with teachers' unions. And it's very difficult work, because it's, you know, it's the height of the adversarial process. But she's good, in that she again has this interesting combination of talented warrior and blue collar work ethic, so she really, truly, generally understands the needs for people to make a living, and doesn't deny them the opportunity to do it, and isn't going to squeeze every last drop of blood of a salary compensation package. And she educates school boards about what they need to do to be smart and appropriate, and legal, and all the kinds of things you would do to try to create harmony in a situation which by definition is disharmonious, given the adversarial nature of the collective bargaining process. So she's excellent in what she does.

I'm not sure if this is really what you're interested in, in terms of my "take" on her work! But it also speaks to our relationship, in the sense that there's a lot of intellectual firepower between the two of us. It's "spark-plugging" between the two of us. Which is fine. The downside of all that intellectual excitement is: We don't have much time for each other, because we're both working far harder than we should be.

That sort of speaks to your second question about Boone; and he suffers from this himself. It's the sign of the times, with dual working couples, and he's fine at the school he goes to, which is a wonderful school, the Marin Country Day School, as I told you. They have a great program there. And he's such an interesting kid, in his own intellectual proclivities. He's a fascinating kid in terms of his interests and the depth of his interests. And at the same time, he has—I don't know if they're really disabilities, but many differences; and they're getting in the way of his success in traditional schools. It will be interesting to see what plays out for him over the next six years, to see what school counts for with him.

FELTON. Any difference having, so to speak, a "boy child" in what you do?

THORP. To be real honest about it, I'm so busy that I'm not a huge part of his life. I don't mean to sound maudlin, but I'm doing this job seven days a week, twelve hours a day, and so I don't have time for anybody else, really. That's a whole other conversation at some point; but in response to that question: Yes and no. He's less boyish than the typical kid in his class, which is an issue for him. And yet I've got to believe in the long run he's going to be the beneficiary of that.

This past Sunday's Magazine Section of the New York Times had an article by Ian Sullivan. He's an active gay writer, a very talented writer. And the reason that I mention that he's a gay writer and why that's relevant, is that his article is entitled "Is there truly a difference in 'female': The role of testosterone in human development." And I'm looking forward to reading that. And Boone is a less testosterone-laden kid than most nine-year-olds.

FELTON. My question actually only intended to refer to the fact that your own children were girls, and now you are a boy's father-figure. But continue.

THORP. Well, this is an issue for Boone, being in a pre-testosterone-laden school, which Marin Country Day is. But I've got to believe in the fullness of his life, he going to benefit from the fact that he's less testosterone-injected than some other kids. I mean, he's a very sweet boy, is one way of summing it up. And some of his friends are *not* sweet kids. He's a very interesting *naïf*, who's always going to be able to stay naïve as long as he can, without suffering the consequences of ridicule by his classmates. He suffers by virtue of his innocence.

FELTON. I think the younger Peter Felton would have recognized what you're describing.

One of my other topics also has to do with gender: I made a visit here on the second half of a half-day, "in-service" day, when students had been dismissed at noon. And of course the regular in-session activity was absent; but there were a number of people buzzing around, using the copier, moving some things out into the hall. All of them, with the possible exception of the receptionist, Iva—all of them were *male.* There was Corkran, the physical education teacher, and Gottlieb, the counselor, and some others. And the entire feeling in the school changed! It really struck me, because it made me think how much of a component of what I feel when I come here is the impress of the nurturing female side. And how much was that element that I felt, in that very brief time that I came in and saw all those guys running around, was the—let's call it the "hunter-warrior" side; but whatever it was called, it was clearly different. It took me immediately back to my youthful summer camp times, which were all male. And yet all that these guys were doing was what they did all the time; it was just that the women weren't here. And it had a profound effect on the place, and on me.

It reminded me of something which I had once noted down because it was so interesting, that the poet C.L. Stand once wrote. And it was something like this—I couldn't remember it exactly:

> *I believe that gender supersedes race, even species.*
> *I believe that a male dog is closer related to me, my nature, my impulses, than a female human.*
> *When I need to imagine a truly foreign being—such as a Martian—I imagine a woman.*
> *And yet—my sensibilities, my artistic explorations, are probably more feminine than masculine.*

And obviously, where I'm leading is: What does an attitude like that—and what do the feelings that I get seeing simply a switch of gender, or an absence of one here in the school—tell us about what's going on here? To how teaching proceeds, given that the age of the people who are being taught makes them particularly sensitive to gender issues? In their own way, for their own reasons. How much does this play in things?

THORP. Well, you can clearly come at that question from such a variety of points of view. The first thing that comes to mind is just the difference in kids. And I know your question began with the faculty; but one observation is that if we filled this school based solely on merit in the application process, it would be ninety-five percent girls. Now, of course, that in some way is stating the obvious, which is: Girls are developmentally more advanced than boys. And it plays out in school, where they're more mature. And some people make the mistake, I believe, of concluding they're more docile, and therefore, they're less confrontational, and therefore they're more successful in public schools because they cooperate more. And when you read recommendations from public school teachers, the extent to which kids are cooperative or not often defines the summative judgment that's drawn in a recommendation of kids. And that's kind of interesting. That in fact, schooling is a *narrowing* experience, rather than a broadening experience. And again, it's easy for me to say, not teaching in a seventh-grade classroom!—but you know, clearly, the value of— "Wow, it's great! This kid really thinks outside the box!" is not something you get too often in recommendations.

So the girls here are not unexpectedly more advanced. The challenge for the boys here is their being asked to do the same program. And by and large, they're less developmentally ready for it. We as the adults and as the teachers need to be somewhat cognizant of the fact that they are, in fact, less developmentally ready for that as a species, than girls are. Again: We need to be careful of "One-size-fits-all."

So, recognizing that girls' language areas are more quickly developed than guys, we need at least to be aware of that in the classroom setting, where that difference gets acknowledged.

It's also the case that explains to some extent the reason why guys dominate conversation through power, because they can't do it through language. There have been all sorts of studies that speak to that. I could look. But there are also studies about the way teachers treat kids differently in the classroom, based on the gender. And the typical study indicates that teachers pay a lot more attention to boys than they do to girls. And there is explication of why that is, and what good a gender-neutral teacher is. That's certainly something that I've paid attention to, and something that I try to model and incorporate.

I don't feel—I'm speaking now about the faculty—I don't feel as huge a gap, as wide a gap in the male teachers-female teachers here at Gateway, in terms of their approach, the way they work, what their goals are, their mission. And I see, to the contrary, much more gender neutrality among the faculty. And I'm only about ninety-percent joking when I say this—that as soon as you throw the physical education teacher in there, it screws everything up, as far as gender-neutrality! Depending on who the combination of people is, as soon as you walk in, and they're talking about—you know—the NCAA basketball tournament, it takes on a kind of jocularity about it that you wouldn't find necessarily in a similar gathering of women teachers.

But it is interesting to me that I don't see real gender division here between the male and female faculty. And perhaps I'm blind to that, to be honest, in your sense. Though for all of us males, we're both blessed by and cursed by the need to solve problems, as you and I have talked before, and that might speak to one of the gender issues here in regard to the pattern of saying, in effect: "Be done with it!" and that's it. And that's not to imply that women are not decisive; for the women here at Gateway are decisive. But they come at it from a different perspective, I think.

So my sense is: You caught a fleeting moment, which was very real in your impression of that fleeting moment. But less so as an indicator of gender at the school. The gender issues at the school are ones in fact that we have talked previously about, and as I've just stated, about kids and conflict, and how young girls deal with conflict, and how young boys deal with that conflict.

FELTON. Yes. Well, good. I think you pegged it. As perhaps that fleeting moment. I think it was that the men were just "down to business"—a bit lost in thought, or taking advantage of the student void to relax the nerves. And when I looked at it, I realized also that normally, even in just in passing through here, if I run into one of the women teachers—I see more teeth! You have more of a rich moment, you know? Brief, but no less interactive. Whereas with the men it's "What's new? What's going on?" And that's it—if even that. It's understandable; I'm probably that way too. Just an old gender truism.

Let me spin on a dime: How's the college prep class going?

THORP. We're a little bit behind where I wanted to be. Also, I had a little bit of a "wake-up" call from a kid. We were talking about the lessons we're learning from college admissions catalogues, and this one kid got teary, and I couldn't understand what the problem was. Now, Meghvi had taken over the class for a while, so she understood. She talked with the kid, and then I talked with her yesterday a second time about it. This student, was very upset that she hadn't yet found a college which she felt was just right for her. And I said to myself: "Whoa! I'm doing exactly the opposite of what I intended to do in this class. Where did I go wrong?!"

Everything's okay, now, we've done some talking about it. She's a kid who's somewhat high-strung in certain ways, and gets easily frustrated. But I'm trying to figure out how to go next; and the very next step is the financial aid part of it. And the next step after that is going to be the college essay. And I'm wrestling—and I'd be curious as to your input—as to whether the essay-writing would *increase* the anxiety or *decrease* the anxiety? I mean, frankly, I don't know anymore. But I have this fear that to have them sit down and write an essay, and then critiquing the essay might sound (a) too much like school, and (b) might increase the anxiety. But I don't know. I've lost my way.

FELTON. Well, I think if you did it, if it was done as a strict academic exercise, it *would* be anxiety-producing. And in fact I think the way—as we used to say in theater—the way to approach that is to "throw it away." It's to do it strictly as casually—not "casually," but as *informally* as possible. So as to open up those kids. And then, all of the things—the things that make kids tense about writing, as I've experienced it, are the fear of meeting structural needs. And performing in some kind of programmatic way that will please somebody else's idea of writing, rather than *just letting stuff come out!*

This is what you were able so well to do that day in class, with the two girls who volunteered—to one of whom you said, after she'd given an idea of an essay: "If we'd tape recorded that, it would be all right there!" And the other girl, who had some experience which caused you to say: "Let's talk!" And that was so wonderful, I thought; because you just grabbed that kid! And that kid was saved for life, because the teacher, and principal, and person whom she's depending on to get her over this burden, was on her side, and taking her hand, held her hand! I thought it was wonderful!

And—that kind of openness and relaxation should be in the essay process. Else, they're going to be deadly.

THORP. Do you think it's "do-able"?

FELTON. Sure!

THORP. Well, then, if you want to get involved, let me know. You can tell, the class hasn't got such a rigid structure to it that—it's pretty flexible.

FELTON. Great. Yeah. That would be fine.

Well, let's wrap up the session by your telling a little bit about the Charter Education Conference held recently, which you and some Gateway students attended. Is there anything that really struck you as noteworthy about that event?—and anything you might care to relate about Erica and Patrick, the students who attended with you?

THORP. They were really incredible. Really remarkable! In the conference each of them was going to say something. And of course, in a situation like that—we did no preparation, and therefore I was pretty nervous, at the beginning of the lunch, having no idea what they would say, and how they would respond. And frankly, I was concerned with how they would stack up against the other kids, there's always that kind of comparative aspect of these things. But they were terrific; I wasn't just saying it to make hay. They were by far the two best kids on the panel. And they were by far the two best kids on the panel because they *are* thoughtful, serious kids—not dour, but serious. The Gateway kids really got the seriousness of the occasion. And by that, I mean, they understood the magnitude of being asked a question. The moderator was Joe Nathan, Joe Nathan, who is from the Humphrey Center at the University of Minnesota, and one of the country's leading charter school figures.

Here were six hundred people—educators—having their lunch, so it was a receptive audience. And these two kids were really *thoughtful* about their responses, to the point where not only were we thrilled by how good they were, but we were really moved by how insightful they were.

You know, they could have answered in any kind of frivolous, expected way. And some of the other kids on the panel did. One of the questions was: "What would you change about the school?" And one kid answered: "We want a pool table." But one of our kids—I think it was Erica—answered: "I understand one of the trade-offs I made to come to a charter school is that I'd be part of this pioneering effort; and yet, I was coming to a school that didn't have everything like a regular school, and I had to make a choice as to whether or not the quality of my education versus the extracurricular things—" It was brilliant!

Another question was: "Why did you choose a charter school?" Erica said: "I love going to school at Gateway because it's safe." And—you know, that was very gratifying to hear. But it was also a very adult perspective. She was saying, "I'm going to the school because it was the good thing to do,' I'm going to give you your money's worth, and tell you my school is safe. And you need to hear from me how important it is to me, as a kid living in the inner city, to go to a safe school." I mean, she didn't say this; but her intimation was: "And you better make damned sure your schools are safe, too, if you want kids like me at your school!"

And Patrick commented on this question "What would you change about charter schools?" or "What would you change about your school?" And his response was: "What I would change is that I wouldn't have to be spending all my time explaining to my friends back home in the East Bay what charter schools are all about." And he said: "I've spent hours talking about charter schools, and they don't get it; and I explain to them again!" It was very humorous, and yet it had a very important point, which is: "Hey, you guys—you know, we are different, and you've got a marketing message to pay attention to, given that my friends don't understand what a charter school is. And if you want people like me, you've got to get the message out about the charter school."

It was totally brilliant! Nathan's very first response—the very first question was: "What are you most proud of?" And Erica's response was: "I'm most proud that I have a 4.0 grade average." And when it came to Patrick's turn, about four or five kids later, I was so moved by what he said right at the beginning. The very first words out of his mouth were: "Well, you know, I'm dyslexic and ADD." And then he went on to say was: "What I'm most proud of is doing what I'm doing at Gateway, and being very successful at Gateway." And he so disarmed the audience by just that statement—"Well, you know, I'm dyslexic and ADD"—and being totally comfortable with saying that, that—and Meghvi and I and a couple of other people really looked at each other, and we immediately were taking the temperature of the room, to see how people reacted. And people were profoundly moved by that statement; I mean, not that they had tears, in that sense; but that clearly, the body language was revealing that they were saying to themselves: "Wow! That's kid's a really-together kid, to be able to say this in front of six hundred adults," and the conclusion from that was: "Wow! That must be a really special school, where he would have the courage to say that."

So they were wonderful! It was really impressive to watch. And very gratifying. And it's a further lesson to me, in talking to the faculty, and talking to the kids: "Let's give the kids more and more opportunities to do this sort of thing. You can't learn—if you don't have the opportunity to do it, you're not going to learn how to do it. So let's make sure that we're doing it."

The conference itself was interesting for me, because I'd been appointed on the board of this organization. So, you know, I'm now beginning to play a role in the charter school movement, and people are beginning to recognize me.

The interesting thing about the charter school movement is that in a conference like this, there are a lot of what I would call "101" sessions. I mean, it's so basic information, for someone like me who's been around all these areas, that—I don't know how you do at these conferences, but I go in and give a workshop five minutes. And if they haven't done anything interesting in five minutes, I'm out of there until the next workshop.

I went to a bunch of them where it was clear that it was pretty "101" stuff; and yet, I recognized that one person's "101" stuff is another person's graduate level stuff. And for me the financial part of charter schools is graduate level stuff. And so I went to some "101" financial things. Which were really helpful, you know, if you come away from a conference with three or four significant chunks of new information, it's been worth the time you give it.

It's interesting to watch the evolution of the charter school movement, because one of the points I was making about this "101" stuff is that there is this combination of relatively unsophisticated but well-meaning folks behind the charter school movement who need a lot of help and a lot of guidance. So one of the sessions was really a "101" course—"How do you build a board of trustees?" And I thought, "Come on!, this is pretty simple stuff." Only it isn't, for somebody who's never been in that circumstance. And then it goes to the other end of the spectrum where you get some very sophisticated people who really are thinking an awful lot about education, and what it means, and the great mass of people who are relatively sophisticated on a relatively small number of issues. And we had a boost in that. But most of the value is in personal connections. In being able to pick up a phone and call somebody.

I was on a panel, on which I was the facilitator. So Gateway actually got pretty good "play." After this panel, we had thirty people come here and see the school. They were here for about forty-five minutes. And they were impressed by what we were trying to accomplish. The kids, again, were just fabulous, and by far the highlight of the conference. It was really great. Both of these kids, at other times, have done similar things in front of different groups of people.

Patrick, in particular, has this marvelous sense of humor. Mel Levine believes that music is the most sophisticated of the neurological functions, that the composer or the musician is "firing on all pistons." My variation on that is: I think stand-up comedians are the highest form of neurological function! And for a kid like Patrick to have a sense of humor, is really a sign of very sophisticated neurological processing, which is so far advanced from being ADD and dyslexic, that it's good we're in an era where he'll get a chance to capitalize on the strengths he has.

FELTON. Was it a full spectrum of people attending, or only school heads?

THORP. No, we had principals, faculty, we had various faculty go at various times. Board people, people from organizations that support charter schools, a lot of "Silicone Valley" types were there, charter school people from Minnesota and Washington, and Florida. The California organization is the second-largest organization of charter schools. And it's probably the most organization as a collective, which says a lot about this organization out here.

I actually have a tricky role to play. I mean, I've actually been intending on playing a tricky role on that board. Some things that we've been talking about previously worked their way into my critique of the charter school movement, both in terms of some of the things it's doing, and some of the things it's not doing. You know, when I feel it's appropriate, I'm a believer in the "back-bench" approach: You keep your mouth shut for a period of time until you get the lay of the land.

But at some point I want to really speak of the question: Is the charter school movement putting out the right marketing message? And if so, how can we reinforce that? I mean, if not, why not? And what *is* the right marketing message?   Obviously, by raising the question I'm making the second question beg the first question. It'll be interesting to see how that plays out; and to be a voice in it. It's really tricky to read between the lines.   The executive director of the organization, I think, is in over her head; and she has a number of talented areas, but this organization has more sophisticated challenges. This way, to be considering legislation is not something that I see her doing. My purpose is not to get on, and eventually to call for her head when I feel the time is right, but to find out whether or not the organization can be as sophisticated as I think it needs to be.   For they're asked to face serious issues.

FELTON.   Well, we'll follow it.

Chapter Nineteen

CURRICULUM VITAE

"So what we're wrestling with is: How do we accomplish our mission? Well, that's exactly what we *ought* to be wrestling with! Every year, every day!—we learn more about what we're doing well, and what we're not doing well. Every year we learn, every day we learn more about what our kids need more of and less of. And we're really looking toward next year, trying to answer the questions that remain unanswered for us. And these are more 'process-related' questions, and from a teacher's point of view, substitute the word 'pedagogy' for 'process.'

"Yes, we have content issues....But the primary issues for us as a school, as a teaching faculty, as a professional group of men and women is: How do we do what we want to do? The pedagogy—what teaching methodologies, strategies, approaches, are effective here, and what ones are ineffective here? And we're doing that in the midst of trying to create the content, and trying to put together lesson plans, and trying to grade kids' papers, and, you know—the list goes on and on...."

11 April—*A young woman sat in the waiting area of the Gateway High School administrative office. Iva, the pleasant receptionist, a Croatian lilt behind her well-schooled English, made the introductions:*
"This is Amy Thorp. She's going to be a student here."

Opposite me was Gateway's latest tenth-grader. With blond hair, a bright look in her eyes, fashionable piercing placements, and a quietude expected from one who was—at a late hour of the year—"the new kid on the block," Peter Thorp's younger daughter appeared to me to be as poised as any new student could be, considering that she'd just left friends behind, and in a sudden move had distanced herself by four hundred miles from the boarding school where her father had been headmaster. Now Amy was enrolled—hastily, there was no denying it—in his new academic province in San Francisco's Inner Sunset District. I exchanged a few words, most of them greetings and welcome, and left her to what had to be an uncomfortable uncertainty about what lay ahead.

Thus my subject had doubled the number of dialogue-participants' family members who were students at this charter school. I wondered if Peter's daughter, like my own son, would become illustrative of personal and school issues which periodically dotted the landscape of our discussions. For now, Amy's resettlement program would need to take its own course, which I didn't envy her. For her dad, as busy as Peter Thorp was with the business of running a charter school, the mixture of parental distress at whatever Amy's difficulty at boarding school had been was muted by his fatherly pride, as his attractive offspring began her new sojourn in his immediate purview.

FELTON.   I guess first in order are congratulations for proving that good looks can strike two generations. I just met your daughter outside.

THORP.   Oh, you met Amy, outside? All right. Yes, the times, they are a'changin', in the Thorp household. Was she looking like a deer in the headlights, or not?

FELTON.   No, no, she looked very capable. I imagine this is a lot for her to absorb right away, of course.

THORP.   She's pretty depressed, pretty nervous. She's lost the thing which was most important in her life, which was friends at her previous school; they're all not seeming now a part of her life. She's uprooted, and moving back to Dad again, and Dad's paramour, and away from her friends. And now she's going to Dad's school, and, you know, not knowing if or how she's going to fit in with Gateway kids. It's every permutation of adolescent *angst* rolled into one. It was tough getting her to come to school this morning.

FELTON.   I'll bet. Tenth grade, right?

THORP. Yes. So—we'll see. We're looking at—you know, this might be a stop-gap measure for us. Although we'll look at other options, there' *aren't* too many other options; which causes one to have an increasing appreciation for what parents in this city go through when you see what it means not to have your kids able to go to private schools.

FELTON. That's true.

In a previous session, you mentioned vocational training. And I'm wondering what your ideas were there? The larger question here is course structure: Whether you're comfortable with the curriculum that's developing, or if you're testy about some things, if you're uneasy, if you have ideas that aren't getting incorporated yet but you project, generally. What are the issues? And, of course, lest we forget!—how does all this gibe with downtown, with the Board of Education?

THORP. This all forms a key question; and actually, we were just meeting about curriculum, so it's a timely question as well. And I'm happy to talk really at great length because it's "*the*" question in terms of school development.

Let me respond to the vocational question first.

Clearly, one of the things you need to learn in schools, and one of the things educators need to learn in general, is: You can't be all things to all people, and you can't do everything. And so you've got to make choices; and the challenge of schooling is that nobody wants to make a choice. Or, in a kind of reverse analogy: It's what I call the "Nuclear waste dump" theory—we've got to have them, but not in my back yard, dammit!

But schools need to make choices, and that's a preface to this: Gateway can't be what it's trying to be and have vocational training, if you will, if we're talking about vocational training as "shop" and preparing for a post-secondary career, rather than going on to college. Now, having said that, I'm increasingly aware that some percentage of our kids probably are not going to go on to college. And the issue might not be finances. On National Public Radio this morning a teacher in Silicon Valley was talking about his two kids, one of whom left college and started working in this "dot-com" company there. And the father said to the kid: "Why do you want to do that? It's a start-up company, and it's only got seven or eight employees; what a risk!" And now a year later, the guy's making six figures, as compared with the man's his second son, who's a teacher, who's still living at home with the father because he can't afford to go out and get any housing.

And of course, Son Number One is probably making twice what the father is, after twenty years of teaching. So there might be some very rational decisions among some percentage of our kids about: "Who needs college? I'm going to stray to the dot-com world. I mean, Bill Gates didn't need it." Or: "Who needs the world of the mind when the world of the hands, particularly in a building boom like San Francisco, is paying eighteen bucks an hour?"

However, what I hope I was making reference to at that point is— and I'm going to stretch my own vocabulary here because I don't know the root of it—it would be great if Gateway produced *a*-vocational training, rather than vocational training. And I'm imagining that the root of that word has something to do with finding one's voice. And if I'm right about that, and I may be totally off my Latin, which is rusty, it sets up one pole—namely, that Gateway can produce avocational training, where kids are finding their voices, literally and figuratively, in addition to finding the voices of their teachers. Of course, the education "game" is outguessing your teacher. A student tries to anticipate what the teacher's going to want, or what homework assignment to do, or especially to outguess them on the test. If you win those games, then you've got it "nailed." That's why education, as I've said before in these sessions, is the world of the logical, sequential, causal—because that's the kind of mind that outguesses teachers pretty quickly. If, however—and here comes the other pole—the focus is to find your *own* voice, rather than the teacher's voice, so to speak, in the avocational training, then, yeah, that is consistent with what I hope we're able to accomplish over time. And that is where that masterpiece program, undefined, ill-defined as it is, and unformed as it is at this point, for all sorts of reasons, will, I hope, play a significant role. It could, in fact, meld in with avocational training: "I just want to get excited about something, and gee, I realize that you have artistic, creative skills, and I found it out through this portfolio I developed working with this guy Felton in Photography Class—and by the way: That might be an interesting career for me!" You know.

So the vocational training might happen as a result of the avocational training at Gateway. It might be a serendipitous result where it puts a kid on a path to something that might be of interest to him or her.

I learned recently of a kid whom I taught in—I'm guessing, 1979; and I introduced him to art history. I just got the word that he now owns his own gallery down in Soho in New York City. He was being interviewed for a video made by this previous school. He made reference to me, stating that it was that course that he took with me that got him excited, and he ended up majoring in art, and then opening up his gallery. Now, I don't say that for *me*; it 's just that those weird kind of things happen in schools, where a kid gets touched by either a program or an educator in a way that suddenly, vocational avenues start showing themselves.

But Gateway's philosophy is more to try to help kids find—again, if I'm using the Latin root correctly—their "voice," therefore their passion, and therefore enable them to act on that passion. Rather than a specific plan such as: "We're going to teach you some skills that you can apply in an area." That's what summer vacation is for.

FELTON. Well, I think that etymologically it really is an interesting concept and word. And it magnifies with all the different prefixes that you have—to "invoke" something; an "invocation" in a liturgical sense. Even to *pro*voke an action. The "voice" idea perhaps needs turning to a similar word: One's *calling*. When I think of the curriculum here, I think of searching for just that kind of spark or impetus that is going to ignite the future art gallery owner, or whatever the choice is. And, as with so many of those things, I daresay, it's not where you think it's going to be.

THORP. Right.

FELTON. It doesn't always come recognizably. It might shoot off from this unit in mathematics, or that unit in geography; but it's not necessarily going to be something immediately derived from the discipline itself. Something will spark there. Do you plan to take it into greater technical areas, that are going to involve more than just the lecture-format kind of inspiration? Are you going to have to get heavy with equipment, and—?

THORP. The easiest area to pursue, in responses to what you just said, is computer-related, technology-related fields. You know—graphic design. One can make a total case for a graphic design course here at Gateway which in no way is intended to be vocational training, when in fact, it is! I mean, not intended to be vocational training; but in fact, it's—you're having your cake and eating it too, so to speak. Film—you know, we could do a course on film here, and video of a variety of capacities. And that.

It happens that this was part of a discussion just before you came in. Philosophy translates into bucks pretty quickly; and my thought is to inject the "buck" issue at the appropriate time, which cannot be too early, because it stifles creative thinking—"Well, we can't afford it"—nor can it be too late, which happens when you let people run with an idea, and then you say: "Well, you know, it's a great idea but we can't afford it." That just ticks people off. So the "buck" issue has to come in at the appropriate time.

Again, revealing a personal bias: One of the things that I'd like to see here in the senior year is an architecture class.

FELTON. Aha!

THORP. And I think, depending on how that goes, the possibilities inherent in that kind of class range from the utterly creative—you know, "We'll run the class with a pencil, and that's it!"—to the utterly vocational—"We're going to teach you drafting and the precision of line; and by the way, while we're doing that, you might be surprised: We're also going to teach you some art history and some aesthetic appreciation, without you even knowing it."

But architecture to me is one of those fields of intellectual pursuit or vocational endeavor, which brings together so many possibilities and so many neurological piston-firings that it's really something pretty cool! It would be great to offer a class—and this is where I have zero expertise, so I'm not even sure I'm going to describe accurately what I should be describing—a class in music, which gets the equivalent neurological pistons firing about music. And if you talk to Mel Levine, he would know how to describe that class. I don't, because I don't know the pedagogy behind that kind of music. I don't know if it's music theory; I don't know if it's music notation. I don't know if it's "improv" in a jazz class. It might be all of the above—to do that sort of thing. So it would be nice to have a series of electives for our kids in the senior year that bring together creative endeavor and vocational pursuit in a way that a kid could really get excited about something. That idea, however, quickly will become a "buck" question. The finances of that will quickly come into play.

Having said that, I've got to believe that we could track down some folks who are interested in doing *pro bono* work at a school like this—you know, an architect who would come in twice a week for an hour, or a couple of hours, whatever, and do an architecture class. Or, a lawyer could come in and teach the kids about the law. And that through that vehicle, teach them about precision in thinking and precision in writing, and where you put that modifier is going to change your case one way or the other. I just read in the paper a couple of weeks ago about Proposition 22—is that the "Gay Marriage" issue?—

FELTON. Yes.

THORP. —That this guy "deconstructed" the proposition. And because they put the word "only" in the wrong place, this guy is saying: "Aha! They didn't do anything in the proposition. In fact, it doesn't ban gay marriage"—and I'd have to see the wording and repeat the article to do it. But he made a point that the whole proposition is bogus because they put "only" in the wrong place. And they modified the wrong word with "only." You know, and that's the kind of great "fun" stuff that I'd get jazzed about, in teaching a class about the law and the precision about the law. And as I think we may have said in a previous session: Kids love studying law. And so if I do in fact teach U.S. History—an Advanced Placement U.S. History course, I'm thinking of beginning the study with the Bill of Rights. Which, you know, lays all sorts of foundations in obvious ways. But it also helps me to teach kids about precision of language. Because kids are really careless with language. And to show them the import of—by putting "only" in a different place, guys, changes the whole meaning of things. And so when you write, there's a purpose in writing with precision. I don't have to tell you that.

So—philosophy first, goals second, bucks third. But they're all interrelated.

FELTON. Good. I've involved myself over a period of years with a variety of arts, and I've always been struck by the fact that each excites the other, even though they appear, simplistically, to be opposite. And the best example of that, in the photography field, is Ansel Adams, who was a musician. Almost concert-level musician.

THORP. Really! I didn't realize that.

FELTON. Yeah. And then when he finally made the decision that he was not going to be a brilliant pianist—that he would have been a journeyman pianist, but not a brilliant one—he started giving his attention to photography, and found so many cognates!

THORP. Yeah. Yeah.

FELTON. You just wouldn't think that. But again: the neuron-firing found their pathways for him, and that's what would happen, I'm sure, here. Well, I hope you can pursue that.

THORP. Yeah. That's on the radar screen. The way you make finances a non-issue is you try to attract people with the idea of public service through a vehicle like this. And again, I've got to believe that we can find enough people in this town who would be interested in doing this sort of thing.

FELTON. Sure! Quite clearly.

THORP. And now, to your larger question.

We're at the point where we're starting planning for next year. Not that planning isn't going on all the time; but when you hit the post-Spring Vacation time at school, suddenly June looks close—which is great, on the one hand, and frightening, on the other hand!

We have a lot of curricular planning to do for many, many reasons which I could rattle off. Not the least of which, and the most obvious of which is, that we have another grade coming next year!—or so to say, the kids will grow into the eleventh grade, as you know so well. And so we've got an eleventh-grade program to develop. That's actually the easy part of curriculum development, because it's—well, you're going to do eleventh-grade humanities, right? Yeah, right—well, what are you going to do, given what we're doing so far in the ninth and tenth grade? Just given the way the world works, the eleventh grade is going to be focused on American History. I said "American" with emphasis, because it's looking like it's not going to be focused on U.S. History.

There is a naming confusion there; and I was actually partly responsible for it a number of years ago. Have we talked about the Advanced Placement program?

FELTON. Not directly; not other than its initials. Take a moment and clarify.

THORP. Okay. Advanced Placement was a program that's been in place now for about thirty-plus years, where kids in high school take alleged college-level classes. And depending on the test they take in May, and how well they do, they allegedly get credit in college for having completed college-level work at high school. You could tell I injected the two words "allegedly" in there. Under the original premise, it was in fact, in the dance program, advance placement for kids to come in and either waive out of introductory freshman-year-in-college programs and go straight into sophomore or junior-year high-level classes, or to get credit.

So I've taught kids over the year, who—one kid, I remember, entered Berkeley as a sophomore. And gained a year, and subtracted a year's worth of tuition; and so there's a financial consideration behind that.

FELTON. I didn't realize it was a formal approach. I knew there were kids who were doing this sort of thing, but I thought it was just perhaps an inspired kid who—

THORP. Like an honors class?

FELTON. Yes. Or even just an ambitious kid, who would find a way to "crash the college gates" early.

THORP. No. There's a difference between "honors class" and "advanced placement." You talk about an AP class—you're following a curriculum generated back in Princeton, New Jersey—you know, this college preparation. Now, again, the reason I injected the word "allegedly" is it's become, in my opinion, a perversion of what it originally was intended to be, which is: Give a kid a challenge, see if the kid passes the challenge successfully, or succeeds in the challenge, and give the kid credit by waiving him out of introductory classes. Well, what's happened in the last decade—and I'm only half-joking when I describe it this way—is that the freshman biology teachers at Grinnell and Williams have stood up in faculty meetings and said: "Ain't no way that this high school biology program is the equivalent of *my* program, and there ain't no way that I'm going to give that kid credit!" And lo and behold, the whole idea has become perverted, where it has now become: "You take the classes to get into college. You demonstrate that you've got the intellectual drive, and ideally the intellectual firepower to succeed in 'AP' classes."

So there is this frenzy, at places like Lowell High School in San Francisco, for example, of kids wanting to take "AP" classes because of course, at Berkeley, you get awarded in the enrollment process, the application process, depending upon how many "AP" classes you take.

And to bring it full circle—I realize this is a transgression; but you can see it gets me going, here—there's a law suit going on right now started by some kids in inner city schools in Los Angeles, suing their school system that they were discriminated against, because their high school had none, or one or two AP classes, whereas some of the other schools had *many*. And the difference in our city is: Balboa High School here in town has four AP classes, and Lowell has thirty-four. So which kid has the advantage in the college application process? It's a scandal, in my opinion.

So the issue for us is: How do we design a program which addresses that disparity? Now, that AP issue was a tangent to—?

FELTON. You were zeroing in on the formalities of adding the eleventh year.

THORP. Right. We were talking about content. So—for example, in humanities, we'll be doing the Americas, "American" history. What I started to say was: I was partly responsible for changing the title of the advanced-placement "American History" test to what it now is, which is "Advanced-Placement United States History," because it was inappropriate, it was a misnomer when it was called "American" history, in that it was only about the history of the United States. And there were a lot of Canadians who were upset about the title. Not to mention anybody south of Tijuana! And so it's now called "United States History," Advance-Placement United States History; and most classes in high school are called "United States History," and most requirements for places like Berkeley call for "A year of United States history." What we think we're going to do is we're going to do <u>American</u> history. So we're going to do "United States history" and—as Carlos Fuentes would say, "Ibero-American" history. And we're going to do our area studies in humanities of Latin- and South-America during next year as well—which might be a really integrated approach to it.

So: The easiest part of curriculum development is the "next layer on the cake"—which is the eleventh grade program. Okay, well—the humanities—you know, you can do United States history, American history. Or United States literature or American literature. And gee, in math we're going to have pre-calculus. Gee, in science, we're going to have biology. And gee—what am I leaving out here?—in Spanish, we're going to add the next level of Spanish.

So that's the easy part. Not to say that it isn't work; and not to say that pulling it all together doesn't require a whole lot of challenge. But here are the challenges for us, and here's where we are, in response to your question: There is this "curriculum development spectrum" where at one end of the spectrum it's a hundred percent *content*, and at the other end of the spectrum it's one hundred percent *process*. Okay. At that end of the spectrum the content is: "I don't give a damn how you learn; this is what you need to know; get it or else." And at the other end is: "I don't give a damn what we're learning; all that counts is how you learn about it,"—and hopefully they would add: "—and how you *feel* about how you learn about it!"

And it won't—I *hope* it won't surprise you when I say: Gateway's position on that spectrum is a little this side, process-side, of center. Which we think is appropriate. Again, we could spend the rest of the afternoon talking about that statement, because the whole standardized test movement belies that statement! The whole standardized test movement is increasingly "content-related." Wait until two years from now, and in the State of California you'll have a high-school exit exam; what's it's going to be? It's going to be content! And what are people going to do, when, as it is with the New York Regents' Test, you teach to the damned test?

So what we're wrestling with is: How do we accomplish our mission? Well, that's exactly what we *ought* to be wrestling with! Every year, every day!—we learn more about what we're doing well, and what we're not doing well. Every year we learn, every day we learn more about what our kids need more of and less of. And we're really looking toward next year, trying to answer the questions that remain unanswered for us. And these are more "process-related" questions, and from a teacher's point of view, substitute the word "pedagogy" for "process."

Yes, we have content issues—and I can talk about that a little bit as well. But the primary issues for us as a school, as a teaching faculty, as a professional group of men and women is: How do we do what we want to do? The pedagogy—what teaching methodologies, strategies, approaches, are effective here, and what ones are ineffective here? And we're doing that in the midst of trying to create the content, and trying to put together lesson plans, and trying to grade kids' papers, and, you know—the list goes on and on. But what we're trying to do is to carve out time, both this spring and especially this summer, outside of the day-to-day grind, to really focus in on that question.

We've received a grant, which is going to underwrite the cost of about eight to ten people locking themselves in a room for a week this summer, to address those questions. And it's as basic as—and I'm not sure those people will come up with the same list—but it's as basic in my mind as: What's the role of homework? Did we talk about this last week?

FELTON. No. You addressed it a little bit last fall in a parents' meeting.

THORP. What *is* the role of homework? Clearly, at Gateway, homework is the biggest obstacle to kids' succeeding. Now isn't that a weird way to put it from a principal of a high school? Because the response to that is: "Well, of course it is! So just sit down and do your homework, dammit!" And there wouldn't be any obstacles. But I'm not sure. And this is where I don't know if I'm right, and if I'm wrong on this, I'm *really* wrong on this—that maybe, schools like this, dealing with kids who don't have the habits and the practice and necessarily the motivation intrinsically or extrinsically to sink their teeth into homework, as we think they should—maybe we've got to look at the role of homework first. Maybe we ought not just to say: "Hey, the solution to life at Gateway and any school like this is, Do your homework, and if you'll do your homework, you'll be okay. I'm not sure it's a good dynamic.

We have seen in the two years of our school's life very few kids sort of say: "Okay, I'm going to do my homework," because the light bulb went off. Others remonstrate, saying: "Goddammit, they're going to drag me kicking and screaming!" As the adults of the school, as the professionals, we feel: "Get them to do their homework and they'll succeed." Or: "The kids who aren't doing the homework—they're just not ready for a college prep program." Or simply, and lamentably: "They're not willing to put in the time and effort."

And maybe that's it, because you've got to be really careful not to be wrong about this; but I'm not convinced that it is, yet. I'm interested in looking at the question: If a school like this looks at the question of homework utterly differently, will we in fact have more success? And may be. That's a question we need to examine. You see, we're a long way away from "What book do we pick in American literature?"

FELTON. It sure is.

THORP. What do you do in a classroom when a kid asks a question that is five steps behind where the rest of the class is? And— you see, the experienced teacher knows which one of those questions falls into that category, and the inexperienced teacher too frequently assumes that no other kid in the room has that same question in mind, when in truth—just to use plausible figures here—two-thirds of those kinds of "dumb" questions *aren't* dumb questions, because three or four kids in the room are sitting there thinking the same thing, or wondering the same thing, but for whatever reason don't want to ask!

On the other hand, when it truly is a "dumb" question—and that's not an expression I feel good about you using in this book, but it happens—how do you handle that as a classroom teacher? What kind of accommodations are appropriate? How do you deal with the testosterone factor? We talked about testosterone. In classes in high school, the animal, the male animal, with a higher level of testosterone, functions in a way differently from his female classmates. And testosterone has a lot to do with bravado, with impulsivity, with quick action—with all the kinds of things that school *isn't*. So how do we address the male issue at this school here? You've seen in the two awards assemblies that you've attended the overwhelming number of kids getting academic excellence certificates are *not* male! Why is that?

Well, the simple answer is: "Because girls are developmentally advanced over guys." And that's true; but don't leave it at that point! Address the cards you're dealt, which requires you ask: "All right, given that—what do we do?" And do we need to be more conscious of how to teach males how to succeed in school when their hormones are working against them? And my answer to that is: "Yeah, we ought to!"

FELTON. You're going to have to.

THORP. Again, that's easier said than done, of course. But if you're talking about accommodations—and this is Andrew Sullivan's

point in the New York Times article I cited before—he began
something like: "So cut through all this P.C. crap about the difference
between sexes, between genders being nonexistent and only a cultural
issue, when in fact, you know—the hormonal difference is very real
and very impacting. Cut through that, and recognize in a school
situation—and you can imagine how "un-P.C." this is!—that you might
have to have a *male* accommodation in addition to the *dyslexic*
accommodation, and that would be very interesting for me to pursue!

There was another piece on National Public Radio this morning,
where they said they'd just recently discovered that males have two and
a half million more brain cells than the average female. And then there
was this wonderful essay by this woman who was sort of making the
point: "Yeah—and what do they use it for? Channel-surfing, or
programming the VCR. So let them have their two-and-a-half-million
brain cells!" Which is true!

So—we've got to look at pedagogy. Okay.

We're also looking at the schedule—every school's anathema.
There isn't a school in the country that's happy with its schedule. And
we're going to have a different schedule next year than we have this
year, and I think I've told you this: We'll never be satisfied with our
schedule. It's a good sign, on the one hand, that we're not complaisant.
On the other hand, we go crazy with it. But our issue with the
scheduling is: Let's make sure the scheduling "tail" doesn't wag the
programmatic "dog." And let's make sure we make some decisions
about what programs we want to have, and then build a schedule
around that.

Do we want to continue to have the lab period, for example? This
has had great success in some areas, less success in other areas. Do we
want to have study halls? That's where we were talking, and saying
that from an administrative point of view, there is no way—it's an
administrative nightmare, it's a total pain in the ass. And it's a total
waste, so to speak, of person-power. On the other hand: Do we want
our kids to go through the day here without having a break? Other than
what they might see as a break—as physical education class, or arts
class—and what does that say about arts class?

So we're going to look at all sorts of scheduling questions.

We're going to look at extracurricular programs. You know, the
kids' biggest complaint about Gateway is lack of extracurricular
programs. Maybe it's not fair to conclude that that is the only issue;
but it's clearly that a complaint about Gateway is the extracurricular
program issue—and they're right! And you know, part of our

frustration is—I was just answering an E-mail message from two of our teachers who are taking a trip this weekend down the Ventana Wilderness, and you know, here they are, two people who are knocking themselves out to do all this planning, and that sort of thing, and as we get close to the weekend, kids start dropping out! Two who had originally said, "Yeah, I'm going." So we're trying to figure out how the schedule will enhance the likelihood that kids will get involved in extracurricular programs.

We're also reexamining the role of the Learning Center. And how do we allocate our finite resources? One of the things that we've done at this school, I believe, extremely well and something we should be really proud of, is that we have supported the most needy kids really quite well.   And those kids who have issues, either specific neurological issues like dyslexia or other neurologically related learning problems, have gotten a tremendous amount of support. However, we've allocated resources toward those kids to such an overwhelming degree, that we've lost track of and haven't been allocating to "middle-ground" kids, for want of a different term. They are students who might benefit tremendously from just a little bit more focus, extra help, support, however you define it, to get them going either in all their classes, or a specific class. This should address the query: "How do I get started on an English paper?" It would give that kind of support.

So we're looking at the role of the Learning Center, both in terms of considering a reallocation of the support services—and having the pendulum swing a little bit back toward the center; or the role of the Learning Center in support of faculty—which brings us back to that "pedagogy" question for the faculty. You know the statement: "No one needs to tell me what book I'm going to choose, and even how I'm going to teach that book." Or, more enlightened: "How do I teach a kid who's got reading problems how to read *Macbeth*'?" I'll put that question to you: What do we do to have kids study Shakespeare who can't read *Sports Illustrated*? Give me an answer to that!

So those are the kinds of questions we're going to be looking at. And in the math area, it's: "How do we get kids to complete Algebra II when they can't do fractions? And they can't understand the difference between positive and negative numbers. Those are the questions that we really need to spend time on, and focus in on. And finally, just from a kind of "task orientation"—next year will be the year that we seek external accreditation/validity, or validity/accreditation through the U.C. program and through what's called the "WASC" –the Western Association of Schools and Colleges Accreditation Process.

FELTON. *That's* a surprise! I thought the school's accreditation was complete.

THORP. Eventually we'll need to get WASC accreditation. That's a time-consuming task. And related to that, of course, is: "What are we going to do starting next year for college prep? What are we going to do in our humanities courses? Are we going to offer Scholastic Aptitude Test prep to kids? And if so, how and in what format, and that sort of stuff.

FELTON. A quick comment, and then I want to go back for a minute. Here are examples of two learning styles: Generation One— Keith Felton: In school I hated to do homework. So I finally, thankfully, resolved that if I paid attention in class, and really listened, and could hang on to it, then I wouldn't have to do so much at home. And I distinguish "at home" between rote homework, and "research," which is reading, or finding and absorbing some resources—which of course was more interesting than the rote part. Then in exams, being articulate, I could roll with just about any idea, and would end every essay with: "If time permitted….," and then list issues that I didn't really know, but that were presumably from my fund of knowledge, to impress the teacher that that's where I would go. My retention was good enough, my short-term memory was good enough; and my on-the-spot "creativity" was strong.

Generation Two—Peter Felton: He goes right home, glues himself to his books, does everything that's asked of him—and I don't think retains very much of it. He has a real retention problem. And fights it. And although he is articulate and creative, he doesn't trust those qualities at all, and doesn't employ them in the pinch!

There are other differences—I invented endless mnemonics, to get through short-term-memory quizzes. But I don't think Peter has that kind of—guile, for want of a better word. So we exhibit two completely different energies and two completely different results. I'm not proud of mine, particularly; I'm *very* proud of his—I just wish he could hang onto more information! He *earns* it, by doing the work. But he doesn't *learn* it—doesn't retain it, or process it into a sufficient permanence.

To me, this means learning style is really critical. And I don't know how you get kids to focus in class—we've talked a lot about that before.

THORP. Does Peter say he focuses in class?

FELTON. I haven't asked him! That's a very good question. I don't know what his answer to that is.

THORP. Ask him those two questions: Ask him, in this order: First: "Hey, Peter, why do you do your homework so thoroughly?" And my guess is, he'll respond: "What do you mean, 'Why do I do my homework'? I'm *supposed* to do my homework!" But press him on that, and get him to talk about what he sees as the role of homework. Because he may be one of those kids I'm sort of hinting at, who understand, either because they inherently understand, or have been kind of "beaten" to understand, that okay, the way to succeed in school is to do your homework! And it's really true here at Gateway. And so he might be saying: "What kind of question is that!" But push him on it, and say: "What's the point?" if in fact, he, too, acknowledges that retention issues are an issue for him as well. So we can come at this in different ways.

And that of course leads to the second question for him, which is: "So what do you do in class? Describe to me Peter Felton in class. Do you focus? Do you daydream a lot? Do you 'zone out' a lot? Do you take notes? Do you not take notes? Do you understand what's going on? Do you ask questions when you don't understand? And I'd be— and I'm sure *you'd* be curious to get those answers.

You know, if I were working with Peter directly, I'd want to know how he perceives himself in that situation. Because, as you say: Your approach has certain strengths; we certainly wouldn't recommend the Keith Felton approach to high school as something that works for everybody. But there are certain aspects that *could* work for everybody, if they balanced it with the Peter Felton approach, which, you know—the two of you together—your grandchild is going to be perfect! Of course, school will change by that point. But—there is a good conversation to have with Peter, about how do things work at school.

FELTON. I will ask him those questions!

The other thing which amazes me—and it may seem like a tiny point, but it's a great example of how Russian kids learn all these declensions or these verbs, or whatever they have to do, without thinking too much about it: The "block" concept of Gateway's daily schedule really throws me! I loved working "flex" schedules; but this endlessly-varied daily scheduling seems insurmountable. And I'm always amazed when I ask Peter, "Where are you third period?" And he answers, with thinly-disguised indulgent patience, "Dad, it's called 'block,' not 'period,' and it's different every day. You gotta get it, Dad." How they manage to coordinate that flexible concept is, I think, laudatory.

THORP. I do, too, because *I* couldn't do it!

FELTON. How was that advised? Is it a Gateway idea, or in general use? And will that be modified? Or will it be continued?

THORP. Well, what will be modified is the unevenness in the blocks, I think, which makes it hard for teachers because there are three different lengths of classes. Our experience over the last two years is that there's value in blocks, more value than in the seven period/forty-five minute period day approach. We think that that's a too-scattered—there's too much syncopation in that day. The block way, which requires fewer mindset changes, has benefit in school. Now, if you ask me for the data to support that, I don't have it; but it's really a function of observation. A year ago our observation was that kids were far more settled on days with blocks. But if you're a teacher who doesn't know how to use the blocks, they can be real challenging. And our foreign language teachers are less the block fans than others, because of the desire for daily use.

FELTON. Right, right.

THORP. And I should mention: I have the highest admiration for quality foreign language teachers, because my experience is the quality foreign language teachers plan their lessons much more tightly than anybody else. And the people who are the least well-planned, in my experience, are historians, who like me, come into a class, and all a student has to do is ask the right evocative questions, and there I go for the next hour-and-a-half. And if you as a student have any sense of listening and Socratic method, you can just keep pulling the questions out one at a time. And it's a fun, but really *lazy* way to teach. And I have to guard myself against doing that, because I can do it. I need to take some inspiration from the foreign-language teachers who know that you have to plan class down to every five-minute unit to keep the kids using the language and make sure that you're developing a habit—habituation, if that's a word, in the acquisition of foreign-language, which is not true in history.

It's fairly interesting to watch foreign languages. It's also much more exhausting to be a foreign-language teacher, in my opinion.

FELTON. I agree. I was a language major throughout my years—

THORP. As in "foreign-language," or English?

FELTON. No, I had two consecutive majors in college, French and theater. Theater finally won out, even though I had literally five times the units in French. And I prepared to go on to teach college French. But one thing I realized, both there and after visiting the country where the language started, was something that I tried later to think of how I could apply it to all disciplines. And that was the simple notion that there's a curve in learning that subject. The pattern is to feel: "This subject is murder, murder, murder, I don't know a thing" — and then all of a sudden, you're there! You arrive at understanding, comprehension, fluidity, mastery. The reason, of course is that your brain, faced with all that information, has been working and processing it for you, and if you're diligent, you've been getting it all along. And there ought to be something like that to offer even a mathematics student, it would seem to me, who can piece together "process," and "schematic thinking," and then have something "catch fire" when he has enough of a body of experience with it and enough just "goods locked in" that it will suddenly make sense. It never did for me in math; it only did it in language, and so forth. But maybe it could happen in math, too.

THORP. And of course, there are high parallels between kids who have issues in math, and kids who have issues in foreign language. At one level, that doesn't make any sense; but when you start to think of math as a language, then it starts to make sense why kids who have problems in math also have problems in Spanish.

FELTON. I can see that!

Let's take up some other problems facing kids, next time.

Chapter Twenty

MANY SLIPS 'TWIXT
FOURTEEN AND EIGHTEEN

"[A]dolescents could be in a sense described as "the mice that roar," in that they get skills sometimes, and attributes, sometimes, that they're wholly unequipped to carry. And it ranges from attitude to cognitive awareness to breasts.

"I think that one of the reasons that [urging them to prepare for college] doesn't resonate with some percentage of kids is: They're not ready—really, internally—to define 'self' as far as 'Who I want to be,' 'What I want to be,' 'What I want to accomplish.' But the more immediate task for them is: 'I want to make sure that I'm *not* this! I want to make sure that I don't have pimples; I want to make sure that I'm not alone; I want to make sure that I'm not beat up; I want to make sure that I'm okay; and I want to make sure that I've got friends.' And—the cap to all this is: 'I want to make sure that I'm pushing my parents away. Because until I push my parents away, I can't become my 'self,' they would say; but in some ways: 'Until I push my parents away, I can't discover my group identity.'"

18 April—*Over a couple of Sunday mornings in the weeks preceding the 18 April dialogue, the Reporter got a chance to wear his teacher's hat. As I had mentioned to Peter Thorp earlier, I had used an approach to Polaroid photography tried by photographer and teacher Minor White at Massachusetts Institute of Technology, and transformed the scheme into what I called the "Minor White Module." With this "module," the Photo Group of Gateway High School did an* *amazing visual reworking of campus walls, driveways, back-alleys, and ivy bushes. The medium was Polaroid film, and the instant-image reward was ideal for young persons interested in photography, some of whom were approaching camera work for the first time. The experience—designed to promote self-insight and socially interactive artistry as well as visual aesthetics—yielded an exhibit-sized rendering of black-and-white images, many of which were utterly remarkable. As instructor, this Reporter was left with a towering feeling about the possibility for creative effort from this group.*

But adolescence has other flavors, other sides to it. And like the taste buds of the tongue, different parts yield, sometimes unexpectedly, some sense bitter, some sense sour, some sense merely salty—but many times tastes distinctly removed from the "sweetness" which was residue from the photographic phenomena of those Sunday mornings.

Two young students brought this stridently to mind, when next I gathered ideas, papers, tape machines, and wits, and sat in Gateway High's front office, awaiting Peter Thorp's attentions, and putting final touches on my querying attentions to him.

*Apparently, computer class had been excessively strenuous for one young man, Ilya, a Russian-*emigré *and now a ninth-grade student. In a class just concluded, he had found it convenient to enlist a friend— another Slavic* emigré, *Gregory—in disruptive experience impulsively fashioned by the two into a more entertaining hour than that planned by the exasperated computer teacher. Invited finally by Lee to entertain their cleverness in the office, the two now sat, in "folie-a-*deux" *states of nervous excitement, and played off each other's energy. Within four minutes, the two managed the following:*

> • *They verbally harassed a second teacher who had come to deal with their misprisions, laughing at her threats of discipline;*
> • *They enraged the receptionist—that former Yugoslav* émigrée—*and derided her limited knowledge of Russian, which language they spoke to each other secretively and teasingly;*
> • *They ignored the Reporter's question about why they felt the need to be rude to the teacher;*
> • *They bragged about their prowess as parental manipulators ("My parents were going to take my ATM card away, okay?" crowed Ilya. "We met last night; I have the ATM card in my pocket. The power of diplomacy!" "You mean you talked them out of it!?" Gregory yearned to know. "The power of diplomacy!" Ilya repeated, with the kind of*

smug expression it is every parent's instant instinct to meet with the full and forceful palm of the hand).

At last, determining that the scene had been drained of any further potential for amusement, the boys preeningly deprived us of their company and sauntered out, taking their full wisdom with them, defying the detention restriction, and leaving the receptionist and the Reporter to deal with a wake of outrage.

I, for one, carried mine into the Principal's office, and decided to update my inquiries about the adolescent experience with the same energies that Ilya and Gregory negatively had updated the good feeling residual within me from the Photographic Weekends.

FELTON. Well, I've prepared a question which I've been holding for a while, which has to do with adolescence. And then a scene outside, just while waiting today, added a quite different dimension to it. There were a couple of guys outside, two Russian kids, Greg and Ilya—

THORP. Ahh, yes!

FELTON. —Who were really generally being thoroughly obnoxious. So that's my immediate past reference before coming in here. I mean, they were both very strongly arrogant.

THORP. That's a modus operandi you're describing.

FELTON. It probably is. Well, when you hear my question, you'll see why they struck a jarring note. My question is—

THORP. "Assuming that all kids are wonderful,—"!

FELTON. Well, actually, theirs was just a level of sophisticated banter and techniques for putting one's own needs forth. And it brought to mind other considerations. I've been having a series of reactions to teenage kids—

THORP. Within the walls of your own home, or—?

FELTON. Some of them within the walls of my own home!— and I've a good friend who's got a kid about this age—ninth grade, tenth grade—who's going through similar experiences. So I'm getting a sort of a comparative here. But most recently, I have had some interaction with my friend Evan, a student here who is my photography tutee. And it's been interesting, and I thought I'd bounce some of it off you, and see what kind of reactions you had.

THORP. Okay.

FELTON. The whole thing comes under the metaphoric name here of "Wet Paint." I've given that little tag to it, to help me understand it. And it has to do with the disparity in development that these kids experience, so that you get these jarring differentials in their stages of development, which seems to affect—this uneven kind of development—seems to affect them at different levels. And here's an example of Evan:

Evan worked beautifully with me on a whole series of photography classes that we conducted. And then right up until a recent Gateway baseball game, he was with me all the way. We were getting things rolling, photographically, in just wonderful ways. And then, I went— my son is on the baseball team—I went to see the game. And while I'm sitting there photographing the game and watching the play, this figure skulked by with his sweatshirt hood pulled securely over his head—and it's Evan!

And rather than approach me—we hadn't expected to see each other, but our last interaction had been just two or three days before— he avoided me; he hid physically more in his hood; and the biggest surprise was that rather than sit with some Gateway folks and watch the game, or talk to the team, he found a couple of young kids sitting with the fans of the other side! And for the entire remainder of the game, he related socially to a couple of kids who were obviously members of the opposing team's school. I thought that was really odd. And at one point, because I was by then jumping all around trying to get the vantage point for pictures—he unavoidably had to go by me, and kind of nervously, awkwardly, said "Hello." And I said "Hello." And then he went on his way.

This incident was followed in the next week or two by the series of meetings of the Photography Group, with Evan in attendance, and once again he was wonderful! He was outgoing, he was friendly, he was "down to business"; his mom brought him, so he had his sort of "Mom-son" time that took him out of interplay for a few moments. But it was egalitarian, and we all got along fine. And the session went well. And subsequently I had another couple of tutorial classes with him and they went well. And he never returned to that mode of being lost, a sort of "waif in the wind," uncertain, scared of his shadow that he'd been at the baseball game. And all this was capped yesterday, when I had my tutorial class with him: He came in and sat down, the soul of authority, looked right at me and announced: "I want to get known for my photography. I want to start selling stuff, and I want you to make it happen!" Out of nowhere!

So we tried to plan out a campaign of how in the world we were going to make a fourteen-year-old into a well-known photographer!

I know that my own son goes through similar rapid back-and-forth changes in apparent level of development. Peter still watches some television shows that are far below his age level. Here is his disparity: He watches the most wry and sophisticated British comedies; and then he'll watch "Sesame Street," or bathetic situation comedy shows, all of which I've come to realize—especially in the situation shows—focus on family life. What he's been deprived of by dint of a quirky social upbringing and split parents, he seems to get in part in the form of nourishment from these shows. And he watches them faithfully. But again, the disparity.

So, this quandary of uneven growth, or disparity in growth between sophistication and some contextual issues that you've talked about before, have come across very clearly in these two young guys. And that's why I tagged the quandary "Wet Paint," because wet paint looks finished, and it looks pretty and ready to go and rugged; but of course, it isn't. It's very much wet just a touch underneath the surface, and it has no ability to withstand the "slings and arrows."

And here is the question I derive from these circumstances: Is growing, for a teenager, doggedly doing what they think is right or told is right—despite how they feel about it? Or do they have a philosophical capacity— "they" connoting a group, which really isn't fair, but just for the sake of discourse—do they have a philosophical capacity to just "keep truckin,'"? That it doesn't matter so much *what* you do; it's just *that* you do? And do you as a teenager have simply to get through the parents' harangue or the teachers' harangue, and at some other stage, in their absence presumably, you can look forward to getting to something that's enriching for oneself?

A final part of this issue:

Meghvi Maheta, the Director of Admissions, added to this discussion when she talked about a disparity I had not known existed, between Gateway's ninth and tenth grade classes. She spoke of there wishing to be an avoidance, one of the other, for some reasons of identification or distraction or disconcert of some degree in which one—and I think it was the ninth—didn't want to relate to the tenth! For reasons that would suggest it would normally have been the reverse, because it was an issue of feeling that the tenth didn't have the maturity on some levels. That's a broad paraphrase of what may have fallen short of expressing her point.

But all of these things come together to make me think about this. And hence ask you about it!

THORP. Okay! The question's been posed?

FELTON. Yes, sir.

THORP. Let me preface a response by trying to make you feel more comfortable, in what I sense is some cognitive dissonance in you about adolescence, by saying the following—and this is stretching the historical metaphor even further than I typically do in this:

One of the reasons why Woodrow Wilson delayed three years in getting involved in World War One is that Americans did not want to sully their hands in the typical European resolution of minor- to major issues through wars. And Americans felt that if we kept ourselves out of what was then called the Great War, we wouldn't get sucked in to become just like "Those Europeans." The Europeans, on the other hand, viewed Americans as these cultural backwoods folks: "How dare they say, 'We don't want to sully our hands by a European involvement!'" And one of the end products of that cultural dichotomy, or that perspective of cultural dichotomy, is Wilson's failure at the League of Nations.

Okay: Why is this metaphor in my head? Because I was in a second-hand store the other day, and I saw this thing—and I'm still thinking about buying it—this kind of plaque, which I think is an original, of the League of Nations, and has the picture of the six leaders, and there is some certificate, and it would be sort of interesting—but my point of this, to set you somewhat at ease, is that at one point, a haughty European said: "Well, the only thing that American culture has ever contributed to this—" and of course, this was much later than World War I, but it ties into the European perspective—"The only things that Americans have ever contributed to world culture are jazz and the musical theater."

Now, to make you feel better about this, I add a third thing to that list of great American contributions, which is: The Three Stooges. This is noted to make you feel better about Peter watching "Sesame Street": I would go home from high school, as rapidly as I could on many afternoons, to watch "The Three Stooges." And I and a couple of my friends, one of whom was probably the brightest kid in my class in a high school of twelve hundred kids, a guy who went on to Harvard and is now a physician, knew every line in "The Three Stooges" that had ever been said. So there's hope!—which is sort of the message I want to give you. Or there *isn't* hope, depending on how you look at it.

So that's the preface to the response, okay? I hope it makes you feel better.

FELTON. I'll call you in the morning.

THORP. As you laid out your descriptor, and I was trying to figure out the "wet paint" metaphor, which I couldn't until you explained it, what came to me was another metaphor as you described it—and I don't know where I pulled this one out; but you remember the movie "The Mouse That Roared"?

FELTON. Peter Sellars.

THORP. Peter Sellars. Do you remember the story of the movie?

FELTON. Not really; I didn't see it, despite being a Sellars fan.

THORP. It was about this little country, I think, Irwan, or some such name, that was "going down the tubes" financially. So they had this Cabinet meeting, and Sellars played one of these *"Die Feuhrer"* kind of guys; and they came up with the brilliant post-World War Two strategy, which was to declare war, as this little European Andorra-like country—declare war on the United States, then lose, of course. But then as a consequence they would have their rebuilt like the Germans and Japanese, so they would become one of the great countries of the world! It was a brilliant strategy, until it got totally blown by the fact that they won! And they won because either they—and I don't remember the movie well enough—either because they really had a death weapon, or because their strategy in declaring war in the first place was to portray themselves as having a death weapon. And the United States believed it enough to resolve a truce.

The metaphorical link here is that adolescents could be in a sense described as "the mice that roar," in that they get skills sometimes, and attributes, sometimes, that they're wholly unequipped to carry. And it ranges from attitude to cognitive awareness to breasts. And I think one of the really tricky things of adolescents is that gifts are bestowed on adolescents sometimes without their desire—it's a lousy way of putting it, but it's like the ugly tie on Father's Day. And—you know—for the young girl who develops at the age of, now, eleven, and ten, in a society where the puberty age continues to lower, it's an horrendous gift! It's the adolescent who develops cognitive insight so that he or she leaps ahead of his or her classmates, and is ridiculed for having that, because it's not okay in this society to be an adolescent intellectual. In fact, it's not okay in many societies.

We may have talked previously in one of our conversations about my theory of America being fundamentally an anti-intellectual society, which I think it is. Well, it's bad enough for somebody who's forty-five to cope with that. Imagine if you're twelve, thirteen, fourteen! In that kind of circumstance. So, part of what's at work, in my opinion, is that adolescents don't have any control as to what's put on them. You know, again, whether or not it's physical changes, or intellectual development, maturation speed, if you will. Or values that get shoved down their throat, either by family or church, or boy scouts or school, or whatever.

Now, again—I'm not going to say that any one of those is shoving inappropriate values; that's not the point. It's the point that values are being crammed in at a time when, by definition, what an adolescent is trying to do is to *define self*—this is what makes adolescence both fascinating and really tricky—that the essential mission of an adolescent is to define self or to define self by establishing one's group. Does that make any sense? I mean, do you see the kind of internal paradox in that?—

FELTON. Sure.

THORP. —That for the typical adolescent, I believe, he or she is trying to figure out, "Who am I?" But it is the *a*-typical adolescent who's able to take that to kind of its logical extreme, which is to isolate himself or herself—isolate the variables, as you were to say, "Okay, *this* is who I am." But rather that "self" is very much a function of "group."

Of course, the paradox is: Well, if it's "group," then it isn't "self!" But to the contrary!—in that the adolescent—much of adolescent definition, self-definition, is more "what I'm not" than "what I am." Does that make sense?

FELTON. Yes. It's the medical research model applied to teendom. But I'd like you to expand on that.

THORP. Okay. As an educator—and one of the things that I experience here at Gateway is this idea "I know the value of a college education!" Okay? "Now's the time to develop yourself in a way where you, too, will recognize that the value of a college education is so worthwhile that you're going to bust your ass and do the homework." I think that one of the reasons that doesn't resonate with some percentage of kids is: They're not ready—really, internally—to define "self" as far as "Who I want to be," "What I want to be," What I want to accomplish." But the more immediate task for them is: "I want to make sure that I'm NOT this! I want to make sure that I don't have pimples; I want to make sure that I'm not alone; I want to make sure that I'm not beat up; I want to make sure that I'm okay; and I want to make sure that I've got friends." And—the cap to all this is: "I want to make sure that I'm pushing my parents away. Because until I push my parents away, I can't become my 'self,'" they would say; but in some ways: "Until I push my parents away, I can't discover my group identity."

And—and this is nothing original to me: What I think is tricky for us as a society is how we recognize that phenomenon and that moment, and how we seize the time with an adolescent—particularly an adolescent male, although I don't think it's in any way exclusive to males—whereby we make sure that the group that they join is not the wrong group, so to speak. And the wrong group can be defined, you know, at some level completely simply and superficially: "Don't get in with that group!" But it's more complex for the typical teenager, which is this interesting combination of your parents saying this might be the wrong group because they dress that way and they "hang out," and you know, they don't share our values, whatever it is. And yet, the kid might be drawn to that group because that group is in fact the one group that's inviting that kid to join!

So—I don't know how well I'm explaining this, and I want you to give me feedback on it. But I mean, to me it's an interesting phenomenon, this—well, here's an image that just came to me, God knows why this did!—you go to Ocean Beach, okay? And at certain stretches in Ocean Beach, you have these rolling waves that almost look like inverse barrel-vaults in a long, Romanesque church where it's really even. There's a very famous painting by Edward Hopper called "The Buoy," I think it is. It simply depicts this big buoy off the beach. And these waves are coming in like tubes in a bobsled run, they're so concrete that, you know, they're just moving in this fixed sense.

Okay, but the image that I'm really thinking about at Ocean Beach are those certain stretches at the beach where you have waves coming in from all angles, and they're crashing together, that sort of thing. And that's where the adolescent is, where the waves are just coming in from all over the place, and they're crashing, and—to keep the image going—there's this tremendous below-the-surface stirring up of the sand, that produces the craziness that is teenagers! And so, if we as a society, if we as educators can recognize that phenomenon, and try to de-personalize it, we'll have improved our odds for making some teenage headway.

Now I want to respond to one other thing you said: It was interesting for me to hear you describe the Evan incident, because you described it in a way that most educators would, because it came from caring, as I interpret it. You *cared* how he reacted to you that day, right? That's the upside of being an educator. But also, you fell into the trap that educators do so much, which is you personalized it in a way that I will guarantee you made reaction so far away from Evan's intent! He had no intent to shut you out! I would bet the ranch that if we had Evan on a lie detector, and really were absolutely sure that he was telling the truth, he would say: "Well, of *course* I didn't mean to hurt Mr. Felton's feelings. Of *course* I didn't mean to ignore him. Of *course*, of *course*, of *course!*"   So you have that most common occurrence—in fact, that's what the group who was meeting here was talking about right before you came in, in this administration meeting— this most common occurrence, where kids mean one thing and adults see it a different way.   You know?   And the most frustrating conversations I have with kids is when the response was: "But I didn't mean it!"   And my response to that is: "I don't give a damn if you meant it or not!—you *did this!*"   You know?   And it's not quite two different value systems going in opposition to each other; but it sure is two different ways of perceiving the world.

Does that make any sense?

FELTON.   Very much! But indulge me to respond to some of the beats in your message.   I had the feeling then, in dealing with Evan—I certainly didn't feel that he was being *rude*.   I thought he was confused and awkward, and simply did not have enough social-grace experience to get over what was a dissonance for him.   He came, expecting one arena; and all of a sudden, there was the guy who does his photo stuff with him, all the way from that other arena, and now right here in this one!—

THORP.   Sure.

FELTON.   —And he didn't know how to deal with it.   And I asked him about it, later, at one of our tutorial sessions: "Who was your friend at the baseball game?"   And it took him a minute.   And then he remembered: "Oh, the kid with green hair."   And I said, "Yeah."   He'd really glommed onto this one boy.   He really acted as if he was seeing a long-lost pal.   I had finally reasoned maybe the other boy was a middle-school chum, who all of a sudden had shown up, and Evan knew that he'd gone on to the opposing team's school.   And the green-haired boy turned out to be a neighbor.   Evan later remembered and described the incident perfectly, as if this awkward boy in the hood who had been himself, or one aspect of himself, was just some totally different person!

THORP.   Yeah, and of course, in a sense he was!

FELTON.   But—to apply here some of the other things you've noted: One of my images of adolescents has always been of them "backing into the future," or rowing, and not quite knowing where they're going but getting there anyway—

THORP. I like that image!

FELTON. —Getting to what's presently out of sight for you. And your point about being different but in a group that will accept you—this was very clear in my youth, typical of me and others, where the "intellectual" who was not afforded the opportunity to be an intellectual because of his youth—

THORP. Because of his peers?

FELTON. Because of his youth.

THORP. Oh. An immature intellectual. Okay.

FELTON. No, actually I meant a precocious one, looking to see if the group—an older group—had room, if there was "a position open," in the group, for a kind of wry, quirky guy, who would then affect a costume, a manner, and ply some reading that he'd done and certainly some natural curiosity. Then if accepted, the niche would have been found, and the role could be established within the group, and he would fill that role. But he is still within the *group's* boundary. And when the group steps into the reality of the larger world, it doesn't work. It's the same dynamic which happens when juvenile gangs are taken by cops into prisons, and asked: "Is this what you want?" And reality comes down like a sledge hammer.

All those realities—I mean, these kids are alive, they look around. They know what's really out there. But they also know they've got to take a certain path—it seems to me—to get there. And it's just—it's very confusing in just the way that you describe.

THORP. Well, we're having this conversation two days before the end of the first anniversary of Columbine. And what I think adults fail to appreciate—and obviously I'm talking about aberrant behavior—I think what adults fail to recognize is just how profoundly tense adolescence can be. Part of the failure to recognize that is the smoky vision of years gone by, and not fully remembering the trauma. Part of it also is that what is considered to be the norm in this society has been established by people who have weathered adolescence, and for the most part have survived it with shining colors, so to speak. And so the people who say "What's normal in adolescence?"—and it's political leaders and educators and church leaders who are the kind of people for whom adolescence for the most part was not so terribly traumatic. I don't think there's an adolescent on the planet for whom adolescence wasn't traumatic in some ways; but you know, for some people it was far worse than others.

It also speaks to why the Columbine incident isn't so aberrant, and why the potential for another Columbine is there because even though the kids' response—the two boys who planned and carried out the shooting—was so beyond the pale, their level of frustration and anger and hurt was far more typical than I think certainly people realized a year and two days ago. And probably understand a little bit better. But what people fail to appreciate is the issue of *power* in this society. And we've touched on this in a variety of different ways.

It's very interesting to watch power groups develop in schools. And I don't think you can criticize a teenager—an adolescent, let me use that phrase—for trying to attack a power center of which he or she is not a member, because isn't that what societies do all the time? Again, this is the social scientist in me speaking. You either can have successful revolutions in France and Russia, or you have—depending again on your definition of American history—an unsuccessful revolution because the people who are running the show in America are just too damn smart, and constantly reconfigure this society in a way where the "outs" get taken care of. And by that, I mean, are given enough—"Let-'em-eat-cake"—that the Revolution dies down.

Part of what you hear is a legitimate position in me; and part of what you hear, I've got to believe you understand now, is just me intellectually postulating here. And here comes one of these postulates, although all of my postulations have some kernel of accepted truth in them.

Yesterday, President Clinton was in East Palo Alto, addressing the question of the "Digital Divide." Okay? And lo and behold: Up popped Carly Fiorino and three or four other heads of big technology companies, who, the President announced, are willing to donate one hundred million dollars to narrow the "Digital Divide." And everybody on the news last night and today is saying: "Isn't this great? A hundred million bucks, hurray!—" Well, crap! Again, this is the cynical part of me. I mean, Great! I applaud any company that's willing to "pony up" and put their money behind the thing. But if anybody kids themselves that a hundred million bucks is going to resolve the Digital Divide, we've got a problem. And of course, the reality is that everybody *will* kid themselves, that that resolves it. And we all go back to feeling comfortable that, "Okay, we've taken care of that!" When, in fact, what's behind the Digital Divide is, in my opinion, an unbelievable, in my opinion, discrepancy between the "haves" and the "have-nots" in this society, that is not only mind-boggling, but so corrupt that it just continues to stun me, generation after generation. Now that I've a few of those under my belt, I still don't comprehend why there hasn't been more of an upsetting of the tradition "apple cart" in this society.

Teenagers, I think, are eminently rational. And these two kids in Columbine, who became utterly irrational, started one day from a rational point of view of: "I'm being oppressed and suppressed by the 'jock' society in my high school, and it's not fair." And one thing led to another.

FELTON. You've made an economic case, and a philosophical case, for the presence of the polarities of the Digital Divide. One real source of the streams of the Digital Divide is also inequitable educational opportunity. There's a phenomenon that I've never seen fail to come up in some way or another. And that is that people who either do not avail themselves or are not availed of the opportunity to go on to college, forever more wear a mantle of inadequacy. And it comes to haunt them. And all of the rather condescending praise of the sort which states: "For a guy who had no background, he's such a smart guy!"—all that kind of talk doesn't lift these people out of their sense of being inferior to the guy who walked through the halls of academe and got the mortar board.

THORP. And who's driving a cab here in San Francisco.

FELTON. Yes, sometimes! But I wonder how much in the kind of school Gateway is—how much of an undercurrent there is, a kind of *sub rosa* notion that a very important part of the mission is in seeing that all these young people never have to have that kind of handicap. That they can self-realize through our group experience here. And how that will prompt them to go on, as autonomous individuals, to gain that kind of recognition for themselves, and hence better meet whatever comes after? Even taxi-driving!

THORP. Well, the simple answer to your question is it's a very integral part of who we are. And it's a combination of *ideal-politik* and *real-politik*. The "ideal" part for us is: All people should have access to great learning. That is intrinsically valuable. The "*real-politik*" part of it, the "realistic" part of it is that you run the numbers, and there you go!—somebody who goes to college is going to make three times in his or her life what somebody will make who doesn't go to college, on average. And of course, the extremes of those averages are even now much greater.

So it's a terribly integral part of our program. I'm doing a job here, in addition to being something that you've given me permission to be, a Philosopher-King here, you know. But I'm still running a school, with very practical issues and practical opportunities, and a real focus to have kids positioned so that, if they choose—and ultimately that's the "baton-handoff" we have to make—if they choose, they'll have the opportunity to seek higher learning, either because it's intrinsically valuable to them, or, I predict, far more likely—they'll seek higher learning because it has a pragmatic element to it. And the intrinsic stuff is just kind of the "gravy."

But I also know that we're going to have a significant—well, we're going to have *some* percentage of our kids who are not going to pursue higher learning. And the Philosopher-King in me has to figure out how to come to grips with that. In some of our previous discussions, I've disparaged some components of higher education where I think the ivory tower is running the risk of such a level of irrelevancy that it needs to be careful.

Stanford just appointed a new President, as you may have read. The Chair of the Search Committee defined their choice this way: He said, "We've hired this person who melds the world of academia and vocation. And it was also very interesting to see what the new President said upon his appointment. He's an engineer professor who states: "My mission is to teach kids to be sure to take advantage of technology." You know: In 1620 when they started Harvard they were saying: "My mission is to teach kids Latin and Greek!"

And Latin and Greek eventually became a few more things in the liberal arts. And all this evolves up to two weeks ago—when that new President of Stanford says: "Our mission is vocational training." Now, he didn't say it exactly that way; but it sure spilled over into a far more vocational construct than I think the typical college president—or at least the typical college president of the liberal arts/Ivy League world—has tended to define education. And I think that world needs to be very careful that it doesn't get irrelevant at some point in the near future. And I think this new Stanford President was kind of an intriguing choice, and I think the choice has taken a huge step toward addressing the irrelevancy question.

Harvard has shut down a thriving student-entrepreneur in recent days, a guy operating a web business from his dorm room. Will Harvard continue to insist that bright, talented people can't make money while they're going to Harvard? What's wrong with *that* picture?, as they charge them thirty-two thousand bucks a year to go there! Well, as a consumer of that, there's a *lot* that's wrong with it!

FELTON. I really would like us to talk a bit—and Columbine invites the opportunity—about security here. Approach it from any aspect that you want; but I wonder if you'd consider this idea:

I sense in every slant of society—certainly, with the help of politics—that not too far beneath the surface of a lot of us, there is an almost-seemingly-natural tendency for polar hatred. Some don't like the Republican point of view, or many didn't tolerate Communism for so long. There's always something that immediately pulls to the extreme. Gore Vidal said not long ago that the Republicans hate Clinton because he's the smartest President of the century, with the possible exception of FDR. And it's this visceral, ugly, unyielding kind of corrupting quality that seems to pervade all public discourse. And—surely as there are no exceptions—it's going to filter down here. How are you—or *are* you prepared to stop the kids who are going to turn into those Columbine kids, those two guys? How will you know that? How much are you banking that there is enough idealism and general happiness with living, amongst your student body population, that they're not going to sink into that kind of despond, so readily that it's going to become, or so inevitably that it's going to become an extremely serious problem for you, and all these other people?

THORP. Well, the simple answer is: There are no guarantees.

I mean, one of the things Columbine—and one has to be careful about making too much of that; but let's use it as the case study that it can be—there are lots of lessons from that tragedy, one of which is: You can never predict. I mean, what were these parents doing!—all these weeks and months when these kids were arming themselves, and planning this? Yet, these were not delinquent parents; these were your average set of parents! In so many ways. So you know—*that* issue is one that I find particularly intriguing in the Columbine event.

It wasn't a school riddled with hatreds, at an obvious level. I mean, if one had said: Name the ten schools most likely to blow up, Columbine wouldn't even have been close to being on that list. But what it *does* speak to is what we were talking about earlier—making sure the adults pay attention to this. And more than anything—and it's one strategy that I support: It absolutely underscores the value in small schools. Given that paradox of adolescence that I described at the beginning of my remarks, about finding oneself in one group, or in a group—the underlying premise behind that is that anonymity is bad. And for an adolescent it's especially bad, because it peels away all sorts of potential support structures. Also, from a schooling point of view, it's bad to put kids in anonymous situations, because they will understandably draw what I think is a totally logical conclusion, that: "They don't care about me!"

And so small schools have value not only because you can hit that many more kids that many more times in a discussion, or in a Spanish class; but to me the real value is because kids are going to get *known*. So, to answer part of your question: The security in a smaller school is higher, I believe, by definition, because the faculty know what's going on that much more. And Gateway is a school, I think, where we really work on that, and we are relatively successful. And when I say "relatively," it means that kids are masters at keeping information away from adults. At least at some level.

So the value of the small school is that the adults are more aware. And the value of the small school is that more kids feel enfranchised. They can say: "This is my school." And when they become aware of aberrant or potentially aberrant behavior, they're more likely to say something about it. And there certainly is a series of movies and books, and the Columbine incident itself, where you know that some percentage of the kids knew that something was going to happen! Either at Columbine, or the incident where teenagers killed a young kid, and friends of the teenagers knew about that. And there was even an incident just last week where two thirteen-year-olds were discovered in an elaborate plot where they were going to stab seven kids. And once again, a certain number of kids knew about it.

Anyway, the point is: In a smaller school, I believe that were there to be a serious security issue about to evolve, the likelihood is vastly higher that some kid would step up in the face of all sorts of pressure not to step up, and say something to the adults. Vastly greater. It's far more likely than it is in a large, more impersonal school, where just the numbers make it far less likely to happen than in a larger school.

But it isn't just the numbers. It's that kids in a school characterized by more anonymity are going to feel less cared-for. And therefore they're going to feel: "If I *do* say something, somebody's going to ignore it." You know, it's the whistleblower in the big company, it's somebody trying to call the IRS and say, "This is crazy!" And not getting any kind of responsiveness to it.

We could talk a lot more about specific security issues, and ways kids treat each other, and that sort of thing. But that's why small schools are better.

FELTON. Let's pursue some of argument. There is a statistic in which it said that in sixty-three percent of high schools, and twenty-nine percent of middle schools, there were law enforcement personnel on the staff and some of them in teaching roles. Some were counseling students, and some were doing mediation; but some were just there as teachers. And I don't know if that meant because it was just a—

THORP. Depends on the question; yeah.

FELTON. —Was it "under-cover," or—what was the identity, to the students, of the individual?—was it "Officer Smith" or was it "my teacher, Mr. Smith"?

THORP. Well, there was an article in the San Francisco Chronicle on violence in the schools. There were a number of statistics about the percentage of kids who have been beaten up, or harassed. Yeah. School's not a safe place!

FELTON. I believe it.

THORP. And when you take adolescence not being safe—I don't know what it was like for you, but I felt safe when I went to school. It's not that I didn't feel safe at home; I mean, I didn't have that difficulty of that kind of a childhood. But school was safe to me. And even for some of our better kids—and by that, I mean kids who don't have to fear safety on a daily basis—schools in general aren't safe. And of course, as we've discussed, one of the real attributes at Gateway that kids appreciate is that Gateway feels safe to them.

I was talking with a youngster yesterday. He was struggling with the answer to my question: "Why are you here if you're not doing your homework?" And his response was: "This is a good school because I get to come here and be in a safe environment. And as soon as I leave this school and go home, I'm hassled constantly. When I walk out my door in the morning to the bus stop, anything can happen to me, in that short walk. And so I'm really glad to get to school, because I know that for eight hours of the day, I'm safe."

FELTON. That's really telling.

You know, when we first started this project, I remarked to you about how amazed I was with the forthcoming quality of the kids. I'd found in them, I believed, a very open, honest and kind of free expression, almost exuberance. I've thought about it since then, because I've seen some examples where the kids weren't quite as "lovely" as I thought; and since that time, I have considered that perhaps what I was feeling and seeing in them, or sensing from them, was just this point. That it was that "safety" coming out, saying, in effect: "Oh, thank God! I have the opportunity now to be exuberant, or just to be myself! Or —you know—to say this joke to somebody, and not be looking over my shoulder, or wondering who's going to grab my stuff!" or whatever's going to happen. I really think it might have been all of that. I don't know.

THORP. The social biologist in me asks: "Is the development of breasts at age eleven and even ten kind of an evolutionary response to the fact that this society is denying kids the full extent of their childhood?" Kids grow up so much more quickly! And I don't know if you meant it this way when you said it; and I believe that a very big part of you didn't; but if, for example, somebody saw your comment about Peter watching "Sesame Street" in addition to "Masterpiece Theater," as critical of Peter—"Why would you watch 'Sesame Street'?"—part of me revels in the fact that he *would* watch "Sesame Street." Part of me says: "Isn't that healthy that here's a kid who can be a child, even though he's learning and tall and growing into adulthood. But isn't it great!" And with a far less prosaic example, it's my "Three Stooges," that—isn't it great that Peter could be happy and content watching a childish TV show? And in that sense, you should feel good!

FELTON. Well, I actually do. And I used to watch with him until very recently. He watched a show made in Canada about a series of tugs called "The Adventures of Theodore Tugboat" And it's clearly made for, maybe, four- to seven-year-olds. And until very recently, six-foot-three-inch Peter Felton was absorbed by that show. We watched that together, without fail, on Sunday mornings; and we would review the elements of the family constellation of tugs. That was the conceit of the show, that familial circle; and I felt it was Peter's "hook" to it. And we talked about the dynamics, and treated it just as if it were "Masterpiece Theater." "What did you think when So-and-So Tugboat did such and such, and how did that make the other tug feel?" So I quite appreciate what you say.

I've always thought, when I see very young adolescent girls who are sporting budding breasts, that they really don't' know how to deal with them yet. I realize it represents a very lovely event in girls' lives; but still, as you say, it's quite a striking difference from what they're accustomed to, and probably comfortable with for a while.

THORP. Yes. And the expectations that accompany all of that. And you look at all these cultures, from "Confirmation" in the Christian religion to "bar mitzvah" to the Sun ceremony, or whatever it was called, in the Sioux, to various mutilation experiences in certain African cultures; they're all assuring: "You're now a man! Or, "You're now a woman!" I suppose on one level, one can be critical of a society that arbitrarily defines manhood, or personhood, with this rite of passage. But now, I realize myself that: perhaps it's worse to have *no* rite of passage. And to a large extent, we have no rite of passage anymore.

And when that happens, kids define their *own* rite of passage. And they shouldn't'. It's kind of "Lord of the Flies," as a rite of passage; but it's more—the lack of ceremony detracts from the kids' greater qualities. And in fact one of the points of focus of our planning for next year is our sense of our own culture. We're going to actively address *Gateway's* culture. And one of the things we talked about, as we began our discussion, is the need to build tradition. This sounds like an oxymoron; but you know what I mean.

FELTON. Sure.

THORP. —We need to build ceremony and tradition in this school. And that's one of the things we're going to be looking at for next year. Particularly as we head toward senior year and graduation. So we will actively and consciously try to create tradition in this school. Because kids don't have tradition in their lives.

FELTON. I think that's important. And if they don't, in each young person there will be a little notation, psychologically, and there will be something needed in that space later.

THORP. We could come full circle about the idea of diversity, for this is one of the problems I have with diversity. Where the goal of the diversity committee is so kids will appreciate diversity, that's great! But if you have kids being exposed to the "multicultural history program," it's really so they will be exposed to many different cultures! And yet, all of that thinking stops short of the question: "Okay, but what *values* do you want your kids to have? What ceremonies and tradition do you want your kids to have? It's important! And although kids resist it like crazy, when you persevere and "ram tradition down their throats," so to speak, they appreciate it. As long as it's not silly and ridiculous, they do in fact really appreciate it. They may call for it in imperfect and inarticulate ways; but they need *and want* it.

And so we're going to look at that.

Chapter Twenty-One

"I'M MAD AS HELL, AND I'M NOT GOING TO TAKE IT ANYMORE!"

"What's the point of education, anyway? Is the point, as clearly it was in McGuffey's Reader, that you would inculcate values thinly disguised as lessons on the alphabet?…[T]he typical education has been designed to transmit values from one generation to the next. You know—'It makes a difference that you know this language. It makes a difference that you study the Constitution. It makes a difference that this curriculum is part of your program.' And I think what's interesting right now, in at least the content side of things, is that the technocrats' role in education is they tend to see it more as a change agent—education as change, as opposed to education as preservation…."

"[I]f you're being accountable in this day and age, to whom and for what purpose? Is it that you're being accountable for state-mandated testing? Or compliance? Or whatever the hell the issue is? Some philosopher-Queen needs to stand up and say: '*This* is the point….'   It's acculturation in a society that's increasingly discultured—or a-cultured, I guess would be a better way of saying it. It's 'Train 'em for the uncertainty of the rapidly-changing world, and just make sure they're risk-takers. You know, the primary goal of education is to take risks.' Now, that's a long way away from stating the goal that the primary goal of education is to be able to read Shakespeare together! At the end of all that is the third goal: 'Train 'em *differently*….'"

24 April—*The unit of currency at Gateway High School—as at any high school—is students. In this case, 192 persons between the age of fourteen and sixteen gathered five days a week, seven or more hours a day, for learning, interacting, growing. Teachers wanted passionately for these students to learn about specific areas of study: Spanish; algebra; Mohammedanism; predicates and reflexive verbs; soccer. Students wanted passionately to learn about—themselves. And each other.*

On Friday, 21 April, three days before this dialogue meeting with the Principal, the student body of Gateway met in its regular assembly. The time, however, was devoted not to routine announcements, or skits to enliven the morning, but to sharing of feelings about the incident which, one year before, had convulsed anyone teaching Spanish, any coach on the soccer field, any student between the ages of fourteen and sixteen. Indeed, the event had added a word to the lexicon of American language, and one with weighted and painful significance: "Columbine."

This first anniversary of the day on which two pained and disgruntled young outcasts in a small Colorado town had carried an armory into their school, murdered a dozen classmates and then themselves, was celebrated thoughtfully at Gateway. As Peter Thorp would allude, students in that assembly, as on the one a year before and only a few days following the event, shared their grief—painful feelings about acceptance, or the lack of it, and hope for the future. Or the lack of it.

To an enlightened and caring high school principal, feeling—even for a moment —that his flock is clouded by doubt about the future, brings its own panic, its own grief. For in such a circumstance, nothing really is working as it should be. No reflexive verbs, no soccer skills, no algebraic equations seem to be serving to teach what everyone in this community has to learn, needs to learn: That to live together requires an unfathomable but unstinting exertion. That to matriculate into maturity means acquiring knowledge and skills— acquiring tools—which dwarf the significance of last night's homework, or next week's quiz. That not to do these things means, quite simply, that we will die together.

FELTON.   I wanted to talk with you about teaching itself, some meanings about teaching; and a way to engage is for me to report in, in a greater depth, about my photo workshops, as I found them ideal tests of "practical pedagogy."

When we set up this Photo Group project, I reworked a group activity which I dubbed the "Minor White Module," because the photographer and teacher Minor White, from M.I.T., got involved with the Polaroid process along about the time Ansel Adams did, in the 'fifties, and really in the 'sixties. Polaroid was established by then, but was in a transition phase from sort of "cutesy-fun," consumer-level snapshots, to real professional use. And he developed this module, and I extrapolated from that and built upon it, which really was based on interaction between students, and the use of the camera and a kind of development of an idea, the execution of the idea, an assessment by the students all along the way of a four-point program, as to how well they were able to realize creatively what was in their minds.

The purpose of our project was to direct students to experience the artistic process, in which photographic expression and interpersonal contact, these two elements, work together to excite both new visual awareness, and new insights about the human social process. Our workshop here produced two sort of conflicting areas. I set up pretty standard protocols, with booklets to follow, and places to fill in commentary before and after processing of the image, with specific instructions for four different levels of "who's in charge" of the image, who's expressing, how is this received by the photographer and the subject, and so forth. And written commentary along the way.

And what I found throughout was that, after the initial "getting-involved," there was inattention to details of the lesson, and a lack of fulfillment of the exact processes in the instruction given. The students instantly seemed intuitively to assess the lesson, and to adapt it to their inclinations. So I let them "run with the ball," and take it where they want; and the results of that were that there was great excitement generated overall. Everybody got really involved, especially when they began to extrapolate and make their own statement of it. An appreciation developed of the photographic vocabulary—vocabulary in the sense of thinking photographically, not merely the language of it. A clear acquisition of technical and aesthetic skills, by learning the equipment, pushing themselves into its development, and seeing the relationship between the two—"When you do this, this happens."

So, I saw that, as anticipated, when they developed artistic and visual modes of expression, their visual acuity enhanced. And a teamwork concept was really nourished—which was one of my two specific goals. Photography is usually a solipsistic effort; and solipsism—loneliness, the state of being alone—is clearly antagonistic to the concept of the class, and by extension the school community.

The other goal I had—and it's a sticking-point for me in photography—is to defeat the rampant and easily-adapted, and even attractive, "paparazzi" idea of photography, which is that you have a camera that advances its film by itself, and you take as many images as you can. Now, there are times when even I find that necessary. But in class I wanted to slow...everything...down! So that at the end of a day's work, or a half day's work, if you've got five or six or seven images, of which two or three are brilliant, and maybe only that many more that ultimately went through your machine, that's just fine. You don't have to go through rolls and rolls of film, because of what that does to denigrate the whole process.

Based on these workshops, I found my group of students greatly open to participation in the group process; eager to learn new skills; willing to take some chances; enlightened and *surprised* to discover their own new personal talents; they felt more secure submerging their "self" into the group; and they took great pride in their artistic achievement, which definitely that came out of this!

I tried to give an overall evaluation to the process. I said: As a measure of whether the assignment was fulfilled on its own terms, how well the kids met the actual parameters I had set forth—it was maybe 40- to 60 percent effective. But as a measure of the assignment as a means to an end—the end being this whole gestalt, and the process, it was clearly 100 percent effective. Or more!

THORP.   So, in sum, the effectiveness of the lesson was what?

FELTON.   I'll rephrase that, so that maybe the percentages—

THORP.   Oh, no. I understand that. I totally understand what you're saying. But what I'm hearing you say is: Given what you set out to do, it was 40 to 60 percent successful, in terms of various criteria. Given observations that you made, and given the big picture, it was 100 percent successful.

FELTON.   Correct.

THORP.   Okay. So now I'm asking you as a fellow teacher, with those pieces, with those two observations in mind: So how effective was the lesson?

FELTON.   Eminently effective, I believe.

THORP.   So what do you learn as a teacher, as a result of that?

FELTON.   Well, what I learned was the lesson reinforced some positive values, or values which are positive to me which I like to impart to students. I felt good to see that this came about, and you can "chicken-and-egg" that point—

THORP.   Right.

FELTON. —But nonetheless, I saw some forbidding initial aspects that happen in a situation like this, about kids—the complete self-confrontation of the young student, who doesn't even want his or her image to be seen. Sometimes that person doesn't even want the picture made, with the individual, with oneself as the focal point. But the lesson proved the student could move away from that, to say: "This is my 'self,' but this is also part of the protoplasmic basis of a learning circumstance, that involves other people as well as me."

This clearly happened, and I was very glad it happened! In fact one of the things that was a testament to the success of the overall project, even though the individual rules were bent, was that the whole module was set up, both with what White did and what I added to it, for two people. Groups, teams of two. And in the second session, a certain four girls immediately wanted to be together, they wanted to operate as a group, and they worked very effectively. Much more than I would have thought. As a team, they got all the values that two people might have gotten. And in fact, in some ways it was enhanced, because some of the diffidence and self-consciousness was removed, by dint of their being members of this group. And when they asked me to interact, as I had to do to take some of those shots of them, because they all wanted to be in them, they were able to set aside the fact that I was coming in to their sphere, their space. They were willing to accept that.

I came out with a different kind of image, that tried to describe this whole process. And the idea I came up with was—this was the Bauhaus! This was taking off the restraints, but with one's own artistic self-discipline driving the vehicle. And what happens when you do that.

THORP. How positively Germanic!

FELTON. Yes, true! I believe the Bauhaus comparison is not outlandish.

So, that was that experience. Since then, the group has had a couple of interesting moments, moments which challenged that community subsuming of the self. At the beginning, I had foolishly told everybody, as a point to quell somebody's tensions, "Don't worry, if we take a bad picture, we're all going to look at them, and we're all going to choose them together, for an exhibit." And then when we went over my cut of them, there was a surprising number of kids who said "Oh—you can't show that. You just can't show that!" And of course, these were all the wonderful ones!—

THORP. Yeah, right!

FELTON. —that they didn't want to show. And of course, there are no terrible pictures, really. So. That's part of this process.

But it was really an interesting process; and part of what is the mystery of photography is involved in all of this, because had I conducted a module in—well, even in writing, or in woodworking, it wouldn't have had at all the same effect. It's still the old idea of capturing the soul, you know.

THORP. Yes.

FELTON. Well, that's the photo group report. But I mention the event, because I'd like you to reflect on some of its tenets—process, pedagogy—community—in a couple of ways: One is: We've talked about curriculum in terms of a kind of hard, cold and formal need to structure every five minutes in a math class or in a Spanish class. And we've talked about what happens—and it's happened to me, and you've mentioned that it's happened to you—when the shrewd student sitting in the front row will say: "Mr. Thorp, what do you think about so-and-so?" And Mr. Thorp's off and running, or Mr. Felton's off and running, or whatever. And it's informative, and it's enriching, but it isn't as rigid as the other.

This was certainly a confirmation to me that I do better in this form than in the other, which might just be—

THORP. "This" being photography, or—?

FELTON. "This" being a kind of go-with-the-flow way of teaching. Which may be a criticism of my pedagogical technique; but it might also suggest a sensitivity to the material, or it might suggest things which are paradigmatic to the different disciplines, that are worth noting.

THORP. So what's the point of teaching?

FELTON. The point of teaching—perhaps—is to take the given and common elements in the universe shared by the teacher and the student, and try and rearrange them again in such a way that yet untold revelations can come out of whatever chemistry or alchemy takes place in the interactive process between the two.

THORP. Because those revelations have equal validity?

FELTON. To what? To each other? Or—

THORP. Well, I don't know. I mean, what I heard you say was that the teacher acts as a catalyst to the process by which new interpretations or new insights come about. And—do each of those insights or revelations or acts of creation have equal validity relative to each other? Or relative to what the teacher thinks ought to be happening?

FELTON. Well—

THORP. In other words, the question is: How didactic is teaching?

FELTON. Right, that is the question. And my answer is: The best teaching *isn't* didactic, I daresay. The best teaching is a private and unspoken covenant in which the preceptor is able to communicate to the pupil: "I'm really just a guide. I know about this a measure more than you do, but I'm older, and I'm going to use some other tools that I've sharpened, successfully, and used before, to move us through this. But you're going to be right there just a second behind me, so that any rocks that fall down are going to hit you, too! They might hit me first. On the other hand, maybe I can see the thing just a split-second before you do, and help redirect you a little bit."

I don't see there being a terrible difference in strata between the two, between mentor and student. I really never have. I mean, there have to be, obviously, informal ways, and we accept the ways parenthetically in which there are differences. But in the best relationships, that's why I think the tutorial approach has real merit.

THORP. And this is why state-mandated testing is such a nightmare! Because it requires a narrowing of education, and a narrowing of lessons, and a narrowing of creativity, rather than an expanding of all that.

FELTON. Yeah. I agree.

THORP. And we do it to ourselves. After all—I mean, I was just reading, this weekend, in one of the journals, the MCAT, which is the Massachusetts testing—they're a couple of years ahead of California in terms of both the magnitude of it and the numbers of students who are boycotting them!—which is going to start happening, I think, in California. I mean, it already has a little bit. In the standards, in the ones that are most under fire, the history standards, and the history component of it, are far too sweeping in terms of the amount of content that kids have to know, and be ready to be tested on. And yet, the standards were developed by teachers, of course. And curriculum developers. We do it to ourselves. But the response to it, at least by one segment, is: "Okay, so we need to cut back on the amount that needs to be covered," without getting at the key issue, which is: "We need to question the fundamental premises."

To me that's one of *the* interesting questions in education, which is: What's the point, anyway? You know—is the point, as clearly it was in McGuffey's Reader, that you would inculcate values thinly disguised as lessons on the alphabet? And so, education was remarkably and typically has been a remarkably conservative phenomenon; that the typical education has been designed to transmit values from one generation to the next. You know—"It makes a difference that you know this language. It makes a difference that you study the Constitution. It makes a difference that this curriculum is part of your program." And I think what's interesting right now, in at least the content side of things, is that the technocrats' role in education is they tend to see it more as a change agent, education as change, as opposed to education as preservation.

And then you have—and I'm obviously putting words in your mouth, but humor me for a moment—you have the educational anarchist like you, who exhorts: "It doesn't really make a difference what the end product is, as long as there's an end product, and as long as the teacher has stimulated the student to generate new insights and new understandings and/or new acts of creation, because that's what it's all about." You would get various people falling into those various camps, from this guy Hirsch, whom I mentioned earlier in a previous conversation regarding "The Cultural Literacy," who would exclaim: "Hey!—the point of education is to be sure that one generation can speak to the next." And so when I say, "Hoist by your own petard," somebody understands what the hell I'm talking about. Another camp says: "The education of the twenty-first century has to prepare people to live in the twenty-first century, and the changing world, and you've got to know the technology, da-da-da-da!" And yet another faction says: "Who gives a damn? Create!" And you have plenty of people falling into each one of those camps.

I think it therefore becomes really interesting to be a teacher, given that range of choices. And it becomes really interesting as a school to decide how much range of choice you want to allow your teachers to have, you want to provide your teachers to have. And then of course, it becomes different in the public sector versus the private sector, again, in terms of how much flexibility one has to do one's own thing, as it were.

There's a teacher in Weston, I think it is—which is a pretty affluent suburb of Boston, with a high-quality public education system, who essentially is boycotting the application of these tests, and rather than get himself fired, he happens to call in sick on those days. And his point is, after fifteen years of teaching the system and after twenty-plus years of him and his colleagues developing this amazing social sciences program with all sorts of electives, they're being forced to jetty those electives to do the "Plato to NATO" surveys, in order to prepare the kids for standardized testing.

So it'll be interesting to see at what point educators stand up and revolt against this, if at all. The estimate in Boston is that had the MCATs been in place–I don't have the statistics accurate, I think I might have them reversed—somewhere around eighty percent of the African-American kids and fifteen percent of Latino kids, or the other, flipped result, would have failed the comprehensive high school exit exam. So eighty percent of whichever group was identified as such would have had to go and spend another year in high school! Talk about a social disaster!

FELTON. How many high schools still have a senior thesis, final comps that have to do with a special project, or something quite apart from the curriculum itself?—or in the university mode? How many still are able to feel it valuable to have that as part of things?

THORP. I don't know. My guess is it's a number that's increasing, in one direction, as schools are turning toward the portfolio reform. And the extent to which the portfolio is consistent with the senior culminating experience, my guess is that number's increasing. The numbers who are doing what you specifically said in terms of the senior comps, is rapidly going down the tubes. Unless those senior comps are tied in to state-mandate testing and/or exit exams.

FELTON. I'm surprised that there's anything in the way of attention to that—to a thesis idea.

THORP. Well, I didn't say that. I mean, a project, yes; a thesis, that's another question.

FELTON. I see. I don't know about you; but I remember the very first programmatic test I ever had to take, one that used computer-scored fill-in-circles forms and so forth. And it was an experience—

THORP. A school test or a state test?

FELTON. No, it was a school—I don't even remember what it was.

THORP. It wasn't the PSAT, or—

FELTON. It might even have been personality tests. I don't remember. I thought they were a battery of scholastic aptitude tests. I don't remember the names of them now. It was in the ninth grade, which in my case means 1957. And everything about their administration was out of the norm. We were all put in the cafeteria, and a man who was a counselor assumed the role of administrator of the test. And all his language was unusual from every other parameter we'd ever known—by which I mean, the entire personality of this heretofore well-known teacher changed! And the taking of the test was unusual and the instructions—which were to help guide us into the kind of mechanistic approach of the testing language—were forbidding. It felt as if we had to spend the morning on Mars.

I'll never forget that. And every other test—the SAT, and every other one I've had to take since then, I remembered back to this experience. It was so different. And not until hitting college and the eternal essay-type "blue book" did I feel comfortable again, in being able to express my expertise. And I'm sure that doesn't happen at all today. I'm sure it would be—the system is "*de rigueur.*" It's the way everything is run. I'm still not quite sure how essay-dependent the classes are here at Gateway, although I think they are, largely—

THORP. Yes.

FELTON. But as I go through—I have a hundred notes in the period of time we've been having these dialogues, and I've probably got ten new ones today, that talk about ways of approaching—ways that school districts and school boards and politicians and everyone else try—to make this whole idea of testing more palatable, more incentive-driven. Some are downright bizarre: "We will give more scholarships if the grades are higher." "We will give the teachers higher salaries if grades are higher." "We will give you, the teacher, a new mortgage!" "We will give you—practically—Depression-era dishes from the movies!—if only your group's scores are higher." And then of course, I see I've got here *another* hundred notes talking about how racially it doesn't make any difference. There's still favoritism toward whites. There's still the widening of a gap. An article I've carried in here several times is entitled: "Race Gap Widens at Lowell." March 10 of this year. "CBST test discriminatory; favors whites." "Diversity—" a reporter heads his piece: "Whites will have to negotiate in a multicultural world in the future." And yet, still showing favoritism. "Segregation: Two-thirds of blacks are still in segregated schools." But it's the year 2000!

I have other stories that we might get into at some point about—and I'm curious about your background in relation to them; namely, what happened in your life around the time of *Brown* vs. *Board of Education.* That whole—especially coming out of Boston—

THORP. South Boston, it happened, yeah.

FELTON. I mean, I'm very interested in some of that. But I don't fundamentally see significant, essential change—in forty years!, when I see headlines like this. Whereas, I didn't think that was a problem. And I promise you, when I walk in and I look at sophomore student Melvyn Thomas, it's very different from when I walked into my eighth-grade class, the term after *Brown*, and looked at a black person, and what happened then. And yet, some of the same problems are still there!

THORP. And what's different?

FELTON. Well, when I walked in—I mean, when *Brown*—when the Supreme Court made its ruling, overnight there was about a fifty percent white flight from the school I was attending. And when I say "overnight," I mean *overnight*.

THORP. Which was where?

FELTON. Webster Junior High School in Oklahoma City. In fact, the decimation from white fear was so complete, that within four or five years of my matriculation from there, the school folded. Closed its doors.

Now, some of the kids stayed after *Brown*, of course. The Felton kid stayed. My folks were old-line integrationists. Rabble-rousing Negro-lovers.

THORP. Border-state folks. Andrew Jacksonites.

FELTON. In spirit, anyway. We were actually San Franciscans temporarily on the loose. And before Oklahoma it was Oak Ridge, where, in 1946, my dad turned the Oak Ridge National Lab on its ear by hiring a new head nurse to take care of all these white folks, and take charge of a hospital full of Caucasian nurses; and by god, this nurse was twenty-six years old, she was a woman, she was gorgeous, and she was black as the ace of spades!

THORP. My god.

FELTON. She was a beautiful woman, named Doris Scott. And, you know, my upbringing went like that. And when I was in the seventh grade at that Oklahoma junior high, I came home from school one day and said to my dad, "Well, I've been invited to this birthday party." And he said, "Oh? Who is it?" And I told him, "Letitia Somebody," I don't remember the full name now. "A Negro girl." And he stopped in his tracks, and looked at me in my face and slowly, emphasizing each word, said: "You're—going—to—that—party!" And he drove me to the south side of Oklahoma City, which was called Niggertown by almost everybody except all the Unitarians I knew. And I knocked on the door, and was asked in, and I handed the girl my gift, and I sat there on the couch, in a birthday party of little black girls in beautiful dresses, very formal, and we all just sat around the living room and they all just stared at me. And then after about half the evening, they tentatively came over to me and they touched my hair.

THORP. How old were you?

FELTON.   Twelve, thirteen.   And then these young girls went back and sat down and sort of giggled with each other, and continued to stare at me, pleasantly.   And then at a certain point I asked to use the phone; and I called my dad, and he picked me up, and that was the end of the party!

And look what happens now!   It's very different.   And yet, it's still dismaying, because what this suggests to me—and this is the thrust of my question—this brings us back really to where we came in on one of our first sessions, which is: So much treading water to avoid a kind of panic.   That's what I feel from all of this.   You know—why should these things be handled this way?   I know we've discussed them; but I see them sort of as a collective problem.

THORP.   One of the great lessons for history is the lesson of what happens to a liberal in the South, in the early 'fifties.   I think I may have said this in a previous conversation, the same lesson of the Populists of the late nineteenth century, who were reformers and who got crushed in Southern elections by not being strident enough on race, and the pendulum swung so far in the other direction that it became these incredibly racist-bating Rednecks, to use the term.   Whereas they had started out where race was not the issue; it was *class* which was the issue for the *populus*, as it was for George Wallace, as it was for Huey Long in some ways.   And people got crushed along the way.   Over the race issue.

With respect to education, in the absence of intelligent leadership, or in the absence of the ability to say: "This is why it's working and this is why it's not working," nature abhors a vacuum.   And the educational world has been unable to agree on why it's working and why it's not working.   And it's not been able to agree using data, in part, because the data is soft data, in most cases.   The variables are so great that it's hard to come up with data that—you know: "Can you conclude that such-and-such place is the best high school system?" if you use this ridiculous poll that Newsweek did a couple of weeks ago, which is, you now, developing this ratio of number of kids versus number of AP tests taken.   A ridiculous way to measure qualities of a high school except for the fact that these high schools have a lot of AP tests, and kids are driven enough to take AP tests.   What does that tell you!

So in the absence of thoughtful self-examination—and what a paradox about the field of education!—which should be all about reflection and self-examination!—then liberally sprinkled with adversarial politics—it's no wonder that nobody has a sense of how to fix what's "broke" and how to say, "Stop! Enough!"   The fact that the "whole-language versus phonics" situation has become a political question, rather than an educational question, so utterly reveals the way it works.

Education is so without the normal gauges of success, be it the "bottom-line" profit in the stock market, and bankruptcy as one way to do it. Or being consumer-driven in terms of "Hey—if you don't like the Chevy, you go for the Ford." And Chevy goes belly-up if everybody goes to Ford. That is just kind of stumbling along, and clearly, folks aren't happy with the stumbling along, and that's where the politicians have said: "Aha! This is an issue. And so I'm going to come up with political solutions (a) to what is essentially a nonpolitical situation, and (b) being a politician, and I can't think all that much with great complexity, I'm going to come up with simplistic solutions to it."

And that solution is: State-mandated testing! We're giving kids that do well on tests scholarships; thanks, Governor Davis, for rewarding those kids who have every advantage as it is already. I mean, it's just—you know, if I had a sense of humor about it, it'd be silly; but because it's such important work, it's depressing to think that there can't be that kind of leadership. Increasingly, the system is broken, and increasingly, I recognize how broken the system is. And that's not—I am not saying that the public schools have failed. To the contrary—I would argue that given the way the system is broken, the public schools are doing remarkable work! And public school teachers are doing remarkable work in the face of ridiculous adversity. But also, it's complex, and I frequently am left to ask: "What's the point of teaching!?"

Come back to the question I asked you: "What are we trying to accomplish here as teachers?" Is it the view of co-exploration, as you suggested, which is to me an eminently admirable rationale for being an educator and approach for being an educator. But I can sure as hell guarantee you that wouldn't sell in Sacramento, let alone Washington! So what's the point?

And to bring you to the grass roots—one of the things we wrestle with here at Gateway is this very issue of "What's the point?" And for our folks, there's the zeal and passion of having bought into a mission. So it isn't so much "What's the point?" about us, as much as: "What's the priority?" What are the choices we make, and if so, why do we make certain choices? That's when education gets increasingly complex. School people are criticized, appropriately so in some ways, for the "I-am-the-Captain-of-my-960-square-feet-in-my-classroom-when-I-close-that-door," and "I'm autonomous, I'm accountable to no one, except, as Miss Jean Brodie would say, : "To me girrlls."

But on the other hand, if you're being accountable in this day and age, to whom and for what purpose? Is it that you're being accountable for state-mandated testing? Or compliance? Or whatever the hell the issue is? Some philosopher-Queen needs to stand up and say: "*This* is the point...." It's acculturation in a society that's increasingly discultured—or a-cultured, I guess would be a better way of saying it. It's "Train 'em for the uncertainty of the rapidly-changing world, and just make sure they're risk-takers. You know, the primary goal of education is to take risks." Now, that's a long way away from stating the goal that the primary goal of education is to be able to read Shakespeare together! At the end of all that is the third goal: "Train 'em *differently.*"

And then you start looking at the European system, which probably has clearer missions, although in a much more—back to our Germanic thrust, back at the beginning of the conversation—is clearer in its mission in that kids get parceled out and separated out to be told: "No, this is your mission, this is your gymnasium, this is your vocational school, this is your university track." In a far more ruthless way than is the case in this country. But—maybe with far better results; or maybe with results that enable the education system to work better for a greater number of people.

FELTON.   Well, in Europe, if I'm correct, the title "Professor" is the highest accolade and sign of reverence one can achieve in the society. Whereas here, "Professor" means either some sad has-been musical impresario, or a faculty person clearly not accorded real respect.

THORP. Yeah.   I clearly see a distinction, though I think a professor in this society has light-years more respect than a teacher in this society. There really is a delineation between those two categories. Whereas, if you go to other societies, including European and especially Asian societies, a teacher, no matter what grade level, has a level of respect that transcends anything. I think the gap gets narrower as you approach post-secondary positions in the society. But it's clearly different; and part of that, I'm saying here, is a function of the question of "What's the *purpose* of a professor?" I mean, what is going to happen to the profession of teaching when, in fact, on-line education becomes the way to get yourself a college degree?

I mean, are you going to want to pay—even in California—eleven thousand bucks per year to go to Berkeley, or sixteen hundred bucks, two hundred bucks a course, for getting through your course work, when the only difference is doing it live or doing it by Memorex? You can't tell me that sitting in a class of five to seven hundred kids in Psych 101 is personal attention!

FELTON. Of course not. Although the Teaching Assistant drawing his little salary check might disagree with you.

To me, probably the most important statement a student makes, is the statement: "I don't know." And to me that's an invitation for everybody. And what dismays me, as we've talked before, about the technological ramifications of education, is that that is not an acceptable statement to make. That from the "get-go," whether you're in the role of instructor or the role of student, you must as quickly as possible get, in the language of the time, "up to speed," and be able to say, authoritatively as quickly as you can: "I *know.*" It's just patently a whole different idea.

And when I think about what you're trying to impart here, and the good attitude you had when you had these waves of people running at you with all kinds of standardized-test necessities, or imperatives—and you're saying, what you've said sounded to me more or less like saying: "I choose to view the glass as half full rather than half empty, and I'm going to work with what I have..." Were I in your role, I clearly would say: "Not only would I look at it as half empty, but the problem is somebody's always trying to spill out the half that's in there! So I'm constantly being set back." And in that respect, I don't envy you your task. And it would worry me greatly.

I've been trying in my mind to imagine a kind of *schema*, a board with strings and pegs, for example, for how you operate, with respect to your teaching staff. And I wondered what freedom you feel, to put true renegades—or anarchists, to use your word—on the faculty, and whether, if you put this anarchist in here, he or she is necessarily attached by this tether to some other privilege or opportunity which, because you're advancing that "freedom," will pull this other one more into the area of restriction. And whether you can visualize that idea, you're constantly having to rearrange things mindful of their total integration with other things that you have to keep your eye on. I don't know if that's the way it is or not. Or whether you staff a "far-out" group, and not really face any serious consequences, lest one of them was a rabid Communist or exposed himself in public, or something pretty bizarre to call school board attention to himself. But if that didn't happen, how long could you do, you know—"Peter Thorp's Private Reserve," best-seller faculty? And "get away with it"? I think that's a question!

THORP. Well, I'll pick up on it about three sentences ago: The extent to which Gateway could tolerate, if not nuture, an anarchist. And the answer is "Not very much." Not, at least, in the short run. This is, in part, because of the reality of being in the public sector.

Also, though—and this is really more the emphasis in terms of my own reaction to that question—the fragile nature of this delicate organism—we had someone on our faculty this year—gone, now—who operated outside the rather expansive boundaries of professional endeavor that one should, in a school like this. To this person's credit, this person realized, halfway through the year, that it wasn't working for him, either! And so, what could have been an unhappy situation, or a long-term unhappy situation, ended soon enough.

It all comes back to: You want to make sure that people "buy into" the mission. And a good mission is, paradoxically, rather narrowly defined, though the methodology of accomplishing that mission might be quite broad. So you can have—let's get away from the word "anarchist"—you can have individualists, in terms of their methodologies. But it's hard in a school, when you have individualists in terms of their goals, their ends. So here at Gateway, a lot of latitude in terms of methodologies, and in fact, we'd like to have this be a cauldron of different methodologies, to—from our kind of "laboratory" approach. But we want to make sure that people are working toward the same goal. And while the goal is not so monochromatic that it's absolutely the same thing—you know, the "dissonance" in that allusion I made a moment ago to that one teacher was that this person's attitude about kids was outside what this school believes should be the appropriate approach toward kids.   That was really the issue, in addition to the methodologies and approaches, being so different that had the attitude toward kids not been out of line, maybe the other thing could have worked. But with the combination of the two, it was not a happy experience.

FELTON. I see. Well, I don't mean this to sound as if it's a "doom-saying" question; but let me preface it this way: What if the legatees of Ronald Reagan and others, like Gray Davis, are successful in putting their concept of education across?   And what if they accomplished this in the same manner that Reagan did it—by lopping off the heads of the important humanistic departments of government? And what if that meant that Peter Thorp and his group of educators felt a loss of a lot of the meaning and the opportunity in teaching, which all of you came into the profession with, and came into this job with, and come every morning into those classrooms with—what if all that energy is slowly degraded and denigrated and degenerated to the point where they suddenly wake up one day and say: "This is totally no longer functioning as I had conceived in myself it could"? Will they—will that point come? Will there continue to be enough inspiration for "fighting the good fight" to avoid that awful confrontation?

THORP. For some people, yes. For more people, no. That time has already come for all of us at certain times and certain ways, where you look at yourself in the mirror and say: "Why beat my head against the wall?" It is, however, more of a phenomenon—well; there is a difference in the impact of that in part depending upon age and experience, and what you're looking to create, and that sort of thing.

It's different for young people, who are having a hard time with this profession anyway. But what's drawing a lot of young people into business are schools like this, where they will be able to say: "Okay—I *can* make a difference!" and "Okay—I *won't* be fettered by the bonds of educational bureaucracy!"

But the reality is, it's not that simple. And it's not—you know; it's not an utter revolution; it's *e*volution, it's educational evolution. And for people who have been around for as long as I have, you understand why it's *e*volution and not *re*volution. For young people who are more revolutionary in their bent, evolution can either take too long—and there's the paradox of the fact that I've got a lot less time than they do on this planet, so you'd think I'd be more impatient. But one develops this perverse patience with older age, I guess. And it may not only take longer, but may result in too many compromises, you know. And those of us who were in the barricades in the 'sixties couldn't understand how one could compromise with the death penalty, or about the death penalty, whatever the issue was—let alone, Vietnam.

You begin to understand the necessity of compromise, or the wisdom of compromise, as you go through certain things and pick your battles. So for schools like this, as I think I've said before: The danger is being pecked to death by ducks. You know, the danger is just being chipped away and chipped away and chipped away. And that's the phenomenon that's taking place. And whether or not it's really conscious, I'm not sure. I don't think it is, actually, because I don't think anybody's really looking at it that way. But the consequence of various battles around the country about charter schools and various issues are fatiguing to the general strength of the greater organism that is education.

I was doing a lot of reading last night in a set of articles about special education and for-profit schools in Massachusetts and this huge argument going back, where this Boston College professor essentially attacked them, saying, you know—they're exploiting the hell out of the kids, and getting rid of the kids who have special education needs, and yet taking the State's money for special education services. And the schools involved came back with all sorts of responses saying: "No, we're not!" This doesn't begin to address collective bargaining; let alone credentialing; let alone financial issues.

So, it will be interesting to see the extent to which the charter school movement gets over Hillary's Step, as it was called, on the way to Mount Everest, or whether or not we get stuck on that wall and can't go any further, because the sum total of the legislative constraints takes away the ability to accomplish what we're trying to accomplish.

I don't think that will happen. I mean, this is to me what still keeps it really interesting, which is that I think the evolution is still taking place, and still capable of taking place. I think where the charter school folks will be intelligent is if they see it as evolutionary, and don't—and I think I've said this to you before—and don't make it revolutionary, in either fact or appearance, thereby putting the status quo on the defensive and reacting to revolution as the keepers of the status quo typically have, historically. But if we evolve, you know, and invade and in fact evolve in a way where some of the good things that we're doing make a difference—I mean, I would be fine, if—pick a number—ten years ago there was no such thing as a charter school, because every public school had adopted the essential premises of charter schools, which is: Parental support, nonadversarial relationship amongst the various constituencies in the school; and the ability for consumers of education to have reasonable access to choice in deciding what school worked best for my kid or me. Then, who needs charter schools in that scenario? So we'll see if the evolution takes place.

FELTON. Let's bring the issue very close to home: How's Amy doing?

And by way of inquiring about her: I don't know if you've been in the situation before, but are there any special things to consider, when one member of the family is in a role such as yours, and another member of the family is in a role such as hers?

THORP. Sure. It's a terrible burden on the kid. There's an advantage in it in that she's got an inside track to the inside dope. She's already been told by some kids that nobody's going to give her a hard time, because she's the daughter of the principal, and the word is spread like fire throughout the school, you know: "No dumping on Amy!, because you're going to have to pay the price." But of course, the fact that that's being said to her singles her out in a way that she'd prefer not to be singled out.

It's not an easy position to be in. And it's not an easy position for the kid, because, based on my first daughter's experience, having gone through this, that the kid also, as any kid does, wants to belong, and become a member; and in order to become a member of a club you have to have something to offer the club. And whether it's your twenty-five-thousand-dollar initiation fee to the Golf Club, or whether it's your brains, or your athletics, or your beauty—there's always some commodity of belonging. And for kids who don't have a commodity of belonging, those are the kids that you read about are slashing their wrists, or committing suicide, or are miserable, or whatever.

Amy's got her own commodities; but a special commodity that she has is if kids wanted to start hitting her up for information about the school—"Go ask your dad, see what you can find out! See what he thinks about it! Are we in trouble? Go ask your dad!" –And my older daughter occasionally used that approach with me, which is, you know: "Tell me something that you wouldn't tell the ordinary kid." I mean, she wouldn't put it that way; but that's the dilemma that she'd put me in. And some of the more difficult conversations I had with her were over that, where I'd say, "I'm not going to tell you, because I wouldn't tell it to any kid, and it's not fair for you to ask me this." And she'd reply: "Come on! I'm your daughter, you know?! You should tell me—what's it going to hurt? I'm you're daughter, come on, Dad, you call tell me? Come on, Dad! I won't tell anybody else!" And they were difficult conversations.

She's doing "fair," is I guess the best way to describe it. She's still experiencing a lot of the trauma of loss and grief and anger for having had to leave her previous situation. And so it's complex. And she's also still trying to figure out what her place is here. And she hasn't yet found kids who seem as if they could make up a group for her. So she's clinging to me. Which is nice, on the one hand. I like that. But it's not a long-term strategy for either one of us.

FELTON. Do you have any sense of how much after-school connectivity the student body here has with each other? What kind of friendships are being formed?

THORP. Not great.

FELTON. Not great, yeah. That fits the bill for my son, I know.

THORP. In fact, less so than I had imagined. Though certainly it's happening in some cases. The stories that I hear from some set of parents are: Such-and-such a kid and another kid really like each other during school, but live on the other side of town from each other, or a lot of them live in the East Bay, so on the weekends they don't hang out with each other. You know. So they're—particularly for our kids in the East Bay, they're back to their old friends on the weekends. Which is good, perhaps; but also makes this "push-pull" experience they're having continue to go on.

Part of it is we need to get more activities going and that sort of thing, and space—we've been down this road before. But it's also that kids go off and go home, and go to jobs, and go to babysitting. So it surprised me a little bit.

FELTON.   That's actually pretty typical of San Francisco.

THORP.   Was Peter here on Friday?   Did he tell you about the assembly?

FELTON.   The Columbine—?

THORP.   Yeah. Did he tell you about it?

FELTON.   Yes.

THORP.   What'd he say?

FELTON.   He—as always happens with Peter, Peter gets stuck on unimportant elements, and it takes two or three "hits" for me to return to the subject to get the real goods. And his "unimportant" elements were that several kids spoke, and he did tell me they spoke passionately; but where he got stuck was a comment on one young girl's typical, as he put it, "diarrhea of the mouth," and how this was upsetting just as a behavior pattern for her, not the import of whatever she said. So I don't really know what happened; I'd be very interested to hear more about it.

THORP.   Pick his brain. Maybe we can talk about it next time. Because I think I've alluded to—a year ago, the assembly we had—

FELTON.   Yes.

THORP.   Also, we had no idea where this one was going. And it was really interesting to see it happen again, for those of us who had been there a year ago. Very few people among the adults in the room had been there a year ago. They were experiencing the phenomenon for the first time, and it was very interesting to see the faculty reaction to it—which was, for the most part: "Wow! Look at these kids—look at them speak with such courage. And I see the kids through a new set of lenses, as a result of this."

FELTON.   Really!

THORP.   —Which was interesting. Again, there was certainly some cause for concern about what they were talking about. But that's another story. So it was reasonably interesting to see the faculty reaction to it.

FELTON.   I will definitely talk with him about it.

One thing I did extract myself from some of the news coverage on it, was that unlike many events which pass an anniversary, the immediacy of this event, and the lack of dissipation of the vibration, was striking.

THORP. I think that's true, yeah. Kids live in fear.

Chapter Twenty-Two

"OUT OF IT": TEENAGERS WHO CAN'T COME IN FROM THE COLD

"[T]here are a lot of kids feeling alienated, I think, in this period and at this age. And even kids who appear to be fine, and in the "in-crowd," are in jeopardy. Maybe the difference again is this power question, that some kids *choose* to be alienated. Some kids choose to alienate others from them. And then there are some kids who are the victims and are forced to be alienated. Some kids have the power to decide how alienated they want to be; and some kids are power-less, to determine that. That might be the great frustration."

<u>5 May</u>—*As a reporter, who by dint of an ongoing assignment had the ear of his son's high school principal on a weekly basis, I felt that some issues concerning my son's current involvement at the school could be seen to serve as more universally relevant to the ongoing dialogue's discussion of questions about adolescent behavior.*

There was no doubt that I felt some natural uneasiness about bringing these matters forth before the Principal; for in all other circumstances in which my son's name had come up as a member of the Principal's school's student body—as it had been when the Principal discussed his own daughter, or his own partner's son—these student-age relatives served as quintessential sentries of exemplary experience, and hence relevant mettle for our dialogue's realm. But it became my belief that more consequential (that is, more deeply personal) issues were legitimate fare as well. Brought to bear on problems confronting the student body at large, the relevance certainly seemed to legitimize inclusion of this also-personal material within the framework of the dialogues we were conducting as Reporter and Principal.

In such a circumstance of consideration did I introduce into the relationship with the school head, the subject of difficulties my boy was experiencing at Gateway. Briefly stated—and with his permission to do so—they were these:

At some time within the two weeks preceding the current session, young Peter was descending a school staircase in the student rush following a class break; in the pushing, his footing slipped. Instinctively thrusting his arms out to brace himself against a fall, his hands inadvertently struck a young female student on the upper torso. When a student next to this girl remarked on his clumsiness, he uttered an inane, embarrassment-covering snarl of bravado—the kind one would not find unusual from a shy, socially awkward sixteen-year-old boy who had just lost his footing and caused inadvertent contact with another student.   Following the foot-slip incident, and despite the fact that the girl's classmate fully acknowledged the innocence of the clumsy event, Peter was first called into the Assistant Principal's office, and told he was on a list of students considered sexual harassers; his advisor, in a parent-teacher meeting, cautioned me that Peter was in a peculiar situation; Peter's mother also had a meeting with the Advisor, the Principal, and another school counselor; and, finally, Peter himself met with the administrative group. At last, a long ten-day period later, Peter was told he was "cleared" of any malfeasance in the situation.

Throughout the events, I reminded myself that this was not Nazi Germany, nor was it McCarthyite America; it was not the San Francisco Police Department; it was in fact an occurrence in the very bosom of trust that I, as an active parent and participant in a special project, was helping to create. Yet I felt it imperative for me studiously to avoid any discussion of the issue with the Principal until its resolution. While counseling my son, and meeting with the Advisor, I determined to hear Peter out on the issue, assess what lengths the school would go toward coloring his name with the charge against his character, and prepare with my son a formal defense and challenge if necessary.

Fortunately, such defense did not become necessary, as Peter was given the "clean bill of health." But the incident underscored certain deep-set problems I felt my boy had regarding his social development, his struggles to reach out to the community of his peers, and his ongoing formation of a sense of self. These issues—discussed with

*Peter Thorp in the form of matters about adolescent behavior in
general, now glowed with the particularity of acute personal meaning.*

*I met with my son, had a conversation with him on these topics,
and brought the substance of our father-and-son exchange to the next
session with Peter Thorp, to add to our larger dialogue on
adolescence's rites of passage. The principal—who had just spent too
much of the previous three days dealing with recurrent plumbing
nightmares in the school—was only too happy to confront some
meaningful problems.*

There were plenty.

FELTON. I understand the assembly just past featured more
teachers' skits!

THORP. Yes, yes. A little variety.

FELTON. You should know that you will forever hold my son
Peter's regard not for your work as Principal, but for a skit you
performed in during assembly. You impersonated, I believe, a little old
lady—?

THORP. I was the old woman running into some of our larger
boys on the street, the charade to demonstrate the intimidation factor
that the little old lady might experience. So: "Be good neighbors," was
the message.

FELTON. I see.

Over the next couple of sessions, I'd like to cover several topics,
all under the rubric of adolescence. One of these issues, which I really
would like to deal with first, extends our discussion about what we
used to call "race relations," and what now emerges in part as the
diversity phenomenon at school, and pull some of this from the point of
view of my son. He is willing to serve as illustrative representative of
class and age here, and I'd like to take advantage of his willingness.

Now, Peter and I spent a good bit of yesterday together, after
school was dismissed because of the plumbing debacle here. Which
was fortunate; I was glad to be able to do that. Not living with him, I
take advantage of every shard of time I can get. And that was a good
example. And he was very happy for that; he initiated it, which doesn't
always happen.

THORP. That's great.

FELTON. He usually just wants to make a beeline for home and
get into reclusive surroundings. He and I went to a huge music store,
and at one point I spotted him away over to one side, looking in bins of

compact discs. And I had this observation that I have from time to time, sometimes out of pride, sometimes out of dismay, really—that, in such circumstances, Peter looks twenty-five years old! And rather than think: "How wonderful, this big strapping boy!," I thought of your comment recently in a session, about how too often kids today are deprived of childhood. And even thought that's not exactly the same thing, there certainly was an element of that, in that, looking so much older than his sixteen years, he creates expectations in others, whether they're just casting a glance at him or dealing with him, where adulthood is expected, or some greater level of maturation is expected.

I personally see part of that deprivation of childhood experience as being one of the victimizing effects of divorce, when divorce hits certain kids. Sometimes either they have to jump into another role, or are just simply inundated with a kind of weight, of worry, that is inordinate for that point. He and I had a long discussion about the baseball team where he felt other teammates had heaped racial abuse on him. They reversed the conventional roles—this Hispanic "gang" singled him out and used epithets and really disturbed him, and he didn't know what to do.

And that's a difficulty with my son, because one of the things Peter tends quite surprisingly to me to do, is to jump to make a racial connection when something doesn't jibe with what he'd like. Quite without any basis. We've almost formed a litany we go through now: "Is that problem from that guy because of his race, or is that because he's a jerk?" "Is that because of his color, or is that because he's on the face of the earth, and odds say there are so many jerks in the world, and he might be one of them?" "And when you think of him, and you dislike him, do you ever think of Melvyn, or your old black buddies Rance and Joseph?" You know—all of those sorts of gambits. And he "comes around"; but the fact that he tends automatically toward the racial slur side is distressing to me.

THORP. Yes.

FELTON. The whole incident last week with the harassment/not-harassment-Peter's a victim of his clumsiness/Peter's a malevolent shark—all of this stuff that flew around really disturbed him, of course. And I felt that it ended in such a way that I hoped he felt victorious, that he gained from it—that he came out of it with not only a sort of "clean bill of health," but feeling that "People were there to support me," but I'm not sure. Maybe down the line, with some help, he might feel that he's got to be more alert to his own behavior.

My whole tack with him on that harassment charge was: "You tell me it was an innocent circumstance; I believe you. Let's talk about the consequences, and how some of the things you do—like quippy, snappy retorts—are misconstrued, because you're trying to cover your bases and look cool. And you step on your own feet that way, and you would benefit by seeing how you might avoid that kind of thing in future." So we dealt with that.

Then I presented the questions you had suggested I ask him about Columbine, and he fielded them with what I thought was intelligence and his customary ease with self-revelation.

But despite his forthcoming responsiveness, and his good nature, to me there's a huge amount of alienation in Peter. He doesn't see always the huge value that he gets from his interaction with classes and teachers, where in large part he's pretty strong. I think he feels tenuous about so much! And while I don't think that Peter's response would ever be antisocial or hostile, I *do* think he feels alienated and torn. And sometimes it slips, as it has easily by the circumstance, into that sort of idea: "Five Hispanic guys versus Peter the white guy" going to the baseball game. And they have come down on him. They've been pretty tough. But—my whole point which I attempted to express to him is that he doesn't have the resilience and he needs to develop the tools. Little bits of insight here and there that he has; but not enough. And kids like that worry me, for their own growth, and for the fact that they can misconstrue the meaning of two, three, four years here, and not really pick up so much that's waiting for them!

Listen to his own statement of his predicament:

"Right now, I just feel more than picked on—I feel hated! Which I'm really ashamed about; because one thing I like to find is the better qualities of people, and I see that these guys are good people, but when they turn bad, they're just awful. And the hard thing is, I can tell they know each other better than they know me. And they'll be friendly with each other. But when I come into a conversation in the group, they'll ignore me. If I start talking to them, or acting in a certain way to be sociable, they'll turn away from me and only speak to the people of their race; and that's why I feel discriminated against. It's almost as if they don't *want* to have anything to do with me, they don't *want* to speak to me, they don't *want* to be around me. And *that hurts me!*"

When he said that, I told him, "What saddens me is that it sounds like a 'done deal'—that your capacity to experience joy, or Gateway's capacity to offer you a 'better deal,' in the form of people you're going to meet and relate with, is not in the cards. And that's devastating to think that you, at fifteen, sixteen, seventeen, would feel so much that this is just the way it is. That nothing seems to give you the sense that there's a capacity for change, in any of these elements."

And he responded: "Maybe I'm just one of those people who sees the world as worse than it really is. I guess just when I see people who are acting in immature ways, and I've seen so many, I feel like 'Is this the end of the world? Am I the only wholesome person in this world?'"

THORP. His is a very powerful utterance. And that sounds too clinical. It's powerful in a number of ways. It's a powerful statement of alienation by a kid. You know, it's a powerful cry for help, it's a powerful wail of injustice. And it's a powerful moment of adolescent reflection, all wrapped up into—you know, as Kermit the Frog would say: "It's tough being green!" And I don't mean that in any kind of frivolous way.

What's fascinating to me about it is that Peter puts it in a racial context. Now, I'm not Peter; and I wasn't there. But I don't think it is a racial issue. And—I think you suggested this in your own comments—it's additionally troubling that Peter sees it as a racial issue. Because I think it's first and foremost an alienation, "You're in/You're not in" kind of exclusiveness that adolescents are masters at. And when kids are vulnerable, they're really vulnerable!

The great part of this story, and the encouraging part, is Peter keeps coming back for more! And at the risk of trying to look for the silver lining, Peter deserves a tremendous amount of credit, praise and respect for the fact that he hasn't quit the baseball team. Many lesser people would have, and should have, in a sense, you know! And the fact that he hasn't is a real credit to him.

Kids who are picked on try to find safe havens. And try to find solid ground and comfort. For some it's family. And as you said, for the divorced family, it's less likely, but not unlikely. Less likely, to find that comfort in the family, because there's the tension there, which doesn't make it easy to make of it a refuge. Kids will find safe haven in music—which I understand is one of Peter's behaviors: "In my room, get the headphones on, and get the stereo on, and I'm safe." "I'm surrounded in a comfortable feeling." Kids will find comfort in activities—and whether or not it's Little League, or rock-climbing, or gangs—and some young people will find in gang activities comfort in action to replace the action that they might really want to do, if given the opportunity, but can't because they're excluded. And so they replace one action with another, and either find it tremendously liberating, feeling: "My God, I didn't realize this was so great anyway! Isn't this terrific!" And that's how you get Rudy Gallindo becoming the National Figure Skating Champion despite his history as a kid whom I've got to believe was picked on and humiliated his whole life. And some other kid becomes a rock-climbing master because it's only him and the rock.

Of course, kids also find comfort in other kids. And it's interesting to see the phenomenon of kids finding comfort in other kids, when— not unlike this situation—the other kids are finding comfort in each other because they, too, are on the "outs." A certain dynamic is created by this phenomenon of feeling, "Well, the only reason we're together is nobody else wants to be with us. And that's what brings us together." On the one hand, there's a very powerful bond there. It makes me wonder what kind of furthering of the anxiety takes place as a consequence: "Well, this happened to me today," one says. "Well, this happened to *me* today," the other says. "Isn't life the pits!" You know, you put all these incidents together, and life can seem pretty terrible.

What I really want to comment on is that my stepson Boone shares some of Peter's quandary. What I think they share in common, and what some significant percentage of kids who are on the outs share, is a very powerful sense of justice. This is because they're being dealt with so unjustly. How do you cope with bullying, or pressure, or being ignored? Usually you make the attempt to mould yourself into something else, something more accommodating: "Okay, maybe *this* is what they want me to be." And usually that path leads to the kid being a class clown, or worse, leads to the kid being the "pet dog" of someone fiercely powerful within the outcast group. But you know, at some point the kids decide either "I can't do that," or "That approach doesn't work, and I'm still excluded!" And then you get the real *profound* alienation, where a kid feels: "I don't belong, period! And so I have to trust myself, or these few friends." I mean, you can obviously run with this analogy and get very quickly, in fact, to those kids at Columbine, who—you know, that's kind of the path that they followed.

But I come back to this sense of *justice*. And again, as I listen to what Peter says, and when I hear him talk in actuality, I don't hear a sixteen-year-old. I hear a much more mature voice in some ways. You know, most sixteen-year-olds don't have the perceptive powers that are revealed in even that brief a discourse. Again, he is misperceived, I think—particularly with the race issue—at least to the degree. Not that he's utterly wrong about that. But he's a very mature kid. And again, what's interesting in my sense is that kids who are picked on from a relatively young elementary school age, from kindergarten or whatever, sometimes will mature much more quickly. Because they have to be. They're forced to be.

How do you deal with pain? That's a maturing process. It's no fun; but you grow up, so to speak, when you have to deal with pain. Again, the divorce analogy that you raised is there. You know, kids grow up when they're parents get divorced; and not necessarily in healthy ways. But suddenly the world is maybe clearer, at least, in its issues. It might not be clear in terms of its solutions.

So you have this interesting yin/yang with Peter, with a kid who's mature beyond his years in understanding justice and injustice. But he's still a sixteen-year-old kid trying to figure out a complex world and trying to make adolescent, almost predictably adolescent bullying—trying to make sense of it. And we might not see it exactly that way: You're the adult looking at it from some context and some perspective. You're not the kid going through it.

So it's—you know, once again, who knows if this think has any kind of psychological validity to it!—but once again, I see the world in terms of a place of power and sharing of power, and exclusion from power. And here's an example where adolescents begin to recognize the role of power, and they begin to recognize it first and foremost from their friends, and then they start recognizing that they have power over their parents as well. And it's a very intoxicating drug, if you will. They might think—"Wow! If I just say to my parents, 'I'm not going to do it,' or if they force me to do it—if they force me to do this, to be perfect, then I won't eat—and I'll show them! I'll weigh eighty-five pounds, and *that*'ll teach them a lesson!" You know. To the kid who says: "Well, I'll fail my classes, and that'll show them!" It's a real intoxicant. And it is to kids on kids as well. Because it is the "high" of: "I'm better, because I'm better than you are." In a time that's full of self-doubts otherwise. You put all teenage kids in a wilderness— and I don't know if this is the basis for the "Outward Bound" experience—but you put kids in the wilderness by themselves, and they can't fall back on injustice. Or they can't fall back on relative power: "I'm stronger because you're weaker." Or: "I'm stronger because I'm going to make you weaker." Or: "I'm weak, because you're stronger." And you really cut to the nub. And that's why I'm such a huge fan of outdoor types of experiences, I would strongly urge the family to pursue that. Because I think Peter could find some solace in a world where justice is elemental. It's either raining or its not. And justice isn't quite as adolescent as this is.

I wish Peter could understand that: One, he's okay. Two: That he does shoot himself in the foot, in part because of his very strengths. He won't go away! You know? And more power to you, Peter!

Certainly Donna's son—and she was just talking to him the other day about this—absolutely gets himself in trouble because he's the kind of kid in some school yard game who'll say: "You can't do that! That's cheating!" You know—to the best athlete on the block who's cutting some corner. "You can't do that—that's cheating! That's not the way the game is supposed to be played!" He says these things, and I suspect Peter has those traits in him. He sees the world very clearly in his own head, in kind of black-white. And kids who are victims of injustice tend to see it in more black-and-white terms, because it's kind of the hand that you're dealt.

Does this make any sense?

FELTON. It's makes a lot of sense.

One thing that concerns me—not only again, to reinforce this point, that we're not only talking about this boy, but about anybody who could be out there in your assembly: I don't quite understand when the concept of empathy forms clearly, and crystallizes to a usable, serviceable functionality. And one of the things that dismayed me a little bit was when I asked Peter to relate some of the events that took place in the Columbine assembly, because I had been primed by you to know that some kids went deep inside, and were very revelatory. And Peter went through those very cursorily. And then he used the other adolescent support, which is: I'm the center of the universe; my ego is the important thing here, so how did that reflect on me? And he borrowed—he sought identification—with someone who had been bullied; but he did not reflect upon the bullied person's experience. Which I know, knowing who the kid was, that it was heart-rending, and brought forth from real depth. And courageous. Now: At what point can a youngster—even someone who has these problems, say: "Gosh, you know—when Melvyn said that, I can really see that! I can feel that! Gosh, what a thing to go through!" Why did none of that happen here?

THORP. Well, I think it *did*. I mean, I think what happened was really varying responses. Peter's response was typical of a lot of the kids, I think. My own daughter being one of them. Maybe not quite in parallel ways. When I talked to her afterwards, and asked: "What did you think of the assembly?"—and I was sort of walking around with this big, beaming, "This-is-what-education-is-all-about" kind of expression—she said: "I hated it!" And I said "Why was that?" And she said: "I just hated it. I just didn't want to hear that, you know?" And so I dropped it. And I think what she was trying to tell me was, given her own emotional trauma, that it was cutting too close to the bone for her. You know: "I didn't want to hear about other kids' troubles, because I've got my own troubles!" So in that way, being unempathetic.

In Peter's case, shared, I'm sure by a number of other kids, was: "Oh, Melvyn......Oh, Peter!" You know. That sort of "being empathetic" to the issue; but quickly internalizing it. Which is, I think, typical of an adolescent. And if I really knew the answer to this question, Keith, I'd be making a hundred and twenty bucks an hour, and having people lying on a couch in front of me. But from an educator's point of view, it's not—it's not surprising that kids would quickly personalize something. It's the great challenge of being a teacher, where criticism—"The paper was excellent, but—" You know. Or: "You really made a great attempt to do this—*but*: ....." You know. And as soon as the constructive criticism comes in, it's: "You don't like me." It's not: "Gee, you're really trying to help me improve," or, to give you a better example: "Don't do that again, that was really out of line!" Okay? "He doesn't like me. He hates me! He's a sonofabitch, too!" It's amazing how quickly personal it becomes.

I had this discussion with my daughter last night: She did something, and I wasn't paying much attention to it, and her response was: "Well, it wasn't my fault!" And I said to her: "I didn't say you did it, or it was your fault. 'Fault' isn't the issue here."

But kids use that language and that posture very effectively. And Peter's language wraps the issue of empathy in ways he—personally can apprehend it, I suspect. Developmentally, when empathy does kick in?—I think probably you and I know a whole lot of adults who are not particularly empathetic. So what is empathy? Do you know when you became empathetic? I'm not sure I know when I became empathetic.

FELTON. Yeah, I have a rough idea. I remember an incident.

THORP. Was it while you were still in school?

FELTON. It was earlier. I think that whatever later veered off into a writer's sensibility started at that point; so it might not have been "hard-core empathy," but it was something that said: "Gee, what's going on there? What's it like to be that person?" So maybe that was it. I was twelve, thereabouts. But I wouldn't swear to that.

THORP. I'm not sure when I became empathetic. I mean, part of me would say I didn't become empathetic until I became a teacher. Which was in my late twenties, basically.

I had a very different high school experience. I mean, I was—you know, if not *the* "BMOC," I was one of the "BMOC's," and so for me, I was always the "in-crowd." I'd like to believe that my "in-crowd" was a lot more gentle than in-crowds of today that you read about.

Language in the common sense is important, as we've discussed. But creative language at Gateway really shone, the other night. And you missed something really revealing, at a Magic Theater presentation of Gateway student-authored one-act plays. It was something, powerfully disturbing.

FELTON. I learned too late! Tell me about it.

THORP. Wow! *Some* of the language would have burned your ears. But the scenarios were disturbing in their misogyny, in their adolescent, girl-against-girl cattiness—forgive the word, but I can't think of another one right now. Racial in their distinction—I mean, some of the writing was really brilliant! In one case—Michael Fountilla—do you know him, the big African-American kid?

FELTON. Pitcher on the baseball team.

THORP. He wrote this piece about being black in America that I turned to Kate Graham, the Academic Dean, and I said: "He *can't* have written that! He had to have gotten that from somewhere!" And so far, I have no reason to believe that he didn't write it. It was incredibly powerful. And then there was this piece done first, written by two of our kids, our two Latina girls were writing about two African-American girls, sitting on a street corner watching the world go by. And it was brilliant, and brilliantly-acted—they wrote the scripts, and professional actors acted their language, their words. Well acted by two guys in drag. It was something really, really special.

At the same time, it was profoundly disturbing. To think that our kids think about this stuff, all the time. I mean, I was still sleeping with my baseball glove at this age; and these kids are talking about oral sex, and graphic body descriptions; the language was unbelievable, and just the viciousness of personal attack. So—and again, not that it's going to make Peter feel any better, but there are a lot of kids feeling alienated, I think, in this period and at this age. And even kids who appear to be fine, and in the "in-crowd," are in jeopardy. Maybe the difference again is this power question, that some kids choose to be alienated. Some kids choose to alienate others from them. And then there are some kids who are the victims and are forced to be alienated. Some kids have the power to decide how alienated they want to be; and some kids are power-less, to determine that. That might be the great frustration.

FELTON.   One of the behavior patterns you just described—someone who purposefully holds people at bay—seems, superficially, to suggest that perhaps it would take a person with great strength of character, who would choose to do that. Someone who was attempting to get some control in the situation, rather than someone who was just lost in the miasma of apartness from people. And yet, I wonder about both of the kinds of estrangement which you talked about—how much that leads to a kind of solipsistic life, which leads, incrementally, to a departure from reality? There is no test-ground anymore. Or is that looking at it too clinically, and too detrimentally down the line?

THORP.   Well—define that reality!?   If I understood the archetype you were describing, yeah—I think you're right; the risk of living in a world that is built upon a foundation of illusion is not so very distant from any one of us, you know.   And—where I'm concerned listening to the excerpts about Peter is that he's building an illusion of racism that has some truth to it, but is giving it a credence that I think transcends the truth, and runs the risk of him being alienated on the basis of race. I know that troubles you—as well it should, I think. Equally, the "excluder" is very easy to delude himself or herself that it's okay to do that thing, or this group that is exclusive and that I'm a member of is something really special.

There was a piece in this student presentation the other night about this, where—it was a kind of "Freaks and Geeks" play—where the three beautiful cheerleaders were dismissing the three "geek" boys. So—one person's comfort is another person's delusion, I guess. And we certainly see plenty of examples of where people have peaked at the age of eighteen. The high school quarterback Bob Marinovich—I don't know if that name means anything?

FELTON.   No, it doesn't.

THORP.   He was a kid from Southern California whose father groomed him to be a professional football player, a professional quarterback.   And it was an amazing example of, well, almost bioethics.   This zealous dad fed him the right foods, and probably married him to the right woman, and I'm not sure what else, but he truly groomed this kid. There was an article about him when he was a kid in high school, about this dominating father doing this. And he had a mixed college career, I forget where it was. And then he got involved in drugs, and all sorts of things. And in fact, the San Diego Chargers are just trying to resurrect him as a backup quarterback, and he's gotten himself in some trouble recently.

FELTON.   So he's current, still?

THORP. Yeah, he's—actually, he's probably in his early thirties now. It's murder to have talent, and subject that talent to one's own weakness and another person's own pathology. There are more people, less well-known, than we think, going through something similar. It's predictable. You see plenty kids coming out of high school who peak at age eighteen.

You know, back in my days heading Cate, when I was talking about the kinds of kids we should enroll in the school for fundraising purposes—and yes, those conversations take place within the world of private schools; Grinnell probably has that as well—actually, even back prior to my arrival, the conversation was always around the children of the well-established families. And my point—usually put a little less subtly and a little more diplomatically than this—was: "Hey!—those families are has-beens. They've used up their nineteenth-century wealth. They've thrown it away on houses and cars and boats and divorces and everything else. So, the people we ought to be admitting are the future Bill Gateses of this world. Those are the kinds of kids who thirty years from now are going to turn back and give your school the big gift for the big building, because they're the ones who are going to be successful. They'll mark a place for the twenty-first century; and we're well-advised to forget about these "landed gentry" types who have essentially given it away.

Well: My statement of insistence, of course, was hardly popular with those landed gentry types that I was telling it to! So there is a lot of illusion, and delusion, taking place.

FELTON. When we next meet, I want to jump to the other half of our concerns about adolescents, moving away from the psychological perspective. Just a little preview of it here: It's an extremely interesting view of adolescence from some of the latest neurological standpoints. I'd like us to discuss some new information that basically has to do with the recent Administration Conference on Teenagers, and some of the material that came out of there about brain cells and connections, and teenagers.

THORP. The new spurt! There's a big conference here next week on a similar topic, and you should try to come. This guy, Oliver Sachs, is going to be there.

FELTON. Oh, really!

THORP. Yeah. I really like his writing.

FELTON. Well, I *will* come—and I'll wear an unmistakable hat.

Chapter Twenty-Three

IS BIGGER BETTER?

"[T]he question we need to ask is: 'How can we keep kids curious? How can we prevent them from being cynical? And how can we encourage them to be risk-takers?' And when you think about it, school is designed precisely to be the opposite of those three!...'"

"[S]chools are not designed to be places that encourage risk-taking, for the most part. And kids are smart! Okay: So what's school, they ask? School is 'plug and chug,' school is 'play the game,' school is 'do it that way.' Don't bug me with things that you're telling me to be curious about, because that's not what education is; education is: Master a certain set of skills, to be able to pass a certain state-mandated test. And the rest of this stuff is crap! And don't try and kid me—you know, the 'rogue' teacher, the rogue—what you and I would describe as the 'rogue brilliant teacher'—would say: 'Forget the standards! Forget this crap! Let's really teach creative thinking!' The kid is going to say: 'You know—I'm smarter than you are! I know better than you; I know that you are a rogue teacher, and you're operating outside the educational establishment, and I, at the age of twelve, I know that for me to get ahead, I need to be operating within the educational establishment. So—out of my way!'

"It's clear what we need to do: We need to enhance curiosity."

__11 May__—*Our next meeting followed another of Peter Thorp's "College Prep Classes." This one—which he felt would be so sparsely attended that we could meet in his office—turned out to have the small but full component of three class members as the first I'd conducted some weeks before. This ideal complement of students—almost a tutorial times three—was much more emotional and much less lexicological in content; for Peter's students, sophomores in high school and still two years away from the dreaded college application process but eager to get a bite on it, had an almost pathological fear of writing in general, and the college admission application essay in particular. My job was to make that pathway easier; and I saw my best opportunity as opening up some feelings in these youngsters (all women, and all "Third-World" members) which we could then harness into language power, and an ultimate acceptance at the institutions of their choice.*

"You'd be wise to remember," Peter told me after it was revealed that my assignment from the previous class—writing a trial essay draft on any subject—had not been met by any student, "that the language skills of all these kids is weak. They don't trust themselves to be expressive, even though they certainly are! It's a formidable barrier. And, at least for today, it's in your lap!"

We managed to carve a good class out of events anyway. And by the end of the session, all three young women were in flood-tears of feeling, and all their rows appeared newly-rained for germination.

"Wow! I guess the Doctor is in!," Peter quipped as we turned next to our own dialogue. We had both noted, with surprise, that one of the students, a girl of East Indian parentage named Amy, had begun the class in one emotional "set," and left the class at its conclusion in quite another. A striking, tall girl, Amy set herself apart from the others by her dress and her manner. She appeared dignified, advanced well beyond high school demeanor; and with great natural beauty, her behavior was distinctly different from others of the jeans-and-sweatshirt crowd of her peers.

Peter commented on the struggle all the students were having with putting pen to paper in thoughtful, organized prose.

THORP. I believe that they now understand what good writing is about. Two years ago they would have had no clue what good writing was about. Now they have a sense of what it is, and we—you and I, particularly in our session of a few weeks ago, had to point out to them that they are eminently capable of writing, but there's even more hesitation, particularly in somebody like Cynthia [a bright and engaging Hispanic girl] with perfectionist tendencies, that writing is now more of an imposing burden. And so the combination of –there are three things at work here. One, vocabulary issues. Two, the intimidation of writing. And three, the complex emotion profiles that linger either just below the surface in some cases—and it doesn't take much to touch that, as we saw. You put those three things together, and writing becomes really difficult for them.

FELTON. There must be someone, some agency—I know there are such people, but to strain the idea of such a profession: A writing therapist, who would function more on the "therapist" than the "writing" side. And I feel, were he in such a position here, he would be faced with the old *cliché* word—the "Breakthrough." What's going to bring the breakthrough to release all that? And what's going to get them, however clumsily expressed, to get them not to care about *how* they say it, but just to get it down! The energy and power is all there! The depth of feeling—it's amazing; and yet they just seize up when it comes to expressing it in that way.

The unfortunate thing about writing, which is maybe why it's a "back-seat" medium today, is that it's linear: You've got to put this word here, and then you've got to put this word on the other side of it, and then you have to put another word on the other side of that one, and it's just—it's hard to think that way.

THORP. Well, that's an area, you know, where you and folks like you who care about writing, and have ideas about writing, could do an immense service to this profession. And that's in trying to help kids get over the hurdle of expression.

FELTON. Yes.

THORP. —Which I think perhaps you're seeing, moreso than you realize, is a trial, and terribly difficult for them. And the fact that they have such amazing stories to tell!—

FELTON. Oh, my God! Yeah! It's astonishing.

THORP. My life as a high schooler pales in comparison, and I wish they could understand that. They have much richness in their lives, to draw from. They should be finding joy and celebration in that, rather than personal defeat and humiliation. It's true.

FELTON. Well, that might come; but it seems now just too early.

It was interesting the direction that Amy Mehta went. When she first made her comments about making her own choices, and being in possession of herself. Then to come back later, and get quite emotional about things—!

THORP. Yes!

FELTON. You just never know. To look at her—I watched her come in the other room where we normally meet. And she walked in—and my God, she looked like a sales representative from somewhere, you know? Not this kid! It's just interesting. Is that her consciously chosen *persona*?

THORP. She's a fascinating student. On the one hand, she's disabled by language, her lack of language. But there's inherent goodness in there. There's strength of character, which is walled in by lack of language, by shyness, by perhaps cultural issues, as well. And so it's easy to dismiss her as not a particularly profound kid. And her troubles here in class—she was having great difficulty for a time, but she's doing very well, particularly recently—now that she has a different math teacher, among other things, because she works so hard. She's so dedicated. She's getting that typical kind of school reward: If you do all your homework, you get rewards. But her level of abstract reasoning leaves something to be desired, as I think you've witnessed, in the group circumstances. And what I can't figure out is to what extent that's simply a function of lacking vocabulary to understand concepts, and to express concepts. Because I think she's eminently capable of having the concepts, if that makes sense. And you heard some of that today. Being able to express them, and being able to relax about "it"—school, is not something that comes easily to her.

So what you see here are three great kids. I mean, if you asked the faculty collectively: "Name three of the best kids in the school," everybody would have them in their top twenty list of kids in the school. But each one of them is pretty well "tightly-wrapped" about one thing or another. It's pretty fascinating.

FELTON. It is, indeed. And I wouldn't have spotted that—to see those three out of the student body—

THORP. The one that really surprised me was Veronica, who is, interestingly, another girl of East-Indian descent. I thought she was relatively carefree, and that's a silly comment; but you understand what I'm saying.

FELTON. Yeah.

THORP. Given the context of that. I knew nothing about her having a temper until relatively recently. I knew nothing about the close-to-tears aspect until relatively recently.

FELTON. Well, console yourself. You're only the Principal, and her advisor, and her teacher. You're not clairvoyant.

THORP. It's amazing. All those tears!—

FELTON. Well. We have to see it as "us males," who will guts it out, no tears for us, by God!—

THORP. Right!

FELTON. Last week I learned through you about the famous Oliver Sachs's appearance at a neurophysiological meeting here in San Francisco. And I want to try to concentrate on one thing simply because of the timeliness of the "Brain Connection" conference that's going on around him.

I think, in anticipation of the conference, I'd like to spend time for a moment with another meeting, a Washington, D.C. Conference on Teenagers, that was held last week, on 2 May. There are two reports on teenagers, and I want to provide you some salient quotes from the National Public Radio handling of the event. For the record, this is some of the work of brain researcher Jay Geed, From the National Institute of Mental Health. Here are excerpts, little snippets, of the lore which emerged from the event:

> The Conference on Teenagers today will highlight research on the brains of health, active teenagers....
>
> It turns out teenagers' brains *are* different!, according to researcher Jay Geed from the National Institute of Mental Health. And he's got the brain-scan pictures of two hundred healthy youngsters to prove how this happens...
>
> It's been widely assumed that the brain's massive overproduction of cells and connections occurred only once, and very early on—in an infant's development. But Jay Geed is discovering that the same process of brain growth occurs again: About a decade later....
>
> We actually followed individual children through their development ... [and] we found there was a second wave of overproduction. This second wave peaks at around age eleven in girls, and about age twelve in boys....
>
> The brain thickens....dramatically in an area right behind the forehead called the "frontal lobes." That part of the brain in charge of planning, judgment, organization—it's as if the teenage frontal lobes are getting ready, bulking up to be able to learn these new, more adult skills....So much like a tree growing extra branches, twigs, and roots, the brain cells grow extra connections, extra branching, extra twigs to communicate with other brain cells....
>
> This second wave of proliferation reaches its maximum—about a twenty-five percent increase—right as the sex hormones kick in, and the kids are poised at puberty. And then, as children become teenagers and experience adolescence, the extensive branching begins to be pruned back....
>
> [I]f children are using their brain at this point, for academics, or sports, or music, or video games—that is what their brains will be hard-wired, or optimised, for....

That's the gist of the report. My own parenthetical question out of all this relates in a way to the odd question I had before, which had to do with Mel Levine.   How do you as an educator, with your predilections and inclinations, most successfully interweave these two strands—the psyche, and the physiology?   I'm interested especially since you and I were brought up in an age of the first, and now have very clearly impressed upon us the emphasis on the second—?

THORP.   I have a stream of reactions, both in terms of that comment, but also in terms of this whole issue.   It's not as well formulated a specific response to that question; but I'll cover it, I think.

To me, this is a fascinating insight.   And yet at the same time, it shouldn't be, I think, in any way surprising.   I'm not a neuropsychologist, I'm not a neurologist;   I'm not a scientist.   But as both an educator and an historian, to me there's logic as to why religions have bar- and bas-mitzvahs, and confirmations in and around this time period.   It is also the case that as an educator—and as a parent, of course—you cannot help observe children pushing away as one of the fundamental phenomena of adolescence.   Arguably the single-most descriptive phenomenon of adolescence is the independence drive.

Now, I'm not a psychologist, and I'm certainly not a Freudian psychologist; but based on the limited study of Freud I've done, I don't remember him listing independence as one of the instinctual drives. Maybe he did, and just did it in a different way in terms of his delineation of the hierarchy of drives. But clearly, it *is* that. And if that is the biological imperative for adolescence, wouldn't it make sense that the brain would have a growth spurt during its most vital moment? The whole organism is saying: "You're on your own, now, kid! You'd better have a brain that's going to help you make some good decisions."   Of course, depending on how far back you want to go, you know—the independence of today, which means to some that you get your own credit card, is a little different from the independence of thousands of years ago, when it was: "Okay, you're on your own, go out now into the desert, and have a good life!"   And you'd better have a brain that is ready to go.

So it's no surprise to me that this has been discovered.   The only surprise to me is that it's taken this long to get discovered.   Because until this, it was: Your brain reached its peak at age two, and it was downhill from that point in terms of brain cell production.

Parenthetically speaking: Even with this spurt here in adolescence, we still are so under-utilized in the brain, in terms of its full capacity. One of the great studies in psychology is this book, *The Mind of the Mnemonist*, by Luria, a Russian psychologist, a classic of the twentieth century about this guy who gets shot in the head during World War One, and has this experience where he has perfect memory.   And one of the points of the book from Luria is that all of us have the capability of perfect memory. But we have selected *not* to have perfect memory, because of the psychosocial consequences of having perfect memory: If you can't forget anything, you're one screwed-up buckaroo! And that was the fate of this guy who had the bullet lesion.

There was also a study of a young girl in England, I think, who was—I believe she was hydrocephalic, and basically had almost no brain. And yet she was eminently capable of functioning at an almost average way, which says—My God!, the capacity of the brain to adapt, even in such a limited manner. A third example: With anybody who suffers serious seizures, life-threatening seizures—and with kids especially, sometimes surgeons cut the *corpus callosum* between the two hemispheres, essentially killing one side of the brain, and then the brain picks up and takes on activities in one hemisphere that typically is assigned to another hemisphere.

And just last week, I read a study—and this shows you that I need to get a life—I read a study on the developing *hippocampi*, the plural of *hippocampus*, a part of the brain—the developing *hippocampi* of London taxi drivers.

FELTON. Really!

THORP. The point of it being that in adults, their *hippocampus* has the ability to grow and expand when you have to past the test, which in London is very rigorous, of spatial relations. These people have to know faultlessly how to get around London.

And so, there is real excitement about the ability of the *hippocampus* to grow. And there has also been some recent work, as you may know, on stroke victims and the possibility of the brain recovering from stroke. So out of all this comes the incredibly good news that the brain is an organic entity, of course, but one that has unlimited potential.

Okay: Back to adolescence. This growth spurt seems, therefore, so natural. Now what to me is interesting, as your article points out, is the growth spurt takes place not in high school, but arguably in middle school. You know, if it's ages eleven and twelve, we're not talking high school.

FELTON. Right.

THORP. And so, the "crunch time" is late-elementary-school / early middle-school, so to speak. And my concern about this is: That age isn't where neurologically-appropriate education is being developed! And so the study I want to get is the corollary of this study, which would posit: "Okay, so what do brains look like at the age of fourteen? Have they, in fact, been hard-wired at the ages of eleven, twelve, thirteen, with video games as just the one example you listed?—so that by the time we get them at thirteen, fourteen, and fifteen, we are either *de*-wiring, or *re*-wiring, or *circum*-wiring, to develop what we believe at the high school level is the appropriate neurological profile for success?"

Now. That idea is quickly followed by my other voice saying to me: "Well, there *isn't* any appropriate neurological profile for success! What it means is, schools need to revamp—high schools need to revamp their curriculum, recognizing that they <u>are</u> getting kids who have some amount of neurological hard-wiring, typical to its culture. Which means: We look at video games. Let's look at video games not only as the cultural trash that they are!—editorial comment!—but let's look at them as the neurological wirers that they are. And my sense is that the use of these games contributes to impulsivity; it contributes to short-term decision-making; it contributes to episodic thinking. And it contributes in all sorts of ways that don't necessarily enhance thoughtful reflection, which the teacher of writing is trying to get kids to do. The teacher ponders: "If they can't get it now, then I'm not doing what I should be doing!" The youngster wails: "If it doesn't come to me quickly, then what is this thing called 'reflection'?"

So: As an educator, it's exciting to know that the brain continues to evolve and to grow. That it really isn't hard-wired. On the other hand: It reaffirms my impression—if I were twins, the next thing I would do is start a middle school right away. And maybe the great frontier of education is middle-schools. I've got all the books here on my shelf about the "shopping mall high school" and that sort of thing. But there isn't a whole lot being written about middle school. And if there is, I apologize that I don't know it; but I—you know, you don't really see this literature about middle schools that you see about high schools. And my point is it might be, if it's not too late—we might be missing a real, or *the* real focus on education.

FELTON. I happen to think you're right about that. Last year I spent a day a week in my other son's fifth grade class. And it was astonishing what I learned, from seeing what the capabilities were, what the openness, the availability in the students was, and at what stage you could begin to see certain development take place. And I think you're right.

But let me react: Some force—God!, Nature—whom- or what-ever—decided that the brain would stop growing at a premature point, so that it could get through the pelvic girdle. The brain had to restrain itself, had to be limited *in utero*. And then it would "catch up" on the other side. So we had a period when we know that a capability wasn't reached, because of another necessity. Is that happening metaphorically somewhere else along here? Is it in middle school? Is it in high school? Is there a place just before the brain is going to take off again? And what is that metaphorical "pelvic girdle" that has to be passed through, in order to allow that second stage to happen?

Another reaction:

In the lore which followed World War Two we hear a lot about what "Rosie the Riveter" did; she got out of the kitchen, put on a scarf, and helped make munitions. We hear about tiny infants, left behind by young men who went abroad to fight. But we almost never hear about the developmental course and the coping problems of kids nine to seventeen, who were left behind when their dad was off at war. There must have been quite a few of those. What did they do to readjust? This surely was similar to what happens as kids today in a divorce have to take a mantle of father-figure. What does that sort of circumstance create in brain development?

Your descriptions of the *hippocampus* and other events, where collateral generation or regeneration has to take place, or generation— is what happens psychologically in those other kinds of circumstances. How do all these interplay with each other in a modern society characterized by early maturation, divorce, and the stresses to succeed as signaled by the pressures of standardized testing?

And, finally, one other notion: Until such remarks as yours, it's very easy to think that advertisers are going to the younger teens simply because they've exhausted the older teens; they've saturated them, and now, they seem to be saying, "We'll start in on this group now." Whereas in fact, might it not be these advertisers' nefarious plan that if they can take a nine-year-old, or a ten- or eleven-year-old and just keep saying, hypnotically: "Pepsi, Pepsi, Pepsi!—" that they will have done what they want to do?

THORP. Well, the better example is: "Joe Camel, Joe Camel, Joe Camel!"

FELTON. True!

THORP. —Because in fact, I would argue that *that* was the nefarious plan, to get an image into kids' heads even before they were smoking, or even before they were considering smoking. That when they had access to cigarettes or, you know, access to that level of rebellion, they'd already have an image in their heads. Nefarious, it certainly is!

Our kids come to us as—I was going to say, "savvy" consumers. It might in fact be the opposite of "savvy" consumers; but they sure come to us as consumers. And they come to us as well-trained consumers. And you know—advertisers are no dummies. I don't have to tell you this; you know that the preponderance of degrees among advertisers are degrees in psychology! They know what they're doing.

FELTON.   Well, I know that—it's interesting again to refer to the three young women here in your class, today. I daresay that those same three, back in the sixth grade, or the fifth grade, wouldn't have been troubled by the reticence that they had today—

THORP.   Correct.

FELTON.   —Those problems just simply wouldn't have existed. There might be other ones. But it wouldn't keep them from thrusting forward—

THORP.   Correct.

FELTON.   —the way there is now a sudden yanking on invisible reins that happens to these kids. Why does it happen now? What is that hesitation, that second-guessing?

THORP.   I've heard quoted a study, and it's one of those that pass through many times, that eighty percent of kids enter school with very high self-confidence, and self-esteem; and twenty percent of kids leave school with high self-confidence and self-esteem. I'm still sitting here, thinking of what I'd said earlier, and trying to come up with this pithy quote as a high school person looking and talking to middle school people—something along the line: "Send me your eager, your curious, your uncynical, yearning to learn!," to come up with a relatively bad paraphrase, and I think that's what you see in the fifth and sixth grade, you see unchecked curiosity, uncynical perspective, openness to risk and failure—each of which, and I could go on, I guess—but each of which tends to dissipate as you get closer to high school. At some point, when it becomes—when the breasts-and-pubic-hair issue takes over, you start this phenomenon where personal judgment comes into play in a way that it can be really damaging. And ten-, eleven-, twelve-year-olds, who are—what?—fourth-, fifth- and sixth-graders, have a real strong preservation instinct. And they will respond to what I would call "psychological lesions" in pretty appropriate ways: Anger—as you saw in one of the class's girls; "waterworks," as Ms. Cynthia called her own emotions; but Veronica has the strength of character to know that she can't lash out in anger in one way, and that's going to be counter-productive.

So the question we need to ask is: "How can we keep kids curious? How can we prevent them from being cynical? And how can we encourage them to be risk-takers?" And when you think about it, school is designed precisely to be the opposite of those three! In most cases.

You don't encourage curiosity if your focus is passing state-mandated testing. You don't prevent cynicism if you provide kids with all sorts of examples of why they should be cynical; that education is political first and foremost; that dollars are allocated for political reasons, and not educational reasons—gee, what a stunning coincidence, that Governor Davis decided to allocate 1.8 billion dollars the day that eight thousand teachers showed up on his doorstep. Totally coincidental! And third, schools are not designed to be places that encourage risk-taking, for the most part. And kids are smart! Okay: So what's school, they ask? School is "plug and chug," school is "play the game," school is "do it that way." Don't bug me with things that you're telling me to be curious about, because that's not what education is; education is: Master a certain set of skills, to be able to pass a certain state-mandated test. And the rest of this stuff is crap! And don't try and kid me—you know, the "rogue" teacher, the rogue— what you and I would describe as the "rogue brilliant teacher"—would say: "Forget the standards! Forget this crap! Let's really teach creative thinking!" The kid is going to say: "You know—I'm smarter than you are! I know better than you; I know that you are a rogue teacher, and you're operating outside the educational establishment, and I, at the age of twelve, I know that for me to get ahead, I need to be operating within the educational establishment. So—out of my way!"

It's clear what we need to do: We need to enhance curiosity.

FELTON. We've been dealing with the scintillating stratospheres of psychological considerations in adolescent development. Let's move, abruptly, to the nadir of our areas—the School Board.

Board member Dan Kelly was interviewed recently, on the subject of San Francisco's threatened charter school, Leadership High. He stated that Leadership's charter was, in his terms, "Open to question." He went on to say that the District "could recall the charter for cause." And then the school's principal was quoted to say, "We have not violated our charter in any way."

Is this a "stalking horse" scenario for the whole shebang? Or are they just—is this a weak link they found, and they're narrowing down? What's going on here?

THORP. Well, what you have is a Board of Education that's split over the question of charter schools. Not helping the situation: A week or so ago, about twenty-five of the thirty teachers at the Edison

Elementary Charter School wrote a letter to the School Board saying that they were going to quite *en masse*, because of working conditions.

These twenty-five to thirty teachers are saying "I quit!"—because of the extra work that's required. And Jill Wynns, the most ardent opponent of charters on the School Board, has seized on this to say, "It is time for us to do an investigation of this school," taking, you know, a kind of "We-told-you-so!" position.

This issue is profoundly troubling to me, because like it or not, in the eyes of charter school critics, for-profit charters and not-for-profit charters are lumped into the same boat, and it's not a boat I want to be lumped into. And so, with the issue of Edison and Leadership bubbling up simultaneously, it results in all sorts of pressure. And the Edison one troubles me because it's going to cause them to zero in on teacher turnover as the primary issue. And charter schools historically have high teacher turnover. We had high teacher turnover at the end of our first year. We don't this year. But you hire great people, and you hire and some people who leave because they don't want that particular challenge of the school or mission, and they don't really realize it until they get here, and experience it. Some people leave because they're so brilliantly talented they have all sorts of other opportunities, and particularly better-paying opportunities. But that's going to be a huge issue.

The Leadership High issue is troubling to me, because politicians often resolve conflict by this statistical phenomenon of regression to the mean, which is political compromise. And more often than not, political compromise results in no solution at all. And if it's: "Well, we don't have a place for Leadership in a building," and then somebody stands up and says: "Well, that's not fair! Gateway has a place.!" Then, the solution becomes: *No* charter school gets a facility." So I'm nervous about this; we've got a lease that takes us through December, and I would wrangle up one side and down the other in the "court of public opinion," as well on that. And if they say, "Well, it's December, time to get out," and here we are in the middle of a school year, where do we go?

But it's distressing for me. I wish I had more time to work on more long-range issues, and more charter-school related issues; and that is something that I'm going to continue to work on. But here in town, we've got to get some important folks lined up behind the charter school movement, so we get *real* support for it. But the superintendent question is a huge question for us.

FELTON. Well, what's puzzling to me about a lot of this, is that just within the scope of my son being here for a year, just within that time frame—it's not even a year yet—in my awareness, which is somewhat late to the game, charter schools have gone from the daring libertine bad-boy to a celebratory welcome of George W. Bush at a school in Mission Viejo, California, where—

THORP. The whole District has gone charter.

FELTON. Yes! Now, if having the Republican nominee saying that charter schools are the way to go isn't enough to qualify as a mainstream idea such that the San Francisco School Board can just relax, thank you, and get off this problem, and onto something real— what can? What will guarantee that this will gain acceptance, and give you a little bit of time and less blood pressure, so you *can* do something else?

THORP. You underestimate the idiosyncratic nature of San Francisco politics. I really do think it follows its own course, weaving in and out of the traffic of national political posture from a libertarian, *laisser-faire* philosophy in many ways, and on issues here in town, to highly arguably socialistic policies.

What the charter school people need to do, both nationally, in the state, and here in the city, is really pull ourselves together and develop enough stories—enough compelling stories, and enough compelling information that it will withstand the attacks that are coming its way. These attacks boil down to three basic arguments: One is—Charter schools cost the District money. It is a drain on the already-precarious financial situation in San Francisco. The second is: Charter schools engage in bad practices, and therefore should be held more accountable for the *quality* of their program. And the third is: Charter schools should be held more accountable for the *results* of their program. Points two and three are related, but are distinct from each other. And what we have to do is to be able to answer each one of those thrusts. We have to be able to answer the financial question to show convincingly that in fact, we're not a financial drain on the system. We have to be able to demonstrate the quality of our program is good, and is consistent with our charter, and three, that through state standardized testing and all that rigmarole, we have to indicate that kids are getting a good education here.

We really have to make a compelling argument for ourselves. And it's hard to do; because all you need is one disgruntled family, or in Edison's case, all you need is one set of disgruntled faculty. You wonder how did they come to this point, when it was made clear from the get-go that this was going to be a 210-day school year, and not a

180-day school year. Knowing of that added stress, all those teachers signed their contracts.

Just parenthetically speaking, yesterday's Chronicle had a classically written article—making the point: "Teachers up in arms, the school board member says 'I told you so,' basically"—and with about four paragraphs left in the article, it says: "Test scores have crept upwards since Edison has been in charge of the school, but it still falls well short of average test scores." Well, it was the worst-performing elementary school in the city—which is why former Superintendent Rojas said "Take it over." And in any other school, they'd be jumping up and down saying: "Our scores have *leapt* upwards! From—pick a round number—from 100 to 104—they have *leapt* upward, our test scores!" Not "*crept* upward," as in this case.

It was a classic example of journalistic writing, in my opinion. But that's what it's all about. They've got people who are just really angry with the way it was done. It's still the debris left from Rojas's tenure; there are certain elements that believe that it was an act against the families that that school had served previously, that they had been squeezed out. There's no real evidence that that's the case; but as we both know, if you've got your story in the press, and the other side doesn't, your story wins.

FELTON. Right.

THORP. So—the next couple of years are going to be critical.

FELTON.   Well, it strikes me that in a sense, there's a name-identity calling problem here. And a name-*calling* problem. It's a question of the big symbolic name. And I mean it in this way:

Take a charter school, a high school, and make it in every respect look just like a public school. You make it pretty, because they have some paint from downtown that they're going to give you. And a gardener will put in a few hours. And you have kids who look like "good little boys and girls" as they're going to and from class, and everything looks clean and bland and nice. And the test scores are high, above-average, whatever is "proper" and acceptable. But—and here's the catch—it's still a *charter* school. It strikes me—given this publicity, this Board's attitude—*that fact* still makes it a *bete-noir*, the bad guy! And yet, the San Francisco *public high school* called School of the Arts—which in *every* respect except nominally, is a charter school—

THORP. Correct. Right.

FELTON.   —is considered okay! So we're down to calling names.

THORP. Yeah.

FELTON. You know. It's "nigger" *versus* "white" again.

THORP. Well, it's also a further example of the degree to which logic, or the lack thereof, governs the political debate in this country. Yeah, you're right.

I got into a "beef" last June with the then-Associate Superintendent, who is no longer with the District, about Gateway's enrollment practices. She was insisting that Gateway could have no kind of enrollment application process. She also insisted that enrollment had to be totally open to anyone, which was inconsistent with our charter; and I kept using both Lowell and especially School of the Arts as examples, saying: "Well, you've got schools in the District that in fact have a screening process, and we're not doing anything—in fact, we're more open than they are, in terms of their enrollment!" "Well, no," they retorted, "That totally has nothing to do with your situation!" "But it does!" "No, it doesn't!"

But it does, you know? And it quickly became—it had nothing to do with logic, it was that she felt she had the power, and I didn't, I was just this little old charter school principal, and so, you know, her attitude was: "You do what I tell you!" As it turned out, she was gone before the issue came to a head. But that's sort of what governs the debate on this kind of issue.

And this is where the national election *does* become interesting; because you have both candidates fully supportive of charter schools. Certainly Gore—you have Gore falling prey to Bush's knee-jerk pattern, seeing education as check-boxes, education as accountability, education as test-scores. He's trying to out-Republican the Republicans on that one! And it's too bad. One of the results of this 1.8 billion-dollar budget allocation to teachers that California Governor Gray Davis is now talking about, is that the CTA—California Teachers' Association—has said, "Okay, we're going to drop our efforts to get this issue on the ballot, now that we don't have to, because we're getting the money, and we're therefore not going to have to spend, as they were quoted, the 'millions of dollars it was going to cost us' to get this on the ballot, and see that this was passed." They're now going to devote their attention to defeating the voucher proposal that apparently is going to be on the ballot this fall.[1]

FELTON. Yes.

---

[1] The voucher initiative was defeated in the California General Election of November, 2000.

THORP.   And once again, this is a question where there will be division between Bush and Gore, I'm assuming that Bush will support it, and Gore won't.   And yet, I'm waiting for either or both of them to—well, I'm waiting for Gore, especially, to come up with a well-articulated, well-reasoned rationale to denounce vouchers.

FELTON.   I would expect that.

THORP.   And again, my point to the CTA is: Then stop beating up charter schools, because if you continue to beat us up, you're increasing the likelihood that vouchers are going to get passed! And you're also increasing the likelihood that charter school people are going to support the voucher movement, which I don't. But you know, again, logic doesn't come to bear.

So—that's where we need national leadership! It can't be said enough. And it certainly doesn't get realized enough!

FELTON.   It's certainly true.

I'm going to jump here, to conclude: You said something in an early discussion, and I didn't pick up on it then; but I made a mental note about it. Now I just thought I'd run it by you. It had to do with Mel Levine. You made the comment—something to the effect, it may not be exact: "I think he needs to realize that he needs us as much as we need him."

THORP.   Yeah, that's exactly what I said.

FELTON.   To me, that rang a bell that said: Something confrontational was going on. And every time his name had come up heretofore, it had been adulatory—not only from you; but certainly generally laudatory. I wondered what had happened to "spoil the party"?

THORP.   It is a reflection of the different universes which exist in education, and especially in educational reform.   And from my perspective that's the big issue. It's also a reflection of a much more pragmatic board-related issue on his end, his board, which is funding him and therefore has some control over how he expends his attention and efforts. And Gateway at that time fell outside that. We were increasingly being invited back into the nest, especially more recently. But—he has been critical of us, not so much to me directly—well, not at all to me directly. People who know him and know Gateway feel that we're really not a "schools attuned" kind of school—this is one of his fundamental concepts. And our point is: Yeah, you're right; but you don't understand why. And until you understand why, my position is your work isn't going to have the potentially broad impact it could as an educational reform movement until you sense this.

And that's where I think we have something to offer; and Levine's organization has this interesting dynamic where they have this guy who's head of the high schools division who loves us and wants us to get real involved and that sort of thing; but he goes back to North Carolina, and gets ground up in the bureaucracy of his own organization, where—you know, that's kind of where we are at this point.

FELTON. I see.

THORP. There's real potential for synergy; it's just me figuring out how to package ourselves, one, in a way that makes that happen; and two, them figuring out how to expend their resources, and their Board figuring out: "Okay, what do we want to do?" And given the people on their Board right now, their issue is: "Let's make sure that kids who have means have access to great services." And I'm on a different campaign.

FELTON. Thank you for clarifying that.

THORP. Yes. Well, it's an ongoing story!

Chapter Twenty-Four

ONE STEP FORWARD, TWO STEPS BACK

"[T]here's some truth to the natural tendency of various dimensions within which teenagers have to operate being increasingly complex; and those dimensions have been made more difficult because the world is more complex. And more fraught with the potential for teenagers to make bad decisions...."

"[I]f we can help kids understand there is a world that exists beyond the force-field six inches in front of their nose—which is about the extent of the global perception of the typical teenager— then we're doing our job. I think. And I think we attend to that, in this school, because we follow up on incidents where somebody has done something that's hurtful, or unthinking, and let them know that in fact, there are consequences. And I think we're raising a generation of kids who don't understand or don't accept consequences very well...."

19 May—*If part of the code of a good Reporter, espousing to produce good Reportage, is honesty, then this is the point for an honest admission: Peter Thorp and this Reporter, many months into our project, were beginning to get just a bit on each other's nerves.*

Thorp had paid me the high compliment of inviting me to teach two of his college preparatory classes; but on the third such class, he brought in a "ringer" from another school—a friend of Meghvi Maheta's—inviting a subtle comparison between what he called this "natural teacher" and the Reporter (whose pedagogy was rougher, more on the order of his idea of the "rogue teacher").   On two occasions, Peter read a newspaper (albeit an education journal) before our sessions would begin. I would wait for this late-hour-discovered Gutenberg broadsheet to be set aside.

This was natural in a process which was months-long and preyed on his limited scheduling time. But I pressed my case, and contributed my own irritations. I began to ask questions designed to force Peter to go back over previous answers, and reflect upon them in new contexts. This was my way, legitimate outside any intemperate use of the technique, to bring new dimensions, new truths to the essential handful of questions we had been positing and facing throughout the year. The Principal was good-natured about this; but after the session about to be set forth—one abridged by a radio reporter's telephone call, which launched the man on his standard "canned" speech about charter schools—I immediately went home and posted to him via e-mail the remaining questions which the radio journalist's questions had foreshortened, and which I asked him to answer by return e-mail. It was too much. He refused to answer the questions until we next met, stating later that he simply "was a better speaker than typist."

Here we now sat, to pick up the pieces of our project. I told him, by way of beginning, that we were entering our third ream of manuscript text. (Most non-writers do not use the concept of word count; but for those who do, we had just entered the realm of 230,000, with about twenty thousand left to create.) I asked him if he would be around during the upcoming summer, if I needed additional contact, and revision recommendations. He informed me he would be gone for about half the vacation.

The issue of safety—a primary question with respect to the Columbine meanings—had arisen, in a lesser strain, in the unlikely subject of my Gateway Photo Group's recent exhibit of photography. A female student had continued to push her objections to the use of her image in an exhibition, fearing its physical (and her psychological?) abuse by others. I would ask Peter to reflect on the issue.

I opened, however, with a return to the "diversity" issue.

FELTON. Flash bulletin—"Blacks fell six percent at the University of California; Latinos are down also at UC, by an unspecified number.
    THORP. When did you hear that?
    FELTON. This was early morning.
    THORP. Today?
    FELTON. Yes.

THORP. Okay.

FELTON. Which could have been a report from—

THORP. The blacks are in this year's entering class?

FELTON. Yeah.

THORP. Six percent?

FELTON. Yes.

A few more wrap-ups on our teen focus. If you don't mind. And then I want to jump in a little different direction, and tell you some things that I—that are more individually oriented.

I'd like to coordinate two different subjects, or areas—phenomena—however you want to phrase it, that relate to this age group, based upon a couple of recent events. I told you last time that we had this issue in the Photo Group; and it evolved this way:

During the course of producing those photos, a couple of the young women in the class said to me: "Now, if we don't like our photos, do we have to have them up? I really object; I don't want any picture of me up." And I said, "Well, look: We're here to learn a lot of things about photography, including aesthetics, and we're here to try and get an objective stance of ourselves as tools of a process, and not as individuals," and all that sort of rationale. And I added, "So, my criteria will be: If a photo is obviously technically deficient, or just totally uninteresting from any aspect, or if it doesn't meet the needs of the assignment, we don't have to consider it." "Well," they countered, "suppose I don't look good!" And I said: "Let's talk about that at the time; because, even though you might think you have an objection, you might find compelling reasons why it makes you look wonderful, in a way you didn't anticipate. So let's wait and see."

Well, Keith didn't exactly wait-and-see. He went ahead. I took the photos that answered all conditions of the assignment, and I put the exhibit up. And I met a wall, a storm of protest from four of the group. And, one protest from another girl, who didn't like the one single shot that I had taken of her that I'd used as a theme for the photo exhibit. I loved it, and really wanted that shot in there; and she was livid that I used it. So there was a long *brouhaha* about it: Failure of faith and trust to come to the fore; I'd stepped on toes; all this sort of thing. We went around and around and around about it.

And I finally got the main objector to agree to negotiate. "We'll take these out, but I really want to leave this one in, because this one is probably the most supreme statement of what the whole assignment was all about." And she said: "I'm really fearful that it will get damaged. People I know will see it, and they'll damage it. I want you to promise me that if the photo is damaged in any way, purposefully, maliciously damaged, that it comes down and doesn't go back up." And I said: "Well, if you can convince me that you'll have no part in its damage, because I can see how strongly you feel about it, then I'm willing to do that. If you're willing to run the risk of having it up." And she said; "All right, let's do that."

Well, we put it up; and within two days, it was damaged. It was damaged very tentatively, with a couple of very light strokes—light strokes over the face, just a couple of very casual ones. Making my private belief that she had in fact just been overcome with humiliation, and done it herself.

The faculty advisor was alarmed. She said: "I'm really worried about this! This says to me that these girls don't feel safe here. That they would not want their image to appear in public." It was smoothed over ultimately. But a number of the girls' phrases stuck in my mind: "You can use it anywhere else, I don't care. But not here! Not where my friends are."

So all that fearfulness was something I hadn't expected. I wonder what you think about that.

THORP. Well, the moral of the story is: Aren't you glad you don't have daughters!

FELTON. Yes! Again, and again, and again!

THORP. I would imagine that there is some truth in the question, or in the statement that the girls must not feel safe here. But as a parent of two daughters, my initial response is that there is a much larger truth in the statement: "Don't put my picture up!" "I don't want my picture up!" "I look terrible!" And much more of the societal condemnation of young women feeling badly about how they look, both in terms of their face, and their body, and that sort of thing. I don't know if I'm right, obviously, but that's my initial reaction, and that may be the reaction of a male, a marginally sensitive male, and much less the reaction of a far more insightful, sensitive female, who says: "No, this is a sign that these kids don't feel safe here." I would be surprised if it was more that than, "Don't put my picture up," which you get invariably when you get these school photo ID cards. You know, it's predictable, what everybody goes through, and the girls all say, "Oh, I hate my picture!"

But what I would suggest is: Ask her. Say, "Okay, here we are at the end of this conversation, we did all this, it was up, and now—teach me, Catherine: Why were you so hesitant?" And see if you can draw from her: "Was the answer to the question because you don't feel safe? Or was the answer because you just didn't like the picture, and you didn't want to have your face up in front of your friends, and subject to the possibility of being teased about having the picture up? Teach me as an adult, what went through your mind as a kid, that caused you to be so reluctant to let it appear?" She might tell you.

FELTON. I will try that.

THORP. Now, is a student named Marina Vance in the group?

FELTON. Yes.

THORP. Did she have any hesitation?

FELTON. Marina—!

THORP. —Doesn't give a damn about anything.

FELTON. Doesn't give a damn about anything, that's right! Marina just brought her—

THORP. —Which is *her* learning disability.

FELTON. What is?

THORP. Part of her learning disability is that she doesn't give a damn about anything. Her particular challenge is a lack of social connectedness.

FELTON. That's really interesting. Because her thrust in our group has been almost totally inwardly-directed. The one thing that excited her about this project was when she could introduce what's been her primary focus, a photographic study of her family history. Not the living; but the dead!

THORP. She's pretty self-absorbed. Which is one way of describing someone, a young person, who's developed a protective device of being able to find satisfaction and comfort in focus on self, rather than focus on others. And she—it is a sign of the resilience of youth that she's "out there," and doesn't care how other people feel about her, because there is certainly some percentage of kids who have been picked on—as clearly, she has, through schooling prior to coming here, where the reaction is either some amount of pathology, or some amount of withdrawal. And for whatever reason, she's decided that "I am who I am, and I want to do what I want to do, and to hell with 'em!"

You know, that's a gutsy, risky decision on the part of a teenager; and she continues to take some amount of grief here for being that way. For example, at the Columbine assembly—and your son Peter might actually have commented about her—remember?—she got up to speak three times. And hogged more than her fair share of air-time. Each of her statements was very articulate, and very much to the point, and not frivolous at all; but she had no clue that maybe, you shouldn't get up this third time.

FELTON.   Interesting. Just parenthetically on her, she was the first student to express interest in the Photo Group. And I've gotten to know her pretty well. And I've never had such mixed feelings about a kid; because she's so bright, and she's got a bubbliness, which is attractive. There's a liveliness about her. But her constant stream of talk is just difficult to take; and I've learned when to interrupt and attempt to restructure it into a *conversation.*

I took her home the other day; she didn't have a ride home. And to my surprise, on the way home, she broke down emotionally, and talked a lot about a very cold father—

THORP.   Yes.

FELTON.   —whose only reaction, when there was any reaction at all, to subjects like her excitement about a possible career pursuit, is a negative reaction—"Absolutely not!" and that sort of thing. And she broke down in talking about it.

THORP.   Interesting.

FELTON.   Yeah. She's got a lot going on there.

The other issue that came up about kids happened recently in a different way. I was sitting in my car, in the parking lot, and had a view of the sidewalk beyond the hedge against the main avenue, where people and automobiles go by. And from a long ways back, out of view, a youngster of maybe three, three-and-a-half, was just zooming down there in a gay, hell-bent-for-leather spree of exuberance. And I followed him with my eyes. Of course, with cars going back and forth, I had that reaction any parent does: "Is he on the sidewalk enough for me not to be worried?" And he kept running. And then, here, a half a block behind this little tike, came Mother; and Mother was a twenty-five-year-old Chinese woman, and she was pregnant.

And in an instant, I could see, in this entire chain of events, fully five and ten years ahead! Here was this woman carrying a new child, with the one already probably not out of diapers; and she was perhaps expecting what's going to happen when this one is born, and the other one goes through all the turmoil—still while in critical developmental ages himself. And this new one is in diapers for a thousand years—and then who knows what's beyond that?

This whole panorama of *time* just went right by; and it was very clearly focused from the mother's point of view. And it made me aware of something: As adults, we have the luxury, the earned luxury, perhaps, of having a time sense.

THORP.   A time sense?

FELTON.   A time sense. A sense of the passage of time, the *weight* and the *feel* of time. And it occurred to me that there are, of course, positive values in our being able to work with time as an instrument of our lives; and it also has negative values, because there's a lot we still don't know about our lives, even though we've learned to control the impact of time to an extent. So, here's the infancy end of the spectrum, operating as I've described. On the other end of the spectrum—the gerontology end—we're blissfully removed from that; because we lose our senses. So we don't have the same kind of time sense. And that brings me to the time-span between the two poles:

This import of time helps us, at our age, to form a world view, in a sense—having that time, that ability to manipulate it in our minds. But—what do *teenagers* have? When does that sense begin to develop? Is it, as I suspect, when first it ran over my mind, that their sense is obliterated, because they don't know what's next? That's a condition which might tend to make them focus on the concrete, or on the present. But yet the future is upon them; and they're warned about it every day: "Do your homework, because you need to pass the test in six months. Pass the course, because you need to get out of school, you need to go to college, you need to do all of that." Which is making the future real by dint of making it threatening, in a way!

And this made me ponder: Since they're not so long out of childhood, do they have the sense from this not only that "the fun is gone," "the fun is over"; but in order to quell the anxiety that they get from positing this, might there be some kind of almost recidivist slide into the areas which would give them comfort, the way a toddler would suck his thumb or grab his blanket? So, all that centered around the idea of expectation, youthfulness, the onset of—and I have another question here about commitment—the onset of these real adult properties, these psychic properties, that are forbidding in some ways, but are there. And are very real. And increasingly real.

Would you like to comment?

THORP. Well, this is the Rod Serling comment: Marcel Duchamps took a set of eyeglasses, once, and held them up and let them reflect onto the wall behind him, and said: "See, here is the two-dimensional representation of this three-dimensional object. Why is it so hard to believe that these glasses are the three-dimensional representation of a four-dimensional reality?"

There are times when I think that teenagers are operating in four dimensions—and arguably even in a fifth dimension, where length, width, and depth, in the context of time, are four dimensions that you and I can operate in, if you will. But for the teenager, there isn't, it would appear to me—that for a teenager, there is not easily categorized dimensional separation, if you will. The youngster is in a kind of Piagetian progression—the youngster has *no* sense of time. And it's like the object-permanence kind of peek-a-boo exercise; at what point does a child realize that when a human figure goes behind the wall and pops out again, that the human figure hasn't disappeared when it goes back behind the wall again? And to be honest, somebody would tell you it's three years, whatever, five years, whatever it is.

So at some point, the developmental part kicks in, where kids can start thinking about the future, and start planning. I'm not so sure that that's a happy moment in child development. Some people call it "the loss of innocence." Or maybe it ties into the loss of innocence. It may also tie into something we were talking about last week, which is the loss of self-esteem, where as one transits from carefree infancy to toddlerhood to early adolescence, to care-filled adolescence—it's not a happy direction. And it may also be a loss of control, where in the pre-teen years you have a better sense of being able to control your environment, because your environment is much more limited. And look what happens to the teenager—and this sort of ties into what we were talking about earlier—look what happens to the teenager's sense of control when they lose control over their bodily functions, if you will—whether or not it's menses, or erections, or pubic hair, or breasts, or whatever. I remember a kid in my gym class who every gym class got an erection right before he walked into the shower. How terrible for his feelings!

So when you think about it, the loss of control is pretty huge for teenagers. And the paradox, something I was talking about with a set of parents and a kid this morning—the paradox is: The kid has total control! The great reality-check of parenting is the first time your kid turns to you and says: "No, I won't." And it's the kind of two-year-old, "terrible-twos" "No-I-wont'!," However, the fourteen-year-old "No-I-won't!" is a whole different level of seriousness! And so there's this amazingly complex tectonic-plate overlap between parents and the burgeoning control powers of teenagers, happening at a time when life seems to be spinning out of control. It may result in why so many teenagers make bad decisions; because now they have the opportunity to make a decision, you know? And if they're moving from an arena where they weren't making too many decisions because their parents were telling them what to do, to a position where they're making a lot of decisions, because, first, they have to, and second, because a lot of parents kind of "cash in their chips" when their kids become fourteen.

Is it any wonder you're going to make a lot of bad decisions? And the consequences of bad decisions increase, as you become a teenager.

If you put them behind a wheel of an automobile, it *really* increases!— in terms of the potential for disastrous consequences, if you make a bad decision.

So, I am commenting about an observation that gets to the point of why at least some percentage of teenagers might feel like three-dimensional objects in a four-dimensional world. Or four-dimensional objects in a five-dimensional world. And not be able to plan—which time is connected to—make appropriate decisions—which time often is connected to; or just to "do the right thing." And it must be enormously frustrating.

One of the reasons I think this may be far from the reality on the question of learning decision-making, is I can't remember my own experiences as a teenager on this issue so much, to know whether or not I'm speaking from experience. What I know is that I sure was operating as a three-dimensional object in a four-dimensional world as soon as I fell in love for the first time! And I made irrational decision after irrational decision as a consequence of that. And my parents were angry, and my teachers were angry; but I was fine! And I do have to believe that this is happening in a time where the kids have the opportunity to make more decisions in this baby-boomer abrogation of the rights of parenthood, either because of increasing divorce, or single-parent homes, or "Here's fifty bucks, go enjoy yourself, kid, while we go to the country club," or "I don't see you because I'm working two jobs, and I can't be your parent because I've got to pay the mortgage, or the rent."

So there's some truth to the natural tendency of various dimensions within which teenagers have to operate being increasingly complex; and those dimensions have been made more difficult because the world is more complex. And more fraught with the potential for teenagers to make bad decisions.

FELTON. Interesting! My dad tells the story of when he was in the army, in a position of authority. And his sergeant came to him and said, "Colonel, should we blue ink here, or black ink?" And my dad said: "Use blue ink." And then he added to me: "It didn't matter what I told him; he just wanted to know that there was a decision! That *this* is what we now do." And that makes me think of this ambivalence for teenagers in getting a foothold in a way that's meaningful at this particular age, then we get to get out, we've learned enough about decision-making to graduate, and we get out, and now we're in the wonderful world where everybody's giving us orders.

THORP. Yes.

FELTON. And we're all of a sudden now *deprived* of our ability to make decisions—except the decision: "Do I keep my mouth shut, or do I not?," basically. Because the world—certainly the corporate world, is "the army." And: If we've done our job, then the kid-become-adult will now know how to function, and his responsible act will be knowing that he's going to pretend a little bit here. He's going to appear to be weaker than he really is. He's going to subvert his will, and subsume it, and behave in a role which, again, is going to be expected of him, because he wants the reward every month.

THORP. I think you'll find that it isn't: The people on the planet for whom I have the least respect, after such obvious targets such as Hitler and the Khmer Rouge—the people on the planet for whom I have the least respect are people that I call "trust-fund" hippies. That people who adopt a "holier-than-thou," "funner-than-thou" philosophy and look down on "working stiffs" because, "Well, you've sacrificed anything because you're working for Philip Morris, or the logging company up in Eureka," and who are able to have such a skewed philosophy in life because they've never had to put bread on the table.

I am at the older end of the baby boom generation, and my parents were very much Depression-era parents. And that "greatest generation," as Tom Brokaw called them, carried with them the scars of a period which even for my parents, were lifelong scars. And resulted in lifelong values. My mother was—well, it probably wasn't fair to say she was a penny pincher, but she sure as hell was conscious of prudent fiscal management! And I think we do our kids a disservice if we allow them to believe that the world is something other than it is.

Now what does that mean? And what is that world? Because the world does infinite permutations, we do the kids equally a disservice if we don't allow them to dream. And so it's not my job to say to a kid: "Forget about it! You can't do that. Forget about it—you'll never get into that college" or: "Forget about whatever—!" That's not my job. What my job is to do, it seems to me—and this is what I was doing this morning with this kid and this set of parents—is to announce: "Hey! You've made decisions all year long, most of which have been not to do any school-related work, and here we are!" And the "here we are" is: "You're going to have to repeat one year if you come back to Gateway. And you're now faced with the fact that you're going to be in this position where the humiliation factor is incredibly high, and my counsel to you is: You're probably better off going to another school where you don't' have to face the humiliation factor."

I told this youngster: "Look—you were, and are, totally in control of this situation. You're the one who decided not to do the homework.

You're also the one who can try to do something within the next three weeks to turn it around, and you're the one who's going to have to make a decision about where you're going to go to school next fall. But whatever you decide, *you're* going to make the decision about whether or not you're going to take advantage of that."

An example: I was really a pretty good athlete in college; and we were playing in this alumni-varsity soccer team, and I was one of the captains of the varsity team.   There was an older guy who was watching the game. He was from the class of '56, and had been quite a soccer player then, and he came up to me after the game and said: "Peter, you're obviously a great soccer player, and you must be a great guy, a real 'Williams man'—I'd like you to think about coming to work for me, and my company"—which was Colgate Palmolive, in Cincinnati. And boy, I look through the lens of thirty years and say: "What an idiot I was!" Because my response was, "No, I don't think I'm going to go into a job in business, thanks." I'd intended it to be, you know—"No, thanks"—but it sure came across in a kind of condemnatory fashion. What a jerk!

FELTON.   What was his response?

THORP.   I don't remember that there was any response other than the end of the conversation. I mean, he was decent enough not to say, "Why, you little snot!" So I don't remember any exchange beyond that.

My point is that what we want to do is prepare kids for knowing consequences of decisions. And the typical "beef" I have with a kid is—you know, the kid does something wrong, and the kid says: "That was really stupid; I didn't think." And my response always is: "You're not stupid individually. So I want you to hear from me that what you did was not stupid. It was wrong! And do you understand the difference between those two things?" And the typical kid can understand the difference between those two things.

But the typical kid doesn't "buy" the difference between those two things; or doesn't "buy" the fact that it was anything other than: "It was stupid; I didn't think." And even now as I'm saying it, I'm looking back over thirty years of giving that counsel, and recognizing that they don't have my perspective on their behavior. They're pondering: "Well, let me think if I'm going to do 'A' or 'B'; I'm going to do 'B' because I think I can get away with it," or "I'm going to do 'B' because I'm really horny and I want to do 'B';" or: "You know, it looks really good, and I'm going to take it!" or "There it is!" You know—they probably don't go through that thoughtful a process to make their bad decisions. But the point I try to make with them is: "Look: It isn't just a question of 'I was stupid, I didn't think, so therefore I'm absolved of responsibility;' it's, 'Okay, you didn't think; you better start thinking, dammit, because here are the consequences: You're in trouble with your girlfriend, or you're in trouble with your teacher, or you're repeating your sophomore year, or you're not getting into college, or you're fired!'"

And if we can help kids understand there is a world that exists beyond the force-field six inches in front of their nose—which is about the extent of the global perception of the typical teenager—then we're doing our job. I think. And I think we attend to that, in this school, because we follow up on incidents where somebody has done something that's hurtful, or unthinking, and let them know that in fact, there are consequences. And I think we're raising a generation of kids who don't understand or don't accept consequences very well.

FELTON. I'm on the floor to hear that, because that's a hugely important statement. I'm distressed to hear it. I also happen to agree with it—which is worse.

THORP. I'll just addend to it by saying: I sure as hell don't think it's all their fault, when they've got Dick Nixon and Bill Clinton to look at as role models—

FELTON. True.

THORP. —Let alone all the other cultural icons who live a lifetime of avoiding consequences.

FELTON. Yeah.

THORP. I don't blame teenagers for that.

FELTON. The kid taking responsibility for his actions, in this scenario—what operates in terms of a kid's rationale, his process, his view, his evaluation? I think about the idea of community service at Gateway; it's going, is it not, from "soft" to "hard"? It was sort of an elective process, and now it's going to be a required—?

THORP. It's—I think there will be a number of intermediate steps.

FELTON. That being the case—when is there, in a teenager's psyche, a sense of readiness to make a commitment? Do we wait until he demonstrates it on his own? Do we make it a requirement so he has no choice? Does he make the decision by thinking: "How will this best serve humanity?" or does he think: "How will this best serve Joe? What's the easiest way for me to satisfy this requirement?" Or is he thinking, as some of Gateway teacher Richard Kassisieh's Amnesty International activist kids are thinking: "I want to get out there because I have a feeling about this important issue"?

THORP.   There's a third feeling. And it's one that's the greatest feeling from a standpoint of community service: Kids will come to it or be dragged to it through the idea of: "This is good for the world; I'm helping out somebody."   Where it becomes really something they commit to is if they are put in the position where they have the possibility of experiencing the profound sense of satisfaction that comes from helping another human being. The school I led previously had a completely voluntary public service program, community service program.   And about ninety percent of the kids participated in it to varying degrees, but they participated in it in a significant way.

And what contributed to that sense of satisfaction was community service to *people* even moreso than *things*. And that's an area were I hope we'll be able to develop more opportunities.   I kick myself, because one of the things I didn't follow through on this year was trying to set up a community service program with the pre-school across the street from Gateway High. And I will do my best to either do it myself, or have somebody else do it next year. But I can assure you that things really click in for a kid when he's put in a service position, a community service position, where you can see somebody else's face change, because you've done something. And to be sure, raking leaves and beach cleanup are important ways of doing community service; but they don't have the visceral reward that that other kind of experience does. And so I want to continue to move on the idea of community service here, not by just requiring it, where kids again are dragged kicking and screaming, as much as building from the ground up and sort of "attacking from within."   Those are the participatory programs where kids come back and say how really cool it is to be working with these little four-year-olds across the street, or an Alcoholics Anonymous program or a senior citizen program on the other side of the church. That kind of effort is how they make that kind of interpersonal connection.

FELTON.   Regarding your meeting this morning with the student and his parents: Recently I picked up this news item: "The three greatest fears for a child—" it wasn't specified what age, but they were talking about younger, slightly younger kids, perhaps middle school— let's just say "a young person"—"The three greatest fears are death of a parent; blindness; and not advancing a grade in school."

THORP. Ah!

FELTON.   So the idea—when I thought about Gateway, and social promotion, I'm interested to hear you tell me that there would even be the possibility that a kid would be asked to repeat. As opposed to telling him he couldn't be here.

THORP. Yeah. And it is that second part of the question I didn't refer to earlier; that 's part of the bigger question, or the bigger picture. If we have a kid whom we believe is demonstrating the kind of potential that we'd like to see if we could continue to try to unlock, and yet falls so way short of the credit requirements that he or she shouldn't be matriculating until the next grade level, we'll consider having the kid back for a second year. That's also a reflection of my, you know— "bleeding heart"-ness, in a sense that I'm willing to give a kid a second year, a second chance, if you will, to try to turn things around. However, I have experienced enough of doing this that the success stories are few and far between. They're great when they happen; but the typical kid doesn't turn things around.

So the basic situation here at Gateway is that a kid could fail the ninth grade year, and be allowed to come back as a repeat ninth-grader, with a different strategy on our part, and different approaches, to assure that the kid might be successful. And we have maybe two or three kids from last year who are repeating the ninth grade.

When you get to the tenth grade, it's more complicated just on the numbers. And it's more complicated in the sense that if you can't pass the tenth grade at Gateway, the likelihood of your passing the eleventh grade at Gateway isn't very high; and the clock is running out, in terms of what you've got to do to graduate from high school on time. But if you had faculty members in this conversation as well, they would ask the same question: If a kid has to repeat a year, why should he be at Gateway? And then we start talking about all sorts of other factors that come into play, in terms of the political considerations of attrition. And I think at that meeting before the Board of Education, you heard one of the board members speaking to that point. The member said: "We want the numbers of faculty attrition, we want to know the student attrition..." But the only thing they *really* want know is: How many African-American and Latino kids don't return to your school the next year? And the basic presumption is: "You're at fault for their not returning, and you've kicked them out." That will be the starting point of the School Board-Gateway conversation.

FELTON. It's a "lose-lose" situation.

THORP. Oh! Totally. Totally. The end of the year, we'll have a faculty meeting, where we will review the plight of as many as fifteen kids, about whether or not they should be able to come back. Last year when we did it, of the first eight kids we talked about, six of them were African-American boys.

FELTON. Wow!

THORP. And if you looked at each one individually, there is no question: They shouldn't come back. But I began the meeting, and it's a touchy meeting as the head of a school anyway, because basically you're saying to the faculty: "Okay, we're going to discuss this issue, but I want to be clear: You're making a recommendation to me, okay?" And the faculty hate that kind of thing! They're thinking: "What do you mean, 'We're making a recommendation to you'? *We're* the ones who are working with this kid every day; who are you?" But I try to explain that, you know, somebody's got to make a final decision, because somebody's got to be looking at the big picture. And then I said: " If we don't ask back six of our eight African-American males, we're going to be in deep trouble. And we *should* be in deep trouble!"

So it's a very complicated situation. I mean, I'm only half-joking and half cynical when I say: "Make sure you're *not* a white kid who doesn't earn enough credits to matriculate to the next grade."

FELTON. The reporter who assessed the failure to advance in grade went on to mention that in all the instances of kids who repeated, there was ultimately a hugely deleterious effect on their lives—they came back in shame, humiliation, they never "lived it down," their growth rate in maturation in psychological terms just leveled off or went down—it was an horrendous situation.

THORP. Yes, it is.

FELTON. Does Gateway participate in any kind of summer school "off-ramp" and "on-ramp" situation? Or is that simply a palliative, if someone is in this kind of straits?

THORP. Well, if I understand your question correctly, basically what the typical kid at Gateway is doing is signing up with the School District summer school. And the most they can get out of that is ten credits, which is the equivalent of two semester-long classes. And they're expected to get sixty credits per year.

FELTON. Oh! That's all?

THORP. They're only getting one-sixth of what they need, by going to summer school. So a kid who fails three or more core classes is behind the eight-ball. He's kind of "behind the eight-ball" anyway.

You know, you ask questions, and I'm sure you can tell—every time you ask a question the wheels just start turning, and some of the wheel-turning is "Let's see if I can come up with an answer to Keith's question," but I trust you know that there are other wheels turning simultaneously, which indicate to me: "Yeah, but what does this really mean? Yeah, that's a good question. And Yeah, have I thought about this? Yeah, if I have thought about this, what *have* I thought about this?" And: "No, if I haven't thought about it, let me think for a few seconds while I'm composing this answer." And even on this question, there's so much here at Gateway that we're doing, that we're accomplishing; but there's so much else that we *could* be doing, with greater resources, greater time, and fewer constraints. And this is an area where I feel under constraint that we can't be a school that just bounces kids—and particularly kids of color.

FELTON. Yeah.

THORP. I mean, the black community continues to need leadership on this issue—over the entire spectrum, from parents to civic leaders. And that's why people like Jesse Jackson are so important, and leave so much to be fulfilled by their lackluster performance. That's where he could *really* demonstrate leadership. I completely understand the challenge of an eighteen-year-old woman who gets herself pregnant and for reasons that are certainly hers to make, decides to have her child and not abort it, and finds herself for the rest of her life up against the wall trying to raise the kid, in a project where there are guns going off, and drug deals going down all along. I completely understand the nightmare of that. But damn it, where are the Jesse Jacksons of this world to stand up and say, you know—"We, the community need to figure out how to raise our babies, we the community leaders need to figure out what to tell our families so that they will feel supported, and will work with those organizations like schools in the interest of our kids." Jesse's a—somebody who knows him, whom I have heard speak about him, says that "If it ain't got something for Jesse, Jesse ain't doing it!"

And such a personal prescription works its way down to this school, and to me!

FELTON. Well, I've written elsewhere about Jackson's speaking power, and its meaning and import. But when he was a younger man, he was not as admirable. Anybody who read enough when King was shot, would've seen that about him. Because he was very concerned with how he would appear, how he would "come off" in that awful episode.

THORP. Is that right?

FELTON. He also may not have read Aretha Franklin's autobiography, where she describes her father, a well-known Bible-thumping minister, who, when his darling *fourteen-year-old* daughter became pregnant, he was just absolutely non-judgmental.—

At this point, that local public radio station interviewer called, to conduct a telephone interview with Peter Thorp. Our own meeting was abridged, while Peter explained to yet another informed and astute individual the rudiments of the phenomenon called charter schools. His responses to her questions indicated not only that a good reporter was probing; it indicated that an education plan clearly the wave of the future—as endorsed by both Presidential candidates, covering the political spectrum—was until then unknown to someone clearly aware of public issues.

At the conclusion of his interview with the reporter, she asked him if he knew of any parents of the school with whom she could speak. He handed the telephone to the man standing in his office winding up tape recorder cables. Then, fulfilling once again that amazing attribute of the busy executive, Peter locked himself next door in the office of Gateway's Academic Dean, and checked off another item on his day's long agenda.

Chapter Twenty-Five

GATEWAY VER*SUS* GROTON!

"Do the benefits of educational opportunity outweigh the costs of educational opportunity? Does the Native American prep school with which I'm associated as a board member, inherently break the heart of a kid by taking him or her away, so to speak, during high school years, away from family, and consciously, unabashedly try to inculcate a set of values that might be counter to the values of that kid's family or community?

It is not dissimilar here at Gateway. Aren't we trying to inculcate values that we, the adults associated with this school, believe are worthy values?....Whose values are they, anyway?

"And unfortunately, to a great degree, schools have backed off from community-wide values at the same time that there has been neither a continuation of nor an enhancement of familial values. So we have this dual phenomenon where kids are increasingly valueless, because they're not getting them at home. And that isn't condemning parents and families—that's not the point. It's just that our society is such that parents have less time to inculcate values, and parents are more confused than they ever have been about what's okay and what's not okay. Kids are growing up so much more quickly— you're having to deal with the twelve-year-old daughter who comes to you not with a question, 'Tell me about the birds and the bees,' but: 'Tell me about sexually-transmitted diseases.' And parents are really confused about how to deal with that."

25 May—*Peter and I were looking ahead to the "final roundup."*

To place the closing parameters on our year of dialogue, I engaged a fundamental pedagogical comparative Peter Thorp had introduced early on in our colloquy: The quandary of tradition-bound Groton Preparatory School. Endicott Peabody's faraway link to a prim New England past, with its rich families and their well-heeled, bushy-tailed progeny, would rise from parenthetical reference to full prominence in our dialogues now. I screened the videotape Peter had lent me early on—a film made fifteen years before—and prepared the next conceptual challenges for the Principal of Gateway High School.

In a real sense, education's multiple problems often come down to the old, tired contest between the "have's" and the "have-nots." Certainly, as Peter had eloquently characterized it, this is the root of the ugliness of the "Digital Divide" problem.

Gateway's students, although not uniformly so, could if need be legitimately be cast in the pole of the "have-nots." I felt it might be instructive here, for the purposes of understanding the pedagogical implications of these poles, to set Gateway on one side of our discussion, and a "have's" school—Groton—on the other side.

Groton's place in the scheme of preparatory schools—self-styled, but eminently-met, was as a purveyor of future world-class figures. On the "Wall of Tiles" on which every graduate's name is emblazoned after matriculation were names like former Ambassador Averell Harriman; Kennedy aide McGeorge Bundy; Reagan Treasury Secretary Douglas Dillon; and—a luminary among luminaries— Franklin Delano Roosevelt. This very roster of greatness made it enticing as a foil in our dialogues for the roster of Gateway High School students. No doubt, Gateway had every reason to expect great things of some of its students; but on the daily calendar, most students were still at the level of meeting learning disability challenges; and being scolded for skateboard riding; and just trying to keep up with the dismaying demands of standardized tests. All the "tiles" were uncut at Gateway, and would remain so for another year. But I wanted the Principal—whose training and professional activity prior to his San Francisco arrival were much more in the Groton mode than the Gateway mode—to confront an educational monolith of power and wealth, and then hold up in comparison his newest-born child: the infant of humility and struggle. Of course, Peter well knew that that "infant" held within it the possibilities of educational reform. And I knew that that fact gave it the edge over Groton. But I also knew that it was salubrious to the soul to stare at all the images of one's product.

I would attempt in this dialogue to help Peter to face, and examine, these variegated offspring.

As always, some preliminary matters got us going first.

FELTON. The new San Francisco Unified School District Superintendent is Arlene Ackerman. As you know, she was the former Washington, D.C. Superintendent of Schools, and you may also remember: She was someone whom we heard speaking with censorious caution of charter schools on the transcript of the earlier MacNeil-Lehrer report on charter schools.

THORP. Read Ken Garcia's column in the Chronicle this morning.

FELTON. Oh?

THORP. It's more of his ongoing "slam" against Rojas, the previous superintendent; and basically he's saying: "We welcome anybody."

FELTON. Well, just parenthetically, they interviewed former Superintendent Bill Hoenig when they took Ackerman on; and they did reveal the little matter of her salary. I had absolutely no concept that that's what—I mean, it's an unenviable job, but is it $192,000-unenviable?

THORP. A hundred and ninety *seven* thousand.

FELTON. A hundred and ninety-seven! Oh, my god.

THORP. Well, the parents and faculty who were at the Board of Education meeting Tuesday night when they announced it booed and hissed and yelled and screamed, and all sorts of things. I don't think it's enough money!

FELTON. Well, it may not be, in the sense that we—we'll see how long she stays. Two years on her previous job is no sterling record. But I don't know her, other than the MacNeil-Lehrer piece; so I will start with Ken Garcia's news piece.

But we've got much new business:

Your background is so heavily imbued with private school—schools of privilege—and I don't really know Cate or the others, apart from your descriptions. But I have had the exposure to Groton through the film you recommended I see; and I'd like its review here to give us insights into Peter Thorp, and more insights thence into Gateway High School. And I believe such a review can accomplish this. So give me a moment to set up our investigation.

We've spoken from time to time about this Eastern "prep" school called Groton. It's what many out here on the West Coast would regard as a traditional, elitist private school, where moneyed families ensconced their progeny, anticipating greatness on a public, political, or philanthropic plane, and where expectations are high in general for these "rich-men's kids."

Some time ago in our process, you asked me to view a film about Groton—Endicott Peabody's original spartan preserve of a nation's most privileged youth, which in recent years has had some reckoning on its way into the modern world. I've found the film illuminating not only about a particular educational institution, but as a foil for much of what Gateway represents. The clashes, or distinctions, are obvious: Money versus hardship; Anglo-Saxon Protestantism versus Latin-African American variegations; the drive for wealth versus the chance to survive. I'd like now, for a while, to use Groton as a paradigm for understanding Gateway better. So I'm going to take moments from the film, briefly describing a Groton protagonist or event, and ask you to reflect upon that person or moment in terms of what it makes you think about Gateway.

I realize that in this construct, "Groton" and "Gateway" have been assigned, for better or worse, the sobriquets of "Rich" and "Poor."

What I'd like to do is read some brief characteristic sections of narrative or spoken material from the film. And what I would like you to do is reflect upon them—not in a commentary way about what you just heard, but rather to take the substance of what you just heard and give a kind of statement about how those issues manifest themselves at Gateway.

THORP.   Okay. Well, let's do the first one as a kind of trial run here.

FELTON.   Here's the first quote—and by the way, all stresses are original:

> Kids who come to us out of a minority background are brought to us out of a really different world. A world where success is assumed. A world in which people are completely different from their experience. What we have to do is to be able to talk to kids. To help them understand who they are. Talk with them about how important their individuality is, while they learn maybe another way of being—another vocabulary of behavior. They're going to have to be something else; just have to be something else. And that's a tragedy.
>
> I'm someone who did this sort of thing myself. I came from a factory town in Michigan, and my father was an auto worker. So I've had to come here and I've, as an Episcopal minister, had to adapt to a somewhat different style, a somewhat different look, and be a somewhat different person. But I'm in touch with my past, and I'm an adult. And that a big advantage. What an impossible task to ask a

teenager to 'pull off that trick.' But many of them do. Many of them do.

We know we have to bring students here from all parts of America. It has to be a school that reflects America. The paradox is that we bring students here and break their hearts.

THORP. It's the Groton reality.

And the last statement, obviously taken out of the context of the whole film, lends a weight to the concept of breaking a heart that is not really what he was saying. Though some hearts are broken in that process, you know—I think constantly it's a question of, at the risk of sounding clinical about it, of a benefit-cost analysis: Do the benefits of educational opportunity outweigh the costs of educational opportunity? Does the Native American prep school with which I'm associated as a board member, inherently break the heart of a kid by taking him or her away, so to speak, during high school years, away from family, and consciously, unabashedly try to inculcate a set of values that might be counter to the values of that kid's family or community?

It is not dissimilar here at Gateway. Aren't we trying to inculcate values that we, the adults associated with this school, believe are worthy values? I have to believe that the overwhelming percentage of the parents associated with this school through their children share those values, values which may be extremely well-articulated, less well articulated values which are still in formative stages, or values which may end up involving us to quite a degree. But the whole benefit of the charter school world is that the clients can vote with their feet. And we certainly tried especially in this past year, to articulate what our values are, through our marketing outreach in a way that has been a not-unchallenging task, which on the one hand is to stimulate interest in the school, and at the same time not to do that as an advertising "schtick."

I believe that one of the Achilles' heels of public education is that people have gone through this wrenching post-sixties process by which schools have become valueless. And schools have relegated the teaching of values to courses. And even that was a reform in the last twenty years when there were not even courses about values. I think it's a mistake to relegate values to classes about values; in that you've got to live the values of your school. And those values, you know—again, as a charter school, we have the luxury of establishing the values that we believe in, and if nobody likes the values, they don't come to school; but if enough people do, then the school should be able to continue, in that sense.

Obviously, the city and state have the right to say that your values are antithetical to public education; and like anything in life, there are easy things at either end of the spectrum—for example, if we were a church school, that would be inappropriate. Or if we believed in corporal punishment as the solution to things, that would be inappropriate. Just as we espouse rigorous education for all kids, everybody goes, "Hooray! Of course!" And of course, the big issues are right in the middle: What is the curriculum of a U.S. history class? And is it bottom-up or top-down? And by that, I mean, what are the voices that you include in U.S. history class? And of course, you choose from all of those; but depending upon one's perspective, one's set of values, it's either a course that is a political-diplomatic-military-history, you know, more or less in its emphasis; or it's a program that is the "bottom-up" or underside of history, as one historian called it. Where the voices of people previously unheard become the focus of the program. And of course, those voices now have to be part of a legitimate program. But what choices you end up making become the values.

As an educator, as the principal of a school, this is a really important question. And for me, the point which has driven all my effort is to provide kids with opportunities, and choices, and to provide vehicles by which they find their potential in their own voices. And the presumption in that is to believe that left alone, they'll have less opportunity to do that. That's why I think the typical educator is at the least skeptical about home schooling. You know, on the one hand, from a practical point of view, let's have everybody home-schooled, and let's get rid of the school system, and we're all happy! Maybe I can get a job in a dot-com world and be much happier than I am. But I think educators have believed since Socrates that extra-familial influence is valuable. And of course, that's the inherent tension in local schools: Whose values are they, anyway?

And unfortunately, to a great degree, schools have backed off from community-wide values at the same time that there has been neither a continuation of nor an enhancement of familial values. So we have this dual phenomenon where kids are increasingly valueless, because they're not getting them at home. And that isn't condemning parents and families—that's not the point. It's just that our society is such that parents have less time to inculcate values, and parents are more confused than they ever have been about what's okay and what's not okay. Kids are growing up so much more quickly—you're having to deal with the twelve-year-old daughter who comes to you not with a question, "Tell me about the birds and the bees," but: "Tell me about sexually-transmitted diseases." And parents are really confused about how to deal with that.

So we have a situation where both at the community level and at the familial level, the anchors in a kid's life have been yanked away, so kids are rudderless and I believe that schools should have rudders to them. And believing that, you know for damned sure that not everybody's going to like it. And what's tricky about it is that in the public sector, when people become critical of that, it takes on a level of entitlement, which is a word that's usually applied in the private sector. A principal would be forgiven for thinking: "I'm tired of dealing with these rich kids, because they and their parents have this sense of entitlement that makes them feel, 'Because we're rich we ought to get this kind of service.'"

The word "entitlement" applies in the public sector as well, which is: "I'm entitled to my rights." Yes, you are. But what rights, exactly, are they? And where do your rights stop? Is there the right, as Jesse Jackson would argue, for those kids back in Decatur, Illinois, to come to school and beat up kids in the stands? And he would of course say they don't have the right to do that; but does the school board have the right to kick them the hell out of school because of what they did? That's where the tension comes into play.

You would hope that schools are clear enough about who they are and who they're not so that kids' hearts are not broken when they go to a school. But they need to know their purpose clearly enough so that kids' values are challenged without being shattered. That they are examined—"the unexamined life is not worth living"—that they are examined without being yanked away. And that the values are therefore reaffirmed, so that when a kid leaves high school, particularly in this era, that kids have what somebody once called an evidential belief system—you know, so that the beliefs are based on either the evidence of reality; or the beliefs are based on an examinatory process whereby the kid says: "Yeah, now that I've thought about this, now that I realize there are other values out there, I've reaffirmed that these are really the values that are important to me." And of course, out of the debris of this challenging process can come the result that some kids are going to change their values.

When I went to college—and in our generation, all this happened at the college level, as opposed to the high school level—when I went to college, I stopped going to church. And it killed my mother! I don't mean literally; but I know it gravely disappointed her. You know, I don't think it jettisoning of that value made me a less-worthy person—

even though it sure as hell did in her eyes!—and maybe God's eyes, you know, I've rolled the dice on this one a little bit!—but that was a value that got jettisoned in my "sort-of-examined" life, as a college freshman.

FELTON. That was a very provocative response!

Your comment about college replacing church is very apropos of something that a Groton student leader says in our film about this Eastern private school. Here is the student, whose name is Wright:

> As you go through here, you learn about all the famous graduates who've done really great service. I think it does make a real impact; at least for me, personally. It has really made me start to think about that as a pursuit in life. It may be one of the best pursuits. I think it's the faculty that gives you that kind of feeling. Because they're all so dedicated to teaching you.

And here is his teacher:

> What we do very well, is we train kids in the academic skills. But if we teach kids anything, I think we have to teach them to have responsibility to the world they live in. I come from the rich and privileged. My name [which was Choate] is a well-known American name. And in the last year, what really bothered me was the whole insider-trading in the stock market. We have kids that come from that environment, we have kids that will eventually go on to it—and I really wonder if we're turning out kids, and turning out kids in society, who would understand that that's a real wrong. I hope we have. And I'm not sure. And it's a battle we fight day after day after day. I want kids to stand for something.

THORP. One of the moments when my heart was broken in education is when I had to stand up in front of the school community at Cate on a Saturday morning to tell them that a classmate had just been killed a half hour before in a car accident, on the way to school. This young woman was a woman of unchecked promise. Unlimited potential. Not that any kid isn't unlimited potential; but this young woman was going to be President. And she was something special. And she had a saying that—and I think it was original to her, but I'm not a hundred percent sure—and it was: "If you don't stand for something, you'll fall for anything." And she was right.

Throughout that time, my own decision-making process as a teacher looking for a path and an identity, I had mixed feelings about working with the children of the privileged. But the ambivalence in my feelings about that is that we are all saddled with the blind spots of our upbringing, whatever they are. And I think it would be a mistake to believe that none of us is biased/prejudiced. I mean, it means that we're brain-dead if we are. And the bias of the upper class, which this film is about, is that service is noble because we as a class have an obligation to serve. And where the blind spot in that is—and there are a couple of blind spots—one is what I'd call an "ecclesiastical blind spot," which is that we are here, as William Howard Taft said, "to take care of our little brown brothers." He was citing *noblesse oblige* to talk about the Philippines.

FELTON. Yes.

THORP. And the consequence of that is the Kennedy approach to life, arguably the Clinton approach to life. Which is: Tremendous caring for the oppressed as a class, but an unchecked willingness to do whatever one wants to do on a one-to-one basis. Locked within this dichotomy is an analogy there about how the upper class looks at service. Which is: "We are privileged to have the opportunity to serve others in a variety of ways." And, you know, from Bill Gates on down, there's incredible generosity and philanthropy in this country, which doesn't exist, really, in any other country in the world, until you start recognizing that in Outer Mongolia, there's total philanthropy, in terms of families taking care of each other, for example.

But what isn't addressed—the blind spot of the upper crust—is the inherent unfairness of a society which produces such a disparity in wealth that we have to have this kind of philanthropy. And the obnoxiousness of the position that "We are therefore better people because we are philanthropic, and you aren't," and the failure to recognize that the vast majority of people in this country, on this planet, have neither the time nor the means to be philanthropic in a way that carries with it the meaning of true philanthropy. This is, you know, the concept in fundraising of the "stretch" gift—it is the value of the unaffordable donation. An example comes to mind from last year's fundraising. We wanted as many parents to give as possible. One parent who had been homeless two years before Gateway, gave us five dollars. You cannot imagine the incredible joy felt among us to receive that gift, when with a three-thousand-dollar gift that we got from another parent there was great gratitude, but it didn't touch the heart strings that the five-dollar gift did.

So my ambivalent feelings in terms of my own professional career is to what extent did I, in my work, try to bridge the gap between *noblesse oblige*, and social reform? And frankly, that's what I'm trying to do now. That's why I'm doing what I'm doing. Take away the college prep, take away the learning disability opportunities, take away everything else, this is what I'm trying to do. And I'm trying to figure out a way that access to unfettered choices will not be a function of one's socio-economic status. And I know that as the head of a school, I have neither the time nor the resources to do that. So my ambivalence is—I mean, my ambivalence about my own job, is this constant weighing of: "Take good care of 185 kids and give them the best you can," or its alternative: "Quit being a principal, run for the Senate, and try to reform education on a level where you hold up such terms as 'gifted and talented' and say, 'Don't you understand, American people, how humiliating it is to use a term like this, and say, 'Oh, by the way, it only applies to ten percent of our children'?"

Now, having said that: Okay, if you have the means, and you don't share it, you're at the lowest end of the phyla system, in my opinion. So, Andrew Carnegie was a noble robber-baron, if that's not an oxymoron, you know—much moreso than J.P. Morgan was.

FELTON. What about people like your interviewer? My whole feeling as I grew as someone with intellectual aspiration—my whole notion was, because I came from a family highly-regarded in society but not particularly wealthy, that it lent—a great significance in my mind to the importance of that other currency which I had, which I wanted to use in my commerce with society, which was whatever brain power could do. I now feel that that is one of the most obviously antiquated, arcane, untranslatable commodities to bring to the current .world, as we've talked about in many other contexts. And yet it's really at the heart in a way of what, if I understand it, what *your* mission is as you've just now described it.

THORP. Well, if there weren't people like you, dressed in the clothing of Irish monks sleeping on a rock in Ireland in the seyenth century, we wouldn't be talking about too much of this. Because, you know, without that kind of commitment to scholarship for its own sake, so much of what had come before certainly would have been lost. And that's not to say that it wouldn't have reflowered, in the Renaissance or whatever; but I think I'm a pragmatic philosopher, if that makes sense, if that's not an oxymoron in thinking. In order for the world of the intellectual, and the world of the pragmatist to intersect, I think the world of the intellectual needs to shift perhaps more than the world of the pragmatist.

And the unwillingness, it seems to me, of the world of the intellectual to do some shifting is unfortunate, because, as it has at various times in world history, it will make the intellectual irrelevant. It was so in 1912 in China, with the overturning of the Confucian tradition of Sun Yat-Sen; and it was so with Spiro Agnew and "effete intellectual snobs." And it is so with "me, as a consumer of college education" where in part I'm driven mad by the tuition bills, knowing that the college is sitting on just a boatload of endowment that could temper the tuition costs of sending a kid to school. And it is with me also in knowing that the personnel costs of the Grinnells and Williams and Columbia Bornans of this world are so high because these college professors live a life of leisure that is scandalous. And this kind of educational profligacy directly has an impact on the cost of education, and that impact further exacerbates social divisions in this country.

The paradox to me is the typical Grinnell and Williams College professor who is a well-meaning liberal, who I'm sure is outraged by the discrepancies between rich and poor in this country! Well, dammit, do something about it at the grass-roots level! Provide more access for middle-class families, to get to colleges like Grinnell and Williams, to have the springboard effect that those colleges have. Stop pretending that you're anything other than, you know, a playground for those "effete intellectual snobs"!

But in saying that, it would be, I think, a tragedy for society to develop to a level of iconoclasm where the value of intellectual pursuit was lost simply because it had no pragmatic or capitalistic ends in sight. Because if we're not a country of dreamers, we're something pretty ordinary.

You've heard me express on a number of occasions my outrage about the discrepancies between the rich and the poor, and the increasing gap, rather than the decreasing gap, particularly in a time of great wealth. I mean, unbelievable! What do we do?—Governor Davis says, "Let's give a tax rebate of a hundred and fifty bucks, or three hundred bucks, per person." You know? We're going to give Gordon Getty a three hundred dollar tax break!? For him that's not even pocket change!

FELTON. That's not one millisecond's interest income from the Getty holdings.

THORP. Right. And another three hundred bucks for a family trying to go to school for a scholarship can make a big difference.

FELTON. Well, let's move on. But when people say, "Where's that money going to come from?"—well, by anybody's calculation, of only a handful of sources, it is clear and demonstrable in any headline today that a billion dollars will have been spent in the Presidential campaign to nominate two blokes who are going to be nominated anyway and more to elect one of them! It's a different perspective; I wonder if that final figure will come out to be about three hundred per family.

Here's the comment of another Groton student—one of the "have's," a rather arrogant young man named Bobby Greenhill:

> Achieving means a lot to kids at Groton. And what makes a lot of them happy, probably talk to their mother or parents, is having a lot of money and being successful. Probably more than making money, as a fantasy, I just want power. You know? I just really want power! I'm not a greedy guy; I just want to be able to run and service a huge corporate structure, and command what happens. The little intricacies. You know, just be—I want to be a shaker!...
>
> I just want to be able to say: "I want to change something, on a wider scale." So I'm probably more hungry for power than I am for social acceptance.

And let me link that with the next one here. It's the minister, the Chaplain of Groton:

> Sure the school has changed. But it still is a school which has that kind of class orientation. There is in fact, something called "Elites." We have a job to do with the Elites here. And that is to sensitize them, to educate them, to bring them fully into the world, and open their eyes....
>
> And we have a lot of work to do with the Elites. We have a lot of work to humanize those people, who can lose their humanity in being entitled. And can lose their humanity and their privilege. And they deserve their humanity, too.

So: Bobby, the salivating student; and then the minister in his rectitude. Comment?

THORP. The one part of the minister's statement I've picked up on is the "We've changed" part: "Groton is a different place now than it was before." Well, what does that mean? You know—"before" was utterly the world of exclusivity and privilege! His point is that as a member of the elite, you had a social obligation to make this a better place. And this Groton ideal really contributed to the thinking of a Franklin Roosevelt, I don't have the slightest doubt about that. And why I respect Roosevelt so much is that he used his power in a way that fundamentally changed some of the premises of this society. That famous New Yorker cartoon, "Let's go down to the Lux and hiss Roosevelt." Do you remember that one?—said by a group of people standing around in tuxedos. It's kind of the classic cartoon of the

1930s and in fact represents the recognition that Roosevelt was changing the premises of this society.

The basic change was the attitude of the 1920s, the laisser-faire, "life-is-tough" social Darwinist approach of Calvin Coolidge, and Andrew Mellon. The interesting figure in all of this, from an historical point of view, was Herbert Hoover.

FELTON. Yes.

THORP. Herbert Hoover was this kind of sackcloth–and-ashes person in history books, but that is in fact a total misrepresentation of Hoover's attempt to change the premises. Without Hoover, there probably wouldn't have been a Roosevelt.

FELTON. Hoover was Harding and Coolidge's Secretary of Commerce, carrying out the national *noblesse-oblige* in post-Great-War Europe.

THORP. Yes, he was.

So what changed at Groton is the interesting evolution in independent schools, which is: "Not only should we take care of these folks; we should now live with these folks, at boarding schools." The non-moneyed Hispanic student, Jo Vega, will figure in this, no?

FELTON. She comes in later.

THORP. Well—do we break their hearts, by bringing them in, and better for Groton to be exclusive, as long as it's teaching the elite who do have the money, the power and the influence, to do good things with their money, power and influence?

That's not an unworthy goal. And the "rich-boy"'s comments were said in the era of Ronald Reagan. You know; greed is good. But there is another context around it, I think—amazingly, what he's saying is: "Yeah! I want to go out and I want to make some money, okay? I want to live well; but I want to use that to turn it, to convert it to power." And he says—I forget exactly the words he uses—but it appears that he wants the power to change things for the better.

And that's no different from the Groton thing. The difference is in the Groton of old, people just took it for granted that they had the money and the power and the influence, which they did. Today, there's at least some increase in the meritocracy in this society, with Bill Gates, who came up from comfortable but relatively modest background, and with Steve Jobs, that we've finally gotten beyond the stage of eighteenth- and nineteenth-century inherited wealth, to some amount of a meritocracy in terms of making money.

FELTON. Groton had a teacher—a woman, a Jew, who stands up in a chapel ceremony, and talks about Passover, and the Groton populace:

> We're talking of people whose values are in some way different from our own. And those values are shaped, in fact, by having more disposable income than we as teachers have. And that we have, for a brief time, an influence, a leavening.

> We all here believe in a time lag, that even if they do not understand now, they might remember at some later time, that there are things that are always right, and there are things that are always wrong.

How influential is a Jew in this environment? Isn't she, in fact a "token" Jew? Isn't she a "token" for all minorities?—the *Ur*-token at Groton? And doesn't she allow the Groton elite to crow, smugly: "How wonderful we are that we would even allow her in the door of Reverend Peabody's hall!,"?

THORP. Yeah. That's both a blessing and a curse. At Gateway, everybody is a minority, so to speak. And that's a function of the diversity of San Francisco. It's a function of the profile of kids that have come our way, where the typical power majority in American society of whites, is certainly not a majority, or power majority in the San Francisco Unified School District. So then, who is the power group, so to speak?

It's also the case that in our still-evolving and unfinished building of school culture, we haven't established power groups. And because of that, nature abhorring a vacuum, certain power groups have filled the role. And it's part of the tension of this school that some of the power groups have gained power in a way that is inconsistent with what we're trying to create here, and what we need to do for next year is address that question.

Read the first sentence of what you just read me, because it really spawned a reaction.

FELTON. "Those values are then shaped by having more disposable income than we as teachers have….. And that we have, for a brief time, an influence, a leavening."

THORP. Yes. A couple of things: One of the things that somebody needs to address is the mixed messages that kids get about the value of education. You know. This is a school founded on the central premise that post-secondary education is valuable. If I'm a fourteen- or fifteen-year-old kid, I'm not necessarily going to believe that, you know. If, first, I haven't already bought into that, because of my family circumstances, or whatever. I'm not necessarily going to believe that, when I sit down and through a thoughtful and rational process I start adding things up and say: "Well, this school Gateway has been in two school buildings in two different years, you know? They're not sure if this is going to be the site forever. Last time I checked we didn't have a gymnasium. You know, they're scrambling in one way or another. And then, we've been hearing all this news about teachers' salaries here in San Francisco—and let me think for a minute—is education really valuable in this society, if our teachers are making less than prison guards? And I'm fourteen, and I'm being taught to be a critical thinker. So let me do some critical thinking about this, and say: Hmm....my conclusion is that this society really doesn't value education. So, why should I? And so—I don't think I will! And so—this teacher who's telling me to do homework because it's 'good for me'—I don't dislike this person, I'm sure this person is well-meaning; but hey! As far as I'm concerned, that's a song-and-dance, that doesn't have any validity to back it up."

That's not an unreasonable or unexpected thought scenario for a student to have! And so, I think we've created our own problem in the sense that I do believe that kids are rational human beings! Imperfectly so, as we all are; and less maturely so. But they're accurately interpreting the handwriting on the wall! They want to adopt an ethic that gives them the power to create the world in which they live.

The Groton chaplain talks about: "We teach them great skills..." Well, you do and you don't. I mean, they come there with pretty good skills. But what they teach them is: Pulling together; hard work and hard play; and converting that into productive energy and productive work and play in later life, is what those schools do so well. And what we would like to think we can accomplish here at Gateway, with greater obstacles and fewer resources. That's why this is not unlike the miracle of the loaves and fishes here.

FELTON. We've talked about the import of place, and I think that figures here, as much as it does at Groton. The point is critically important, when you reflect the way you did in introducing that last imagined student commentary, about: "Gee, this is our second school in two years, and—where is the 'there' there?" What you obviously have done, instinctively if not consciously, is given them transitional guideposts to begin to lay down feelings that will establish the same bond until the physical plant is resolved. There are, after all, other ready touchstones here. And I would imagine, I would daresay that one of the most important of these is that at some point, for a majority—I don't know how many, some kids will never get it; but most of the kids—when they sit in your assembly, there will be some point when the now-ritual-energy of the assembly hits a certain point when there's real connectivity—between you and these kids. And the impress of that moment is so strong, that it will replace all of this temporary "up-in-the-air-about-place" stuff, until it all settles down and you can look back on a history, in a similar way to what Groton does. You can say, "Ah, yes; there's the "chapel," and there are the "tiles," and so forth. There'll be moments like that for Gateway, too!   Because these kids want them.

THORP. Yes. And they have them.

FELTON. Sure. I'll bet so.

In the Groton experience the student Jo Vega appears. Hispanic, female, artistic, of modest means, bewildered—Jo Vega has lots of issues!   Here she meets with her counselor, a very understanding woman: "When you first came to Groton," the counselor says, "you felt vulnerable. And you also acted as though you were. The major difference is that you can now feel vulnerable without being vulnerable."

And Jo says: "I kind of feel like I've shed some skin. And I've become this new metamorphosed person. It was really in adapting to the people around me. Here, it's a different world. I felt very insecure.

She went home for solace, and ethnic food, and Spanish. She says she came back to Groton

> …stuttering in English. It wasn't Spanish any more. That made me feel in despair. I thought: I have to go home—I have to speak Spanish! I have to do something. I have to be around my people! I felt like some kind of captive on a strange island. It was important to be around the other girls; but after a while, it was kind of like I was leeching. I was not going to leech! I was going to be Jo Vega! I was going to find my own little niche here; and for four years, that's been my struggle. I'm not a part of anyone here; I'm me.

And my question to you is: How easy is it at Gateway for a student to be oneself?

THORP.   Well, I'll give you a quick response to that one, which is: Very easy. Too easy.

FELTON. Explain.

THORP. The issue for us is far more: How do we have Gateway kids feel their part of a group? And what groups are those? You know;

can we develop greater affinity groups? We started to develop this in a kind of ad hoc way, ranging from Peter Felton's lunch group to the Photography Club, to outdoor interests. But we've a different challenge; Our far greater challenge is making students feel part of the group.

The sense of belonging is a critical stage of adolescence. And it's this tension between separation and individualizing with parents; and at the same time, getting a different family, which is these "affinity groups" that kids develop. Of course you hope that they're the right affinity groups, and not the wrong ones. Isn't it too bad that Jo Vega wasn't able to see her experience as one of gain rather than one of loss? As somebody who is bicultural—has that person gained or lost? I think schools, most schools, would answer the question with "One has gained."

FELTON. Agreed.

THORP. But clearly, for the Jo Vegas of this world, it's pretty easy to understand how that person could feel that he or she had lost, rather than gained. You're faced with an untenable choice. Walking in one of the worlds means you have to reject the other one. And that was so hard for her. Hard for various people over the years who have chosen to take advantage of the opportunities that have been presented to them; but in doing so have been faced with this very difficult choice, this very difficult reality.

I still tend to believe—and of course, as a white male, I can't fully empathize with the pain and *angst* of that choice—but I still believe that the alternative is worse than that. I still believe that giving kids an opportunity to live in a bi- or multi-cultural world, is a positive opportunity. I guess I have to respect those people who reject that as an opportunity and say: "That's too costly. And my culture is too fragile." And clearly not unlike extinct species, there are extinct cultures. One ramification of this dilemma is the tension we see here at Gateway between this generation of Russian kids and their parents. They have really different values! And we perceive internal familial tensions that play out in those circumstances.

FELTON. Let's return to the first student we heard. Young Mr. Wright is on the crew team, and he makes one of his many wonderful comments. He says:

> The best times rowing that I had were actually in practice. And so for me, it wasn't always beating the other team that was the most important thing. The most important thing that you can get is more a

feeling of accomplishment for yourself. But for a lot of people here, I'd have to say: What it takes to win is a real cutthroat attitude. Everyone is very clear about what it takes to win. You can see it in their fathers. And usually, it means a lot of money. But you'd like to think that that's not all there is.

Actually, that observation was followed by the contrasting notions of young ambitious capitalist, Bobby Greenhill, again:

Nowadays, I really think that more and more people just want to go to college and get a good job, and have a happy marriage, and go crank for a large corporation. I don't think people are willing to spend a lot of their lives contemplating about giving to charity, about helping the community. Now, obviously, there are a few exceptions, because it's the "in" thing to care about human life. It's the "in" thing to be generous and giving. And I think it's probably the "in" thing to care and to go to Ethiopia and give up your salary for something like that. And I think most of the school doesn't want to do that, you know?"

I'm sorry that Bobby isn't here so that he can be the first student in your Gateway community service pre-school work program over at that church!

THORP.   Well, can't you say: "And what's wrong with that?" I don't see anything inherently wrong with that being a life plan. "I want to go to college because I want to get a good job, I want to live comfortably…" whatever he said; "I want a happy marriage." I don't see anything wrong with that. And of course, it would be nice, if that same person was generous philanthropically, and was a good citizen, and so on—

FELTON.   He said: "People don't want to spend their lives giving charity." To me, he was saying: "I don't want to do all these things that I don't like; so I'm going to say that everyone else doesn't want to do that." A very underdeveloped, under-evolved point of view, even for a prep school kid, no?

THORP.   Actually, I think he's accurate! The typical person doesn't want to do those things, in part, because the typical person has no ability to comprehend that kind of a life. Because it's so reserved for such a privileged few, to dedicate my life to others means you've got the trust fund that enables you to do it, or you become a priest.

FELTON.   Yeah.

THORP.   And so, I don't quarrel with that perspective, as much as to me, it's a reflection that at Groton you're taught to aspire to that, given the tradition of the school, which is great and noble; but irrelevant to most people. And when things start getting to be irrelevant to different groups of people, communication breaks down in a way where a different way of looking at the world becomes pejoratively cast. You know—"You're less worthy as a human being, because you're not giving to charity and you're not doing this...." Or: "You're less worthy as a human being because you're this effete intellectual country club snob, who isn't willing to mix it up."

So I think if schools can help to bridge the gap of perceiving the world, they have something to offer. The irony of the focus on standardized testing—this seems like a nonsequitur, but it isn't—the irony of the focus of standardized testing is that by definition, it's further exacerbating social division, or just division, period. Okay?

FELTON. Yes.

THORP. Because the last time I checked, any standardized test has a normative basis to it, where some kids are going to fail, and some kids aren't. And so if it becomes a perfect world, where the quality of education improves much greater than it is, you're still going to have winners and losers, based on standardized testing.

Now, the average SAT score may go up from, you know—431, to 461, and it isn't that great; but it's the wrong issue! It's "Who's at the tail end?" and "Who's at the upper end?" and "Why are the kids at the upper end?" and "Why are the kids at the lower end?" And the kids at the upper end are there because they come from families where language is used a lot, and they come from families who can support them in SAT preparation courses, and whatever the hell it is. That's scandalous, as you've heard me say in other commentaries.

So—you know, I guess I think that if a secondary school can influence a kid in an everlasting way that is positive, then we've done our jobs. We can't mold kids into becoming something. We can't assign to them—and this is really the independent school person speaking!—we can't assign to them goals of service and make them feel less worthy if they end up rejecting those goals, or make them feel necessarily more exalted because they establish a family foundation which, you know, is "chump change" from their end. I think we simply need to say: If we can ensure that kids go out the door wiser—I didn't say smarter—wiser than they walked in the door, more compassionate than when they walked in the door, in possession of a greater sense of empathy than they had when they walked in the door, greater clarity of their own ambition, both purely individually and in the context of other ambitions, then I think we've done our job. And if all that adds up to

the kid goes to Harvard, or Stanford, or Berkeley or a city college—
well, then: Whatever works!

FELTON. Well, Principal Thorp, our ride to Gateway will take
us again to Groton.

Chapter Twenty-Six

GROTON LOVES GATEWAY!

"[P]arents with means, our generation, baby-boomer parents [are] doing everything they can to protect their kids from failure. And it's such misguided parenting! I'm not recommending you set a kid up to fail; that's not the point. But if your essence as a parent is to do everything to prevent your kid from having a bad experience, that is bad, bad parenting! Because if a kid doesn't have a bad experience at some point—I mean if a person does not experience failure at some point in his or her life, it means that they're not doing a hell of a lot. And either it's because they have the inherited wealth that they don't have to do a hell of a lot, or it's because they end up not doing very much. And so the kinds of parents who encourage work, or help kids understand the congruence between hard work and opportunities, are the parents who are preparing their kids for survival in the twenty-first century, and to thrive in the twenty-first century...."

"[T]he overtures made by me, and by our faculty, are often viewed with suspicion. Some students here feel: "What do they need to know that for?" "What is he asking me that question for?" "No, I won't take advantage of this opening I'm being offered by this adult, to know him better, or to spend time with him." And it's just a realization to me that we've got a lot more thinking to do, and work to accomplish, to figure out how to get kids to understand where we're coming from. But we're heading in the right direction, given the faculty we have here, who are eminently attractive to kids who will be open to them. And a lot of our kids are getting the hang of it."

5 June—*As we pressed to finish a comparison of the Groton model of school with Gateway, the swirl of school's end came upon us. Peter*

Thorp's schedule became crowded;   teachers' meetings, final examinations, and a process called the Humanities Portfolio descended upon Gateway's young population.

A high school equivalent of an oral thesis defense, each student's "final exam" in Humanities class was a ten-minute presentation of aspects of that individual's chosen high points from the year's study. Panels consisted of the teacher, a parent, and another student. While far from a cogent expression of a year's learning, it did carry out one of Thorp's goals: to create more opportunities for public presentation by students. Setting aside the natural inhibition, the discomfort with this kind of personal attention, and the general lack of cogent organization of a year's pursuits into a brief revisiting, the three students who presented during the panel which included this Reporter demonstrated that the important part of learning was, simply, doing.

In our work, Peter found a pocket of time for our penultimate session which enabled us to begin to bring our process toward its close.

FELTON.   Before we return to our Groton extrapolations—just a little parenthetical note: I don't know if you picked up on this report, but a study that was conducted in England, where apparently at long last, after two millennia of elitism on behalf of the "Oxbridge" families, the people there in England are finally beginning to say, "Wait a minute!: Only seven percent of students are going to either Cambridge or Oxford, and ninety-three percent of what's important is given to people who come from there. How are we going to enable anybody to go to these places?" Which of course, hearkens again to the problems facing Groton.—

THORP.   Who was asking that question back in England?

FELTON.   A young woman from the public schools—as they call their private schools—had been refused admission to Oxford, when her record clearly showed that there was no reason to do so. And she contested it. And they came out with the usual throat-clearing sort of generalized rationalization afterwards, to describe why they didn't take her. But the reason that finally could not be denied is that she did not come from any family of distinction, and—

THORP.   Was she white?

FELTON.   I don't know, but I think so. They interviewed her, and just judging from the limited evidence of inflection of voice, and so forth. They were circumspect, if not.

THORP.   I ask, because it's doubly complicated in England. It sounds like the report, which I didn't hear, was primarily focused on class, which of course, we have in a sense, in this country; and thus the Groton experience. They're more overtly class-ridden, in England; but it's going to get further complicated by race. At least in this country, it's been a mixed phenomenon. The Jo Vega of Groton represented a class and race issue; and what they didn't focus on was "Joe Palooka" at Groton—you know: A white, middle-class, blue-collar kid, which category in fact has been a phenomenon at some of those boarding schools, but less of one than the Jo Vegas of this world.

But the Oxbridge system is going to blow up over race, before it's going to blow up over class. And my prediction is that they'll figure out a way to get over the class issue, because of kids like this. And they'll côme to some realization that—Oh!—they'd better lighten things up. And Tony Blair would support that, I think. But where it's going to get difficult is when they start getting all these applications from all these incredibly bright Indian kids, for example; then we'll see! Then we'll see what happens to tradition!

FELTON.   Well, I haven't been in England since 1976; and at that time, the East Indian contingent was still driving the buses. And I imagine in that quarter-century they've worked their way up at least to the middle-bureaucratic level. And I don't who has replaced them on the lower echelon; but—yeah, clearly, there's a knock at the door.

There are a couple of notes where we'll touch on that again. Now, to the Groton materials.

The school minister offers this pertinent comment:

> What people don't understand is that at a school like this, many schools are not interested in training people to be in the Establishment. That isn't what we're about! But in fact, everything, almost everything we speak of as important is not what people ordinarily think of as important in America. We don't honestly think that money is important. We don't honestly think that gaining power is important. We honestly think that service to people is important.

The minister wasn't the only pious figure at Groton at that time. The headmaster was also the Bible teacher, and he led a special class, a class on ethics. He had entitled his class "Trust and Cunning." And a girl in the class says: "I think you need love to get by. Because if you love other people, they're going to love you. They're going to take care of you and help you, and you have to be smart, and you have to be the best at everything. Other people are going to be there for you."

And a fellow in the class responds: "You can say that it's love, you can say that all you want. But if it comes down to you and one other person left on earth, and only one apple left, you'd fight for your life for that apple."

The teacher-headmaster asks this boy: "If you're going to work for someone, would you rather work for someone on the basis of trust, or on the basis of cunning?" And the kid says: "Honestly?" "Yeah." "Probably," the kid says, "the one that paid more money."

So those two sorts of ideas play out in the class discussion. And the headmaster gives a kind of coda, a little voice-over wrap-up statement:

> Kids today get very conflicted messages on what values besides competition do you need to be successful. What will be important in their lives? When I was a child, I sat on my father's knee; and he told me what life would be like in the future. And what values would hold me in good stead. That was entirely credible. He believed it; I believed it. And that's the way life was. I don't think that happens anymore.

THORP.   I have three related statements, although each with its own distinction: The first comment is: The minister is absolutely sincere. And absolutely befuddled, in my opinion—or absolutely wrong-headed about it. He is totally sincere when he says that Groton is absolutely committed to a world of preparation which is not so cunningly Machiavellian in preparing them for power, so to speak.

Now, there's a whole wing of people who look at independent schools and particularly independent boarding schools, and particularly independent boarding schools of the tradition like Groton, who would say, "That's crap!" And in fact, there is a book, written not shortly after this film, called "Preparing for Power," whose whole premise is: That's what these schools are all about. And there's no question that that's what those schools used to be all about. There is, however, in the last generation, the last twenty years' evolution in boarding schools, the emergence of the fact that the Jo Vegas of this world are now that much more prevalent than they were even as recently as twenty years ago. That is no longer the mission of those schools, per se, and precisely the opposite; if you read their mission statements, and they're all alike, they do not include preparing for power and maintenance of the status quo, and the class structure as part of the mission statement, as you might imagine.

But the truth of the matter is, they still do. And that's where one has to be honest at a level that is productive, and doesn't rent a community asunder. I have a special perspective on this, obviously, given my new position and my former background, and I think I've alluded in other comments that I've made in our conversations to various times when I tried to get the school community, either directly or less directly, to focus in on some of the issues, I remind you of comments I've made about the difference between nineteenth-century wealth and twenty-first-century wealth, and what that's going to mean in terms of power.

If you honestly examine the facts, though, you must conclude that there's a great deal in this society, and a great deal in the English society, and a great deal in the Japanese society—to pick three distinct but industrial, post-industrial states—where education is designed to ensure that the power elite continues its position of elite. Of course, it would appear that the people with more money in this society have access to the better education! And it would appear that access to better education would mean that you're likely to get more money! Now, doesn't that seem to be preserving of the upper class? And the answer is: Damned right it does! And it ranges from access to schools, through available finances, to access to SAT prep classes, to access to neighborhoods where they have umpteen Advanced Placement classes being offered. And when you put it all together, you have an educational system that in fact prepares people for power!

If the assumption is that power is socio-economic status, where one can choose to exercise power if one happens to do it—I don't think it would be fair to condemn boarding schools—and in fact, the point of the Groton film is that they try to teach how to use power in a noble way. And I don't criticize that. I think they're naïve, if they expect a fourteen-year-old kid not to say, "Well, I want this to prepare me for a job," you know, "—and to make a lot of money." Because that's what they're looking at: They're looking at the Douglas Dillons of this world, whom they see as people of power and influence, because of their socio-economic status, and eventually they'll become mature enough to recognize that you can be Rupert Murdoch, and have all the money in the world, but you might have less power and influence over noble things in this society than even renegade rich men. It speaks to having equal power—but different use of the power. And clearly, it's to me the most interesting thing about Bill Gates. Who's the real Bill Gates?—is he the overbearing CEO of Microsoft, who knew damned well what he was doing with all these steps to try to eliminate competition? Or is he the person whose established the richest foundation in the world, and who's doing things that could have worldwide impact? Or is he both?—and if so, how does he reconcile those two parts of him?

So the Groton minister is absolutely sincere. He fails to publicly acknowledge, however, the abject reality that the consumers of that kind of education, particularly the parents from the upper class, or the parents of new wealth who have the means to send their kids to these schools—they're no dummies. They certainly see that access to privileged education means access to ongoing privilege in life. That's just the way it works.

And you take the Japanese example, which is kind of intriguing, because on the face of it, it seems less class-structured because the ticket to success is just gaining admission to Tokyo University—namely, if you can get in, your life is set. You don't have to do a lick of work while you're there. It's the getting in part that counts. And the getting in is purely on a test. So there's more of a meritocracy in that sense. But again, I'd have to look at it carefully just to know what advantage there is for people with wealth in terms of getting access to the test. And all the kinds of tutors that come into play.

So Quote number one about the minister is that. The second one was the headmaster and the girl—?

FELTON.   Yes, in the ethics class discussion.

THORP.   The balance between "trust" and "cunning": The girl said love, and the guy said money. He responded to that. And then the third—

FELTON.   He wraps it up, and talks about being on his father's knee—

THORP.   Right, right.

FELTON.   —That those values were holding in good stead.

THORP.   Yes. And again, for me, it's autobiographical in a sense that having taught in a world like that, what some of those folks don't understand is the basic premises upon which they operate hold true only for a very narrow range of the population. And they fail to recognize that. This isn't to say that their premises are wrong, or anything like that; it's just that they're not universally attributable. I mean, one of the quotes that you read me was the headmaster's condemnation of competition. Well, that's easy to say if you don't have to worry about competing! So—whether England, or Japan, or Groton—it's a matter of class!

To me, what is interesting about all this technology is what's it going to do to class? What is it going to do to race? What is it going to do to nationhood? And that to me is going to be the story of the twenty-first century. And it'll be really intriguing whether or not—it's kind of the "big-brother" version of events, where you have this super-power, super culture, if you will. My prediction is: It's going to go the opposite direction, in a circle, which is that it's going to Balkanize the world, into equally well-informed, but infinitely less-cohesive small groups. And we're going to go back to the Stone Age, in terms of people's cultural isolation from each other.

FELTON. Well, let me quickly ask about that: How do you reconcile that prognostication, with the shibboleth about people in the twenty-first century, that we will all be "coffee-colored"?

THORP. In terms of actual racial development? Well, I think there'll be truth in that. Of course, traveling around San Francisco, the future is now!

FELTON. Yes.

THORP. But I don't think that that means that culture will be universal. And I think that all being coffee-colored, it will be very interesting to see which societies hold out the longest. And some theorists, I would imagine, would venture to speculate that those societies that do hold out the longest will be the strongest societies. If you take Arthur Schlesinger's thesis, in his book of a couple of years ago, talking about what's happened to our culture and the loss of common bonds in our culture, and how we are now a divided country, it would be interesting to see if some countries who remain more culturally cohesive are in fact going to be able to weather the storms of the twenty-first century in a stronger fashion, because other ones will get ripped apart. I mean, it's not unlike what's happened to the Soviet Union. And this country certainly has the potential to get Balkanized. One of the things I do in teaching AP U.S. History is just wrestling with the question: Is it conflict, or it is consensus? You know—what is the essential theme of this country?

Gore Vidal observed: "America is a great country really for two reasons: Cheap natural resources, and cheap labor." And when that runs out, as according to the gas prices in San Francisco it apparently has!, it will be interesting to see just how cohesive we're going to be able to remain.

FELTON. In fairness to the general tenor of Groton's "upper crust": When I first saw the film, even though the hair went up on the back of my neck at the attitude of some of these wealthy kids, I felt general beneficence from most throughout the film. I mean, these were decent human beings—

THORP. They sure were.

FELTON.   —Even if some had blinders on, they certainly were trying their best to move through what they saw.

THORP.   Totally!

FELTON.   —And when I heard comments like the minister's, during their first year, about how they didn't want something that was dark and ugly, and they really wanted something that was positive and hopeful, I had a sense either that these people are totally sincere, with whatever degree of self-deception there might be there; or, they are people who are saying, "I've got to believe this, or I'm going to take a .38 and do myself in."

THORP.   Richard Cory.

FELTON.   Right.

THORP.   And it's neither.   It's a third, which is: There is absolutely sincere belief in the mission being appropriate and worthy, and recognition—especially in the last twenty years, and the Groton one was kind of right at the cusp of the evolution—and a recognition as to some of the inherent tension within the mission of those places.   I think there probably is some semantic gymnastics that allows people to fall asleep at night, on the one hand; but there's no doubt in my mind, that there is utter sincerity, in the belief that these schools can maintain tradition, promote service—a key to it—and at the same time be so dramatically less elite than they used to be, and therefore contributing to the society in a way that they didn't before, and a way that's really important and really healthy!

We now need to move away from that film, or just a perspective of Groton, and put it in the context of other schools.   There needs to be a film about Lincoln High School in San Francisco, the American dream at Lincoln High School, and it sure as hell would be interesting to see what kind of response you'd get if you posed those same questions to those kids.

FELTON.   That's a good point.   Well, just to draw it to a conclusion, with Jo Vega's help:

Into Groton, as we know, came an idealistic, artistic, "little brown sister," named Jo Vega.   And Jo has a trial of her early years.   She says:

> As the years would pass, and I would assimilate, I'd go home, and my friends would say, "Hello Jo.   You know, when I think of you,   I think of a white girl."   And all that work, all that self-realization had gotten me nothing!   On the outside, I looked white, and who knows, maybe on the inside I *was* white.   I don't know.   And that was scary.   The moment my brother's friend called me a white girl, I realized I'd never be a part of home. I realized I'd never

be a part of Spanish culture. And that that's when I saw the doors closing in on me....

Her language is so emotional, so emotive. She also talks about the defense mechanisms of a Puerto Rican woman, where the husband can't find a job, and ends up in madness and drinking. And such a woman has to be a strong force to bring her family up. And then the film shows other students attacking her. She's given a chance for an exhibit of her art; and she is forced to defend it as the work of an outcast. "Everyone came from somewhere else," they counter, to diminish her uniqueness. "Everybody has to get a job, everybody has to defend himself against madness, as you put it, and against alcohol!" Yet she vigorously sticks up for herself: "But this is my problem, and I've had to live with it, ever since seeing my father struggle. I've seen him struggle, and try to assimilate and fit into society. Being told, 'You're going to make it in the land of opportunity; and if you don't make it, it's because you aren't worth anything!'"

Another critical student says to her: "Most people deal with these problems so they won't build up and explode into an expression of art."—As if art is some kind of embarrassing filth! And Jo, in growing frustration and indignation, says: "You guys see the exterior of me, but there's a lot more inside." And another student says: "Hey, come on! Everyone deals with isolation and alienation. Ever teenager in the United States and all over the world feels isolated and alienated."

A black girl in the group begins to side with Jo, saying: "I have to deal with color of skin!" "Sure," the same white guy goes on, "there are categories. You're a black. You're a Spic, in negative terms. Everyone is put into some kind of category that we don't want to be put in. When that happens, they feel uncomfortable." And Jo says: "I can never be accepted in the Groton world, because I don't have a long line of, shall we say, 'educated ancestors.' At Groton, I'm Puerto Rican, and that's not good. At home I'm white; and that's not good. So what's good?"

When I first saw the tape, I took Jo's side, and I hated those kids; and the second time I heard it—even though I still thought the boy looking at her art exhibit was a little insensitive and obnoxious, his arguments were far less assailable. You know?

THORP. Well, that's only one or two sentences away from the affirmative action debate. I have sat in my office, as a head of school, listening to a kid say: "I didn't get into the college of my choice, because I'm white." The argument goes: "—And this other kid, in a small graduating class of fifty or sixty kids, did get in; and he's black, and I'm white, and I had higher grades, I did more, and I had higher SAT scores, so let's cut through the crap, Mr. Thorp: Why did he get in and I didn't?"

The most poignant—and maybe you have this, in one of your next pages—the most poignant moment in the film, for me, was the moment between Jo and her mother.

FELTON. Yes.

THORP. And I won't anticipate your question on that, but it ties into this in a sense that you know—and again, it's one of the themes of teaching U.S. History, it's the story of the American dream. What comprises the dream? What's worth it to achieve the dream? And the dream comes at what cost? Those are the questions that every person, every family, every race, socioeconomic class needs to answer. It's truly the story of Gatsby. And for Jo Vega and Groton, it's the "We-bring-them-here-and-we-break-their-heart" idea. I think there has not been an adequate voice addressing Jo Vega's question, which I would paraphrase as: "Must I give up who I am, to seek the American Dream? Must I shelve my heritage to seek the American Dream?"

FELTON. That surely is her question.

THORP. For some number of years, people on the outside looking inside had to make the decision to talk like this, to ask those questions! You know. Rather than what their heritage might have encouraged them to speak. And so the issue here, of "What do you have to give up to get something?" is one of the big questions. And I'd like to hear Jesse Jackson speak about that, and Colin Powell speak about that. And Henry Cisneros speak about that. And Maya Angelou speak about that. And is it giving up?, or is it gaining? And what is the heritage that we want to preserve after all? To me, it becomes intriguing, because once again in this culture of cowardice that exists in this society, to avoid talking in productive ways, and meaningful ways about difficult questions, we're not getting at the key questions, I think. And again, what was so poignant about the conversation between Jo Vega and her mother, is her mother was asking the key questions! Making the key point: "We came here for the land of opportunity"—I forget what were the words she used, and you probably have them there; but—

FELTON. I do. And we'll get to it.

THORP. This is a piece of that, and if we jump ahead to the graduation, and then come back and find Jo in a quandary earlier on, let's give her the benefit of being out of sync, here. She's talking with her parents, and she addresses her father: "A tribute," she says, "to the special courage of those parents who point their children toward the cultural divide they cannot cross. It's a present, to you and mom, for your courage in sending me to Groton. Thank you!" And Mrs. Vega says: "America means a lot to me. And Groton is an inspiration. Words cannot express my gratitude." And Jo says: "Mom, don't you think it's more difficult for Latinos to move ahead?" And the mother says: "Not if the Latin-American is determined. In America, nothing is difficult." And Jo says: "But we're a special case! There are a lot of Puerto Ricans living in Harlam there." And then the mom says: "But in America, there's opportunity for everyone! You must be determined. Opportunities call out; I am grateful to America. I am proud to be an American citizen."

FELTON. After I heard that, I put this question. I asked: Who will succeed?—You're going to take me as a muckraker throughout all this, I'm afraid, but I'm really looking for the dark side of this—as an impetus. Who in Gateway's context—which student will succeed, who will get the job, or the college admission: The mild-mannered Latino Federico, or the tall, smiling white Student Body President Gus? In other words, what is the picture of America, in the year 2000, to Americans?

THORP. Why did you pick Federico?

FELTON. Because I would say that he has two wonderful qualities, wonderful in the literal sense of things to think about, that I believe make it easy to put him in a certain ethnic group. One is that his appearance varies from day to day between looking like a gang kid, and just looking very Hispanic. And the other is that he has an unbelievably searching earnestness in his gaze. And when he looks at you, you can read so much in that face! It's a very ingratiating face. It's an attractive face, in many senses; it pulls you to it. So he's a kid with a lot of contentious forces going on inside. It comes out in his body language, that says: "I'm beaten down; I'm a member of a beaten-down group. And I don't know how I can stand up all the way." It reveals his feelings of weakness—and that vulnerability is affecting. And then you compare the other kid—white, here, despite all Gateway's goals, still has a superlative power.

THORP. I disagree. I mean, if I had to pick between Gus and Latina Erica Goncalves, I would have said: "Erica, in a heartbeat!" And as I think I've said to you before, the most immediately interesting set of kids here, to me, are the Latinas, the young Hispanic women, who in many cases are the most feisty kids, and to me most interesting. And I'm hoping to teach a bunch of them in this class next year.

These are kids whom I think have all the potential in the world to go as far as anybody in this school. And Gus is this really interesting combination of talent and yet talent realized in an unorthodox root—home schooling, in particular. Which means there's a level of ambition there that is so attractive because he's had to make choices sooner than the typical kid, who just kind of goes through his grade, and goes to the next class, and so on. He's learned about goals and ambition a lot sooner than the typical kid.

Did you see the National Spelling Bee that just finished?

FELTON. Yes.

THORP. The kid who won was a kid from Missouri, I think. But the top three kids were all home-schooled. Interesting.

FELTON. Yes, yes. As also was Gus Porter! And I believe one of the winning youngsters spoke a different language at home.

THORP. Why not create an educational system where the content and standards are available on a website, and kids just stay home and to keep the State happy they take standardized tests whenever they have to take standardized tests?   It sure would make things a hell of a lot easier, and cost a lot less money, if that's the way they want to do it! And it rubs my grain, because to me, rightly or wrongly, there is a personal connection between teacher and student which is very powerful.

Somehow, we need the leadership from the leaders of color, frankly—to help kids sort out what ambition is; what goals are; what I need to do to accomplish these, and why, in fact (I guess and believe) having goals and ambitions are eminently worthy and in fact will change the society, so there is a more even distribution of wealth in this society. I think that would be a good thing for this country.

And I'm not sure that it's happening in most schools. You know— the boarding school Groton is doing it, I think, as well as anybody— and that's why even though the school is easily criticized as a result of the exposure through this film, the intent of the school and schools like that is absolutely worthy. But of course, it touches a small number of people; and, to bring it back to ground level here, it's the schools like Gateway that have both the opportunity and I venture to say the obligation to try to figure out how to make this work. And believe me, I don't have time to be teaching this AP U.S. History class; you probably know that better than anybody. But I'm doing it for precisely this reason: I'm using the vehicle of this history class to get at the kids' ambition.

FELTON. Expand on that idea.

THORP. To discover it within, assuming it exists. I've got to believe it exists or they wouldn't sign up, because I've made it very clear that they're signing on for extra work. To help them figure out ways to act on that ambition and to reveal their ambition, and to peel off the layers in a way that I hope will result in opening up all sorts of new channels and opportunities to them. And that's why I'm doing this.

FELTON. Back to bedeviled, reviled Groton.

Homecoming Weekend concludes the film. It reminded me—in its cocktail-hour ambience, how many such events the head of a school must attend!

THORP. Well, what most people don't realize about me, is what hard work that is for me.

FELTON. I know it is.

THORP. I don't know if we've talked about this, but I'm a very shy person. So I don't do this easily.

FELTON. That makes doing that sort of thing a gift of extraordinary reach on your part, I know.

One of Groton's old alums is talking about Endicott Peabody, the school's legendary first headmaster. And he says—I thought this was very interesting: "I remember a sermon Peabody used to give, in which he would describe the unethical practices of American business, illegal rebates given by railroads—"

THORP. That's Rockefeller.

FELTON. Yeah! "—adulteration of food and dishonest financial practices by brokerages and that sort of thing—" and that of course was the impetus for Upton Sinclair's literary focus—"And we thought that was a little bit quaint at the time. But what he was trying to do was to tell the future leaders of corporate America, the future chairmen of J. P. Morgan, what values he really ought to be working for."

And another old alum walks by, who happens to be C. Douglas Dillon, former Secretary of the Treasury under Reagan. And Dillon says: "What I think Groton stands for is service."

THORP. "Service," yeah.

FELTON. "—That was one thing that was preached to us the whole time we were here, by the Rector." Does he mean Peabody? Was he of that era?—I guess he was. "—by the Rector. And our motto was 'He who serves reigns.'"

And my question—well, I had two questions. One was how did the powers-that-be, the governing boards at the time, allow Peabody to get away with that scalding kind of acrimony about the wealthy? I mean, I think it was amazing: Either they said of him, "the dear old soul, just let him go on," you know—or they weren't listening. Because that's clearly outrageous, socialistic alarm being sounded by the guy who's in charge of their kids' lives!

My second question is: What would you say is Gateway's 'motto'?

THORP. Hmm! It will take me a while to come up with that.

Well, the first response, and the reason I'm leaning back—I don't know if you can see it from where you are—this is my Cate seal on this chair, see?

FELTON. Yes.

THORP. At the bottom it says, "Servons," in the French—"Let us serve."

FELTON. "Let us serve," yes!

THORP. That's the motto of Cate. So you get it on both coasts! There were two kinds of boarding schools founded over the course of time—the schools that were founded in the "cult of personality" of which Groton was one—the personality being Endicott Peabody; a guy named Frank Boyden at Deerfield; a guy named Louis Perry at Exeter—all of whom were the quintessential heads of schools and defined their schools and defended them—and Cate, Mr. Curtis Cate, founding what was called the Santa Barbara School until he retired, and then they called it the Cate School.

So you had schools that were created through the power of the individual. And you had schools that were founded by churches, and by organizations, or collectively founded. I don't know either Endicott Peabody well enough, or Groton's story well enough to know what kind of response that sort of statement would have engendered among the very people in a sense against which it was aimed. I will, however, share my uninformed personal bias, in this, which is: The value of these guys like Peabody is, I think, that they had insights about class structure in this society, and were trying to tell the elite: "Look, you turkeys—if you want to maintain your status, you've gotta throw them a bone once in a while!" That's, again, the cynical Marxist point of view.

I think once again of the book I told you about called Captains of Consciousness, about advertising in the 1920s, and again, the whole thesis being if you give enough people enough access to the American Dream, but not too much—you're okay. And so, returning to Peabody—he was absolutely sincere in wanting to help people say that—and it's a very Christian view, that along with wealth and power comes the opportunity and the obligation to make a difference, you know? It's very much Episcopalian wealth and power, as opposed to Catholic wealth and power, in that, you know—there isn't much quoting of "It's easier for a rich man to pass through the eye of a needle in a High Episcopalian church" than there is in some street-corner Catholic mission! But—again, he was utterly sincere in this kind of *noblesse oblige*. And to their credit, I believe, it produced Franklin Roosevelt. I mean, he's the epitome of the Groton graduate. And he's the epitome of somebody who acted in a way that capitalized on wealth, power and influence to make the society a better society.

When I teach the history of the 1930s, I actually argue that Roosevelt was more conservative than people give him credit for, because if you didn't have Roosevelt, you would have had a revolution! And, where I hiss back at the Republicans is: Roosevelt saved American capitalism.

I think it was the Grotonian view of the world that enabled people to recognize that humane capitalism plays a role, and you don't have to sacrifice your wealth and power to have other people be part of the American Dream. That's Roosevelt's great contribution, I think. And I think it is absolutely connected to what he became at Groton. Because I've got to believe that had FDR not gone to Groton, his crazy mother would have driven him in much different directions, and he would have been a far more avaricious human being than he ended up being. And of course, his bout with polio also produced an ethic that would not have been the same without that experience.

FELTON. A very complicated man.

THORP. Yeah. But there's a real connection between Roosevelt and Clinton, I believe. I have no doubt that Clinton is utterly sincere in his views about race and class and the promotion of equal rights among gender and that sort of thing. And I think the same is true of Roosevelt and Teddy Kennedy; I don't have the slightest doubt about that. But they treated individuals very badly. And there is this interesting, mostly Democratic viewpoint on life which feels: "let's make the world better for peoples, and in the meantime I'm going to screw over whoever's close to me and not give it a second thought."

And the typical person in this country can't figure out Clinton—how can he do that?! And in doing that, and in having himself be revealed, unlike Roosevelt, whose affair wasn't revealed during his lifetime, have caused people to be totally cynical about Clinton. And all this other stuff must just be going through the motion. I don't think so; not for a second! I think he must be totally sincere. But the price in his mind, the price of doing good is "I get what I want when I want it." And that's kind of how it's been.

FELTON. Yeah.

THORP. And that's why Al Gore's going to lose.

FELTON. I'm not sure I get the connection.

THORP.   Because Al Gore, to his credit, is a much more decent human being—

FELTON. You mean, he's not torqued by that sort of sentiment?

THORP.   Yeah, he doesn't have the—I don't think he has the passion to be a leader. And that's not to say therefore he wouldn't be a good leader; that's not the point. But at least as of yet, he hasn't been able to get people excited about something that he could do. Now, in Roosevelt's case, he didn't really either. And he got elected because it was "anybody but Hoover!" But obviously then, he was presented with an opportunity that he totally capitalized on.

Clinton, on the other hand, had passion. And people responded to that. And as I think we both know, there is a relatively thin line between political passion and sexual passion. And I've talked to women who have been in Clinton's presence, and they just go weak at the knees with this guy! And it has a lot to do with the kind of passion that he reveals.

FELTON.   You're the head of an institution, a community. Do you think these terms apply to you? Your behavior? Your own feelings?

THORP.   I had somebody this weekend describe me as a passionate person. And that probably comes as some amount of a surprise to you, because I'm not the kind of "passionate person" as in, say, a Latin-lover stereotype. But in a sense, passion is passion—and I do get passionate about teaching.

FELTON.   Let's return to the school we're setting up here as a foil for discussion of Gateway.

The new generation, the graduating seniors are having an informal colloquy on the grass. It features Wright, the sensitive and bright kid who's on the rowing team; Greenhill, the little dollar-gleaming guy who wants to make money—whom you insist on defending most of the time; and some others. But—would it surprise you, Teacher, that one of Groton's moneyed youths makes this comment?

"Most people in the past had their life set out for them. It's not too easy for us. We've not had that opportunity. We've had to work for what we do."

Another student echoes this sudden discovery of their awful travail: "It was very easy for Averell Harriman to go into all those service positions because—" and he's interrupted by another kid— "Because his father was a robber baron and he'd already made all that money! And exploited the poor people. And it was very easy of him to go and put a little back into the system." And another student says: "I think Mr. Polk is sincere when he gives a chapel talk about service and injustice in the real world. And I think there's something there."

Finally, Bobby Greenhill, the money-for-me boy, says: "My dream—" he just cuts right to it!—"My dream is to get a townhouse on Beacon Hill, a BMW, and just live in perfect—that would be heaven for me. I would work my tail off, and I'd probably be pretty slimy. And that's what Groton—that's what Groton—" And then the other kid asks: "Did you say 'slimy'? Would you break the law?" And Bobby retreats: "I don't mean break the law. I wouldn't do anything illegal. I mean, I would do whatever I had to. That's life."

Yet another kid in this group continues the first theme:

> There's not the comfort with privilege that I think there used to be. What was easy for the previous generation is very difficult for us. And yet, the outside world has very little sympathy. Because they look like they're on 'Easy Street.' There's a lot of tension in their lives, whereas maybe Daddy came here, and as long as you enrolled in Groton, you'd go on to Harvard or Yale by virtue of your name and your birth. These kids realize that's not the way it is.

Any comment so far?

THORP. Well, probably to your chagrin, I agree with the kids totally. One of the big gaps in the generation is that the Averell Harrimans didn't have to work, and so could get into a life of service. It's the story of the CIA. And if you go back into a pre-World War Two period and look at a typical CIA person, it was somebody coming out of Princeton, who, you know, didn't really need to work for a living, and was really excited about this Graham Greene life overseas. And as a result, we missed the whole Iranian revolution, and the Guatamala revolution! Because these guys are too busy drinking Diaquiris in a bar downtown. So I agree with these young wide-eyed lads totally. And to me, it is also a tension between inherited wealth and this Bobby-Greenhill generation of kids where their parents are not preparing them for a life of competition. And that's why the Bill Gateses of this world are blowing them off the screen, so to speak. Because these are kids—not that Bill Gates was anything other than quite upper-middle-class, if I remember correctly; but he certainly was not coming from an extraordinarily wealthy family. And certainly Steve Jobs at Apple wasn't. So these kids are dramatically underprepared for a world of competition.

However—the benefit of going to a place like Groton and then going on now to a place like Princeton, is that they are now increasingly exposed to kids who wouldn't have been in those worlds previously. And they're beginning to get the picture that—whoa!—I need to do my homework! Or, if I go to law school, I can't just march in the door as Averell Harriman's generation could, whenever they wanted to go to law school.

So I agree with those statements exactly. You know, the question to Bobby Greenhill about being slimy and breaking the law—John D. Rockefeller said once, "I didn't break any laws...but they sure made a lot of laws because of me!" And, you know—that's kind of the Bill Gates. I don't think he broke laws; but they're figuring out how to deal with what he's done in this world.

It's the difference as I said earlier between nineteenth-century wealth and twenty-first-century wealth. It's parents with means, our generation, baby-boomer parents doing everything they can to protect their kids from failure. And it's such misguided parenting! I'm not recommending you set a kid up to fail; that's not the point. But if your essence as a parent is to do everything to prevent your kid from having a bad experience, that is bad, bad parenting! Because if a kid doesn't have a bad experience at some point—I mean if a person does not experience failure at some point in his or her life, it means that they're not doing a hell of a lot. And either it's because they have the inherited wealth that they don't have to do a hell of a lot, or it's because they end up not doing very much. And so the kinds of parents who encourage work, or help kids understand the congruence between hard work and opportunities, are the parents who are preparing their kids for survival in the twenty-first century, and to thrive in the twenty-first century.

I look at some of these sets of parents—not here at Gateway, really, but at other schools; and I just say, "You know, if you only knew what you were doing to your kid. If you only knew how you were setting your kid up for a life of disappointment and a life of just not being able to *carpe diem*, so to speak." But when you've got the means, that's what you do for your kid.

And happily, here at Gateway, that's much less true. Now for a lot of our kids, the pendulum's in a lot different direction.

I'm conscious that I'm still avoiding your question about what Gateway's motto is. And it's really a great question, because we ought to come up with one. And I haven't thought of it! Besides, my Latin isn't good enough to come up with them quickly. *Arbeit macht frei*!?? You know, there's actually some wisdom in that—unfortunately it was subjected to the ultimate perversion of the Nazi madness. Maybe I can do some sort of play, "Abandon hope, all ye who enter," and I can say: "Gather hope, all ye who enter!" Actually, I'm not being frivolous in saying that.

Maybe we can come up with something that has Biblical roots in some way or another.

FELTON. Maybe the motto ought to incorporate some of the Hippocratic Oath, which you may remember, begins: "First, do no harm."

THORP. Yeah! That's right!

FELTON. Let's seek inspiration from dear old Groton:

We're into the phase of our overview now where the students are getting their college acceptance or rejection letters. A teacher, in voiceover, relates: "We're not here simply to crank out smart kids to get into Ivy League colleges. It's very odd when a person has worked hard, when a conscientious student does not get into the college of his or her choice. But that's not the end of the world; and I speak as someone who did not get into the college of his choice. And it was easy to get into colleges [back then]."

Then we cut to a girl on the telephone, talking to her girl friend. She says revealing things: "Can you believe that only six people got into Princeton! In Princeton they want smaller classes. Twenty-four! ....I don't know, most kids are pretty happy. My roommate's taking next year off and going to England....But then again, I think that's because she said that Yale was her definite, absolute first choice. And that was like the first day she heard from Yale, and boom! She got into all three! She was celebrating!...."

And then we cut to Tim Wright, the crew team man: "My father went into a room with a guy from Princeton. And you talked to him, and you were admitted to Princeton!" And then the voiceover teacher says: "There was always the assumption that a certain number of 'Grotties' could get into Harvard and Yale, and perhaps a few into Princeton. And if you weren't a hard, or a stupid, or an incorrigibly lazy person, you could go to any school that you wanted. You really could!"

My question for you derived from this phase is: What would be the choices for your students at Gateway—what schools will they get into? And I mean that both in the general sense of what kinds of schools; and I mean it in a categorical sense, which is to ask: "Who amongst them will go to no school? What percent will go to a tech school? What percent to City College for an Associate of Arts degree? What percent to a state university? What percent to UC? What percent to a prestigious college like Williams, Grinnell, Whitman, Oberlin, Reed, Swarthmore, Lewis and Clark, Antioch, Harvey Mudd, out here? Who will go to an out-of-state big school?

And—equally if not more important: Who will fall through the cracks? What number who should be in college just won't make it there?—at least not right away?

THORP. Well—I don't think any of them will fall between the cracks. That's my goal. Partly because the list of options you listed was so comprehensive you didn't leave any cracks! I don't know; and that's a good question. And I'm going to be really curious to see what happens. I certainly have modified my original thinking, which was, we're here to have one hundred percent of our kids go to four-year colleges. First, I know that's not going to happen; and second, I'm not sure it should happen. If Federico, to use him as an example, goes to City College for two years, and enrolls and attends, and then decides to go to UC Davis or some other school, to get a BA, I'll be thrilled. In fact, I'd be thrilled if he went to City College for two years!

On Friday, I'm going to talk at the assembly, to bring the year to a close, and come a little bit full circle from my remarks at the beginning of the year. I don't know if you were there or not, for my opening-of-the-year convocation speech?

FELTON. No.

THORP. Next year we'll publicize it more.

FELTON. Yeah. I wish I'd known.

THORP. And I talked about—it was my "Just Say Yes" speech. One of the things I concluded is being kind—what's the choice? I say, Just say no, and I talk about taking drugs and that sort of thing. "Just say yes—say yes to risk-taking." And then in the end I talk about "Just be kind," as kind of words to live by. In a world that isn't very kind. And I'm going to talk about it on Friday, I'm going to say, "We haven't been as kind to each other as we should have been."

The more I'm beginning to figure this all out, the more in part I'm recognizing that a lot of it is the journey and not the destination. And a lot of it is getting kids to believe in themselves, and believe that they can do things, whatever the "thing" is, it is more necessary and more primary than what it is they are going to do. Again, the luxury of the Groton experience is there was never any doubt that, especially in the earlier generation, that you will go on to Harvard or Yale or Princeton, and that was just not a question! And the question in part then became,

"What are you going to be able to do with this wonderful education you've had?" "Well—serve."

For our kids, that isn't a given; and so the whole idea of taking pride in seeing to it that they develop some amount of ambition and goal-setting and then act on that is, to me going to be very satisfying to watch. And I'm really concerned about it—which is yet another reason why I'm teaching this history class. Believe me, I thought a lot about this before I threw my hat in the ring, so to speak. Because it's going to be tough. But—my hope is that there is going to be a real ripple effect in the school as well. And I say all this with some amount of understandable humility, so recognize that I don't think I'm going to change the world through this class; but I am trying to set a tone and spread the word and have, I hope, some of the leaders of the school walking around and talking about how cool it is to work their butts off for a class. And maybe that'll rub off a bit on some of the others.

This past weekend I attended the second graduation of the Native American Preparatory School where I'm on the Board—fifteen graduates in the class. Four are going to Stanford.

FELTON. Is that right!

THORP. Four will go to Stanford. One to Cornell. One to Barnard. Two or three to Whittier. One to McAllister. And the list goes on. A couple of kids will go to Colorado College. I'll talk about that in my remarks on Friday, as well. And so what's interesting is that—and to me kind of fun, in terms of being provocative—is that the tables have turned. And instead of "You went to Harvard and Yale because you went to Groton and because your name was Peabody, or because your name was Smyth-Smyth," four kids are going to Stanford because they're Native American kids. To be sure, they are Native American kids who did well; but come on already, let's be honest about it: Schools are just dying to get well-educated Native American kids who have been away at boarding school, and who have been away from home and dealt with their issues of departure and division, the Jo Vega issue, before they got to college! Again, the boarding schools are providing a service for the colleges and universities by helping to prepare these kids—not just for the rigors of scholarship, but for the tough thing, about going to a different world! You know—that's where they serve, a lot! And four kids out of fifteen, going to Stanford!

It was interesting to watch the reaction of these Native American families, being so proud of their kids, most of whom were first-generation college kids. But every kid's name was announced, and that person came up and got the diploma, their tribe was announced, and what tribe they represented. And where they were going to college was announced. Which was a little bit unusual in the typical boarding school, because you don't do that; if you do, the kid who's going to go to the University of Arizona feels a little bit bad. But they did; and that's the way it would go. And every time Stanford was mentioned, the place went crazy! And for people who know nothing other than Stanford, it was the whole caché thing.

So that's the solution. And later, at one of the meals a person said to me, "My family really does have Native American blood in it; so I probably ought to put that on my application to colleges?" And the answer is: "Damned right, you oughta!" You know, if you want to play the game, here's a game you can play!

FELTON. The Native American School's college-admission experience forms a different dimension for measuring schools like Groton. Here's how one of the Groton teachers characterizes the problem:

> How do you keep the kids from coming here and saying, "I'm going to use this to get into Harvard?" You've got to work to get beyond that. That's the real work I think we do here. Why I like teaching here—you know, you're in the athletic fields, you're in the classroom, you're in the dormitory—there are all sorts of contexts, and you've got to keep coming back with that message. The whole point of a Groton education isn't just the next step; but there's something far greater beyond that. You have to keep coming at it, and at it, and at it.

And young Wright adds:

> The real problem is that some of these kids have old families that have gone to these Ivy League institutions for years and years and years. And those kids tend to get into the Ivy League schools more often than ones whose families didn't go to these places. I didn't think the legacy was that important; but it was really poignant, when I saw all these people out in the hall; those whose families had legacies got in—and those who didn't, didn't. It's not what everything's supposed to be about. It's supposed to be if you work hard, and you get good grades, you can get into one of these good schools. And here are these kids who didn't, and didn't get in.

Illuminating variant points of view, no?

THORP. Well—where's our college system in this country? Our meritocracy? Again, there is another side to that. And I've been on that other side, as the head of a boarding school—making decisions, or being involved in the decision-making process, about who would get in, and who didn't get in. And it's tough. Tonight I'm going to a board meeting of this school that I sit on here in San Francisco, Berk's School for Girls. And—though we're past the admission season, they've got a quandary: There are twenty-three spots in their Kindergarten, and they probably have sixty to eighty applications for these twenty-three spots in Kindergarten, and whom do you pick? And of the sixty applications, fifteen of them are from younger siblings. Do you take them? It's not a great example, because sometimes it's hard to make qualitative judgments about five-year-olds—but I certainly have been in that circumstance, where there would be one seat left in the class; and on one hand you've got the kid you know nothing about other than an unbelievable transcript, and on the other hand is the kid who had a much more modest record of accomplishment, but was coming from a family that had been a part of the school—either because the kid had an older sibling who was in the school presently, or because the kid was a legacy, and had a long history with the school.

So the initial reaction was: Hey, this is a meritocracy; why should a kid get in school just based on the name? But then, it starts getting a little more complex; and to get down to the ugliest part of it: Schools like that offer programs that don't pay fully through tuition, so you've got to raise money to make it happen. And yeah, some kids walk into schools because their families are wealthy. Some kids walk into schools, especially at the University level, because they can jam a round ball through a round hoop. And what kind of meritocracy is that? You know—tell me about Indiana University and Coach Bobby Knight's basketball preciousness. I mean—that really defines what American higher education is all about!

FELTON. I am afraid it does.

THORP. For me, one could say: "Well, what kind of hypocrite were you in promoting the class structure by letting kids in?" But the interesting thing about it is, if you talk about school as community, and if you talk about school as family, as these boarding schools do, and as Gateway is trying to do, in a language that's less familiar to the typical Gateway family, then you've got to "walk the walk." And if you walked the walk, you talked about how when your kid is admitted, the family is admitted, to become part of the Gateway family.

It's now being balanced out by the fact that Stanford took those four Native American kids—most of whom probably didn't have the track record. Some other kids got turned down. So. Turn-about, fair play in my book!

FELTON. One could say that.

THORP. And, of course, it's the argument: Why should I, young master Wright of Groton, seventeen years old, have to pay for the sins of my forefathers? That's the way it works, kid.

FELTON. The informal lawnside colloquy of seniors continues a moment more. All the school's student elements that we've viewed come together to talk about graduating and learning. Here are Latina Jo Vega, the young, arrogant, money-grabbing Bobby Greenhill, and philosophical rower Wright.

Jo talks about Columbia, her choice of college:

"I think there's always something pulling me home, for better or worse. I mean, something at home that I'm always attracted to. I don't know what it is. But there's a strange feeling that I'm always going to be something completely different; like, sort of a—well, I don't know how they'll think of me anymore."

My question here: Will Gateway students emerge having made a major change of form, as did Jo?

Jo goes on:

"I think the hardest thing for me was that I have to sum up four years. I want to make peace with Groton at this point."

Again, I ask: Are there Gateway students who have operated in this kind of opposition / conflict-ridden relationship with the school, and still, as she did, maintain themselves?

Greenhill says:

"I think I want to be remembered as somebody who wasn't too goal-oriented. I think I want to be remembered as—sort of a, you know, a good guy."

And Wright says: "Graduation is something I've eagerly anticipated for five years. I'm looking forward to college. But at the same time, talking to graduates of this place, I don't see how it's going to be as big an experience as the one I'm leaving behind here."

THORP. Totally true!

FELTON. And my question here, in the broader sense: Is high school, in critical and fundamental ways, actually more important than college?

These students have just a couple of more remarks. Wright—fully in character— says: "I knew that my ideals have changed since I was younger; but I don't want to just find a job that's going to pay the most. Maybe everyone does feel that little tug to try and achieve for the rest of the nation, the world."

And Bobby Greenhill—also in character!—says: "These are the people who are intelligent here. And these are the people who will probably influence the world that I'll travel in. And so I think I'm fortunate in a way that I'm becoming acquainted with these people." Boy, you've got to hand it to him—he's just saying it the way he thinks!

THORP. Sure!

FELTON. And sweet, artistic, Hispanic Jo Vega—completely true to character!—says: "The most important thing that I could do would be to take what I've gotten here, turn it around, and make it work to benefit minorities. I don't want security; I don't really need it. I've seen enough of the bad in life that I can live without security. And I realize that your part in the scheme of things is to make that world a little better for other Puerto Ricans and blacks and Asians. And in fact, I've been given a chance, now, to do that."

FELTON. So....three students, three futures. Three ways of viewing the results of American education?

THORP. Well, just as an editorial comment: There is some reason to believe that Bobby Greenhill was "putting the filmmakers on." Which is one of the side stories in this—I mean, how straight were these kids being? This was one of the questions. And my sense is that this was a revisionist history on the part of the Groton school alumni, about Bobby as being so out-of-character from the typical Groton kid. My sense is he was probably being totally who he was. And there certainly are kids like that, and a lot of kids like that. But in fact—and this is a very timely question, given my experience at the Native American School last weekend—people who have not had that kind of educational experience can't understand the power of that kind of experience, and can't understand how fundamentally life-altering that kind of an experience is, or the power of the memories that stay, even if life isn't necessarily altered.

It enforces, for me, unequivocally, the importance of having kids feel like adults care for them. And about them. That's what we're trying to do here. And yet, it's an alien concept for a high percentage of our kids.

And so the overtures made by me, and by our faculty, are often viewed with suspicion. Some students here feel: "What do they need to know that for?" "What is he asking me that question for?" "No, I won't take advantage of this opening I'm being offered by this adult, to know him better, or to spend time with him." And it's just a realization to me that we've got a lot more thinking to do, and work to accomplish, to figure out how to get kids to understand where we're coming from. But we're heading in the right direction, given the faculty we have here, who are eminently attractive to kids who will be open to them. And a lot of our kids are getting the hang of it.

It's been a pointed message to me a few times this year. Your choice for Mr. Modesty, Federico, actually said to me just a week or so ago: "Hey, where you been, Mr. Thorp? Don't see you too much." And teachers need to listen to those kind of statements carefully, because he's telling me: "Hey, you haven't been around. And you set up the school in a way where you told me you were going to be around, and you're not around. And so I'm starting to fall back and think, 'Maybe it was a pile of crap!'" So I listen to those kind of comments.

Again, you feel flattered that a kid like that would say that to you. But there's a lot more to it than flattery. And keeping track of that kind of statement is important. Federico's comment to me really prompted me to think: "Okay, I want to end the year in reconnecting with the kids."

So that kind of educational venue ought to be able to be experienced by every kid. And it isn't that green lawns are absolutely essential—although I'll tell you it makes a difference, particularly in those schools, the two that I've worked in, represented by these chairs that we're sitting in: There's no question that place affects one's soul, if you're open to that. And there's no question in these two schools, that coming back to a certain space carries with it all sorts of meaning and welcome memories. It's an incredibly powerful reality. Moreso than just the triggering of memories by familiarity. I'll presume to comment, and I hope I'm wrong. My guess is the typical Grinnell graduate isn't bound to the physical space at Grinnell; that there was something else there, not in lieu of, but in addition to; the physical place. At Williams, there definitely was this sense of the place pulling you back. And without having intended it, I think, it's been interesting that my educational life has been spent in educational institutions after high school where place plays such an important role. And now I'm in this job where there ain't no place!

So only you know how fully frustrating this whole Gateway site dilemma is for me; because I really see the value in place. It's place and people. At Groton, for a few kids, it is. But it's the place that they have grown up in. And having been given the opportunity to have grown up away from their parents, that reality makes that place immeasurably powerful. And the people, some of whom you saw in that film—even Bobby Greenhill—will carry these things with them for the rest of their his lives. And I'm hopeful that Gateway kids will come back twenty years from now and will be able to say, "You know, Miss Kini, when you taught me in class, I just want you to know how much it meant to me. Because I was working with you on a common endeavor that just changed my life." That's where that kind of independent school education makes such a difference.

FELTON. It's interesting you should use that teacher as an example. I ended the section on the first semester here with a reference to her class one day after school, when I stuck my nose in there because I thought we were supposed to use that space for the Photo Group. She was working with a student; and they were—you could see them together at the desk, with their backs to the door, where I was; they were not even aware I was there. And the intensity and the togetherness of those backs bent into the project was so wonderful; and her caring was palpable.

THORP. It would have made a good photograph.

FELTON. It would have made an incredible photograph. It said a lot about that teacher. I think you're absolutely right: I think that student, or others like that student, will remember her.

Your comments about Federico gently taking you to task will relate to some of the issues I want to bring up next time. For now, I'd like to get any commentary or offering that you have about the District's hiring the new Superintendent. And I'd like to explore whether that choice of theirs will affect you in any respect. I'd like to point out that Ms. Ackerman's views were presented by her in at least one national news program; and she was not shy in her commentary about charters.

THORP. Well, I will preface it by saying this is one where I would want to make sure that the remarks didn't hurt the school. So I'll be utterly candid; but I reserve the right to review what I said on this one.

FELTON. Absolutely.

THORP. The word on the street is she's not a big fan of charter schools.[1] And lo and behold, I confirmed that this weekend, so your timing is great, as always, in that one of the alumni at Fountain Valley is a black kid from Oakland who ended up at Colorado Springs, but

---

[1] See Chapter 15: "A National Awakening to Charter Schools." Arlene Ackerman appears in the cited MacNeil-Lehrer News Hour feature on charter school, and is critical of Washington, D.C.'s encouragement of charters. She was then that city's Superintendent of Public Instruction. Hers is the voice saying "We have to move slowly," to which Thorp took exception.

who now has developed a career as a politician in Washington, D.C. And he's now a district councilman or assemblyman in D.C.

FELTON.   A fortuitous find!

THORP.   "Ward Five Counsel Member, Counsel of the District of Columbia," to be exact.   And so I picked his brain a little bit when I saw him.   And as I suspected, one of the reasons she's leaving Washington is that she got undercut in decision-making over a charter-school related issue.   So we're working upstream.   And with that in mind, now with having made the connection with him, I'm going to begin a conversation with him to see how he might be able to be helpful to us, and communicate a few things before she leaves town. And while he still might have an "in" with her a little bit, to at least say: "Give this guy at least a listen-to, because he's okay."   But we'll see. And there's no question that we're at a critical junction in the life of charter schools here in San Francisco.   Once again this is over this facilities problem.

Now, again, we're okay for the next five years as far as having a charter, assuming we don't do anything so stupid that we would have it yanked.   But the facilities sword is hanging over all of our heads.   And it'll be interesting to see the extent to which we're just going to have to keep plugging along.   I've come to some peace with the thought that this building is probably going to be as good as it gets.   I don't think there are going to be other options for us out there.   And that means all sorts of things in terms of enrollment and facilities, and investment and time and all that.   So assuming that's the case, and assuming somebody doesn't drop fifteen million bucks on us so we can go buy another building, we're going to have to make do with this.   And make it happen.   And we're going to have to figure out how to stay in here. And that's going to become political, very quickly.   It's going to be "squatters' rights."   And it's going to be tapping into our parents to say: We need you to write letters now, for our lease is up for renegotiation, and the School District doesn't want us to extend our lease beyond next year, and so we're going to have to start going to the press and mount our campaign.   And I'm ready to do that.   I mean, I've tried for two years to show the Board that I'm genuinely interested in working with both them and with the School District, to help the students of San Francisco.   And I think all of them understand, but I think few people accept it.   And there are other people about whom I need to come to my senses, and realize that they aren't going to change.   And if that's the way it is, then I've got to play the political game the way it needs to be played, and in an urban city, to get what you want.   Everybody else is playing it; so if I don't, I'm not going to be effective.   I might be less tarnished; but I'll be less tarnished without a roof over my head. Which I don't want to see happen.

FELTON. Well, you know, every time I go by that huge old high school building which is now the Board's temporary quarters, on Van Ness—

THORP. At 135 Van Ness?

FELTON. Yeah—the same thought goes through my head, which is that every charter school in the city, as presently constituted, would fit into that one building! And I'm not suggesting that that's ideal; but just the fact that there are—I personally know maybe six such schools, not so large, that are just sitting in San Francisco, gathering dust. Did I whiff some poison once which makes it impossible for me to see the logic in letting those buildings just sit there?

THORP. Well, regarding the huge school building at 135 Van Ness, the logic there is that that building's promised to SOTA, School of the Arts.

FELTON. Oh, it is! I didn't realize that. That's a coup for them!

THORP. Yeah. SOTA's going to go in there, when they raise the seventy-five million bucks they need to renovate the building. And that's why we're not in there this year. We were scheduled to be in there this year; but when the SOTA people got wind of it, they mounted a campaign against us, and it was painful for me, because the SOTA people assumed things about us that were not true. They thought that we'd go in and never let it go, and they never would be able to claim it. And my response to them was: That isn't going to happen. Of course, my assurance was ignored.

Now, in retrospect, they were probably more right than not, because had we gotten in there and not had this building, what would we be doing now? We'd be in that circumstance of saying, "We need to be in there one more year," and we said it was only going to be one year, but here we are asking for one more year. I think it's at least another couple of years before they break ground. But squatters' rights is—well, I just commented that I'm going to act on the squatters' rights principle if that's what I have to do to stay in a school building.

FELTON. Who hires the superintendent?

THORP. The Board of Education.

FELTON. So you don't really have to look further than that to get the coloration of the decision-making.

THORP. Right. Ackerman is an impressive educator, from everything I've heard. I mean, you'll hear no complaints that they've hired some flunky. It's just that she's apparently not had a good experience with the charter school situation. So I'm very nervous about that; and as I say, I'm going to pick Vince Orange's brain to see how he would advise me to approach her initially. So we'll see.

FELTON. Yeah.

THORP. On the other hand, with the departure of Rojas, who was very supportive, it's not like we've been getting a lot of support this year.

FELTON. I've just one other question on that line: Somewhere— when everybody starts to have the idea that this is such a radical idea, somewhere in that meeting a few weeks ago, where George Bush went down and was welcomed by that Mission Viejo school, there was some commentary about charter schools. It was one of those enthusiastic, slightly forced set-up statements, where somebody was saying: "Yeah, those charter schools are great! I mean, they can do all kinds of things." And this charter "fan" started naming things. And one of the things in this litany of charms ascribed to the charter schools was: "Yes, and some charter schools are going to be setting up where you don't even need grades. We might put somebody in because he's at a certain level, or not at a certain level—why worry about the distinctions?" Now, to me, that's a very radical idea! And how anybody even remotely connected with the Republican nominee could come up with that, surprised me. Fine idea, as far as it goes; but I don't know how practically it could be implemented, especially with all the other turgidity about testing, and all that.

THORP. Well, I know you don't mean to imply that radical conservatism is an oxymoron. I mean, it can very much be that; that was Barry Goldwater's whole thrust! So in fact you should not be surprised by that; certainly, one of the great accomplishments of Clinton—whether one thinks it's a good or bad one is irrelevant— certainly one of his major accomplishments was to bring the Democratic Party back into the center. His legacy will be that, from a political standpoint. And it's a remarkable and brilliant legacy. I mean, think of where he started. Think of the shape of the Democratic party prior to his arrival. It's an incredible legacy.

And particularly with education, there should be no surprise in Republicans supporting that, because Republicans see education as the monopoly of government, and they see education, just like the postal service, and just like welfare, and just like other examples which escape me right now, but just anything that the government runs is a mess. And so the only solutions are radical solutions. No, the Republican support for radical reform is both not surprising and extremely broad and deep.

The real question will be the voucher movement. And that will divide Republicans and Democrats, because the Democrats don't want to do something that promotes private education, whereas the Republicans are beyond that concern. And again, I don't question their motives. I don't think they're trying to keep the Grotons in business by supporting the voucher movement. I think they're simply saying that families ought to have choice. They're a little bit blind about how much choice a family can have with a voucher of—whatever it might be: twenty-five hundred, or three thousand bucks, when, you know, the cheapest parochial school here in the city, I've got to believe, is at least five or six thousand bucks.[1] But, they're coming from a radical reform. I mean, all these venture capitalists down in Silicon Valley, most of whom are Republicans, know that the only way to reform the school system is through radical changes.

And that's why, ironically and frustratingly to us, there's not as broad support for increased funding for education in this state as one would think, just given the miserable funding there is. Because certainly some people believe—and there's ample evidence for support here in San Francisco—that more money is just going to mean more waste.? More janitorial overtime, is how they see it. So their point is well-taken.

But it will be an interesting fall, both in local elections, the School Board, and the national election in terms of education. Both parties are outdoing each other in support of charter schools. But I hope that—I'd like to see a debate about education on one of the televised debates. And have somebody ask some really thoughtful questions about what is your party's educational program? And really find out: Is it simply more money and more tests? In which case, forget about reform coming. But if it's—there are plenty of things that one of the two candidates, or both of them, could say that really would revolutionize reform—one of which is: Pay teachers more, and in an exchange for that, teachers would forget about collective bargaining—

FELTON. Pay teachers more!? Pay those Communist slackers more!??

THORP. —And we'll set up a system whereby you can have teachers do their own evaluations, you know? We'll pay you more—but you're going to be held accountable for the pay that you deserve. Just like anybody else in the real world. So we'll see if somebody has

---

[1] The November 2000 Ballot Measure Proposition 38 sought approval for vouchers of $4,000 per family.

the courage to say that. And the answer is—it won't be Al Gore! Too much Teacher Union money behind that. Now, that's radical reform! You know? Just get rid of grades. Or who do we think they're kidding with 180-day school year? You know—fix the damn building. Or it's—the one that I would start with, is: Get rid of schools' comprehensive social services. If kids need social services, they ought to get social services. But not in school. So schools that run teen pregnancy centers and schools that run all these other social service programs make the running of school so much more complicated! And set up different agencies—let the schools be schools. I'd like to see somebody say that.

FELTON. Good.

THORP. My next career will be as a Presidential speech writer. I write the speeches in my head, and every time I take a shower; but I don't seem to be able to follow through and actually do it.

FELTON. Don't worry: Maybe the next President's speech writer will be a "Grottie."

Chapter Twenty-Seven

VALEDICTORY

"One of the problems in education is that people have underestimated the strength of the status quo. And certainly some educational reforms have expanded the strength of the status quo; there's that Vietnamese proverb about how that blade of grass bends in the wind, and when the wind finishes, the blade of grass becomes upright again. And I think that's an apt metaphor for educational reform in the second half of the twentieth century."

—Peter Thorp, in looking back on his career.

22 June—*For the first time since the inception of our year's look at the life of a charter school principal, Peter Thorp and I sat not in his office, but in a nearby coffee shop. At his invitation, we'd left the surround of the busy high school office, and retreated to "Tart to Tart," the San Francisco Inner Sunset District's older but wiser version of Starbuck's. Trading the Captain's chairs of Cate Preparatory and Fountain Valley School for well-used bentwoods, we sat at a small square table along a dark side wall. The environment for our last talk featured not Peter's time-punctuating secretary's knocks, or Meghvi Maheta's large-eyed entry for occasional inquiry, or even Peter's own younger daughter, checking in with Dad before going home, but the overly-loud voice of a cellular phone user, pumping up his business voice with caffeine, a pair of young women priming each other for a job interview, and the other ersatz patrons of Irving Street's favorite daytime dive.*

By the time this last session had arrived—changed several times, to meet the fast-paced schedule of a school principal's summer concerns—much had happened in a short period. *The humanities students had undergone and survived their ten-minute trials-by-fire in the portfolio presentations. The entire school underwent, and survived, an almost-three-hour awards ceremony, during which Peter Thorp and team found every possible way to make as many students feel good as they could. And the beginning encroachment of summer proper, with its pressing plans for many, made its way into the present: Iva, the Croatian receptionist, left her station to try her fortune in Los Angeles' young filmmaker community. Bonita Dunning, Peter's talented aide-de-camp, saw her own daughter through a high school matriculation, and sent her off to college. And Tara Kini, the ninth grade humanities teacher who wore the same purple backpack every day to her Gateway teaching room as she had worn every day since the seventh grade, made the final preparations for a wedding, up the coast in Sonoma, to her young man Josh.*

Peter continued to have meetings; summer was no respite for him. But with this final session, our work of documenting "a year in the life of a charter high school principal" was brought to a close.

This was a time, I told him, for any kind of notion, of remark, of commentary, of observation that he wished. Perhaps it was the time to tell the mysteries of his sins, as he'd alluded in one session. Perhaps it was simply a time to let himself relax, a little, from even the routine tension of our sessions, in which a conscientious professional had wanted to be at his best. We had the luxury, now, of not needing to be our best. We'd done that, we both felt.

Reflections? Peter was, indeed, reflective; a little wistful, even— not, I thought, from the occasion of our last meeting as much as from the still-rippling recent shock of a school without students, a string of meetings unbroken by that sharp-edged, uplifting challenge—the adolescent face with its thinly-masked angst, come to the principal's office, for good or ill, at his beckon or one's own desperate compass direction, seeking redemption or redirection or the sandwiched praise-and-chastisement which, coming from Peter Thorp, always seemed to result in a better feeling about things. Even the desperate things.

So: Reflections?

I had one of my own:

FELTON.   This is troublesome for me, for I'm having to shift all my natural impulses now, the series of sort of ongoing procedures this process has generated, with it in mind that I'm not going to have this opportunity any more. We'll live with that.

THORP. Well, we want to talk about that. I mean, in terms of whether or not you see the need or the desire to continue the conversation. That's a thing that we could talk about. I'm not sitting here thinking, "Okay, this is Keith's last hour-and-a-half with Thorp, and never again!" So....

On the other hand—if the focus is "A year in the life"—

FELTON. That's right—

THORP. —Then we're almost there.

FELTON. We're almost there; and I'm fudging a little bit here and there; but I really think we've got it. And my actual idea is next year, to try and follow, if it can be worked out, try and follow a likely candidate for student, with parents—

THORP. Somebody other than your boy Peter?

FELTON. Oh, yeah, yeah. I think so. There are some problems with having my own son be the student.

THORP. Sure.

FELTON. I don't just mean that he's my son; I mean—Peter's—Peter has a really interesting—the word which came to mind was peculiar—a unique way of thinking and interpreting. He's really an artist who hasn't yet discovered a solid art form other than his love of music.

In fact, speaking of him, there are two things that happened last week that are so unusual, from students. One was that girl I mentioned at the Parent's Meeting, that girl named Maya who came up and sat down next to me and just talked, and talked, and poured her heart out.

But another thing happened in that event, that I didn't anticipate. I was there to start my Photo Group, and the only one who had showed up so far was Evan Alsnauer. And Evan was sitting on one side of me, and Maya came and sat on the other side. And after a while, after listening to this deluge of self-deprecation, Evan started pitching in! He said, to her: "You know, I was in that boat. And you know what I did? I kind of did *this*, and I found that after a while, the other thing wasn't so bad..." And he really entered into it! He wasn't embarrassed, he wasn't scared off. He brought himself out, for a fellow student's benefit, in a way that I thought was wonderful.

THORP. Great, great! That's something he wouldn't have done a year ago.

FELTON. I believe not.

THORP. Photography has given him a voice in a number of ways.

FELTON. That's just great! I'm really glad to hear it.

The other thing: Peter—my son—is a very sentimental human being. And romantic in all the senses of the word. So when the yearbooks came, he wanted to get people to sign his yearbook. And I asked him if he'd mind if I looked at the signatures. And he said, "No." There were only a couple there. And one kid had written this— and it was astonishingly on target. He wrote: *"Peter—you are kind of weird, and in your own little world. But you FIGHT for it!"*—with FIGHT capitalized— *"You FIGHT for it. And I respect that. Keep on fighting!"*

THORP. Wow!

FELTON. Isn't that interesting?

THORP. That's really profound!

FELTON. It *was* really profound. Yeah, for one kid to write to another—to see that, and to be comfortable enough to call that to the person's attention, and put it in that positive light. I thought it was great.

THORP. How did Peter take it?

FELTON. Peter liked it—as much as he was able to share. I read it and said, "Well, this is astonishing!" And he said, "Yeah," and then went on to something else. He didn't reveal too much at the moment. But I know he feels it.

I had a thought that I wanted to talk with you about. It just recently occurred. Do you follow the NBA at all? Did you follow the recent playoff games? The whole time the games were going on, I was thinking, "Damn it, I'm a Laker fan, and I really want these guys to win, but nothing is happening out there! They all look sort of drugged; they all look—they all move only at the very last minute, when the opposing player, Miller, has destroyed all their self-respect, and they finally will win by one point, you know! And it was ticking me off.

And then toward the end of the games, and after the games, there were some interviews, including on the News Hour, with the Laker coach Phil Jackson. He, as you may know, is a Zen practitioner, and one who espouses some of those principles to his players. And even during the games, some commentators would interview Jackson. Unlike the News Hour gang, who took his Zen seriously, the commentators on the regular network sort of made a little bit fun of it. But when Jackson talked about how he would give some player a book, and how, when challenged by the interviewer who suggested that that player laughed at the book and never read it, and went on playing basketball the same way, Phil Jackson said: "Yeah, but there's a little seed there; and maybe twenty years from now it will mean something."

And given his low-key Zen style, I started thinking about it. And I thought: "Wow!—I got sucked in. I, who am not a competitive person, who doesn't really move with those energies, nonetheless wanted the team to do the conventional thing, and come out charging. And now, here's a guy who apparently is saying: "You can do it a different way, even at that level, in that kind of competitive arena. With the world spotlight on you, you can still do it a little bit of a different way."

And I'm wondering what is in that message that students can begin to pick up on, because this particular coach will only have so much influence. Can we hope that this is as trend? Can we hope that this is going to move in and replace some of the other narrowly-viewed competition goals?

THORP. Here's where you need to talk to a sociobiologist. Because I grew up in a world where competition was one of the more highly valued aspects. And for two primary reasons: One was I was able to compete, and you were drawn to a world where you could be successful. And so as an athlete, I could play a lot of sports, and so my world was the world of competition. And I received a lot of rewards from that.

I also went to a camp from the ages of eight to eighteen, run by one of the great people in my life. But the ethic of the camp was competition. You earned points for everything! And you eventually became a "chief" in the mock-Native-American culture that this camp espoused, based on a certain number of points that you earned through competing.

It worked for me. And it was only later in life, when I looked back at that camp experience and said to myself, "How many kids were miserable there because they couldn't' compete?" Or: "How many kids are miserable at Columbine High School because they can't compete?" Ratchet ahead, speed ahead full-forward to today, to educational reformers, the Silicon Valley types, or the venture capital types, or other schools of educational reform, and they're saying: "The fundamental flaw in public education is that it behaves like a monopoly, and the worst kind of monopoly is: There's no accountability, in the public sector monopolies, or even in the post office. Microsoft at least had some accountability, in terms of its customers and stockholders. And so what public education needs is more competition."

I'm not sure where I fall on that question. If, because one person displays an ethic of competition and therefore everybody grows and improves and gets more out of it as a result, that's one effect. Another person's competition based on the "zero-sum" idea, that there are basically winners and losers, is not something that I think will be good for education. And I think that's at the heart of the question.

I was at a meeting yesterday for two hours at the San Francisco Foundation, a local foundation.

FELTON. Yes! I know them well.

THORP. They brought in about twenty educators from the Bay Area in various programs, and they wanted to talk about the state of the world, so to speak, through the eyes of educators, and what the Foundation could do to apply some of that thinking. And we talked about a whole range of issues; but for me, this question of trying to find a right balance—well, one of the questions which comes up a lot in education is this word "equity." And I think a lot of jargon mistakes take place in society because people assume that the common definition of "equity" is "diversity"—when in fact, I think that we all know that there aren't common definitions of it. And that's a huge part of the problem, because people aren't willing to go to the next step, to thrash out and find a common definition of diversity.

But a notion on the question of equity speaks to this competitive matter: If one means by "equity" that one will have the same experience, that's one thing. If one means, on the other hand, that everyone will have equal opportunity, that's another thing. It's sort of Teddy Roosevelt's philosophy in what he called "The New Nationalism"—which is reformed Darwinism. You're not trying to make everybody have the same experience. You are trying to tear away the barriers for equal opportunity. And in that sense, schools need to be more competitive, and fight more, if you will, to wrestle with what those barriers are. And they are ranging in the Affirmative Action programs up or down, depending on how you look at it.

I think one of the problems in the last quarter-century in American education is that the term equity has been interpreted to mean "equal experience." And that's why you have people going after "Gate" programs, which is a concept I despise. I don't think it's taking education in the right direction to get rid of advanced, more challenging programs, because every kid can be successful, and therefore it's not equitable to have that. That's junk. And that's one of the issues that I think educational reform will need to deal with.

The competition issue is a tough thing. I am a product of competition, personally, and yet in my arguably more mature days, I've really backed away from competition, and am disgusted it by what's happened in professional sports. It has even taken the essence of pure competition—almost an Olympian mentality, in my mind, and perverted it into this world of entertainment and/or selfishness. And that to me is extraordinary.

My last commencement speech at Cate had as its theme, "Humility." And I picked that for specific reasons. I may have used this expression before with you, but Cate is an arrogant institution. And as I paraphrase Winston Churchill, "arrogance with good reason."

FELTON. Yes! Attlee's legacy.

THORP. —They have a lot to be arrogant about! But in fact one of the great things about this group of kids that I was speaking about, who were sitting on the stage graduating, is that they were humble. And I talked about how being humble doesn't mean that you are less competitive or less aggressive, or less good or less ambitious or anything like that. And I espoused the virtues of humility. It's the quality that I think is essentially absent from professional sports. And it's one of the reasons why professional basketball's Shaquille O'Neill is more impressive to me now than ever before. In seeing that he is a reasonably humble person. And perhaps some of his colleagues in business might take some lessons from him.

FELTON. I think you're absolutely right. It was impressive to me, once during the Championship, and a couple of times in the playoffs, to see, on a break, or a time-out, to see the cameramen home in and stay on player Ron Harper talking with player Scottie Pippin, old friends and teammates now wearing different uniforms and playing in this game on opposite sides. And the implication of that shot was so clear; it was: "Wait a minute—these guys are supposed to hate each other, and look, they're not!"

THORP. Yeah.

FELTON. And I thought that kind of image might be part of introducing a different aspect, a new way of looking at competition-cooperation. And I hope you're right. Because that takes—maybe humility isn't the word there, but it certainly takes having a whole different view and mindset.

I wanted to tie that in, in a way, with the major change you've made during the last two years—from a Cate to a Gateway. I see it in part in terms of a kind of egalitarian matter, in a way, regarding the classes. And though you speak with quasi-Marxist tongue, and legitimately and compellingly when you do, you also give the boarding school elites their fair shake—this was clearly the import of our vetting the Groton film—and you always have. And when I see that in operation, I see somebody striving for a different dimension than any apparent to anybody else. Someone who can "lay in" something, some promise, that might later come to fruition. But my specific question here, is: Is there any kind of handicap in that? Or is there the possible germination of something that would "do you in" later, as a result of wanting to be fair to both, or having both be legitimate in your eyes, when in a sense, you have a kind of forced partisanship here, at Gateway, as you did there, at Cate?

THORP. Yes. When you say "both," do you mean, both classes? Or—?

FELTON. Both classes, or an extreme making of opposites there. For the sake of the point. I suppose I'm asking, does this constitute a "double loyalty"? And, to use the vernacular, does it make you feel at all "schizy"?

THORP. Well, if your question speaks to one's life's choices— you know, you make your choices and you pay the price. But you must make your choices thoughtfully; and sometimes you have the fortune of making the choices thoughtfully and sometimes you don't. You know—sometimes other people make them for you. Those thoughtful choices are, in my case, professional and personal choices all wrapped into one. It's also, as we look toward the future again, reading in your question that you're sort of looking ahead some number of years, that as I look back, the choice to come here—even though I made a choice dramatically under-informed about what it really was going to entail—I don't look back for a second on the choice.

Somebody at this Foundation meeting yesterday said: "You know, one of the real crises in education is we can't get principals, nobody wants the principal's job." That gave me the opportunity to say that I love every minute of my job here at Gateway, and I explained why.

The one dark cloud on the horizon for me, *vis-à-vis* Gateway, is— I'm not twenty-five, or thirty-five, or even forty-five. I'm not that far away from fifty-five. And one gets more impatient the older one gets—actually, there's probably a bell-curve on that. But you know, I need to be sure that I'm seeing satisfactory results soon enough, and next year's going to be a real test for the school, I think, and for me, in terms of assessing whether or not I accomplished what I set out to do. And again, I will obviously not be doing this by myself.

A year from now, if we could have a conversation where we look back and say, "Yeah, now we're really heading in the direction we want, and now this learning community that we've established is really functioning—" then I will be able to take great satisfaction in what I've accomplished, and be able to continue improving upon that.

In another sense, if a couple of years down the road, I'm beating my head against the same walls, then I've got to go through some serious reflection: "Is this 'do-able'?" Or, perhaps: "Is this 'do-able' by *me*?" And maybe this job requires somebody with different approaches and skills than I have.

So I'm the kind of person, as I'm sure you know by now, who's a pretty reflective person, and probably reflective to a fault, in some ways. So I'm constantly reflecting about what we've accomplished, and what we've not accomplished. And recognize that I can't do it all, nor should I have the hubris to think that Gateway's going to rise or fail on my shoulders. On the other hand, somebody's got to be at the tiller, and I am. So next year is a key year for us.

One decision I push at our end-of-the-year faculty meetings is something that no other member of the Gateway community knows about yet. You and I talked about community service, as part of this springtime reflection that the faculty and I were feeling in a variety of ways. And the recommendation from this committee of the faculty was that we would continue the community service program as-is, to offer interesting opportunities for kids, and if kids signed up for it, then great. But now, I've decided we can't do that. It is time for us to act consistently with our mission. And so, at some point within the next few weeks, and certainly by early August, you and Peter will be getting a letter crafted by me, which says, "We go into next year with a community service requirement." And we're going to get a lot of squawking from kids about it—

FELTON. Are you so sure?—

THORP. From kids, yes, and arguably from parents in some cases. But I've learned that in the world where I came from, a voluntary community service program which was something that ninety percent of the kids really "bought into" terrifically, is not a world which exists at Gateway, and isn't going to exist unless we require it. This will be maybe five years down the road, when we have the culture created, and we can make it voluntary again, because it will have worked.

So I feel we have achieved a certain stability in the school, and I can really now turn to the more fundamental schooling aspects, or educational aspects, which is what school should be about. Now, if I can get this building we're in taken care of, and get settled on that, and now that we have our charter, and so on, we can get going and really develop the community service program that I want to develop.

But there is an "aside" in this: Next Tuesday night, you might want to attend the last Board of Education meeting of the year, which will be interesting for all sorts of reasons. For one thing, it's the budget meeting, and so it's guaranteed to go until three o'clock in the morning. But also: There are resolutions that are going to be voted on—board-authored resolutions, one of which is to take away the charter from Edison Academy—which comes as no surprise, because they've been—

FELTON. They've been screwed up.

THORP. —beat up on since the day that they got established. And perhaps you read about this situation where the whole faculty of that school sent a letter to the Board saying they were going to quit. But—here comes a "knock-your-socks-off" matter: There will also be a resolution to yank Leadership School's charter!

FELTON. You mean—I knew they were their losing their physical plant—but kicking them when they're down—?!

THORP. That's it. It's based on the fact that the charter was approved with the understanding that they would occupy quarters within Golden Gate University, and now that they are no longer at Golden Gate, we're going to yank their charter.

FELTON. But that is specious! It's astonishing!

THORP. At least it emerges out of the woodwork short of where we are. Not that it comes as any great surprise in one case. It was co-authored by two of the board members, whereas the Edison one was co-authored by four of the board members. And if you've got four votes, either for you or against, you—

FELTON. —That's it!

THORP. So I think they're cooked. I think they're toast. And Don Fisher, who pumped in twenty million bucks to the Edison Corporation, probably isn't going to be all that happy. And I've got to think that at least one phenomenon at work is their sitting there saying: "Why should we invest money in a school which we think is great, but which is part of a movement which is on such rocky soil here in San Francisco?"

I can't believe it. So I'm going to be at that Board meeting, because my guess is that Leadership's charter will not be yanked, and what you will have is two board members carving out publicly their position on charter schools, as they go into the fall election.

FELTON. Board members Wynns, and—?

THORP. Dan Kelly. But in the latter case, with Kelly, I'm going to try and get a meeting with him this summer, to see if he's just waiting in the bushes for Gateway to make a mistake, or if he's willing to help us succeed. Not that we don't want to be held accountable, and not that we shouldn't be criticized where we deserve to be criticized— but, does he want us to succeed?

And that will be an interesting conversation. Because if he declines to support us, I'm going to marshal my parents to do everything we can to defeat him in the general election.

Of course, then, if he wins—!

FELTON. Will the new Superintendent be in place then?

THORP. She's coming in mid-July, we meet with the new Superintendent on August 16, I think. That sort of takes us off track, but—

FELTON. Well, it's alarming. It does happen to raise a fantasy that I had during those first board meetings, 'way back in March. And the fantasy was: "All you're doing is playing a bunch of games, and we're trying to do something worthwhile, here! So the hell with you! We'll go it alone!"

Leading to the question: What's a ballpark Gateway "nut"? What's the yearly cost? I mean, if the parents, and the patrons of Gateway had to bootstrap it—would that be possible?

THORP. Well, I should note that nothing is impossible. But what you're really talking about is one of two approaches, which is to take the Gateway idea, and go find a school superintendent that's more receptive to the idea of a charter school carrying it out. Or, to become a private school.

FELTON. Yes.

THORP. Those are really the two venues that we have.

FELTON. When Lisille Matheson and her group of founding mothers were doing their initial work, and you came on board, was there any view—just for whatever could have been gained from it—in looking at the Albany school system? Do you know about that?

THORP. No.

FELTON. It's just a little chunk of real estate between Berkeley and Hayward. It has its own school system, and it is a plum! They run it from a humanitarian point of view, the community is limited—and it's a pretty affluent community.[1] I don't know if they'd welcome an outsider charter or not. They can do what they damn well please, although it's their public school system. And it's just been wonderful for some of the parents I used to know there. But then, it's easier to

---

[1] At year's end—21 December 2000—students at Albany High School moved a strike force onto school grounds protesting that teachers' salaries were too low.

get things done when you don't have, you know, gargoyles sitting in a Board meeting every month telling the parents what to do.

THORP.   But I don't know; maybe there is a third path, and maybe what you're suggesting is that Gateway could get itself rechartered outside the confines of the calculating San Francisco Unified School District, and remain in the Bay Area and be successful at it.

FELTON. Yeah.

THORP.   I suppose it's as simple as thinking: Can we do it in San Mateo, for example? Or Marin? But the real question is: Could we stay exactly where we are, and just have our chartering agency be in the state. And I think there is a provision in the state law that allows that. But of course, in the meantime, you know, you've got to deal with what's here. With my competitive juices, there are parts of me that, if put to the wall, would do everything I could to create that.

FELTON.   I know that's so.

THORP.   We'd need to start with temporary restraining orders. That would be my first step—to enjoin the School Board from yanking our charter. That's why I'm keeping track of the screw-ups that they make. We may have to use them.

FELTON.   Your "South Boston scrapper" side is coming out!

THORP.   You'd better believe it.

FELTON.   Well, I would definitely try to get to that meeting.

THORP.   You could also listen to it on their radio broadcasts. It might be less—at least, you could sit there and drink beer—

FELTON.   —And keep my blood pressure level from hitting the roof!

Well, that brings us full circle. And I want to take a bit of a look back. Let's go from the School District and the Charter School to the Leader. In some senses we started with you, and needed to get to know about you. And a couple of things jumped out in the process.

Just for starters, in the sense of names, the sense of identity: My opening question was: "Who is Peter Cahill Thorp?" I found out that he's an athlete; he's a precocious student; a world scholar. He's a young art history teacher, and later a school administrator; still later a headmaster and a school principal. Lastly, he's a participant on boards of governors of several other academic institutions. That's illustrious just by itself; certainly it's a strong achievement by your young age.

What's ahead?

—And, before you comment, let me summarize your options, as they've emerged in our dialogues. Here's what you've suggested so far, just as "asides"—and you've thrown them all out as "asides," except one. The "asides were: One—The regional leader of a charter movement, a school movement. Two—Possibly the national leader, coming from that experience, of the same movement. Three—A U.S. Congressman or even Senator!—that's come out as well.

But the one that was not an "aside"—the one in which I seemed to catch the greatest gleam of sincerity in your eye—was: Teaching the first grade! At the end of all this career.

What's ahead, promising, attractive—likely—as of today?

THORP. I would say the most likely scenario, looking at it from "likely scenario," as opposed to your "wave-your-magic-wand" and tell me what you'd like to do. The probable scenario is that I will finish my career in education, and most likely in the classroom. Then at some point, I will make a decision—for all sorts of reasons, my needs will be met, my personal needs and my vocational satisfaction needs will be met, by going back to where it all started, and teaching kids. And I say that not as: "Gee, my life kind of devolved back to where it started!" but with the excitement of making a difference.

But I would like to be in a position where I could effect change a little more broadly. I'd like to be Gore's education speech writer! Or President Bush's, more likely. And, I would like to think of making a difference. But certainly one of the things—I said this in that foundation forum yesterday—is the fact that one of the problems in education is that people have underestimated the strength of the status quo. And certainly some educational reforms have expanded the strength of the status quo; there's that Vietnamese proverb about how that blade of grass bends in the wind, and when the wind finishes, the blade of grass becomes upright again. And I think that's an apt metaphor for educational reform in the second half of the twentieth century. There are a few exceptions—it might be as specific as foreign language labs; go into a school and see if you can find a foreign language lab anymore, where you and I experienced them when they were all the rage. It might be the phonics-reading debate, which became political. And the list goes on and on.

What education needs is an educational messiah. Now, it's not me. But I sure would like to be the speechwriter for the educational messiah! Because somebody has to come up with the simple, clear, courageous message about what education is all about. And there isn't anybody in the country right now, in my opinion, who's really doing that, though there are people who are capable of doing it—but they're fighting so many entrenched status-quo battles that in a sense they made the decision, and understandably so, that if you're going to make improvement, you've got to do it by steps. And so, I'm going to take it one step at a time.

You think of people like Ralph Nader, who although not an educator, takes the kind of approach that I'm talking about. I think more specifically about a guy like Jonathan Cosal, who wrote *Death at an Early Age* many years ago when he was a young English teacher in a black school in Roxbury in Boston. He's written a series of books, one called *The Irreconcilable*, which was written about three or four years ago, which talked about essentially the poverty gap, and what remains in education. And his new book which has just come out is called something like Resurrection of Hope, which is a modestly hopeful message and analysis of schools in the South Bronx.

Anyway, there's somebody we'll need to find who has the voice of a Messiah. Or even William Bennett, the former Secretary of Education, and fellow Williams alumnus—whom I'm not sure I would agree with politically, but at least he's got a pretty clear message about who and what he thinks is important in education, and the values in education, a moral education. And I agree with him. I might not agree with him on which values, or when, and how much; but a valueless education, to me, is not an education.

There is also a guy named Alfie Cohn, who is an interesting guy not too many people know about, whose most recent life's work in the last fifteen years has been attacking competition in schools.

FELTON. Ah!

THORP. He's a pretty interesting guy; and again, there's another book you can throw on your bedside table. But the reason he's interesting is because he talks about how schools are fundamentally flawed by this aspect of competition. And as you might imagine, he's hugely critical of standardized testing.

In this meeting yesterday, I met the Dean of the School of Education at Berkeley, a guy named Gil Garcia, whom I was prepared would impress me. And to be fair to him, he was just responding to other things; but he didn't impress me based at least on what he said, because his whole point was that the way to solve the educational problem is get rid of emergency credentials.

What he was actually saying, of course, was: "Get rid of inexperienced teachers, particularly inexperienced teachers in the lowest-performing schools, where you have this cycle of bad performance." And he's totally right about that, in terms of the result. But on the other hand, we can't get enough teachers anyway. And as you can imagine, the question I wanted to ask him, and I decided that I couldn't do this in front of the crowd, was: "Well, wait a minute—your premise is that we've got to have credentialed teachers in the classroom, because that's the only measurement of quality people in the classroom. And I'd like to question you about that premise. Let's throw the private schools into the mix, where you have zero teachers with credentials, and see that they seem to be performing pretty well! So let's look at your data set based on that. Is having a credential the right variable? Or is it finding quality and experienced people the right variable? Obviously, you know what my answer to that question is.

Wouldn't it have been great if this important guy had said, "Yeah, I'm here to say that as the Dean of a School of Education, I'm willing to admit publicly that all schools of education are credential mills, and that's how we all keep our jobs and make our money. And if any of us think that we're affecting the world of education, well, I'm telling you up front that we're lying to you; because we know that we're not affecting the world of education!" But somehow he didn't muster up that statement.

FELTON. You dreamer, you. You optimist, you!

THORP. So—you're most likely to find me in the classroom. However: If I have the opportunity to work in a public policy arena in education, I would leap at that opportunity.

FELTON. Is there any that you would combine—since you're not going to be a former Cabinet official, which is a logical stepping-off point for being a Fellow at a think-tank—is there any way where you could operate in such an institution, being effective in coming up with legislative policy, or something?

THORP. Well, one of the things I should do is, I should start writing more. And I just don't have the time. Also, unlike you, writing does not come easily to me. I mean, I write well, but it's labored writing, and I really have to work at it. Not that you or anyone else doesn't have to work at it! But I really have to be in the right place mentally in order to sit down and write something.

I do need to write more, and I should start writing letters to Education Week, and the other important journals of education.

FELTON. That would be valuable. For you and education.

THORP. However, if I do write, I'm going to tick a lot of people off. Because I'm not going to write pabulum, I don't have time for that. So it's going to be provocative writing. And again, before I expose myself as the Marxist that I am, I want to come to some resolution as to where we really stand with the School Board here. And I want either to continue to try to navigate the minefield of local politics, which I've done relatively successfully so far, or just say,

Screw it. I've got to do what I've got to do, and let the School Board votes fall where they may.

FELTON. Well, the San Francisco political parochialism is astonishing! And whatever happens with Arlene Ackerman in harness here, it's worth comparing, for a moment: I'm very eager to see what happens when former Governor Roy Romer takes over the Superintendent's job in Los Angeles. And I noticed that in some newspapers a couple of weeks ago, Jerry Brown announced a new charter school for Oakland, which is a military school—?

THORP. Yeah. A boarding school.

FELTON. What's the story there?

THORP. Did you hear what happened to it?

FELTON. No.

THORP. It got defeated.

FELTON. Oh, it did!?

THORP. It "tied" five-to-five, and this tenth person on Oakland's School Board—it didn't pass. And the debate was unbelievable! In fact, one of the people in this meeting yesterday made it appear that he was opposed to it, and he made it clear that he was not at all a fan of charter schools as well.

FELTON. Gee! What was Jerry Brown's problem?

THORP. The debate was: He was at one level, in terms of the idea, as he might have put it: "Ain't no damned military school going to be that close to Berkeley!" I also heard of another point of view that I find extraordinary, which was: "It is racist to create a military school for black kids."

FELTON. Really! And what did His Honor think of that notion?

THORP. I'm amazed that he couldn't get this through, particularly since a couple of people that he just appointed to the School Board, under the legislation that passed last March, which enabled them to add some people to the school board, and they voted against the proposal. The very people he appointed voted against him!

FELTON. That's the Saga of Seminarian-Governor-Presidential Candidate-Mayor Jerry! He's really a phenomenon, a unique story.

THORP. That may be so; but once again, here it's a function of the forces of the status quo.

FELTON. That's right. That's part of the saga. And now that story includes charter education development.

THORP. Now, here was a guy, who got Gray Davis to pony up 1.8 million bucks, and he hasn't given to any other charter schools. And you know that Jerry Brown wasn't going to do anything second class, and you know that five years from now parents and kids would be thrilled with the opportunity to have this kind of school in Oakland. But he couldn't pull it off.

FELTON. Well, I'll be damned. The Priest's magic fails.[1]

THORP. So as you've seen, just in yesterday's paper, in fact, the ballot measure for the voucher will now be on the ballot. It got certified by the Secretary of State, that they had enough appropriate petition signatures. So on the November ballot is going to be the voucher issue. The vouchers would give four thousand bucks a family!

FELTON. Is that right?

THORP. Which is bigger than most places. Four thousand bucks, and you can take the money and put your kid in any private school you want.

FELTON. Gee! Amazing!

THORP. And between you and me? I think it's going to pass.

FELTON. Do you? Yeah, it probably will.

THORP. Now, everybody including myself is going to wind up against it. But I think people underestimate the frustration of families—

FELTON. Which is higher than most places.

THORP. It's not going to make that much of a difference, because how many people who are given four thousand dollars are going to be able to go to a private school that costs twelve thousand or fifteen thousand, as is the case in San Francisco? Or how many parochial schools that might cost five thousand, which in fact then, somebody could afford—how many openings are they going to have?[2]

FELTON. Yeah. Now, in my novelist's mind, I see that as prodromal Bush. Just kind of building that side of the ideological bank up.

THORP. In which case, then, we constitute ourselves as a private school, and then could get four thousand bucks per family, then some schools which were much closer to an independence—

FELTON. Yes—?

THORP. —We could take off from there. But there is a part of this notion that, from an ironic point of view, the voucher movement could make Gateway work.

---

[1] In mid-December, 2000, California Governor Gray Davis—himself a military school product—successfully assisted Brown to create the military academy.

[2] California Proposition 38, the voucher initiative, was defeated on November 7, 2000, by a wide margin.

FELTON. Well, it's a peculiar community that allows all that to happen. But, then, it means that the ultimate is undecided; It really could go your way.

I wanted to refer to Peter Thorp's final comments in the Gateway assembly that went forever recently. So I don't know what you said, as I needed to leave before the awards were all given out, and before you spoke; but I had a question that might elicit the same response from you.

Incidentally, I posited this question in my notes almost when we started the project, because it was very easy to do But its bell is now tolling, all these months later:

In a couple of years from now, this day will be Graduation Day— the first graduation of the full-complement four-class Gateway High School. In the Multi-Purpose Room, or some other auspicious and meaningful locus will sit Freshmen, Sophomores, Juniors—and Seniors!—surrounded by the charter parents who gave birth to these youngsters a bare decade-and-a-half before.

There will also be the people who counted on the place, and the teachers who pushed them on, and shaped the raw material into better-formed, advancing scholar-citizens with what I think surely will be firmer inner compass. This is the goal for which you have worked so hard.

So: What do you say to them? And what would you say to them if today were that day?

THORP. Having given as many Commencement speeches as I have, I recognize, or I acknowledge that it is probably the most ignoble form of speech, and probably the most inappropriately exalted form of speech, at the very least. And speaking of humility: I am humbled aplenty, when I talk to people, or when it's made clear to me somehow that such a speech of mine was forgettable within minutes. Most recently this news has been brought to me by my younger daughter, who would make a point of showing up at graduation after I spoke! She would say: "Oh, I know what you were going to say. It's just the same stuff you say to me all the time."

And the reason I think that is this: I would say two utterly different things, sort of a halfway commencement speech, in light of the school now. It would not sit well with my thinking about what commencement speeches should do, to do otherwise. I couldn't give the kind of pompous "words-to-live-by," sentiment now. If I did, I won't be able to understand myself entirely two years from now. But what I would like to think I would be able to accomplish is more an acknowledgment of what the kids have accomplished. And it's premature right now to say anything of great meaning, because—it's just premature!

But two years from now, I hope to be able to speak about the accomplishments of this group of kids; and obviously, just given my inability to resist some lightness, I will try to weave that into a theme, not unlike what I did a year ago at Cate. Basically my point was: "You guys have been blessed with all sorts of things, and wealth"—although I didn't quite put it that way—"And yet, you have maintained and discovered a sense of humility that really speaks well for your ability to go through life and seek its opportunity. But don't forget to be humble about it."

So my words will be very much formed by what the kids here at Gateway accomplish and create within the next two years, and by what the school becomes within the next two years. And—who knows? I mean, it'll be kind of fun on the one hand, because it's utterly unpredictable as to what we'll be able to say! I won't speak to "achievement," so much, though the pressure will be there to do that. I won't do as the Native American School did, saying: "Look at all the kids who got into all these colleges!" But my communication will be more designed—this is just the way I look at the world—to speak to what they have become as people, or how they have grown as people, in the last four years.

That's what I'll speak about. And were I able to do so now, I would speak about that. In my remarks, at the end of this year, I was critical of the kids. I mean, I think they felt *criticized*. But I made the point—I brought my remarks back in a circle to what I said at the opening Convocation, which was: "Be kind." You know, "Live your life being kind. Make a difference." And I pointed out that in my opinion this year, we haven't been kind to the extent that we need to be, and I asked the kids to think about that over the course of the summer.

FELTON. Actually, Peter mentioned that.

THORP. Oh, did he?

FELTON. Yeah. That impressed him.

THORP. He listened! Peter's my best audience! It runs in the family.

FELTON. *Apropos* of that, in a way: You mentioned the San Francisco Foundation; let me take advantage of your contact with them to describe one of my own. It illustrates a point which might relate to your struggle, and certainly the students' long effort ahead:

Years ago, in the mid-seventies, they'd set up a fund—using trust moneys left them by famed San Francisco Mayor James Phelan, to reward young writers, native California writers. So I applied with a book that I'd done, and they turned me down. The next year, I wrote and sent in another book. And that book didn't win that year, either. So the next year, 1977, I wrote and sent in yet another book, and it won. It won the Prize. They brought me up here from Los Angeles, we had a ceremony, and it was very lovely. But at the end of it all, I turned to the host from the Foundation, and said: "Look: I sent you a book two years ago which was every bit as good as the one I just won with. And I sent you one last year which was just as good. And then I sent you this one this year. Why didn't those others win?" And he just smiled, and said: "We wanted to see if you had 'legs' on you."

I thought that was very interesting. But—with kids, you can't let it hang there, to see if they have that assiduity, you know? They need more immediate, pronounced support. It does, however, form a worthwhile tenet for the process: "Are you going to hang around? Are you going to keep working?"

THORP. That is the point, indeed.

FELTON. Let me close with a couple of little "Rorschach" tests, in a way—

THORP. Free association—?

FELTON. Yeah. I'm curious what you think about a page out of the PBS catalogue which advertises video tapes designed to improve a student's performance in one area or another. A number of these products are portrayed, and purveyed, in every publication promoting such media collections.

THORP. Well, it's certainly a statement on the plight of children in today's society.

FELTON. When I see such things, I wish I wasn't so cynical that I don't automatically say: "Man, it doesn't take them long to see if they can get a buck out of 'em."

THORP. I don't think it is that. But you need to look at it through a physician's eyes, so to speak. And decide to what extent—to decide the relationship between the cure and the disease. And I think in social services, that some of the "cure" exacerbates some of the disease.

An example of that question—and I'm not even sure how I feel about that question—is the methadone plan. You know—is that the right way to go at the same quandary concerning drugs? A more politically-defined question along those lines is the whole concept of welfare: Did that cure the problem, or was it simply addressing the symptoms of the problem? More recent legislation will answer that.

But I think on some of these kid-related issues: The fact that a fourteen-year-old girl can make reproductive decisions without parental consultation is to me mindless by society, utterly mindless. And yet if I were to say that in public, I would be ripped to shreds by child-rights' advocates, and others. And so, the solution to give kids rights, and to reckon with them—well, we're not getting to the fundamentals of what the issues are. And you look at those video programs—I think at least in some of the cases they're good. Richard LeBoy makes one we use in school, which is really trying to get at some of the fundamental issues in schools. And perhaps these others are, too.

FELTON. There are other products advertised in similar veins, which to me represented perfect symbols of what ambivalence this country feels about its educational process. I'm thinking of a picture of students at a blackboard which I've seen used in test-score-boosting programs. Now, in one sense, this blackboard in the picture says: "Isn't it wonderful, we have blackboards in our schools, and therefore our schools are great." But in fact, they're not saying schools are great; they're not saying, "By God, this is where we ought to be focusing!" They're just saying: "Well, we better get something out on the market which has to do with schools. That's the big seller coming up." And it feels very lukewarm to me.

THORP. There's a lot of ambivalence about schools, I think. We've talked on many cases about the proper role of school systems in a democracy, and also the inappropriate role. And too often, I think we fall back on inappropriate assumptions.

FELTON. One of the spaces which needs to be given here, even if only for a minute, is this: What, through my incessant badgering, have I kept you from saying that you might have wanted to say?

THORP. Great question! I've no real answer, off the top of my head. You've given me more than both adequate time and leeway to do essentially a year-long word-association, to give me a topic and then let me talk for seven minutes about it, which might have been extraordinarily frustrating to you. So really, nothing.

The only question I have, the only untouched pocket that I have is this enormous sense of you having whatever number of hundreds of thousands of words our dialogue has become now, and not really much to pull together to write the monograph you want to write. What you have is ramblings of another person. But my question—to you— is: How are *you* feeling about this?

FELTON. Well, there's an answer that has been so consistent. And I've asked myself that in a different way. Not from the doubting stance, but from the positive stance.

My process on this forum of ours has always been to meet with you, to go home, secure the tapes, punch them out to protect them, prevent mishaps, put my security tape somewhere else—and then let it sit, until just a couple of days before we would meet again. And then I would transcribe that last week's session. And doing it that way, it had a wonderful quality of allowing me to hear it fresh. And every single time, I found what you gave out had incredible richness and value. And I'm not saying that to flatter; there would be no point in doing that. I truly felt that there was a huge amount of material there, and my positivism was confirmed in transcribing it. Also, sometimes, I would be totally surprised. It was as if I had never been in that room, that I was hearing this for the first time; and it was really compelling!

There were a lot of things going on that I wouldn't be aware of at the time, because obviously, I can only listen to you with one ear, and I've got to pull things together for the ongoing questions with the other ear. And that's distracting, and probably seemed to you second only to drooling as an inadequate response to what you were saying! But it never failed that the transcript revealed you would come up with something absolutely cogent.

It's interesting: People who aren't full-time writers, such as yourself, often worry beforehand about content. Just before I came down to your office today, I went up to say hello to Meghvi Maheta, Gateway's Admissions Director whom I'd interviewed earlier in the year. Meghvi wants to do a book about her father. And she and I are going to meet a couple of times to talk about it. And she—so earnestly this morning, she got out a piece of paper for a list, and said: "What do you want me to have prepared when we meet? What do you want to know about? What should I make note of?"

And I said, "You don't have to make note of anything! If you really want to do that book, sit down and brainstorm every tiny little thing you can remember about your father. I don't want to know his political theories; I want to know how long he kept a pair of shoes. And what his speech mannerisms were. And any things which bothered you—you know, did he have any embarrassingly vulgar mannerisms? Just put down everything you can think of, and let them all flash through your mind, just little vignettes. And out of all that, you'll begin to get a picture of things. And then you can move into his environment, and social position, and all the other things that you'll want to do to frame that. That way, each note you'll then have, in some little way, will have an element of truth about him."

And she was perfectly happy to do that and in a way it was a relief for her to contemplate approaching her task in that new way. I really think it takes the onus off a lot of writing. Your stuff—the material you presented here—I mean, you're thinking! You were thinking, and it was the product of a lot of time; I don't mean now, or these past months of our sessions. I mean the last thirty years of time!

THORP.   But the question I ask—and I appreciate your making me feel it wasn't a waste of your time—have I taken away from your original purpose, in a sense that I don't think this has been a balanced story about a year in the life of Gateway, as much as it's been: "Here's this guy Thorp." And I don't know if that's what you set out to write. Gateway has become a context within which you've heard a lot of political and/or educational philosophy, from just one person. So—?

FELTON.   Well, I understand what you mean by that. I haven't ever seen it as really about you. In fact, sometimes I had to focus on that just to get a view of you as a person. I see it as a story about young people and growth. And what the learning process is. And about human capability. And that just comes shining across. I know those are interests of yours; and they really jump out of this process.

My whole experience of junior high and high school was cut in such a different way. All the student issues that are of paramount interest and occupy front-row attention, so I imagine, in your faculty meetings and elsewhere today, are issues that were at most parenthetical or personal asides that an administrator probably thought about for a minute and then got away from, back when I was going through it all. And the Principal was some austere figure off somewhere greeting public officials with an egregious grin, or sitting behind his desk with his hands clasped, wearing a face of insufferable rectitude; and the Vice-Principal was a bully and a "cop"; and it was a whole different kind of feeling. I think what we logged in our process here is really about what really happened in that school called Gateway, and what happened to the people inside it. And looking at this year embodies how they got there, and where they're going to go.

And I just got lucky! I got a highly intelligent, articulate guy. I mean—my fear was—until that first Parent Night, where you came in and straddled a chair and just talked for about twenty minutes—until then, I wanted to do this, but I thought: Jeez, suppose I get some guy who thinks that what I want is just for him to go down his calendar, and tell me what teacher he chewed out, and what memos he was going to issue. And instead, you took every one of those opportunities where you were worried about things, and made them into a philosophical precept, and reflected upon the policy imposition alternatives, and then showed the impact of all that upon the kids.

Always, the kids. With Peter Thorp, I found, again and again and again, it always came down to the kids.

What more can you want?

Coda

VOICES IN THE QUIET
OF A DIALOGUE'S COMPLETION

Any poor country replaces the "poorness" of the people with the richness of the art, the food, the life!

—Mark Rabinek of New Orleans, Louisiana
(known as "Dr. John the Night Tripper")

Lemuel P. Garrett, in name, appearance and manner, gave off every air of being a small-town Southern sheriff. The year was 1953; and this physically handicapped, huge-bellied, over-compensating, puffily unhealthy turn of a man lorded what authority he could muster over the teachers of Pleasant Hill School, a rural "K through 8" grammar-and-junior-high grade facility outside Oklahoma City. He did so, however, not as a Southern, or even a Southwestern, sheriff, but, rather, in the equally dictatorial position he had held for years; for Garrett was Pleasant Hill's Principal.

At Pleasant Hill, the word "Principal" conjured up a maelstrom of meanings, all horrific. His office and person formed a stern and definitive apex of authority.

In this role, which he hewed daily to meet his own concept of its own perfection of cruelty and unquestioned rule, Lem Garrett gave this reporter (then a young boy bored with Tina Freed's sixth-grade class) a firm point of departure for measuring future Principals. And, amongst

Garrett's other contributions, in retrospect he has given considerably to the rationale for seeing Peter Thorp in such a favorable light.

Pleasant Hill School carried out the State's intentions of providing elementary education for its rural citizens, by serving as a locus for indigent farm children, Native Americans (1953's "Indians"), a wretchedly poor band who did not have benefit of autonomy or today's endowed and supportive tribal communities, and a smattering of other children from the outskirts of the still-geographically-contained Oklahoma City. Amongst those communities was the developed, exclusive area—polar in character— surrounding Twin Hills Golf and Country Club, which provided mansions and great rolling lawns to comfort the outreaching professional families of the area.

The University of Oklahoma Medical School's new associate professor had brought his family of five to their new capitol-city Oakwood Drive dwelling near Twin Hills, just a few months before school started in that year during which Frank Sinatra proclaimed in song: "Fairy tales can come true; it can happen to you, if you're young at heart." The forced conscription by a small, country school held no allure; but then, I was the new kid on the block, without privilege or choice (despite 16 Oakwood Drive's three floored manse and three-acred park-like grounds).

Lem Garrett's uniform as Principal was unwavering: A starched shirt and tie on top, light tan linen trousers which bore a neat crease, and dropped the viewer's eye, with their slope, down from the forty-six-inch beer-belly they contained to the white-on-top-of-brown loafers at Lem Garrett's feet. (One did not allow one's gaze to tarry at Lem's feet, however; for the man had suffered some form of polio earlier in life, and walked with a cane and a pronounced, limb-dragging gait. To stare—even for an instant—was to invite big trouble.)

The Principal looked, in effect, like Col. Harlan Sanders without goatee-and-string-tie. He lacquered a few strands of remaining hair hard over his bald pate, which shone above rimless glasses. The face below wore a perpetual, malevolent little smile. And there was no crime in any of this; except for the fact that the cane did more than prop up a recovering crippling virus' victim: it perched in his hand, ready to threaten a beating at the slightest suspicion of juvenile infraction.

I would encounter Principal Garrett caning about the school, for he micro-managed the place long before the term was known. He rang the bells for the classes, by pushing a button on the wall bordering a little stage in the school's gathering room. He carefully monitored the use of the one school luxury—a celadon-green soft-drink dispensing machine, which only purveyed one beverage: The popular green-bottled "Dr.

Pepper." "It's got prune juice, y'know," Principal Garrett was fond of saying. "Prune juice is good f'r ever'one!" But Friendly Pepper-upper Garrett was not. *Ten, Two, and Four*, each bottle's clockface logo, became for me an ineradicable way of measuring a day's passage at age eleven.

I never suffered a caning from this strange, irksome man, for I would never have allowed him the pleasure of becoming aware of any infraction I had been foolish enough to commit. And pleasures for me were rare in that sixth-grade year—the only year I allowed Pleasant Hill to exact from me, changing to a city-side junior high two years earlier than the little grade school's top-end eighth grade. In fact, the daily lunch of canned government-surplus spinach, which I spiked with vinegar from a condiment jar in the little ten-feet-by-fourteen-feet "cafeteria room" in the school's midsection, provided the only pleasing diversity I can remember from that year (other than Carolyn Jones' expressed sexual curiosities which lured me twice to the class cloakroom, and twice met with her change-of-heart lack of intention to satisfy that curiosity).

Every day at about three o'clock, teacher Tina Freed would wind a small, ancient hand Victrola in class to provide a "musical interlude." Once, I witnessed Miss Freed (whose class combined the school's fifth- and sixth-graders into a group of fifteen or twenty) approach Principal Garrett and nervously ask permission to enhance her class's patently limited music program. "Nothin' wrong with what you got," he proclaimed, and noticeably, I thought, restrained his urge to cane a woman who, sadly, could boast no physical appeal, being bone-thin, overbite-burdened, and who had the indignity to tower a good eight inches above Garrett. This rebuke caused Tina to return to the classroom, in tears she did her best to hide, but which I discerned; and, administering the "music program" she already "got," wound again the little portable Victrola with the replaceable sewing-needle stylus, and forced upon us children for the thousandth time Bing Crosby's 78-rpm recording of "Carolina In The Morning."

Had Peter Thorp been at Pleasant Hill School in 1953, he actually would have been in an even earlier grade than I. And, with his blue eyes and sweet face, I suspect that he would have been either passed over by Lem Garrett as being too innocent, or might conversely have become a focus for the strange man, as a likely, helpless target for his cruelty. Garrett, like so many men in positions of dubious authority, didn't want anyone to achieve more in life than he had. And, since he couldn't inflict a polio germ upon them and make them need the use of a cane, he simply made their life as quietly miserable as he could. And gave them the cane the only way he could. (Except at ten, two, and four, provided they had a nickel.)

This experience comes to mind, not simply because Peter Thorp's far-thinking and inspired energy is so many galaxies away from this pathetic Principal-figure of my youth; but because it is an alarming measure of how much is accomplished by time's passage. This almost fifty-year jump seems like millennia, given the concerns on Thorp's list. But every passing day distorts time: Only forty-two years separated Lindbergh's flight from Apollo 11's; a mere eighteen years separated Roosevelt's death from Kennedy's; less than nine years separated Reagan's tag-along Falkland adventure from Bush's Desert Storm; and a miniscule six years divided the halcyon young Turk Clinton from his own besieged paramour-antics with a calculating brunette adventuress.

The moral of these calendar-musings is this: Time is "moving faster," and time is running out in so many ways—time to patch the ozone hole, time to strip fat from the diet and smoke from the lungs. Time to quit coddling nonacademically-motivated athletes; time to turn attention from the demands of standardized testing and back to the nonstandard urges of each single student in every American school.

Lem Garrett's cane (surely sinecured now for doubtless decades) will strike no more children, nor will it even strike fear in their hearts. Surely, its wielder must have died some time back, or else he would be a centurion (doubtful, with that waistline and that cerebrum full of vengeful stress). (Young Tina Freed herself, barely in her second year of teaching in 1953, would now be in her seventies!)

But the threats from the other end of Lem Garrett's support cane— the threats from men who lack such wisdom and insight in brain and heart that they would take a walking stick and turn it into a device of ill-conceived pedagogical policy—are ever there. The threats are subtler now; they're the metaphorical stick with which school boards beat principals who advance ideas not vetted by aeons of insensate repetition. They materialize every time a Peter Thorp needs to defend his Gateway against the rumblings of the local power structure; and they materialize every time a Conservative politician invokes the latest fear tactic to keep the electorate from releasing funding into education.

And if the threats continue long enough, and are directed toward those of lower threshold for tolerance than Peter Thorp, perhaps once again, in the name of a school program, some Principal will decide to use his cane for more than ambulation; the music program will retrench to the scratchy strains of Bing's warbling whistle; and the lunch will hit its throwback stride as an offering of vinegared spinach, washed down with Dr. Pepper's juice of prunes.

People like to say that the schools aren't what they used to be. The truth is, they're much too much like they used to be.

We must make standards meaningful by holding students, teachers, principals and everyone else accountable.

—William Jefferson Clinton
Newsweek Special Issue,
December 1999-February 2000

POSTSCRIPT

During the summer between the close of school in the 1999-2000 school year, and the beginning of the 2000-2001 school year, some changes happened at Gateway:

Peter Thorp let his beard grow.

Math teacher Taimi Barty quit to become a woodworker deep in the California Redwoods.

Gateway's beloved athletic coach, "Corky" Corkran, left (with two dogs and VW van) to pursue a graduate degree.

Two teachers celebrated summer marriages.

In July, a news clipping on the faculty bulletin board stated that the entire teaching staff of thirty at Edison Elementary Charter School resigned in protest to that school's inadequate management.

Incoming instructor Amy Meuller practiced the vocal exercises she would teach her drama classes the coming fall.

Two young immigrant students—Anna of Ukraine, and Ivor of Croatia—moved smoothly into the fuller womanhood and manhood of junior class status.

Newly-hired Spanish instructor Carlos Roig pondered whether he would teach his minor subject with as much conviction as he had for his first love, anthropology.

Tenth-grader Kelly Allegretti made plans to get a new wheelchair.

Gus Porter, Student Body President, added to his already great height, bringing him to six-foot-six-inches.

Many members of the junior class (Gateway's highest) mourned the loss of the intimate feeling of the old, smaller, one- or even two-class school they had been.

With the help of a reconstruction crew, Gateway High School claimed new third-floor space, and took on more feeling of having been a school forever.

And your reporter joined the school faculty.

"The more things change, the more they remain the same," Voltaire pronounced.

(Maybe he should have said it the other way around.)

ABOUT THE PARTICIPANTS

PETER C. THORP (subject), founding principal at Gateway High School in San Francisco, has been an educator for the past twenty-five years. Before beginning Gateway's exciting project, he was headmaster at Cate School, near Santa Barbara, and taught and served in administrative capacities at a variety of schools, among them Fountain Valley School in Colorado Springs. In addition to his leadership at Gateway, he currently serves on the boards of several schools both in and outside California.

A Williams College graduate in art history, Thorp earned an M.Ed. at Boston State College and has done additional postgraduate work at the University of Colorado and Harvard Graduate School of Education. Although the study of history is, by his avid proclamation, both an academic and personal calling, Thorp broadened and deepened his love of the interconnectedness of learning by a Fulbright Scholarship in China in 1983, and five summers spent working on a medieval dig in Southern France. His teaching expertise covers U.S. foreign policy, colonial history, Asian studies, and American art and architecture.

Thorp is the father of two daughters. The elder, Elyssa, attends Barnard College; her sister Amy will be in the first graduating class at Gateway High School.

KEITH SPENCER FELTON (author) passionately believes that a dimensional education involves intensity and virtuosity; his focus on the literary, graphic and performing arts has underscored this belief. An acknowledged author, photographer, filmmaker and playwright of almost forty years' experience, he received a Bachelor of Arts degree in Theater Arts and French from Grinnell College, and earned a Master of Fine Arts degree from UCLA. His writing, photography and film work have garnered prizes and recognition in both the United States and Western Europe, among which honors is the James A. Phelan Prize in Literature. For many years a regular contributor to the Los Angeles *Times* Book Review, he is also the author of *Warriors' Words: A Consideration of Language and Leadership* (Praeger, 1995).

Felton is the Study Center Counselor and Photography Group Advisor at Gateway. His older son Peter, a budding musicologist, is a member of Gateway's junior class; his younger son, Lars, studies Mandarin, science and mathematics at San Francisco's multicultural Chinese American International School.

INDEX

Note: A year's canvassing—of an educational movement, a school's emergence, and its leader's interests, impulses, and actions—produces incalculable indices. Those listed here represent only a partial overview of some of this text's broad areas of concern.